Mary Telfair

Best wishes

Charles J. Montgomery Jr.

Carl Ludwig Brandt painting of
Mary Telfair

Mary Telfair

The Life and Legacy of a Nineteenth-Century Woman

CHARLES J. JOHNSON, JR.

FREDERIC C. BEIL

SAVANNAH

Copyright © 2002 by Charles J. Johnson, Jr.

Published in the United States by
Frederic C. Beil *Publisher*
609 Whitaker Street
Savannah, Ga. 31401
http://www.beil.com

LIBRARY OF CONGRESS CATALOGING-IN-PUBLICATION DATA

Johnson, Charles J., 1932–
Mary Telfair: the life and legacy of a nineteenth-century woman/
Charles J. Johnson, Jr.
p.   cm.

Includes bibliographical references (p.   ) and index.
ISBN 1-929490-12-7 (alk. paper)
1. Telfair, Mary, 1791–1875. 2. Savannah (Ga.)—Biography.
3. Upper class women—Georgia—Savannah—Biography.
4. Women—Georgia—Savannah—Biography.
5. Children of governors—Georgia—Biography.
6. Savannah (Ga.)—Social life and customs—19th century.
7. Women—Southern States—Social life and customs—19th century.
8. Women—Southern States—Social conditions—19th century.
9. Sex role—Southern States—History—19th century.
I. Title.

F294.S2 T455 2001
975.8'72403'092–dc21
[B]
                                        2001025822

First edition

This book was typeset by Nangle Graphics, Savannah, Georgia;
printed on acid-free paper; and sewn in signatures.

The frontispiece is from a posthumous portrait (1896)
by Carl Ludwig Brandt
of Mary Telfair at about seventy years of age.
Courtesy of the Telfair Museum of Art, Savannah.

Printed in the United States of America

For
Peter, Casey, Lucy, and Stella Rose

Contents

CONTENTS

Illustrations

Preface

Mary Telfair—everyone in her native Savannah has heard of this nineteenth-century woman, and visitors to the city's Telfair Academy of Arts and Sciences can see her portrait by Carl L. Brandt in the rotunda of the museum that she founded. It is common knowledge on Bull Street, and Broughton and Bay, that Mary Telfair died an "old maid"; that she had the reputation of being proud and aloof, eccentric perhaps; and that she left to charity her considerable fortune, including the family mansion that was to become the Telfair Academy and the funds to build the Telfair Hospital for Females. The knowledge of most Savannahians ends there, however, and outside of Georgia she is largely unknown. This is understandable. Although Mary Telfair's legacy vastly enriched the culture and well-being of the low-country South, her life was not marked by notable achievements. She did not work to bring about social change; nor did she espouse any great cause. She did not wield power or exert intellectual influence. She authored no published works. She is not one of those "women worthies" that history has neglected.[1]

Yet Mary Telfair was a woman of no small consequence. The daughter of a wealthy merchant-planter and three-term governor of Georgia, she belonged to a privileged class, an elite circle of urban Southerners who felt as much at home in the drawing rooms of Philadelphia and New York as the parlors of Charleston and Savannah. She was part of the social set that dominated Ballston Spa, Saratoga Springs, and Newport in the first half of the nineteenth century. Like others of her class, Mary Telfair took enormous pride in her family name and colonial heritage. Being a Telfair defined her identity. As a member of a cosmopolitan society more closely connected with the port cities of the East Coast than the red soil of the rural South, she bore no kinship to the plantation mistress living in isolation, alienated by paternalism and male domination, on widely separated agricultural units throughout the South. As in the case of other Southern women, there is much that is wonderfully ordinary in the life of Mary Telfair—long walks, a game of battledore, needlework, restoring an old desk, choosing a gift of a jar of figs. As she observed herself—paraphrasing a line of verse by Hannah More—"Trifles make the sum of human life." Telfair's privileged status, however, provided her with opportunities for travel, cultural enrichment, and self-fulfillment far greater than those afforded most other women and particularly those from rural communities in Georgia and the Carolinas.[2]

Mary Telfair is a model of the educated, independent-minded woman, raised in the era of the early American Republic, who was not willing to accept fully the gender role assigned to her by the male-defined norms of the day, but still was bound by convention and good breeding to function within the system rather than defy it. The nineteenth-century "cult of true womanhood" demanded of women piety, purity, submissiveness, and domesticity.[3] Pious and pure she was, but it was not in Mary Telfair's nature to be submissive or to find satisfaction in domestic pursuits. She was intensely inquisitive about the world around her and was not content to sew in the chimney corner while the outside world beckoned. Management of the household was left chiefly to her younger sister, Sarah, who fit the ideal of domesticity quite easily.

To Mary Telfair, intelligence was an attribute to be valued above all others save piety, and much of her life was devoted to intellectual pursuits. But the intellectual woman in the nineteenth century was an object of suspicion and even scorn. Young women were warned to suppress an interest in books and to avoid literary discussions lest beaux run from them as if they had the plague. Telfair ignored these warnings and went so far as to display an interest in politics, a subject clearly outside the sphere assigned to women. The expectation that a woman be an informed, vivacious conversationalist did not extend to knowledge of political issues. Yet Telfair formulated strong opinions on world and national affairs and openly expressed her convictions. How many other women would have ventured to debate with Supreme Court Justice James Moore Wayne the merits of renewing the national bank charter?[4]

Mary Telfair's unwillingness or inability to conform to the early nineteenth-century female model created internal tensions with which she was forced to deal. In this respect she was not alone. Along with thousands of seemingly quiet and accepting women, there were thousands more who resisted the model. Some openly exhibited and discussed the tensions that they felt in attempting to function as unique individuals while fitting themselves, however torturously, into prescribed gender patterns. Telfair and other like-minded women might chafe under the strictures imposed by a male-dominated society, but few well-bred women of her generation were sufficiently rebellious to protest openly and strike out into the public sphere, as did so many women later in the century. To do so would have run counter to the nature and upbringing of a woman such as Mary Telfair. The Grimké sisters of Charleston, abolitionists and advocates of women's rights, were the exceptions that prove the rule.[5]

It has been suggested that a "culture of resignation" existed among many women from property-owning families in the Old South, a culture based on the premise that women should accept inequity, not resist it. Mary Telfair was her own woman, but she affirmed her identity within the framework of good manners, decorum, and taste demanded of women of her station. To the extent that she remained within the private sphere and bowed to convention where it was not too inconvenient, her experience partially supports this thesis. Historian Gerda Lerner takes the position that the ongoing and continuing contribution of women to the development of human culture cannot be found by treating them only as victims of oppression. Rather, the true history of women is the history of their "ongoing functioning in a male-defined world *on their own terms.*" Mary Telfair succeeded in living her life on her own terms, in measuring her worth by her own standards, but she did so by adapting to gender conventions or carefully skirting or evading them, rather than openly defying them.[6]

Little has been written of those Southern women of Mary Telfair's class who came of age in the post-Revolutionary period. Mary Boykin Chesnut, well known for her diary, belonged to the Charleston elite; but she was of a later generation, and her world was defined by the Civil War while Mary Telfair was well into her forties before regional self-consciousness and the institution of slavery became serious national issues. We learn something of the Southern elite of an earlier period from the study by Wylma Wates of the Izard family of South Carolina. Although her view of the world was more limited than Mary Telfair's, the letters of Maria Bryan of Mount Zion, Georgia, also paint a picture of a cultivated woman's life in the nineteenth century. Women, including Alice Izard and the Manigault sisters of Charleston, figure prominently in Daniel Kilbride's study of the relationship between the Southern elite and their counterparts in Philadelphia. But the literature to date on wealthy, urban women in the South is exceedingly thin.[7]

Mary Telfair's long life (1791–1875) spanned a significant period in the history of our country. As a member of the Continental Congress, her father participated in the birth of a new nation, and his avid patriotism in the struggle against King George III helped to shape hers. Mary shared the fear that gripped Savannah during the War of 1812. She and her friends suffered through the economic crises that plagued the country during the nineteenth century. She followed closely the great events and issues of the day: the Napoleonic Wars, the attempts to expand slavery into the territories, the election of Abraham Lincoln as President, the establishment of the Confederacy, and the progress of the Civil War. Telfair and her family were in Savannah during the city's occupation by Sherman's troops, and they suffered with other Southerners the indignities of Reconstruction.

Many of the country's leading figures passed through the lives of the Telfairs. Edward Telfair entertained President Washington at his home in Augusta while serving as governor. William Few, one of the two original senators from Georgia, was Governor Telfair's close friend. Mary Telfair lived with the Fews while attending school in New York. With the fluid networking among members of the privileged class that took place along the East Coast of America and even across the Atlantic, it is not surprising that the Telfair family knew Thomas Paine, the author of *Common Sense*, and Albert Gallatin, secretary of the treasury under Presidents Jefferson and Madison. Mary Telfair was a good friend of Nicholas Biddle, the well-known financier. She witnessed the pomp and ceremony accompanying Lafayette's visit to the United States. She and her sisters were presented to President John Tyler and had an audience with Pope Pius IX in Rome. She was received in Bath by the Reverend William Jay, the famous dissenting preacher. She watched Louis Napoleon review his troops on the Champs de Mars in Paris and saw Queen Victoria in London and found her a coarse-looking woman.

The Telfairs were related to, or close friends with, most of the prominent families in Savannah and the Georgia upcountry. Mary's mother was a Gibbons, and her cousin was Thomas Gibbons, the fabulously wealthy steamboat magnate who made history in breaking Robert Fulton's monopoly on the Hudson River. Another cousin, William Gibbons, was a neighbor of General Nathanael Greene and his wife, the enchanting Caty, on whose plantation Eli Whitney invented the cotton gin. The descendants of Noble Jones, one of Georgia's original settlers, played a significant role in Mary Telfair's life. The two families became related when Mary's aunt, the sister of Sarah Gibbons Telfair, married Dr. George Jones. The Habershams were the Telfairs' factors as well as their friends and confidential advisors. Other well-known Savannah and upcountry names that appear in Mary Telfair's story are Berrien, Bulloch, Campbell, Cecil, Clay, Cumming, Cuthbert, Terrell, and Wayne, to name but a few. William Jay, Savannah's favorite architect, designed the Telfair mansion. Though a committed Presbyterian, Mary often attended services at Christ Church to hear the sermons of Dr. Stephen Elliott, the first Episcopal bishop of Georgia.

Despite her reserve and proud veneer, Mary Telfair was a woman of great personal charm. She made wonderful, lasting friendships; she loved nature and adored flowers; she was well versed in literature and history; she read and wrote poetry—Byron was her beau ideal; she had a keen appreciation of the visual arts—she was moved to eloquence in describing the marble figure of Byron's Medora by the sculptor Horatio Greenough; she was able to draw beautifully; her curiosity drove her to travel extensively in Europe. Mary Telfair's values shine forth from her letters and journals, revealing a mind of deep sensitivity that abhorred pretension and show, greed and insincerity, and that revered beauty and truth. Mary had little regard for worldly goods and valued wealth chiefly as a means of aiding the less fortunate. She had nothing but scorn for the trappings of fashionable society. Mary Telfair loved jokes, enigmas, and humorous verse. She had an acerbic wit. She could laugh at herself. She was not above fibbing about her age. She had her problems and sorrows, but faced them with courage. She grieved deeply over the deaths of loved ones. She loathed the disgrace to the family name caused by the scandalous behavior of her great-niece Alberta. She frequently was ill in an age plagued by illness. But she found comfort in her strong Christian beliefs and, with God's help, managed to cope with adversity. Her faith was at the core of her very being.

Mary Telfair and her friends provide insights into life in nineteenth-century America. It was Mary Telfair who introduced to New York society her cousin Ward McAllister, the social arbiter who created the list of "the 400," those members of society who could fit comfortably and feel comfortable in Mrs. Astor's ballroom. Mary Telfair's letters contain accounts of family dinners and long carriage rides into the countryside. We can picture her writing letters by the fireside in the Telfair residence or being served tea in the oak room by her servant Friday. Mary Telfair wrote of the intellectual climate of New Haven, where she met the formidable scientist Benjamin Silliman, and of visits to the Shaker Village in New Lebanon and the mills of Lowell, Massachusetts, where young women toiled long hours for a subsistence wage. She described the charms of the towns along the Hudson River, the realm of Rip Van Winkle and the Headless Horseman. We view the institution of slavery through the eyes of the Telfairs and their neighbors, slaveholders who saw no evil in their ownership of other human beings.

Mary Telfair corresponded with her friend Mary Few on the subjects of mesmerism and phrenology as well as on the propriety of dancing. From her quill pen we learn something of what it was like to sail in a sloop from New York to Savannah in the early 1800's or to travel by stagecoach over the rutted roads of the eastern United States and endure drafts, filth, and greasy food in primitive inns along the way. Through her travel journals, we share Telfair's excitement in visiting the great capitals of Europe and her enchantment with the ruins of the castle of Roland and the palace of the Black Prince. We can feel the tingle in her spine as she stood on the site of the Battle of Hastings, where Taillifer the minstrel, a Norman hero with mythic Telfair ties, lost his life in 1066.

Mary Telfair never married, and her single state was another defining feature of her life. With her inherited wealth, she was not a woman for whom marriage was an economic necessity. Nor was she one of those women who made a rigorous assessment of the marital institution and found it wanting and in conflict with female autonomy, self-development, and achievement. Mary Telfair was not achievement-oriented. She had no need to establish a vocational identity. Although she strove to realize her full potential as a person, there is no evidence that she consciously rejected marriage as inconsistent with her desire for self-actualization. She knew quite well the shortcomings of "single blessedness." American ideology demanded "Republican Mothers" whose primary task was to train sons for future citizenship and daughters for future domesticity. She could not have failed to observe the glorification of marriage and motherhood that emerged in the early nineteenth century as the "cult of domesticity." So long as she remained a single woman, Mary Telfair failed to meet the expectations of the society into which she had been born. The stereotype of the ill-humored "old maid" carried strong negative connotations that she and every other woman found distasteful.[8]

Certainly Mary would have preferred to remain single than to marry a man who was not her intellectual and moral equal. Certainly she agreed with the cultural convention of the day, "better single than miserably married." Certainly she enjoyed the intimacy of a close circle of female friends and could be more open with other women than with men, but so did many other nineteenth-century women who ultimately married.[9] Mary might make sly jokes about the opposite sex and insist that she was not the marrying kind, but she would not have filled her letters with talk of love and marriage, as she did, if she did not take a romantic interest in men. There is no evidence that Mary Telfair ever received a proposal of marriage. Nor is it likely that she ever went out of her way to seek one. She had too much pride and self-esteem to play the coquette or to use feminine wiles in an attempt to snare a husband. Her refinement and reserve would not allow it. Marriage was not a necessity for Mary Telfair. She could function quite well in the single state. It is likely, however, that she would have found greater satisfaction and fulfillment in a happy, companionate marriage than in her life as a spinster, and that in her heart she knew it.

Mary Telfair and Mary Few became best friends during their school days in New York. They maintained a close and loving relationship that lasted a lifetime and kept up a correspondence that was warm and intimate. In her letters to Mary Few, Mary Telfair found emotional release. There was no one to whom she could pour out her affection more freely. Much has been written of the "romantic friendships" that existed between women, including married women, during the eighteenth and nineteenth centuries. It has been posited that it was virtually impossible to study the correspondence of any nineteenth-century woman and not uncover a passionate commitment to another woman at some time in her life. There also are innumerable fictional accounts of such female love relationships, all without any hint that they might be considered abnormal or even unusual. Intimacies and expressions of love between females that to the twenty-first-century mind would be considered erotic were not viewed as such in a pre-Freudian age.[10]

Mary Telfair's story does not end with her death. The Telfair will contest was one of the epic legal battles of the late nineteenth century, and no book about Mary Telfair would be complete without an examination of the struggle to thwart her testamentary intent that continued for eight years and was resolved only by a decision by the Supreme Court of the United States. It is an extraordinary tale. At one point a jury held Mary Telfair's will invalid on the ground that she had been a monomaniac on the subject of her great-niece Alberta Wetter and Alberta's children. The judge set aside the finding, but the lawyers fought on, raising every possible legal challenge from conflicts of interest on the part of the witnesses to the rule against perpetuities. It is a tale, however, with a happy ending for those who benefitted from Telfair's charitable bequests.

In writing this book I have quoted from a number of sources, including the letters of Mary Telfair. These letters, taken together, constitute a unique expression of a nineteenth-century female point of view and an enlightening record of female experience in the context of the American urban elite. I have quoted extensively from Telfair's letters because I believe that her story is best told in her own words. All of the nuances are there, and her character and wit come through most clearly when we read her thoughts as expressed through the medium of her own pen. Moreover, Mary Telfair's own words are the best evidence of her keen intelligence. Mary learned to spell at Miss Dow's school in New York, and she learned to do so quite well. On the few occasions when she erred, I have made the necessary corrections in order to avoid the intrusive "[sic]." Archaic spellings such as "shew" have been retained. As adept as she was at spelling, Mary Telfair was impossible when it came to punctuation. I have added some commas and semicolons and have broken sentences in two where essential to clarify the meaning of the text.

I first came to know Mary Telfair when my friend John Luck asked me, in his capacity as president of the Telfair Museum of Art, if I would write a history of the museum. I am grateful to John for getting me started on an endeavor that has resulted in this biography of that fascinating nineteenth-century woman who made the museum possible. My thanks also go out to Dr. Diane Lesko, the executive director of the Telfair Museum of Art, for her unfailing encouragement and support. This book could not have been written without the resources of the Georgia Historical Society, that vital organization serving the public throughout the state under the able direction of Dr. W. Todd Groce. I spent many hours pouring over documents at the Historical Society's library at Hodgson Hall in Savannah, a building erected as a memorial to the husband of Mary Telfair's sister Margaret. The staff at Hodgson Hall never failed to provide assistance with enthusiasm and good cheer. I also appreciate the help provided by the staffs of the Georgia Department of History and Archives in Atlanta, the Special Collections Library at Duke University, and the New-York Historical Society as well as the wonderful professionals at the Telfair Academy of Arts and Sciences. I am grateful to Professor Nancy White of Armstrong Atlantic State University for allowing me to audit her course on nineteenth-century women as I sought to gain insights into the world of Mary Telfair. I owe a particular debt of gratitude to my friend, historian Christine Jacobson Carter, who read my manuscript and made valuable suggestions. I am also grateful for the suggestions of Dr. George Fenwick Jones, who likewise read the manuscript from beginning to end. My thanks go to Deric Beil for his keen editorial eye. My wife, Chris, as always, has been a source of inspiration. I thank her for her patience and love and especially for her willingness to make room for another woman in my life, albeit one who has been gone from this earth for over a century.

Savannah, Georgia
June 2002

I

The Legacy

People will not look forward to posterity who never look backward to their ancestors.

Edmund Burke, *Reflections on the Revolution in France* (1790)

On June 1, 1875, shortly before 10:00 A.M., General Alexander R. Lawton, a senior member of the law firm of Jackson, Lawton & Basinger, arrived in his carriage at the stately Regency-style mansion on Savannah's St. James Square that was the home of Mary Telfair. He climbed the eight steps to the portico, knocked, and was admitted by a servant. Mary Telfair was seriously ill, and he had come to supervise and witness the execution of her last will and testament. Lawton, at age fifty-six, was a much admired member of the Georgia bar. He had recently completed a term in the Georgia General Assembly as a representative of Chatham County and was now concentrating on his law practice. He was pleased to have as a client one of the wealthiest women in the city, but in the tight society of upper-class Savannah, Mary Telfair was a friend as well as a client, and he feared that the end might be in sight for this grand lady. Lawton was familiar enough with death. He had seen some of the best young men in his brigade struck down in Virginia in the Second Manassas Campaign. He had faced his own death when his horse was shot from under him in the bloody Battle of Antietam and he himself was severely wounded. Lawton hoped and prayed that Mary Telfair would be spared, but he knew that it was important for her to execute her will promptly lest her illness prove to be as serious as he feared.[1]

Mary Telfair was advanced in years (she was eighty-four), but she had been quite chipper until just recently. She had been well enough to attend church the preceding Sunday. But now she was confined to her bed. Three days earlier she had realized that she was not feeling at all well. Her physician, Dr. James B. Read, was called in the following day. Dr. Read was a distinguished member of the medical profession, professor of materia medica and dean of the faculty at the Savannah Medical College. He had been Mary Telfair's physician for about two years. During this time he had been called in occasionally for slight ailments. He generally stayed for an hour on each visit, for he enjoyed his conversations with his patient and found her to be a most entertaining lady with a fine mind. This, however, was the first time that he had seen her in two months. He examined her carefully and did not find her condition to be serious. The following day she took a turn for the worse, however, and Dr. Read examined her once again. This time he found cause for alarm. She had developed pneumonia. The doctor called on her five times that day. He prescribed a mild dose of anodynes to ease her cough. He advised her that she was very ill. "If you have any arrangements to make, you had better make them," he suggested as gently as he could.

Mary Telfair appreciated the importance of keeping her affairs in order and of assuring that her substantial estate would be disposed of in accordance with her wishes as they might evolve over time. She had never married and thus had no children of her own to whom she might leave her wealth. One of her brothers had died in infancy, and another at the age of sixteen. The three that reached maturity, Josiah, Thomas, and Alexander, had died years before, leaving no descendants bearing the Telfair name. Her sisters, Sarah (Mrs. George Haig) and Margaret (Mrs. William Brown Hodgson), had predeceased her as well. As neither had a surviving child, Mary inherited their estates. Alberta Wetter, the granddaughter of Mary's beloved brother Thomas, had caused her great pain as a result of her disgraceful behavior in eloping at the age of thirteen with a man beneath her station, divorcing him, and then marrying the German immigrant Augustus P. Wetter. Mary Telfair could never understand how a girl with Telfair blood could have lowered herself to such an extent. It was mortifying. Alberta had died in 1866, and Telfair had no intention of doing anything substantial for her children. Indeed, she barely knew them.

2

In April 1874 Telfair had signed a will that General Lawton had prepared for her, but by early 1875 she had decided on additional bequests and other revisions. She arranged for an interview with Lawton and advised him that it was her wish that a codicil be made to her existing will. She had with her memoranda that she had prepared setting forth the changes that she desired. Lawton did not like the idea of drawing up a codicil to the will. "It will append badly," he told her. "All the changes of property made to different persons will appear." It would be better to draw up a new will. It would be just as easy to do so. Telfair accepted her lawyer's advice and instructed him to go ahead and prepare the document.

General Lawton proceeded to draft a new will for his client using the 1874 will as a base. The changes that he made were taken from the memoranda that Mary Telfair had left with him. One memorandum provided for a modest trust for the education and support of the two daughters of Alberta Wetter. Their father, Augustus P. Wetter, had once been one of the wealthiest men in Savannah, but had recently fallen on hard times. Mary Telfair's friend and cousin George Noble Jones had persuaded her to make some provision for the girls. She agreed to do so, but made it clear to her lawyer that she wished to be entirely sure that their father would have no control over the corpus or income of the trust or be able to reach it in any way. She made no provision for the girls' brother, Edward Telfair Wetter, for reasons known only to herself. A second brother, Conrad, had died in 1874 from drinking contaminated water from an old well while on a hunting expedition.

It was the middle of May before General Lawton completed drafting the revised will. At that time he turned over the draft to his client so that she could read it through and make sure that it met with her approval. As she read over the document, written in Lawton's strong hand, Mary Telfair could see that he had followed her instructions. The will provided that several parcels of real estate in Savannah would go to George Noble Jones. He was the grandson of her mother's sister and Dr. George Jones and was the son of Noble Wimberly Jones II, her first cousin, who had died in 1818. There were gifts of cash and railroad shares to cousins and friends, including her cousin Mary E. Thompson and Mrs. Thompson's niece and adopted daughter, Margaret Ewing Ritchie. Mrs. Thompson and Miss Ritchie had been staying at the Telfair residence for some time and were devoted to the old lady. They both were descended from William Telfair, the brother of Mary Telfair's father. Mary Telfair specifically requested in her will that Mrs. Thompson stay on in the mansion after her death to assort and arrange the furniture and other articles of value. There was a gift of twenty-five shares of railroad stock to Mary Telfair's "faithful colored servant George." George always was at hand whenever she needed him, and she wished to remember him in her will.

Mary Telfair had decided that the bulk of her estate was to go to charity. There was a devise of a commercial building to the Independent Presbyterian Church, where she and her family had worshiped for so many years and whose spire she could see from her bedroom window. General Lawton had followed her instructions and had clearly specified that this gift was made upon the condition that the church trustees would never authorize any material alteration to the pulpit or galleries of the church. The gift was made upon the further condition that they would keep in good order and thoroughly clean up each spring and autumn the Telfair burial plot in Bonaventure Cemetery and that no one else would ever be interred in the vault or within the enclosure. The last thing that Mary Telfair wanted was for the remains of Augusta Wetter or her children to be buried with the Telfairs. There was a bequest to the Presbyterian church on Telfair Street in Augusta, a street named for her father. There were gifts of land to the Union Society and the Widows Society for the benefit of their charitable causes.

It was very important to Mary Telfair that her home on St. James Square never again be used as a private residence. She certainly did not want any of the Wetter children living there. It was equally important to her that the memory of the Telfair name be preserved. She was the last of her family to bear the name, and she knew that the only way that it could be carried forward was through her charitable bequests. To this end she decided to leave the mansion in trust to the Georgia Historical Society, together with her books, furniture, and works of art, upon the stipulation that it be maintained as a "Library and Academy of Arts and Sciences" open for the use of the public. The will, as drafted by General Lawton, also provided for a bequest to the Georgia Historical Society, in trust, of 1,000 shares of capital stock of the Augusta and Savannah Railroad Company to provide income for the repair and maintenance of the mansion and the management and care of the academy that Mary Telfair wished to establish. To assure that the family name be given the recognition that Mary Telfair believed it deserved, the will clearly stated that the devise of the mansion to the Georgia Historical Society was made upon the express condition that the Society, as trustee, "cause to be placed and kept over and against the front porch or entrance . . . a marble slab or tablet, on which shall be cut or engraved the following words, to-wit:—

Telfair
Academy of Arts and Sciences,

the word 'Telfair' being in larger letters and occupying a separate line above the other words." General Lawton had graphically shown in the will how the engraved tablet was to appear, so that there could be no question as to the prominence to be given the name of Telfair.

The bequest to the Georgia Historical Society of the Telfair mansion and its contents for the purpose of creating the Telfair Academy of Arts and Sciences was no dying whim on the part of Mary Telfair. Some ten or twelve years before, Mary's sister Margaret had told a friend, Margaret E. Harden, in Mary's presence, that their dwelling always had been used by their family as a home, and that they did not wish other persons to live in it after their death, but desired it to be used as an art gallery or something of that kind. In June 1866 Mary Telfair had executed a codicil to a then existing will in which she stipulated that, should she survive Margaret (her sister Sarah Haig had died in 1845), the lot and residence left to her and her sisters by their brother Alexander, and her paintings and statuary within the house, were to go to the Historical Society on the condition that it would be a "Public Edifice" and be used only for a "Library, Academy of Art, and Museum." She stipulated in that codicil that a marble tablet was to be placed on the front of the building inscribed with the words "The Telfair Institute." Telfair's testamentary intent in 1866 with respect to her residence was quite similar to that expressed in the will that she signed in 1874 as well as in the new will that General Lawton had prepared for her.

The limitations that Mary Telfair wished to impose on the use of the building in 1866 also were similar to those set forth in her last will and testament. In 1866 she wrote, "I require that no music, dancing, public speaking, public meetings, nor exhibitions of any sort be

5

permitted within its walls, neither can it become the private residence of any Person or Persons." The 1875 will stipulated that "no part of the buildings shall ever be occupied as a private residence or rented out for money, and none but a janitor and such other persons as may be employed to manage and take care of the premises shall occupy or reside in or upon the same, and that no part of the same shall be used for public meetings or exhibitions, or for eating, drinking, or smoking."

The residue of the estate was to be used to establish and endow in Savannah a hospital for sick and indigent females. The will went so far as to name the initial "Directresses" of the institution. To further honor the family name, it provided that the hospital was to be chartered as the "Telfair Hospital for Females."

After reviewing the document prepared by General Lawton, Mary Telfair remembered that there was a little village called Telfairville that she had completely forgotten. It had been named for her father and was near the site of his old sawmill in Burke County. Just as she had made provision for the church on the street in Augusta named for her father, so too she wished to make a bequest to the church in the village that bore his name. She asked General Lawton if it was too late to make a change, and he assured her that it was not. He took the last two pages of the will back to his office to make the necessary revisions and to add the attestation clause that he had not as yet prepared. He left the other pages with his client. As revised, this would be the document that Mary Telfair would sign on the morning of June 1, 1875. As General Lawton later recalled, never before had he drawn a will where such exactness was given and required by the testatrix.

Upon his arrival at the residence on the morning of June 1, Lawton mounted the stairs to the second floor and entered Mary's bedroom at the front of the house. The old lady was propped up in bed with pillows behind her back. She was perfectly at ease. After exchanging pleasantries, General Lawton said that all was in readiness to have the will executed. Telfair called for a servant and asked for the small tin box in which she kept her important papers. She had stashed away there the pages of the will that General Lawton had left with her. The lawyer had with him the final pages on which he had added the bequest to the church in Telfairville. The document that General Lawton had prepared for Mary Telfair's signature was written on 8½-by-14-inch legal foolscap, the same type of lined, wide-margined paper used by lawyers today. General Lawton was not one to engage in waste. By writing on both sides of all but one sheet, he would use but eight sheets of paper for the fifteen pages of writing that set forth Mary Telfair's testamentary intent.

Lawton looked over the sheets of paper that Mary Telfair extracted from her little box. He found that they were indeed the pages of the will that he had prepared. "You know all about this; it is not necessary for me to read it over," he assured his client, not wishing to put her to any unnecessary trouble or strain. "I prefer—I *prefer* to hear it all," was her response, as full of starch as ever. Sitting up in bed with one hand cupped behind her ear in order to hear better, Mary Telfair listened intently as Lawton read the document aloud. She was still as sharp as a tack. She interrupted the reading occasionally to question the meaning of a clause. When Telfair was satisfied that her will was as she wished it to be, Lawton said that he would call in the witnesses. He placed a small desk on his client's lap and laid there the pages of the will.

General Lawton had arranged for Dr. Read to be one of the three subscribing witnesses. When he had received Telfair's approval of the document, but for the addition of the clause relating to the Telfairville church, she had been perfectly well. Upon learning that she had taken ill, Lawton inquired of Dr. Read as to her condition and was assured that she was entirely capable of making a will. "Won't you be a witness to the will?" he asked the doctor. Dr. Read replied, "I will, but had you not better be a witness yourself?" After his visit with Dr. Read, General Lawton went to the office of William Neyle Habersham, who, along with William Hunter, was named as an executor of the will. Neyle Habersham's father, Robert Habersham, had been designated as sole executor in wills executed by Mary Telfair during his lifetime, and it was quite natural that his son would be her choice after he succeeded his late father as her principal business and financial advisor. William Hunter was a prominent Savannah businessman and civic leader. He came from one of the city's leading families. Mary Telfair knew that he was the kind of man who could be trusted to work well with Neyle Habersham in administering her estate. Upon arriving at Habersham's office, Lawton asked William J. Marshall, Habersham's bookkeeper, to be the third witness. Lawton chose Marshall because the young man knew something of Mary Telfair's business affairs. Marshall agreed to be at the Telfair residence at ten the following morning. General Lawton thought that this would be an appropriate hour as his client might be a bit drowsy earlier in the day.

When summoned, Dr. Read and Mr. Marshall entered Mary Telfair's bedroom. It was then about 11:00 A.M. General Lawton presented Mr. Marshall to his client as she did not know him well. She wished him a good morning. Then, referring to Dr. Read, Mr. Marshall, and himself, General Lawton asked Mary Telfair, "Do you desire these three to be witnesses to your will?" Looking at the three men, she nodded and replied, "I do wish them." One can picture General Lawton as he leaned over the old lady's shoulder gently pointing out where she should place her name for identification in the margin of each sheet of paper on which the will was written. Dr. Read was standing nearby, and when he saw that she was not in a position to write with ease, he pulled up a chair and, sitting beside her, held her propped up in a comfortable position. When Telfair finished signing each page for identification, General Lawton showed her where to place her name at the end of the will and how to make the mark that would constitute her legal seal. In a hand that displayed her illness, Mary Telfair did as instructed. After doing so, she held up the will and noticed that she had not dotted the "i" in Telfair. Lawton was about to take the document from her hand, but she held on and placed a dot over the letter before releasing it. Lawton later noted that this little incident "almost produced a smile." Then, in the time-honored words of the attestation clause, "in her presence and at her request and in the presence of each other," first General Lawton, then Dr. Read, and finally Mr. Marshall signed their names as witnesses to the last will and testament of Mary Telfair. According to General Lawton, everything that the lady said and did with respect to the execution of her will was conducted with "the greatest coolness and exactness."[2]

After the gentlemen had taken their leave, Mary Telfair could close her eyes and contemplate what she had accomplished that morning. If her condition was as serious as Dr. Read seemed to think, she would soon be going on to a better world. She had done all that she could to assure that the Telfair name would be remembered. This was of crucial importance to her. With its wealth, political power, and colonial roots, her family had been part of that genuine, if small, aristocracy that existed in the low country from Charleston to Savannah, a world of "silver and carriages and courtliness and manner."[3] The name Telfair was every bit as distinguished in Georgia as the name Bulloch, Clay, Habersham, Houstoun, or Jones. Hers was a proud heritage deserving to be honored. Other women of her class felt much the same way. For example, her close friend Sarah Cecil could trace her lineage to English nobility. Through her father, Leonard Cecil of Burleigh Hall, Wilmington Island Plantation, Sarah Cecil was a direct descendent of William Cecil, who as Lord Burghley was secretary of state and lord treasurer to Elizabeth I, and of his younger son and political heir, the hunchback Robert Cecil, who as earl of Salisbury became lord treasurer in 1608. Family membership defined a Southern woman's place in the world, and if one's family was of the aristocracy it was a matter of considerable pride.[4]

Mary Telfair had good reason to take pride in her family, and especially in the achievements of her father, Edward Telfair, a patriot in the revolutionary struggle against Great Britain, a member of the Sons of Liberty, a delegate to the Continental Congress, and governor of the state of Georgia. Although she was only sixteen when her father died in September 1807, Mary knew much of his background and his illustrious career. Edward Telfair was one of the many Scotsmen who settled in Georgia in the eighteenth century. He had been born in 1735 on his family's ancestral estate in southwestern Scotland near Kirkcudbright, a village located on an estuary of the River Dee some six miles north of its junction with the Solway Firth. The Telfairs were Scottish lairds, landowners of substance with strong family pride. Young Edward Telfair attended a grammar school and then was employed by a firm of merchants. In 1758, when he was in his early twenties, he set sail for the English colonies with his brother William and a cousin. Edward first settled in Virginia, where he represented the Scottish firm that employed him, then moved to North Carolina, and finally joined William in Savannah in 1766. He formed a partnership with his brother and with Basil Cowper, another Scotsman, and became one of the most successful merchants in colonial Georgia. He also acquired substantial holdings of land in Christ Church Parish (later Chatham County) and elsewhere in the Savannah River basin. In time he became the principal owner of land in Burke County in the area along the Savannah River near the present town of Waynesboro. He was a planter, as well as a merchant, and as such the owner of many slaves. He also had a water-driven sawmill in Burke County, which was supplied from his vast holdings of timberland.

Two years after his arrival in Savannah, Edward Telfair entered into the political life of the Georgia colony. In 1768 he was elected to the Commons House of Assembly as a delegate from St. Paul Parish, where he owned land. During 1774 and 1775 he attended the meetings at the tavern in Savannah operated by Peter Tondee and his wife, Lucy Mouse, at which efforts were made to compel Great Britain to show proper respect for the people of Georgia. Edward Telfair was slow in advocating independence. He was a British subject and merely sought to have his fellow Georgians afforded the full rights of citizenship. He was a member of the Provincial Congress, which met in Savannah in January 1775, and joined with other members to form an association designed to curtail Great Britain's economic hold on Georgia by means of nonimportation, nonconsumption, and nonexportation agreements.

In May 1775, when news of the battles of Lexington and Concord reached Savannah, Edward Telfair joined with Noble Wimberly Jones, Joseph Habersham, John Milledge, and other Liberty Boys in breaking into the royal magazine and making off with six hundred pounds of powder. Telfair was named in June 1775 to the Council of Safety, a body formed to supervise the enforcement of boycotts and to seek solutions to the growing crisis between the colony and the Crown. One of his acts as a member of the council was the removal of the Reverend Haddon Smith from the pulpit of Christ Church for refusing to participate in a day of prayer and fasting declared by the Continental Congress.

Outright rebellion by the more radical members of the independence movement occurred in January 1776, when Joseph Habersham and a small group of revolutionaries arrested Royal Governor James Wright and held him prisoner at his home for a month until his escape to a British ship anchored at the mouth of the Savannah River. This brought to an end for a time the king's authority in the Georgia colony. Then came the Declaration of Independence on July 4. This was a difficult time for Edward Telfair. His brother William resolved to remain loyal to the king and later moved from the colony, leaving his property in Edward's care to be reclaimed when peace was restored. Edward's other business partner, Basil Cowper, also chose loyalty to the king over independence. Edward may have wavered, but in the end he remained committed to the cause of freedom and performed valuable services throughout the war. His partnership with Cowper was severed.

Telfair was elected to the Continental Congress in 1778 and was reappointed each year until 1785, when he decided that the state of his health and the severe winter climate in the North precluded him from serving any longer. While in Congress, he was one of Georgia's signers of the Articles of Confederation. In July 1780 a bill of attainder was passed naming certain rebels against the Crown who were declared guilty of high treason and were barred from ever afterwards holding any office of trust, honor, or profit in Georgia. Edward Telfair, as a member of the rebel Congress, was among those named.[5]

Mary Telfair's lineage was equally distinguished on her mother's side of the family. Her mother was a Gibbons. The Gibbons family was one of the most prominent in the Georgia colony and extremely wealthy. Its roots went deep into the soil of the South. Mary's grandfather, William Gibbons, had been born at Bear Bluff in South Carolina in 1726, some seven years before James Oglethorpe first sailed up the Savannah River. He married Sarah Martin in November 1752. Their daughter Sarah (she was called Sally) and Edward Telfair were married on May 18, 1774, a time when revolutionary fervor was at its height in Savannah and Edward was deeply involved in the controversy. Edward was almost forty when he married; and his bride, a girl of sixteen, was more than twenty years his junior. The wedding took place at Sharon, the plantation owned by Sarah's mother some five or six miles out the Louisville Road in Newington Village. Sarah's father was not there to witness the happy event. He had died four years earlier.[6]

The couple's hopes of beginning a family were dashed in the year after their marriage when their first-born, a little girl named for her mother, died in the same month as her birth. It would be five years before Edward and Sarah would have another child. Edward Jr. was born in South Carolina on March 13, 1780, while his father was serving in the Continental Congress. William, born in Philadelphia in 1782, died in the year following his birth. Three sons were born in succession: Josiah on June 24, 1784, Thomas on March 2, 1786, and Alexander on January 25, 1789, the year that the Paris mob stormed the Bastille and President Washington began his first term in office.[7] The three younger sons, unlike Edward, who died in his teens, would live to become men of considerable prominence. Mary Telfair could take comfort as she lay in her sickbed that in honoring the Telfair name she would be honoring the memory of her beloved brothers as well as her father.

Edward Telfair maintained cordial relations with his wife's brothers and cousins. William Gibbons, the son of Sarah's uncle Joseph Gibbons, had been a member of the Sons of Liberty and had participated with Edward Telfair in the raid on the British powder magazine. He went on to become one of the leading lawyers in Georgia. He was made an associate justice of Chatham County in 1786 and was named speaker of the Georgia House of Representatives the following year. He was president of the convention that devised the new Georgia Constitution of 1789. General Nathanael Greene died from sunstroke incurred while taking a walk on the rice dikes on Gibbons' plantation. William Gibbons' brother Thomas was another outstanding Georgia lawyer. He served for a time as mayor of Savannah. Born in 1757, Thomas Gibbons had been a Tory during the war. After the British defeat, he was banished from the colony and his estates were confiscated, but he stubbornly fought back and regained his position and lands on the ground that he had used his status as an influential Tory to relieve the suffering of the patriots in Savannah. Thomas' father had been granted a thousand-acre pine-barren tract by King George II, and this land was incorporated by Thomas into his 2,820-acre plantation later known as Fair Lawn and still later as Whitehall. Whitehall Plantation became famous as one of Chatham County's greatest agricultural units in the nineteenth century.[8] In later years Thomas Gibbons would be a party to one of the most famous cases in the history of constitutional law.[9] Mary Telfair's relationship to such towering figures as William and Thomas Gibbons did much to cement her position as one of the country's elite.

Sarah Telfair's brothers were considerably younger than her husband, as was she. William Gibbons, Jr., the eldest son of William Gibbons and Sarah Martin, had been born in 1754. Not to be confused with his cousin of the same name, he devoted his time to his plantations. His principal holding was the Beach Forest Plantation in Chatham County adjacent to Sharon. Edward Telfair's two other brothers-in-law were even younger. Joseph Gibbons had been born in 1766, the year that Edward Telfair settled in Savannah. He pursued a career as a lawyer and lived and practiced in Liberty County. Barack

Gibbons was born three years after Joseph. He too became a planter and inherited the Sharon Plantation.[10]

Mary's extended family had been important to her, and she had always taken pleasure in her relationship with the Joneses, the descendants of Noble Jones, who came to America aboard the *Anne* with General Oglethorpe, and his son Noble Wimberly Jones, her father's fellow Liberty Boy, friend, and physician. Dr. George Jones, the son of Noble Wimberly Jones, was married to Mary Gibbons, Mary Telfair's aunt, who was known to her friends as Polly. Dr. Jones was a physician, but most of his life was spent in public office serving the city of Savannah and the state of Georgia. He belonged to a generation younger than that of his distinguished brother-in-law Edward Telfair. His marriage to Polly Gibbons joined together two of Georgia's most prominent families. The first child of George and Mary Jones died in infancy. Noble Wimberly Jones II was born on January 2, 1787. He would become Alexander Telfair's closest friend, and his son George Noble Jones, who was born in 1811, would always be a help and comfort to the Telfair family. Sarah Gibbons Jones, who married Alfred Cuthbert, was born in 1789 and was a lifelong friend of Mary Telfair. Mary never really knew her Aunt Polly for she died in 1792 while Mary was still an infant.[11]

As much as Mary Telfair took pride in her father's role in the Revolution, she knew that his greatest contribution had been his service as governor of Georgia. Edward Telfair was first elected to the governor's chair by the legislature in 1786 and again for two-year terms in 1790 and 1792. In May 1791 President Washington visited Georgia. When Washington came to Augusta, which was then the state capital, Governor Telfair, George Walton (then attorney general), and most of the principal men of the city officially greeted the President on the road four miles outside of town and escorted him to the capital. That afternoon Governor and Mrs. Telfair entertained the President at an elegant dinner at the Grove, their residence at the eastern edge of town. There Washington admired the "many well dressed ladies." Mrs. Telfair was the hostess at a ball at Richmond Academy that evening, which the President attended.[12] Mary knew that events such as this had added luster to the Telfair name.

Throughout her lifetime Mary Telfair had maintained a deep attachment to her colonial and revolutionary heritage. She revered the great men of the past who, like her father, had been responsible for the creation of the American Republic. She had experienced a sense of sadness one spring day when she and her sister Margaret were looking over some old papers and came upon a letter to their father from Patrick Henry. She thought that it "combined so much talent, integrity and enthusiasm." She mused that all of the "high toned in character" had passed away. There was no longer anyone around to compare to the great men of the past. "I have always found," she wrote, "that the truly great in real life seize upon the imagination with a stronger hold than all the fine spun characters of romance."[13]

As Mary Telfair lay in her familiar room attempting to suppress her cough, she could take satisfaction in the full life that she had made for herself. There had been sorrows and disappointments to be sure. Her brothers had died too young. She would have loved to have had a child of her own. Her two nieces and her great-niece could never fill the void. She would carry to her grave her distress over Alberta's scandalous behavior. Then there had been that frightful war that took the lives of so many gallant young men and left the South in a state of subjugation. But there had been compensations. There had been her wonderful friends—Mary Few, whom she loved above all others; the other Few girls, Frances and Matilda; Anne Clay, a woman of strength, independence, and intellect; Catharine Hunter, whose marriage to Jones Bulloch had been a disaster; and Eliza Terrell, a dear friend in later life. There had been her sisters, her closest companions. It had taken some getting used to, but she was pleased that Margaret had found happiness in her marriage to William Brown Hodgson. He had enriched her own life as well.

There were so many wonderful memories to balance against the sorrows. There was the blissful childhood as a schoolgirl with Mary Few. There was her first view of the Hudson River. There were the early-morning fogs that rolled in from the sea at Newport. There were the four trips to Europe—the canals of Venice, the French Alps, the paintings at the Uffizi, the Paris Exposition of 1855. How she had delighted in tracing the footsteps of the poets, statesmen, and heroes of the past.

Books had filled Mary's life. She was proud that she had always kept her mind active and was grateful to God that she still retained her faculties. "I never expect to reach what is termed old age," she once wrote, "but if it should be the will of Providence to protract my days I hope the mental infirmities of age will not seize me with their ruthless grasp."[14] Her hope had been realized.

Mary Telfair's strong Christian faith had prepared her well for this day. "I think that the afflictions & cares & vexations of this life would sit very lightly upon us," she once wrote, "if we could constantly realize that this is not our home and that we are rapidly passing on to 'a City that hath foundations eternal in the Heavens.'" Throughout her lifetime she frequently returned to the theme that her real home was not in this world but in the world beyond:

> If we did not frequently meditate upon our own short & un-certain existence here, and realize our connection with the world of Spirits, we could not under some trials bear the burthen of existence. Every thing here seems dark & mysterious—there is no resting place for the affections upon Earth and yet how prone are we to expect comfort from the creature. We need con-tinued admonitions to remind us that this is is not our Home and that perishable is inscribed upon all terrestrial objects.[15]

According to family lore, the Telfairs bore a mythic relationship to Taillifer the minstrel, a hero of the Norman Conquest. During the Battle of Hastings in 1066, in the first of several decisive cavalry charges leading to the death of Harold of England, the young min-strel, singing all the while in Latin the stirring battle songs of Char-lemagne and Roland and tossing his sword in the air with one hand and catching it in the other as he rode into the fray, was mortally wounded on the field of battle. William, the duke of Normandy called the Conqueror, who witnessed his prowess and courage, knighted Taillifer as he lay dying. His last words, "Je suis pret" ("I am ready"), became the Telfair family motto.[16] Like the legendary minstrel, Mary Telfair was ready. Mrs. Catherine Few, the mother of the Few sisters, had written in Mary's commonplace book when Mary was a young woman that there was no peace but in the enjoyment of God's love here and in the anticipation of everlasting blessedness in His pres-ence above, where there is "fullness of joy."[17] Mary believed this, and she was ready to move on. She died the following morning.

2

Building Minds
for the Republic

Studies serve for delight, for ornament, and for ability.
Francis Bacon, *Essays* (1625)

On January 28, 1791, in the seventeenth year of her parents' marriage, Mary Telfair was born at the Grove, the family's residence in Augusta. Her father was serving his second term as governor and in a few short months would be entertaining George Washington during the President's trip through the South. At the time that their baby sister entered the family, the four Telfair boys were of an age marked by rough games and scraped knees. Edward was ten, Josiah six, and Thomas four. Alexander had just celebrated his third birthday. Now that a baby girl was in the nursery, the boys would have to be more subdued in their behavior. Another sister, Sarah, was born the following year, on September 28. With four older brothers and a father who expected nothing but the best of his children, Mary and Sarah would learn early in life to assert themselves in a male-dominated world.

Mary's childhood was not unlike that of other young girls of her class. As the daughter of a wealthy merchant-planter and political leader, she lacked for nothing. Looking back upon her early years, she recalled that "the promptitude with which my wants were satisfied prevented me from expressing them." It was a childhood of ordinary pleasures. Mary and her sister often would frolic in the garden at the Grove and swing under the clustering grape vines that grew there. When in Savannah, the girls would occasionally be taken to play with their little friend Ann Wallace, who lived in Montgomery, a community on the Vernon River twelve miles from town. Mary remembered playing there on the village green and had fond memories of a childhood tea party at the Wallace home: "I remember Sarah & myself playing *Mams* with Mary McLeod at a little table—our Hostess handed us some tea in tiny cups of pewter—it was cold water, brown sugar & milk—Sarah spit hers out. I *swallowed mine*—my ruling passion the fear of offending being strong even in childhood."[1]

Colonel William Few was a dominant figure in the lives of the Telfair children. He was one of Governor Telfair's closest friends, and his family became a second family for Mary Telfair. Few was a Marylander by birth and a Georgian by adoption, an upcountry Georgian who settled in the area close to Augusta. During the British occupation of Savannah, he and his brother Benjamin Few were leaders of the Richmond County militia that conducted partisan attacks against the enemy in the Georgia-Carolina back country. After holding a number of political posts, he was chosen as one of the six Georgia delegates to the Constitutional Convention that first met in Philadelphia in May 1787. He was there on opening day and remained throughout most of the long hot summer's debate. Although faithful in his attendance and in recording his votes, he was one of the few delegates who did not rise to speak on the floor of the convention. He and Abraham Baldwin were the two Georgians who signed the federal Constitution. William Few and James Gunn were the first United States senators from Georgia. Colonel Few was described as tall, slender, and erect. His demeanor was said to be grave and dignified. In 1786, at the age of thirty-eight, he married Catherine ("Kitty") Nicholson, a young lady of twenty-two. Kitty was from New York and was the daughter of Commodore James Nicholson, who had the first command in the United States Navy. Few at the time was serving in the Congress in New York. Kitty would give birth to three daughters, all of whom became fast friends of the Telfair girls.

During most of the 1790's, William Few and his family lived at Hesperia, his plantation in the Georgia upcountry. He was a member of the Georgia legislature that declared null and void the fraudulent Yazoo Act. In 1796 Few offered himself again as a candidate for appointment to the United States Senate, this time to fill the vacancy caused by the resignation of James Jackson. His rejection by the legislature was the greatest humiliation of his political life. He accepted a judicial appointment, which he held for three years. In 1799 Few moved with his family to New York, where he pursued a successful career as a lawyer and banker. For several years he served in the New York State Assembly. He was a director of the Bank of Manhattan from 1804 to 1814 and was the president of the National City Bank from 1814 to 1816, the second person to hold that office. He also was president of the Bank for Savings in the City of New York. The Fews "moved in the higher and more polished ranks of society," as Mrs. Few's obituary would state many years later.[2]

Grief came to the Telfair family on January 18, 1797, when Edward Jr. died. He was only sixteen. His sister Mary was six at the time. It was the second time that Mary had seen death strike her family. Her mother had given birth to a stillborn son three years earlier. Young Edward's last illness and death must have been particularly hard on his mother, for at the time she was seven months pregnant with a baby girl whom she would name Margaret. Edward's obituary referred to him as an "amiable youth," who "beheld, with the firmest Christian fortitude and resignation, the slow and gradual approaches of his dissolution." There was little more that could be written of the death of a person so young except that it had "deprived his country of the hope of so promising an ornament of society." He simply had not been given the time to live up to his potential. He was buried in the family vault at the Sharon Plantation.[3]

Edward Telfair was determined to have his children receive the best education available. He and his friends had helped to create a new nation, and he believed that the future of his country depended upon well-trained young men committed to public service, men such as his three surviving sons. The governor also was concerned with the education of his daughters. The importance of female education was repeatedly emphasized in the new Republican Age. The ideal republican woman was an independent thinker and patriot, a virtuous wife, competent household manager, and knowledgeable mother; and improved academic training was necessary for this ideal to be realized. While members of the previous generation of women, if they were so fortunate, had received advanced training only in such ornamental accomplishments as music, dancing, French, and fancy needlework, republican girls from middle class and well-to-do families could attend schools at which they were taught grammar, rhetoric, history, geography, mathematics, and some of the natural sciences. They would form the first generation of educated female Americans.[4] Mary Telfair would be among their number.

The College of New Jersey, as Princeton was then officially named, was the college of choice for young gentlemen from the South, so it was quite natural that Josiah and Thomas Telfair would be sent there. Colonel Few kept an eye on the Telfair boys while they pursued their studies in the North and from time to time would issue reports to their father. After one short visit to the governor's sons at Princeton, he reported that Josiah was very well, but "Tommy was a little indisposed—he had taken cold and had been afflicted with a cough and a spitting of Blood, but was getting better." The young men promised to visit the Fews during vacation time.[5]

There were female academies and qualified schoolmasters in Georgia at the turn of the century, but Governor Telfair was not satisfied to have his eldest daughter educated in Savannah. As his son Thomas would write of the governor, "He holds Savannah rather unhealthy in the mental qualities."[6] Mary's father decided that she should attend school in the North, and when the time came he turned to William Few for advice. As far as Colonel Few was concerned, there was no school for Mary but Miss Dow's classes, the academy in New York that his two older daughters attended. He so advised his friend in July 1801 as the ten-year-old girl was about to sail for New York with her brother Alexander. Colonel Few informed the governor that Miss Dow was a young lady from Scotland of the most polished manners and finished education, that she employed masters to teach the various branches of education that she could not attend to herself, and that she would take girls to board with her or otherwise as the parents chose. He acknowledged that the tuition at Miss Dow's was quite high and that there were other respectable schools for girls in New York that were far less expensive, but he felt that Miss Dow's school was well worth the price. He assured Governor Telfair that "this school is sanctioned by the upper class of citizens." He explained that Miss Dow taught her classes near his home in the Village of Greenwich during the summer "for the better security of health" and in the winter moved the school to the city. Colonel Few offered to have Mary stay at his home should the governor choose to have her attend Miss Dow's school: "If you should incline to send little Mary, Mrs. Few will be happy in paying her due attention. She can stay with us during the summer, where we have the best prospects of health, and attend the school with great convenience." Alexander and Mary left Savannah in July 1801 and arrived safely in New York in good health after a sea voyage of seven days.[7]

The New York at which the Telfair youngsters disembarked was a far different place than their native Savannah. The population of the city stood at sixty thousand, and the city was busy, bustling, and noisy. Carriages drove through roads as deep in sand in Savannah, but in New York there were paved streets and sidewalks. The houses were packed close together, and everyone seemed to be in a hurry. The city was confined to the tip of Manhattan Island. It extended from the Battery about a mile up the Hudson River and two miles along the East River. Broadway, aptly named, ran up the spine of the island and turned into a farm lane when it reached the country. The web of cross streets with names such as Maiden Lane and Pine, Wall, Beaver, and Pearl streets went in every direction, in contrast to the neat grid pattern of Savannah that had been laid out by General Oglethorpe and his surveyor Noble Jones. Wharves lined the waterfront along the Hudson and East rivers. Alexander and Mary must have gasped with astonishment as they walked down the gangway from their ship. The two young people were taken immediately to the Fews's spacious home in the Village of Greenwich. Greenwich Village at the time was a community of wood-frame houses on tree-lined mud streets just to the north of the city. The road that led out to Greenwich ran along the Hudson River. On the other side of the island was the highway to Boston. The Boston road could be reached from Greenwich by way of a sandy cross-island track that ran through the countryside.[8]

Alexander and Mary were welcomed most warmly into the Few household. "I am extremely pleased with Alexander," Colonel Few told the boy's father, "he is one of the finest best behaved boys I have seen." Alexander left shortly for the preparatory school that he was to attend in Princeton. In Savannah he had been tutored by a Mr. Davis, and this was to be his first experience boarding away from home. His two older brothers were at Princeton attending college, so he would not be alone. Colonel Few wrote to the governor concerning the arrangements that had been made:

Alexander stayed with me a few days and has gone to Princeton, as Dr. Jones [Alexander's uncle] is not going that way until towards the last of the summer I thought it was best to send him with Mr. Ralph Clay [the fifth-born son of Joseph Clay and Ann Legarderé Clay]. I have wrote to Josiah and enclosed him fifty Dollars to make the necessary arrangements for tuition, accommodations &c, with instructions to render me an account of the expenditure, and call on me for Cash when necessary. I have opened an Acct. with you and have given you Credit for Cash received 300 Dollars, and will occasionally render you accounts of the disbursements which will enable you to judge of the supplies necessary. Be assured the business will give me no trouble, but on the contrary it will afford me real pleasure to render you, or the dear little ones any service.[9]

Governor Telfair was insistent that Alexander learn French, but beyond that he had not given Colonel Few any guidance as to the course of study that he wished his youngest son to pursue. Few had some ideas of his own and put them into effect pending any contrary advice from the governor. He tried to lead his friend into sharing his own views as to how Alexander's education should be structured:

I wish you had been a little more explicit respecting Alexander's education; you have only desired that he may enter Academy, and attend to French; but as a boy cannot pursue his studies to the best advantage by only attending to one branch at a time, I have advised him to appropriate some part of his time to Reading, Writing & Cyphering, until we hear from you. If it is your intention to educate him for a Merchant, perhaps it will not be necessary to make him go through that irksome and laborious business of learning the dead Languages; but if it is your intention to give him a complete Classical education, he must begin with the Latin Grammar & that language being obtained the other languages are more easily acquired, and such is the method, or routine of education, that the French is generally taught towards the last.[10]

Colonel Few continued to urge Mary's father to have her study under Miss Dow. "We have not yet made any arrangements relative to her schooling," Few advised the governor upon Mary's arrival in New York, "but think it will be best to send her to Miss Dow the Tutress I mentioned to you in my last—it is true her terms are very high but it is generally believed there is not a more respectable or better school for young ladies in the United States." In any event Miss Dow's school would begin an eight-week vacation in August, so Mary would not be able to matriculate until the first of October. Colonel Few proposed that Mary enter as a day scholar and continue to live with his family. In the meantime Mrs. Few would see to it that she attended to her writing, drawing, and music along with the Fews's little girls. Colonel Few made arrangements for music lessons during the summer. A music master lived next door to the Fews, and Colonel Few employed him to give lessons to the girls twice a week for seventy-five cents per lesson. The two little Marys were about equally advanced in music, and Few was certain that they would stimulate each other in their efforts and would show rapid improvement.[11]

Mary entered Miss Dow's school in the fall. The Fews's daughters, Frances (sometimes called "Fan" or "Fanny") and Mary (sometimes called "Molly"), joined her there. Frances Few was two years older than Mary Telfair and Mary Few a year older. According to their mother, Fanny was "remarkably giddy" though sweet in temper, and Mary was the mildest child she had ever seen and "one of the most thoughtful & grave." They were bright little girls. Fanny had learned to read and Mary to spell words of four syllables before they had ever gone to school. They both had lively imaginations. While still living in Georgia, they would take imaginary trips to New York and pretend to be their grandma or one of their aunts. Frances and Mary Few, and later their younger sister Matilda, became Mary Telfair's close friends. They remained staunch friends throughout their lifetimes, and Mary Telfair and Mary Few developed a special relationship that was intensely close and meaningful to both of them. The Fews were pleased to have Mary with them. Writing to the governor, Colonel Few said that "dear little Mary seems to be one of the most amiable and lovely little girls." "Already she has gained the esteem and affection of the family," he assured her father. "She is beloved as a sister by our little Girls, and Mrs. Few and myself feel a Parental regard for her."[12]

In later years Mary would remember the first school that she attended "where it was customary for the pupil who misspelt a word to give place to the superior Orthographer and go down one lower." Mary did well in her schoolwork relying more upon natural quickness and memory than serious study. She remembered how she and Mary Few would meet on Saturday evenings at Greenwich Gate to talk over the "weekly troubles" at Miss Dow's. She liked to think back on the times spent with Mary Few in the room on the third floor of the Few house and the "soul enlivening" conversations that she shared there with her "philosophic friend." The spot before the garret window, out of which the two girls gazed and dreamed their "airy visions," was to Mary Telfair a place "consecrated to sober sentiment as well as elevated mirth." She could become a bit carried away when sharing with Mary Few her memories of that "halcyon period" when "the heart promised what the fancy drew." She remembered their own special garret window: "Cowper celebrated a Sofa, Gay a Fan and why should not *we* (who to be sure are geniuses of a lesser order) do justice to a *window?*—particularly as the *prospect* from it was so rich, so variegated, so full of all that could *fascinate* the eye alas!"[13]

The two Marys had wonderful conversations whenever they were together as schoolgirls. Years later, in 1819, Mary Telfair reminded Mary Few of a conversation firmly implanted in her memory:

> Do you remember the walk we took at Morristown on our way to Schooleys Mountain when we seated ourselves on a timber to watch the reapers scythe and enjoy the scenery that surrounded us. I believe the conversation of that hour is more firmly impressed upon my memory than any we ever had—you complained of feeling too old, and I of feeling too young—the effect upon us was directly opposite, it inspired you with gloom, and I with gaity. Since that period I seem to have passed over twenty years of my life, so very different does every object in the world appear to what it formerly did.[14]

Mary also would remember the "childish sport" engaged in with the Few sisters and the days spent walking with Mary Few in the woods of Richmond Hill, singing of "over the hills and far away" and "laying plans for futurity which *alas!* have never been realized."[15] These woods, "which witnessed our sports," were to Mary "Childhood's Eden bower." She remembered her rivalry with Mary Few in "the art of sliding upon the roof of the ice house at Richmond Hill." She thought back on how her friend had laughed at her plight when she fell over a fence eluding "the Cow with the crumpled horn." The girls were somewhat impish in those days, tomboys of a sort. Mary Telfair remembered Mary Few as her "Hoyden companion at Richmond Hill." The two Marys were not above engaging in pranks. Mary

Telfair remembered the "terror and remorse" she felt when she and Mary Few stole some forbidden fruit from a little peach tree that Colonel Few had carefully cultivated. Mary had felt "like Mother Eve" every time she passed beneath the tree, and finally the two girls succumbed to temptation and decided to pluck a peach. They stood "petrified with astonishment" when a limb came down along with the fruit.[16]

Mary Few's young cousin, Ignatius Few, who also was studying in New York and would go on to serve as a Methodist minister in Savannah, delighted in tormenting Mary Telfair while she was living with the Fews. In retaliation, Mary ran over his foot with a wheelbarrow, and the "Ruffian Boy" beat her for the act. "I believe it was the first and only hostile act I ever committed," Mary wrote years later, "and elicited the only *banging* I ever received." Despite her banging, Mary Telfair always would look back at her years as a schoolgirl as the happiest period of her life, and she and Mary Few agreed that their happiest days were those "spent among the shades of Richmond Hill."[17]

While Mary Telfair was enjoying her happy days as a schoolgirl and thriving in her studies, her father was becoming increasingly dissatisfied with the academy that Alexander was attending in Princeton. It did not have the best reputation in Savannah. In January 1802, when Colonel Few recommended that Alexander transfer to an academy closer to New York, the governor readily agreed. For one thing, he preferred to have Alexander near to Mary. "You will see her once every week at least," he instructed the boy. When advised that he was to transfer to Bergen Academy, Alexander may have protested that he liked it in Princeton, for his father wrote to him, "The sooner that you qualify yourself for College the sooner you will return to Princeton."[18]

In April 1802 Colonel Few wrote to Governor Telfair from New York to say that Mary and the boys were well, that Josiah and Thomas would set out for Princeton in the next day or so to resume their studies at college, and that Alexander would leave the following day for Bergen Academy. Mrs. Few, he wrote, "intends to send Mary to New Ark [Newark Academy] the first of May." Bergen Academy was a relatively new school, but the governor did not consider this to be a disadvantage. "I hope that your exertions will be great," he wrote to Alexander. "The institution of which you are a member being new, and your tutor little known at Princeton, will I flatter myself act as a spur on your part. I make no doubt of the Bergen Academy rearing into reputation and that its Rector will send forward young men that will do him credit."[19]

Shortly after Alexander's arrival at Bergen Academy, his father (in a letter carried to New Jersey by cousin Thomas Gibbons) wrote to inquire how his studies were progressing:

> I hope that you are settled at Bergen to your satisfaction and that your application to your studies will be such as will enable you before very long to return to Princeton to enter College. I do not expect this from you in a few months. Much will depend on application. You will soon be a big Boy. It is not tutors that can force the elements of the language. It arises in a great measure out of the student from two sources, genius and application. If a Boy be even deficient in the former it may be acquired by the latter.

The governor requested an immediate reply to his letter giving details as to the number of tutors and the manner of teaching at the academy. He closed by reminding Alexander that he must learn French, whether it be at Bergen Academy or in college.[20]

In 1802 Mary Telfair was studying French under the tutelage of M. Francis T. Berier, professor of the French tongue, as well as attending to her studies at Newark Academy. Her mathematics exercise book bearing the date 1803 indicates that during that school year she was struggling with such problems as "How many minutes since the commencement of the Christian Era allowing it to be 1792 years?" Another problem that she was able to solve with ease was "If from Dublin to Cork be 101 miles I demand How many Barley Corns will reach between the two Places allowing 3 Barley Corns to make an inch." Her father was pleased with the regularity with which she wrote home to her parents. As for Josiah, he wrote home only when he needed money.[21]

Governor Telfair did his best to impress upon his boys the value of a dollar. He was wealthy to be sure, but he was not about to raise his sons to be spendthrifts. Before Alexander entered Bergen Academy, his father advised him, "Col. Few will advance for Pocket Money one Dollar per month. This sum will be as much as will be of use to you." Alexander assured his father that he would curtail his expenses as much as possible, "so not to appear extravagant on the one hand— nor niggardly on the other but to keep a mediocrity." The governor required of his sons a strict accounting of their expenditures. He believed it to be good discipline.[22]

As frequently as Governor Telfair would instruct his sons in financial matters, he would never speak or write to his daughters of anything as crass as money or business. These matters lay outside the sphere of female concerns. Mary would remember in later years a teacher at her school in Newark who asked her if her father was a planter. Such was her ignorance of her father's affairs that she replied, "I do not know." "In fact," she recalled, "children knew no calculation then but what their sums in arithmetic taught them & Parents never talked before them of money, crops, and Bank stock."[23]

Edward Telfair could be as pompous and condescending as Lord Chesterfield in writing to his sons. "Take care when you read that you understand and do know what you read," he wrote to Alexander shortly after the boy first entered school in the North. "Fast reading without understanding what you do read will not carry you within the walls of College." On another occasion he urged, "Above all take care to read Books of instruction & morality." In his view novels were a waste of time.[24] Mary was undoubtedly influenced by her father's opinions on matters literary for throughout her lifetime books of religious instruction and morality dominated her reading and, but for the tales of Sir Walter Scott, which she found irresistible, she read little fiction.

Telfair advised his sons to avoid going in debt, advice that Alexander would ignore. The governor could be hard on his sons. One particularly harsh letter was written to Alexander from Savannah the July following his entering Bergen Academy:

> I received a scrawl from you dated at New York said to be a letter. In it you mention your studies. They appear to me to be outdoor ones, for certain it is that you are losing fast what you acquired here. You wrote correct far more so than either of your Brothers. What then can be the cause of your falling back in your English. If you do not attend a bit more to it you will make a poor figure with your Latin. Perhaps your mind is at times engaged in speaking and writing French. This you ought to do—you are not to enter College until you are master of French. You have no doubt tutors at hand. You are not to be left to your own choice in this regard. If your old master Davis

were to see your Letter with the following words as they stand in your pretty epistle: *herd, fruite, duch, Bred, handkershiefs*, what would he say to it.

As demanding as Edward Telfair could be with the boys, there were times when a gentle tone would creep into his letters. Alexander must have yearned for home when he read these words penned by his father: "Your Colt is a fine one, and you and Tom have one each of the present year."[25]

Upon his graduation from the College of New Jersey in 1803, Josiah Telfair turned to the study of law in Savannah. The governor was as insistent that his sons pursue a profession as he was that they study French. After Josiah spent six months reading law, his brother Thomas thought him better prepared for practice than half the lawyers in the city. He intended, however, to study for another year and in 1804 was attending lectures at the Litchfield Law School, that distinguished institution in Northwestern Connecticut founded in 1784 by Tapping Reeve. Reeve himself was a graduate of the College of New Jersey (class of 1763), and many of his students came to him from Princeton. His was the first law school in the United States, and for many years it would have no equal. Aaron Burr had been a student there, and in later years it would number among its alumni John C. Calhoun and Horace Mann.[26]

Josiah's real love was the soil. His father had presented him with 1,500 acres of land in Columbia County, and it was there that he liked to spend his time, determined to make a success of his own plantation. He did, however, return to Princeton to receive a master of arts degree in 1806.[27]

Alexander joined Thomas at Princeton for the 1804 fall term, which began in August. He was only fourteen. He had taken the entrance examination, had passed, and was now a Princeton man. The college that the Telfair boys attended had been chartered in 1746 by King George II. It had been founded by Presbyterian divines who were members of the "New Light" faction of the Calvinist faith, followers of the evangelist George Whitefield, who felt the need for a college for the training of young men for the ministry in the Middle Colonies. The college was permanently established in the village of Princeton in 1756 after the construction of Nassau Hall. By the time the Telfairs arrived at Princeton, the undergraduate population was no longer dominated by students of theology. Only a handful of pious young men destined for the ministry were being graduated each year. Instead, the college had become a place for the sons of wealthy planters and merchants.[28]

Young men from some of the leading families in Georgia were at Princeton with the Telfair boys. Some of them would go on to achieve prominence in the state and on the national stage. Alfred Cuthbert, who would become a United States senator despite his eccentricities and would marry the Telfairs' cousin, Sarah Jones, was in the class of 1803 with Josiah Telfair. His younger brother, John A. Cuthbert, who achieved equal prominence in later years, was a member of the class of 1805, along with Thomas Telfair. The Cuthbert boys were the sons of Colonel Seth John Cuthbert, a soldier of the Revolution, and grandsons on their mother's side of Joseph Clay, who had once been Edward Telfair's business partner. Richard Wylly Habersham was another of Thomas Telfair's classmates. A son of the patriot and financier of the rebellion James Habersham, he became a lawyer of some renown and was elected to the twenty-sixth and twenty-seventh congresses. The Telfairs' first cousin, Noble Wimberly Jones II, was in the class of 1804. Another boy from Savannah, James Moore Wayne, was a year behind Alexander in the class of 1808. Wayne was appointed an associate justice of the United States Supreme Court by President Andrew Jackson in 1834 and would serve on the Court for over thirty years.[29]

Governor and Mrs. Telfair and the three girls passed the summer of 1805 in Savannah. The governor commented that this was the first summer that the family had spent in the lower country for the past twenty-one years. There was much sickness in the city, but the family remained well. It was mid-September, and Thomas would be leaving Princeton in a few days. Alexander would continue his studies there without the company of his brother. Edward Telfair was coming to sound more and more like Polonius as he poured out advice to his youngest son:

As your mind expands write on various Subjects taking special care that before you commit to paper that you have for your guide a studious attention to the subject on which you comment. Without this be done you will make a poor figure on paper. From what I can learn you may acquit yourself with some degree of Credit as a Speaker. Oratory alone will do but little without the groundwork is well supported in *science*. Without this the mind will be barren and the imagination weak.[30]

Thomas returned to Savannah after his commencement exercises in the fall of 1805. He would spend the winter there. "Savannah is more gay this winter than it has been for many past," he wrote to Alexander in January 1806. "Balls in profusion, I went to three in one week." The young ladies of Savannah had their eyes on the Telfair men. Thomas reported to Alexander that one appeared to be out to capture Josiah: "Josiah is at present up the country at a place of his. He has been there one week & we do not expect him down for one week yet. Miss Cpl. delays giving a ball until his return. How does that look?" Alexander had asked Thomas to describe "the characters of those who move in the fashionable sphere of Savannah." Thomas replied, with a smile as he wrote, that this would be an impossible task:

> Some there are I was about to say who have no character at all, others the features of whose characters are so inexpressive, so void of variety that it would puzzle the acuteness of Plutarch properly to define them. At the same time it must be confessed that others there are who unite intelligence of mind with elegance of manners. You seem to wish a particular description of S.C. but indeed she has made so slight an impression upon my fancy that in endeavoring to paint her to you I should be too mechanical & artificial, entirely deficient in nature & accuracy. However this one general remark I can make, that I am able to discern but a very slight difference either in the manners or appearance of Southern girls from the Northern, except that the first are more fond of dress & shew.[31]

During his winter in Savannah, Thomas spent some time in the courts taking in the eloquence of the leading lawyers of the day. Governor Telfair wished to have him study law in Virginia, and he was inclined to do so for his father had promised him a substantial allowance if he did.[32] Instead, Thomas began the study of law at the Litchfield Law School, the same law school attended by his brother Josiah.

By 1806 the pressure to excel that Edward Telfair was placing on Alexander seems to have caused a serious strain in their relationship.

Alexander must have flinched when he read these words from a disappointed father:

> Some months have elapsed since I have had a line from you. I begin to see that you are doing but little for yourself. The idle talk of Boys appears to be gaining ground fast upon you. Letters & Science will be neglected, and without a speedy change, you will at a future day lament a waste of time. When with Davis [the Savannah tutor] your hand writing was good. You could *spell*. What are your letters to such of the Family as you write to. They are without arrangement, scrawls without meaning, dashed off without reflection and form, a composition of nonsense & absurdities.[33]

The seventeen-year-old college student continued to receive the same old admonitions from his father:

> You are approaching to that period when you are to leave College. Under this impression ought not then your mind be devoted to study and when your Paper, Pen & Ink are before you and when you are about Letter writing pause a little and be circumspect in every word that you commit to paper. Let not the mind be shackled with trifling matters. Draw forth the powers of the mind on a large scale. Think of the subject well before that you place any part of it on paper. By this means you may acquire a style in Letter writing. Your Pen ought to be considered as your chief *Weapon* in this regard. To write well and correct can only be done by writing much. Quires of paper will be a profitable measure.

Governor Telfair demanded an immediate response from his son listing the books that he was reading and informing him of the time spent each day in composition.[34] Alexander did not respond. A month later, his father, deeply upset, penned a short note to his son accusing him of "indolence & neglect." The governor did evidence some understanding of his son's position: "It is a difficult time of life, the one that you have arrived at. It is between the Man & the Boy, looking up to the former at the same time conducting yourself with the folly of the latter."[35]

Alexander finally answered. Although his letter has not survived, he must have explained politely to his father that there were just so many hours in a day. If he were to spend as much time as the governor expected on composition, reading history, and studying French, there would be no time left for his studies. He had not been neglecting his college courses, and indeed he was doing quite well with them. Governor Telfair's reply indicates that he was somewhat chastened by his son's response:

> I take up my pen to make a few remarks on your late Letter to me. I do not mean to draw from your labours as a student in College or to rebuke on the score of neglect. If you continue to do as you have done for the year to come you may take your farewell of College perhaps with some credit to yourself. I say by doing this you may be able at some future period in life to distinguish yourself in the service of your Country.[36]

Alexander's father still thought that he should learn French. He even was willing to have his son forego the reading of history to do so:

> I have exercised my pen to your Brothers whilst they were in College to set apart some portion of their time to obtain some knowledge of French. I failed, and they will feel the loss of it. Would it not be more ornamental to the mind to acquire French than reading Books that any Rice or Cotton Planter can read at his chimney corner after the arrangements of the day are brought to a close. Let me enjoin you to set apart the reading, *even useful history,* whilst in College and apply your surplus hours to the Study of French.[37]

Governor Telfair, for the first time, tried to explain to his son why he placed so much importance on the study of a foreign language. The old Liberty Boy who had worked so hard for the cause of freedom wished his country to develop a national character of its own, one separate and apart from that of the country of which it had once been a colony. A more cosmopolitan outlook on the part of its citizens would go far in this respect:

> On the acquirement of our independence and upon the formation of State & National Governments I had reason to believe that our American Seminaries would have made some variation from the Old School. For as matters now stand the young mind of the American & English are one & the same. This position in my mind may in time prove fatal to the liberties

of America. Our National characteristic ought not to be held as the offspring of any Nation. It ought to be selected from the *Many* of such as have materials to conform with the genius and spirit of our Government. Few if any of such materials can be drawn from what is said to be the Constitution of England.[38]

As the time approached for Alexander to graduate from college, his father worried about his future. He urged Alexander to plan for a career in a learned profession and offered any required financial aid:

> You are arrived at that stage of things as to enable you to reflect and think a little for yourself. In a work of this nature any aid that I can afford will not be withheld. Delicacy on the present call forbids any interference on my part. After a College Education a profession must follow for future support. To it you must look forward. Make your election and I will contribute toward its acquirement. My mind will be relieved on this score as soon as you communicate your choice to me.

In a letter transmitted a few weeks later, enclosing a draft for $250, "your last supply in College," Governor Telfair pressed the issue: "After your farewell you will no doubt incline to be a few weeks here to visit the family and your friends here. After which you must take a fresh departure in quest of a profession."[39]

In the meantime Thomas Telfair was pursuing his studies in Litchfield. The work was hard. It was time consuming. But in November 1806 Thomas did find time to spend four or five days in New Milford "not without a little dissipation" followed by "that depression which naturally succeeds a great deal of amusement."[40] In April 1807 he wrote to Alexander at Princeton apologizing for his inability to find the time to ghostwrite a proper speech for his brother to deliver. Thomas was considered an accomplished orator, and his younger brother had turned to him for help. But Thomas simply did not have the time. His plan was to return to Savannah in the fall, and there was so much to do in the meantime. He explained his position to his brother:

> I have resolved upon returning in the fall unless my Father objects, & from my Mother's letter I am inclined to believe that his objections will be feeble—Now from calculation I find that in order to take with me a complete course of lectures I shall be under the necessity of writing between 12 & 14 pages a day,

besides reading that portion of Law which probity assigns me. Now after performing this I have but little time; this little I have hitherto devoted to the study of history & N. philosophy, but now I must be swallowed up in Law for upon the return of a Student from this place he is supposed to have Law at his fingers end.[41]

Part of Thomas Telfair's education came from exchanging with his father opinions on national and international affairs. In corresponding with the governor, he knew that he had best think a matter through carefully before venturing an opinion. Writing from law school of the outrageous boarding of the frigate *Chesapeake* by the British, Thomas exhibited the flair with words that would stand by him in his later political career. In July 1807 he wrote to his father:

> Being so much nearer the seat of action than I am, you no doubt have long before this heard of the insolent outrage, which one of his Britannic Majesty's ships of war has committed upon an armed vessel of the U. States—The heroic conduct and noble spirit which the Virginians have exhibited on this occasion exhibits an honorable proof that the heaven born spirit, which gave life & vigor to the Worthier of '76 still animates the breasts of their Sons.

It seemed, Thomas felt, that Britain still viewed the United States as a colony. "What can impel this misguided Nation to hazard a war with America?" he wondered, particularly while "France is perpetually holding over her the sword of destruction—while Bonaparte is constantly exhibiting to Europe the melancholy sight of prostrate Kings." He went on to speculate: "It seems possible (but I spurn the idea while I suggest it) it is possible that her conduct arises from a supreme ignorance of America—England may still think, as she once thought, that with a handful of men, she could quietly take possession of our Country."

Thomas was convinced that war with England was imminent, and if it should come, he was prepared to forego his recently made plan to study in New York and "bear a portion of the burden of War." He believed that war was "replete with evils" for the nation. In particular, he felt that war was inconsistent with liberty for "the mind accustomed to obey the supreme command of a General will not always be able to distinguish between civil liberty & oppression." Thomas assured his father that "with such ideas as these, which I believe are correspondent with your own, I have heretofore been an enemy to War." At some point, however, the line must be drawn:

> But repeated insults will rouse to anger & resentment the most torpid or philosophical mind—the American Citizens have shown themselves too wise to plunge head long into an unnecessary War—But when roused by a repetition of injuries, they will shew to the World that the Wrath of a free and offended people is terrible as the thunder of heaven.[42]

The old governor must have been proud of the wisdom and eloquence of the son who perhaps was most like himself. If only Alexander would show the same good sense. He was delighted to discover that Alexander's outrage over British infamy was equal to that of his brother. His own outrage knew no bounds:

> I have a letter of you of the 12th [illegible] and am pleased to observe the indignation that you express on the brutal & infamous attack on the Chesapeake Frigate by the British King's Ship of War the Leopard in sight of our Coast. When we were reposing in the bosom of peace the arrows of war were piercing the hearts of our Fellow Citizens. This atrocious and malignant crime is calculated to excite the warmest sentiments of hatred and contempt to a Nation whose ambition and views are and for many years past have been to reduce the people of these United States to their ancient line with that Nation.[43]

Alexander's final months at Princeton were months of personal turmoil. He had fallen into debt, despite his father's warnings, and he found it necessary to call upon Thomas for help. In a letter written in late June 1807 Thomas expressed sympathy for his brother's plight: "I am sorry for your sake, for the 4th of July is an unpleasant season to find a Princetonian out of pocket." What was worse for Alexander was that his father was constantly on his back. He refused to let up for a minute. The old man's letters were filled with lectures on the evils of dissipation and demands that his son choose a profession. Alexander's emotions were in a confused state as well, for he believed that he had fallen in love with a girl much older than himself. "Pretty fellow" was his brother Thomas' comment upon hearing the news.[44]

Most disturbing of all was the student rebellion at Princeton in the spring of 1807. The suspension of three students from the college for various offenses, including "cursing and insulting some of the peaceable and orderly inhabitants of the town," led to a student petition in protest that included the signature of Alexander Telfair. The rules of the college expressly prohibited "combinations" challenging the authority of the faculty and the trustees, and the president of the college announced that those who did not withdraw their names from the offensive document would be suspended as well. Alexander was one of the students who marched from the prayer hall shouting and yelling, and he and the others were suspended. Following the events from Litchfield, Thomas Telfair was disgusted with the lack of backbone on the part of those students who capitulated. With biting sarcasm, he let his brother know how he felt:

> I suppose the heroes of '76 were but pygmies in comparison with those of the College. For the first two or three days after the College was dissolved no doubt more heroes stalked the Streets of Princeton than in Paris after the memorable Revolution of France—but now without any great effort of fancy I can see them moping about with broken spirits & relenting hearts.[45]

Alexander wrestled with himself over whether his honor would permit him to reenter college and graduate with his class. By late April he had pretty much made up his mind not to do so on the terms set down by the faculty. The governor intervened. He wrote to his son in June: "I have at length seen the Petitions of the Students and have only to regret that your name is to it. The composition is small and weak, it breathes little of matter & less of Science. If your name not be expunged from it I trust that you will apply to the Faculty for permission to do it." Alexander must have found a way to submit without violating his honor as a Southern gentleman, for he did graduate with his class the following September.[46]

There is no hard evidence to indicate how long Mary Telfair continued at school in the North. There is some indication that her sister Margaret may have continued her education at Newark Academy under the watchful eyes of the Fews until she was seventeen. A reference to her in an October, 28, 1814, letter from Mary Telfair to Mary Few hints of a schoolgirl recently returned home from the North: "Margaret has improved very much, she appears to be very

35

amiable and well informed for her age. She is very fond of you & talks incessantly of the whole family. Accept our grateful thanks for the attention extended her by every individual that bears the name of Few."[47] Among the Telfair papers is a vade mecum or, "Friendly Remembrancer," presented to Margaret by the Reverend Timothy Alden upon her graduation from Newark Academy.[48] It is dated 5 October, but the year has been intentionally obliterated, perhaps in later years by Margaret herself for the purpose of destroying evidence of her age. There is no documentary evidence relating to Sarah Telfair's education. One thing that is certain is that the formal education of the Telfair girls did not go beyond Newark Academy, for there were no colleges for women at that time. The first college chartered to confer degrees upon women, the Georgia Female College in Macon, afterwards known as Wesleyan College, did not open until 1839; and Mount Holyoke, in Massachusetts, an academy offering courses equivalent to those offered by the men's colleges, did not come into being until 1837.

Although Mary Telfair did not enjoy the advantages of a college education, her academic interests never flagged. In the fall of 1808, a year after Alexander was graduated from the College of New Jersey, Mary was in Princeton at the commencement exercises at Nassau Hall listening to the orations by the candidates for degrees. Frances Few was in town at the same time on her way to spend the winter in Washington as the guest of the Gallatins and was disappointed that her friend was too engrossed in the academic exercises to spend time with her.[49] As much as she liked to trade jokes with Frances, for Mary Telfair the life of the mind took precedence.

3

The Torch Is Passed

The old order changeth, yielding place to the new.
Alfred, Lord Tennyson, "The Passing of
Arthur," in *Idylls of the King* (1869)

Governor Edward Telfair died on September 17, 1807. According to
the Chatham County Register of Deaths, he died at his Savannah
town house of "Old Age, etc." after a two-day illness. A few months
before, he had written in a reflective mood to his son Alexander: "It
has been my endeavor to do everything in my power for my Children. I am aged and must soon return to my Father who sent me
here. In the interim I shall persist in doing them all the good that I
possibly can." On balance, he had done very well. The governor's
wife and children were not at his bedside when the end came. Mrs.
Telfair and her daughters were still in the upcountry, and Josiah as
usual was at his plantation. Alexander was in Princeton about to
attend his commencement exercises, and Thomas had come down
from Litchfield to New York with plans to go on to Princeton for
the ceremonies.[1]

Governor Telfair's body, attended by a large body of citizens, was
taken to the Colonial Cemetery in Savannah, where church services
and military honors were performed over it. One can only hope that
those who attended the body carried out the direction in a codicil to
the governor's will that "my remains be placed in a rough wooden
coffin with common nails in it, with black crape only for such as may
incline to mourn." The body then was taken to the family vault at the

Sharon Plantation. In the year of Governor Telfair's death, Telfair County was created and named in his honor. Years later, the governor's remains would be removed to Bonaventure Cemetery, where in 1860 his surviving daughters had erected a fine monument to the memory of one of Georgia's most prominent citizens.[2]

With the governor gone, it was incumbent upon his sons to carry on the family business. In his simple will, written in his own hand, Edward Telfair left his entire estate to his wife and six surviving sons and daughters, "one seventh part to each." The executors named in the will were his brothers-in-law, William Gibbons, Jr., and Barack Gibbons. In a codicil to his will he appointed as executors, in addition to those already named, his three sons as each of them reached the age of twenty-one.[3] Josiah and Thomas were already of age at the time of their father's death; and Josiah, as the elder, took the lead in managing the estate. There was plenty for Alexander to do as well, and no further thought was given to his late father's wish that he pursue a learned profession.

As ships of the Royal Navy continued to violate American territorial waters and impress American seamen, the threat of war with Great Britain hung over Savannah. In April 1808 Thomas Telfair helped organize the Georgia Foresters, a volunteer infantry company based in Savannah. He was commissioned an ensign in the new company, and the following year he was promoted to the rank of lieutenant.[4] The Telfair brothers, like other young men of their generation, felt strongly their duty to defend their country. Their father had impressed upon them the obligation that they owed to the memory of those heroes of the Revolution who had fallen in the fight for liberty. The old patriot had expressed his feelings eloquently in a letter to Alexander written shortly before his death:

> It may come to the turn or tour of duty of the Young Americans to exchange English Powder & Pomatum for Powder & Balls. Their Fathers have left them a valuable inheritance, one superior to Gold or to Silver. This gift handed down to them was acquired with the blood & loss of nearly one hundred thousand men to acquire our independence. The present times will probably bring us to the test. It is the duty of one and all to contribute to maintain and defend our National Sovereignty that it may be handed to posterity unimpaired.[5]

had been scalped. She was not happy with President Madison's conduct of the war. She thought that his approach was lacking in energy. She wrote to Mary Few that she wished that she were a man "possessing talents either for the cabinet or the field" for "I think I should be very active." She was so critical of the administration that Alexander laughingly accused her of harboring Federal sentiments.[10]

In the spring of 1813 ships of the Royal Navy based in Bermuda undertook a raid on Norfolk, Virginia. An American battery on Craney Island held off the landing force and sank the barge of Admiral Warren, the commander of the fleet. The second in command, Rear Admiral Sir George Cockburn, retaliated by devastating the country around Hampton, sailed up the Chesapeake Bay, and raided Havre de Grace. It was generally thought that Savannah would be next. Mary Telfair, writing to Mary Few, said that "the Women receiving a general lesson by the attack on Hampton are all removing into the Country while their Fathers, Brothers & Husbands are determined on wielding their swords in defense of their City should their fears be realized." She reported hearing a few days earlier a "heavy cannonading" from "that quarter where Beaufort lies." She also advised her friend that her brother Josiah had "a fine troop of Horse ready for action whenever the governor chooses to accept his services." Alexander too was serving in the ranks of the Savannah Heavy Artillery.[11]

The war stirred martial passions in Mary Telfair. She admired the great heroes of the war: General William Henry Harrison, the victor of Tippecanoe, and General Zebulon M. Pike, the great explorer who lost his life in a powder explosion while advancing with his troops against the city of York in upper Canada. "I feel as if I could idolize Harrison and venerate the memory of Pike," she wrote. She despaired of the apathy of the women in Georgia with respect to the war. As much as she would have liked to have joined in the fight, she recognized her own timidity:

> Among my numerous *female* acquaintances I find none who enter into the feelings which at present occupy my breast. I know not whether it is the case in the North but the southern Ladies are so much engrossed by *domestic concerns* that they seldom think and talk of their Country and except with my Brothers I can never give scope to "*the unruly member*" and exercise it on *politics*, however yours and Frances's letters are a never failing

treat, and whenever I read them I wish we *were all three men,* that we might fight our country's battles, say Molly how would you like to be a General and have your old friend for an aid. I would promise never to *desert,* or let you *surrender to an inferior force.* But as a woman I am the verriest coward in existence and tremble at the sight of a wasp, how then could I brave the cannon's roar, or the savage yell. I believe I should have to serve my Country in the Cabinet instead of the field, notwithstanding my predilection for the latter.[12]

Alarming news reached Savannah in January 1814. The British had landed two thousand black troops on Cumberland Island. In all probability they were "maroons," slaves who had escaped from the United States. The people of Savannah feared that an attack by the British was imminent. Mary expected the worst. "It is reasonable to expect," she wrote, "that Savannah the emporium of the State will not escape." She noted that "the inhuman Cockburn" was in command and expressed the belief that "everything is to be dreaded for no doubt a number of slaves will flock to his standard." She felt that the Southern states were in a more perilous position than the Northern ones, but took some comfort in the fact that her family had an upland retreat. But yet she realized that "lives which we hold as dear as our own will be exposed." She could not bear to think of it.[13]

Mary Telfair was intrigued by Napoleon. His reign as emperor of France and the Napoleonic Wars had filled the news during her teenage years. Mary had followed with interest Napoleon's campaigns in Europe. She found that he had just the romantic touch that appealed to her. Napoleon was forced to retreat from a deserted Moscow in October 1812, and when his forces were defeated by the allied armies a year later at the Battle of Leipzig, his grand empire collapsed almost overnight. On March 14, 1814, the allies entered Paris, and Napoleon, who was a few miles away at Fontainebleau, agreed to abdicate. The French Senate decreed the restoration of the Bourbon line in the person of Louis XVIII, brother of the unfortunate Louis XVI, who had lost his head on the guillotine in 1793. The deposed emperor was granted a pension of two million francs per year and sovereignty over the little island of Elba, near his native Corsica in the Tyrrhenian Sea. Mary Telfair shared with Mary Few her bemused surprise at this turn of events:

You are such an able Politician . . . that I am almost deterred from expressing my opinion on the late revolution in Europe, scarcely can it be realized, my sympathy for Bonaparte is not half as great as it would have been had his reign been less brilliant but more virtuous, but I cannot at all reconcile the idea of such a conqueror submitting so quietly to his fate and receiving a pension from the very family on whose ruin he rose, do not think me immoral when I say he ought to have followed the example of Cato; it is better to die gloriously than live *meanly*. What an asylum does the Island of Elba afford to one long accustomed to the splendors of a court and the din of arms; his mind must be as much tortured in retirement as the Body of a victim extended on the rack.

Mary thought it "unwomanlike" of the Austrian Archduchess Marie-Louise to have abandoned her husband in his time of distress, particularly as he had "reposed so much confidence in her and treated her so much as his equal (a thing by the by very rare with *great* men)." Mary guessed, however, that "there exists but little affection among crowned heads." They are, she supposed, "the mere creatures of ambition or interest."[14]

Mary speculated on the effect that Napoleon's abdication might have on the prospects for peace with England:

I hope my dear Mary the olive will be extended to us, but I very much fear Great Britain will be more unwilling than ever *now* to accede to our terms and should she remain inflexible what a long and dreadful war this will be the thought of it makes me shudder, still I cannot bear that our national honor should receive a stigma by yielding to her.[15]

Napoleon, of course, would return to have another go at conquest, only to be defeated by Wellington at Waterloo on June 18, 1815. He would then be imprisoned on the lonely island of Saint Helena in the South Atlantic, where he would spend the rest of his days.

An invasion of Savannah by the British was expected at any hour in the fall of 1814, and there was nothing but confusion in the city. Fortifications were progressing too slowly, and Mary observed a lack of public spirit. She despaired over the lack of leadership in local government and had no confidence in the mayor, Matthew McAllister, the brother-in-law of Thomas Gibbons. He was too puffed up with his own self-importance for her taste. In November, Mary heard cannonading offshore and received the sad report that the USS *Wasp* had been captured by HMS *Lacedaemonian*. But, in Mary's words, "our infant navy was destined to prop the glory of the nation." Savannah never was attacked. By then the forces under the command of Admiral Alexander Cochrane and General Robert Ross had retired to Jamaica to refit for an attack on New Orleans. The politicians were at work as well, and the peace treaty was signed at Ghent on Christmas Eve. It was followed by Andrew Jackson's decisive defeat of the British in the Battle of New Orleans, a massacre of British soldiers that took place before news of the treaty reached the opposing commanders. Mary Telfair thought General Jackson a "peerless Hero" and "Valour's favorite Son." Mary Few believed that the country had been under the "peculiar care of Providence."[16]

The extended family was extremely important to planters in the antebellum South.[17] Familial relationships beyond the nuclear family were important to the urban elite as well. Mary Telfair and her brothers and sisters had strong ties to uncles, aunts, and cousins, and these relationships were a source of great personal satisfaction. "I wish I had a *land of Cousins* to go," Mary Telfair wrote, "for I have a *large* heart which could contain as much love again as at present fills it." The Telfairs had cousins living on an estate called Belfair in the Beaufort District of South Carolina. They were ladies by the name of Eliza G. L. Telfair and Margaret Telfair. They were daughters of William Telfair, the governor's brother, who in 1769 had married Miss Elizabeth Bellinger, daughter of Edmund Bellinger, a wealthy South Carolina landowner. The name of the Beaufort estate was a combination of the names Bellinger and Telfair. Mary kept in close touch with her Carolina cousins and exchanged frequent visits with them. Mary spent the summer of 1804 with her cousins in South Carolina while her parents and her sisters were in the upcountry. A third daughter of William Telfair, Mary Laura Lucia Telfair, married one Alexander Ritchie in Nassau, the Bahamas, in December 1799. The couple were living in England when Mr. Ritchie died, and his widow came to Belfair to live with her sisters. The Ritchies had four sons and one daughter, Mary Ewing Ritchie, a girl who in later years would play a large role in Mary Telfair's life.[18]

William Telfair had died in 1812 in Surinam, Dutch Guiana.[19] His wife returned to the low country to be near her one daughter who was in residence there at the time. It was of them that Mary wrote to Mary Few:

My Aunt at present resides in Savannah. You have often heard me speak of her and my Cousin. They are both elegant Women possessed of an uncommon share of intelligence & taste and prove a valuable accession to our circle. I wish you knew them for I am sure you would pronounce them to be quite above the common sphere; their information has been gained as much from Society as Books which gives a pleasing variety to their minds & conversation.[20]

Mary Telfair was happy to entertain another branch of her extended family, her brother's wife and in-laws. "I am in hopes that Mrs. Telfair will spend the Winter with us and her *beautiful Cousin* who Sarah Jones portrayed in such glowing colours," Mary Telfair wrote in October 1816. "We also expect Colonel & Mrs. Long, so we shall muster a strong family retinue. I love a large circle round the hearth in winter." Despite her disapproval of Thomas' wife, Mary Telfair had a high regard for his in-laws, Colonel and Mrs. Long. A gallant soldier, Colonel Long had come to Wilkes County from Virginia, where as a mere youth he had served in the Revolutionary War as a dragoon officer, first in the Virginia and then the North Carolina line. Later, in the War of 1812, he would serve as colonel of the Forty-third Regiment, United States Infantry, which was organized to defend the coast of the Carolinas and Georgia. Mary would say of Mrs. Long after her death that "she was an excellent woman and her loss will be felt by her family and society at large for her house was the seat of hospitality." Mary admired the calmness and serenity with which she faced her death after three years of gradual decline.[21]

After their father's death, the Telfair brothers remained close to their surviving maternal uncle, Barack Gibbons. Joseph Gibbons had died in 1794 and William Gibbons in 1804. Both were bachelors and died without lawful issue. William Gibbons, however, had maintained a relationship with a mulatto woman named Sally, whom he emancipated in 1796, for whose maintenance he provided handsomely upon his death, and to whom he bequeathed "one old mahogany bedstead, one feather bed, one mattress, all my coarse sheets, all my coarse pillow cases, one bolster and two pillows, one pavilion, one large hair trunk, one set of common castors and the sum of ninety dollars." There can be little doubt that he fathered Sally's three children, Maria, Emma, and John Charles, for whose use, education, and maintenance he established substantial trusts and to whom he bequeathed many fine items of personal property. In the penultimate item of his will Gibbons appointed his executors guardians for Sally, Maria, Emma, and John Charles.[22]

When Barack Gibbons died in 1814 at the home of Dr. Lemuel Kollock on Broughton Street, a victim of dysentery, Josiah Telfair was at the bedside of the forty-five-year-old bachelor. It was Josiah who made the arrangements for his uncle's burial at the Sharon Plantation. Barack Gibbons was the sole owner of Sharon at the time of his death. It then consisted of some 928 acres. He devised the entire property to his sister, Mrs. Edward Telfair, for life and upon her death to his four nephews, Thomas, Josiah, and Alexander Telfair and Noble Wimberly Jones II, and their heirs and assigns as tenants in common. The four nephews were named as executors.[23]

Thomas Telfair was elected to the United States Congress in 1813. He and the other members of the thirteenth Congress from Georgia —William Barnett, William W. Bibb, Alfred Cuthbert, John Forsyth, and George M. Troup—served in that august body with such worthies as John C. Calhoun of South Carolina, Henry Clay of Kentucky, John Randolph of Virginia, and Daniel Webster of New Hampshire. When the fourteenth Congress convened, Clay was elected speaker. Telfair remained in congress until 1817. Shortly after he first took office, his sister Mary expressed disappointment that she had not seen a specimen of Thomas' eloquence in print: "He wrote me word that he had delivered several speeches, one I understood was published in a *Federal* paper and as we do not deal in *such stuff* never saw it." One year while her brother was in congress, Mary considered spending the winter with him and his wife in Washington, but her mother was not very anxious that she should do so, so she returned to Savannah instead. Of Thomas' political career Mary wrote, "I hope he will distinguish himself, his ambition is great if his pride does not interfere, it is rare in this state for a politician to succeed without suing for popularity and that does not accord with his ideas, he is for being sought." A trait that Mary admired in Thomas was eagerness, an eagerness, as she put it, "connected with great sensibility and disinterestedness." This combination of virtues, she thought, gave "a deep interest to his character."[24]

Josiah Telfair had political ambitions as well. At the same time that his brother was beginning his term in congress, Josiah was a candidate for the state legislature. Mary said of her eldest brother, "Josiah combines the character of Legislator, Planter and Soldier." Josiah, however, did not have the same force of personality as his brothers. Mary noted that he resided chiefly on his plantation. He preferred life in the saddle to the social life of Savannah or the cities in the North. Referring to Josiah, Mary found it "a hard matter to move *old Bachelors* particularly when *crops* are in the way." She could never live as Josiah did. "I would almost rather be a Millner or Mantua Maker, or a *School Mistress* than a *Planter's Wife*," she declared with fierce conviction.[25]

On April 25, 1815, Sarah Telfair was married to Captain George Haig, U.S. Army, a soldier and a planter. The previous October, Mary had insisted to Mary Few that reports of Sarah's engagement were entirely without foundation for "her heart if analyzed would be discovered to be of more adamantive material than mine, which you well know is perfectly impenetrable to the wiles of sly little Cupid." But Mary was wrong. Captain Haig returned from the War of 1812 to claim Sarah as his bride. As could be expected, Mary Telfair had formed an opinion of the gentleman, and she was happy to share it with Mary Few:

> Sarah's Hero, as you style the gallant Captain, has not yet returned—he left Washington about ten days ago, my Brother Thomas wrote me. You would not admire him very much, he is amiable, handsome, and very genteel, but you I believe do not like *fashionable* men, he is exactly what the generality of Women admire, for he is fond of the society of the Fair and very respectful in his attentions to them, he received his education in Edinburgh but is a *good Republican*.

When Sarah married Captain Haig, Mary was happy for her sister but knew that she would miss her company. Life went on, however, and even as Mary was contemplating her dependence on Sarah, she was planing to sail for the North, under the protection of her uncle George Jones, and to join the Fews on a trip to Niagara Falls.[26]

A son was born dead to Sarah Haig in May of the year following her marriage. Her sister conveyed the sad news to Mary Few: "Sarah was confined the 23d day of May but was so very unfortunate as to lose her infant." Sarah conceived again, but Captain Haig did not live to see the son he so sorely wanted. He died on December 4, 1816, after a painful illness during which he was bled and blistered by Dr. Lemuel Kollock. Her husband's death so affected Sarah that she neither wept nor spoke for ten days thereafter. Mary wrote to Mary Few of Captain Haig's death:

> I am happy to inform you that Sarah's health has not suffered materially from her late affliction, although her early prospects of Happiness are so blasted. I believe few Persons knew more happiness than they did, they were united not long enough to experience the cares of the married state and the separation appears more melancholy on that account.[27]

In the meantime Josiah Telfair had fallen seriously ill. Mary was greatly distressed by her brother's condition:

> When I view my Brother's situation and see him daily declining it makes me feel very melancholy; it is eight months since he was first attacked; his tour to the western country was of great benefit to him but he returned too early in the season and in consequence was very ill with a billious fever when Alexander arrived at his Plantation. I yet hope that the mild season of Spring may produce the same effect on him as it does on the vegetable creation.[28]

This was not to be. Josiah Telfair died in March 1817 at the age of thirty-two.

Sarah's baby was born on May 10, 1817. He was named for his father. Mary found her nephew "the sweetest little Boy I ever beheld." "I am sure I could not love this little fellow more if he were my own child," she wrote to Mary Few. But tragedy struck again. Sarah's son died the following November at the age of six months. Sarah was crushed for she was devoted to the child. Mary was devastated as well: "Little George, the most lovely & interesting child my eyes ever beheld, is now an Angel in Heaven; he has made a happy change but has left a void nothing can fill." "Oh! how I loved him," she wrote, "it was sinful really for I forgot that he was only lent to us . . . it will be a useful lesson to me I hope, never again to place my affections too much on any thing in this world."[29]

Alexander had not been well himself that winter, even as he nursed Josiah in his final illness. In the spring of 1817 he went on an excursion to Cuba in the hope that the trip would be good for his health. He found the island an enchanting spot and returned to Savannah feeling much better. He concluded, however, that the Spaniards were an indolent, avaricious, and bloodthirsty race. Upon his return he told his sisters that for the Spaniards no tie is held sacred and no crime is too enormous for them to commit. Mary was shocked. "If any other person but my Brother had related some anecdotes of Spanish treachery & cruelty," she wrote, "I should have deemed them fabulous and only calculated to figure in the pages of a romance."[30]

Alexander's health took a turn for the worse. He came close to death in late 1817 while at his plantation near Louisville, Georgia. His sisters Mary and Margaret were there to nurse him back to health, a duty that they often were called upon to perform. Mary had put off writing to Mary Few until Alexander was out of danger and called upon her friend to "think of his being ill for four weeks on a Plantation with no white Being on it but Margaret and myself." Caring for Alexander during his illness was a duty that required a devoted effort on Mary's part: "I sometimes think I was endued with uncommon firmness to have gone through what I did, but I was so constantly engaged that I had no time to reflect. I only felt as if my existence hung upon his, and feel grateful to the supreme Being for preserving a life I value so much more than my own." Mary was called upon to nurse Alexander on another occasion during a sea voyage from New York to Savannah. Although seasick herself, she managed to provide her ill brother with the care that he needed and "succeeded in not only *dosing* but keeping the Hat & Cloak on in the Cabin & prohibiting Lemonade & indigestible food." Mary recognized that her solicitude could have been embarrassing to Alexander: "I believe the Men set me down as *a Shrew* and pitied Alexander for being under Petticoat Government."[31]

Thomas Telfair died on February 18, 1818, at the age of thirty-one. An affidavit presented to the Court of Ordinary of Chatham County by Noble Wimberly Jones II, Thomas' cousin and lawyer, described the circumstances of the young man's death. Jones drew up a will for Thomas and read it to him clause by clause in the presence of his mother, Mrs. Sarah Telfair. Thomas approved each clause as correctly drawn, except the last, which Mr. Jones changed in accordance with his client's wishes. Then, the lawyer stated, "while this deponent was annexing the usual attestation the testator was suddenly seized with a spasmodic affection, which terminated so unexpectedly & suddenly his life as to prevent the regular execution of this said instrument." The unsigned will was admitted to probate in reliance upon this affidavit. Thomas' widow, Margaret, was left with the care of their two little girls and the management of their Savannah residence and three plantations—one in Wilkes County, which he devised to his wife; another in Columbia County, which he devised to his daughter Mary; and a third in Screven County, which he devised to his daughter Margaret.[32]

To Mary Telfair, Thomas' death was the severest loss she had ever sustained. "You knew how beloved was the object I lament," she wrote to Mary Few, "how much I estimated his virtues, and how I delighted in his conversation; he was Brother, friend, & instructor, indeed every thing to me *and the separation was hard indeed.*" Mary Few wrote expressing her condolences, and Mary Telfair responded with the assurance that "to meet with sympathy from those we love is one of the greatest sources of happiness in this world." Mary sought solace in her Christian faith: "I reason with myself and am reconciled to it for he has been saved perhaps from much misery in this world, and I trust that he is happy; we cannot penetrate the ways of providence but of this I am convinced that every thing is wisely ordered."[33]

Alexander, the youngest Telfair brother, found himself at the age of twenty-nine as the patriarch of the family, responsible for the welfare of his widowed mother and his three younger sisters, Mary Telfair, Sarah Haig, and Margaret Telfair, aged twenty-seven, twenty-six, and twenty, respectively, as well as the business affairs of his brother's widow, a young woman with two little girls to care for. Thomas' widow was pregnant with another child at the time of her husband's death. In May, as the time of her confinement approached, she went to be with her father at his plantation in Wilkes County. Sarah Rebecca was born in May 1818, three months after Thomas' death, but would live to be only seven.[34] Colonel Nicholas Long, Mrs. Telfair's father, died of consumption on August 22, 1819, a year and one-half after the death of her husband.

There was another death in the family in 1818. Noble Wimberly Jones II, the Telfairs' cousin and Alexander's Princeton contemporary and closest friend, died in the fall of that year. Mary Telfair wrote to Mary Few in December that breaking the seal of her letter was the first thing that had afforded her delight for several weeks "for we have since I last wrote to you met with a sad shock":

You have heard before this of the death of our Cousin Noble Jones an event which has cast a gloom over us all, he was the only friend of my Brother and except him the only male relation we had in this world. The resignation and piety displayed by him in his last moments afforded consolation to his surviving relatives but poor Mrs. Jones almost sinks beneath the weight of her sufferings, the rest of the family bear this heavy affliction with great fortitude.[35]

The Telfairs' cousin, Thomas Gibbons, had become an established figure in the North, as well as one of the leading lawyers, planters, and political figures in Georgia. He passed his summers in Elizabethtown, New Jersey, in elegant luxury. Gibbons had amassed a fortune, and he believed that he could turn it into an even greater fortune by operating a passenger steamboat between Elizabethtown and New York City. In 1818, at the age of sixty-one, he embarked on his new venture. He purchased a steam-powered vessel, the *Bellona,* and hired as its captain a young sailor by the name of Cornelius Vanderbilt. A second vessel was put into service at a later date. Both boats were enrolled and licensed to be employed in the coastal trade under an Act of Congress of 1793. The problem that Thomas Gibbons faced was that the New York legislature had granted to Robert Livingston and Robert Fulton the exclusive right to employ steam vessels in the navigation of the waters within the jurisdiction of the state. These gentlemen had assigned their franchise to Aaron Ogden, with whom Gibbons had recently been associated, but with whom he had had a falling out. Ogden did not take kindly to the ferry service being operated by Gibbons in total disregard of his monopoly. So he petitioned the New York Court of Chancery and obtained an injunction against Gibbons. The injunction was upheld on appeal, with Chancellor Kent writing the opinion holding the New York statute to be constitutional.[36]

Gibbons hired the great Daniel Webster to argue his appeal before the Supreme Court of the United States. The result was the landmark decision in Gibbons v. Ogden, in which Chief Justice John Marshall defined the scope of the Commerce Clause of the United States Constitution.[37] The Constitution granted to Congress the power to regulate commerce among the several states; the term "commerce" includes navigation; carrying passengers is as much a part of the coasting trade regulated by Congress as is carrying goods; and where Congress is regulating an aspect of commerce among the states, a state may not interfere by imposing its own regulation. So reasoned the great chief justice in upholding the right of Gibbons to operate his steam ferries. The decision was greeted with wild huzzahs throughout the country and resulted in an increase in steamboat traffic in the United States.

Alexander Telfair was the owner of Trust Lot Letter N on St. James Square in Savannah's Heathcote Ward. The lot had once been the site of Government House, the official residence of Royal Governor James Wright. The building that would serve as Government House was originally constructed as a residence for William Clifton, who had been appointed to serve as attorney general of the Georgia colony under the first royal governor, John Reynolds. When Clifton came to build his house, all of the residential lots had been built on or granted away, so he was granted a dispensation and was permitted to build on one of the so-called trust lots reserved for public use. By 1818, through a series of land transactions, Alexander had acquired the entire fee simple interest in this choice parcel of real estate.[38] Alexander, still unmarried, decided to build there a mansion that would be suitable for himself and the ladies under his care. It was thus that he came to know the architect William Jay.

William Jay, at the age of twenty-three, arrived in Savannah from London on December 29, 1817, a passenger aboard the clipper ship *Dawn*. Born in the English city of Bath, Jay was the son of the prominent nonconformist minister, the Reverend William Jay. Inspired, perhaps, by the architectural beauty of the city in which he grew up, young Jay decided upon architecture as a career. He was apprenticed to an architect and surveyor in London and there learned to design the Regency-style buildings, with their simplicity of form, that came into vogue during the Regency (1811–1820) of George, Prince of Wales, later George IV. When Jay arrived in Savannah, he carried with him the still uncompleted plans for a home for Richard Richardson, the president of the branch office of the Second Bank of the United States, which had opened in Savannah in 1817. Richardson was related to Jay by marriage, Mrs. Richardson's older brother having married Jay's sister. It can be surmised that this connection had something to do with the young architect's commission. Jay completed the plans for Mr. Richardson and supervised the construction of his first building in America, that dignified mansion on Oglethorpe Square now called the Owens-Thomas House. While working on the Richardson project, Jay received the commission to design a home for William Scarbrough, a wealthy merchant, born in North Carolina and educated in England, who headed the syndicate that launched the first transatlantic steamship, the SS *Savannah*. The Scarbrough mansion, on West Broad Street, was completed in time for the reception on May 18, 1819, at which President James Monroe, accompanied by Secretary of War John C. Calhoun, was introduced to Savannah society.[39]

Alexander Telfair was not to be outdone by the Scarbroughs, and the Jay-designed home built for him and completed in 1819 was every bit as grand as the two other Savannah mansions designed by the English architect. The Telfair mansion was a two-story structure with the first floor set high above street level to avoid the dust thrown up by the horse-drawn carriages that passed by on the sandy road in front of St. James Square. Like so many other buildings constructed after the great fire of 1796, it was made of brick covered over with stucco. One entered the residence through a portico, adorned with four unfluted Corinthian columns, with steps on either side. A low ceiling covered the portion of the entrance hall at the front of the building. Plaster decorations rounding off the corners of this ceiling created the illusion of a dome. There was a nonfunctional, or "blind," door on either side of the entrance hall. Beyond these was a door to the left that entered into an exquisite octagonal reception room grained to simulate oak paneling, called by the family the oak room. Behind it was the dining room, and on the other side of the hall was a large drawing room, rounded at both ends (a Jay trademark). By closing the pocket doors at the center of the drawing room, it could be converted into two smaller parlors. This room had two marble fireplaces carved and signed by the sculptor John Frazee of New York.[40]

A wooden double staircase ascended along both sides of the entrance hall beginning immediately beyond the entrances to the oak room and the front parlor. The two sections met at a landing, and from there a single staircase continued to the second floor, where the family bedrooms and guest rooms were located. At that time these rooms (six in number) were entered from a balcony that surrounded the upper part of the entrance hall. The basement contained the kitchen, which opened to the garden, a laundry room, other rooms used for similar domestic purposes, and Alexander's wine cellar. Alexander had one of the best cellars in Savannah. An inventory taken after his death listed over seven hundred bottles of fine wine, principally Madeira, port, and old sherry, and casks holding eighteen additional gallons of wine.[41]

A stable and carriage house stood at the rear of the lot, above which were the servants' quarters. The old-fashioned garden between the two structures was enclosed by a high brick wall. A stately live oak grew at the center of the garden. Mary Telfair loved to sit on the portico on warm evenings "inhaling the sweet South and watching the soft dews of twilight steal over shrub and flower."[42] In their new home Alexander and his family were surrounded by lovely things: fine china and silverware, damask tablecloths and napkins, and exquisite carpets and furniture. It was a fitting home for a young man who was one of the wealthiest and most prominent in Savannah.

Alexander Telfair was one of the founders of the Savannah Theater, another building designed by William Jay. He served as chairman of its five-man board of trustees. The theater first opened on the night of December 4, 1818, with a performance of *The Soldier's Daughter*, a patriotic drama by Andrew Cherry, an actor of some note on the London stage. As Alexander's mansion was being built, another building was rising in Savannah that held deep significance for the Telfairs. The Independent Presbyterian Church, which had been founded in 1755, consecrated its new place of worship on Bull Street in May 1819. It was a wonderful structure, its spire a Savannah landmark. When Mary Telfair lay on her bed in her brother's new mansion, she was able to see the spire "peering in solitary grandeur above the trees." She was able to hear from the house the church bell pealing in the warm spring air. President Monroe attended the consecration service during his visit to Savannah as well as the christening of the steamship *Savannah*. To help finance the church's construction, Alexander purchased the fee to Pew Number 6 for the not insignificant sum of $1,170.[43]

As the people of Savannah looked forward to the decade of the 1820's, the city's commerce was at a standstill because of high protective tariffs and a national depression. And there would be more troubles to come. In January 1820 fire ravaged the city, wiping out two-thirds of its homes. Then came the plague. A tenth of the population died of yellow fever.[44] There were no further commissions in Savannah for William Jay, and in 1821 he abandoned the city. Savannah languished over the next decade. Its population would decrease from 7,523 in 1820 to 5,215 in 1830.

4

A Coastal Aristocracy

One country, one Constitution, one destiny.
Daniel Webster, Speech (March 15, 1869)

The Telfairs usually spent the early summer in New York or Philadelphia or part of the time in each of those cities. The family cus-
tomarily moved on to one of the fashionable Northern resorts during
the latter part of the summer. Alexander had his own place at Bristol
Banks, on the Delaware River in Pennsylvania, and his sisters enjoyed visiting there as well. Savannah was not considered a healthy
place to be during the warm months, and it was the custom for those
who could afford it to spend that time of the year in the North. The
period of good health could be expected to resume in November with
the first frost, viewed as "the harbinger of health," and it was then or
in October that the return trip was made to Savannah.[1]

It was not only health concerns that motivated the Telfairs in making the long journey up the coast each year. They and other members
of the establishment from Savannah and other urban centers in the
South were part of an East Coast society that transcended sectional
differences. Mary Telfair's father and other political leaders from
Georgia had spent months in Philadelphia as members of the Continental Congress and had come to know and respect their peers from
the other American colonies. The networking continued as their sons
went to college in Princeton, Cambridge, or New Haven and then
went on to study law in Litchfield or medicine at the University of
Pennsylvania or the Jefferson Medical College. After graduation

some traveled to Washington to represent their state in the United States Senate or House of Representatives. Many contemporaries of the Telfair brothers at Princeton were building careers in the Northern states. The trips to the North provided opportunities to see old friends and classmates and to participate in the rich intellectual and cultural life of the country's major urban centers.

There were close ties between the privileged classes in the North and the South during the Republican Age. Georgians such as William Few and his family had settled in New York before the turn of the century. Merchant-planters such as Alexander Telfair had agents in New York and could carry on business during their summer travels through correspondence with their factors and overseers at home. Mary Telfair had many friends in the North in addition to the Few sisters. Ann Wallace, her childhood playmate, had moved to New York. Newport had been a favorite resort for Southerners as early as the late eighteenth century. There they spent the summer months with their social equals from Northern cities as they did in Saratoga and Ballston Spa.

The elite of Savannah often found mates in the North. Dr. George Jones's third wife was a woman from Philadelphia. His grandson George Noble Jones married Delia Gardiner of Maine, a young lady he had met in Newport. Mary Telfair's friend Mary Clay married William R. Gray, a gentleman from Boston. "It is said we have another northern Lady transported by Hymen to our land," Mary wrote upon learning that a Savannah gentleman of her acquaintance might be engaged to a girl from Philadelphia.[2] The wealthy, well-connected Savannah resident, operating plantations in the Georgia upcountry on a semi-absentee basis, had far more in common with the elite of Philadelphia, New York, and Baltimore than with the Georgia planter and his wife bound to the soil by economic demands.

The social and cultural flow moved in a North to South direction as well. Most of Savannah's reading matter came from Northern cities as did visiting lecturers, actors, opera singers, and minstrel shows.[3] The Southern elite ordered the latest books from dealers in New York or Philadelphia. They subscribed to newspapers published in New York. Pierce Butler had his principal residence in Philadelphia, but was one of Georgia's wealthiest planters. Mary Few's nephew married a girl from Augusta. Northerners, with letters of introduction in hand or preceding them or with invitations from friends in the

South, enjoyed the social life of Savannah and Charleston during the winter months. "I have had a consignment from Mrs. William R. Gray," Mary Telfair wrote, "a very pleasant couple from the land of steady habits. I took them to Bonaventure yesterday afternoon—they were charmed with the druidical Oaks."[4]

All of these people, whether from the North or the South, moved in an East Coast society, an aristocracy defined by class and not constrained by state boundaries or marked by regional differences. Those differences existed to be sure. A Federalist could not be found on a plantation in the South, and the tariff was a divisive issue between Northerners and Southerners. But nationalism was stronger than sectionalism in the decades before the 1850's, when the issue of slavery drove a wedge through the heart of the nation. The Spirit of '76 prevailed in the early decades of the century; and Mary Telfair, the daughter of a Liberty Boy, would copy into her commonplace book the lines of "The Star-spangled Banner," written by Francis Scott Key a few years earlier (1814) during the British bombardment of Fort McHenry, as well as the patriotic words "Breathes there the man with soul so dead who never to himself hath said this is my own my native land" and the poem "Columbia," with the stirring refrain: "For oh! her sons are brave and free / Their breasts beat high with liberty."[5] National pride stirred hearts in the post–Revolutionary era, even those of women from the deep South such as Mary Telfair.

Historian Daniel P. Kilbride points out that Spruce Street between Ninth and Tenth in Philadelphia was known as "Carolina Row" in the early decades of the nineteenth century. Philadelphia, the cradle of American liberty, was the center of what he calls an "Atlantic aristocratic community." He supports the thesis that a mobile East Coast aristocracy existed during the Republican Age. "Throughout most of the antebellum era," Kilbride writes, "the mental boundaries of wellborn men and women followed not Mason and Dixon's line but the peaks of the Appalachians —not North and South, but East and West." This "urban community" was one "united by bonds of common intellect, taste, kinship, and friendship."[6]

Richard H. Shryock, in his 1929 introduction to the letters of Dr. Richard D. Arnold, described the close ties among the elite of the port cities. He writes that "the picture of cultural connections between Savannah and the northern ports" is one of the most significant features of Dr. Arnold's letters:

It suggests, not the general "Eastern" sectionalism which historians usually recognize in this period, but the persistence of an even more restricted sort of coast-line sectionalism, based upon common colonial traditions, and the relatively intimate communication afforded by marine transportation. Dr. Arnold, and many of the other "people of consequence" in Savannah, felt at home in New York and Philadelphia. They were strangers in an alien land—culturally speaking—fifty miles up-country in their own State!

Shryock also observes that in the process of illustrating the close connections existing between the Northern and Southern ports, the letters also picture "an urban culture common to both sections."[7]

In his memoirs, published in 1898, Judge Richard H. Clark made a similar observation with respect to Savannah at the middle of the nineteenth century: "Savannah fifty years ago saw nothing of interior Georgia, except the people in the surrounding counties. She was much better acquainted with Boston, New York and Philadelphia than with our interior towns and counties."[8]

Wealthy women from urban centers in the South were familiar with the current fashions in dress. The Telfair ladies had many of their clothes made in New York; and Mary Few was kind enough, when requested, to make arrangements with dressmakers and for the shipment of garments. "You were good enough to offer to transact any piece of business I left unfinished," Mary wrote to Mary Few, and then went on to outline her wishes:

> I want something warm & genteel for cold weather, either a bombazine or Poplin whichever you think most suitable & do not think me stingy if I add *most reasonable*. I can procure it here but cannot have it made up and do not like to *butcher* it myself; therefore I will get you to procure as much as will make Margaret and me a Dress & suitable trimming whatever Madame George thinks best. I think satin of the same color would do— she has our measure.[9]

On another occasion Mary asked Mary Few to "enquire of Madame George respecting a Box she has with our Winter Clothes, which Sarah Jones got her to make for us." She assured her friend that they were all paid for, but by some mistake had never been sent.

Acting on behalf of her cousin, Mary asked another favor of Mary Few:

> Sarah Jones sent me a small trunk with 5 yds. of muslin to make a morning dress & begged me to ask you to receive it and have it made up for her by Miss Marshall in Cedar Street in the most fashionable style & trimmed with the most fashionable trimming. She has sent an old black dress by way of guide to know her size. She also begs you to get her a handsome dress Turban either of crape or of silk lace & a morning cap of muslin. She begs if there is any money left after getting those things that you will get a painted velvet Card Case & a painted ditto box, and that you will pay the freight of the Trunk out of the enclosed & ask Miss Marshall for the paper pattern.[10]

New York also was the place to buy fine furniture, and Duncan Phyfe was the cabinetmaker of choice among the elite. "I must trouble you my dear Mary to call on Phyfe," Telfair wrote to Mary Few; "you recollect I paid him sixty dollars for my work Table & $1 50 cts for boxing it. He never sent it on board the *Tybee* as he promised and if any accident happened to the Table he will be honest enough to return you the money." Imported works of art could be purchased in New York as well, as indicated by Telfair's words of thanks to Mary Few: "I thank you for the trouble you took to procure the engravings I sent for—it was the price that attracted me at Burgess's—It was an english set & I was sure such a bargain would not remain long unsold."[11]

Mary Telfair turned to the shops of New York for her Christmas shopping whenever the holidays rolled around. Mary Few, with her base in the city, was a big help. Mary appreciated her assistance:

> Thank you for all the trouble you have taken in procuring our things and in shipping them. The Hobby Horse is a beautiful one and little Telfair Habersham was delighted with it—he could not realize it was for him. He said pointing to George Jones when it was opened, it must be for that little boy—he evinced the family trait disinterestedness. The Gentleman's Portfolio or traveling writing desk is just what I wished for George Jones; indeed we are perfectly satisfied with every thing.[12]

Before the advent of the steamboat, the annual sojourn to the North was made by sailing vessel, whether a sloop or a brig. The overland journey by stagecoach was most arduous, especially for the ladies. Frances Few described "a most perilous journey" in March 1809 on roads that were "almost impassible" between Washington and Philadelphia. One female passenger kept squeaking as the coach lurched along, "We are over." At length, the road became so bad that the gentlemen had to climb down and walk beside the coach. "Just as it began to be dark," Frances wrote, "a part of our harness gave way. The gentlemen were all called upon to help fasten it. After many efforts they got it together and we were ready to start, but to our great surprise we found that the horses could not move the carriage. The gentlemen pushed behind, the ladies all got out, the coachman whipped the horses—but all was in vain. The carriage had stuck so deep in the mud that it was immovable and we had to walk a mile and a half over our shoes in mud before we came to a house. I do not know how I should have got along if it had not been for the little Quaker [a young man by the name of Palmer]; he helped me over the bogs and threw rails over the worst part of the road."[13]

The accommodations along the way were dreadful. Frances Few described an inn on the road between Washington and Baltimore: "One Tavern that we stopped at really presented a deplorable scene —we looked in at one door and opposite it on a bed lay a child apparently three years old emaciated and very ill—near the bed sat a tall meager miserable looking woman with an infant in her arms—in the same room was a black woman and half a dozen little blacks and in the room joining were eight or ten drunken men gambling."[14]

In traveling to the North or returning home, good time could be made under sail if the winds were right. On one return trip to Savannah, the *Aurora*, with the Telfair ladies aboard, made the voyage in five days. On another voyage, which took twelve days, Mary spent three of them confined to her berth with seasickness. It would seem that Mary Few rather enjoyed voyaging under sail. Thus she described a trip aboard a sloop in October 1812:

Two doleful nights have passed and we are again preparing our beds for a third while sighs & groans are echoing throughout the Cabin at the dismal prospect of a head wind and contrary tide present. Pigs squealing, children crying and mothers complaining form a concert truly musical—poor Mr. Appleby and Grace are almost sick from want of sleep, but for myself I sleep soundly, eat heartily and laugh most merrily.

The merry laughter all but ceased the following day when the weather turned nasty:

I had written thus far dear Mary when a violent breeze from the South sprung up which made the Sloop rock us all deadly sick. It was laughable to see the poor creatures rolling from one place to another in vain endeavouring to breathe the fresh air on deck, one woman would seize the arm of her next companion and almost reach the steps to ascend when a sudden blast would turn the Sloop on its side and cause us all to run in that direction. With the assistance of Mrs. Appleby, Grace & myself reached the deck where we vomited most freely—after which we retired to bed, and before daylight awoke and found ourselves at the Dock.

Some voyages truly were disasters. Mary Telfair compared one trip under sail to "the voyage of life" for "it was a succession of storms & calms, of hopes and fears."[15]

Alexander could enjoy himself on the high seas, although he was not a particularly good sailor:

We had a very pleasant passage of four days to the capes and two from thence to the city [Philadelphia]. Notwithstanding the shortness of our passage, we had the usual vicissitudes of calms & head winds, but they were of short duration and rather gave variety to the voyage. Upon the whole I have never had a more agreeable time at sea, tho seasick as usual.[16]

Mary Telfair thoroughly enjoyed her visits to the North. They gave her the opportunity to be with the Few sisters and exchange serious thoughts with Mary and jokes with Frances. They brought back the happy memories of her years at school. Mary Telfair loved the beauty of New York State and New England. As a child of the low country, she remembered her first visit to the Hudson River valley in the vicinity of Rhinebeck. When she first sailed up the Hudson, she was like a "child in a toyshop." "Never shall I forget," she wrote as a young woman of twenty, "my emotions on first viewing the mountains, there was something so grand (and to me) so novel in the appearance of them, that my eye was quite enchanted, and I thought I could never tire of viewing the lovely scenery that surrounded me." In the spring of 1815, after an absence of several years, she wrote of an impending visit to the North: "I should be almost afraid to revisit those delightful regions, for the attachment I formed during my stay there for the Country, the climate, and above all for the Friends, rendered me so perfectly happy there that I could never like my native state afterwards; the only solitary charm it possessed was that of containing near & dear relatives."[17]

Mary marveled at the mountains, green valleys, and winding streams of Connecticut and Massachusetts. She fell in love with Boston:

> Boston is a Century beyond any City that I have visited in improvements. The buildings are splendid and things look permanent here.[18]

Mary liked the people in the North as much as she liked its scenery and cultural attractions. "The manners of the Eastern people I decidedly prefer to the Northern or Southern," she wrote, "they are so social & conversible." On another occasion she wrote:

> I am fascinated with the Yankees—they are the best educated, most hospitable, and agreeable people in the United States. Their manners are an improvement upon the Southern—they are quiet, animated & social. Alexander was apprehensive that I would fall a victim to their "cheek music" which is the most melodious that I have ever been serenaded with.[19]

Not only did Mary think that Southerners had inferior manners; she also found them to be too mercenary, an opinion she was willing to share with Mary Few:

> The Southrons have already begun to flock to the North to inhale your delicious breezes and gaze on your wild romantic scenery, as well as your cultivated farms—How provoking it is that you should have so greatly the advantage over us in every respect. I think between you & I the Southward is only fit for money making Geniuses but this you must keep profoundly secret.[20]

Mary had some very definite ideas on the characteristics of the peoples of the several states in the South:

> I do not generally like the South Carolinians, they are too fond of pomp and parade & pride themselves quite too much on their wealth indeed they think themselves the nobility of America. The Virginians appear to possess their foibles but are so greatly superior in point of talents that there is no comparison between them. But I like the Kentuckians, they pretend to nothing, and are capable of every thing they have certainly evinced more patriotism this war [War of 1812] than the citizens of any other State indeed they seem to be soldiers by nature.[21]

Although Mary thought the Northern states superior to her native Georgia, she felt that none of the Southern states surpassed it. With reference to Richmond, Virginia, she wrote, "I see nothing in it to admire, nothing to awake the Song of the Poet." Indeed, she was "dreadfully disappointed" in every part of Virginia for "every thing wears the air of decay." She thought this "ruinous looking country" inferior to her state of Georgia and that it ought to be called "the ancient dominions." "I acknowledge the superiority of the northern states over it [Georgia]," she added, "but not the southern."[22]

In thinking one spring of her forthcoming trip to the North, Mary wished that she might stay longer than just the summer. She knew, however, that Alexander could not stand the rigors of a Northern winter: "I was in hopes that we should have remained eighteen months but I should dread Alexander encountering a Northern winter, his constitution has received such a shock that he could not live in a cold climate and we could not separate from him."[23] There were times when Mary thought of making her permanent residence in the North apart from her family. Her love for them prevented it, however:

> I left Philadelphia with the deepest regret. It suits my taste in every respect, and if it rested with me to make choice of a residence I would select that place in preference to any in the whole world. I never had such a struggle between duty & inclination for I was half disposed to stay—but they would have missed me so much at home where (between you and me) I am a very important personage & then I am never happy separated from my own family any length of time. I doubt whether this state of

mutual dependance is not productive of more misery than happiness. I am sure living in an unhealthy climate creates great timidity of character & weakens our energies not a little. The deathlike stillness which reigns throughout our streets and the languid air & silent tongues of many of its inhabitants afford a striking contrast to the animation & spirit left behind.[24]

On one occasion while in the North, Mary confided in Mary Few her determination to have a residence there where she could spend at least half the year:

> I mean to manage matters so as to have a little spot some-where in the north and if I cannot have you to visit me in Geor-gia must have you in this (to me) far more agreeable land, this last trip has completely subjugated my affections, and I am wholly disposed for a northern residence for half the year at least, and now much as I hate responsibility all my energies shall be exercised to accomplish it if Sarah will cooperate with me.[25]

Mary felt that she was a different person during her summers in the North than when she was at home in Savannah:

> I fear I have two characters—a northern and a southern one— You see me only as a dissipated creature, luxuriating on fine scen-ery and talk—apparently without habits— You ought to come to Georgia to see this picture reversed. Here I am cheerful and domestic surrounded by my Books and work—drawing as much society as I can to my own home, and seldom straying from it.

Mary Telfair and her sisters were a bit too partial to the North to suit some of their Savannah friends. "Sarah Cecil & Margaret are en-gaged in a violent debate," Mary wrote to Mary Few. "I believe the former thinks we are too northern in our taste & habits. She thinks Georgia a Paradise." Sarah Cecil simply could not understand how the Telfair sisters could prefer the cities of the North to their native Savannah.[26]

When Mary and her sisters visited the North, they generally stayed at a hotel or boarding house. They usually traveled with servants, and they preferred not to take them into a private home. Mary frequently visited Mary Few at her father's place at Sing Sing. She had several chuckles on one trip down the Hudson River to the city after a visit to the nearby town of Fishkill:

> We had a tedious time of it returning from Fishkill. We stopped three hours at Haverstraw for the accommodation of the camp meeting folkes who swarmed like bees on the deck of the *Franklin*. I played solitaire; not one female phiz invited me to sweet converse but [I] was amused by overhearing the remarks of some of the Methodist sparks and sparkesses. One man accosted a woman in the following style—"Do you remember me?" After receiving an answer in the negative, he replied, "That is very strange for I made your Mother's Coffin." To my amazement the Dame brightened up and a long confab ensued. Such melody burst upon my ear for the good folkes sang hymns until they exhausted themselves. An old woman opened her stock of goodies near me. When I espied the great pound cake and saw the slices circulating I became fierce for some but the stingy old thing skipped me to the no small amusement of Alexander tho I believe he was as fierce as myself.[27]

Colonel and Mrs. Few were well connected politically and socially, and through them Mary Telfair came to know a number of public figures during her sojourns to the North. Thomas Paine, the author of *Common Sense*, often visited the Fews. The Fews were close friends of the great patriot, and he had a home not far from theirs in Greenwich Village.[28] Mrs. Few's sister was married to Albert Gallatin, who had served as the Republican minority leader in Congress and from 1801 to 1813 as secretary of the Treasury under presidents Thomas Jefferson and James Madison. He later would head the peace commission assigned to negotiate the Treaty of Ghent that ended the War of 1812 and even later served as American minister at Paris. Mary Telfair received intellectual stimulation from her friendship with Nicholas Biddle. This Philadelphia gentleman was director of the Second Bank of the United States and president of the Bank of the United States from 1823 to 1836. A man of great wealth, Biddle was a fastidious dresser and was considered something of a ladies' man. An acquaintance described him as "a handsome man wearing a blue coat with brass buttons, yellow nankeen pantaloons, canary colored gloves, and a glossy beaver." It was he who said that "the world was ruled by

three boxes—the ballot-box, the cartridge-box, and the band-box."[29]
Mary Telfair apparently rented quarters from Mr. Biddle one summer, and the condition of a staircase led to this lively exchange of
verses between them:

> O dear Mr. Biddle!
> O pray, Mr. Biddle,
> Your carpenter speedily send:
> Our lives are at stake,
> Our necks we shall break,
> If these horrible stairs you don't mend.
> Each day I will call;
> And that is not all:
> Your house we will live in rent free;
> So a mechanic pray send
> Our ways to amend,
> And regain the good-will of
> M.T.

A reply was promptly improvised by the great banker:

> Why, dearest Miss Telfair,
> My zeal for your welfare
> Is shocked by the state of your stair,
> Which I'll hasten to mend,
> For fear it should end
> In a false step you ne'er could repair.
> But I'll send, and not go,
> For the danger I know
> In which all who approach you must be;
> And I'd much rather cease
> To have rent than have peace,
> So my heart, like my house is rent free.[30]

After the War of 1812 began and travel by sea became dangerous,
it was not possible, or at least not advisable, for the Telfairs to attempt their annual journey to the North. To escape the heat and evil
humors of Savannah, the Telfair ladies spent the wartime summers
in the Georgia upcountry. Mary found it rather dull. Writing to Mary
Few from the vicinity of Waynesboro in October 1812, she explained
that she had not written earlier because of "a want of subjects for a

letter in this remote place." Mary and her sisters had been in the country for close to four months. "Here we are immersed in a wilderness far removed from the vortex of business and pleasure," Mary wrote, "and the only pleasure we enjoy is looking and talking to each other." She had read nothing but newspapers that summer and had been engrossed in her needlework and in "inventing little trifles by way of amusement." She said that their life was "similar to a monastic one only we have no Nuns or confessors, and we are permitted to range unmolested through the gloomy pine trees whose dark green tops cheer the eye, and whose hollow murmurs enchant the ear." The family would return to Savannah on the 28th of October. "I always return to town with pleasure, and never leave it with regret, for even the most solitary abode where Hygieia dispenses her blessings is preferable to remaining in a place where the mind remains dormant from excessive heat and the body liable to be effected with sickness."[31]

As venturesome as Mary Telfair was and as much as she loved new experiences, the independence that she craved was not possible in an age when women could not travel alone. This could be frustrating. At the end of the War of 1812, after several years of confinement to the South because of the hostilities along the Atlantic coast, Mary yearned to visit Mary Few and other good friends in the North. She despaired of making the trip, however, for it would be unthinkable for a woman to travel such a distance without male protection, and none of her brothers was willing or able to accompany her:

> If I could prevail on that Bachelor Brother of mine Josiah to escort me as far as New York I would then give him a Furlough to seek his pleasure, to roam at large oh! that I had 'the eloquence of Cicero I would employ it on this occasion, but I fear it would take a *smoother* tongue than mine to induce the Hermit to leave his green fields, he promised Sarah & myself last summer to escort us to the Virginia Springs but when the time arrived his affairs required his presence and you know we women cannot move *without a man.* Alexander cannot leave Mamma & my Brother Thomas is a *married man*, so with three Brothers I have not one at my service is it not provoking?[32]

Ballston Spa in New York State was a favorite resort of the Telfairs during the years following the War of 1812. Sans Souci was the hotel of choice for the elite, and many Southerners flocked there.

This large wood-frame building, with an inviting veranda facing on Front Street, was the first of its size anywhere in the United States.[33] The Telfairs often stayed there, although Sarah Haig thought that "all the evil passions have their play at Sans Souci." Mary Telfair and her party would get to Ballston by taking the overnight boat from New York to Albany and then the stage the next morning to Schenectady and on to the spa. By the time they arrived there at twilight, they would be fatigued and covered with dust. Sarah doused herself with the sulphur waters every day, but Mary had little faith in their curative powers. "I find they have no effect on me and have given them up," she wrote. Mary believed that half of the people who came to Ballston were there "more with a view to shew their smart clothes and dashing figures than to benefit by the waters." There were balls to attend every other evening, and at these affairs the ladies could show off their finery. "There is to be a Ball tonight at Lows," Mary wrote, "the Belles here are preparing their dresses which I dare say will be wondrous fine for silks, crapes and costly trinkets are displayed in common." Mary observed that there were some excellent dancers among the gentlemen, who chiefly were Carolinians. However, she preferred the more simple pleasures that she described to Mary Few:

> Last evening the Ladies all appeared dull for want of some amusement. I proposed a game of Blindmans Buff which was seconded by an old lady from Philadelphia. She is a little of an oddity—very eager to promote amusements for the young people. You will be astonished when I tell you that her age is sixty-five and as active as a girl of fifteen—rides on Horseback every morning before breakfast ten miles. When it came round for her to be blindfolded I never laughed so much in my life. Alexander being the only Gentleman in the room she made a determination to catch him—and she did, to the diversion of all present.[34]

A young woman dubbed by Mary Telfair as the "Belle Esprit of Saratoga" arrived in Ballston and captured Alexander's fancy. According to his sister's account to Mary Few, "Alexander who you know is rather stoical in his taste admires her face excessively." Mary despaired of getting her brother to "act the Beau," however. "He will not dance or even admire the fair assemblage who dance so gaily through the maze of pleasure," she complained to Miss Few, but "his notions respecting women are as *fastidious* as *ours* respecting men therefore we cannot in justice blame him." "I am afraid this visit will make him a *Woman Hater*," Mary wrote of her brother, "for he thinks *Delicacy* almost banished from Ballston Springs and will not *condescend* to talk to any but *old Dowagers* & young married Women; he really handles the Belles most unmercifully." Mary found her brother to be exasperating at times. On one occasion he admitted to her that he has "*almost* lost his heart." "I was ready to give him *a thump* for not quite doing so," was her reaction. The way Mary had her brother figured out, he was "fated to live in 'single blessedness' *from choice and not dire necessity.*"[35]

Members of the Telfairs' circle of friends at the Northern spas might come up with a poem to brighten an evening's entertainment. Mary and her sisters must have enjoyed reading "Lines written on leaving Saratoga Springs and addressed to Three Sisters—Miss Mary Telfair, Mrs. Haig, and Miss Margaret Telfair" by Major John Michael O'Connor, dated August 21, 1822, which included this tribute:

> Amidst the crowds three graceful sisters moved
> By all most Honored, and by many loved;
> In their sweet converse days have fled like hours,
> And life has sparkled neath their magic powers!
> Oft shall my thoughts on these Three Sisters dwell,
> Recalling Hours they could adorn so well!
> And while Remembrance passes in Review
> Life's fleeting pleasures which are ever few,
> My warmest wishes shall for them arise
> To Him who rules the Earth and Seas and Skies;
> Invoking on these Sisters every Blessing,
> Which Heaven delights for ever in dispensing.[36]

A supper party inspired another poetic tribute to the Telfair ladies:

> The Wits and the Graces, the Muses and all
> Concluded because they couldn't give a Ball
> That a Supper they'd have of choice viands & wit
> And I pledge you my work the repast was *a hit*
>
> For the senses were greeted with every thing fine
> The Men they were witty—the Ladies divine

The jest & the toast—the champagne & the cobbler
Went round till every one limped like a Hobler

There was Mary the delicate, refined, and genteel
And Sarah the dauntless—as true as the steel
And Margaret the lofty refinements own *cretur*
And Margaret the haughty—particular Meta.[37]

Not everyone in the spas of New York found Mary, Sarah, and
Margaret to be congenial companions. Robert Mackay, the non-
fictional hero of Eugenia Price's novel *Savannah*, wrote to his wife
from Saratoga Springs of an encounter with Sarah Haig:

> Since writing the above I have dined at the large Table,
> which consists of three long Tables spread as long as an im-
> mense room will admit of, by accident I got the head of the
> middle one, & who by me but Mrs. Haig the only Georgia
> female at Table or in the house, she was as communicative as
> usual, & did at length venture to say that Captn. Haig was in
> very bad health & hoped I intended to drink nothing but the
> Saratoga Water while I remained at the Springs for fear of her
> husband joining me.

Later, Mackay wrote to "My Dear Eliza" from Ballston, "No Georgians but Haig & Wife & ourselves at Saratoga & no company *her*."
And once again he wrote to his wife from Saratoga: "Mrs. Haig sits
by my side at every meal & her husband also, she is a poor creature
as I ever met with & has not made one acquaintance among the
crowd male or female, Capt. Haig is I think in a bad state of health
and the waters appear to do him no good."[38]

The ability to blend comfortably into the social life of Philadelphia, New York, and Baltimore and to converse easily with the best
and the brightest in the new capital city of Washington placed the
Telfair sisters and other wealthy, well-educated women from the
urban South in a class apart from the plantation mistress whose
world did not extend beyond the nearest market town. Visits to the
Telfair plantations in the upcountry made Mary Telfair particularly
"sensible to the changes effected in the southern character by frequent visits to the North." If she had lived all her life in the South,
she mused, she should have been as helpless as "the Infant muling &

puling in its nurse's arms." Mary believed that her frequent visits to the "Northern World" had made her "only half a Southern." "My habits, views, tastes, feelings have all been changed by Northern association," she wrote.[39]

Travel had broadened the outlook of the Telfair sisters and had made them relatively liberal in their thinking. Mary felt that her view of life was much different from many of her Southern contemporaries, even those living in urban Savannah: "They have such strong prejudices and are so *local* in all their feelings—they seem to miscall things—self possession is boldness—social feeling toward strangers love of novelty."[40] Mary, on the other hand, was cosmopolitan in her view of the world, sophisticated, curious, and venturesome. As one of the coastal aristocracy, she had every opportunity for self-fulfillment and intellectual and cultural enrichment. The nineteenth-century notion that a woman's interests should be restricted to the domestic sphere might have been be acceptable to the plantation mistress, but not to the likes of Mary Telfair.

5

Single Blessedness

I have met with women whom I really think would like to be married to a poem.

John Keats, Letter to Fanny Brawne (1819)

By the time that Mary Telfair had moved into her brother's new mansion, her life had fallen into a pattern typical of many well-to-do young women of the early nineteenth century. It was a life of relative ease, with the mundane aspects of everyday living left largely to the care of household servants. Mary was close to thirty and unmarried. She had reached an age when the prospects of marriage were becoming increasingly dim. As she put it to Mary Few, "We are rare instances of two Ladies arriving at a *certain* age without feeling the influence of *la belle* passion." The two Marys were quite reconciled to a life of "single blessedness."[1]

Men controlled courtship and marriage in the antebellum South. Upper-class men tended to marry late while choosing young brides. The younger the girl, the more malleable and less self-assertive she was presumed to be. Mary was well aware of this male preference. Her own father was close to forty when he married her mother, a girl of sixteen. The older the man, she thought, the greater value he placed on youth: "Depend upon the truth of my remark that *old men* admire youth & beauty more than young ones in *every clime*." Many women also placed a premium on youth. Indeed, Mary would comment that her friend Mrs. Richard Habersham thought every woman "antiquated after twenty." Clever women were not in much demand. Mary could understand this. "Superiority of intellect is no safe guard to domestic happiness," she acknowledged. "Sweetness of temper, ingenuousness & disinterestedness are the qualities which throw a charm around the domestic circle." She wrote that "it is only the beautiful, languishing and gentle Fair one who undermines the citadel of a Man's heart and finally makes him a captive." Money, of course, figured in the marital equation, as Mary Telfair understood quite well. "The beautiful Miss St. George is regaling the eyes of the beaux," she wrote, "but as she is not rich her charms do not produce an *indelible* impression." Many women resented the passive role they were forced to play in the rituals of courtship. One woman wrote, "The inequality of privilege between the sexes is very sensibly felt by us females, and in no instance is it greater than in the liberty of choosing a partner in marriage; true we have the liberty of refusing those we don't like, but not of selecting those we do."[2]

Mary Telfair had no need of a husband to provide her with financial security. The pursuit of economic independence that consumed so many spinsters simply was not a factor in her life. She had all the money she could possibly spend. Nor is there any evidence that Mary was one of those women who made a conscious choice to remain single in order to maintain personal autonomy. She firmly believed that a woman could find happiness in a companionate marriage. When her friend Mrs. Richard Habersham, who was "insane" on the subject of marriage, expressed the hope that her daughter would "never be the *drudge* of any man," Mary "shocked her *delicacy*" by saying that she "hoped she would be the friend, companion & wife of some excellent man." There is nothing in Mary's writings that comes even close to the passionate declaration of the young woman who wrote:

> "Wedlock, wedlock is a strife," never never marry never!! I want to find friends but I don't want a companion for life. I'm afraid of having my wings clipped instead of "stretching away, stretching away, On the wing, Ever & aye, Ever & aye as I sing." I have a dread of settling down to a stated round of earthly duties, I want my heart ties to be spiritual ones.[3]

Mary admitted that as a girl she was a romantic when it came to matters of the heart. At "thoughtless yet happy seventeen" her life was "full of poetry." She had formed her notion of the ideal man. Her reading led her to a vision of perfection. Sir Philip Sidney, the English poet, scholar, soldier, and courtier, indeed the very model of a Renaissance gentleman, was the beau ideal of her youthful imagination. On occasion she had met such a man. Referring, as a young woman of twenty-two, to a "beautiful youth" who had won a poetry contest, she wrote, "I was introduced to him at a Ball two years ago & danced with him. He resides in Charleston bids fair to be a fine Poet." As schoolgirls, Mary Telfair and Mary Few might develop a crush on a man and discuss his virtues long into the night. Mary Telfair would remember one object of their interest: "Mary I long to know whether you are as taciturn as ever although I confess I never found you so *in private* particularly when *our* friend Mr. Wright was the subject, even now the remembrance of his *courteous manner* and our *violent predilection* for him makes me smile."[4]

One gentleman, referred to by Mary Telfair only as "Cousin Joe," was much admired by the young women in her circle. "I was charmed by your description of a *female* Paragon, she must be for a woman as incomparable as 'Cousin Joe,'" Mary wrote to Mary Few. "I should like vastly to see this 'most captivating of human beings.' I have often heard Mrs. Bryan speak in raptures of him; how fortunate it is that he is a married man or all hearts even the most *adamantive* would yield to the power of so much perfection."[5]

Mary thought her sister Sarah quite unlike herself in her approach to romantic love: "She never had any romance in her nature, never dreamed of ideal perfection but calculated on pursuing the *beaten* road to Happiness." With the passage of years, Mary's romantic sentiments dimmed. She confided in Mary Few that "the early mist which romance created around me has for several years past been dispelled and I wonder how I ever *drempt of perfection*." On another occasion she related that the sight of a man and woman together carried her back to her childhood and made her think of "the loves of youth that are no more."[6]

Despite her romantic bent, Mary Telfair had claimed from an early age that she was not the marrying kind. Her sister Sarah had married before her twenty-third birthday; but Margaret, her other sister, would not marry until much later in life. The Telfair girls were not exactly the type that the beaux flocked to at a ball. John Wallace, a young acquaintance, wrote to his sister from Augusta in September 1814, "The pumpkin faced Telfairs were here a few days since,—they cut so many high flourishes, I could not refrain from comparing them to some of the country wenches I have seen in their Sunday gowns."

If a gentleman did come to call, the conversation could become strained. Mary reported to Mary Few on a "long visit from a new acquaintance, a *Northern* Beaux inclined to be *dandyish*." "I have talked myself *hoarse*," she confessed, "my words did not flow *sweetly*. Margaret however relieved me from the task by making her entrée." The picture that Mary paints of herself is that of a young woman, shy and unsure in the presence of a possible suitor, talking incessantly for fear of an uncomfortable silence and finding it a "task" to deal with a difficult social situation. Even if Mary Telfair was not a noted beauty and as a young woman was somewhat awkward with men, she was not alone in these respects, and other girls who were not considered belles went on to become good Republican wives and mothers.[7]

Mary Telfair had too much self-respect to go out of her way to pursue a husband. She had too much dignity to play the coquette. It would have been out of character for her to attempt to do so. She had no use for the typical Southern belle. These girls were selfish and vain. "If I were a man I never *never* would marry a Fashionable Belle for they seldom feel for any one but themselves," she wrote. Mary was of the opinion that a girl ought never to love first. Her friend Mary Clay, whom Mary thought rather susceptible to men, strongly disagreed. Mary admitted that a girl might "accidently conceive a partiality for a gentleman." If so, however, she should never reveal it, "But let concealment, like a worm in the bud / Feed on her damask cheek." Mary's brother-in-law was sure that she would behave accordingly: "Captain Haig says that were I so unfortunate as to *tumble* into love I would disgust the object by my hauteur, so great would be any endeavors to conceal it." Not only was Mary Telfair reserved herself when it came to men, but also disapproved strongly of women who were aggressive:

> Savannah has been in an *uproar* at the arrival of a fashionable London Belle who plays off her airs & graces inimitibly; she not only *shakes hands* with the Beaux but sports her figure in the Waltz with a young Prussian. She abuses us all for being distant & reserved says in England it is customary for the Ladys to make the first advances but I hope that custom will never (for the honor of my countrywomen) be introduced here.[8]

Mary had little interest in parties or balls, the kinds of occasions where courtships could begin. She wrote in 1816:

Savannah has been gay this winter if the idea of gaity can be associated with *Tea Conventions, Public Balls & Card Parties*. I have partaken very moderately of them, for they excite so little interest in me that I always rejoice when the toils of the evening are over and never fail to wish that I could form a little society of those I admire for their mental endowments, and love for their amiable qualities, I should then be so selfish that I would never roam beyond that sphere.[9]

Mary's lack of interest in living the gay life of a belle was a theme that she would return to frequently in her letters:

What is called gay life is everywhere the same. Dressing & feasting, lights, music and *heartlessness* compose it, but rational society—the conversation of animated intelligent people possesses a charm superior to any other in this world. The eye may rove over the beauties of nature or rest upon the treasures of art with delight, but *companionship* is wanting.[10]

Mary Telfair and her sisters were thought of as proud and haughty, and this may have been viewed as an unattractive trait by the young men of their acquaintance. Mary was aware of her reputation and commented on it in a letter to Mary Few:

I am sorry to hear that the Miss Fews have established the same character for Pride in New York that the Miss Telfairs have in Savannah. It is unfortunate but I know from experience that it is impossible to do away public opinion; it is very *inveterate*. I like to think myself destitute of *false pride;* it is a mean contemptible passion; but there is a proper pride which every human being ought to possess, a pride that deters us from committing a little action and which I hope never to lose. Perhaps your unpopularity arises from the same cause of ours; you have not a general acquaintance and are not deceitful enough to appear interested in people whose every word is calculated to create a *yawn.* There is not a greater *bore* than to be compelled to associate with beings who awaken no faculty of mind or soul.[11]

Mary's proud demeanor may have been a cover for a lack of self-esteem. She considered herself unattractive to men. When a friend who was off on a trip offered to lend her a beau, Mary protested, "I am sure that he would *refuse* me particularly as he once bowed lowly at the shrine of *Beauty, Wit & Fashion*." She promised Mary Few that she would try to summon the courage to sit for a portrait to send to her, "notwithstanding my aversion to seeing my own ugliness." In thanking Mary Few for the gift of a bonnet, she could not resist poking fun at her own appearance. She liked the bonnet, she wrote, "because it conceals or rather shades an ugly face; I am in hopes it will *frighten the pimples away as well as the freckles*." Perhaps she could have used herself some of the "rouge and pearl powder" that she recommended to a friend to regain her husband's lost affections. She had a question for Mary Few: "Cannot we find two *intellectual Slovens* with spirit enough to amuse our solitary hours who will be satisfied with *the old & ugly club*?" Telfair also was inclined to deprecate her own personal qualities. "I often wonder at the interest some people take, or *appear* to take, in me," she wrote, "as I do not possess that sort of fascination they value." Similarly she lamented, "I have not the qualities to excite devotion." She was only half joking when she wrote, "If the first step towards improvement is to distrust ones self I must be on the rapid march to *Perfection*." She minced no words when she declared, "I sometimes think I am the *queerest* animal in creation and feel not a little elated when I meet with one as *queer* as myself."[12]

Mary Telfair also refused to accord the "Lords of Creation" the respect they thought they deserved. While the belles stroked the egos of the local beaux, Mary could be downright rude. The word probably was out that Mary Telfair was not the sweet, deferential type who would make a submissive helpmate. Consider Mary's disdainful treatment of Jabez Jackson, the son of James Jackson, the Revolutionary War general and governor of Georgia from 1798 to 1801. Jabez had developed a romantic interest in Margaret Telfair. Margaret and the Telfairs' friend Catharine Hunter were themselves rude to the young man during his frequent visits to their Philadelphia boardinghouse in the summer of 1818, and Mary found it all quite amusing: "Jabez is not exactly like the ague & fever for he does not come *every other day* but every day to see us. I am seriously afraid Catharine Hunter & Margaret will offend him. They have taken it into their heads to quiz him & he to be a *professed Beau*. You would smile to witness his *evolutions*." Mary assured Mary Few that there was nothing to the rumor that Jabez and Margaret were romantically involved:

As for the foolish report about Jabez I never give it a second thought. To be sure he lived almost at Mrs. Frazier's and behaved *so foolishly* as to create a laugh among the borders whenever he made his bow. Margaret and Catharine Hunter actually outraged decency in their behavior towards him, they *quoted* from him to his face, he really is something of a spaniel he bears ill treatment too patiently to induce one to think he is made of *sound* materials.[13]

One problem that Mary had with her sister's suitor was the peculiarity of his language. Undiplomatically she let him know what she thought of this eccentricity:

I gave him to understand his language was too high flown, for positively at times it baffles me to find a meaning. He says New York is a *fungus a heterogeneous mass, an insupportable influx.* Ask Frances to translate it into common sense for me. He is too *wise* for my poor brain; I can't stand such a volley of hard words—speaking of a Gentleman of superior mind he said his *ramifications* were characteristic.[14]

Mary became even more certain that nothing would come of the match when Jabez's visits became less frequent after the sisters returned to Savannah in the fall:

He ought to like me for I was very *kind* to him, however his penchant for Margaret if he ever entertained any has *cooled off;* he has been to our house only three times since our return. . . . I tried to study Jabez's character, but it defies *my speculations.* I think he is cold and I suspect *calculating.* Margaret has as great an antipathy to a man without manners as I have to a man without mind, so there is not the smallest chance of Jabez proving an accepted lover if he was to come forward as such.[15]

It is easy to see why Jabez Jackson stopped calling on Margaret. When he did, he had to put up with her elder sister who thought "a little *seasoning* of common sense would strengthen his mentals and a *good drubbing* render his body more supple." Mary admitted that she was not very polite to the young man:

I am afraid I have given offense to his *serene* highness, he spent an evening here about a fortnight ago and was in *fine spirits,* he actually made himself a complete Buffoon. I not only roared in his face but I exercised my tongue with some severity; I made him both *feel and hear*. We had a most tremendous argument. What do you think were the subjects—*Love & Marriage*. He says it is very hard that a Man cannot fall in love with a woman of fortune without being called a Fortune Hunter and I told him it was equally hard that a Gentleman could not visit a Lady without a report ensuing—he is certainly a very strange Being. I sometimes think he is a quiz. I am certain that he is a *Gossip*; he knows a great deal of scandal and loves to deal it out with a bountiful hand. I really thought highly of him notwithstanding his want of refinement until last summer, but now he is no favorite of mine.[16]

Although Margaret would profess a "singleness of heart" and claimed that she would not be won by "stratagems or spoils," one must wonder whether Mary ever listened to her younger sister's opinions before conveying to Mary Few her own version of Margaret's feelings:

As to his getting into our family *I* never drempt of such a thing, for I knew his want of *fashionable* consequence, *air* and *manner* would be an insuperable objection with Margaret who likes the society and attentions of men but I am convinced that she is as indifferent to changing her name as I am, indeed we are all so happy in each other that we desire no change.[17]

George Glen was another young man treated shamelessly by Mary Telfair. Writing from Philadelphia, she joked with Mary Few over one encounter with the gentleman:

Thanks to my dear Mary for her letter which was handed to me this morning by Mr. Glen accompanied by an *explosive* smile. I mean to make him *useful* as no danger can result from *propinquity* therefore dear Molly I will follow your *good* advice. I wished to know what effect the air of Park Place had on the *nerves* of Mr. G. whether he "shook from the turret to foundation stone" or "philosopher like viewed thee unmoved, but those were questions I could not put to him."

Writing again of George Glen, this time from Ballston Spa, Telfair demonstrated once more her fondness for making men the object of ridicule: "We took a long walk this morning to the Lovers leap. Mr. Glen was of the party. I tried to persuade him to leap but he was too wise."[18]

Mary's women friends were all too aware of her harsh treatment of men. While her friend Catharine Hunter was still unmarried, Mary criticized her for being too hard on men. "I never heard her speak well of more than two men," Mary told Mary Few. "She is very difficult to please—she has not an eye to popularity, she smiles graciously on those she likes and treats those she dislikes very rudely." Mary did not fail to recognize the irony in her comment. "I undertook don't laugh to *lecture* her upon the subject," Mary related. Catharine Hunter, however, thought that Mary was no one to lecture *her*, "She seemed to think my precept better than my example."[19]

Mary admitted that she was "not a general admirer of the ruder sex." "I have never seen one that could cause my heart to palpitate one moment," she told Mary Few, "all my affections I have to spare to that sex are centered in my Brothers." "I sometimes meet with one who can talk so as to induce me to listen but very, very seldom." Frances Few sometimes would express exasperation over her friend's negative comments about men. It was "the old theme," which grated on her "like a piano out of tune, not quite so discordant as the cry of the boding owl." One gentleman with whom a friend was in love was described by Mary as belonging to "a class of men that you meet with every day—there is nothing in his manners, conversation or appearance that would distinguish him from the common order." And a man of her acquaintance in New York she dubbed "His Serene Dullness." Yet she preferred a man who was reserved in manner. "I have come round to Madame de Staël's way of thinking, that reserved men possess most sensibility—Shewy men are almost always hollow-hearted."[20]

Even Mary's dear brother Alexander could be maddening at times, especially when he played the patriarch or flaunted his role as the protective male. On one occasion when Mary passed along to him Mary Few's remembrance, he "made some gallant speeches" in reply. "He says you are *endeared* to him by Canada associations," Mary reported to her friend, "that you were one of his charges & he loves every one who is dependent on him." "Just like the Lords of Creation," Mary sniffed, "but I say they depend more on us *frail* beings than they are willing to acknowledge." Alexander needed to be put in his place on occasion, and his sister was just the one to do it. On the other hand, Mary was always happy to defer to Alexander's wishes. He was the head of the household, generous and kind to be sure, but in family matters he was not to be pushed:

> I sometimes think the difficulty we encountered two summers ago will induce my brother to decide on a northern trip—he is so considerate and makes so many sacrifices for our happiness that I do not like to draw too largely on his indulgence. I never mind seeing selfish folkes put out of the way, but I cannot impose on disinterested ones, so, anxious as I am to visit the North I have never expressed my wishes on the subject.[21]

Although Mary appreciated good looks in a man, a gentleman need not be handsome to be pleasing: "Looks go but a little way towards happiness—the *inward* man is more important than the *outward* and as Shakespeare justly observes 'Tis not the front and visage of a man that stamps his merit.'" Yet she was not above commenting unfavorably on a man's appearance. Of one gentleman of her acquaintance she wrote, "The Judge has returned from Washington as fat as an Alderman who lives on Turtle Soup." Another she thought "as fat as a summer fig." And still another she put down with the comment, "He looks as if he wanted small change to buy shoe strings." Some men she thought rather strange. Of one she wrote to Mary Few, "I think *entre nous* (for walls have ears) that with his black gloves on that he might pass for a Jesuit—and his noiseless step seems to suit the aisle of a *Gothic* Cathedral."[22]

One would expect that Mary Telfair would have found romance at one of the fashionable spas that she visited during her summer sojourns to the North. Not so. The beaux at Sans Souci in Ballston Spa, she thought, "do very well in a Ball-room but they do not possess the art of pleasing in conversation." Upon arriving at Ballston one July, she expressed her disapproval of the company in a letter to Mary Few: "There are very few ladies—and those few appear to be very sociable —but the men oh! they are a terrible looking set—both ugly & ungenteel." "I will except one who is really a charming looking Fellow," she added. As usual, there was one major problem: "Sarah and I were both delighted with his appearance but fortunately before our hearts were quite captivated we discovered that he was a married Man." Despite the gentleman's marital status, Mary could not resist describing him to Mary Few and adding a comment on the wife:

I will describe his person and if your ideas of beauty and mine coincide you will admire the description. He is of the middle size rather above than below—neither too stout or too thin—dresses very plain & genteel—has a beautiful intelligent pair of black eyes, fine forehead & eyebrows—good nose and very pretty mouth, chin & teeth—his features are perfectly regular & countenance uncommonly expressive, complexion dark, & no colour that may be occasioned by ill health—His Wife is here she is neither pretty or agreeable—very awkward in her manners.[23]

Many of the attractive men that Mary Telfair met were indeed married. She described to Mary Few a man she had met in Madison Springs: "I have been very much pleased with his conversation; he is called a man of superior talents, and appears to possess a good deal of feeling, without much refinement—he is . . . *married.*" Mary Few accused her friend of admiring only married men. Telfair laughingly denied it. "As I am not a *marrying* character, it is immaterial to me whether a man is old or young, married or unmarried, so as he has the powers of entertainment." On an earlier occasion, however, she admitted a preference for the company of married men for with them she need "entertain no notions of being pleased or pleasing too much"[24] In a word, she was more comfortable in the company of married men, for with them she had no need to go out of her way to be charming.

If a man with interesting possibilities did show up at a summer resort, Mary's sense of refinement would keep her from joining in the chase. One gentleman described to Mary as "a Lawyer above the drudgery of the law" made an appearance at Ballston one August and caught her attention. "I am not well enough acquainted with him to discover whether he belongs to the order of fine spirits," she confided to Mary Few, "but hear from those that are intimately acquainted with him that he possesses *genius & refinement.*" Would she pursue this fine fellow? She simply could not bring herself to do so. "I find that I am more reserved here than any where because I see every one laying themselves out to attract and hear the censures passed on them." When Alexander was on hand, however, he could be a useful intermediary. Writing from Schooleys Mountain one July, Mary described one such occasion:

> We had *one Agreeable* here for ten days but he could not, or would not, talk to Ladies, but I always contrived to get near so

as to enjoy his conversation as Alexander was his constant companion it afforded me an excuse of being an *Eaves dropper*. Politics, Agriculture and Character seemed his favorite topics—the latter of course was more *musical* to my ear.[25]

The women at Ballston vied with one another for the attention of the gentlemen and the admiration of other women. One star would be eclipsed by another as new arrivals appeared on the scene: "Miss Rutledge I hear has eclipsed the Beach's. Her polished surface is no longer overwhelmed by the waves of admiration, her tide I fancy is ebbing fast and if Miss R and Miss Thomas continue to rise in favor she will be soon deserted." Mary was not about to enter the competition. Certainly she was not willing to make a fool of herself like the Morris girls. "The Morrises *grin* in vain, they can't be Belles however they *make a great noise* and aid Tom Smith and his followers in their orgies." Mary was "quite sickened with the scene."[26]

On one occasion Mary was pursued by a man she believed to be of low moral character. She did everything necessary to avoid his company. She described the unseemly circumstances to Mary Few:

> I assure you that Mr. Ebenezer Harlow Cumming was not the person I alluded to, for he is not personally acquainted with either Sarah or myself. How came you acquainted with that Gentleman? I know him too well from character and when he solicited to be introduced to me at a Ball I refused the Gentleman thru whose medium the request was made for I had often heard him spoken of as an artful, unprincipled Man perfectly regardless of truth. I could tell you a great many anecdotes respecting him that would excite your contempt, ridicule & abhorrence, but I find he is a Man of some consequence at the Northward and it would be a pity to mention any thing that would injure him yet probably he has *reformed* perhaps pique at our refusing to become acquainted with his Lordship has induced him to register us in his *scandalous chronicle* for he claimed us in Georgia to be *proud & satirical* moreover declared me to be an *intimate acquaintance* of his.[27]

Mary was always quick to put down gossip concerning her purported romantic involvements. She expressed surprise to Mary Few that a mutual friend had passed on a rumor that she, who was "such an admirer of the Christian faith," was engaged to be married to an "elegant Jew." Few reported to her friend that she had denied the rumor. Mary wrote back:

> I am glad that you contradicted it for neither *Jew* or *Gentile* has any chance of drawing me as a prize in the grand lottery of matrimony. I am too great a lover of *liberty* to resign it particularly to an Israelite besides I belong to a family devoted to "single blessedness," therefore my dear Molly believe anything you hear of me sooner than that I am going to be married, not that I am enemy to the *holy institution*. I approve highly of the state when two persons enter into it from disinterested affection and where there exists a congeniality of character, but I have always thought the number of happy matches considerably less than unhappy and always conclude that there are faults on both sides. Among the whole circle of my acquaintance I know of but one couple who come up to my ideas of a rational pair.[28]

Mary liked to joke with Mary Few about marriage and men. An unmarried man was an "unappropriated sweet." "So you really believe I have experienced the pangs of Cupid's dart," she teased, "the very idea of it makes me laugh." Mary Telfair had received from Frances Few an amusing missive that referred to "Old Maid's Alley, Courting Corner, and the Temple of Hymen." Referring to this piece in a letter to Mary Few, she wrote: "Tell Fan I admire her wit and should like to know which of the three is her shrine. I suspect she means to slip into the latter with some *dear creature*. I hope she will give me timely notice and not take me by surprise for the *shock* will be almost too much for my nerves." Telfair expressed the belief that she and Mary Few would become old maids and that they could be content in the single state. "I think Molly you and I could joy through life without an *incumbrance*, which most women think absolutely essential to happiness." Mary Few might fool her, however: "But Mary what report is this you alluded to for I am all curiosity to know who you have been flirting with. Oh! you are a sly girl and betrayed yourself without intending it, however I will not believe it as you say there is no truth in it."[29]

In reporting to Mary Few that her cousin Sarah Jones had danced with Alfred Cuthbert at her brother's wedding, Mary Telfair referred to Alfred as her friend's "old flame." "Don't be jealous of Sarah

Jones," she joked. "Have you lost your heart yet?" she asked in the same letter and went on to nip in the bud a rumor that she herself was engaged. "A report has been circulating here (& believed by many) that I am engaged to a young Gentleman in this Place. Should you hear it believe it not as my heart continues the same as when we separated no *new emotion* has caused it to throb and nothing short of a *Clem* ever will."[30] Presumably Clem was a young man who had caught Mary's fancy at an earlier time.

Mary Telfair felt it right that her friend not make any "rash vows" against marriage "in this *Chivalric* age." She teased Mary Few that she thought "some dauntless son of Mars might prove your heart not invulnerable, and by his graceful evolutions induce you to surrender after a *short* siege." On one occasion when she suspected that her friend might have been attracted to a young military officer, Mary was quick to offer encouragement: "Were your *blushes* called forth by the appearance of *a certain gallant Hero* or were you provokingly tranquil, take care that my predictions are not verified as I think Frances's judgment in most instances correct and as she approves highly of this Son of Mars *I will give my consent.*" In one of her letters to Mary Few expressing disappointment that she had not been able to persuade her friend to summon enough courage to leave home and cross the "vasty deep" for a winter in Savannah, Telfair wrote that it would have been "only for a winter unless some *eloquent* Son of the South could have prevailed upon you to remain here *for life.*" "I would for selfish reasons espouse his cause," she added. One young man who had been pursuing Mary Few with no success was cut to pieces by the sharp point of Mary Telfair's quill pen. Referring to a trip to Niagara Falls that the young ladies were planning, Mary wrote to Few: "I know *who* would be very glad to join the party but I will not venture the name. I leave it to your ingenious fancy to devise *who* I mean—poor fellow I am seriously apprehensive that he got *frost bitten* walking so often to Richmond Hill that combined with the *cold looks* was enough to convert him into an Icicle."[31]

Lighthearted banter concerning men was sometimes exchanged between Mary Telfair and Frances Few through the agency of Frances' sister.

But a word to Miss Frances—call her to an account in my name for *daring* to predict that my *fair* hand *impressed with the signet of liberty* would be bestowed eventually upon some *"good, easy cake loving mortal"* alas! I could never exercise my talents in behalf of such an animal—he should *starve* or feed upon *hominy & corn bread* the best food for people of *leaden* minds—I must have my retort, however—Tell her *the oracle* tells me that instead of a *tall, thin Cassius looking* fellow with intellectual attractions (that is more mind than heart) she will fancy some *fat, merry faced* Being, with *kindness* stamped upon his brow, who will prove as *jolly* as he is *good*—I draw my omen from this—Women always marry the reverse of what they most admire in imagination.[32]

Like Mary Telfair, Mary Few enjoyed teasing friends about the young men that passed through their lives. Her friend Mary Garrettson was on the receiving end of a few barbs when the rumor mill revealed that she was interested in a gentleman from Georgia:

> And who is this wondrous Georgia beau? Sister mysterious is at her old tricks again. Do you remember the horned son and the beau who came at ten in the morning and staid till ten at night. I suppose the sugar and molasses beau is near a kin to him. Henry Algernon!! expressive hazel eyes! noble contour! what a fascinating creature! No wonder your tender heart was moved. . . .
>
> I wish I had some charming Algernon to descant upon—but alas! alas! they do not abound. It is only by such rare damsels as sister mysterious and sister curiosity that they are to be found. As for poor me the only fascinator I have seen since I have been in Maryland was a married man!! Do you not pity me? Well it is really a pitiable case.[33]

Much as she might protest that her heart was "impenetrable to the wiles of sly little Cupid," one suspects that Mary Telfair once harbored hopes of finding her "charming unknown." It is doubtful that she really meant it when she wrote, "I never *have, could, or will* see a *Soul* in a man worth loving." If she really had so little interest in marriage, why did she dwell on the subject to such an extent in her letters? It is revealing that as a young woman she owned a small book entitled "Practical Hints to Young Females on the Duties of a Wife, a Mother and a Mistress of a Family." Her name appears on the flyleaf along with the date 1816. Perhaps at the age of twenty-five she had met a young man whom she hoped might ask for her hand in marriage. A decade later, when an acquaintance, newly married to a Mr. Davis, sent Mary a message through a friend expressing the hope that she, Mary, would soon follow her example, Mary asked the friend to "tell her I will do so if she can provide me with a Mr. Davis."[34]

Mary was well aware of the social disadvantages of spinsterhood. She agreed with Mary Few that a mutual acquaintance "ought to have had a *Pilot* to have directed her *light* barque and sheltered her from the *Rocks* and *quicksands* of single life." She also wrote, "Very few women can grow old *single* without being soured by the mortifications and disappointment attendant on the state of *solitaire*." In a reflective mood, she mused, "Pascal says we ought to learn to live alone for we must die alone. It is easy to talk but difficult to act." She knew that those in "old maid's alley" must stand "the world's dread laugh." She realized that a single woman must take care not to become self-centered: "I have so often heard that single people become absorbed in self that I am very vigilant for fear that I may fall into the error of studying my own comfort and ease more than that of others." But then, a single woman might become too absorbed in the lives of her family and friends. "I think (entre nous) that there is very little medium in unmarried women," she wrote to Mary Few. "They are apt to sink into entire listlessness, or to be too busy in the concerns of others." "Woman is an odd compound," she wrote on another occasion, "she must be restless or listless." "I try to steer between Scylla & Charybdis, and find myself very near being wrecked upon the latter," she continued, "And yet I am always occupied." "My choice is made to be an amiable and if I can a *useful* old maid," she wrote. "I am not afraid of possessing either the *envy, hatred & malice* usually attributed to that class of females, as I feel no *glimmerings*. The sparks of those evil passions will never I hope be kindled in my heart."[35]

Mary believed that "a married woman is always of more consequence than a single one" and that "it requires a vast deal of Independence for an *old maid* and a variety of resources to bear up against the neglect of an unfeeling world." But then, too, life was difficult for women in general: "The lot of woman in this life is a hard one, and it requires instead of *a Coat of Mail* a *Coat of Independence* to shield her from the shafts of envy, malice and all uncharitableness." The life of a woman in the South was particularly hard. "You must read the Southern Matron," she urged Mary Few, "it will give you an insight into the cares and perplexities of a Southern Woman."[36]

Whether she harbored hopes, no proposals of marriage came Mary's way, or at least none that she found acceptable. Her lack of suitors does not seem to have bothered her greatly. If men, uninteresting and unrefined as so many were, preferred empty-headed belles to women of intellect, so be it. The disdain that so often surfaced in her treatment of beaux such as Jabez Jackson and George Glen is reflected in this bit of verse found in her commonplace book:

> So sir you really do declare
> You'll dance with none but who are fair
> Suppose we Women should dispense
> Our hands to none but men of sense
> Suppose . . . Well Madam & what then
> Why sir you'd never dance again.[37]

Spinsterhood was a matter to be treated lightly, at least on the surface. "I have never viewed the state of 'single blessedness' with horror," Mary insisted. Her resignation as she grew older is found in these lines copied into her commonplace book:

> Retire with decent and becoming grace,
> And leave to younger Belles your former place.
> Thus prudent Generals weakened troops withdraw
> And leave the field of action with *éclat*.

Mary must have expressed polite amusement when a woman friend copied into her commonplace book a piece from Hannah More's *Moral Sketches* that she called "advice to old maids by one of the sisterhood." And Mary herself copied into her book the lines, "How happy is the blameless Vestal's lot! The world forgetting, by the world forgot." Humor also tempered Mary's thoughts in this comment on the subject of love:

> I cannot coincide with "Cousin Joe" in [the] opinion that there is no happiness without love. Indeed I think the *Belle Passion* productive of more misery than felicity however I am only a *Theorist* on that subject, never having bowed to the dominion of "the Felicitous *Tyrant*" consequently [I] am a very *negative* character.[38]

Mary had some very definite ideas on the suitability of the marriages of her friends and acquaintances as well as on the way that some of her contemporaries approached the holy institution. She wrote in 1814 of the relationship between Mary Few's cousin Ignatius and his wife:

> Your cousin Ignatius, now Colonel Few, is stationed here; he commanded the militia in this district and is said to be an excellent officer. Do you remember what *bitter foes* we were and how he delighted in tormenting me? He married about two years ago a beautiful girl of Columbia County but a *terrible vixen*; she has made him lead a terrible life ever since.[39]

Cousin Ignatius went on to become a Methodist minister and a founder in 1836 of Emory University. In later years Mary mellowed a bit when it came to his wife, the vixen: "We received a visit from Mrs. Few this morning. She improves upon acquaintance, but I still think Mr. Few merited a different *Help Meet*." On another occasion Mary wrote to Mary Few concerning her cousin's "Help Meet": "His wife has been a *Beauty* and a *Shrew*—Time I presume has robbed her of all claims to the first, and religion tamed the latter."[40]

Mary had no time for mothers who insisted on brilliant matches for their daughters:

> Mrs. L must find it a Herculean task to make up her mind to *settle* Cora—She is too ambitious to be satisfied with any but a splendid alliance—What an error in Mothers to look for that which cannot confer happiness! *Companionable* qualities with the gentler virtues united with a *useful* intellect is more to be appreciated than all the glitter of wealth or allurements of fame; but people who live in the gay world continually must marry as well as every thing else to please that world.

Marriages that were nothing more than a "match of calculation" met with her disapproval as well: "If we had mirrors to reflect *hearts* as well as faces we should find many bowing before the holy altar with hearts unoccupied by that affection which seems necessary to bear a woman through the cares, the duties & uncertainties of married life."[41]

Mary was surprised to learn of the possible split-up of a married couple of her acquaintance, particularly in view of the lady's mercenary tendencies:

> I thought her just heartless enough to sail through life with a man she did not care a sou for, and he seemed a mere *Lackey*

—She needed no *Pilot* but gold—no anchor but silk—it needed not this example to convince me that *sterling principle* is more requisite as a bond of union in married life than *sterling pounds*. Have you heard the cause of this projected separation? He must have played Truant to *Love* or *Money* to have tempted one so ambitious of the world's approbation to take such a step. I heard it whispered when they were at Ballston that "*Separate Apartments*" were requisite, and I am old fashioned enough to condemn that modern innovation.[42]

Of one potential attachment Mary wrote, "He is very rich and a very good man that is all I can say in his favor—I am still *romantic* enough to think that it is better to marry a poor man for love than a rich one for money." Worse yet was to marry a poor man simply for the sake of getting married:

> Mrs. Genl. Wayne has taken her spouse to Charleston to live. He had not the means of supporting her here. What a miserable match—She leaves him and his children there and goes to her Mother for the summer. Poor soul her aim was to be married and his to get a fortune—I wonder when we look into the motives that lead half the people to assume the matrimonial yoke that there are as many happy couples as we meet with in the world.[43]

Even worse for a woman and her family was a marriage to a man who turned out to be a scoundrel:

> You have heard of Miss Early—she was educated at Mrs. Grelaus and after receiving a winters polish in Philadelphia came out here last winter and was much attended to on account of her musical talents. She is the child of adoption and was led to believe she would be a great Heiress. Owing to the unprincipled conduct of Mr. Early who defrauded his wife of an independent property settled upon her, they are reduced to want and this poor Girl just seventeen gives a public concert in order to purchase the necessaries of life.[44]

In an ideal world, Mary believed, a woman should love a man for himself and enter into a marriage without regard to his wealth or social position. The world was far from ideal, however:

I do not pretend to be a diviner into *les affaires des cœurs* for it is hard to tell the state of feelings from the manners, but I used to think in my young days of Romance that if I was a man gifted by fortune & fame, I would play Burchell in the Vicar of Wakefield and win some unsophisticated heart that could love me in an *old coat* and love me for myself. I fear Le Count never could have succeeded in such a disguise and few men of the present day could. It is certainly the fashion to be heartless. The engagement between Le Count & Eliza Hunter is dissolved. I have not heard the particulars of the affair. I only think he shewed a *dreadful* want of judgment in thinking of her and she a terrible deficiency in delicacy in engaging her hand, where she could not bestow her affections. I am a firm believer in *presentiment.* I always predicted she would break with him, for she is an ambitious Girl and wishes to make a display in society. A man of some fashion & a fine establishment is what she requires to make her happy.[45]

As far as Mary Telfair was concerned, for a marriage to work, harmony was required:

Two people coming together in holy wedlock always reminds me of two Birds in a Cage. Unless they sing in concert, what *discord* ensues—far better to *chirp* & tune their notes on some lonely spray, *unseen unheard* in "single blessedness," for a *solus* well performed, is preferable to an indifferent *Duet.*[46]

When Telfair disapproved of a match, she could get rather worked up about it:

What does Ann Wallace think of her Uncle Stiles's dereliction from common sense? He is in a few days to become a married man—His choice a young silly girl who I suppose is dazzled by his *filthy* lucre, for I can think of nothing *clean* attached to him—We have often discoursed upon the *insanity* of widowers but this exceeds all that has ever occurred in the annals of foolish matches—I understand he is *a devoted Love.* A man who for forty years has never left his own domicile except to walk over his fields & attend Church drives up daily in his Barouche to the door of his *fair Enslaver* and basks the whole morning in her smiles. Have I been too severe upon the old Man dear Mary?

After the wedding Mary began referring to the bride as "old Mrs. Stiles." As for old man Stiles himself: "I hear he goes to *Roost* with the Fowls at seven o'clock—how terrible to be condemned to the pillow for so many wearisome hours."[47]

Mary Telfair could be rather catty. It is easy enough to figure out why she was not invited to this wedding:

> Last night "the rich Mr. Potter" led Miss Grimes to the altar. It was an inauspicious day, it stormed violently and Sol did not smile upon them for a moment. I have seen no one who was at the Wedding, but presume it was a splendid affair—The Bride glittering in Topaz and smiling without meaning—The Bride Groom displaying the poetry of *motion* for he understands all those graceful evolutions which distinguishes a man of fashion, and yet (entre nous) I always feel inclined to yawn when he talks to me—next to George Glen he is the greatest *mental anodyne* I have ever encountered—So much for "the best match in Georgia," and yet he is a *superexcellent* match for Sarah Grimes—But stupid men are often *the best matches*.[48]

Mary wrote to Mary Few of "a very singular marriage" that was about to take place in Savannah. There was a good deal of buzzing over the match among the members of the church. One of the more pious members remarked that the church would weep over such a marriage. "It does not strike me as a criminal connection," Mary opined, "but one highly revolting to delicacy." Yet, she thought that their minister would not refuse to perform the ceremony. What were the circumstances that caused such a stir? The prospective bride was Mrs. John Elliott, a woman of exalted piety. As Mary explained it:

> She married in the first instance a Man old enough for her Father and no doubt sacrificed feeling to ambition. She made a most exemplary Wife & (hardest of all duties) an excellent Step Mother. For four years she has acted the part of a dignified Widow which of all characters (Step Mother excepted) is the most difficult to support, and now she is about marrying her husband's daughter's husband—he has been living in the house with her ever since the death of his wife and I thought viewed

by her with sisterly regard. I begin to think with Miss Edgeworth that *propinquity* is dangerous and beyond the relationship of Brother and Sister mutual dependance is apt to create sentiments more tender than platonic.

The late Mr. Elliott's surviving daughter's feelings were, according to Mary, "very much enraged." "She was devotedly attached to her Step Mother," Mary wrote, "but refuses to have any intercourse with her or her Brother-in-Law." Mary felt very sorry for Mrs. Elliott.[49]

Mary claimed to find marriage customs ridiculous. She could not believe her ears when she learned that an acquaintance had paid ninety dollars for a wedding gown. Her comment on a newly engaged couple "sitting up for company" was, "What an odious practice!" She would never engage in such silly behavior: "It is lucky I have never been a Bride or I should have trampled on all bridal laws—married without spectators and disappointed the gourmands of their cake. I very believe that if some women married Methuselahs they would have Brides Maids and cover their *night caps* with a veil and attend to all the etceteras of the business."[50]

Mary felt elaborate weddings most inappropriate when a woman married a "Methuselah." It was not that she objected to people marrying late in life; it was only the manner in which the wedding was carried out:

> There is no folly in marrying late if people marry suitably and observe no more form than in *walking to Church*. It is the pomps & ceremonies attendant upon a wedding with the *billing* and *cooing* that succeeds it which makes it appear ridiculous for those who are not young to marry.[51]

Mary found it unseemly for a newly married woman to go on at great length about her marital bliss:

> I have a strange sort of feeling that I do not like to hear a woman directly after she is married dwell with rapture on the happiness of conjugal felicity—No doubt every woman who marries from affection & is not disappointed in the object must be a great deal happier but let it be a *silent* happiness until time & experience justifies her talking of it.[52]

In an age when disease was rampant and childbirth fraught with danger, a man frequently would marry a second or third time. So too might a woman whose husband was stricken in one of the plagues that descended so frequently without warning. Mary Telfair sometimes would reflect on this subject:

> There is no connection so close as that of Husband & Wife and yet generally speaking it is sooner forgotten. I think the reason is it is the only tie which death dissolves that can be renewed. It is taking a melancholy view of the inconstancy of the human heart when we reflect that a few months after the most devoted Wife & Mother is consigned to the dark & lonely grave, she is scarcely remembered, and in a year or two another fills her place—Alas! poor human Nature![53]

It was a theme to which she would return:

> It is indeed "the fate of Woman to be forgotten." The conjugal tie though the closest is the only one which (when severed) can be renewed—to that we may ascribe the facility with which the most beloved husbands, and wives, are forgotten after death. It is wisely ordered for were it otherwise, how desolate would be homes and how neglected would be children! I think it requires great singleness of heart to love *devotedly* and peculiar qualities in the object beloved.[54]

Mary Telfair's attitudes with respect to men and marriage bear a striking resemblance to those found in the correspondence of Mary Adelaide ("Addie") Dogan (1830–1873) and her twin sister, Caroline Dogan (1830–1881), of Unionville, South Carolina, of which Joan E. Cashin has written. One thinks of Mary Telfair upon reading that "only once did they even describe a man of their acquaintance as attractive, and he was safely married to one of their friends." They used military imagery similar to Mary Telfair's in describing encounters between the sexes: a suitor preparing to "besiege and attack" and attempts to dodge Cupid's "fatal arrows." They believed that married couples rarely were happy. When one of their relatives married, they wrote that she had "resigned her single blessedness for a name and a ring." Although they had made a "resolution against matrimony," the Dogan twins, unlike Mary Telfair and her friend Mary Few, did eventually marry, Addie at age twenty-six and Caroline at twenty-eight.[55]

Joan Cashin found that the Dogan sisters "always felt far more comfortable in the company of other women than they did in that of men."[56] While Mary Telfair could be shy and awkward as a young woman in the presence of a potential suitor, as she grew older she became more at ease with men and enjoyed dealing with them on their own terms. Some of Mary's happiest hours, however, were spent within her circle of female friends, where conversation flowed lightly and freely, accompanied by the click of knitting needles. Even greater satisfaction came from the exchange of serious thoughts in conversations or correspondence with women friends to whom Mary felt particularly close. The bonds of friendship that Mary forged with members of the "Sisterhood" enriched her life beyond measure.

6

The Sisterhood

[I]f one asked me to what do I think one must principally attribute the singular prosperity and growing force of this people [the Americans], I would answer that it is to the superiority of its women.

Alexis de Tocqueville,
Democracy in America (1840)

Mary Telfair valued most highly her friendships with other women, those members of the "Sisterhood" with whom she maintained warm, caring relationships. At the top of the list, of course, were her two natal sisters, cherished companions with whom she shared life's joys and sorrows. They had shared with her, as no one else could, the grief that came with the death of close family members. Mary and Margaret had been at Sarah's side when her husband's life came to an end and later when death took her infant son. It was Sarah and Margaret with whom Mary would spend quiet evenings by the fireside, reading aloud and sewing. It was they who would cheer her during her blue moods. They were her traveling companions on journeys to the North, sharers of the same adventures, bearers of the same memories. The Telfair sisters were a trio. They depended on each other for mutual love and for mutual care, both physical and emotional.

Many of Mary's dearest friends were ladies in the North with whom she associated during the summer months, including the Few sisters, her friends from childhood. Mary and her sisters also had a congenial circle of friends in Savannah. During the winter months there would be visits by female friends to the Telfair mansion and return visits by the Telfair ladies. Mornings would be spent in good conversation accompanied by the play of needles. There were afternoon teas and family dinners to share with other women, principally ladies of the best families who shared the Telfairs' colonial heritage and personal refinement.

Historian Carroll Smith-Rosenberg contends that between the mid-eighteenth and mid-nineteenth centuries "American society was characterized in large part by a rigid gender-role differentiation within the family and within society as a whole, leading to the emotional segregation of women and men." She argues convincingly that during this period a specifically female world developed, "a world built around a generic and unself-conscious pattern of single-sex or homosocial networks." The female relationships so formed, she observes, "were frequently supported by severe social restrictions on intimacy between men and women." "Within such a world of emotional richness and complexity," she writes, "devotion to and love of other women became a plausible and socially acceptable form of human interaction." Suzanne Lebsock found in the Virginia town of Petersburg a separate female culture, a body of values and attitudes distinctive to women. This culture, she maintains, had its foundation in the manner in which women of similar backgrounds identified with each other and offered each other practical assistance.[1]

Joan E. Cashin, in her study of the Dogan twins of Unionville, South Carolina, while stopping short of concluding that a separate women's culture existed in the Old South, found that elite Southern women in cities and towns formed close personal bonds with each other and enjoyed rich, distinctively female social relationships unknown to their more isolated plantation counterparts. Cashin observed that the Dogan sisters often took part in social events reserved for women only. Young women might be invited to arrive early at a party in order to talk and work on a quilt before the male guests arrived. At one party the Dogans had more fun dressing, talking, and joking with the girls before the festivities began than in the parlor where the men were assembled. The Dogans "took great satisfaction in the emotional intimacy they enjoyed with their close circle of female friends."[2]

The Telfair sisters and a few selected women friends formed a club one winter to formalize a social relationship that already existed. The conversation and activities at the weekly meetings were distinctly feminine in character:

Our coterie has been unusually flourishing this winter. We meet once a week at each other's houses. Oyster suppers introduced which promote sociability—and our knot is the envy of the Town. People who shun the gay world require the stimulus of social intercourse. Home is the center of attraction to me and I never wish even for a day to leave it. Still I like to be enlivened very frequently by some cheerful faces besides my own family. We have hitherto introduced only needlework into our club. I have proposed reading a short piece each time by way of furnishing a new topic of conversation even if it gives our conventions an air of pedantry alias *bluestockingism.*

Scandal was prohibited at the weekly meetings, according to Mary. "We talk sentiment, tell anecdotes and make puns," she reported. The Few sisters had formed a similar sorority some years earlier, a study group that met mornings on a regular basis. Matilda Few described it to Mary Garrettson: "Three Miss Lewis's, Maria Laight, Frances, Mary & myself have formed a reading party, one sews while the other reads, every day from 9 to 12 in the History of England. We have reached the fourth Volume and are very much interested in the life of Henry 8."[3]

There were occasions when the conversation at gatherings of the sisterhood might become mildly risqué in a girlish way. One evening, the ladies became "very satirical" and began relating "Saratoga anecdotes." Swearing Mary Few to secrecy, Mary Telfair related to her "a *bon mot* of Sarah's": "A lady with a tremendous *frontpiece* called on us. It was a perfect fortification alias *breastwork*, to complete the scene she wore a *point* in front to a very full body. Sarah said there was *quarts* under the *pint*. What a lawless creature she is?" Bodily functions, too, were an acceptable subject of banter among the ladies of the Telfairs' set: "Sarah heard a cart *rumbling* while she lay in bed a few mornings since and mistook the sound for one emanating from her *own lower regions.*"[4]

The refined evenings that Mary Telfair enjoyed with her women friends were quite different from a "sociable evening" that she spent at the home of the Richard Habershams. Men at a social gathering could change the tone of an evening and interject a certain coarseness that was not entirely to Mary's liking. Mary and her sisters had declined several invitations from Mrs. Habersham, but finally decided that it "seemed selfish to refuse" and that they "must brave the rude attacks of Boreas who whistles a perfect tune in her drawing room." Mary sought refuge in a corner with Anne Clay, a close friend, and Mrs. Cutler, "the finest model of a Clergyman's wife I have ever encountered." The party became spirited: "Richard took the men in the backroom several times, I concluded to give them a little *beverage*. It reminded me of a driver taking his Horses to water. If I was *yoked* to such a man I would change his habits if I could not improve his *morals*."[5]

Most of Mary Telfair's close female friends in Savannah were unmarried. To marry was to "desert the Sisterhood." When a young woman in Mary's circle did take a husband, she generally became less accessible to her unmarried friends, and they often resented it. "Margaret apprized me of her intention of visiting Mrs. Montgomery who I have scarcely heard of since she entered into the *silken* state of matrimony," Mary wrote to Mary Few. Then following up with a reference to a private joke that they shared and a dig at the new husband, she inquired, "Has she been made happy yet? I never think of your objection to Mr. M. without smiling, it certainly was a very formidable one." Sometimes the resentment ran deep, as indicated by a confidence that Mary Telfair shared with Mary Few: "I once had a friend that I adored, she married and forgot me, and all the protestations of friendship she so often made; if you knew the whole story you would think I displayed too much pride on the occasion, but I have never been accustomed to slights and can illy brook them." Mary had particular difficulty adjusting to the marriage in 1815 of her sister Sarah:

> Although I was happy to see Sarah united to the Man of her choice (who is amiable, generous & affectionate) still there was a void created in my heart by her marriage which I never before felt, she had been my constant companion for so many years and although our dispositions were dissimilar, I always rested on her for support in all my little *troubles & difficulties*. She never encouraged me in the *sombre*, her raillery never failed to extinguish gloomy feelings, and I may in truth compare myself to the *ivy* and Sarah to the *sturdy* oak. Time has already reconciled me to the separation for I am certain that her happiness is augmented by it, *new ties* will weaken *old ones* and it would be unreasonable in me to expect to retain that portion of her affections which I once possessed.[6]

Sarah Jones and her half-sister Harriett Campbell had been very close, and Harriett felt most keenly the loss of their intimate companionship when Sarah married Alfred Cuthbert. Mary Telfair turned to biblical imagery in describing her friend's plight:

> I predict that Harriett will follow Sarah's example. She feels the loneliness of her situation now more than ever. Sarah's stealing a march upon her has saddened my poor little friend very much, for she calculated that Sarah and herself would gently glide along the vale of life hand in hand—but alas! alas! human hopes & prospects are in vain! Hal [Harriett] was about creating a little Paradise, she commenced building a House, designed a spot for a garden and looked forward to Sarah & herself inhabiting it like our first Parents in blooming Eden culling flowers and enjoying a life of ease and tranquility but the *tempter* came—remember I do not say he *quoiled* himself into the heart of one—for believe me when I say Sarah's happiness will be greatly increased by the change.[7]

One of Mary's closest friends was Anne Clay, a woman characterized by her as "a charming union of dignity, grace, intelligence & vivacity." Mary found her conversation "both a moral and an intellectual treat." "I have seen Anne Clay several times," Mary wrote on one occasion; "she is very much admired & will prove to be the most brilliant star which will illumine the southern hemisphere this winter." There was no one among her Southern friends for whom Mary had greater admiration. "I never see Anne Clay without thinking of Queen Elizabeth and how well a crown would suit her head," Mary wrote of her regal friend. Perhaps she was rather too austere, however. "I think her more formed to command esteem & admiration than to be beloved," Mary wrote. "She belongs to that class of women who Alexander says are better calculated for Queens than Wives." Despite Alexander's opinion, Anne Clay, in contrast to Mary Telfair, was actively courted, but rejected the married state. She was a woman who made a conscious choice to remain independent. Referring to one of Anne's suitors, Mary Telfair wrote, "I give Anne credit for treating him with such civility. It requires amazing self control to keep *the Lover at a distance* and yet retain him as a friend."[8]

Anne Clay shared the same colonial roots as Mary Telfair. She was the granddaughter of Joseph Clay, who had been Edward Telfair's business partner and a strong supporter of the Revolution. His wife, Anne's grandmother, was Ann Legarderé Clay, who came from a French Huguenot family. Anne's father was Joseph Clay's eldest son, Joseph, Jr., and her mother was Mary Ann Savage, the daughter of Thomas Savage, a merchant who left Bermuda before the Revolutionary War and settled in Charleston. Joseph Clay, Jr., was a brilliant man. He was graduated from college at Princeton with first honors. He read law under Chancellor George Wythe in Williamsburg, Virginia, was admitted to the bar in Georgia, practiced with distinction, and was appointed a judge on the United States District Court for the District of Georgia. He was a planter as well. He cultivated rice along the Ogeechee River in Bryan County not far from where Fort McAllister later stood. Above all, he was a devout Christian. He resigned his judicial post in 1801, was ordained a Baptist minister in 1804, and wound up as pastor of the First Baptist Church of Boston. Anne had a brother, Thomas Savage Clay, and two sisters, Mary and Eliza. Like their father, they were tall people, or as one commentator put it, "Socially high, these four Clay children were also physically high, both the son and the sisters being of commanding bodily proportions." Their friends must have found amusement in seeing Anne Clay and Mary Telfair walking together along Bull Street with the statuesque Anne towering over the five-foot-tall Mary. Joseph Clay, Jr., died in 1811 while his children were still in school in Medford, a Boston suburb. Thomas was eight at the time. The family stayed on in Medford until the children completed their educations. Thomas went on to Harvard, from which he was graduated with an A.B. in 1819 and an A.M. in 1821. In 1809 Mary Clay married William Rufus Gray of Boston. After Thomas' graduation from Harvard, he resettled with his mother and his sister Eliza at "Tranquilla," the family plantation in Bryan County. In 1821 Thomas purchased, through his father's estate, the 487-acre rice plantation on the Great Ogeechee River, known as "Dublin." Anne Clay renamed the plantation "Richmond." Anne, it appears, spent as much of her time in the North as she did in Georgia.[9]

Despite Anne Clay's roots in the South and her frequent visits to Bryan County, the Few sisters thought of her as "a young lady from Boston." Mary Telfair was delighted when Mary Few and Anne Clay had the chance to spend some time together. It gave her pleasure to think of two of her favorite people becoming better acquainted:

I am glad that you had the opportunity of enjoying the society of Anne Clay. I know no two people better calculated for each other & yet you are very different—She is all energy & you are all humility—She brings forward all her stock of information you keep yours as a Miser does his hoard—Much as I admire her, I could never love her as much as I do you—for this reason, I suspect she wants tenderness & sympathy.[10]

Another good friend in Savannah was Catharine Hunter. According to Mary, she was "the most satirical woman I know" and yet "her society is so amusing that I am willing to forgive all her sins." "She is nothing without excitement," Mary wrote of Catharine, "and it is only when we are gay & happy that we are capable of enjoying badinage." Catharine was one of the members of the club. She was fortunate to be able to attend the weekly meetings, for at about the time that the club was formed she had narrowly escaped losing an eye. As Mary Telfair related the incident, "Her fille de chambre instead of rubbing her head with camphor out of mistake rubbed it with Bug poison." At one point Mary Telfair was called upon to deal with Mary Few's prognostication that her brother Alexander would marry Catharine Hunter. Mary assured her friend that "it will never, *never* be accomplished":

Catharine Hunter will no more be my sister than Jabez Jackson my Brother. The world often selects for people against their will, a few *trifling* attentions not exceeding the bounds of civility are often converted by some people into a proof of attachment. Miss Hunter possesses many pleasing qualities but she has made not the slightest impression on a heart which has never yet yielded to the power of female charms, besides I know several girls who Alexander prefers to her, but as to marrying or soliciting the hand of any woman at present he does not dream of such a thing. I sometimes doubt whether an angel's form & angel's mind could tempt him to wear the chain of Hymen.[11]

Other female friends in Georgia were cousin Sarah Jones, the sister of the second Noble Wimberly Jones, who married Colonel Alfred Cuthbert in 1823, and Sarah Cecil, another member of the club with whom Mary often stayed up chatting until midnight. At one point Mary suspected that Miss Cecil was about to desert the sisterhood, but she never did and remained unmarried throughout her lifetime. There were several families in Augusta that were considered the social equals of the leading families of Savannah. The Campbell family was one. Telfair numbered among her close friends Harriett, Sarah (called "Lillie"), and Maria Campbell, the daughters of Macartan Campbell and Sarah Fenwick Campbell (who in 1795 became the second wife of Mary's uncle, Dr. George Jones). Lillie married Noble Wimberly Jones II, the son of George Jones, but was widowed in 1818. Maria married Dr. Lemuel Kollock in 1802, shortly after his arrival in Savannah from Rhode Island. Another of Mary's friends with roots in the Augusta area was Anne Cumming, the daughter of Thomas Cumming. She married General Peter Smith and joined him at his post in St. Augustine. Mary thought that Anne Cumming "possessed a mind uniting uncommon powers of reflection & observation with a lively imagination."[12]

Mary particularly admired the Campbell ladies' sister-in-law, Sarah Hull Campbell, the wife of Edward F. Campbell. Mary thought Mrs. Campbell "lovely in mind and character" and her conversation "equal to a sermon." Mary quoted to Mary Few a line of poetry applicable to Sarah Campbell, "Like Ships on Seas, while *in* above the world," and then paid her the highest compliment by comparing her to her best friend:

> You must not think it flattery when I say that Mrs. Campbell continually reminds me of you—her mind is cast in a different mould from yours, and yet her sentiments are in accordance with yours—her views of life the same. Education & self-discipline have done every thing for her mind—it is brilliant by nature, but pure & elevated, enjoying every thing that is intellectual and bringing Religion to bear on every thing.

Telfair described Sarah Campbell as a "most amiable, pious & benevolent woman," a person "who sympathises deeply with the afflicted and is more frequently to be found in the haunts of poverty & distress than in scenes of (what the gay & thoughtless call) pleasure."[13]

Mrs. James Hunter was an older woman whom Mary considered a valued Savannah friend. She was a woman loved by her "almost better than any one in Savannah," a woman described by Mary as "all softness, tenderness & feeling." Mary enjoyed the company of Mrs. Henry Kollock, the minister's wife, and found her "very pleasing in her manners" and "lively in the extreme." "I find her much improved," Mary wrote of her friend Harriet McAllister, "she is not very interesting, but she is very discrete, she is liberal of praise, and seldom censures, her appearance too has improved, she has a good figure and dresses with taste." Mary enjoyed the company of women who were quite different from herself so long as they were interesting. She thought a Mrs. Bryan of Wilmington Island "one of the most fascinating women I ever met with." "She possesses those masculine traits of Character which render her more pleasing to Women than Men, she is endued with almost Spartan courage, independent in her ideas and eccentric in her manners with a great deal of candour and vivacity all this is united to a flow of language rarely to be met with."[14]

Friendship, to Mary Telfair, required sharing difficulties and lending support in times of grief. Eliza Terrell of Sparta, Georgia, was a good friend of the Telfairs. She and her husband, Dr. William Terrell, a physician, United States congressman, and agronomist, had two daughters, Louisa and Lucy. When Louisa fell ill, Mary was there to nurse her:

> Dr. & Mrs. Terrell left their daughter a lovely girl of fifteen to pass the winter with Mrs. Telfair [Thomas Telfair's widow] for the purpose of taking lessons in Music & French. She was endowed with a singular degree of beauty, good talents, and an angelic temper. She was taken sick about a week since. Her Father & Mother arrived to see her in a Delerium from brain fever. She was the idol of their hearts and for 12 years their only child. It was too affecting the night before their arrival, while I was giving her medicine she took me for her Mother and I had to answer her as such to appease her. Her reason returned the day of their arrival. She recognized them and relapsed into a state of insensibility and is now hovering between life and death.[15]

When Louisa died, having never recovered from her illness, Mary was there to offer sympathy and spiritual encouragement to her parents:

> Poor little Louisa whose situation I mentioned in my last letter is no longer an inhabitant of this Earth. I was by her when she breathed her last—it seemed like one sinking into a

sweet sleep, and she had that angelic look that seems a promise of future happiness. Her Parents were inconsolable. I have known Woman's grief equal to the Mother's, but never Man's like the Father's—it was overwhelming. I trust that they will derive support in this deep affliction from the only true source and that we may all devine a salutary lesson from it. When we see the young, the beautiful and the promising snatched away suddenly by the hand of death, we naturally ask ourselves the question why are we spared?[16]

Mary Telfair tried to exercise care in forming friendships with other women. "I begin to view things as I ought," she wrote, "and instead of being charmed with *tinsel* I await until a long acquaintance unfolds the merits of persons, for I have been too frequently deceived." She found it necessary to be cautious in her dealings with other women: "I have been so often deceived in my own sex, I have seen so much petty contention for superiority, so many little arts practiced, and so much envy fostered, that I feel under more restraint in the society of Women than Men." She believed that "injudicious friends injure us more than malignant enemies."[17]

At times Mary would be mildly critical of her female acquaintances. In commenting upon reports that she had been charmed by a certain young lady, she admitted that the person's appearance and manner were pleasing and that her movements were graceful, "but she wants vivacity," Mary complained. "Her conversation is too sentimental for my taste," she said. "I believe I should weary of angelic sweetness if unconnected with animation—A human being without it is like a body without a soul." She agreed with a comment made by her sister Margaret that "softness of manner in Woman was a cover for art." Mary could be a bit rough on her acquaintances, at least when sharing a confidence with Mary Few. An anonymous character who frequently turned up in her letters was "the little witch of West Point." Of another acquaintance she wrote, "She is the greatest oddity in existence and her very countenance has the power of exciting one's risibles." Commenting on a lady recently arrived from France, she found her "unlovely in face & form." "I think her stiff & awkward but she is called elegant by that Connoisseur in the school of fashion Robert Patterson." "She is a girl without mind—and I think her insipid," Mary wrote of another acquaintance. "Her appearance will interest as long as she is pretty and young—but there is nothing for middle age—a mere *spring flower* which summer will wither, and autumn blast."[18]

As a paragon of nineteenth-century Southern propriety, Mary Telfair could not abide the thought of a woman compromising her virtue. As far as she was concerned, sexual indiscretion by one woman was a reflection on the entire sisterhood:

> I felt a little anxious to know the object of the Slander in New York. Sarah *guessed* Mrs. Astor. I am at a loss to imagine who it is but hope the unfortunate Woman has been able to prove her innocence. I feel when one Woman strays from the path of virtue that she not only disgraces herself but implicates her whole Sex.[19]

Mary did make an effort not to be openly critical of others. It was a trait that she did not appreciate in her friends. She found Ann Wallace "too prone to unveil the weaknesses of people." When Ann told Mary that she felt complimented by Frances Few's remark that she was an admirable judge of character, Mary replied that "others were as quick sighted as herself, but they were restrained by various motives from *publishing* the failings of their fellow beings." "Whenever the failings of others come across me very much," Mary wrote of herself, "I always endeavor to pallitate them by saying to myself, if I do not possess that fault I have others perhaps as obnoxious to them as theirs are to me—I find it a never failing antidote to ill humor."[20]

The friendship that Mary Telfair shared with Mary Few was a very special one. It was a friendship that was intensely loving and emotionally fulfilling. Mary said of the other Mary that she had never known anyone "whose heart beat more responsive to my own." "I feel that you are my *second self*," she told her friend. She called Mary Few her "Siamese twin" and said that the fact that they often saw "with the same eyes" was proof of their twinship. They were "the only female Castor & Pollux in the world." "I think we ought like Damon & Pythias to be immortalized in verse," Mary wrote to Mary Few. On another occasion she wrote, "Whenever I stroll alone I wish that you were my companion, & I never see a beautiful flower expand to the warm sun, but I wish that Mary Few had it." Mary named a rosebush in her garden "Mary Few."[21]

Mary Telfair's deep affection for Mary Few was reciprocated in full. "You once told me (in a pleasing tête a tête)," Mary Telfair recalled, "that you would always recall the *absent* Mary to your mind *reverieing* and when you view her in that abstracted state you may imagine yourself the presiding Goddess of her *golden dreams*." Mary Few wrote in Mary's commonplace book in 1818 that when "like the evening Sun comes the Memory of past times o'er my soul" then "is my dear Mary associated with the pleasant recollections of my life—the Companion of thoughtless childhood—the chosen friend of my youth—and one to whose friendship I still look forward to smoothe the downward path of life; and when all its Sorrows, its Hopes, and its fears are past may we be seen in a world of rest where Hope shall cheat no more and Disappointment cease to follow in her train." Mary Telfair needed frequent reassurances of Mary Few's love. In agreeing with her "Friend so beloved," that it was "one of *your rights*" to hear from her frequently, Mary wrote that "to receive your opinions on various subjects and above all to know that *you* still love me will ever cause the chords of joy to vibrate through my heart."[22]

The only opportunity that Mary Telfair and Mary Few had to share one another's company was during the summer months at the Few's residence in New York, at their country place in Fishkill, or during trips together in the Northeast. "It is a cruel destiny that separates us," Telfair wrote one December day. Her infrequent meetings with her dearest friend were like "little spots of verdant sunshine scattered along the dreary wastes of existence." "I am glad that we met before I left the *dear North Countrie*," she wrote to Mary Few one fall, "as it served to cement more strongly that affection for you which time only serves to strengthen." After one extended visit that Mary Telfair made to the Fews in New York, during which she wore out Mary Few with shopping, Mary Few wrote to Mary Garrettson, "The Telfairs sailed yesterday for Georgia. I cannot tell you how much I miss Mary."[23]

On the occasions when they were together, the two Marys would have warm and intimate conversations as they had as schoolgirls dreaming their childish dreams. Mary Telfair wrote that upon receiving a letter from Mary Few "what an irresistible desire do I then feel to *chat* with her who was my Hoyden companion at Richmond Hill and afterwards my philosophic friend in the garret in Robertson Street." "You always make me a *Raconteur*," she teased her friend. On another occasion she wrote that "we never *flag* in the tongue when together." One winter while "ailing as the upcountry folkes say" and confined to the house, Telfair wrote to her "dearest tête a tête companion" that she wished her "on the opposite side of the chimney corner, that like Darby & Joan we might *codge* in our old way." "A little of the flow of soul would act as a sovereign balm," she added.[24]

The two Marys kept up a lifelong correspondence that was warm and intimate. Miss Telfair assured her friend that "rather than forego the pleasure of *confabulating* with you, I would employ a *rusty nail* as a pen." Another time she wrote, "A letter from you my dear Mary is like a benefit night to a poor actor; it gives me something to *live on* for several days." Apart from Mary Few's "siren tongue," there was nothing that she "appreciate[d] more highly then the *outpourings* of [her] heart on paper." "To hear from you always *warms* my heart," she told her dear Mary, "and makes me wish that I could grasp the reality instead of the shadow." In her letters to Mary Few, Mary Telfair found emotional release. There was no one to whom she could pour out her affection more freely. "I am never happier," she wrote, "never feel my heart glow with more warmth than when engaged in writing to my beloved Mary." Of their correspondence she wrote, "The feelings are less constrained than in conversation and we pour forth our whole heart without knowing it." Mary Few's letters had a "magic influence" on her and would cause "little brilliants to flutter around and support [her] spirits." She wrote to her friend, with feeling, that "there is a magic charm in receiving letters from those we love."[25]

There was a yearning for exclusivity in Mary Telfair's feelings for Mary Few. One December day, shortly after leaving New York and becoming separated "from one in whom I take such deep interest, and who occupies so large a portion of my heart," she wrote to her friend from Savannah, "When eve arrives and you all encircle *the dear delightful stove* do you not think of me far away, but in every corner will my heart flutter and *to you* will be as warm as the friendly stove though *cold as ice* to the world in general." The depth of feeling was intense when Mary Telfair wrote to Mary Few, "Oh! how I wish you were with me that we might *talk walk eat & sleep* together." The twinges of jealousy that Mary Telfair experienced when she felt that Mary Few was neglecting her suggest feelings of love more intense than mere friendship:

> What dear Mary has been the occasion of your long *very long* silence, two letters of mine still remain unanswered. Must I acknowledge the truth and tell you that I have felt a little *piqued*

at your neglect of an old and sincere friend. I have repeatedly intended writing to ascertain the cause of your silence but my *predominant passion* pride deterred me, for I really sometimes think and *fear* that you have forgotten me and unless you answer this immediately and tell me that I still retain a little portion of your heart I shall conclude some new friend has totally supplanted me and I am so *selfish* that I wish to monopolize as much of your love as can be spared from your own family.[26]

Mary could become poetic in expressing her longing for an even closer and more permanent relationship with her friend. She despaired, however, that this could ever be achieved:

> *Our Willows* will never be *twined together* except in imagination—what a delightful Bower might not *our useless* hands form. *Such a union of tastes* could not fail to produce one of *Arcadian beauty*—you may realize your plans while I only peep occasionally at them. I am doomed to wither and to die in this sultry clime, while you may flourish in a more genial one—our meetings are indeed like "little spots of verdant sunshine scattered along the dreary waste of existence"—All our enjoyments are transitory.[27]

Passionate female friendships were common in the eighteenth and nineteenth centuries. They were casually accepted in a pre-Freudian society as entirely normal, indeed spiritually uplifting. Historian Nancy Cott relates that Catherine Sedgwick wrote in her diary entry upon meeting Fanny Kemble in 1834, "Ours is nearest to the love of angels." She records another nineteenth-century woman's reflection on an intense and enduring female friendship: "Love is spiritual, only passion is sexual." Christie Anne Farnham echoes the theme: "The ideology of separate spheres also encouraged women to think of their love for their closest female friends as being on a higher plane than heterosexual relationships because there was no carnal passion." Mary Telfair would not have disagreed with this assessment: "Men are strange creatures they do not love like women. I sometimes think the attachments of most of them founded on passion or interest. Is this a misanthropic idea?" Mary believed that men were lacking in perception when it came to women, "for the best of men are ignorant of the *intricate* winding of the female heart." "We are better judges of each other than men are of us," she wrote. "We see our own sex with minds *undressed*—They see them decorated for conquest." In the eighteenth century the term "romantic friendship" came to be used to describe loving relationships between women. It is a term that Mary Telfair used herself in writing of a female relationship that she admired for its lack of self-interest: "Mrs. Coke spoke to me of her romantic friendship for Miss Teller, who it seems resembled an only sister of hers who died early. Such evidences of a romantic spirit in these days would appear ridiculous, for self interest appears the order of the day."[28]

Carroll Smith-Rosenberg, in her ground-breaking study of loving friendships between women, based on correspondence and diaries between the 1760's and 1880's, found much that was sensual in women's expressions of devotion to one another. She argues, however, that the essential question is not whether these women had genital contact and could therefore be defined as heterosexual or homosexual. Rather, she contends, "The twentieth-century tendency to view human love and sexuality within a dichotomized universe of deviance and normality, genitality and platonic love, is alien to the emotions and attitudes of the nineteenth century and fundamentally distorts these women's emotional interaction." With respect to two pairs of women who "were lovers—emotionally if not physically," Smith-Rosenberg writes, "There is every indication that these four women, their husbands and families—all eminently respectable and socially conservative—considered such love both socially acceptable and compatible with heterosexual marriage. Emotionally and cognitively, their heterosocial and homosocial worlds were complementary." Smith-Rosenberg discounts the possibility that the letters that were the subject of her study were "but an example of the romantic rhetoric with which the nineteenth century surrounded the concept of friendship." Not so, for "they possess an emotional intensity and a sensual and physical explicitness that is difficult to dismiss."[29]

Christie Anne Farnham, in attempting to assess how important physical affection was to romantic friendships between Southern schoolgirls, observes that the antebellum South accepted as quite natural the free expression of affection in public between women while frowning on the same behavior between members of the opposite sex. Mothers and daughters, aunts and nieces, cousins, and female friends often hugged and kissed. Hand-holding on the streets was widespread. The public display of affection between males and females was another matter, however. Modesty and purity were essential characteristics of the nineteenth-century Southern lady, and any hint of sex outside of marriage would ruin a woman's reputation for life. In contrast, because a sexual component was not a recognized possibility in same-sex relationships, women were free to openly express their love for one another. Smith-Rosenberg makes much the same point: "While closeness, freedom of emotional expression, and uninhibited physical contact characterized women's relationships with each other, the opposite was frequently true of male-female relationships. One could thus argue that in such a world of female support, intimacy, and ritual it was only to be expected that adult women would turn trustingly and lovingly to each other. It was a behavior they had observed and learned since childhood."[30]

Despite the pervasiveness and openness of physical affection in female life in the South, Farnham raises the question whether any of the romantic friendships that she studied should be characterized as lesbian. She points out that the label is the product of sexologists intent on developing a new field of inquiry at the end of the nineteenth century and that accordingly the concept of lesbian sexuality would have been unknown to antebellum girls. While finding that one young woman's interests "clearly focused on women, not men," she found that most of the young women eventually married and that a subculture of lesbian experience never developed in the antebellum South. Bertram Wyatt-Brown made a similar finding in concluding that "Boston marriages," with their hints of lesbianism, was more a Northern than a Southern phenomenon. "There was no comparable term in the South," he writes, "no 'Charleston marriages' of paired female friends."[31]

While Mary Telfair might express a wish to monopolize Mary Few's love, she insisted that she was not selfish in this respect. She assured her friend that "as proof of it I would willingly see you united to a Man deserving of you." Indeed, Mary came up with the notion that brother Alexander might be a good match for Mary Few. What could be better than to have her best friend as a sister-in-law? Alexander had an eye for the ladies. His sister knew that he was a passionate admirer of "soul beaming eyes, rosy cheeks, and coral lips." Actually, brother Tom would have been Mary's first choice for Mary Few. The trouble was that he already was happily married. "Brother Tom thinks you a *Prodigy*," Mary wrote to her friend. "If he had been a *single* Man I would have given him to you provided you would have deemed him worthy of acceptance." She did not even consider Josiah, for he was interested only in riding, hunting, and cultivating his land. But Alexander was available and would do quite nicely: "I think you would like Alexander he is handsomer [than Tom] and more polished in manners with more versatile talents, but he is not *half as interesting* because he has less enthusiasm but I forget that I am talking of relations, but I have no reserve towards my dear Mary."[32]

Whether or not an erotic element entered into Mary Telfair's feelings for Mary Few, and there is no evidence that it did, it does not appear that their friends found anything unusual in their relationship. Indeed, Telfair mentions to Few that "Sarah Haig, who has but a poor opinion of Human Nature, not only of the Lords but the *Ladies* of Creation, says we furnish the only example of *female friendship* that has ever cheered her orbs in her sojourn through this vale of tears." Sarah called the two "the Siamese Twins" just as they did themselves. On one occasion when Mary was under the weather, her sister Margaret commented, "When you get with Mary Few you will be quite well."[33]

For Mary Telfair there could be no love without respect, and Mary Few was a person that she respected most highly. On one occasion she assured her friend that "there is not a Being in existence who I esteem more than I do you." She admired Few's character:

> I often wish dear Mary that I possessed some of your *rationality*, you view everything so calmly and dispassionately, you act so entirely from the operation of judgment that you ought to be better satisfied with yourself than certain wayward folkes who are forever erring and repenting.[34]

Telfair believed that she and Mary Few had been drawn so closely together in part because their situations in life were so much alike:

> I was thinking a day or two ago dear Mary that it was not only congeniality of feeling alone that drew me so closely to you. Our situations in many respects are similar and there cannot be full sympathy in this world where there is a wide difference in situation. We cannot expect the gay votarist of fashion to sympathize with the Anchorite in his cell, or the married friend surrounded by lisping Bairns and involved in numerous cares to sympathize with the unmarried one.[35]

As tokens of their affection, Mary Telfair and Mary Few delighted in exchanging small gifts. Other family members shared in the joy of giving. On one occasion Colonel Few sent down on a schooner to Savannah two barrels of New York State apples. A box of oranges, which Mary packed with "my own little hands," was sent north on the schooner *Othello* with instructions to wipe them with a dry towel and lay them out on the pantry or closet shelf. Another gift was a jar of marmalade, another a bag of dried peaches, and yet another a barrel of potatoes that Mrs. Telfair sent to Mrs. Few. Mary intended to accompany a barrel of grits that she sent to Mary Few's mother with some Georgia hams, but could not do so since their stock had not yet "descended from the Highlands." In another shipment Mary packed a pair of French China bottles of cordial beneath the grits. Mary much admired a French handkerchief received from Mary Few. "The pattern is quite in demand," she wrote, "and I am much obliged to you for *smartening* me." The tongue that Mary Few sent down to Savannah was greatly appreciated: "Your *tongue* arrived most opportunely. Alexander had a few Gentlemen to dine and it was introduced as a New York tongue to the Epicures, who enjoyed it more than an *eloquent* one."[36]

In one of the boxes sent to New York, Mary enclosed for Mary Few a "fortune teller" to amuse her visitors. "You twirl the circle round and wherever the *witches* stick points is the fortune," she explained, and added, "I met with it at the last Fair." In one "box of souvenirs" sent down by the Fews there was an exquisite lamp, a cap for Sarah, and engraved vellum notepaper for Margaret along with some manchettes. Mary passed on to Mary Few Sarah's comment that the simplicity of the cap suited her taste and Margaret's and that "if she had an elegant she would be tempted to put her manchettes on him, but being beauless she will sport them herself." A gift of a penknife elicited another joke: "Sarah desires thanks to Matilda for the beautiful penknife she sent her & says there is no danger of its *cutting love*." One gift from Sarah Haig to Mary Few was a pair of india rubber garters. A jar of figs that was sent to Mary Few was followed by an observation that her Mamma would enjoy them for they are soft and well suited for those whose "grinders are few."[37]

Mary Telfair's relationship with the sisterhood and her special love for Mary Few reflect her feelings about friendship found in these words copied into her commonplace book:

Happiness is the natural design of all the world and every thing we see done is in order to attain it. My imagination places it in Friendship. By friendship I mean an entire communications of thoughts, wishes interests and pleasures being undivided; a mutual esteem which carries with it a pleasing sweetness of conversation and terminates in a desire to make each other happy without being forced to run into visits, noise and hurry which serve to trouble, rather than compose the thoughts of any reasonable creatures.[38]

It was in the close and intimate friendships that she formed with other women and the rich female culture that these relationships fostered that Mary Telfair found a happiness and contentment rivaled only by the joy that came from intellectual pursuits, those matters of the mind that filled and enriched her life.

7

Matters of the Mind

Absence of occupation is not rest,
A mind quite vacant is a mind distress'd
William Cowper, *Retirement* (1728)

Mary Telfair had wide-ranging intellectual interests. She believed
that "intellectual resources are essential to unmarried women" and
that next to religion nothing was more important to them than "that
cultivation which strengthens the mind and places it above those
petty feelings which are so much indulged in by the ignorant." Mary
and her brother Alexander differed on the importance of intellect.
Alexander thought his sister had one "insane point," the undue value
that she placed upon intellect and "the advantages resulting in private
life from the cultivation of the mind." "We have had almost a *Quar-
rel* tonight upon the subject," Mary wrote. "I tell him he is just as
insane upon the qualities of the heart as I am upon the mind."[1]
   Although she had a deep and abiding attachment to matters of the
mind, Mary did not wish to be considered a bluestocking, one of
those female pedants who ostentatiously placed their literary knowledge and intellectual accomplishments on public display: "There is
something in the term blue stocking that conveys an idea of pretension to the mind and I hate *pretension* in all its grades."[2] In the early
nineteenth century, "intellectual woman" was a phrase of derision.
Bertram Wyatt-Brown writes that in the nineteenth-century South,
"A ladylike humility about mental agility, creative talent, and other
marks of distinction beyond domestic skills earned a girl and woman
praise." Mary was well aware of this. For example, she recognized

that her intellectual friend Anne Clay was "the sort of woman that men would *fear*—her mind is cast in just the mould to interfere with theirs." "They prefer the clinging ivy to the oak which resists the tempest," she wrote. "Not being a man, I cannot help wondering at their preferring tenderness & gentleness to the union of solid intellect & strength of character." Mary knew that "the Lords of Creation," as men were sardonically called by her set, "admire generally passive minds in womankind." Hers was far from passive, and this could be intimidating to many men. Mary understood the necessity of maintaining her femininity while pursuing her intellectual interests and admired a woman who could combine "the delicacy of female refinement with a masculine understanding."[3]

Mary Telfair's intellectual development was influenced by the romantic movement in literature, music, and the visual arts that began at the end of the eighteenth century and emphasized the imagination and emotions over pure reason. It was during her formative years that the rationalism of the Enlightenment philosophes, who sought to reduce the universe, society, and even mankind to a set of rules, was yielding to the individualism of the Byronic hero. With the emergence of romanticism, women as well as men began to think in individualistic terms about the uniqueness of personality and the importance of exercising one's own will, about fostering self-awareness and encouraging self-expression, about promoting self-reliance and the need to develop a personal identity. Mary Telfair, like other women of her day, was devoted to the writings of Madame de Staël (1766–1817), the French-Swiss belletrist renowned for her glittering salons as well as her charm and talent for conversation. This most intellectual of women symbolized the vigor and energy of the romantic temperament and spread a new gospel of selfhood. She created in her novel *Corinne* a heroine whose life matched her own in terms of great expectations and who embodied her ideal of a life of the mind.[4]

Mary Telfair's intellectualism was closely linked to her independence of spirit and her need to assert herself as an individual. They were two sides of the same coin. Mary knew that a woman in her position must be discreet in pursuing her independence. Pejorative labels were attached to independent women. They were called "amazons," "hermaphrodites," and "mannish maidens." One small step that Mary took in asserting her independence was to prove that she was capable of caring for her own personal needs:

I have abandoned the old fashion of having a waiting maid the first step towards a reform. Alexander seems to think I will be too *independent* for a Lady but I already experience the salutary effects of running up and down stairs and *waiting upon myself* so do not be alarmed if you should chance to hear you have a *bustling* friend.[5]

Mary had a burning curiosity and delighted in new experiences. With no husband to concern her or children to care for, she was free of domestic restraints. "*Novelty* is certainly the charm of life," she wrote; "its attractions are all powerful to *womankind* and in many things I am *very woman* but most of all in this." Pity the woman who found more satisfaction in domestic trifles than in savoring the many wonders that the world had to offer. Mary Telfair knew that Mary Few would share her contempt when she wrote, "I have seen some women derive as much satisfaction from sorting clothes and wiping cups as we did from mounting the ramparts at Quebec." Women consumed by domesticity could be total bores:

> Women I think taken en masse are far more wearisome than men. We have to contend with *a host* of tedium in one little body, fine clothes, fine furniture, the annals of the nursery and kitchen are *ably* discussed for our edification and although these things are interesting enough in their proper places it does not do to introduce them into drawing rooms.

As for herself, she could take no interest in the details of housekeeping. "I could keep a house well from duty," she wrote, "but my *Heart & soul* could not be engaged in it."[6]

In her search for new experiences Mary was treading on dangerous ground. Convention required that women stay within their separate sphere. As Bertram Wyatt-Brown has put it, "The sexes differed. They lived separate lives—one in the world, the other in the home, one in exterior circumstances, the other in the inner sanctuary that required vigilant safeguarding." Mary Telfair accepted the conventional wisdom, in theory at least: "The best wives are those who combine sweetness of temper with cheerfulness and energy. I begin to think more depends on the woman than the man. Home is the sphere of one—while the turmoil of business occupies the other."[7] She was determined, however, to live in the larger world to the extent possible without directly defying male-defined conventions.

Alexis de Tocqueville wrote in 1840 that while Americans "do not think that man and woman have either the duty or the right to perform the same offices," they nonetheless "show an equal regard for both their respective parts; and though their lot is different, they consider both of them as being of equal value." Indeed, the great French observer of life in America went so far as to say, "As for myself, I do not hesitate to avow that, although the women of the United States are confined within the narrow circle of domestic life, and their situation is in some respects one of extreme dependence, I have nowhere seen woman occupying a loftier position." Not all women agreed that they were considered the equals of men. Mary Few believed that women in the South were held in less regard than in the North. Mary Telfair thought that her friend "would suit Massachusetts," for, as she pointed out to her, "like Emerson you think female intellect is only appreciated in Northern latitudes." Mary disagreed with Mary Few's assessment. She thought that women were not sufficiently appreciated either in the North or in the South: "I know you think Woman less valued in Southern than in Northern regions. I do not—Human Nature is the same every where."[8]

The independence and self-fulfillment that Mary Telfair sought could be difficult in an age when convention required that women travel only under male protection. Mary was not constrained by convention alone, however. Living the active life required a certain strength of will, and in one aspect of her nature Mary was a procrastinator. "If I had no one to depend upon me," she wrote, "I should do nothing, for I feel strongly disposed to fold my arms in listless repose." Sometimes she was embarrassed by her own timidity. She was never too embarrassed, however, to joke about such matters with Mary Few:

I returned on Friday from a visit to my Cousins [in South Carolina] where "rural quiet" is enjoyed in perfection. If you had been gifted with second sight you would have pitied me on my *little* journey. My fears (which you know seldom slumber) were awakened first in the ferry boat by a passenger loudly calling out that there were too many persons on board. The next cause of fright (for as an ugly & timid French woman once said, "I am very *frightful*") was occasioned by the war of elements—We were overtaken by a storm of thunder, rain, and lightning—We had to *draperize* the Barouche by pinning my cloak in front, and covering with Alexander's *fearnaught* [an outer garment of stout woolen cloth] which proved more impenetrable to the rain than *uncle's*, which covered me during our memorable *trudge* at Quebec. The third and last fright was caused by the tricks of one of our Horses—Matilda's acquaintance Harry, to me he seemed as formidable as *old Harry*, when he began to rear and run backwards at the sight of some rails in the road I was keen for jumping out. Alexander lost his patience and said, "You ought never to leave your own fireside." I thought so too, and feel fully convinced that cowardice with me is a vice which neither reason, reflection or time can eradicate for it has "strengthened with my strength." I hope that I have moral courage sufficient to atone for my physical deficiency.[9]

Mary Telfair loved good conversation. She believed that this was an art in which women excelled, an opinion shared by some men as well as by other women. These words in Mary's commonplace book on the subject of women and conversation were composed by a man:

> Nature has fitted Women for conversation. Their minds are more refined and delicate than ours; their imaginations more vivid; and their expressions more at command. When sweetness and modesty are joined to intelligence in this composition, the charms of their conversation are irresistible.[10]

Mary wrote in a similar fashion after commenting on the superior intelligence of her friend Anne Clay:

> I do believe some Men are jealous of female talent. I do not think it very desirous to possess it unless it is usefully employed —Women *fear* it in their own sex though they profess to *idolize* it in Men.—And yet I love it in all its variations—It is music to me from the *loud swell* to the *low warble* and there is no accomplishment equal in my estimation to talking well.[11]

Mary Telfair purported to abhor gossip, which she called "the daily mental food of uncultivated minds." "Some Women would consider a letter without that specious article [gossip] as uninteresting as a Romance without love," she wrote to Mary Few, "but you & I can do without either." Telfair, however, was a bit of a gossip herself occasionally, and Mary Few's gossip was somehow different: "When you condescend to gossip I enjoy it for it has a *peculiar flavor.*" Mary liked people who were frank in their speech and simple in their manners. "*Great* and *loud* talkers are my aversion," she wrote to Mary Few. "When in the society of a person of this description, I always sigh for taciturnity, and feel every inclination to silence them." "The fact is," she wrote, "people who talk for talk sake must say much that ought to have been *unsaid.*" "What a pity," she continued, "that blowers could not be invented for the mouths of the indiscreet as well as for the grates. Some of our friends would be too much muffled. The *blower* would never be off. I begin to think that good sense consists more in holding one's tongue than in talking well."[12]

Mary Few found it difficult to cope with people who were not natural and sincere, while Mary Telfair could still admire a person although studied in manner and conversation. Alexander shared Mary Few's feelings:

> I wish you could hear Alexander & myself quarrel on that subject—He is such an advocate for Nature & sincerity that he will never listen to my eulogies of any one who wants it—Mrs. Gray is a wonderful favorite because she is animated & natural —I like her very much & appreciate those qualities in her but I prefer Anne Clay with all her *studied* charms. I never myself sacrifice at the shrine of Insincerity and yet I have enjoyed the society of persons who I know to be insincere.[13]

Mary Telfair was not always consistent in expressing her opinions, however. On another occasion she condemned insincerity: "If I know myself I would not resort to subterfuge to gain all that this world could bestow. To affect what we do not feel ranks next—how few think it a sin to appear through life in a fictitious character—*always masquerading.*" And in a similar vein she wrote: "There is something inexpressibly delightful to me in *single hearted disinterestedness,* even if *martyrdom* should be the result of it. When I meet with *unalloyed sincerity* I *almost* worship it." Likewise, "Defend me from a *Machiavellian* character; I fear them as I would pestilence." Actions, of course, always spoke louder than words: "There is nothing more offensive to me than a worldly religious person—talking *good* and *acting bad.*"[14]

Telfair found bright, interesting people stimulating, but there were many in the parlors of Savannah who had the opposite effect on her mind, as she explained to Mary Few:

Some folkes have the art of dissipating the mind much more than others. Your favorite C. Hunter is one of them. I took tea with her en famille last evening and went *fierce* for a little *desultory* conversation but *my opiate* Mr. G was present, consequently my ideas instead of running in a clear stream, became *stagnant*, and my whole mind a *muddy pool.* What a treasure a sprightly mind is, not only to the possessor, but to all who come within its sunny influence!

At parties Mary tried to steer clear of those she called "the Insipids." She refused to engage in idle conversation with those who did not interest her. She knew that she became "exceedingly talkative and gay" when she came upon a character suited to her taste, but felt that she had to wade through a "*muddy* stream of insipidity" before arriving at "*the fountain* of *intelligence* and *sprightliness.*"[15]

Mary recognized one of her faults when she confessed to being lacking in prudence. "I wish I had a little of it," she wrote, "for my tongue must always give vent to my thoughts." Although her tongue might cause offense on occasion and some of the insipids might recognize that they were being ignored, for the most part Mary believed that she was able to conceal her disdain for those who bored her: "I do know some *Flats*, as Alexander styles the *genuine Insipids* that baffle human efforts to elicit one ray of animation. When they cross my path I give them a cordial shake of the hand—a gracious smile—inquire kindly after their children; that is quite enough to satisfy them & gain their good will for life." "I really am *panic struck* when an *idea killer* sits down by me to *prose* for I cannot call it talk," she wrote to Mary Few, and one must wonder whether she really could conceal her feelings from a "flat" of that high order. Mary felt sorry for the "flats." "I verily believe the dissipation of Southern Men may be attributed to the depressing influence of such *help mates* who are incapable of enlivening a domestic fireside—of reasoning or being reasoned with." She felt even more sorry for their children. "How terrible that such irrational and uncultivated minds should have the direction of others," she wrote. "Ignorance is the parent of conceit and prejudice," she believed. She had an admission to make: "This is a subject upon which I am not *sane.*"[16]

Mary Telfair loved books. "I wish I had all the tears back that I have shed over fictitious woes," she wrote. On one occasion she shut herself up in a snug little room for two rainy days and "had a rich mental banquet" in Sir Walter Scott's *Ivanhoe.* She found Rebecca, the beautiful daughter of the Jew Isaac, to be a "noble creature," but thought that she ought to have been a Christian. She had not enjoyed Scott's earlier novel *Waverley,* published in 1814. "I think it unworthy of the pen of Walter Scott," she opined, "indeed I doubt whether he really wrote it." She wondered whether Mary Few had read *Kenilworth,* another of Scott's novels. "We have all *feasted* upon it," she wrote. She thought that her fellow lover of books would approve of the character of Edmund Tressilian, adding "as for me I am half in love with it notwithstanding my predilection for *dashing talents.*" Mary also spent some time "feasting upon" Scott's *Legend of Montrose.*[17]

Mary read *Glenarvon,* the novel written by Lady Caroline Lamb that was published anonymously in 1816 after the author was thrown over by Lord Byron. Alfred Cuthbert had admired the book and had lent it to Alexander, but Mary found it a "vile production." She could not find any resemblance between Glenarvon and Lord Byron, on whom the character was based. She was struck, however, by the originality and force of the line: "He has an imagination of fire playing around a heart of ice." Telfair read a collection of short stories by Mrs. Amelia Opie, wife of the painter John Opie. "There are two that I think will please you," she told Mary Few. These were "White Lies" and "The Confessions of an Odd-tempered Man." "The rest are romantic *love sick* things, which *you & I* ought not to *patronize,*" she warned her friend.[18]

Mary enjoyed biographies. Shortly after its publication in 1825, she read Thomas Moore's life of Richard Brinsley Sheridan, the Irish-born English playwright and statesman, of which she wrote:

> I have just finished Sheridan's life—poor Sherry! I love him with all his faults; the romance of his life & character awaken the deepest interest—the best traits of his character are delightful and recalled some to my mind who like him seemed destined to delight and interest—I was foolish enough to weep over several pages—What a finished creature she was, the very wife for a man of Genius & feeling. She had, as Moore justly observed, intellect to appreciate his talents, and sensibility to enjoy his success.[19]

Telfair enjoyed the memoirs of interesting historical figures and frequently could be found reading the memoirs of women:

I am now reading the "Memoirs of the Princess Lamballe." I have *a passion* for court scenes and court characters but the age of Louis the Fourteenth furnished the most brilliant subjects for the compiler of memoirs. There is something so harrowing to the feelings in every thing connected with the French Revolution and something so melancholy in the fate of the beautiful Marie Antoinette that our sympathies are too much enlisted in her cause.[20]

Mary read Josephine's memoirs and found the consort of Napoleon to be "too charming and disinterested and above all too unfortunate not to enlist the sympathies of every reader of her biography." She told Alexander that some of Josephine's traits of character reminded her of her own. "Name one," he said. She replied that she was always ready for everything proposed and so was Josephine. Soon after, Mary remarked to her brother that if she had been Josephine, she never could have tried to conciliate Maria-Louisa, but instead would have hated her. He replied gravely, "That is very unlike Josephine and very unlike *you*." At that, Mary was reminded of a favorite saying of Catharine Hunter: "We never know how high we stand until we lower ourselves."[21]

Collections of letters could often be as revealing as memoirs:

I have just finished Lady Russell's letters, the style of them is rather too quaint for my taste, but her character which almost every line develops must have been a very lovely one, and her views of religion so elevated, her foretaste of Heaven so pure and simple, that it was difficult to realize that one so deeply involved in the affairs of this world and whose high rank compelled her to mingle with the vain & frivolous could have attained to such a state of Christian perfection.[22]

Mary was "bewitched" by Lockhart's life of Sir Walter Scott. "I feel as if I had known him intimately from my childhood so familiar are some traits of his character to me." She enjoyed the biography of the Christian soldier Colonel Hutchinson, written by his wife during Cromwell's Civil War. She recommended to Mary Few the letters of the English essayist Charles Lamb. "You will be charmed with the beautiful simplicity of his character and the overflowings of a heart full of affection for his Sister and his friends." Telfair became deeply engrossed in the *History of the Life and Voyages of Christopher Columbus* by Washington Irving. "There is something original & bewitching in his style," she wrote, "perhaps a little too smooth and polished." But she found Irving's *Tales of the Alhambra* a bit too racy for her taste. "They are very voluptuous—quite unworthy of the pen that sketched the character of Columbus and Roscoe."[23]

Mary felt that she owed it to herself to become familiar with the classics. "I have just commenced reading Josephus with a determination to go through with it," she wrote to Mary Few with reference to the author of *A History of the Jewish War*. "His style is admirable for the age in which it was written—very very superior to Bunyan and I only wonder that I should have deferred so long the perusal of a work so very interesting."[24]

Mary was inspired to wade through three large volumes of the life and writings of Robert Burns after hearing a lecture by James Ogilvie, the itinerant and opium-dependant "Hero of the Rostrum." On another occasion Mary heard "the interesting & eloquent Ogilvie" deliver a lecture on dueling, in which he traced its origin to single combat in the age of chivalry. "He drew so *exquisite* a picture of a Tournament, his language was so elegant his description so glowing, that I was lost in admiration," she wrote. Mary yearned to become acquainted with this romantic figure, yet she was sure that she could never summon the courage to enter into a conversation with him. Ogilvie was staying at the inn on St. James Square, and Mary and her sisters sometimes would have "a view of his emaciated Figure walking to & fro in the Balcony." "He must be a miserable Man although so eminently gifted by Nature & Education," Mary wrote, "for he exists on opium and unless under its influence is perfectly melancholy & abstracted." Ogilvie had been confined to his chamber owing to the exertion he made in delivering his "strains of eloquence." Mary summoned up her courage and sent over some "*delicacies* fitted to the palate of an Invalid." She did not have the nerve, however, to use her own name; instead she sent them in the name of her mother.[25]

Poetry played a major role in the lives of Mary Telfair and her friends. Mary's commonplace book is filled with the verse of well-known poets, such as Robert Burns's "Sensibility" and "Highland Mary," and a number of pieces by Lord Byron, who was a favorite of hers. After reading Byron's poem *The Giaour*, a tale of love, violence, and remorse, she decided that this most romantic of poets rivaled Scott "although his Muse is if a different cast, the one is wild & playful following nature in all her rambles, the other dark, gloomy, mysterious and often grandly sublime." "I scarcely know which to give the preference to I *adore* the one and admire the other."[26]

Mary thought Burns "the sweetest Bard that Nature ever formed." She found Alexander Pope "divine," though satirical. After all, Mary knew that it was he who wrote that some women cannot take their tea without a stratagem. Coleridge was "too mystical" for Mary's taste. "I cannot enjoy what I do not perfectly comprehend," she confessed. "Life is too short for *refined subtleties.*" Mary had read her Shakespeare and copied into her book Hamlet's soliloquy, "To be, or not to be, that is the question." She predicted that a young friend's "*ideal* sorrows" would commence with the reading of *Romeo and Juliet.* There also appear on the pages of Mary's book poems by William Cowper, the pre-Romantic who suffered from a morbid religious mania. Mary was quite taken with Cowper's line of verse, "The only amaranthine wreath on Earth is Virtue, the only lasting treasure Truth."[27]

Mary not only enjoyed the novels of Sir Walter Scott, but also delighted in his poetry. It epitomized the romantic revival that had such an influence on her taste. Mary found delightful the "wildness and enthusiasm" of Scott's verse and approved of his "amour patrie." Her favorite poetic work by Scott was "The Lady of the Lake," portions of which she knew almost by heart. Much as she loved the poem, she did wish that Ellen had married Fitz-James instead of Malcolm. "What a captivating fellow is Fitz-James," she wrote, "so much of the elegant man of fashion combined with a mind full of chivalrous deeds & romantic ideas, a heart replete with sensibility." She believed that Ellen must have been attracted to him. "Ellen, *woman like*, notwithstanding her predilection for Malcolm, could not see him unmoved and refrain from bestowing a parting glance a little of the coquette in that."[28]

The subjects and themes of many of the anonymous poems copied by Mary Telfair into her commonplace book are sentimental and romantic. There is a poem about a "lovely dark eyed maid" and a tear-inducer entitled "The Blind Mother." One of the verses in the collection of poems sent to Mary Telfair by friends and preserved among her papers is a highly romantic piece entitled "Lines occasioned by the sight of a lovely but miserable Girl." Another romantic poem,

"Lines supposed to be uttered by Mrs. Bolton on the receipt of her Mother's likeness sent to her by Mrs. Ashton," bears the ascription at the end "By Mr. Jay of Bath," undoubtedly the famous divine who was the father of Mrs. Robert Bolton as well as the father of the architect who designed the Telfair mansion.[29]

The art of writing letters was held in high esteem by ladies of Mary Telfair's class. Letters written by Sarah Haig to her sisters while on a visit to Charleston were "excessively amusing, *full of satire* & her Portraits true to life." They made Mary roar with laughter. Catharine Hunter's comment after reading excerpts from Mary Few's letters was that her letters ought to be published. When Mary Telfair showed a gentleman acquaintance, a "man of sense," a scenic description in one of Mary Few's letters, "he would scarcely believe that Woman *poor weak Woman* could feel, and write so well." He "declared it was written in a *masterly* style." When Catharine Hunter read one of Mrs. Catherine Few's beautiful letters, she allowed that she had never read anything except Washington's farewell address that had touched her heart more.[30]

Mary enjoyed playing with the English language in all its richness and variety. After reading a particularly delightful letter from Mary Few, she wrote in reply, "I feel as if you were very near 'within hail' as the crackers say." When Mary Few owed her a letter, she complained of her "delinquency in the epistolary way." The soirées that a Mrs. Helms held in New York were "yawnees" to Mary. She described herself as "a perfect solitudinarian." She asked Mary Few to "pardon the *stupidozas* for they seize me with as much violence at times as the *penzirozas* do the poor Italian Cicisbeo." Some of her word-plays called upon classical allusions. "Does he retain his *Anacreontic* penchant for the Vine?" she inquired concerning an acquaintance who enjoyed a nip or two. The letters that Mary wrote by the chimney-corner were "lucubrations," and when she and Mary Few corresponded they "confabulated." Some words she simply invented as when she asked of Miss Few, "When do you commence your perigrinations?" We can only wonder what she meant when she wrote that she was convinced that life was an "Ignusfatuus." "As I am an American," she wrote, "I am privileged to use a *big* word and say my pericranium is often in a state of *conglomeration*."[31]

Mary had a deep appreciation for the visual arts. A lovely painting or a beautifully executed piece of sculpture could move her intensely.

After viewing the marble figure of Byron's Medora by Horatio Greenough in the collection of Robert Gilmor, Jr., in Baltimore, Mary breathlessly described the work to Mary Few:

> Nothing that I have ever seen from the pencil or the chisel can compare with it. The shroud is perfect—so transparent that the knees were seen through it. I felt disposed to say, *this cannot be marble*. The whole figure was exquisite more touching by far than the poetical description. Even the roses in her hand were exquisitely chiseled, and the ringlets hanging carelessly from her forehead and clustering around her throat—the dimpled hand and arm so beautiful and so natural but I will say no more and only wish that you could see it.[32]

Mary Telfair was a skilled artist herself—not a creative artist, but an illustrator who could fashion a floral wreath or a basket of fruit with precise strokes of a pen and, with a delicate brush, fill in the lines with rich colors. Lovely little drawings adorn her commonplace book. On one page there appears a bow with a quiver of arrows and on another a bouquet of flowers. Among the Telfair family papers are pencil drawings, landscapes for the most part, including one of Scots Pond in Lenox, Massachusetts, and another bearing the notation "From Miss Fairman's." Another example of Mary's work is a tempera painting of a castle in Scotland. The "human face divine" eluded her grasp, however. "Sarah Haig says all my attempts at sketching phizes terminate in producing an *old French face* that I cannot give an English expression to my heads."[33]

Music does not appear to have played an important role in Mary Telfair's life. She had taken music lessons as a girl, and an inventory of her father's personal property shows that the family had a "Piano forte Grand" in the parlor, but Mary never mentions a musical evening at home. "We have no music but cheek music," she wrote. Apart from an occasional musical evening hosted by a friend, Mary makes no mention of ever having attended a concert. Surely she considered the visual arts more significant than music: "I attended a Conversazione last week in Mrs. McAllister's parlour. The subjects *debated* were Music and Painting. The Question—which was the most extensive in its influence over the minds of Mankind. Mr. Eastburn was one of the *debaters*. I think he advocated Music, Mrs. Mac the same—Mr. McAlllister Painting which I *silently* advocated."[34]

Mary Telfair had little interest in science. "Have you been to any more lectures upon Geology?" she inquired of Mary Few. "I do not like the subject for I am told that it has a tendency to *bewilder* the brain & create a belief that five worlds existed before the present." When it came to philosophy, Mary felt that close reasoning was more suited to the Northern than the Southern mind. She thought Thomas Carlyle and the French philosopher Victor Cousin "quite too metaphysical for my *unmetaphysical* mind."[35]

Mary Telfair's life was not lived exclusively on an intellectual plain. There was much in her day-to-day existence that was ordinary and mundane. A good part of her life involved, as she put it, "the dull monotony of every day actions." Mary kept her hands busy with her needlework and her ebony work. Frequently, of a morning when she called on a female friend or when one called at the Telfair mansion, conversation would be accompanied by the play of needles. "I find the needle a grand solace this winter," Mary wrote. "It keeps off that Vulture of the mind—Ennui, and does not banish that *'soft soother'* *talk.*" Mary might be found by the chimney corner in the evening employed in "coarse work." One evening, for example, she made a flannel shirt. On occasion she might be found making gifts for friends. She described this activity to Mary Few one day in June just before leaving for the North:

> This morning I cut out ten waistcoats & expect to continue the trade for several days. You will think that I take Time by the forelock when I tell you all these waistcoats are for *Christmas presents* and are to be made by one of our Femme de chambre during our absence. I never plan for myself but my life would stagnate if I did not employ my head & fingers a little for others.[36]

Mary claimed that she had no hobbies. "Every body has their *Hobby* but me—I candidly acknowledge that I am *Hobbyless.*" But she did like to take on small projects. One December found her busy restoring a desk that she had used in her student days:

> I found an *old, maimed thing*, which was my juvenile companion and after cleaning it of the rubbish of *the olden time*, sent it to a Cabinet Maker to get its *joints* mended and to acquire a

little *modern polish* so as to be able to *grace a drawing room* after slumbering in a Garret almost as long as Rip Van Winkle did on the Catskill mountain.

This old piece probably afforded as much pleasure as the secretary that Mary had purchased from Duncan Phyfe in New York City some years earlier.[37]

Mary appreciated the benefits of sturdy exercise. She enjoyed long walks and loved riding in her carriage through the countryside breathing in the good air away from the dust of Savannah's sandy streets. "There are cares & troubles which seem to have a momentary suspension when we can actively engage our bodies & minds," she wrote, "and I sometimes think, in my twilight musings, that if I lived in a large City whenever I felt oppressed by despondency I would put on my bonnet and take a long walk. If I lived in the Country I would order my Carriage and take a long ride—for Nature soothes, when Art has ceased to please." Mary could take pleasure in a game of battledore on a cold day. She found it to be good exercise. She wished that she had been "trained to row a boat and ride on horse-back." She blamed her own "effeminacy." Although for diversion Mary might sit down to a game of solitaire, "active industry" provided far greater rewards.[38]

Mary had a charming if quirky sense of humor. She collected humorous ditties. "The Knight's Lament" begins with the stanza:

> I sing the fate of a hapless knight
> Who was nearly killed last Saturday night
> But what nearly killed him, no one could find out
> whether love for his Lady, or a twitch of the gout.[39]

A combination of piety and impishness led Mary to copy a bit of doggerel composed by a clergyman to assist in memorizing the names of the books of the Old Testament. The first stanza is sufficient to convey the gist of this ditty:

> The Great Jehovah speaks to us
> In Genesis and Exodus;
> Leviticus and Numbers see,
> Followed by Deuteronomy.[40]

The couplets of "The Omnibus," however strained the meter, have an amusing ring:

> The praises of the Omnibus I sing,
> Tis such a glorious independent thing
> And all who patronize it must declare
> That tho' a cheap conveyance, it is *dear*.

This poem does, however, demonstrate the disdain that some members of Mary's social class felt for those whom they considered their inferiors:

> The dashing belle with velvet hat and plume
> In all the pride of early youth and bloom
> Is seated next the Emigrant from Erin's shore
> Whose tattered garb proclaims him very poor
> And misery is stamped on every feature
> She shrinks from contact with the *awful* creature.[41]

Mary and her friends traded funny little riddles called "enigmas" that took their humor from puns and word plays. These are some of the more dreadful of them:

Why is a vain woman like a music book? She is full of airs.

Why is a man upstairs beating his wife like a man of honor? He is *above* doing a mean action.

Why is a widower who marries a second time like the captain of a ship? He has a second mate.

What is the difference between a good soldier and a fine lady? One faces the powder and the other powders the face.[42]

Mary could take a simple item such as a goose-quill pen and make it the subject of her humor. "Geese are not favorites of mine in *every sense of the word*, but I *venerate* their snowy *plumage* as it affords me an opportunity of conversing with those I love at a great distance—so when I *sacrifice* it shall be to a *Goose*." Puns were not off limits: "We have had melting weather but I have *weathered* it extremely well." Mary took umbrage at a gentleman who described her as a little romantic and "very satirical": "Is it not provoking that we cannot be estimated as we merit. I *once* was strongly tinged with romance but any thing but romantic now, and though I do make puns sometimes

& love ludicrous associations they are presented in an amiable garb—
I *am not satirical.*" Mary's humor could take an odd twist at times.
One must bring some imagination to the shared joke referred to in
this excerpt from one of her letters to Mary Few:

> The Valentine (which is a secret between us) was after being
> revised & corrected sent to the Post Office and duly received—I
> have been exceedingly amused by the criticisms passed upon it
> —A Lady quoted from it a few days ago and asked me if I did
> not think it *very smart*, another remarked when it was handed
> to her—It sounds like Mary Telfair but she never wrote it—Like
> Junius I have escaped detection and am still the *little* instead of
> the great unknown. The irony contained in it must have been
> very *artfully* veiled as I understood the receiver was much flat-
> tered by it.[43]

Mary found humor in a visit to the Supreme Court in Washington
to which Justice William Johnson of South Carolina had been appointed by President Jefferson in 1804. Thus she wrote to Mary Few:

> Tell Matilda *Capt. Smith's* seat in the Supreme Court was
> pointed out to *Pocahontas*—in case this should appear enigmati-
> cal I will inform you that Mrs. Dr. Jones proposed celebrating
> at her country place (where Oglethorpe landed) his birthday.
> Mrs. Campbell proposed that characters should appear and that
> Judge Johnson should go as Capt. Smith and I as Pocahontas.[44]

Mary had the good humor to be able to laugh at herself. She loved
a good story even if it was at her own expense:

> Margaret & myself were on our way to a party—the streets
> were deluged by rain. Our Horses took fright at the reflection
> of a lamp on the water & attempted to run. I was agitated to
> *fainting* pitch and our footman who is a Hercules in strength
> took me in his arms & bore me to dry land. Margaret perse-
> vered in riding while I determined to *foot* it. After trudging a
> little way I was arrested in my pedestrianations by a pond—my
> faithful escort bore me over it and several others I encountered
> before I arrived at my journey's end. In the midst of *my feat* the
> ludicrous figure I cut enveloped in an immense cloak & hood in
> the arms of a little fellow who might personate the Black Dwarf

shot across my brain and I roared until I lost my strength—
what with fright and laughter my poor nerves were shaken to
their centre."[45]

Mary Telfair had a deep-rooted set of values that remained consistent throughout her lifetime. As she grew older, she did not lose any of her appreciation for those aspects of life that really mattered to her. She wrote in her early thirties, "I enjoy some things in this world as much as I did at sixteen—The beauties of Nature, the works of art, friendship and *good* society have greater charms for me now than they ever had." Mary often pondered moral and behavioral questions and frequently turned to her books for guidance in formulating her thoughts. She respected the opinions of Miss Jane Taylor (1783–1824), who along with other accomplishments was the author with her sister of the nursery rhyme "Twinkle twinkle, little star." Mary decided to avoid a tendency to bandy words about in her conversation after reading one of Taylor's letters: "Miss Taylor in one of her letters censures that style of conversation so much, and presents the dangers attendant upon the indulgence of it in such a new light that I determined to conquer my 'taste for drollery' and I perfectly agree with her in thinking that humorous associations often interfere even with our most serious engagements."[46]

Mary dipped into Taylor's *Contributions of Q. Q.*, published in 1824, and found there ideas of great interest if not entirely in conformity with her own:

> The essay on the government of our thoughts I read with great attention for I have never been able to govern mine and the less I am interested in passing scenes the more they rove—a brain of this order or rather a brain of disorder makes the possessor of it very humble. I cannot however agree with my paragon in thinking that the individual who cannot govern his thoughts has no control over his actions, so far from it that I think an undisciplined mind governed by steady principles may act very consistently.[47]

Mary pondered whether it was better to confine oneself to a limited number of intimate friends or to seek broader associations as a means of self-improvement. It was a matter that she would discuss with Mary Few on an intellectual level:

I scarcely know how to decide upon the important question you proposed in your last—whether the cultivation of general society is calculated to improve our condition or not. It is hard to determine—it is frequently a subject of debate with Sarah & myself, and we usually conclude by acknowledging that it is a *heartless* enjoyment, but an evil which people who have not a great deal to occupy their minds with must resort to by way of escaping the shackles of that fiend Ennui.[48]

Mary's intellectual and spiritual life was enriched by her extensive reading on religious subjects. In writing to Mary Few, herself a woman of deep spirituality, Mary had a kindred spirit with whom to share her reflections:

I read Baxter's Saints Rest five years ago. I will read it again as you recommend it, perhaps I shall enjoy it much more now than I did then. The old Writers upon sacred subjects are more spiritual than the new & for that reason their conceptions of Heaven and heavenly things are more distinguished for purity & sublimity—but I confess my ear is more in harmony with modern style. I have tried to cultivate an interest in *the quaint*, but in vain. I fear my taste was too early corrupted to enjoy what people of fine taste prefer. There is something ludicrous at times in it— even Matthew Henry when he is most disposed to be impressive weakens the force of his argument by quaintness which borders upon drollery. I am at present engaged in reading a very interesting work "on the divine attributes." I think it would interest you.[49]

Mary read numerous other religious works. One summer, her constant companion was *Keith on the Prophesies*. Sarah Haig became attached to *Wayland's Sermons* and prevailed upon her sister to read his sermon on the abuse of the imagination. This led Mary to observe, "I have for several years past considered it wholly unprofitable to cultivate the imagination, and I now think with Mr. Wayland that it is a sin to indulge in those visions which have a tendency to unfit us for two worlds by teaching us to create one of our own." Mary thought that the hymns and letters of Reginald Heber bore "the impress of his pure and lovely character." Legh Richmond (1772–1823), the rector of Turvey, had a strong influence on the religious thinking of his time. His moral tract *The Dairyman's Daughter*, published in 1809, had a circulation of two million copies. Telfair was familiar with his writings: "Leigh [sic] Richmond beautifully remarks that there are three places where the rich & poor meet—The house of Prayer—the house appointed for all the living, and the house not made with hands eternal in the Heavens—it is in the last only that we can hope to be reunited to those beloved ones who have preceded us on their journey home and prepared the way for our departure."[50]

For Mary Telfair there was nothing more important than her belief in God and her Christian faith. She could empathize with the words of Chateaubriand when she copied his lines, "The religious soul like an aromatic plant of the mountains, seems to raise itself towards Heaven, to make to it an offering of its perfumes." She agreed with Hannah More that "Genius without religion is only a lamp on the gate of a Palace; it may serve to cast a gleam of light on those without, while the inhabitants sit in darkness." Many of the poems in her commonplace book have a religious theme. One entitled "Our Father who art in Heaven" begins, "Art Thou my Father? Then no more my sins shall tempt me to despair." Another extols the power of prayer.[51]

Mary despaired of becoming as strong a Christian as she would have liked. She felt that she was lacking in piety. Unlike Mary Few, she never underwent a conversion experience or made a public expression of faith. Writing to Few in 1828, she compared the depth of her religious faith to that of her friend: "I was happy to learn from your last letter dear Mary that you have chosen the better part and united yourself to the church. I wish I was worthy of following your example but though my most ardent desire is to become an exemplary Christian, I feel that I have made very little progress towards it."[52]

Mary Telfair strove for moral perfection but believed it an impossibility because of man's sinful nature:

> There would be very little incentive to act always from principle if we looked only to this world for reward—and yet there is something so soothing in the approvals of conscience that I wonder how we can so often do that which awakens its remorse. There can be nothing so delightful as "a conscience void of offense." The best rule by which we can attain it is to "do unto others as we wish they should do unto us." We can aim at it but to arrive at any thing like perfection is impossible our natures are *too too* sinful.[53]

Telfair's Christianity was the Christianity of Calvin. Not only did she believe that mankind was sinful by nature as a result of Adam's fall, but that the elect were saved by God's grace alone. "I am very sensible of the fact that we can do little for ourselves," she wrote. "Grace is the gift of God & we can only pray for it. We may read and be convinced of the truth of the gospel, and our hearts may continue uninfluenced by the holy spirit." Mary's sturdy Calvinism even crept into her humor: "Transpose the word Presbyterian and what does it make? Best in prayer."[54]

Mary Telfair had no use for the Roman Catholic faith. The pomp and ceremony of the church were not to her taste. Nor did she approve of the more evangelical Protestant sects. "Your description of a camp meeting interested me very much," she wrote to Mary Few. "I have never attended one, objecting to the manner in which they are conducted in the interior of our state." The idea of an established church was anathema to her, having come to appreciate the principles of religious freedom embodied in the United States Constitution: "I am as much opposed to the union of the religious with the worldly Man—as the union of church and state."[55]

Mary, at times, might express a philosophy of life that was practical, down-to-earth, and secular: "I have lived long enough to know that good useful practical people are the only ones fitted to buffet with the cares, the sorrows, and disappointments of a world where unalloyed happiness is sought, but never found."[56] More often, however, her faith in God was the rock on which she would lean in times of trouble and sadness:

> Submission is the lot of Mortals and I acquiesce in all the dispensations of Providence for I know that they are wisely ordered.[57]

> Since I have reflected on the mysterious workings of Providence I have become more dependent on His will and as a principle of duty reconcile as much as possible the changes of life—I have learned to be grateful for little blessings as well as great ones and to sigh for nothing beyond my attainment.[58]

If we could only realize that we are under the guardianship of Providence always, we might rest secure amidst pestilence & peril, but we are so short sighted that we require to be continually reminded of our dependance upon him who is the arbiter of our destinies as well as the ruler of the Universe.[59]

Contentment is truly a blessing from above, for the natural man cannot possess it—the want of it caused our first Parents to transgress and we have daily instances of the evils springing from discontent. I believe that we never learn to live in the present until the future and the past are veiled in impenetrable clouds—When we look forward and look backward only to regret misspent time—then we are improving.[60]

There is no balm for a wounded spirit in earthly comforts & consolations—Peace has not its origin *below*, it comes from *above—Perishable* is inscribed upon every object in this visible world from Man down to the humblest insect that sports the summer breeze.[61]

While Mary Telfair accepted the Calvinist doctrine of salvation by grace alone, she devoted much of her life to good works. With her nieces, Mary and Margaret, she assumed the role of the wise aunt, becoming their counselor and tutor. She sought to aid other young women, particularly those she believed could benefit from the advice of a wise-aunt figure, and on occasion would emulate the efforts of other women in the South who sought to provide a Christian education to the slave children on their plantations or in their households.

8

The Wise Aunt

Delightful task! To rear the tender thought,
To teach the young idea how to shoot.
James Thompson, "Spring," in *The Seasons* (1728)

Although Mary Telfair had reconciled herself to the unmarried state, she yearned to have a child of her own. "If the little creatures dropped from the clouds I should be apt to snatch one up but as that is impossible and they are articles too precious to be given or sold I must covet them in vain," she admitted to Mary Few. "I never envied any woman *her Husband,*" she continued, "but I have seen several children that almost made me wish to turn Gipsy that I might steal them." Even though children were too precious to be given or sold, Mary could still beg for one while engaging in banter with a friend:

> I have seen Mrs. Howard and her *little Colonels.* They are fine children and will no doubt be instructed in *the art of happiness* by their Mother, who is better fitted to steer her course *happily* through the vast ocean of human life than any woman I know. I will venture to say she will never be *shipwrecked* on Cape *Fear* or the shore of *fastidiousness.* I begged her to give me one of her little heros. She gave me a very impudent reply. I cannot venture to insert it in a letter. I covet her petit enfants as much as I do *her art of enjoying life.*[1]

Mary, at least, had opportunities to play with the *petit enfants* of her friends. It gave her real pleasure to do so:

In a garden and a nursery of *human* plants I take a retrograde step and find myself again a child charmed to enthusiasm. Our neighbor Mrs. Howe has a sweet little child of seven months old & I go much oftener to see her than I otherwise should on purpose to kiss and play with it. Our love for Bairns is so well known that they collect here in groupes.[2]

"I prefer the company of children to uninteresting adults," Mary wrote. "I can even join in their sports." She enjoyed observing how friends took renewed pleasure in life through the enthusiasm of their children. Through their young charges, they could relive their own childhood: "An advantage that Matrons have over Spinsters—the former may return to *second childhood* in the meridian of life the latter can only do so in *dotage*." Mary's love of children may have shown through in her demeanor as indicated by this anecdote:

A poor french Emigrant came this morning to receive a piece of linen from me to make up. She could not speak English and I in *broken* french tried to hold a conversation with her. At length I discovered she was deaf and commenced *screaming* which brought two of the servants to witness our parley which was interrupted more than once by their bursts of laughter. At length *Mamselle* rose to depart after asking me if I had a *Baby*. There must be something *anti spinsterial* in my *looks* as I invariably pass for a *Matron*.[3]

After the death of Thomas Telfair, his widow and her two little girls stayed for a time with her in-laws in Savannah, another example of the Telfairs' willingness to welcome to their hearth members of their extended family. The visit afforded Mary Telfair the opportunity to become better acquainted with little Mary and Margaret, namesakes of herself and her sister. She was particularly taken with Mary, the elder of the two. She described the child to Mary Few:

The eldest is a child of uncommon capacity we all think her a prodigy her appearance too is uncommonly interesting. I have sometimes thought her a little like Frances she is excessively pale with a roman nose, dark blue eyes and very red lips either very animated or unanimated no medium about her very apt to take violent fancies or aversions. Alexander is the only being she fears she was very fond of me but never obeyed me.[4]

Although little Mary was not yet five, Mary Telfair was ready to assume the role of the nurturing maiden aunt and take the girl under her wing. If she could have a positive influence on her late brother's elder daughter, it would be some compensation for not having a child of her own. Historian Lee Virginia Chambers-Schiller tells us that in this period of the country's history there was a "reserve army" of unmarried, available women who moved in and out of the homes of relatives performing various tasks, including the nurturing of motherless nephews and nieces. Although her nieces were not motherless, Telfair felt responsible for their well-being. Their mother, so she thought, was so completely lacking in good sense that she could not be trusted with the upbringing of Thomas Telfair's daughters. The woman was totally lacking in intellectual curiosity, and her world was limited to Wilkes County and Savannah. Mary worried over the effect on Mary and Margaret of continued exposure to the Georgia up-country, an area that she considered an intellectual and cultural wasteland. She owed it to her dead brother to do what she could for his girls. "I do not think my affection for Mary & Margaret proceeds from any peculiar qualities they possess," Mary Telfair wrote. "They are the representatives of a beloved Brother for whom I would have made any earthly sacrifice and whose untimely loss I shall never cease to deplore."[5]

Service to others was a major tenet of the nineteenth-century cult of domesticity, and Mary Telfair hoped to find fulfillment in the instruction of these fatherless girls. Chambers-Schiller has found that popular nineteenth-century literature portrayed the maiden aunt as a wise counselor and family advisor, a person who embodied the qualities of "true womanhood" while remaining unwed. This was a role that Telfair was ready to undertake. She was determined to be a "useful old maid." Although it would call for self-sacrifice, she was prepared to work hard with young Mary: "She requires very peculiar management and unless her mind is cultivated and her feelings properly directed will make an unhappy Character. I have sat for hours and listened to her with more interest than many grown persons."[6]

As the girls grew older, young Margaret joined her sister as a student of her aunts, and the instruction of Thomas' daughters became a joint enterprise of two of the Telfairs sisters. On a visit to Wilkes County in the summer of 1826, while the girls were on vacation, Mary and her sister Margaret kept themselves busy with their nieces' education. Margaret worked with young Mary and Mary with the even younger Margaret. Mary found that her charge had a quickness of mind rarely met with in a child of ten. "She has imagination without much sensibility," her aunt wrote, "easy to acquire but difficult to retain a mind full of vivacity and associations and delights in the ludicrous." The latter propensity was one that Mary was not inclined to encourage. When the girls were obedient they were rewarded with games in the evening calculated to awaken their intellectual powers. Mary believed that "enigmas benefit the mind as much as wrestling and running do the body—both are a play that prepares the mind and body for serious labour." Mary Telfair was able to win the affections of young Margaret. "She is very anxious to be christened over again that I might be her *God Mother* and begs me to *adopt* her," Mary wrote with considerable pride. "It is a singular whim but shews that the little thing has warm feelings." Mary had hopes that young Mary's mother would become sufficiently sensible to the importance of a good education as to allow her elder daughter to go to school in the North the following summer. She realized, however that she and her sister could not push the issue: "We feel the delicacy of our situation and cannot *urge* what we feel."[7]

Mary's position was indeed delicate. In her own mind she knew exactly what was best for the girls, but her strong feelings on the intrinsic value of education and the superiority of female academies in the North were viewed with indifference by their mother. The values of this woman from Wilkes County, who had once been a belle of considerable renown, bore no resemblance to those of the intellectual Mary Telfair. If her daughters were pretty and charming what more was required? Mary had always been outspoken in her views. She recognized in herself a lack of prudence.[8] She knew that she must bear in mind that she was not the girls' mother and that there was a real risk that she might say something that her sister-in-law would find offensive. The situation called for discretion and tact.

The occasional visits that Mary Telfair and her sisters made to Thomas Telfair's widow and her two daughters in Wilkes County convinced Mary that this rural area would have nothing but a stifling effect on her nieces' development. She found the place to be uncommonly dull: "A march through the deserts of Arabia can alone compare with it in solitude and dearth of interest." She thought the women in that part of the country totally lacking in responsibility.

"Here they do not even keep their bodies sweet and clean—to *glut the appetite* is all they do."[9] These visits convinced Mary of her need to persevere in her efforts to instruct the girls and ultimately to remove them to a more stimulating environment.

During the winter of 1826–1827, when both girls were studying in Savannah, their aunts worked with them on their homework. "No galley slaves ever toiled more faithfully than we did," Mary Telfair wrote in retrospect a year later. In the process Mary found herself going over her own earlier education. She was able to revisit geography and grammar, for the girls' teacher "gives them tremendous lessons." Unfortunately the girls fell short of what Mary expected of those with Telfair blood in their veins:

> Poor Mary from possessing a slow mind, finds committing to memory an Herculean labor, while Margaret acquires her lessons with astonishing ease. I am quite satisfied with her mind, but she is careless, volatile, and indolent. The independence of her Nature revolts at Discipline—in fact she is the most singular child I have ever known and will unless *properly drilled* turn out *a mere woman of the world*. She has a great deal of Sarah Haig's drollery, and is often witty, but I never encourage her propensity for satire for she will never have prudence to balance it.[10]

Mary's work with her nieces led her to read books written for children, including tales designed for moral instruction: "I have been reading children's books for the last three months with an intensity of interest which surprises me, and in that respect entered into a state of *second childhood*—The valuable morals which these books contain are of as great advantage to old heads as young ones." Mary would read some of the stories aloud to the girls with mixed results: "Little Margaret (who is full of faults) was so struck when I read the history of poor Constantia to her that she conceived an aversion to hearing it—the parallel was too great between the spoiled child & herself."[11]

Mary Telfair had very definite ideas on how a child should be raised and educated. "The mind of a child is like a clear stream," she wrote, "impede its progress and it becomes a stagnant pool." She believed that a child's mind was a tabula rasa to the extent that if Lord Byron "had been blessed with a Mother capable of directing his infant mind and subduing his turbulent passions, his virtues might have been as transcendent as his genius." The women in the South, and particularly in the upcountry, had no idea of how to raise children as far as Mary was concerned. "The children in this part of the world are so *dragged* up, and neglected, it is a mercy when they are cast upon strangers for instruction." A child must be subjected to proper discipline. Mary was told of one mother whose strongest reproof to her young daughter was "Julia Frances, you will make Mother cry—you don't love Mother." "What imbecility!" was Mary's reaction. Mary felt strongly that a child should not be allowed to become selfish:

> Children ought early to be taught to make sacrifices to others. If there is any thing odious to Character it is that of selfishness. Parents often sow the seeds of selfishness, vulgarity and ill-breeding in their children by indulging them in every whim. You know I look upon infancy as a blank sheet of paper upon which any impression may be made although I admit the doctrine of innate depravity.[12]

Moderation was the key to a child's proper upbringing:

> If I was the Mother of children the first lesson I would teach them would be *moderation*. It should be the watchword that should echo from the Drawing Room to the Nursery from thence to the Kitchen—how can any one leave human plants to Nature to be the sport of feeling, and nursed by *Accident*. It is better to undergo the severest discipline which *English* systems can devise than to be the creature of impulse.[13]

Children must be taught at an early age to tell the truth:

> I have arrived at the conclusion that a boy may get along, if the natural temperament is right, with the education Walter Scott gave his. Do you remember the remark to Irving, "I teach them to shoot, to ride, and to tell the truth the rest I leave to their Tutor." To speak the truth is the basis of every virtue, and if that is early implanted the fruits will appear in after life.[14]

Referring to a young mother of her acquaintance, Mary Telfair wrote:

> I am glad to hear she is so devoted to the interests of her children for to me it seems natural that a mother should forget herself in her offspring—Some have an *animal* attachment to their bodies, keep them clean & caress them without seeming

to remember that they are immortal beings, and susceptible to every improvement which education can bestow—Others allow them (the *Housekeepers at home particularly*) to wallow like "pigs" in dirt, and to grow up like the trees of the forest, without culture or pruning—Observers on the Theatre of life, who have had full time for *Study* without a great deal of occupation understand better how to train children than those who early undertake maternal cares & duties—Becky Smith made a very sagacious remark to me upon her first acquaintance—She said she never saw a child that required whipping, but she had seen a great many mothers who did.

Mary's much-admired friend, Mrs. Edward F. Campbell, who was a great teacher of children, also believed that the young could be trained without punishment.[15]

Mary would not have minded administering a whipping to those mothers who "allow their children to domineer over others from the want of energy to control them." She shared with Mary Few her strong feelings on the subject:

> We may be *spinsterial* in our notions but we both think the relation of parent to child is an awfully responsible one—and yet how little they feel it. Some appear to me than to have no other delight than in humoring their whims—and *glutting* them with improper food—I hope I am not too severe—but the inanity & blindness of those who ought to be as vigilant as sentinels on their post provokes me to wrath.[16]

Mary recognized that she and her sisters could find the behavior of children a bit annoying at times:

> To take a deep interest in children and be *soothed* by their noise they must be your own—Mrs. C. thinks we are *Phenomena* in Nature to put up so quietly with children, but I think my *tolerance* is altogether cultivated. Sarah says their very questions excite her nerves, and Margaret's *love of order* makes "the playful children just let loose from school" a little annoying.[17]

On another occasion she wrote: "Sarah's & Margaret's nerves are more sensitive to the noise of children than mine though I cannot say it is *music to my ear*." She added that one young mother of her acquaintance deserved "a patent" for the system she had devised for the training of her child:

> The little fellow is an only child three years of age; he winds his Grand Mother's worsted, feeds his silk worms and arranges the flowers in the flower pots with his own little hands; is put to bed at sunset—Such obedience I never saw before—We received two parcels of flower seeds picked and put up by him & nicely stitched.[18]

Through her patient efforts, Mary Telfair was able to bring about substantial improvements in her nieces. "Mrs. Telfair is now on a visit to us," Mary reported to Mary Few. "She thinks we have *worked wonders*—We certainly have made her children very obedient without inflicting any punishment." Mary regretted, however, that neither of the girls had what she called the "Telfair temper." She found young Margaret "uncommonly attractive." "I never saw a child win hearts with so much ease," she wrote. She initially found Margaret "self willed and unamiable," but by "never overlooking a defect in temper" and by "never allowing her to *command* a servant," she worked positive changes in the girl. She reached a point where she could say of Margaret, "She has talent & vivacity, some beauty, and a great deal of manner for a girl of eleven."[19]

Mary Telfair continued to believe that her nieces should be educated in the North as she had been. Those years as a schoolgirl in New York and Newark had been the happiest of her life, and she wished the same for the girls. She had her wish, and young Mary Telfair went to New York to study during the winter of 1827–1828. Telfair was gratified that Mary's mother had allowed her to leave Georgia. She believed that her niece was a girl who required "early discipline." "Her capacity is very good," she wrote, "with more originality than any child I ever knew—but she has no application, and quite too many of the *eccentricities* of *Genius* which I am no friend to either in *Man* or *Woman*." Mrs. Green's boarding school was chosen for her by her Aunt Mary and her Uncle Alexander. Alexander had first consulted with Mrs. Catherine Few, the mother of the Few ladies. "We wish to put her where the solid branches of education are attended to," Mary wrote, "where there is tuition for the head & heart." She believed that she had found the right place for young Mary:

> This morning Alexander & myself visited Mrs. Green & entered Mary as a Scholar. She commences her boarding school career tomorrow. I am very much pleased with Mrs. Green. She seems to be a rational, well informed judicious woman & I trust *past neglect* will be repaired as far as she is capable of doing it. We accomplished so much in the way of subduing the temper last winter that I am in hopes, though the materials are not of the brightest order, good principles will be a foundation to build upon. Awkward as Mary appears now she is *highly polished* to what she was last summer. Anna Stiles was *a fine specimen* of a southern child—coarse & undisciplined. If she is *civilized* there can be no higher proof of the capacity of Mrs. Green for training young ladies properly. We at first thought of the Misses Delavan but upon reflection thought a city held out greater advantages for a shy backward girl whose manners require as much cultivation as her mind.

Mary hoped that the schoolmistress was a good disciplinarian. She believed that young Mary needed "firmness & consistency" to govern her. "She requires urging on," Telfair wrote, "as much as a lazy Horse requires a spur."[20]

"Ask Mary Telfair if her fingers are frost bitten," her Aunt Mary suggested to Mary Few that winter. She requested her friend to tell the young Mary Telfair to direct her letters to her sister Margaret to Washington, Wilkes County, for that winter Thomas' younger daughter was "digging learning out of a hollow tree." Mrs. Green's school was near to the Fews's house, and Mary Telfair was pleased at this for she thought that their advice and example would be of advantage to her niece. "I wish her to love you all as much as I do," she wrote to Mary Few, "but that is impossible for she is of a colder temperament consequently a great deal more prudent than I was at her age."[21]

Mrs. Catherine Few looked out for the interests of Thomas' daughter while she was in New York, just as she had looked after the elder Mary Telfair years earlier when she was pursuing her studies at Miss Dow's classes. When Mary Telfair sent a $200 check to New York to defray her niece's school expenses, she sent it to Mrs. Few. Mrs. Few took young Mary into her home and nursed her back to health when she fell ill during the late winter of 1830. Mary realized that her advice to her niece was not always well received. "How is Mary Telfair?" she wrote to Mary Few in New York. "She does not deserve a kind word from one of us for she never writes and I presume never thinks of us. I suppose she did not relish my letter of *advice*. I always felt gratitude to those who gave it to me and I hope she will yet learn to value it."[22]

The close tabs that Telfair kept on young Mary Telfair through Mary Few suggests that her relationship to the girl was becoming increasingly parental. Referring to her niece, she wrote in December 1828:

> If we could have sheltered her in our own Domicile I never would have given my consent to a Boarding School but she is better under Mrs. Green than she would be any where else—I never thought I had firmness of character until she called it forth—The love of pleasure with her is so strong that I fear the sympathies of her character will be destroyed by it.[23]

Educating a girl in the North was expensive, and Thomas Telfair's widow was not one to handle money well. She had squandered much of what she had inherited from her husband. Alexander, however, was willing to provide the funds required for his niece's education. Mary explained the situation to Mary Few in the utmost confidence:

> I am now going to tell you *a secret*. Her Mother by her specu-lations & ridiculous extravagances has involved herself & her Children so that neither of them can afford to spend any thing but my Brother will not allow them to feel it so that Mary's real wants will be supplied and no economy where education is concerned will be practiced. I wish Mrs. Telfair had the same ideas on that subject that we have—then instead of her children running wild she would have devoted her time, her income, her all to their improvement. But *up country* notions are the *antip-odes* to ours. They seem to think a *little shew* all that is necessary in living & in education.[24]

The surveillance continued into the spring and extended to young Margaret, who by that time also was studying in New York under the watchful eye of Mary Few:

I am happy to hear that Mary retains her high reputation at school. Her principles were always good but she had faults which Mrs. Green seems to have corrected. I am sorry to perceive that an aversion to writing still exists with her. I fear she will be very, very inert. I am as you imagined very glad to hear of the decline of Margaret's popularity with her schoolmates—her principles are by no means fixed and her influence can be of no advantage now to any one—I wish she could be influenced by her superiors—but the *upland* spirit (our friend Mrs. Skinner excepted) the desire to be looked up to is a powerful feeling with her. I wish you would give me an insight into their conduct, etc.—You are an impartial judge and never exaggerate.[25]

Mary Telfair continued to worry over her nieces, but found comfort in reports from Mary Few:

Your letter dear Mary arrived here I presume about the same time that mine reached Park Place—I need not say how cordially it was received, and how much I felt obliged to you for the intelligence you gave of Margaret and the kind interest you have taken in her—Our anxiety respecting her was very great, and I confess that until your letter arrived I thought of her incessantly, and my busy fancy conjured up a variety of disagreeable images—therefore you can imagine the relief which your communication afforded. It is not necessary to be a Parent to feel the responsibility and anxiety of one. I *pity* the Mother who feels more than I have of late.[26]

Mary Telfair wished to have young Margaret continue her studies in New York until she was at least fifteen or sixteen. She expressed her concern to Mary Few in January 1830 that the girl might return to Georgia prematurely:

Alexander thinks I am very proud of the talent which I appropriate to myself of reading character. Certain it is that I am seldom deceived now a days. It is one of the advantages we derive from an increased knowledge of the world. You, dear Mary, have read little Margaret's with *my eyes*. She is a great cause of anxiety to me. I hope my Brother's influence will detain her in the North a year or two longer. Inevitable ruin will be the result of her returning next autumn. The idea of her being launched at fourteen upon the wide world with unformed principles makes me shudder. I grieve at the thought of their being doomed to the *land of traffic* for *cleverness* at Wilkes consists in making a *good bargain*. *Speculation* is the Genius of the Place. Women enter into it with the same spirit that Men do. Providence often befriends the Orphan and all things are ruled by him. We can only rely on his guardian care.[27]

While Mary Telfair's principal concern was the intellectual and moral development of her two nieces, she believed that a woman's obligation to serve others extended beyond the confines of family. Christian concern and a natural inclination to help those in need, particularly young women who could benefit from the advice of a wise-aunt figure, sometimes led Mary Telfair to place less fortunate women under her special care:

> Now Mrs. O'Connor weighs heavily upon our minds. You recollect Mrs. McAllister brought her out from *pure compassion*. We have provided her with an asylum across the street in the house of a Dyer—an Irish Widow *with an only son*—We are to furnish her with food & to have her washing done & she is to work to pay for her room 2 dolls. per month. She ought to lay by 10 dollars a month at least. I intend giving her wholesome advice. She is so full of romance & poetry that I fear she will look upon me as a *Calculating Monster*. She is much given to "*the melting mood*" and is a *facsimile* of Miss Powell. I have been weaving in the loom of fancy as brilliant a destiny for her as your mother did for Peggy, instead of *a Fountain* I have pitched upon a Son of Erin who happens to be her Landlord. Some "*white winged messenger*" whispers in my ear that he will elevate "*the lovely* pale O'Connor's Child" to his Cara Sposa.[28]

The O'Connor woman did not marry the Son of Erin or find another acceptable husband in Savannah, so Mary Telfair, ever vigilant in her concern for the less fortunate, found her a position as a seamstress in Augusta.[29]

It was one thing for a poor Irish widow such as Mrs. O'Connor to contemplate marriage with an Irishman of the same social class, but it was shocking for a young woman of good family whom Mary Telfair had befriended, indeed a person who had been to tea at the

Telfair residence, to go off and marry an Irish-Catholic lighthouse keeper. The woman, who had moved to Savannah from Baltimore ostensibly to teach music, came to Mary with a letter of introduction from her aunt in Philadelphia, a person for whom Mary had the highest respect and admiration. As Mary related the story:

> I invited her to tea & to dinner; the former invitation was accepted, the latter rejected. I sat two hours with her on Tuesday morning listening to her *fine sentiments & fine language*. On Friday I learned that the following morning she was to plight her faith at the Altar of the Catholic Chapel to a Mr. Ramsbottom, a *low irishman* whose wife was killed last winter by being thrown from her Gig. An hour after the ceremony was performed he bore her off in his own little sloop of which he is the *commander* to an uninhabited island where he dwells as *Light house keeper*. What a rash act on her part! What an era do we live in for *matrimonial exploits!*[30]

In another example of her reaching out as a caring aunt-figure, Mary Telfair sought to assist the Misses Livingstone, ladies from New York who had fallen ill after moving to Savannah and found themselves without a friend in a strange new city. Mary Few had written to Telfair of their plight, and the latter had promised to call and see if she could be useful to the ladies. After all, she thought, "The sick & afflicted have always claims upon those who have known suffering themselves." There was little that she could do for them, however:

> As soon as I received your letter we went to see the Livingstones and have been repeatedly since. I was there this morning and saw the only one who appears except a child who she told me was her youngest Sister. She interests me very much. She seems to feel very deeply her Sisters' situation but cannot induce them to see any one, not even a Physician. I am going again tomorrow to urge her to get medical advice. Her Sister she thinks becomes worse every day. She eats indiscriminately and never leaves her room—her cough is dreadful and her fever constant. I wish we could do more than send them delicacies and give them our sympathies.[31]

It also was the duty of Christian women to offer solace to the aged poor. On one occasion Mary went with a friend to visit an impoverished woman of ninety-four, a Swiss Protestant who had been bed-ridden for four years. She had been in her early years a governess in an English nobleman's family and had become dependent upon the charity of a few acquaintances. According to Mary, the woman was "more grateful for a little *talk* than for 'the crumbs that fall from the rich man's table.'" "Her memory is unimpaired and her spirits good," Mary reported. "The poor generally speaking are happier than the rich."[32]

Christian concern led some women of Mary Telfair's class to attempt to instill religious principles in the black children under their charge and to provide them with a rudimentary education. Despite legal restrictions based on the belief that education would only make slaves more discontented than they already were, underground schools were prevalent in the South. Anne Clay spent many hours teaching the slaves on her family's plantation. In answer to the question whether she had seen Miss Clay, Mary Telfair wrote, "I have not but hear that she is engaged in improving the minds & morals of their slaves —her success I believe is not equal to her exertions. She is one whose mind & character fit her for an extensive sphere of usefulness." In her efforts to educate her family's slaves, Anne Clay was supported by her brother Tom, who authored a detailed plan for the moral improvement of Negroes on plantations that he read before the Georgia Presbytery and was printed at the request of that body under date of 1833. Anne Clay's work with the slaves also received the support of the Reverend Charles Colcock Jones, the well-known Presbyterian minister from Liberty County who in 1842 wrote *The Religious Education of the Negroes in the United States* as part of a movement to bring Christianity to more blacks in the South. He, Bishop Stephen Elliott, and Bishop Meade of Virginia once met at the Clay plantation to confer on the religious responsibility of the South with respect to the black population.[33]

Mrs. Edward F. Campbell was another close friend who exerted serious efforts in an attempt to give black children a Christian education. Mary Telfair visited Mrs. Campbell's school one Sunday afternoon and found her instructing some forty-five or fifty children. "Her method is a very happy one which is exemplified in the improvement they have made in the space of two years," Telfair reported. "She uses the scripture cards and the infant school books, gives a great deal of oral instruction, and teaches them to sing hymns." Telfair found that

Mrs. Campbell possessed "a great deal of quiet energy," and like Anne Clay had "both a passion and a talent for pouring instruction into the minds of children." "Her benevolence is of the most active character," Telfair wrote, "she keeps a set of bed linen and ready made garments for the poor, and I have heard from good authority that she goes herself and has them changed and not only administers food for their bodies, but their souls." Sarah Haig thought her equal to a missionary, and Mary thought so too.[34]

Inspired perhaps by the efforts of Miss Clay and Mrs. Campbell, Mary Telfair spent some time giving lessons to the daughter of one of the servants at the Savannah residence:

> I am giving oral instruction to a little *sable pet*, the most gentle and affectionate little creature. I asked her a few days since who was the first man; she replied *Uncle* Adam. In teaching her the four Seasons I asked her where I went in Summer; she said *to Heaven*. I laughed for I thought it a heavenly change in hot weather. She is too *refined* to say Hell—she says that wicked people go to "*the bad place.*"[35]

While Mary Telfair frequently played the role of the wise aunt with less fortunate women outside of her family, and even with the slave children, her main concern continued to be her nieces. She took the girls with her on summer trips to the North and did her best to have a positive influence on their lives. When her niece Mary married and had a child of her own, a little girl named Alberta, Mary Telfair tried to take on the role of the wise great-aunt. Unhappily, Alberta would be Mary Telfair's greatest disappointment. Mary would come to bitterly reject Alberta, her way of life, and her children, with consequences that would reverberate long after Mary's death.

9

The 1820's

There is a pleasure in the pathless woods,
There is a rapture on the lonely shore,
There is a society where none intrudes.

Lord Byron, *Childe Harold's Pilgrimage,*
Canto iv (1818)

Frances Few spent the winter of 1819–1820 with the Telfairs in Savannah. Mary Telfair was thrilled. For years she had been trying to persuade the Few sisters to come south for the winter, and now Frances had sailed into town. During her visit, Frances and Mary were inseparable, and Frances charmed the household. She totally captivated Mary's uncle, Dr. George Jones. Mary and Frances tried reading together the life of Lorenzo de Medici, but made little progress due to constant interruptions. There were calls to be made, for social convention of the early and mid-nineteenth century required that young, unmarried, middle- and upper-class women spend part of every day in social visiting. The ladies spent an entire day at Wormslow (the old spelling), the country estate of Uncle Jones. The yellow jasmine was in bloom, and the two friends enjoyed a walk along the "moss grown alley." Frances was delighted with the ruin of Noble Jones's old fortified tabby house, which remained on the grounds. She reveled in the excitement of her visit to the South in describing to her friend Mary Garrettson the cedar tree growing within the moldering walls, the wild flowers and weeds covering the tabby, and the nearby graveyard with its slabs of marble. Most of all, she marveled at the beauty of the moss-covered oaks:

But nothing struck me more strongly than the venerable old trees which everywhere adorn this desolate spot. They were covered with a species of moss a light brown color which hangs about a yard from the branches; it waves with every breeze & reminded me of the gray hairs of nature. We approached the place thro' an avenue of live oak whose branches formed a complete arch where the moss waved in solemn grandeur.[1]

The evening before she left for a month's stay in Augusta, Frances attended a ball accompanied by Margaret Telfair and their friend Harriett Campbell. They walked about from room to room, engaged in small talk, and returned home at midnight, much fatigued by the scene. Mary and Sarah Haig stayed up to hear how they had enjoyed their evening. Mary scolded Frances for making no effort to detain by her side a gentleman who had stopped to chat. Mary related the tale to Mary Few in the bantering tone she so often adopted when alluding to men and romance: "It was cruel in my *Protégée* to blast the *brilliant* hopes of her Protectress, was it not Molly?—particularly as I with the true spirit of a *Duenna* charged her to look animated and display the powers of her mind."[2]

Mary Few spent the winter of 1821–1822 in Paris with her Uncle Albert Gallatin, then serving as minister plenipotentiary, and her Aunt Hannah. She sailed for Portsmouth in November 1821 and traveled in England and Belgium as well as in France. She had a most pleasant visit, thoroughly enjoyed seeing foreign lands, and felt fully repaid "for all the suffering and sickness of a sea-voyage." Most of all, she enjoyed the pleasure of returning home.[3]

Frances Few was married in 1822 to Albert Chrystie, a prosperous New York merchant and farmer. When some years earlier Mary Telfair heard that Frances was interested in Albert, she made no secret of her amazement:

My astonishment at hearing of the situation of Frances with regard to Colonel Chrystie was very great. I knew that he was attached to her but was so certain that it was not reciprocal that I once got angry with Sarah Haig for saying she was fond of him. Their characters were certainly dissimilar don't you think so Mary? I believe he had some fine qualities but the thoughts of Frances's uniting her fate to his never once entered into my head.[4]

After his marriage, Chrystie built a mansion in Fishkill, where in 1823 Frances gave birth to their first child. The little boy was named William Few Chrystie and would be called "Willie." When Mary Telfair first learned that Frances was pregnant, she expressed her approval to Mary Few: "I always told Frances she was *cut out* for a Mother her love of children, her matronly air and figure united to a total indifference to the empty joys of the world admirably fitted her for the nursery." After the birth of the "little bairn," she sent a bundle of baby clothes to New York in the care of a friend with instructions to leave the parcel at Mr. Chrystie's store on Maiden Lane should the family be out of town. "I expect Frances will be too much occupied with nursery cares to enjoy any old jokes," was her smiling comment to Mary Few. She longed to see Frances' baby. She requested Mary Few to "kiss little Willie who I hear from various sources is quite a beauty." "I think I could devour him with kisses if I could only see him, for my foolish fondness for sweet children continues undiminished." Little Mary Chrystie was born the following year.[5]

In September 1822 Mary Telfair was with her brother Alexander at his place in Bristol Banks. Her mother and sisters were there as well, and Dr. John Cumming and his wife came for a two-week visit. Dr. and Mrs. Cumming were frequent traveling companions of the Telfairs. On one journey, when cholera was raging all about them, Mary took great comfort in having a physician as a member of their party. Mary also felt very comfortable in the company of Mrs. Cumming. "Mrs. Dr. Cumming is one I am never afraid of—she has so much discretion and Christian charity that I feel a greater degree of confidence in her than most women."[6]

In October 1822, Mary traveled to Philadelphia from her brother's place in Bristol to be present at the marriage of her uncle, Dr. George Jones, to Eliza Smith of that city. Dr. Jones was in his mid-fifties at the time and had buried two wives, Mary Gibbons (Mary Telfair's aunt who had died in 1792) and the widow, Sarah Fenwick Campbell, by whom he had no children that survived infancy. Mary reported that the company at the wedding was "small and select." Dr. Jones's daughter Sarah was present, as was Harriett Campbell, the daughter of his second wife by her first husband, Macartan Campbell. Unfortunately the son that Mary Gibbons had borne Dr. Jones was not there to share his father's happiness, for George Wimberly Jones II had died in 1818. Mary observed that the bride "was much agitated at first," but she was pleased to note that "her tremors soon subsided into a calm." Mary admitted that she trembled as well, as she always did at weddings, for she considered them "solemn affairs." Mary felt that Sarah and Harriett behaved extremely well: "the former looked like a Nun about to assume the fatal veil, the latter wore an air of despondency which as she is seldom animated only a nice observer could have discerned." Mary expressed the belief that Sarah would soon become reconciled to her father's marriage and predicted that it would be "the means of her taking a similar step." Mary was "not seer enough to discover who will be her Companion to the Holy altar."[7]

Mary was correct in her prediction. The following fall, Sarah Jones was married in Philadelphia to Alfred Cuthbert of Savannah, Thomas Telfair's eccentric Princeton classmate, who by that time was making his mark in politics. Cuthbert had served in the Georgia legislature from 1810 to 1813 and at the time of his marriage was a member of the United States Congress. He would go on to serve as a United States senator from 1835 to 1843. Mary Telfair was in Philadelphia while plans for the wedding were under way. "Sarah Jones is still preparing (alias) shopping for the *great event*," she wrote. Mary did not entirely approve of the match: "I feel for Sarah as the *solemn* period approaches and yet (tell Matilda) he is 'a Man of Talents' what *poor comfort* in this case." Mary attended the wedding and continued to harbor reservations concerning Cuthbert, as evidenced by her comments to Mary Few in a letter written after her return to Savannah: "I am wearied with the questions put to me about the Bride Groom —he certainly behaved with great *decorum*; if it was any body else I would say *delicacy*—but prejudices cannot vanish in a moment."[8]

Actually, when her cousin became engaged to Cuthbert, Mary found that she liked him better than she had thought she would. Perhaps she had been too much influenced by Thomas' tales of his classmate's odd behavior. Mary did find Cuthbert to be "artificial" but nonetheless "a most agreeable companion." But he was as different from Sarah Jones as was Conrad, the corsair, from his beloved Medora in Lord Byron's poem, *The Corsair*. One problem was that Alfred Cuthbert was not much to look at. In commenting to Mary Few on the man's appearance, Telfair tried to recall the words of Diana Vernon in Scott's *Rob Roy*. She could not remember them exactly, but set forth their import in a letter to her friend: "If he could meet with a *blind* mistress never was man surer of a conquest—

but the charm created by the eloquence of the tongue was dissolved by the eye." "This is precisely the case with Mr. C," Mary opined. "He converses delightfully but his air, look, and manner were not formed in Nature's finest mould." Sarah Haig, always one to speak her mind, put it more bluntly. "He is too ugly to love" was her comment.[9]

Marriage seemed to agree with the new Mrs. Cuthbert, and even Mary Telfair, who seldom had anything good to say of the married state, was able to recognize it when next she saw her cousin:

> Sarah looked so gay and happy after the *affair* (as Miss Oliver styled it) that I began to think marrying *could not* be such an awful piece of business as our imaginations have presented it— Sarah must have met old Hymen with more *hardihood* than Frances did from your account of her—for she looked days after as if she had been married twenty years.[10]

Nonetheless, Mary continued to have doubts over her cousin's choice of a husband. Her comments to Mary Few on the match reveal more of the writer than the subject:

> I have not received a line from Sarah Cuthbert since our separation. I unite with you in hoping that "Cousin Alfred" may continue to fascinate her. I do hope she will not settle down into her former state of listlessness for if I have a knowledge of his character which I tried to gain by *study*, she must be on *the alert*—"Her hand is on a Lion's mane" he will either be her *slave* or she his; no medium can exist with a man of his eccentric habits and wild imagination. I think a mind like his would have dazzled both *you & I* some six or seven years ago but I have become so *tamed* that I prefer a solid judgment, useful intellect & cultivated taste now to the excessive flights of fancy and vagaries of genius. I believe I am *half* indebted to Alexander for this taste for he thinks a mind without judgment like a character without principle and both pardon a vulgar comparison like a coach without Horses.[11]

Mary was with Sarah Cuthbert in Philadelphia the year following her marriage. Sarah had just "ushered a little Daughter into this world of trouble" and had "made light work of it." Mary thought the child the "softened image of its noble Sire." She found that Sarah's happiness had not paled: "What an astonishing change the double state makes in some women—With her it is a new being, the *Penseroza* has entirely given place to the cheerful and never have I seen her look half so happy—She talks too of the superior happiness of married life which I think will influence Harriett." Harriett Campbell never did marry, however, and when Cupid's arrows pierced the heart of Sarah, her constant companion, she was left in a state of loneliness.[12]

After the death of his brothers, Alexander took over the management of his father's estate, including the River and Mills Plantations in Burke County and the Smithfield Plantation in Richmond County. He had his late brothers' estates to manage as well and had much to say in the operation of the Sabine Fields Plantation, twelve farm lots in Chatham County six miles to the west of Savannah to which his mother held the fee. Alexander carried out his duties with the utmost care and precision, meticulously keeping his books of account in his own neat hand. His father's admonitions with respect to the importance of accurate records that were pounded into his head while a schoolboy obviously had their effect. Alexander was a man of considerable complexity, but in his own mind he was primarily a planter. In his will he referred to himself as "Alexander Telfair, Planter." In addition to the properties left by his father to his wife and children, Alexander had his own plantations: the Retreat in Jefferson County and the 850–acre Thorn Island Plantation across the river in South Carolina in the Barnwell District.[13]

Slavery provided the economic underpinning for the Telfair plantations, just as it did for the estates of every other planter in the South. Georgia was the only English colony in which slavery originally was prohibited, but it was only a matter of time before the prohibition eroded away. Southern Christians had no problem reconciling human bondage with their religious beliefs. A fundamental tenet of the ideology justifying slavery was that the institution was ordained by God, a part of the natural order of things. Even after the Civil War, a clergyman would write of Joseph Clay's grandson, "If it ever could have been really doubted whether a slaveholder could be a Christian, we think the caviler would have found himself by the side of Thomas Savage Clay. He was a slaveholder not from covetousness, but from conviction." He did not call his slaves "slaves," but "his people." When he died, one of his slaves said that he had lost not a master but a father.[14] It would have been difficult for Alexander Telfair and his sisters to have escaped the same self-delusion.

The Telfairs would have scoffed at the suggestion that the institution of slavery bore the seeds of its own destruction. When Mary Telfair complained that "nothing prospers at the South," she blamed it in part on the purported laziness of the slaves: "The sloth of the sable population and the heat mar against improvements physical, moral and intellectual."[15] It did not seem to occur to her that the fault might be found in the institution of slavery itself, the South's "peculiar institution" that undermined the spirit of the master as well as the slave.

The day-to-day operation of each of the Telfair plantations was under the supervision of an overseer. Most of the acreage was planted with upland cotton, but some of the fields were used to grow feed corn, rye, and oats. Livestock was raised on the plantations as well: cattle, sheep, and hogs. Chickens gave the eggs that were shipped to Savannah, and there were cows to provide milk. The sawmill at the Mills Plantation provided the lumber that was sent to Savannah by barge and sold at Telfair's Wharf or exported. The overseers gave written reports to Alexander on a regular basis, sending them through the postal service to Savannah or the North, or by a worker riding to Savannah. Usually the overseer reported that things were going "tolerable well," but frequently there was either not enough rain or too much rain. It was good news if the slaves were reported obedient or if the cotton crop was better than expected, but Alexander must have felt concern when a letter arriving in Saratoga Springs one summer reported that lightning had struck the house at the Retreat and had killed two calves. Then there was the time that Eland, one of the field slaves, was bitten by a snake. Decisions had to be made. Was it worth the cost to have the slaves inoculated against smallpox? One of Alexander's problems was an overseer who was constantly threatening to quit. There were constant annoyances as indicated by the $20 reward that Alexander offered for information concerning the person who had shot and bagged his domestic ducks at the Sabine Fields Plantation.[16]

Periodic visits were made to the plantations. "Margaret & Alexander leave us next week for the upcountry," their sister Mary noted in December 1823. During the winter of 1825, Alexander was absent from Savannah for six weeks while on an upland tour. Sarah Haig accompanied him while Mary and Margaret stayed at home to manage the house. "My butter was pronounced excellent, and so were my puddings & cakes," Mary bragged in the absence of the sister who usually took charge of domestic matters. Sarah met with an unfortunate accident while on her journey. The horses ran away with the carriage, and she received a cut on her forehead. She suffered a great deal of pain at first. She decided to wear a black band to cover the wound and later the scar, which according to her sister, gave her a "very quizzical look."[17]

Sarah undoubtedly coped well with her accident for she was the stoical type. She had lost her husband and two babies, and nothing could bother her very much after that. Mary Telfair envied her sister's equanimity:

> Behold me in fancy's mirror seated in your favorite nook the chimney corner toasting my toes and scribbling, while Margaret is adjusting her night cap, and *Madame Utilite* in an adjoining apartment laying plans I suppose for future usefulness. What an enviable being she is to pursue the quiet tenor of her way so *philosophically*, seldom sad and never gay, and yet when the club meet, we elicit occasionally a brilliant sally from her. I despair of ever reaching the same state of *equanimity* tho it is my constant aim to do so. Nature made me of more volatile materials; therefore my task is a difficult one—I have to climb hills, and approach precipices, while she treads the smooth and level lawn.

Sarah was indeed a wonder. It was she who ran the household with energy and efficiency. She could stay up until late in the evening, her needle flying with the dexterity of a mantua maker, while Mary tried to keep her eyes open in order to finish a piece of correspondence. Mary admired her sister's domestic qualities, although she herself despised drudgery.[18]

Alexander and Sarah made another trip to the upcountry during the winter of 1828. Mary found amusing Sarah's preparations for the journey through "the region of gloomy pines and druidical oaks": "You would laugh to see the *Ark*-like preparations for the *grand tour —A wadded hood to sleep in*—Two extra Petticoats, and double garments. I tell her she will be an admirable personification of Atlas. I should not only *bend*, but faint under such a load." Sarah wrote to her sisters of her adventures during this excursion. They learned that she had traveled through a dismal swamp on horseback, crossed a river in a frail barque, and had spent the night in a hovel. When Alexander and Sarah returned home, Sarah had the opportunity to embellish upon her adventures, which led her sister Mary to describe them with historical and literary allusions: "Sarah imagines herself a Heroine— a second Catharine of Russia in boldness and enterprise because she waded through a swamp on a grey Palfrey; and Ellen Douglas like was paddled in a little skiff across the willow bordered stream."[19]

During their tour, Sarah and Alexander received some respite from the rigorous life when they paid a visit to one of the elegant up-country plantations, an oasis of refinement in the midst of an otherwise bleak cultural desert. Sarah described her stay to her sister, who in turn described it to Mary Few:

> However all these *horrors* were exchanged for the elegant and hospitable abode of Mr. Urkhart who is something like Mr. William Wallace in character—he is eminently pious, very literary, and a devoted admirer of the Arts. How delightful it is to find religion blended with general information and a refined taste—it seems all that we can require in this world and makes people *too interesting*. Sarah says their manner of living reminds her of some *Lord and Lady of a Manor*. While he was discussing the beauties of sculpture, poetry and painting she was giving a score of *recipes*. I never knew Sarah pour forth so much enthusiasm before. This venerable pair seems to have bewitched her— even the melody of the sable tribe as they *chanted* after the evening service was portrayed in glowing colours. I think it would *do me good* to spend a week with such people. I have as great a desire to meet Mr. Urkhart as Anne Clay has to make a Pilgrimage to Rhinebeck to hear Mrs. Garrettson talk.[20]

Mary did get the chance to meet this venerable gentleman and found him a person who appeared "to live above the world and yet in it." She discovered that he was acquainted with the Fews:

> We made a delightful visit on the way from Jefferson to an elderly Gentleman & Lady. I dare say your Father recalls Mr. Urkhart for he enquired after you all—he is united to a very fine woman and they seem as happy in their embowering shades as our first Parents in Eden. I was charmed with their style of

living, so rational and simply elegant, their hospitality seemed
to flow from the heart alone—and they seem fitted by Nature
and education for a country life, which after all is the happiest.[21]

Mary herself made a "tour of duty" with Alexander which lasted
five weeks. Unfortunately it took place in the cold of winter, and Mary
was not as much of a heroine as Sarah Haig:

> I wish you could have seen me getting into bed in an upcoun-
> try *Auberge* with even my shoes on and a shawl over that vulner-
> able part the head. The crevices around [were] wide enough to
> admit an Astronomer to watch the movements of the celestial
> bodies and admire the starry firmament. Such weather never
> was known in Georgia. The water in our guglet [goblet] which
> stood by a *rousing* fire was frozen in the morning—and for four
> days a pan of milk continued congealed.

"The only gleam of civilization that irradiated our path was a visit of
two days to the Urkharts," Mary wrote of the trip. "The Lord of the
Manor was absent—but we were entertained by the Lady of the
Manor. You will smile when I tell you three waiting maids appeared
in the morning to aid us at the Toilette—which of course we dismissed not being accustomed to even one at our Plantation."[22]
The "housekeepers at home," as Mary called the farm wives in the
upcountry, were far from congenial company:

> The Housekeepers at Home think only of entertaining with
> their *colloquial* powers. I felt inclined to *cork* one Woman's
> mouth when I espied a filthy table cloth and were compelled to
> shiver by the side of a clay chimney as wide as the entrance to
> the Cave of Trophonius. The windows open & both doors, in
> order to afford free access to Boreas. Alexander was obliged to
> put his hat on & by way of *hint* I got my plaid cloak & wrapped
> myself in it at the same time giving a *satirical* groan.[23]

A trip to the upcountry was for Mary "a sojourn to Crackerland."
The people with whom the Telfairs were obliged to deal on their
plantations were not the most refined: "Our Overseer's Wife paid us
a visit with an *Ayah* beside her—who she immediately called upon
for a glass of water—We afterwards learned that she never combed
her own hair or washed her feet. The indolence of that class of

people in this country is unexampled." When visiting rural Georgia, Mary was forced to suffer not only inelegant speech but also rough slaps on the back:

> I am an *excitable* being and often *flag* when some folkes are always "*pearte*" as the "*Housekeepers at home*" elegantly style that charming word vivacity. A Parisian bel esprit would *faint* at a sound so inharmonious to a polished ear, but we sojourners over wild lands learn not only to listen to rude sounds, but sometimes to bear hard thumps over our delicate shoulders.[24]

Mary found the South Carolina uplands as unattractive as rural Georgia. She complained that "*fragrant* beds and uninviting meals characterize both." There too the "housekeepers at home" failed completely in the discharge of their domestic duties. Mary concluded that "industry and management are only to be met with among the *Ladies* of our land—the *Women* are too, *too* lazy like the Medes & Persians they are so wedded to their habits that it is impossible to revolutionize them." She was inclined to say, "let them alone they are joined to their idols."[25]

Mary had mixed feelings about plantation life. She loved nature and the quiet that could be found in the upcountry, but it was lonely there. Writing from the Retreat Plantation on a July morning, she shared her feelings with Mary Few:

> You have often heard me deprecate *Plantations* and contrast them with the fine comfortable looking Farms and elegant Country Seats at the North, so rich in all that can delight the eye or satisfy the taste, but I always contrive to make myself *contented* wherever I am. Retirement accords with my taste, it is friendly to the growth of virtue, there all our best feelings originate and are nourished; but *Solitude* I detest, we were formed for *social intercourse* and a human Being who seeks delight in *woods* and *wilds* is one degree higher than a *Quadruped.*[26]

Alexander set down strict rules and directions for the operation of his plantations. Those for the operation of his Thorn Island Plantation, which the overseer was enjoined to strictly attend to, were set forth in Alexander's handwriting in a small notebook. These terse directions covered every aspect of plantation life, including the nature and amount of food and clothing to be allotted to the slaves, procedures for their discipline, the regulation of their coming and going, the manner of planting, picking, and packing cotton, and the maintenance of records.[27]

Transportation to and from the Telfair plantations in the uplands and in the Savannah River basin was by road or by river. The Burke County properties, which were the most extensive of the Telfair holdings, bordered the river and were bisected by the old stagecoach road that connected Savannah with Augusta. Prior to the advent of steamship service on the Savannah River, the standard means of shipping cotton downstream to the wharves of Savannah was by cotton boxes. Bales of cotton were loaded into wooden containers that were carried along by the current to the port. There the cotton was unloaded, and the boxes were broken up and sold for lumber. The Telfairs also owned a fleet of barges. Manned by slaves, the loaded barges would be guided down the river to the port. The return trip was more difficult, for it would take days for the men to pole their way back to the plantation. Steamboat service was inaugurated on the Savannah River in 1816, after the War of 1812 came to an end. In time Burke County became the largest producer of cotton in the antebellum South. The stagecoaches that carried passengers from Augusta to Savannah and from Savannah to the state capital in Louisville passed through Burke County. The large vehicles, pulled by four or sometimes six horses, traveled at the rate of ten miles per hour. By 1822 there were three roads through Burke County, the 126-mile direct route from Savannah to Augusta (the old Savannah Road), a branch of the same road that led to Augusta by way of Waynesboro, and a route from Waynesboro to Greensboro.[28]

The firm of Robert & Joseph Habersham was the factor for the Telfairs through which they sold their cotton and had other business dealings. Founded in 1744 under the name Harris and Habersham, it was the oldest and most highly esteemed business of its kind in Savannah. The firm had been responsible for the establishment of Savannah as a trading port when it made the first shipment of cotton to England in 1749. It had constructed the first wharf on the Savannah River capable of handling seagoing vessels. The Robert Habersham with whom Alexander Telfair had business dealings was the son of Edward Telfair's fellow Liberty Boy, Colonel Joseph Habersham, and the grandson of James Habersham, president of the Georgia Provincial Congress and acting royal governor during Governor

Wright's absence in England.[29] Alexander had such faith in Robert Habersham as to name him as one of the executors of his will.

The state of the cotton market was a matter of constant concern to Alexander Telfair and other planters in the South. Writing from Philadelphia, Alexander passed on to Robert Habersham the latest information on the subject:

It is said that Pilot Boats have been dispatched from New York with very extensive orders for the purchase of Cotton at Liverpool. Whether this speculation is founded upon an actual deficiency from the increased consumption of the article, or the uncertain conjecture of the Crop of the next year being short, from the inundation of the Mississippi, I do not know: it is probable that these causes combined have occasioned it. The Fall Market will in all probability open at a high price, & I shall give orders to my overseers to forward my Crops in small parcels as it is prepared for transportation.[30]

A letter to the Habersham firm, sent from Bristol, demonstrates the extent to which Alexander was able to direct his business affairs even while absent in the North:

You will direct Shaw to repair my Wharfhead. Direct Jack to do the digging, and if more force be required order Isaac to come in for a day or two with his men and do it. Jack will work with Shaw thru out at the carpenters and you will pay him *One Dollar & twenty-five cents a week* to supply himself with provisions, whilst so engaged; after which he will return to the Plantation if he has not finished then, or work out, if he has. If Shaw can get Cyprus logs, I prefer them, otherwise the best light-wood sticks he can procure. . . . My overseers have been very regular in communicating with me except the one at Bertrand in Effingham County of whom you reported so unfavorably. You were right in not supplying him with either liquor or money. I shall write him tomorrow to your care & request that you will get the Letter conveyed by some market cart to the Widow London's on the Louisville Road.[31]

Alexander Telfair had numerous business interests in addition to the plantations and his mercantile operations. For many years he was a director of the Savannah branch of the First Bank of the United

States, which had been established in the city in 1802. He was president and a director of the Savannah, Ogeechee & Altamaha Canal Company. Alexander retained his position with the canal company until his resignation in January 1831 shortly before the celebration of the opening of the canal between the Ogeechee and Savannah rivers, a link that, as Telfair put it in his toast at the opening ceremonies, "united the Wood Nymphs of the Ogeechee with the Water Nymphs of the Savannah."[32]

Alexander had a keen sense of civic duty and involved himself in community affairs. He served as an associate justice of the Inferior Court of Chatham County. He was a member of the Union Society, one of Savannah's oldest charities. In 1821 he joined the St. Andrew's Society, that venerable Savannah institution for Scotsmen organized in 1750. Dueling had for many years been a serious problem in Georgia. Lives were ruined or destroyed because a man was required by his honor to accept the challenge of an adversary. In one of the most famous duels in Savannah's history, Lachlan McIntosh and Button Gwinnett, firing from the traditional ten to twelve paces, wounded each other in the leg. McIntosh survived, but Gwinnett did not. In another famous duel James Jackson and Thomas Gibbons missed each other three times. By 1826, the Anti-Dueling Association had been organized in Savannah. Mary's uncle, Dr. George Jones, was its first chairman. Alexander Telfair was an active member.[33]

In the fall of 1824, plans were proceeding apace for the visit to the United States of the Marquis de Lafayette. He would be entertained in New York, Philadelphia, and Washington and would be in Savannah in March 1825 to dedicate the monument in Johnson Square honoring his comrade-in-arms, General Nathanael Greene. That September, writing from Philadelphia, Mary Telfair observed the excitement gripping the people of New York and Philadelphia and thought that it had gotten out of hand:

> The Lafayette Mania has not seized me so far as to pay my devoirs to the Hero—I am glad to see the Enthusiasm of '76 rekindled and I feel a *tender interest* for his health for I am sure he will be feted to death. Here [in Philadelphia] they mean to *outshine* New York with a general illumination and (what a farce) they are practicing six cream Horses (with sweeping tails) in order to have him drawn in a coach & six; this is aping royalty

—How much better it would appear in a Republic to preserve more of republican simplicity, for the greatest display here falls so far short of European splendor. I dread poor Savannah for the southerners are famous for overdoing matters—Sara Haig predicts his neck will be broke before he gets there for no *drilling* in this part of the world can make six Horses draw a coach—she mournfully predicts that the tomb of Washington which is prepared for his *inspection* will be for his *reception*—poor old Gentleman. I really think the hard service of the revolution *light* to his present campaign—the excitement is enough to give him a fit—but I sincerely hope he will live through all the efforts that are made to destroy him and that he will return to the land of his sires to breathe his last.[34]

Remarkably Lafayette arrived in Savannah in one piece on March 19, 1825. The week before his arrival by boat from Charleston, Mary Telfair wrote to Mary Few:

> The Nation's Guest or as Geo. Cumming styles him the Nation's Jest is to be in Savannah on Monday next; every thing and every body is brushing up for Lafayette—I am very lukewarm; I saw him in Philadelphia and do not feel that enthusiastic glow of amour patria that some talk so loudly of—I am afraid it is the first step towards a "waveless calm" but not the "slumber of the dead."[35]

Most of Savannah did not share Mary's lack of enthusiasm. Governor George M. Troup proclaimed Lafayette "thrice welcome" to the State of Georgia. Alexander must have found his sister's cynicism somewhat annoying for he was a member of the committee that had made the arrangements for the hero's reception in Savannah. From the graceful balcony of the Owens-Thomas House (then Mary Maxwell's boardinghouse, where Lafayette was staying) the hero of the Revolution reviewed the city's militia as it marched by, the soldiers resplendent in their colorful uniforms. The first night, there was a great banquet with endless toasts (the guest of honor slipped away before midnight), and the following morning, with school children strewing petals in his path, the marquis made his way to Johnson Square to do the honors for General Greene. Lafayette and his entourage went on to Chippewa Square for speeches and the laying of the cornerstone of the Pulaski monument. Alexander Telfair, as a member of the monument committee, delivered an address in which he told of the bravery and untimely death of the gallant Polish count at the Siege of Savannah. He then called upon Lafayette and his Masonic brethren to set the cornerstone in place. In reply to Alexander's address, Lafayette reminisced of how it was he who, some fifty-eight years earlier, had presented Pulaski to General Washington and the American Army upon his arrival in this country. There was a Masonic banquet that afternoon, after which the marquis and his party steamed up the Savannah River for another two days of festivities in Augusta. Upon leaving Georgia, the sixty-eight-year-old hero suffered from a fatigue that caused a momentary inquietude among his staff; but, as Mary Telfair had hoped, he did manage to return to the land of his sires to breathe his last nine years later.[36]

John Macpherson Berrien of Savannah, then representing Georgia in the United States Senate, was Andrew Jackson's choice for attorney general when the new President named his cabinet following the election of 1828. Berrien had been born in New Jersey in 1781 and had come to Savannah with his parents in 1783. He received his bachelor of arts degree from the College of New Jersey in 1796 and was admitted to the Georgia bar in 1799 after reading law in the office of Joseph Clay, Jr., a federal judge and the father of Anne Clay. As a lawyer, Berrien's oratorical powers had earned him the title the "American Cicero." No less a figure than Chief Justice John Marshall had dubbed him "the honey-tongued Georgia youth." Berrien was a state senator for one term before being appointed to the United States Senate in 1824 by the Georgia legislature. As respected members of the close-knit Savannah community, Judge Berrien and his wife, the former Eliza Anciaux (she would die in 1828), were friends of the Telfairs.[37]

Alexander Telfair frequently was called upon to serve on committees relating to civic matters, and in the spring of 1831 he was a member of a committee that organized an entertainment in honor of Attorney General Berrien.[38] Unfortunately Berrien would serve as attorney general for only a few weeks after the toasts had been raised in his honor, for on June 22 of that year he was forced to resign from the cabinet because his refusal to support the President in his crusade to make Washington society accept Margaret Eaton, the daughter of a Georgetown tavern keeper and the wife of Secretary of War John H. Eaton. When Mrs. Eaton's virtue was questioned, the President declared her "as chaste as a virgin," which led Henry Clay to quip, "Age cannot wither her, nor custom stale her infinite virginity."[39]

Alexander took an active interest in the Independent Presbyterian Church. The Reverend Henry Kollock was a favorite of the Telfairs. Mary thought that there was no one who surpassed him as a preacher. When the Reverend Kollock was charged by the presbytery with habitual intemperance and deposed as a minister of the gospel, Alexander Telfair was one of a committee that handed down a report in 1814 concluding that the church in Savannah was an independent organization, free from the authority of any presbytery, and that accordingly the act of suspension was unauthorized, illegal, and not binding on the pastor. In 1823, when the Reverend W. D. Snodgrass, the minister at the time, accepted a call to a church in New York City, Alexander Telfair, Dr. John Cumming, and Benjamin Burroughs were named as a committee to call a new minister. Later Alexander served as chairman of the church's board of trustees.[40]

The call to the Independent Presbyterian Church to succeed the Reverend Snodgrass was accepted by the Reverend Samuel B. How. Mary Telfair found him a "very zealous animated Preacher and gentlemanlike in his manners." Dr. How remained in Savannah until 1827, when he became pastor of the First Reformed Dutch Church in New Brunswick, New Jersey. While there, he wrote a tract entitled *Slaveholding Not Sinful*. The Telfairs' church was without a stated minister for a year after Dr. How's departure, and in the spring of 1828, the Reverend Daniel Baker accepted the call to Savannah. The new minister had been born in the Midway settlement in Liberty County in the year of Mary Telfair's birth. Mary did not think much of the choice:

> We have got a Pastor for our Church—A man without refinement or education—A native Georgian—He is said to be a man of some genius & great piety. I love to see the Christian & Gentleman combined. I fear in Mr. Baker that union is wanting —The Trustees thought it important to fill the Church—its present condition is truly forlorn and as they could not command talent, eloquence & piety they determined to get who they could—so Mr. Baker is Hobson's Choice.[41]

Shortly after taking up his duties in Savannah, Mr. Baker wrote to one of the elders of his old church in Washington, "My congregation is the largest in Savannah and embraces a great portion of the wealth and intelligence of the city. . . . Our prayer meetings are crowded. I have a very flourishing Female Bible Class." Mary Telfair, however, preferred the Bible class at Christ Church to the one now conducted by the unrefined Mr. Baker:

> I went Sunday week to the Episcopal Bible Class & am delighted with the way it is conducted. They draw Questions & write Essays which are read aloud by the Clergyman—As it is an *Incognito* business one feels secure of not being discovered— Louisa McAllister transferred her Question to me. It was— "What attestation does Christ bear to the Character of Nathaniel." I did not attend to hear it read but Sarah went and returned highly delighted with *Nathaniel's success.* The credit was due to Alexander as he gave the *finishing touch* to the Portrait. I think writing Bible answers more improving than attending the best sermons that can be preached. The research that is required gives one such clear views of scripture.[42]

When Mr. Baker went off on a two-month tour distributing Bibles, Mary became enthralled with the sermons of the minister occupying the pulpit during his absence. Mary Few was given a taste of her enthusiasm for the visiting minister along with a hint of her feelings toward her brother:

> You will smile with your usual leniency when I tell you I go three times a day on Sunday to hear him, and attend his weekly lectures constantly. He is giving a course of lectures on Our Lord's Sermon on the Mount and also on his Parables. I have found them extremely interesting & instructive. Last Sunday He gave us a beautiful Portraiture of the young Ruler. I could not avoid drawing a parallel between it and our young Ruler at home. I found several persons had discovered the resemblance besides myself so I was very much pleased with my own sagacity. Alexander thinks I am very proud of the talent which I appropriate to myself of reading character. Certain it is that I am seldom deceived now a days. It is one of the advantages we derive from an increased knowledge of the world.[43]

Like their brother, the Telfair ladies took an interest in community affairs and charitable causes. Mary described to Mary Few a benefit for the Bethesda Orphanage in which her sister was involved:

There is to be a fair on Tuesday given by the Ladies of Savannah for the benefit of the Orphan Asylum—All the talent & industry of the *fair* Ladies has been elicited on this occasion. Margaret is immersed in gold paper & paste. In my next letter, if I attend it, I will give you a *faithful* description of it—I go as a *Purchaser* not as a *Worker*. If *cobbling* had been required I could have furnished some able specimens.[44]

In July 1827 Mary Telfair, her sisters, and their friend Sarah Cecil spent three weeks in Saratoga Springs. Earlier in the summer they had been to Canada. July was not the fashionable time of year to take the waters at Saratoga. "The fashionables wait for the last of August," Mary explained. But the Telfairs had no interest in that crowd. "As we intend to be *hard drinkers* we will commence our *libations* while the weather is hot," Mary joked. Mary had seen enough of Saratoga at the height of the season in earlier years, when all was gaiety and a woman was judged by the size of her fortune:

Here I am still sheltered by the Pavilion which is nearly deserted. The tide of fashion has ebbed here & flows rapidly towards Ballston, and Sans Souci is the region of delight. The eyes of the Belles sparkled with new lustre at the prospect of achieving fresh conquests, and the *dear* beaux skipped & hopped like "Peris just released from their cages" as they in "fancy fond" reckoned over the Catalogue of *Specks* which flourish around them. Wealth is the idol here, old & young pay due homage to its glittering charms. I never am so *painfully* sensible of my want of interest in this World & its *goods* and *chattels* as when I visit these famed springs.[45]

After leaving Saratoga, Mary and her party moved on for a stay in Lebanon Springs in the Berkshires. It had been ten years since Mary had been to "sweet Lebanon," and she found it much changed. The countryside remained lovely and reminded her of the area around Quebec City. But, wrote Mary, the society where they were staying "generally does not look exactly comme il faut." Matilda Few was expected to arrive any day, and Mary vowed to watch every post coach that drove up the hill. An excursion was made to the nearby Shaker Village:

We have just returned from the Shaker Village where we made a few purchases and went through their dairy and feasted on their nice bread & butter and cheese—they are the neatest people I have ever seen—I wish the *"Housekeepers at home"* could take a few lessons of them; however they are so *conceited* & incorrigible in their habits that I doubt whether Quaker neatness could produce even a *burst of admiration.*[46]

Mary Telfair enjoyed sightseeing and making new acquaintances on her travels. In a letter written on an August day in Lancaster, Pennsylvania, she described to Mary Few a journey that she and her sisters had taken through that state escorted by her brother and Dr. Cumming:

Dr. Cumming & Alexander united in the purchase of a Post Coach and four and hired a good Driver so we commenced our Travels under favorable auspices. The ride thus far has been beautiful and I wished for you to admire with me some scenes that a Claude Laurraine would have gloried in sketching. I was charmed with Bethlehem—it is full of romantic interest—the Town so neat & well built. We took the Physician of the place for our guide. He was very gallant, he told us he would like to travel with us as we were single Ladies—he was an old Bachelor. I tried to comfort him by telling him that no wife was better than *a bad one*—a curious dialogue to pass between two people after half an hour's acquaintance. . . . I think the scenery as we approached Reading was transcendently lovely—and the Farm Houses and the Barns look as if they were built for Posterity. We calculate taking the mountain route and hope to enjoy the sight of the Natural Bridge and Harpers Ferry, both so celebrated in the annals of our country.[47]

Illness was a constant threat. It was a reality to be dreaded, and one that could fall upon a family at any time. Yellow fever had plagued the people of Savannah going back to colonial days. The epidemic of 1820 was particularly severe. It would be many years before Dr. Walter Reed would demonstrate that the disease was transmitted by a particular species of mosquito. The prevailing theory in the 1820's was that the epidemics were brought on by miasma, or vapors carried in eastern winds caused by decaying matter. The Telfairs arrived in Savannah by ship in the fall of 1827 in the middle of another yellow fever epidemic. Mary related the news given to them upon entering the port:

This has been a very fatal season in this place and those lives that have been sacrificed were valuable indeed—the heads of families. Mr. [Abiel] Carter the Episcopal Minister & his wife died within three days of each other—both in the prime of life and the parents of three helpless little children—What an awful and mysterious dispensation of Providence! how wonderfully mysterious to us short sighted mortals. They were both resigned and willingly exchanged the world for a better—Mrs. Sorrell, also the mother of a young and helpless family, took Mrs. Carter's infant to nurse and two or three days after fell a victim to yellow fever—I cannot express to you my horror upon hearing this report from the Pilot—The weather was & still is exceedingly warm—Seeing several of our friends—meeting the servants who seemed to feel so much—produced in me such a state of nervous irritability that I could not sleep for several nights and still feel very wretched—Alexander forbids our using any exertion for fear of producing fatigue—If we could occupy ourselves actively we would feel better but I think the more quiet we keep the better for our bodies.[48]

The Telfairs' mother, Sarah Gibbons Telfair, died in Philadelphia shortly after Christmas of 1827. She was buried at the Christ Church graveyard in that city. She was sixty-nine years of age at the time of her death and had been a widow for twenty years. She had suffered the pain of having babies that died in infancy and of losing three sons in the flower of their young manhood. Yet she had led a good life and had spent her last years in the warm presence of a loving family. The Telfairs had lost their mother, yet life went on in the family circle much as before. The following year, the Telfairs suffered the loss of a beloved friend. Colonel William Few died on July 16, 1828, at the Chrysties' residence in Fishkill. Mary Telfair had long held him in high esteem as the only surviving friend of her father.[49]

The winter of 1828–1829 was brutal in Savannah with an abundance of snow and ice. Without the luxury of central heating, it was difficult for the Telfairs to cope with the freezing weather that sometimes blew down from the North: "We have been *writhing* with cold for the last weeks," Mary complained one January day. "Every thing has been frozen even eggs in their shells. Alexander has been obliged to keep his room it affected his breast so much, and Sarah from sheer inability to stem its severity shrunk into the chimney corner." In February 1829 Savannah was ravaged by another of those fires that plagued that city of wooden houses. It was not as extensive as the great fire of 1796 or the holocaust of 1820, which consumed 463 buildings, including the Bank of the United States, the public market, the customhouse, and the police station, but it was serious indeed. The Telfairs had a close call:

> We have recently gone through a fiery *ordeal* and narrowly escaped conflagration—forty Houses in our immediate neighborhood were consumed and nothing [saved us] but the great exertions of our friends & servants who were indefatigable until all danger had subsided. If I know myself my besetting sin is not a love to worldly *goods & chattels;* I was perfectly composed & only dreaded the consequences of exposure to wind & water —Alexander had been confined to his room for a week with a severe cold and would wander about to give directions for keeping the flames out of the windows—Sarah was weighed down with thirteen garments and still felt the cold—None of us have suffered any inconvenience from our *extraordinary energy.*[50]

Mary and her family had another close call which she described at length to Mary Few:

> We were all prepared dear Mary to commence our journey tomorrow but a circumstance of a most unpleasant nature occurred two evenings since to frustrate our plans and induce us to embark in the course of a week for the North. We were returning home from a friends with whom we had passed the evening which fortunately for us was a fine moonlight one when in a state of intoxication our Coachman dropped from his seat. We never missed him but happening to turn my head I discovered the seat vacant, the Horses keeping a straight course. Alexander endeavored to stop them by his voice. The Carriage being closed in front he could not get the reins—fortunately I had (though dreadfully alarmed) presence of mind enough to order our footman to run & stop them which he did to my surprise—If the other pair of Horses which we use quite as much had been in (it

was a mere matter of chance that they were not) we must have been dashed to pieces. A kind Providence alone seemed to have protected us. The wheel ran over the legs of the driver without seriously injuring either of them—I know nothing that could have depressed me so much but the death of an intimate acquaintance.[51]

Mary's description of the incident led her into a rambling digression on the treatment of servants and the evils of overindulgence in drink:

Alexander to gratify us purchased very lately the Servant— He once belonged to our family and we placed so much confidence in him that it was a terrible shock to find him unworthy of it—Our best intentions often are productive of evil consequences—Alexander would not consent to have him wait in the House though a complete House Servant & elegant waiter—because he wished him to lead an easy life—Every indulgence was granted him—whereas if he had been kept constantly employed he would not have had time enough to engage in that fatal propensity—however when Men of Genius are sacrificed to it we cannot wonder at those who have no intellectual pursuits.[52]

Matilda Few visited the Telfairs in Savannah early in 1831. It snowed while she was there. Mary thoroughly enjoyed the visit. She felt that during the stay she had really gotten to know Matilda for the first time. She realized that she had always been so occupied with Mary Few during her visits to New York that she had never taken the time to cultivate the friendship of her younger sister. "Matilda and myself have become *quite well acquainted*," Mary wrote, "and to my amazement I find she is *a great Talker* when we are alone. The only fault I find with her is that she is too reserved with Strangers, the very reverse of myself for my friends tell me I am too fond of *new* acquaintances." Matilda, however, did become well acquainted with Catharine Hunter and found her company fascinating. Mary confided in Mary Few that her younger sister reminded her continually of Frances Chrystie. She thought that Matilda resembled Frances "in mind and face—a little too in manner, and *love of a joke*." "We have had one that would make Frances crack her sides with laughter if she could hear it."[53]

While in Savannah, Matilda got in touch with her cousin, the Reverend Ignatius Few, and made frequent visits to his parsonage. Writing to Mary Few, Mary made reference to the Methodist divine:

> Matilda I suppose gave you an account of *Saint Ignatius*—He stands very high in his church both for talent & piety. Sarah went last Sunday with M to hear him preach and was delighted with his sermon. I must judge for myself. If tomorrow is a fine day we intend calling at the Parsonage. I hope Mr. Few will not recognize in me the rude child who ran over his foot with a wheel barrow in Greenwich Garden.[54]

In the middle of March, Mary and Matilda engaged in a "religious dissipation" when they stayed until 11:00 P.M. at the McAllisters listening to Mr. Wilder, a visiting preacher, and Anne Clay converse on the subject of religion. Mary then gave Matilda a "furlough of three weeks" during which she went to Augusta and visited a friend living on the Sand Hills. Mary then "ordered" her back to Savannah. Upon her return, Mary planned to go with her to Belfair to visit the Carolina cousins. Matilda left for home in May, sailing on the *Tybee* in the company of the Habershams, the Joneses, and Mary's cousins. Matilda's visit had been a great success according to Mary's report to Matilda's sister:

> I hope the South has left a pleasing impression upon Matilda's mind—it has certainly benefitted her health and I was delighted to find that we could make her happy at such a distance from Home—She was thrown in social contact with a variety of characters, and I hope she reciprocates the friendly feeling which she excited in some—Mrs. Cumming and Catharine Hunter are her warmest friends. We cannot boast of fine scenery, neither can we exhibit any of the treasures of art—but we have much as regards soil and character that is valuable, and I have always maintained that the North has more to attract the mind—the South the heart.[55]

Alexander Telfair was known as a scholar. According to his obituary, "His mind, trained to instruction, in earlier life, was improved and expanded in his leisure hours by study and reflection."[56] He was chairman of the board of the Chatham Academy and gave the commencement address there in April 1830.[57] He loved books and art and had the means to purchase whatever works caught his fancy. During the summer of 1831, John James Audubon, the famous naturalist, visited Savannah. There he solicited subscriptions to his series *The Birds of America* (200 sets were issued, each consisting of eighty-seven numbers of five plates each), and Alexander Telfair was one of a handful of Savannah gentlemen to come up with the $1,000 subscription price.[58]

Articulate and assured on his feet, Alexander was chosen to deliver the oration at the centennial of George Washington's birth, which was celebrated on February 22, 1832. Mary worried whether he was up to the task as his health had been less than robust. He did just fine, as she assured Mary Few:

> I have *worried* and *flurried* for the last fortnight. Alexander delivered the centennial birth day Oration, and as I always identify myself with him I was nervous and miserable until it was over. I was afraid his physical strength was incompetent to the undertaking but he agreeably disappointed me; if he felt mauvaise honte he did not shew it. I will not say what I think of it, as he says it is very indelicate to extol the virtues or talents of relations but I have *stolen* the manuscript and when you come to Georgia you shall read it.

Actually, the speech was well received by all who heard it, for Alexander was accorded considerable praise for his delivery by the members of the committee in charge of the celebration.[59]

The trip to the North in the summer of 1832 was made by the overland route. The Telfairs were accompanied by their friends, Dr. and Mrs. John Cumming. They took the steamboat to Charleston by way of the inland passage. This presented the opportunity of seeing from the water a number of fine low-country plantations, deserted by their owners at that time of the year. "I think the lower country of South Carolina a century in advance of her Sister State," Mary wrote. Part of a day and a night were spent in Charleston. Mary took a moonlight carriage ride through the city and into the suburbs. Her guide was an old lady of seventy and upwards who put her to the blush by riding without her bonnet while Mary wore both a bonnet and a shawl to protect her from malaria, for, she wrote, "we Georgians have as great a dread of their climate as they of ours." Mary was pleased with her visit:

I was very much delighted with the situation of Charleston; it is like that of New York. Some of the private buildings are immense and have a very venerable appearance. Except Boston I know of no City that contains so many *lordly mansions*. The people appear to be very gay. I believe their strong local feelings and prejudices give a perennial flow to their animal spirits; they seldom travel, consequently see no deficiencies in themselves— they imagine that their City unites the advantages of Rome and Athens.

The travelers hired two carriages in Charleston and proceeded northward on the great state road to Camden, South Carolina, and on to Baltimore and Philadelphia. It was not the most pleasant of trips. But Mary and her party made the best of it for, as she observed, "as the Camel is constituted for the Desert, so are we Southerners for *marooning* and *roving.*" The cholera epidemic in New York forced the roving Southerners to alter their plans of going to Newport. The daily reports of cholera in the cities of the Northeast had the same effect upon Mary as "ghost stories upon children." The family spent the bulk of the summer at Schooleys Mountain enjoying the pure air and lovely scenery.[60] Little did Mary then know that her summer in the North, spent so pleasantly, would be a prelude to a season of sorrow.

10

A Season of Sorrow, a Time to Heal

Death rides on every passing breeze,
He lurks in every flower.

Reginald Heber, *At a Funeral*, No. 1

Tragedy struck the Telfair family on October 9, 1832. Alexander Telfair died at nine in the morning in Winchester, Virginia, following a summer spent in the North. He was forty-three at the time of his death. Alexander suffered an attack of pleurisy upon the family's arrival in Winchester, and for weeks his life seemed to hang upon a thread. His sister Mary was gripped with fear during her brother's last illness. The violence of the disease and the harassing cough that it produced placed her in a state of despair. "The effort to conceal my anxiety and misery from him is very great," she wrote, "and I scarcely sleep at all." Mary was pleased, however, with the excellent physician who attended Alexander and the black male nurse who cared for him. Sarah was a source of strength, and Mary took some consolation from knowing that every effort had been made to bring about Alexander's recovery.[1]

Alexander's remains were buried in Winchester, and in 1844, when the graveyard was incorporated as Mount Hebron Cemetery, the pamphlet containing the dedication orations was sent to the family in Savannah. Mary kept the little booklet among her cherished possessions.[2] The bereaved sisters made their way south under the protection of Dr. George Jones, who was returning home with his family. Mary was consumed with grief. Alexander had been "the dearest object of [her] affections." She tried to find solace in a little volume by a clergyman entitled *Thoughts in Affliction.* "The hope of a reunion in a future existence is all that sustains me," she wrote to Mary Few from an inn in Winton, North Carolina. "We should never allow ourselves in this world to love our nearest relatives too much. We naturally infer when they are taken from us that if they had been less of idols they might have been spared."[3]

For Mary, the time following Alexander's death was a "season of sorrow." When she arrived back in Savannah, she had a horror of entering the house now that "the glory of it had departed." She was totally despondent: "All my former pursuits are tasteless, and I feel that there is no enjoyment left for me in this world—All that I desire is to be able to perform my duties here and prepare for an eternal Home." As much as Mary had grieved over the death of her brother Thomas, her sorrow now was even more intense. Thomas had been married and a father at the time of his death. He had his own home and was living his own life. Alexander and his sisters, on the other hand, had lived under the same roof. Mary had shared her unmarried brother's everyday experiences. She had participated vicariously in his triumphs, had cared for him when ill, and had identified with him emotionally, becoming "worried and flurried" on such occasions as his delivery of the Washington centennial oration. Now there was a void in Mary's life that never could be filled. Mary's friends tried to console her. Uncle George Jones and his family stayed with the ladies for a week following their return to Savannah. Sarah Cecil then came and remained for three weeks. Catharine Hunter's visit followed. "Our friends are devoted to us," Mary wrote, "and if their affection and sympathy could alleviate our sorrow, our tears would cease to flow." During this time of deep mourning, Mary's thoughts turned upon Mary Few "more frequently than upon any one in this world." Shortly before Christmas, Mary Few sent Mary Telfair a meditation on the word "home" that concluded that a person's true home was the place prepared for him or her by God. "Shall we not all meet there one day sooner or later?"[4]

The winter passed "like a dream." Stillness reigned throughout the house. "To mourning now is chang'd our mirth, the glad smile to a tear," Mary quoted. Mary continued to grieve deeply throughout the spring. She felt that it was wrong to yield to her depression and made every effort to cultivate a spirit of resignation and to "look beyond this troubled earth for consolation." "I know that I have many more blessings than I deserve," she wrote, "and have been supported through a trial as great as human nature can sustain." Still, as late as April, she was having periods of mental suffering that nothing could mitigate. She struggled to be philosophical over her great loss:

> Though we feel the unsatisfying nature of all things temporal yet we need the rod of affliction to wean us from a world which we know is not our rest, and to which we are too prone to fix our affections upon & cling with idolatrous fondness to the creature instead of elevating our affections and placing them supremely upon the Creator.[5]

The summer after Alexander died, Mary Telfair and her sisters did not take their usual trip to the North. Without Alexander's support, they lacked the energy to make the journey. Mary explained their predicament to Mary Few: "We deeply regret dear Mary that we cannot be with you this summer. The inconveniences attending leaving home seem so great—we have no one to depend upon, and you know it is a great distance to go. We have no enterprise and our feelings revolt at the idea of throwing ourselves in any way upon strangers." As an alternative, the sisters leased a house in Summerville, a resort village in the Sand Hills outside of Augusta. They planned to spend a few quiet months reading, sewing, walking through the pine barrens, and riding in the countryside. The upcountry was considered a healthy retreat, although at the time scarlet fever was ravaging some of the towns and villages in the Georgia interior. This epidemic led Mary Telfair to recall the lines of the English prelate and hymn-writer Reginald Heber:

> Death rides on every passing breeze,
>   He lurks in every flower,
> Each season has its own disease,
>   Its peril every hour!

The Telfair ladies could have their own domestic servants with them in the Sand Hills and be as retired as they wished. Most appealing to Mary was the ease with which the trip could be accomplished with "no land traveling and no ocean to traverse."[6]

Catharine Hunter agreed to join Mary and her sisters for the summer. Sarah Cecil was to have been there as well, but was obliged to remain in Savannah owing to the forthcoming marriage of Eliza Cecil Hunter, her niece, to John Macpherson Berrien, the former attorney general. This was another match that met with Mary's disapproval: "He is a Grandfather and the father of seven children, a difference of thirty years in their ages—She seems insensible to every thing but the glory of being his wife. Ambition is a rock upon which too many women split and what different views people take of Grandeur." Apparently Eliza created quite a stir at the wedding. "Matilda knows Eliza Hunter," Telfair wrote to Mary Few, "tell her that she is married—that her wedding was a very public one—that she was so overcome as to drop her head upon the Bridegroom's shoulder during the ceremony and at the end of it fainted away & was bourne in the arms of her husband to the sofa. When she recovered, he lifted her veil and kissed her (*between us*) what a scene!"[7]

Mary and her party took the steamboat to Augusta on June 18, 1833, and soon were ensconced in their summer quarters. Mary, still grieving deeply over the loss of her brother, described their arrival: "We are settled down here in a comfortable well-furnished house removed from the sight of any other habitation, and embowered in Trees & Shrubbery—Sarah turned immediately to her domestic avocations, and in two hours we were *to rights*. I was glad to make up beds to divert my thoughts from dwelling too much on the loneliness of our situation." It took a while for Mary to become accustomed to her new surroundings, but then she never did feel at home in or about Augusta. Catharine Hunter said that this was because of her love of high masts and that indeed she had noticed that whenever the newspapers arrived Mary always looked at the shipping list before turning to the poets' corner. Soon the ladies fell into a routine. One day did not differ from the next. Mary described their situation during this period of mourning:

> The Sandhills are superior to what I expected as regards cultivation—the white cottages have a sweet appearance surrounded by trees and flowers but you who have been accustomed to the sublimity of mountain scenery and Fishkill cultivation could admire nothing here—Health & retirement are the objects we seek—if we obtain them we shall be quite satisfied, for we cannot enjoy society. Several families have called but as we do not visit we cannot expect them to visit us.[8]

One friend that the Telfairs saw frequently that summer was Mrs. Edward F. Campbell, the lady of the school for black children. Mary was fond of Mrs. Campbell's children and particularly her young son Edward. He helped distract her from her grief:

> Little Edward is devoted to us, he is the companion of our walks and rides—our Pioneer through the pine barren. He points out the houses, tells us a little of the owners and is a most intelligent guide for four years of age. Sarah Haig says he is the only being on the Hill whose society has any power over me. When we are laboring under a depression of spirits nothing so soon causes a momentary forgetfulness or cheers us but Nature and an artless intelligent child.[9]

Mary's occupations that summer were "of a sedentary nature." They consisted of "reading, sewing, writing & thinking." "We usually ride or walk every evening," she wrote, "but there is little pleasure in either, so heavy are the roads that we, as well as our cavalry, are much incommoded by the depth of the sand." One day while in the up-country, Mary and her sisters took a nostalgic trip to the spot where the home of their mother and father once stood. Edward Telfair and his family had lived at the Grove while he was serving as governor of Georgia, and it was there that he and Mrs. Telfair had entertained George Washington on his visit to Augusta in 1791. It was at this place that Mary and Sarah Telfair had been born. It was now a dead place:

> We drove last week to the spot where the light first dawned upon Sarah & myself—the hand of desolation had swept away every trace of former grandeur—the venerable grove where Druids might have worshiped and the clustering grape vines under which we used to swing in the sunny days of childhood were all gone—The garden too where Nature & Art had lavished their choicest gifts converted into a meadow—I thought how changed! and yet how analogous to the fates of those who were once the possessors of it. Changed as it was I felt that in me there were changes quite as great—though spared myself I had seen those cut off who gave to life its every charm.[10]

Mary had a pleasant brush with the past that summer when she received a visit from a lady of her parents' generation. She was impressed with her guest's quiet dignity:

An old lady who was the brides maid and contemporary of my Aunt (Sarah Cuthbert's Mother) passed a day with us not long since—it was the hottest of our hot days. I felt the debilitating influence of the weather so much that she several times said to me "something ails you" for even my voice seemed to sink under it. I proposed to her to lay down. She said I never approach a bed in the day time. She would neither sit on a sofa or rocking chair neither did she lean back but sat like an arrow. I may add of reproach to us for she had numbered seventy-one years and had been familiar with sorrow and yet active, cheerful & resigned. I never met with more purity and simplicity of character. When she spoke of Polly Gibbons I felt as if I was living in a past age. I had never found it difficult to sympathize with the old and now I feel more drawn towards them than the young whose thoughtless mirth depresses far more than it cheers.[11]

Other friends came to visit bringing both happiness and some strain:

We had a visit of a day & night with our old friends Mr. & Mrs. Urkhart—they too are blessed with vigorous constitutions. They rode 21 miles from their Carolina residence here rising with the dawn. We were delighted to see them—it so happened that we had given our Man Servant permission to go for several days to visit his sick father and had only two children to take his place in consequence of which Sarah & myself had to *work* behind the scenes—which united to the excitement of talking with them made us so nervous that we lay awake all night. I believe Telfair nerves are differently strung from other folkes, for our old friends were as bright as larks the next morning—while we were wretched.[12]

During the cool days of August, Mary Telfair and Catharine Hunter would take a walk each morning at ten in order to warm their feet. On one such occasion they strolled to the former residence of Governor Milledge, which was not far from the house they were renting in Summerville:

It is a lovely spot, the only place that excites me on the Hill. The view from it is richly variegated & extensive. The lawn studded with here & there a venerable tree and sufficiently beautiful to attract the attention of a Painter. The distant view of Augusta and the wooded heights of Carolina contrasted strongly with the silence & desolation which reigned within the Mansion, once the seat of hospitality. There is something particularly affecting in visiting a deserted place particularly when those who once animated it with their virtues and their talents have gone "where the wicked cease from troubling, and the weary are at rest." After strolling through the neglected garden, we paused at the melancholy spot where repose the remains of those whose souls I trust are rejoicing among happy spirits in "a land of pure delight where saints immortal reign," and where tears and sorrow are unknown.[13]

As the summer wore on, Mary Telfair became increasingly comfortable with her isolation. She seemed quite content when she wrote to Mary Few after five weeks in the Sand Hills, five weeks that seemed to her five months:

Our days are unmarked by incidents, and our present mode of life foreign to what we have been accustomed to. I can only compare it to yours at Sing Sing as regards retirement. The comparison extends no farther, for we have no lofty range of Mountains to contemplate, tinged with the crimson rays of sunset—no dark rolling Hudson to wash with its murmuring waves the base of *our Hill.* All is dreary stillness—except when the mocking bird pours forth her matin song or moonlight serenade, or the watch dog disturbs our slumbers at midnight. We are so embosomed in trees that we have not even a *vista* view of our nearest neighbor—but we have pure air and quiet, and I have learned to appreciate those simple blessings. When I first arrived the deep solitude of our situation, connected with painful associations and sleepless nights, made me feverish and wretched. I could not summon *one home feeling* to my aid. The strange portraits that cover the walls, and the melancholy fate of the family who so lately occupied the house, increased my sadness and I wished myself again at my own home where habit had made objects familiar to me, but now I am better satisfied with this barren hill than I should be with vine clad France or classic Italy. We occupy ourselves with reading, sewing, walking

& riding. Sarah keeps house and every Saturday winds up the decent clock that clicks behind the door.[14]

As the fall approached, Mary's interest in reading had begun to revive, and she found the books sent to her by Mary Few a "delightful treat." Nonetheless, constantly distracted by her grief over Alexander's death, she felt that reading could never be an absorbing feeling again. "Indeed," she wrote, "all keen enjoyment in every thing in this life is passed away." Far more time was needed for her spiritual wounds to heal. Notwithstanding Mary's despondency, the summer in the Sand Hills had been a success. She was grateful for "an exemption from sickness." "Sarah & Catharine Hunter ought to speak well of the Hill," Mary wrote as their visit drew to a close. "It has dealt kindly with them—they have both fattened—Margaret too has improved in her appearance." The ladies returned to Savannah the first of November.[15]

After Alexander's death, Mary and her sisters were required to take on his role in supervising the operation of the plantations. He had left the Retreat Plantation jointly to Mary and Margaret and the Thorn Island Plantation to Sarah Haig. The slaves were divided among them. He devised his interest in Sharon to Thomas Telfair's two daughters. The sisters relied on the overseers for the day-to-day operations of the plantations. Elisha Cain, the overseer at the Retreat, reported to Mary Telfair that they were "suffering for rain," that mules were dying of colic, and that he could make do with the old cotton gin for that year as there had been no complaints on the quality of the cotton. Later Cain wrote to Mary suggesting that the family get out of the business of spinning and weaving, for eight hands were engaged in this activity and it was "very ungaining." A few years later, the overseer at the Thorn Island Plantation warned that the land was wearing out and that it was essential to follow a strict system of treating the soil with manure.[16]

Mary concerned herself with the welfare of the slaves. She required detailed assurances from the overseers that the Negroes were being furnished with sufficient blankets, and she instructed them that her slaves were not to be treated with severity. Mary had always been considerate of the house slaves in Savannah. "I could spin out my letter," she once wrote to Mary Few, "but our valet is waiting to out the candles & I am not so much of a *Southron* as to trespass on the time & patience of a domestic." Women on plantations would often plead with planters for the humane treatment of slaves. The slaves understood this and frequently would appeal to the mistress to intercede with the master on their behalf. Mary occasionally found herself in an analogous position. When one of the plantation workers, on a trip to town, complained to her of being mistreated, she took up his cause, only to be told by the overseer, most politely of course, that she should not believe all that she was told by these people. Mary found that, as a woman, it was difficult for her to command the overseers to do anything that they did not approve of. She found some of them "pretty conceited." Nonetheless, she persevered in her efforts to run a major agricultural business while maintaining humane living conditions for the slaves: "I have turned *Architect* and am building new houses for our people and superintending a vegetable garden." "I sometimes think I should like to be a *Farmeress*," Mary had written while Alexander was still alive, "but upon mature reflection I think I am better calculated for a *Town Lady.*" Nothing that Mary was experiencing was likely to change her mind.[17]

George Noble Jones, Mary's cousin and friend, helped out when he could and from time to time would look in on the Telfair plantations and confer with the overseers. George Jones was twenty years younger than Mary. She was of his father's generation. But he served as a friendly advisor to her and her family. For example, on one occasion he wrote to Mary from Olivinia, his plantation in Jefferson County near the town of Louisville, suggesting that she agree to her overseer's request that a slave driver be appointed at the Retreat Plantation and offering, upon her authorization, to select a man for the post.[18]

The Habersham firm continued to handle business matters for the Telfairs. The genial Robert Habersham, senior partner in the firm, not only looked after the ladies' financial affairs but also took a deep interest in their personal well-being. In 1836 the "Son" in the firm name was William Neyle Habersham. Neyle, as he was called, had been graduated that year from Harvard College, where he had been a member of the Porcellian. He was nineteen when he entered the family business. He would become one of Savannah's most prominent citizens, respected not only for his business acumen but also for his proficiency as a fisherman, his knowledge of fine wines, and his skill on the flute. After the death of Robert Habersham, Neyle became the business advisor to the Telfairs. He later would serve as one of the two executors of Mary Telfair's will.[19]

The process of healing that Mary was undergoing following Alexander's death was furthered by her empathy with the joys of her friends as well as their troubles. She learned in January 1834 of Matilda Few's marriage to John Tillotson. Mary Few had sent down to Savannah a piece of the cake with its bridal decorations. Tillotson was Mary Garrettson's first cousin, the son of her "Aunt Tillotson." He was a widower with children, and Matilda had known him for most of her life. Mary approved of the match, but could understand Mary Few's feeling of loss now that she and her sister would no longer be living under the same roof:

> Your last letter My dear Mary was received a week since, and I am truly happy to learn that the wedding is over and that Matilda's prospect of happiness is so bright. May it continue unclouded. I think (as far as human foresight goes) she has every thing to make her happy—an amiable husband, sweet children and a home endeared to her by the associations of childhood, of youth, and of maturer years surrounded too by her most valued friends. I am sure you felt the separation deeply and believe me I have followed you through it all.[20]

Mary Telfair's nieces had grown to be young ladies. Young Mary married Pierce Cobb of Columbia County in 1832 and the following year gave birth to her daughter Alberta.[21] When her elder niece was first engaged to be married, Mary Telfair shared the news with Mary Few. She was shocked to hear shortly thereafter that a rumor was in the air that young Margaret also was engaged:

> I hope my dear Mary that you kept the secret I confided to you viz Mary's engagement. Eliza Hunter has just returned from a visit to Augusta and brings a report that Margaret is *also engaged*. I really hope it is a mere report, poor child! I should grieve over such an event, but her Mother would approve of it for she says every girl ought to marry at sixteen—do not think me satirical but she reminds me of Gay's fable of Hymen and Death. "Sixteen, d'ye say nay then 'tis time,"—"Another year destroys your prime"—but seriously speaking it *is an awful thing to marry at fifteen*.[22]

Mary Telfair had invited young Mary and her baby to visit her at the Sand Hills during the summer of 1833 while Mary's husband was traveling for his health. The invitation was declined. "Mr. Cobb is said to be both amiable and intelligent," Miss Telfair wrote at the time. "Mary is devotedly attached to him." Travel did not improve Cobb's health. "He has a settled cough and I fear is far advanced in a consumption," Telfair wrote of him after he stopped by to see the ladies at the Sand Hills in September 1833 on the way to Columbia Court House. "I believe it was altogether a love match on Mary's side," she continued. "She seems unconscious of his situation."[23]

Thomas Telfair's widow, her two daughters, and baby Alberta were in Savannah in the spring of 1834. Young Mary's health was wretched. She had decided indications of consumption. Mary Telfair tried to persuade her to go north with her that summer, but she refused. Her husband's health was very bad. "She seems very much attached to him & her child," Telfair wrote. "It was an unfortunate marriage—It was formed too early." "Margaret is adverse to returning to Wilkes," Mary wrote of her younger niece. "Her Mother thinks her much improved and I am glad that she thinks so. Poor child she requires a judicious counselor & good examples. I tremble for her future happiness. If her sensibility equaled her pride she would be miserable, but she seems as happy as one could desire."[24]

By the time that Margaret did return to Wilkes County at the end of May, it was clear to Mary Telfair that she was not going to be able to turn the girl into another Mary Few or Anne Clay:

> Mrs. Telfair & her children left us a day or two since. Margaret left Savannah with great regret. She has an aversion to the up-Country. I gave her a letter of advice how to pass her time & a list of books to read. But Pleasure is so much her idol at present that I fear she will laugh & sing the hours away. How completely certain traits of Character descend—it may be the influence of example but I trace much of Mrs. Telfair's Mother & herself in Margaret—and only one solitary trait of her Father & that is the love of variety and eagerness of disposition. With him it was interesting for it was not in the pursuit of trifles. Margaret is too much puffed & flattered it will be her ruin. Few youthful minds can resist the siren song of flattery and she receives it from both Sexes. I cannot divest myself of great anxiety respecting her.[25]

By May 1834 Mary and her sisters had regained sufficient enthusiasm for life to enable them to make plans to spend the summer in the North. The previous March, Mary had written to Mary Few that her energies were "so benumbed" that she had "a horror of moving." "Some of our friends recommend us to go to Newport—and try the benefits of sea bathing and riding," she advised her friend. "I leave it entirely to Sarah & Margaret to decide—Even our short removal last summer gave us so much trouble that I hardly know whether it is worth while making efforts even for health." Mary managed to pull herself together, however. She and her sisters sailed for New York on June 1 in company with Harriett Campbell and Mary Fenwick Kollock. She asked Mary Few to book accommodations for them at Cowlings on Murray Street near to the Fews's residence. Mary Few had extended an invitation to the ladies to stay with her family at No. 10 Park Place, but Mary politely refused: "As we take on two servants, and *it is a principle* with us never to take them into a private family, we cannot *all* stay with you but I will be with you if not all part of the time that we remain in New York. Indeed the only comfort that I anticipate is from your company."[26]

While Mary Telfair was in Newport in July 1834, she received a major setback in her struggle to put her life in order. A letter from Sarah Campbell brought news of the death of Sarah Jones Cuthbert. Mrs. Cuthbert was forty-five at the time of her death.[27] Mary had been close to her cousin, and the news came as a great shock. Mrs. Cuthbert had been out for her usual ride the day before. She was expecting her second child. As her confinement approached, she complained of some pain. She was dressed and sitting up when the pain increased and a premature birth occurred. The baby was born dead. Sarah seemed fine at first but then suffered a convulsion, continued insensible for half an hour, and then breathed her last. Edward F. Campbell was not surprised by the death of Sarah Cuthbert: "Col. Cuthbert and Alfred left us on Tuesday last for Jasper. The death of his wife, though sudden, was not unexpected by me. I anticipated the issue whenever her confinement took place. She had a presentment of it herself and begged that her Father should not receive too flattering accounts of her health."[28]

Mary wondered how Uncle George Jones, then at Ballston Spa and in poor health, would bear up under the weight of sorrow occasioned by the loss of his daughter. George Noble Jones went immediately to the side of his grandfather. He later reported to Mary Telfair that at first the shock to the old man was very great and his grief very deep. By the time that George left him, however, he was composed and resigned. He felt it his duty to be so and also felt "his pilgrimage near its end." "How many buoyant hearts has he lived to see the clods of the valley press upon!" Mary wrote of her uncle. As she did so often when faced with tragedy, Mary turned to her faith and observed that sorrows and disappointments are "purifiers of the soul" and prepare it for a "house not made with hands eternal in the Heavens."[29]

Mary worried about Sarah Cuthbert's son Alfred, as did other members of the family. Mary Fenwick Kollock wrote to her brother that "the loss of such a wife and Mother is irreparable." She believed that Colonel Cuthbert truly felt the loss of his wife for, she wrote, "with all his eccentricities I am convinced he was sincerely attached to her." Miss Kollock did not believe, however, that Cuthbert should undertake the care of his little son: "I hope Alfred will be left with one of his Aunts, for his Father, engrossed as he is with his plantation, cannot bestow that attention on him which he requires. Poor little fellow! He is just the age that I was when I lost my dear Mother."[30] There was agreement on the part of Mary Telfair:

> Harriett Campbell writes me that little Alfred returned with his father to Jasper. I hope he will be sent away to school—any situation would be better for him than the one he is now in. His Mother to him is an irreparable loss, for she was devoted to him. I never think of the poor little fellow without the lines of Savage occurring to me: "No Mother's tender care shielded my infant innocence with prayer."[31]

Mary Telfair received word of the death of another friend while at Newport that summer. Associate Justice William Johnson of the United States Supreme Court died in Brooklyn under unhappy circumstances on August 4. It was he who had played Captain John Smith to Mary's Pocahontas at Dr. George Jones's masquerade years before. A Jefferson appointee, he had served on the court for thirty years and had established himself as an independent thinker rendering numerous dissenting opinions throughout his long career. Mary reflected upon his death in a letter to Mary Few:

On our way to church last evening we met Mr. Bayard who informed us of the death of our old friend Judge Johnson—he died under a surgical operation—he refused to have his limbs bound with cords and the effort he made to bear up under his agony was so great that Nature was exhausted. I fear he was too much absorbed in the enjoyments of Ambition and Society to reflect upon a future state. He was certainly a gifted being, and more calculated from the brilliancy of his intellect and the native unaffected elegance of his person and manners to adorn society than any man I ever saw—Calculated too for domestic life in all its relations. But alas! What are those gifts at the close of life? As Cowper says the only "lasting treasure is Truth."[32]

Despite the sad news of the deaths of Mrs. Cuthbert and Mr. Justice Johnson, the Telfair sisters spent the summer in Newport most pleasantly. The serenity of the place brought a peace that helped heal the wounds that had been reopened by her cousin's death:

We *pedestrianize* twice a day and have *ferreted* out every green lane and fine prospect in New Port and its lovely environs. Mr. Schroeder's Cottage would realize your *beau ideal* of rural taste and beauty—Nothing can transcend the bright verdure of the grass here—it is *emerald green* and must look like that which carpeted Eden before our first Parents ate the fatal apple. The fogs and saline air nourish its growth, and the frequent ambience of the sun vivifies it. The rides about this Island are beautiful, and the ocean is visible from almost every point. The harbour too presents a scene of picturesque beauty. In our drive this morning we had the rich variety of hill & dale and cultivated fields, and flocks & herds reposing in the latter on one side of us, and on the other the beautiful bay whose unruffled waters looked like a mirror. The town is not devoid of interest to admirers of the *antique*. The number of its old Mansions *respectable even in ruins* awaken a *mysterious* sort of interest and I often stop the little boys to inquire "*who lives there?*" The house in which Mrs. Bayard boards was once occupied by Genl. Washington. And the house in which Mrs. Evans lives was once owned by a cousin of Mrs. Aneiaux—a great belle in her day and now reduced to beggary—chiefly supported by the crumbs that fall from the table of the house she once called her own.[33]

In response to Mary Few's question in a letter addressed to New-port, "What are you carrying on?" Mary Telfair answered, "I carry my frame (which is increasing in *bulk*) twice a day to walk." "Every green lane and street in New Port has been explored," she continued, "and my interest in surrounding scenes, which are imminently beau-tiful, is a *growing* one." It was particularly lovely to take a drive in the cool of a Newport evening:

> We took a drive two evenings since to the fort—the road is extremely rough, and rocky, but the prospect wild and pictur-esque beyond description—On one side lay the bay with its unruffled waters dotted with Islands and the Town of New Port looking like a City rising from the waves—On the other side was the boundless Ocean—the view of the beaches recalled *the rapids and the noble St. Lawrence* with which Mary Few is ever associated.[34]

Mary loved the "primitive simplicity" of Newport. She thought it would suit the taste of Mary Few. Every day she would observe, "Mary Few would admire this." "*Simplicity & Antiquity* are stamped upon this unenterprising place," she wrote to Mary Few. "I should like to introduce you to *the old tower* which tradition says was in the olden times a refuge for Buccaneers—it stands in the center of a verdant field and only wants the creeping Ivy to give it the air of a classic ruin."[35]

While at Newport, Mary was treated to a visit from Mary Clay Gray, the married sister of Anne and Eliza Clay. "She heard of our being here while she was on a visit to Providence and came accompa-nied by Tom Clay and Mr. Arnold to see us," Mary related. "She stayed a day and a half—We took a walk and a ride together and talked until I was exhausted." "She is a most improved character," Mary wrote of her friend, "She was always lovely and attractive but now Religion has given the finishing touch to her character."[36]

The best news that summer of 1834 was the forthcoming marriage of George Noble Jones to Delia Gardiner, the daughter of Robert Hallowell Gardiner and Emma Jane Tudor Gardiner of Gardiner, Maine. Upon learning of the couple's engagement the previous May, Mary had expressed her approval to Mary Few:

> I believe I have not mentioned to you the engagement of Geo. Jones to Miss Gardiner of Maine. She is of the *House of Tudor*

a fair branch of it. She is said to be pious, amiable and intelligent—interesting in her appearance without being pretty. I am glad he has made so judicious a choice for he is a most deserving young man.

Jones had met Delia during a summer sojourn at Newport. "I take the earliest opportunity to acquaint you with my plans," the young man wrote to his cousin George J. Kollock from Oaklands, the Gardiner estate in Maine. "It was yesterday [July 25] decided that the 2d September should be the wedding day!" Jones and his bride-to-be hoped that Kollock would be able to attend. "Delia desires me when I write to remember her to you & to say she hopes you will be on in time for the 'event' as your presence cannot be dispensed with." Delia had been in poor health at the time of her marriage, but her mother and father thought that a winter in the South would probably restore her to health. Mary Telfair became better acquainted with Delia the winter following her marriage: "She is a very interesting woman, and only wants health to be a treasure to him. There is a fitness and propriety about her that shews *education*." On another occasion she wrote of her cousin's wife, "She interests me deeply. She is very pious, amiable & intelligent in fact one of those pure spirits that seem to be fitted for a happier world."[37]

The summer had been a success. Mary and her sisters had grown to love Newport. Mary was particularly impressed with Trinity Church:

> I strolled into Trinity Church yesterday afternoon—the most ancient Church in New Port. It is as large as the Cathedral in Quebec. The organ has the crown upon it and was presented upwards of a century ago to the Church. The monuments bear equally the stamp of antiquity, some are crumbling in ruins, while the hand of time has effaced the inscriptions from others.[38]

Mary wrote of her newly found contentment near the end of August:

> We feel quite at home in New Port—its green lanes are daily trodden by us, and we continue to admire the beautiful turf which seems independent of dews and showers for its enchanting verdure. Sarah & Margaret are as much pleased with this emerald isle as I am. We all equally admire the beauties of

cultivated nature. I feel no inclination to become a permanent New Englander, but if my lot had been cast in it I believe I should not have been a stranger to *local attachment*.[39]

The season of sorrow following Alexander's death and the two years of healing that Mary Telfair and her sisters had struggled through during that saddest of times had been punctuated by the joys of marriage and birth and the agony that came with the deaths of other relatives and friends. Peace had come to the Telfair sisters at long last as they spent the last crisp days of summer walking the green lanes of Newport and watching the fog roll in from the ocean that churned beneath the cliffs. Alexander would always be in their thoughts, but they had finally come to terms with his death. The sisters would return to Savannah in the fall and would settle into their customary winter routine. They did not anticipate that upon their arrival in Savannah there would be a major surprise from one of the Sisterhood.

II

So Many Changes

There is nothing stable in the world—
uproar's your only music.
　　　　　　John Keats, Letter to George and Thomas Keats
　　　　　　　　　　　　　　　　　　(January 13, 1818)

Upon returning to Savannah in November 1834 after a stormy four-day passage, Mary Telfair learned to her surprise and dismay that Catharine Hunter had been married on October 29 to her first cousin Noble Wimberly Jones Bulloch. Jones Bulloch was the second son of Archibald Stobo Bulloch and Sara Glen Bulloch. His grandfather was the patriot Archibald Bulloch, who was named president and commander-in-chief of Georgia in 1776 and died in office in 1777. His uncle (his father's brother) was the distinguished Georgian William Bellinger Bulloch, who served in the United States Senate. Jones Bulloch's father had a far less distinguished career. He lost his considerable fortune in the difficult economic period of the early 1820's, being required to sell all his property to meet his obligations, including his mansion on Orleans Square (since demolished) that had been designed for him by William Jay in 1818. With no family backing and with a clerk's pay to live on, Jones Bulloch had little going for him. He was twelve years Catharine's junior. For Catharine Hunter to leave the sisterhood of unmarried ladies was a development too radical for Mary Telfair to comprehend. For Catharine to have married Jones Bulloch was even more incomprehensible:

Women are Enigmas, few of them *solvable*. She who was such a slave to the world's opinion and who ridiculed unequal mar-

196

riages even when the disparity was on the right side to take such a step. Sarah Cecil tells me that the devoted attachment on the young man's part brought it about, that when he first proposed she laughed at it, but *propinquity* says Miss Edgeworth is dangerous—She saw no one else last summer and *it was to be.* The public I understand deal *unmercifully* towards her—she stood very high both for intellect & character, when that is the case *men, women & children* unite in condemning an unequal marriage. I hope she will be happy, but I doubt it.[1]

Catharine's relationship with Jones Bulloch developed at a time when she was most vulnerable, and Mary Telfair was convinced that her friend had been driven to marriage "as a refuge from accumulated sorrows." The chief of these sorrows was the suicide the previous March of Catharine's brother, Wimberly Hunter. He had been in poor health, and before putting an end to his life had shown strong marks of insanity. "His wife is inconsolable," Mary wrote, "his Mother bowed down by it, and poor Catharine who loved him very dearly is in the deepest sorrow." Mary believed Wimberly to have been a sincere Christian and trusted that "he is now a happy Spirit in a world where changes are unknown and where sin & sorrow never enter." It appears that Jones Bulloch, a very religious man, was a comfort to Catharine in her bereavement and that his efforts to console her blossomed into a romance.[2]

Mary Telfair's curiosity concerning the strange union of Catharine Hunter and Jones Bulloch continued to gnaw at her. In December 1834 she finally sat down with Catharine and tried to uncover the real story. She was not entirely successful, as she confided to Mary Few:

> Mrs. Jones Bulloch & myself (entre nous) have had a *talk.* I cannot ascertain whether she is the happier for her alliance.... Mrs. Hunter I think is *satisfied* with Catharine's choice—her ambition has been subdued by affliction. I really think this step of Catharine's will improve her character—her humility is already increased by it & her Husband is one of your *duty* Men & a most sincere Christian—he dislikes society & I am inclined to think she will not try to draw him into it. Sarah Cecil is *unreconciled* to the marriage. She viewed Catharine as a Madame de Staël. We never know how high we stand until we fall. I had no idea her reputation for intellect was so high. I have never

thought her mind soared above mediocrity except as regards originality & humor—as a companion she was delightful.[3]

A bit later, Sarah Cecil would express the opinion to Mary Telfair that Catharine was much happier for the step that she had taken but was unwilling to let it be known. Mary's comment was, "Women are enigmas not only to their friends but to themselves." Mary reported to Mary Few on another visit with Catharine that winter:

> Catharine *Hunter* Bulloch paid us a visit yesterday. She *looks* happy but to my surprise feels no more interest in life than she did previous to her union. I have had her matrimonial *experience*. I begin to think there is such a thing as *passive* happiness in the married state. The young and ardent do not admit it but the staid, the sober & the experienced think it possible.[4]

During the fall of 1834, the painter Richard West Habersham, then in his early twenties, returned to Savannah after spending the preceding three years as an art student in Paris. Habersham, who had been born in 1811, was the eldest son of Richard Wylly Habersham, the grandson of James Habersham, Jr., and the great-grandson of James Habersham, who arrived in Georgia in 1738 with the Reverend George Whitefield and who served as acting governor of the colony while Governor Wright was absent in England. The young artist was the eldest son of the eldest son of the eldest son of the first Habersham to come to Savannah. As a boy he attended Partridge's Academy in Middletown, Connecticut, and then went on to study mathematics at the United States Military Academy at West Point. Art was his real love, however, and in 1831 he went to Paris to study at the atelier of Baron Gros.

In Paris, Habersham made the acquaintance of Samuel F. B. Morse, a man twenty years his senior and by then an established artist. They met at the Louvre while Morse was making a copy of a painting by Rembrandt, one of the many copies of paintings that he made and sold to enhance his income. For a time Habersham and Morse shared quarters in a house on a street near the Madeleine. Cholera was raging in the city, but the occupants of the house escaped the disease purportedly due to Habersham's insistence that they ingest a tea-spoonful of charcoal every morning. Habersham and Morse counted among their friends the novelist James Fenimore Cooper, who was then living in Paris and who enjoyed strolling to the Louvre to watch Morse paint after a day spent writing. It was during this time that Morse completed his most famous painting, *Gallery of the Louvre* (1833), which represents an imaginative view of the Salon Carré lined from floor to ceiling with masterpieces of sixteenth- and seventeenth-century European paintings. But Morse was not just laying paint to canvas. He also was formulating the concept of the electromagnetic telegraph, and his ideas on this subject frequently were tested in conversations with Habersham.[5]

The Telfair sisters commissioned Habersham to paint their portraits, and in December 1834 Mary Telfair was busy with sittings at the artist's studio. Never happy with her own appearance, she found it something of an ordeal. She described the process to Mary Few, who apparently was well acquainted with Habersham:

> We have patronized the young Artist Richard, which gives us a daily walk to his room—Sarah's Portrait is completed & pronounced a good likeness—Margaret's will be, but he cannot catch my ugly phiz. After five sittings he erased mine and commenced another, which looks so cross that I flatter myself it is unlike me. Sarah says mine is no face for Painting—too much I suppose of *abstraction & distraction* in it. You have made quite an impression upon the artist—to use his own phrase, "Miss Mary Few realizes my beau ideal of female character; if she had been some years younger or I some years older I would have been captivated by her." I need not say he took the *broad* road to my heart by his commendations, which I am certain will not please you as much as they did me.[6]

Mary Few must have responded with a quip upon learning that young Habersham was painting her friend's portrait, for Mary Telfair fired back in late January with a few quips of her own:

> I knew you would not approve of an *old* face being taken by a *young* artist. He says the tournure of my "Pieter" (as our old cook calls it) resembles Miss Mary Few, which induced me to examine closely & I do think the *head* quite as much like yours as like mine. I am inclined to think the *huge*, I might almost say the *suspicious* bust, would tempt you to pass a brush over it, or reduce it in some other way.[7]

While painting her portrait, Habersham engaged Telfair in a discussion of the importance of the fine arts to the acquisition of knowledge. He told the older woman, who had become his friend as well as his patron, that his highest ambition was to aid in raising Georgia from its provincialism "brought on by devotion to cotton, horses and dogs." Telfair offered encouragement in words that the artist would recall in later years: "Great artists and the martyrs of science and religion have made the world what it is, and to your generation will be entrusted the making of the next step onwards and upwards."[8]

Habersham would recall years later that "externally the three Telfair sisters were not *beautiful*." They had certain appealing qualities, however, that set them apart. In describing the ladies, Habersham did not identify which one was the object of his comment:

> One was pretty, amiable and intelligent; another was possessed of a face which, when fixed upon canvas, was said to be *very like*, but *very much flattered* (which *flattery* is generally due entirely to the artist's skill in drawing out any fixed beauty that lies deeper than the skin), while the manners and intelligence of the third made those who could appreciate and enjoy her conversation and friendly unreserve forget all else to feel, and afterwards to wonder at, the fascination exercised over them by her.

The artist was particularly taken with Mary, who probably was the third-mentioned of the three sisters:

> Miss Mary, especially, was imbued with the poetic and artistic spirit, and possessed a fund of curious and interesting traditional, mythical and antiquarian lore, so that while the spirit of the ancient Troubadours remained in the breasts of the descendants of the cavaliers and Huguenots, it is not wonderful that there were youth in Savannah who looked to her and her like as did "Dunois, the young and brave," to the Virgin Mary when he prayed before her shrine.[9]

Habersham had moved in with his parents upon his return to Savannah. They lived in a spacious house on the southwest corner of Barnard and Perry Streets. His younger sister, who was living there as well, was the most intimate friend of young Margaret Telfair, then a girl of eighteen. Soon after the first frost that fall, with the return of her aunts to the city, Margaret the younger came down to Savannah from Wilkes County, having just recovered from an attack of "country fever." She had changed dramatically from the awkward country girl that Mary Telfair had worked so hard to train. Richard Habersham would recall in later years that Margaret did not strike him as beautiful, but that "as she recovered her health she showed signs of what she afterwards was, a most stately, dignified and attractive woman." His description of the Telfairs' niece was altogether positive: "Unusually tall in stature, very amiable in manner, tolerant of the peculiarities of others, and although full of humor and occasionally satirical, she was to all a pleasant drawing room companion, and to those who knew her intimately a reliable friend and charitable dispenser of her superfluous wealth."[10]

By this time Mary Telfair had resigned herself to allowing her niece to do as she pleased: "I am determined to let her have her own way and never to intrude advice, although sensible that she requires a great deal. Her temper is a very peculiar one so peculiar that I think she dislikes every one who endeavors in any way to control her and I have a horror of being hated by any one." "Our secluded and desolate home seems a happy one to her," Mary wrote of her niece. "She goes out a great deal and we allow her to have her own way. Experience must be her guide and counselor. Amusement is the idol to which she bows. She is very eager in the pursuit of pleasure. When the Spring arrives and the period of her return to Wilkes arrives she will not relish it much—her dislike of the up-country is very great." By giving Margaret some breathing room, Mary found that her relationship with the girl was improving: "I thought when she first came to us she wanted ingenuousness but every day I perceive her confidence in us increases, and I am in hopes she will yet feel that we are her best friends."[11]

Mary Telfair might not have been so tolerant if she had realized the extent to which Margaret was being pursued by the young men of Savannah. As the elder brother and "traveled man of the world," Richard Habersham became the repository of all his sister's secrets, at least those which, as he put it, "it was proper for me to know." One of those secrets was the story of the pursuit of young Margaret Telfair by the French consul in Savannah.[12] According to Habersham, "He was a dainty little gentleman, short in stature, slim in body, and so studiously neat and unruffled in his dress that the girls said he looked as if he kept himself in a bandbox." He was the nephew of Casimir Perrier, prime minister to Louis Philippe, and had been given a consulship to keep him out of the snares set in Paris for young men of family and small fortune. In Habersham's opinion he had been posted to Savannah, first, because it was the only consulship vacant at the time; second, because it was "a place of old-fashioned morality—free from gamblers and demi-monde"; and finally because it was "the winter headquarters of the rich planters of rice and cotton" whose daughters would be glad for "an alliance with the nobility (old or new) of glorious France and its splendid civilization." Habersham had little use for the gentleman, viewed him with some amusement, and "knowing his antecedents and not particularly pleased with his quiet, unobtrusive assumption of superiority, was content with recognizing him with a civil bow and otherwise leaving him alone."

The little Frenchman chose Margaret as the object of his affections and carefully planned his approach. The siege went on for two months and by the end of the third the assault was made. In Habersham's view, Margaret at the time was "as yet a mere novice in the ways of the world." Apparently she was oblivious to what was going on. When the Frenchman finally came forward and asked outright for her hand, she was shocked and refused him in no uncertain terms. She immediately rushed to the Habershams' house in a state of excitement to tell her dearest friend what had transpired. Richard, reading in his study on the second floor, could hear the chatter of the girls below "ending in a musical burst of merriment." He described what happened after Margaret left the house in a fit of laughter:

> She was scarcely out of sight before my sister ran up to my room in high glee, saying: "Dicko, I promised not to tell, but if you promise not to repeat it I will tell you! Monsieur le Consul has declared himself, and gone off mad as a hornet as his repulse. You know Margaret is not the least bit of a coquette, but the confident manner of his approach left her no opportunity of showing the estimate she put upon his attentions. She could only treat him like she did others, and he mistook her manner for encouragement; so this morning he declared himself in form. She received him with courtesy, and, taking her seat on the sofa in the alcove of the reception room, invited him to a chair. But he sat down by her side and, O Dicko, you ought to

hear Margaret mimic the little man and the confident and condescending air he assumed in declaring himself."

Richard's sister, being no bad mimic herself, went on to repeat Margaret's imitation of the Frenchman as he took her hand and poured forth his proposal of marriage:

> Eet is not necessaire for me to tell you, what you must have long seen, the consuming fiare which burn me up and combust me heart wid de warmth of my feelins for you! And now, mees, I come for you to give me your heart for de one I gives you, or to leave me a breast without a heart, empty as an exhausted air poomp.

When Margaret withdrew her hand from his and expressed her surprise, the Frenchman accused her of leading him on and then begged her to think of what she was throwing away if she refused him: "A life in Paree! Ah, what a life it would be in dat centre of civlizashong! What glory would surroun' de bootiful and riche Americaine, de wife of de nephew of the Prime Minister of France and a queen in de societay of Paree, la belle, la magnifique." When Margaret assured her unwelcome suitor that she had no ambition other than to be an American lady, he accused her of having a lover. "Dat I will not permeet," he said, "and I will speet him on my sword!" When Margaret denied his charge, the Frenchman clumsily persisted in his quest until Margaret finally was reduced to laughter. Insulted, the little man backed to the door, bowed, and cried out in a loud voice, "Adieu—adieu—for a very long time—adieu forevaire."

Habersham reported on another of young Margaret Telfair's encounters with a gentleman.[13] He observed, first, that from frequent contact with her aunts she had taken on something of their manners. He went on to elaborate on this observation and to attempt to explain the type of behavior that was expected of members of Margaret's circle:

> The consequence was that in the privacy of domestic intercourse there was none of that artificial bearing which she was sometimes obligated to assume towards strangers and to her mere drawing-room acquaintances. To understand this, it is necessary to say that the circle of Savannah society in which she moved

was remarkable for its absence of rivalry and gossipry, its freedom from personal allusions and its cordiality—going, generally, only properly short of familiarity. This cordiality existed notably among the families of the ante-Revolutionary generation, but it extended naturally to those of later date, and especially to strangers. Among these, natives as well as strangers, there were individuals who appeared not to understand this unusual state of things, and therefore there were occasional approaches to familiarity which were distasteful to our ladies, especially to the elder ones, who were invariably present at a large proportion at all our parties.

In a word, familiarity was considered vulgar. With this introduction, Habersham went on to relate Margaret's reaction to what she considered undue familiarity:

Among our fashionable youth of the time was a student of law, an intelligent, pleasant fellow, only son of a revolutionary distinguished father, and well received by all. His manners were perfectly good but a little bluff, while his portly person gave him an air of self-importance which he really did not feel. At a party one evening he approached Miss Margaret, intending to invite her to dance, and began: "Miss Margaret," when she interrupted him with a quiet "Mr. W. *Miss Telfair,* if you please." At this he drew himself up to his full height and replied: "So be it! *Miss Telfair* it shall always be hereafter!" and then bowing very low he turned on his heels and strode away.

Habersham, who was present, followed the young man to the piazza, where he was walking with a swelling breast and a flashing eye, proud that he had put this haughty young woman in her place. Habersham could not resist pricking his balloon and asked how "such a woman-killer let slip such an opportunity for securing the largest fortune and fairest lady in Savannah." With an "Humph!" the fellow replied, "I can't conceive how I could have done it better than I did. How *should* I have done it?" Habersham, toying with the proud young man, countered, "Oh! I do not say how *you* should have done it," and displaying his keen wit went on to relate how *he* would have done it:

Ah, fair lady! how little do you know what there is in a name or why I call you by your Christian rather than by your surname! Margaret means "pearl," and I never gaze on your fair face

and softly beaming eyes that I do not think of Moore's lines—
"No pearl ever lay under Oman's green water/ More pure in its
shell than thy spirit in thee." And how different the image that
rises at the name Telfair in the form of the gigantic Crusader
who split helms and cut through maces with such ease that the
name of Taliaferro, "the cutter of iron," has descended from the
Middle Ages as *Tolliver* in Virginia to *Telfair* in Georgia! Which
now shall I call you?

Habersham then suggested that the fellow might even have gone
on to evoke the memory of the minstrel Taillifer:

> I even prefer the associations of ideas connected with the pearl
> to those that arise from the tradition which tells of the brave
> warrior and noble minstrel, who sung the song of "Roland" with
> such effect at the Battle of Hastings that it was said the victory
> was half owing to the enthusiasm breathed into the Norman
> chivalry by him!

All of this left the young man sputtering that he had none of the Blar-
ney stone that Habersham had inherited and that he was not one to
flatter and lick the hand that strikes him. "But it was a woman's hand,"
Habersham countered. Thus did the young artist amuse himself.

Young Margaret, or "Margaretta" as she was then being called,
"who goes the nightly round," was a puzzlement to Mary Telfair. So
were the girl's friends. There were so many changes in the attitudes
and behavior of young people from the days when Mary Telfair and
Mary Few had been girls that Mary found them incomprehensible.
The previous spring, she had written of her niece and her crowd with
a touch of disapproval mixed with a forty-three-year-old spinster's
wistfulness:

> I have seen more of very young persons this winter than for
> years past owing to Margaretta being with us. And I must say
> either the world has changed or I have been *asleep*. I have listened
> with amazement to their opinions—so much calculation and
> worldly knowledge. They begin life with more of a *certain sort of
> prudence* than some end it. Perhaps they are happier for it, they
> build no Castles of Romance to be dissolved like Catharine's
> Palace of Ice. I think like Mrs. Jamieson that "there are young
> persons now a days, but no such thing as youth." The bloom of

existence is sacrificed to a fashionable education and where we should find the rose-buds of spring, we only see the full bloom precocious roses of the hot-bed.[14]

Mary despaired in particular of "the troop of boarding school girls who seem to think dress, fashion & beaux all that is worth living for." "I dread the influence of fashionable associates," she wrote. "The youthful mind is so open to impressions and so apt to be dazzled by the glitter of haute ton. If Mothers took the same view of gay life that I do there would be no *bringing out*,' and *Belle* would be an obsolete word." Mary had nothing but disdain for the emptiness of fashionable society. On another occasion she expressed her views to Mary Few in even stronger terms:

> I was amused by a New York *exclusive* asking if we visited such a Person she met at the Springs, for if we did not she would not continue the acquaintance. I very frankly told her that we were no standard, that we lived out of the fashionable world therefore could give no *weight* to any body in it. Defend me from the notoriety of a fashionable *stand*. The society and the good opinion of the pious and the intellectual is to be desired —but nothing more.[15]

Pierce Cobb died in February 1835 in Marianna, Florida, shortly after arriving at his wife's uncle's place following a trip to New Orleans.[16] By then, Mary Telfair had formed the opinion that he was "a very cold and indifferent Husband & Father." Young Mary's mother felt that the girl's marriage was "productive of unhappiness to them all." Having failed to fit her nieces into the mold that she had created for them, Telfair had sought to distance herself from their concerns. "You know," she confessed sadly to Mary Few, "I disciplined myself early not to look to my nieces for happiness."[17]

Mrs. Thomas Telfair, young Margaret, and little Alberta were staying with the Telfair sisters at the time of Pierce Cobb's death. Mrs. Telfair rushed to her elder daughter's side upon hearing the sad news. Left with Alberta under her care during Mrs. Telfair's absence, Mary Telfair had the opportunity to once again assume the role of the wise and nurturing aunt, or now the wise and nurturing great-aunt. Perhaps she could be more influential with this girl of a new generation. The little girl's grandmother treated her as a pet and allowed her to get away with all sorts of misbehavior. It was the same story all over again. Mrs. Telfair would spoil her granddaughter, just as she had spoiled her daughters, unless her sister-in-law intervened. The first step would be to try to bring some discipline to Alberta's life. "I wish you could have witnessed my first lesson of obedience," Telfair wrote to Mary Few:

> I wanted to take her measure for an apron; she got into a rage and a *scuffle* ensued. I tried by gentle means to subdue her as the old man in the fable did the rude boy who went up the tree to steal apples. I found harsher means requisite. I told her with *a look of Thunder* she should stand still & when she found me resolute & on my way with her up stairs she consented to behave well—after that nobody had any trouble in managing her, and all the credit was accorded to *my commanding air.* My brief experience impels me to echo the words of an old Clergyman— "The first lesson that a child ought to be taught is obedience— the second lesson obedience—the third obedience."[18]

As the world changed around her, Mary Telfair sought stability in her books. That winter she was treating herself to a rich intellectual feast. The letters of Hannah More (1745–1833), the English reformer and author, had been published in 1834, and Mary was spending hours pouring through the multivolume work. "I have just finished the first volume of Miss More," she wrote to Mary Few in January, "and think her the *greatest* as well as the best of Women. She certainly did more to promote the interests of Religion & virtue than any Woman that ever lived." Hannah More was a friend of the leading intellectual figures in eighteenth-century England: Edmund Burke, the actor-playwright David Garrick, Samuel Johnson, the clergyman John Newton, Sir Joshua Reynolds, Horace Walpole, and Mrs. Elizabeth Montagu and the other ladies of the bluestocking coterie. "I think her friends were all interesting," Mary wrote. "Newton's letters pleased me more than any of her male friends. Mrs. Kennicott's among her female bear the palm in my humble opinion—Lord Oxford (alias) the gay & witty Horace Walpole leaves a sad impression upon the mind. I think his inscription upon the blank page of a Bible presented to Miss More proves his respect for the sacred volume as well as for the Receiver of it."[19]

The following March, Mary Telfair was still deeply engrossed in the writings of Hannah More:

I am still reading Miss Hannah More and am nearly through the second volume. I have read it with mingled feelings of pleasure and pain. How her later years were clouded by sorrow for the loss of beloved friends! and with what pious resignation she bore her accumulated trials. She was a rare exemplification of the following remark made by her to Newton—A Christian ought not to live so much out of the world as *above* it. She certainly took an *elevated* view of Christianity, and rested as little upon her own works for salvation as if she had never performed one good action. Her humility was deep and her charity boundless & those may be called the fruits of Faith.[20]

Several years later, while reading a biography of Hannah More, Mary became effusive in extolling the virtues of this remarkable woman and reflective on the insignificance of popular acclaim:

I look upon Miss More as the greatest Benefactor to the human species that ever existed. Garrick's death seems to have been blessed to her. He seemed the link that bound her to that society which seemed to worship her talents. His death seems to have awakened her to a sense of danger of applause & determined her to consecrate all the energies of her powerful mind to the interests of religion & virtue.[21]

As spring arrived in Savannah in 1835, following a fierce winter that killed all of the orange trees in the yard of the mansion on St. James Square, Mary Telfair was feeling listless. "I have with mental dullness been very dyspeptic," she wrote to Mary Few, "the *union* a miserable one." She finished the first volume of the memoirs of George Crabbe, the English poet and clergyman. "I think for a Minister of the Gospel he wanted religious fervor," she wrote, but she was intrigued by his account of five single ladies of independent fortune who established a nunnery in England. This led Mary into a conversation with Sarah Haig: "Sarah & myself were saying a few evenings since (by way of furnishing a topic) that we would like to establish *a Protestant Convent* composed of Mary Few, the Demeres & a few others." They decided that Anne Clay would not be invited to join. "Anne Clay is too active for a conventual life." The sisters also discussed where they should stay in New York the following summer: "Sarah thinks we would be more quiet in a private boarding house. She is a horrible coward about Hotels, imagines them as much the resort of *Banditti* as the Alps & Apennines."[22]

In a world filled with change there was always a new fad. The big fad to hit Savannah in the spring of 1835 was phrenology, the pseudoscience based on the theory that character traits and mental facilities can be determined from the configurations of a person's skull. Whether there was any truth in the doctrines of phrenology was an issue mooted by the Savannah Young Men's Debating Society. An interested observer, Mary Fenwick Kollock, wrote to her brother in Savannah to see whether he had been caught up in the craze:

> I understand the good people of Savannah are *Phrenology mad;* have you become infected? There is scarcely any other topic of conversation here among the elite, and I feel quite like an ignoramus among them. I should like to have heard Dr. Barber's lectures, very much, as I wish to understand something of the science and I am told he makes the subject very interesting. If it be true, however, that the character can be ascertained by the developments on the head, it will be rather unpleasant to be in the society of these *wise folks* as we are unwilling that our *weaknesses* and *infirmities* be held up to *public view*. I must say I am very incredulous although I have had some points in my character told me by those, who have studied the science, and who knew nothing of me previously, which I know to be true.

As for Mary Telfair, she had "no faith in the science" and considered phrenologists to be rogues and cheats.[23]

The summer of 1835 approached, and the world of George Noble Jones was about to crumble. He and his bride returned to Maine following a winter in Savannah. When Mr. Gardiner saw his daughter, he was struck by "the hectic flush in her cheek." He consulted his family physician, who examined the young woman's lungs very carefully and expressed the fear that the disease in them had made so much progress that there was little hope of its being arrested. The doctor advised that another voyage or journey would only tend to aggravate the complaint and would add greatly to Delia's discomfort. Mr. Gardiner, believing it his duty to tell her the truth, communicated the doctor's views to his daughter. The shock at first was very great. "Her prospects in life were brilliant," Delia's father wrote, "With a husband devoted to her, and with his family feeling strong affection for her, with his large fortune, her own personal beauty and very pleasing manner, all that this world can give seemed at her command." He lamented, "All these were to be exchanged for the prospect of an early tomb." Mr. Gardiner described the final months of his daughter's life:

> The first day after I spoke to her she shut herself up and saw no one but her husband, but she soon became reconciled to the will of her Heavenly Father, and frequently expressed to me her thankfulness for my letting her know her real situation. We were then living at the cottage. Delia and her husband came down there, and Mrs. Jones and her daughters, and his sister Miss Campbell, took lodgings at Mrs. Gay's, half a mile above, in order to be near. It was an inexpressible comfort to us to have Delia with us, to watch the growth of her Christian character and her gradual preparedness for her Heavenly Home. The sympathy and loving attention of so many devoted friends made her last days serenely comfortable, while, as she approached the termination of her course, she could look upon death not only without terror, but as the gate of everlasting happiness. She died on the 8th day of January 1836.[24]

Mary Telfair admired the Christian resignation with which Delia Jones had accepted death:

> She early, very early felt the insufficiency of earthly joys & placed her hopes upon "the evidence of things unseen." Her piety & resignation were remarkable in life & in death. Though all was bright before her in this world, she was willing to exchange it & leave all she loved behind for a Mansion in her Father's house. She took an affectionate farewell of all her friends, recommended religion to them & while her spirit was engaged in prayer it left its tenement of clay.[25]

As Christmas of 1835 approached, the Telfair sisters were passing their time in their usual quiet fashion. Mary Ewing Ritchie was spending the winter with them. As always, Mary's world became brighter when a letter arrived from Mary Few:

Your long expected and despaired of letter my dear Mary shed its lustre on our trio three evenings since, and I can truly sympathize with you in the chimney corner for I never leave mine except to take a walk *from duty*. We like crickets live in it but no "sympathetic mirth, no kitten its tricks to try" but "the crackling faggot flies" for we pile the wood up in opposition to modern Anthracite. Sarah insisted on my reading aloud Master Humphrey's Clock *precluding* it with a compliment by saying she could never listen to anyone's reading but mine—it is a family vice not to listen to reading.[26]

Thomas Telfair's widow, her two daughters, Mary and Margaret, and Mary's child Alberta also were staying at the Telfair mansion in January 1836. Miss Telfair reported that the "little doll" was "very tractable," a "source of interest" to its mother and grandmother, and a joy to her Aunt Margaret. "Mary lives just for her child," her aunt would later write. The South Carolina cousins were at the residence as well, having sold all their possessions. Cousin Margaret's health had been in decline for some time, and she and her sister soon would seek a healthier climate by establishing their permanent residence in Philadelphia.[27] The move to the North by her beloved cousins was another change to which Mary would have to adjust.

Although in the nineteenth-century scheme of things, politics lay outside the sphere assigned to women, Mary Telfair could enjoy a good political debate with James Moore Wayne, an old friend who in January 1835 was sworn in by Chief Justice John Marshall to fill the vacancy on the United States Supreme Court created by the death of Justice Johnson. He paid one of his frequent visits to the Telfairs shortly before Christmas in 1835:

> Judge Wayne broke in on the monotony of an evening lately. He got upon politics—a violent follower of Van Buren. I told [him] my politics embraced but two subjects having very limited ideas. I was for that Administration that would terminate the Florida War and give us a National Bank—I am afraid that he thinks my head runs upon lucre—He says that a National Bank would ruin the South—make it more tributary to the North— You see I am willing to be under Northern government—The Judge & I seldom agree but though he is the antipode to my great men I like him for auld lang syne.[28]

As for Mrs. Wayne, Mary Telfair thought her "the Madame de Staël of Georgia" and paid her the ultimate wry compliment: "She even gossips in an elegant style." "I should like to hear your opinion of her," Mary wrote to Mary Few. "We are wonderfully sociable when we meet, but not at all intimate. I admire her mind excessively—her character has no very high claims to superiority—she is *too worldly* to interest one who does not enter into her views of human life."[29]

It was a mild winter, and the jasmine was blooming in January. Mary thought this a blessing for the sake of those detained in Savannah due to the war with the Seminole Indians in Florida. She found the Indian War a cause of great anxiety and worried over the "young men of promise" who had gone to Florida as volunteers. "The Indian War is the all exciting subject," she wrote, "I feel for the poor deluded creatures and for the brave spirits who have gone to subdue them but I cannot *dream of laurels* as some do & talk of it as a thing of wondrous pomp and circumstance."[30]

The institution of slavery, which Mary Telfair had always taken for granted as a way of life in the South, was increasingly coming under attack. The work of the abolitionists commanded Mary's attention. Nat Turner's rebellion had taken place in Virginia in 1831, and plantation owners in the South were imposing harsher codes of behavior on their slaves. The American Anti-Slavery Society had been founded in 1833, and despite intense harassment, the Boston firebrand William Lloyd Garrison was demanding immediate and uncompensated emancipation. The abolitionists were petitioning Congress to abolish slavery and the slave trade in the District of Columbia, over which it had exclusive jurisdiction, and the underground railroad was operating with some effectiveness. Mary Telfair read an antislavery tract by William Ellery Channing, the Unitarian clergyman, and was not at all impressed: "I have read Dr. Channing's work on slavery. It is as feeble as his own little body. I cannot imagine from what source he drew his information. The reply to it by Austin of Boston I admire exceedingly. It displays more depth of argument as well as intellect than the production of 'the Addison of the Age.'"[31]

During the spring of 1836, Mary was finding pleasure tending her garden:

> We have had a Northern Spring cool & verdant and the roses have been as abundant as when Thompson painted them de-

scending in showers—My plants flourish without an *awning* and invite me to shelter them in a green house, but I have not *energy* enough to provide them with so troublesome an abode— My plants are my only recreation. Sarah has taken to Birds— She commenced with a pair, like Adam & Eve, but single bless- edness prevailed—Adam eloped—Since then *wooers* have come to Eve in the form of three Nonpareils & been admitted into the Cage—Our garden is a natural Aviary—And yet like the Master of Lee Place we leave it for New York.[32]

Plans for the annual trip to the North got under way that spring. Mary and her sisters would sail on the brig *Madison* on the last day of May 1836. They were forced to make a change in their usual prac- tice of having several slaves accompany them on their travels for, as Mary explained to Mary Few, "A late law passed in the Legislature prohibits both slaves and free coloured persons from being taken on." The ladies planned to go directly to New York, where George Noble Jones had arranged for them to have accommodations at the Astor Hotel. They would be within walking distance of the Few residence on Park Place. Their niece Margaret would accompany them. Her mother was most anxious that she should do so. As they did not plan to visit any public watering places, Mary felt less the responsibility of having a girl of twenty in her charge. "She is very gay and fond of pleasure," Mary wrote, but added, "I find her much improved, her faults are those of youth."[33]

The reason for the law prohibiting travel by blacks to the North was that abolitionists in that part of the country had been inducing slaves to leave their masters. George Noble Jones reported on one such incident in Boston in May 1836: "The abolitionists still continue their diabolical deeds. A negro girl belonging to a Southerner who had been putting up at this house [the Tremont Hotel] was last night enticed away." Jones believed that he knew how to deal with abolitionists: "They have been having a convention here and I am told that they are much provoked at not being noticed in any way. I believe neglect will more effectively destroy them than opposition or strong measures."[34]

After spending some time in New York, Mary and her party traveled through Canada and New England in the company of George Noble Jones and his family. They went first to Montreal and then headed for

Maine traveling through the Green Mountains of Vermont and the White Mountains of New Hampshire. Mary marveled at Franconia Notch and the granite profile of the Old Man of the Mountains described by Hawthorne in his short story "The Great Stone Face":

> We visited the Franconian Notch and galloped up the mountain with six horses, at first I felt a sensation of fear, but it soon subsided and I was lost in admiration and wonder at the contemplation of that great natural curiosity the profile in the Mountain. It is a perfect Roman head, even to the swell in the throat, the lips apart, as in the attitude of speaking. There is something very solemn in the sight.[35]

"How I wished for you during my sojourn," Mary wrote to Mary Few in August. "There is nothing half so sweet as the society of a *contemporary* friend—I begin to think people must number the same years to think alike and feel alike." The travelers spent upwards of a fortnight in Gardiner, Maine, a spot "as quiet as if we were in a *Convent* instead of a Hotel." "The independent habits of these regions would delight you," Telfair wrote to Mary Few. Much time was spent with the parents of George Noble Jones's late wife. "The Gardiners call every day to see us, and contrive to shew us all the beauties of the surrounding country." Mary found her visit to Maine to be most pleasant. "Imagine me seated in an old fashioned Chaise with an *Antiquarian* of a Horse, Emma Gardiner driving to the abode of an humble neighbor to afford me a view of the Kennebec & transact business for herself." On another drive along the banks of the Kennebec, Mary was amused to see a man "navigating the river on a log & paddling all the way" and another "in a boat with a tree instead of a sail to catch the breeze." "Well may Yankee enterprise become a *proverb*," was her reaction.[36]

"The country here is very sweet," Telfair reported to Mary Few. "The Kennebec is a beautiful river, and its shores smiling." When he came of age in 1803, Robert Hallowell Gardiner had inherited a hundred-thousand-acre tract of land on the Kennebec from his grandfather, D. Silvester Gardiner, a leading surgeon of Boston who had amassed a fortune delivering medical supplies to the frontier. Mr. Gardiner rebuilt the mills and wharves originally constructed by his grandfather and turned a remote trading outpost into a thriving town. "This was a wilderness when Mr. Gardiner came to it," Mary wrote, "now it boasts a flourishing village & the surrounding country studded with cottages." It was here that Delia was buried. "I understand he [Mr. Gardiner] gave the ground and ten thousand dollars towards the erection of a church which is a beautiful little gothic building. There poor Delia & George were united, and there her mortal remains rest."[37]

Mary Telfair took an older woman's interest in the Jones girls, who were part of her party that summer. They brought to the surface her nurturing-aunt instincts. "Mary Jones is the very personification of innocence," she wrote. "She seems to extract amusement from a country life. She learned to milk the cows & to row a boat last winter. I hope that a winter in Boston will not *fashionize* her too much." Mary believed that time spent with Mrs. Gardiner was good for Fenwick, the other Jones girl, who, according to Mary, "was at one time devoted to fashionable pursuits." "Emma Gardiner's influence over her is a very happy one; she directs her reading, and her example must have a salutary effect." Mary thought the world of Mr. Gardiner:

> He is quite a model for a Gentleman, so perfectly unpretending and refined, omitting no duty and uniting sterling virtues with excellent sense. How delightful to see such a head of a family. How few men *shine* in that capacity. They seem to think if they furnish *food & raiment* it is enough, without regard to the minds and souls of their offspring. I have found that superiority of character in *real* life gives one a higher standard than any furnished in History or Romance. I think the Gardiners must contrast their Father with the *Insignificants* who cross their paths in the forms of *Dandies* and *Money Makers*.[38]

The party headed down to Boston, and Mary wondered how the noise of the city would agree with her after weeks of quiet and seclusion. They first stayed at the Maverick Hotel on Nahant Island overlooking Boston harbor and then took private apartments at the Tremont Hotel. Anne Clay was staying for a few days in Boston with her sister Mary Gray. Anne joined Mary Telfair's party on a drive to Cambridge. Harvard College had been founded in 1636, and the bicentennial celebration was in progress. The senior Mrs. Jones attended and gave the others a full account. Mary enjoyed her stay in Boston. She shared her reactions with Mary Few:

I am very anxious for you to visit Boston & its charming environs and to know some of the people—they understand how to shew kindness & attention better than any people I have ever known. If we had not taken our stand to remain in *home bred* retirement we should be whisked in every direction—Tomorrow we are going with a pleasant old couple to Salem to visit the Museum there—the next day we go to Lowell to visit the Manufactories and then we shall wind up with a visit to Mr. Lyman's Garden. Mrs. Campbell is to act as our Pioneer.[39]

The Lowell textile mills that Mary and her party visited thrived through the exploitation of female labor. The system was not far removed from the South's "peculiar institution." There is no indication whether Mary was appalled or was taken in by the painted roses over the factory gates. The hours were unbearably long at the Lowell mills, the working conditions abysmal, and the pay a mere pittance. The overwhelming majority of the workers were girls in their early twenties recruited from the farms. The young women lived in company-operated boardinghouses where they were required to be in bed by 10:00 P.M. and to observe specific rules of Christian decorum. After paying for their bed and board, there was little left over from their pay. Church attendance on Sunday was compulsory. The hours of work varied somewhat with the season. In winter the morning bell rang at 5:00 A.M. The girls dressed and took breakfast quickly and began their tasks by lamplight. They stood by their machines for the entire long day. The factory rooms were stifling, and motes of cotton befouled the air. The midday break for dinner was limited to one half-hour. Work continued until 7:00 P.M. Most girls left after a few months to be replaced by other innocents from other farms, but those who did not give the requisite notice could be blacklisted and thus precluded from obtaining another job.[40]

While Mary was staying at the Tremont Hotel in Boston, she received a letter from Mary Few relating a dream that seemed to portend Mary Telfair's marriage. Mary assured her friend that this was not to be the case:

Your dream my dear Mary proved indeed "the baseless fabric of a vision," for no congenial spirit in the form of man or *sprite* has crossed my path of single blessedness—We need a Joseph to interpret such a brilliant assemblage of images. Thank you for your consent to the dream's fulfillment—it would be all important to have your support in conjunction with Mrs. Campbell's on such a momentous occasion, as one of her *cherished hopes* is to see me *yoked*, even if it be *unequally*.[41]

The six-day sea voyage from New York to Savannah that fall on the *Ocmulgee* was enlivened by the company of the Clays and their neighbors, the R. J. Arnolds of Bryan County, who were traveling with their children. Anne Clay would sail some days later aboard the *Louisa*. Mary particularly enjoyed her conversations with the senior Mrs. Clay. She sat for hours with the older woman in her stateroom and enjoyed her company immensely. Mary was unreserved in her praise of Mrs. Clay: "She has natural eloquence & more originality than any one I have ever known; in fact I cannot find words to express my respect & admiration." Thomas Savage Clay was on board with his new bride, the former Matilda Willis McAllister, a girl from Bryan County. Some thought her pretty, but more important for Tom's family, she was very religious. Eliza Clay was a passenger as well. Mary liked Eliza, but could not get close to her. "Eliza I could love *if she would let me,*" she wrote to Mary Few, "but she retreats from my advances and you know I am more of a *retreating* character myself than an *advancing* one." Mary thought Eliza Clay to be "one of the most disinterested of human beings," as evidenced by her attention to her sister-in-law. "Her devotion to Tom's wife was unwavering —poor soul I never saw such a sufferer from sea sickness—she was reduced to the helplessness of infancy." Mary did not think much of Tom Clay's bride. In reporting on the wedding to Mary Few the previous spring, she said of the rather listless young woman, "I hope that she has a *teachable* spirit—if so Anne may do much toward her improvement. It strikes me that she is a *Lapitudenarian.*" The sea voyage did not change Mary's opinion of Tom's new wife. "She is so entirely different from his Mother & Sisters," Mary wrote to Mary Few. "Why did not he take Eliza for his pattern; such a woman would have made him so happy." Tom deserved much better, Mary believed: "He has intellect enough & character enough to have obtained the highest prize in the Matrimonial Lottery, for a lottery it is at best, how could such a man *choose* a blank!"[42]

Shortly after arriving home on November 10, Mary came down with influenza. "I am of such a *sympathetic* temperature that I catch every passing epidemic with as much ease as the canvas receives the breeze," she told Mary Few with good-natured resignation. She was confined to her room for a week. "My Physician recommended abstinence from animal food and tea," Mary wrote, "the former was no hardship but my *mental* nature is so dependant upon the latter that I cannot relinquish it."[43]

During the spring of 1837, Mary was busy with gardening and other domestic pursuits and, as indicated in a letter to Mary Few, was disturbed by the changes in her life wrought by the marriages and deaths of friends:

> What a climate is ours! Yesterday we had summer heat today a winter storm which excludes us from our *Jardin des plantes*— We have a little spot in front of our house which is visited by the early sun that occupies Margaret and myself an hour or two every day—Your Geranium is in full blossom and attracts much admiration; it occupies the most conspicuous place in our little verandah—I am training a hedge not such a one as we saw at Miss Gibbs's farm near Newport, but an humble privet instead of a poetical hawthorn. I wish I had more resources to gild (if possible) the evening of my days. As our friends drop off by marriage & by death, and society loses all its attractions, which it has with me, we require the varied occupations of domestic life to keep us from listlessness and despondency.

The ladies' efforts at gardening were successful, as Mary was able to report later in the spring: "Our shrubbery is the admiration of every body and they come to look at the Dahlias—The grass from being constantly watered has an emerald hue. Some people think us crazy to leave such a spot." Having a bit of ground to cultivate was important to Mary: "I would rather live in a cottage with extensive grounds than in a Palace without it if I were a Lady of high rank instead of simple Mary Telfair."[44]

One day during the spring of 1837, Mary, then past her forty-sixth birthday, became especially introspective:

> The natural indolence and independence of my character keep up a continual warfare almost equal to that of the flesh and the spirit—I never look into myself & see the *compound* of contradictory qualities without feeling an increased indulgence

towards the failings of my fellow mortals. I have lived to find every thing earthly fade before my eyes and to feel that the world contains nothing but my own small family and friends to cheer the dreary waste. I can truly say with Cowper that "the only amaranthine wreath on Earth is Virtue, the only lasting treasure Truth."

She continued her reflections in a similar vein:

> I often dread *stagnation*—We must live *out* of ourselves in order to promote the flow of the benevolent affections—Ennui is woman's direct foe—Nothing I believe but religious principle combined with active duty & bodily exercise can allay its subtle inroads—Intellectual pursuits are no ramparts to protect us from the attacks of that merciless enemy.

At this stage in her life, Mary preferred the simplicity of family gatherings to the trappings of fashionable society:

> The only way to cultivate society naturally is to bring people into your family circle without any parade. I leave it to the gay & fashionable to entertain them with numbers and all the etceteras that follow in the train of tea parties & dinner parties. How could I ever have enjoyed those unmeaning things? But we must go through an ordeal to learn what true enjoyment consists in—We must spend half of life, and be schooled and disciplined by sorrows and disappointments to know how to spend the other half.

"If I were a Catholic," she wrote the following year, "I would desire no greater penance for my sins than to go to a party."[45]

In June 1837 William IV of England died and was succeeded on the throne by his niece Victoria, a girl of eighteen. Her coronation at Westminster Abbey marked the beginning of one of the longest reigns in the history of Europe and the onset of the age that would bear her name. The year 1837 also ushered in a period of economic turmoil that brought financial ruin to many in the United States who theretofore had enjoyed comfort and wealth. While the Telfairs would not be materially affected by the depression, many of their friends would feel its impact most seriously.

12

Financial Panic and Tragedy at Sea

The human species, according to the best theory I can form of it, is composed of two distinct races, the men who borrow, and the men who lend.

Charles Lamb, "The Two Races of Man,"
in *Essays of Elia* (1823)

The financial panic of 1837, which erupted shortly after Martin Van Buren assumed the Presidency, had a heavy impact on Savannah as well as the country's financial centers. During the depression that followed, many of Georgia's banks shut their doors. "I regret to hear of the pecuniary distress in New York," Mary Telfair wrote to Mary Few in the spring of 1837, "they are also very great here." Telfair, unlike Mary Few, was not personally hurt by the depression to any significant extent and could afford to stand above the debacle: "As a nation we are too devoted to money making and needed a check to that all absorbing spirit of the times." Greed was a dreadful vice, in Mary's opinion. "I wish Banks could be torn up root and *branches*," she wrote, for "they have been powerful auxiliaries in producing the present state of morals." As far as Wall Street was concerned, it was "the infected district." Mary wrote from Savannah in June: "The depression here is very great—The Planter as well as the Merchant feels it—the incomes of the former will be diminished one third of what they had been, so much the better for them. The high price of cotton for the last three years was an injury to the seller as well as the buyer."[1]

Mary believed that retrenchment was necessary for everyone. When she expressed this view to her sisters, Sarah replied that if Mary had to retrench, the last thing she would give up was her carriage and horses. "It is certainly the only luxury I enjoy," she admitted. "There is something so soothing to my mind in driving through the woods, listening to the carol of birds as I go along and 'The Harp of the Woods' alias moanings of the Pines." Mary did not believe herself extravagant: "I have to *create* wants & find it as difficult as some to restrain them." Mary's depression reading was most appropriate. She reported on reading a piece on three experiments in living by a Mrs. Lee of Boston, "Below one's means, up to one's means, and above one's means." The Telfairs had no need to retrench. Although Mary was tired of hearing people say to her, "You can afford anything," it appears to have been quite true. Some tried to take advantage of the Telfairs because of their wealth. Mary related one such incident: "I hired an English Gardener who proved a disciple of Bacchus—cheated me and took umbrage because he could not exact more money than he got from others."[2]

Mary placed little value on money as such. "Not that I am a Chameleon and can exist upon air," she wrote, "but I can always accommodate myself to circumstances and be as happy without money as with it." Money could not buy the things in life that Mary cherished most. "It cannot buy friendship, sympathy and a thousand nameless things more to be valued than fine gold," she wrote. "It is *power* to some, but it is *Powerless* to me. I have been shocked at even religious people attaching so much importance to it. The self-indulgence it leads to is so injurious to character. The only balm it brings is when it affords us an opportunity of relieving the indigent." In the same spirit she wrote, "I think that we were a happier & more virtuous people before wealth & luxury poured in upon us—before the revolutionary spirit was extinct." Of course, with her wealth, Mary had the luxury to feel as she did.[3]

Mary Telfair had a number of examples on which to base her opinion that money cannot buy happiness. One struck her as particularly poignant:

I was forced into a train of reflection by the history of a Lady in Carolina who was adopted by the friend of her Mother—this Lady was immensely rich—a widow without a child but confined to her bed for years with an incurable disease—her adopted daughter watched her and devoted her time, thoughts & affections to her afflicted friend. She died lately and left a splendid establishment & *fourteen* servants, 170 thousand dollars in Bank Stock to this adopted daughter—who lives *alone* and whose grief is so great for the loss of her *only* friend that she shuts herself up in her splendid mansion and her fourteen Plagues annoy her incessantly. During a violent thunderstorm last summer she seated herself on the stair case as a place of refuge. What is wealth but an evil to such people; those who earn a scanty subsistence by the sweat of their brows are far more to be envied than the forlorn & solitary possessor of wealth without the talent of diffusing it —for it is a talent to know how to distribute it judiciously.[4]

The Telfairs had other problems to contend with along with the state of the economy. "We have had our share of losses," Mary wrote. "An epidemic upon one of our places swept off many lives & a conflagration lately consumed our Mill & all the lumber ready for transportation; the latter I did not feel but the former was most distressing." The depression continued; indeed economic conditions would not begin to improve until 1840. Mary wrote in the spring of 1838, "Planters quake for their crops—Though I am so unfortunate to be a *Plantress* I am never troubled about *failures* in that line. If like the Patriarch I can find food & raiment for them [the slaves] I never trouble myself about *money*." Here Mary evidences once again her belief that the family's ownership of slaves did not constitute the exploitation of human beings against their will. As far as she was concerned, she and her sisters were there to care for these people, to house them, clothe them, and feed them. They were to be treated kindly, but of course they must work. As Mary had heard so often from the pulpit, this was in the natural order of things.[5]

Economic woes gave rise to materialism on a national scale, an obsession with wealth that Mary deplored. She found that it had even rubbed off on the very young. She commented on this situation to Mary Few:

I never talk of the degeneracy of the age except to one or two of my contemporaries—You & I can look back to our Greenwich days when *Calculation* was only understood in Arithmetic; now children lisp (not in numbers) but such a one is so *rich*—Last winter a little child at school said Alberta need not *learn fast*—she was so rich that she might be a long time at her studies. Have you ever known such an instance of *precocity*—It is enough to make the rich envy the poor whose children may escape contamination in one way.[6]

Mary was struck by another instance of precocity in the very young: "A child called here the other day about 8 or 9 years of age—crossed his legs like an old man and asked me the following questions: Have you made a good crop—How many bags of cotton? I *was confounded*, and resisted my natural inclination to tell him those were improper questions."[7]

Dishonesty went hand in hand with materialism, and to her dismay, Mary Telfair found dishonesty all about her:

> If I were a "*Coelebs in search of a Wife*" I should be almost afraid of making a selection from the circles of haute ton for fear of not getting an *honest* woman. There was a time when I thought stealing and lying confined to the uneducated, but I have lately become so enlightened as to find the latter very common among some persons who stand very high in society—Alas! poor human nature it is "frail as the leaf upon the stream"—"and changeful as a summer's dream."[8]

Frances Few Chrystie had given Telfair much to ponder with her account of thievery and excess among the fashionable set in New York even as the depression continued to plague the country:

> I hear & see & know enough of what passes to fill me with astonishment—*gentlemen* putting their fingers into the Basket & helping themselves to money and *ladies* going from house to house and stealing silver & whatever else they can lay their hands on!!!! What will not the extravagance of a fashionable life lead to? Mrs. Brevort the beloved friend of Mrs. Marsh had a fine fancy ball the night before last—800 people were invited & all that went were in assumed characters. There were queens, Cupids, Paul Prys, monks, nuns & I know not what. Josephine says it was delightful & that nothing could be more entertaining; some of the characters were well sustained & very witty & the costumes of the days of Louis 14 & 15 generous and elegant. Even great grandmothers were there with hair craped, fuzzed &

powdered & raised half a yard above the head—& there was vanity & folly & nonsense enough. Mrs. Marsh was to have made one of the company but her evil practices were detected a fortnight beforehand. Her friends are endeavoring to make it appear that she is deranged. She has avowed herself a Catholic & they have taken her to a nunnery in Maryland. One of her sons is so much afflicted that he will not leave the house.[9]

The economic disruption that hit the country did not interfere with the Telfairs' plans to spend the summer of 1837 in the North. Their financial position remained sound. Mary Telfair wrote in June of the family's intention to leave for New York later that month. The sisters had made arrangements to take rooms in a small establishment in accordance with Sarah's wishes:

Sarah's physical temperament shrinks from an *airy* boarding house. Mrs. Helmes's *long table* connected with the clatter of knives and the play of the breezes does not suit her, and my *mental temperament* is opposed to a crowd. I am never so much alone as when surrounded by merry faces. I cannot be cheered by what cheers most people, and when I see people growing old clinging to a certain sort of excitement it fills me with wonder & compassion.[10]

With the advent of the coastal steamers that sailed from Savannah to Charleston and then on to Philadelphia and New York City, these vessels became the preferred means of transportation for those who made the annual sojourn to the North. Mary Telfair made her summer voyage by steamboat at least as early as 1822. The vessels were large and comfortable, and some found the trip pleasant and restful. Mary did not. She and her sisters traveled to the North by steamboat in June 1837 in the company of Uncle and Mrs. Jones and Anne Clay and her family. "I have never been to sea with Anne," Mary wrote, "I know her only as a *Lands Woman* of the highest order." There was a crowd of four hundred on board. "I think the *evils* of traveling greatly increased by its facilities," she wrote of the voyage. "When people depended upon sloops & stages for transportation they were not likely to be jostled out of their existence."[11]

Before going to New York City that summer, Mary and her sisters spent some time in Philadelphia. Their cousins from South Carolina had moved there permanently. Mary perceived that they took little interest in Philadelphia society. Indeed, she thought that they lived as "cloistered nuns." She realized that it was difficult for people who were not young to form new friendships. Yet they were strong women, the kind that could be in imminent danger from a fierce storm at sea and bear it with tranquility. Mary admired their *"strong nerves* and *masculine courage."* The lodgings that Mary and her sisters booked in Philadelphia that summer were in Gerard Row behind Chestnut Street. It was a long walk from there to their cousins' house and an even longer one to the Marshall House, where the Jones party was staying. Their accommodations were quite pleasant, however. "We have two delightful bedrooms communicating," Mary reported, "and this petite Maison is as clean & quiet as if the Shakers presided over it."[12]

Mary Ewing Ritchie was living in Philadelphia with her aunts. While in Philadelphia, the young woman developed a devotion to the sermons of the Reverend George Washington Bethune, the pastor of the Dutch Reformed Church, who had become popular for the power and devotional quality of his orations from the pulpit. Bethune was not only an inspiring preacher; he also was an exact student of theology, a poet, and the author of several well-known hymns. He was a devoted fisherman and in 1846 edited and published anonymously the first American edition of Izaak Walton's *The Compleat Angler* (1653). Mary Telfair had attended one of his talks in Savannah when he was a young man just beginning his career. Mary Ritchie persuaded her to go to hear this remarkable clergyman. After all, she did enjoy a good sermon. Mary would hear Bethune preach several times that summer and would come to know him socially. They became sufficiently well acquainted to exchange visits and dinner invitations. It was only natural that the Telfairs, as members of the East Coast aristocracy, would be welcomed into the home of Philadelphia's leading churchman.[13]

In the nineteenth century, cemeteries had become places of recreation and reflection. While in Philadelphia, Mary and her friends visited Laurel Hill:

> We have taken a drive to Laurel Hill Cemetery—The situation is lovely on the serpentine Schuylkill but it is not to compare to Mount Auburn [Cambridge, Massachusetts]. There is

something though saddening yet salutary to the mind in viewing those mansions of the dead. They speak loudly to us of our
own mortality and we know not how soon we may lay our heads
beneath the cold earth's silent breast—"Where sorrow's tears no
more are shed no more the ills of life molest." The group at the
entrance representing old Mortality on the tomb his Poney and
Walter Scott contemplating both is very affecting—it carried
me back to the happy days when I read that beautiful tale and
caused me to contrast the present with the past. Sculpture is
certainly an ennobling art and ought to be employed only on
elevated subjects.[14]

Mary planned another bucolic visit while in Philadelphia, this time
to the *Jardin des Plantes*. She was sure that Mary Few would enjoy
the gardens and commented, "Our early propensity for flowers fostered in Greenwich Garden seems to cling to us." She later noted
Hannah More's observation that "the last feelings that linger around
the hearts of old persons are the love of flowers and of children."[15]

Mary Telfair could not make up her mind whether she preferred
travel by sea or by land. The discomforts of the overland trip to and
from the North were great, but Mary seemed able to bear them.
"Give me Terra Firma with wretched accommodations, dreary pine
woods & dilapidated towns in preference to steam upon the briny
waves," she wrote on an occasion when travel by land seemed the
lesser of two evils. Mary's description of the discomforts of a trip by
private carriage to Savannah in the fall of the year in the company of
her sisters and cousins (the Carolina/Philadelphia Telfairs) seems to
have been written with a sardonic smile on her face:

> For the three last nights I have slept in my clothes so *airy* were
> our apartments. Cousin Eliza compared me to a Sister of Charity
> with my black shawl over my head, closely pinned under my
> chin. The Fleas lacerated my body and the filth set me on a regi-
> men not the most favorable to the improvement of a Dyspeptic,
> viz Eggs and Potatoes. Margaret says nothing can be eaten with
> safety upon this road without a *case*. I proposed to her *Sausages*.
> My *genius* has been *disciplined* my memory exercised by count-
> ing miles by day & counting hours at night and keeping upon
> the alert to read sign boards and inquire about cross roads.

There were two frights during this trip that Mary felt worthy of note:

> The night we slept at Suffolk we were aroused at nine o'clock from our slumbers by the sound of the drum & fife. Presently we heard the Virginia jig struck up, and such a *pounding* in the room below, screaming, etc. etc. They continued their revels 2 hours & then went to the next Tavern. The extremes of society meet—for instance the Virginia jig & Mazurka & "the swift Gallapade." Fright the second—In crossing a dilapidated bridge over a river the boards with *chasms* between, Cousin M & myself got *the shivers*—We both felt faint at the height & looking at the water below—Our Carriages went through the ford—However we did not tumble—I never can look down from an eminence without being giddy.

Mary wished that she were stronger and braver:

> I have felt more than ever on this journey my want of *manly* qualities. I have often regretted that I was not trained to business & I now add to that regret that I did not learn to manage the restive steed & to fire a pistol. I never had a horror of masculine women being always sensible of my want of physical strength & courage and to quote from Miss Goddard & Anne Clay, "I have passed the age to care about being called a lovely woman."[16]

In November 1837 Mary Telfair was in Savannah enjoying the company of old friends. "Sarah Cecil is living life over again in her great nieces & nephews—*lucky for her,*" she reported. "Catharine Bulloch is absorbed in her adopted children. I expect Mr. B & herself here this evening to eat oysters with us." "We have some one stepping in every evening to see us," Mary wrote. "Ours is a *harbour* for married men and we have concluded that they are a great deal more agreeable without their wives than with them." There was a visit from Justice James Moore Wayne and his wife and son that was worthy of mention:

> The Judge and *Judgess* with young Harry came a few evenings since & passed it with us. Mrs. Wayne & myself talked of Mary Few. I like her all the better for *understanding* and *appreciating*

you. I told Catharine Bulloch it was a proof that she was not thoroughly a *Woman of the World*. I do think her a woman of excellent mind and temper and eminently fitted for society.

There were other quiet evenings such as the one in December that Mary described to Mary Few: "I have just finished a letter of three pages to Geo. Jones and with tired hand and exhausted intellect I again wield my pen in your service. The trio are seated around a wood fire, Sarah *ruminating*, Margaret reading, and I scribbling to one who I know excuses all *blunders* and *blots* as well as crooked lines."[17]

As Mary Telfair entered her late-forties, she seemed to take less interest in life. It was a constant struggle to overcome listlessness and despondency. Laments such as these crept into her letters with increasing frequency: "Frances writes me that she feels too old to make new friends, and so do I. She has spirits to recommend her and what a powerful recommendation it is. I feel mine ebbing every day, and the want of interest in every surrounding object increasing." Periods of depression were nothing new to Telfair. Often in past years she would have a "deep fit of the Blues," or as one of her friends called them the "azure Daemons." Mary called them "sombre fits." On one occasion as a young woman, she sought Mary Few's understanding for not having written. "I felt dull and spiritless and I was aware that my feelings would have imparted a melancholy hue to my pages" was her excuse. There were times when her pages were indeed melancholy. Once, upon learning of the death of one of Mary Few's friends, she went on at great length to bemoan life's trials:

> How many changes take place in a few months, and what melancholy ones! But it is necessary that we should be weaned from this world; after all there is no happiness, no substantial enjoyment to be found in it, often, very often when I reflect on the mutability of human affairs, the trials and sorrows we are subject to in our earthly pilgrimage, I feel ready to exclaim, "how weary, flat, stale, and unprofitable, seem to me all the uses of this world."[18]

Medical wisdom in the nineteenth century, such as it was, held that maiden ladies were more prone to physical and mental illness than women who married and bore children. It was believed that there was a special interconnection between the female reproductive organs and the functioning of other parts of the body. The womb, it was thought, was somehow tied to the central nervous system. Motherhood was woman's normal destiny, and a woman whose reproductive organs remained unfulfilled could expect to suffer various ills. Perhaps Mary Telfair's single state did have something to do with her dark moods. She herself believed that the cares of unmarried women were much lighter than those of married women and that this gave them "more time to brood over ideal misery."[19]

Mary could be subject to wide swings in her mood—one day somber, the next gay. She had been subject to mood swings even as a child. On one occasion she wrote to Mary Few, "I cannot say with you that childhood was not a happy period with me. I was *too happy*, and yet I was subject to extremes of gaiety & sadness." She admitted to having "fits of giggling" and to be "full of extremes either *crying* or *laughing*." Mary thought that the best antidote for the blues was to keep busy: "I pursue my avocations with unremitting ardor—it is a maxim with me here if I am not amused to be employed, for I find when idle my thoughts take a melancholy turn." "Active employment" was the remedy that she prescribed for Mary Few when Few had her own periods of depression:

> I am concerned to hear that "Mr. Blue Devil" has been exercising his despotic sway over you of late; do endeavor to resist his powers, as Sarah Haig declares that his *wand* is so *magical* that one wave of it over a *sunshine* face transforms it immediately into a *dismal cloudy* one—whenever I am seized with a *gentle* fit of the blues she inveighs so bitterly against my *hideous* aspect that I am compelled to look *serene* although all within be *dark & troubled*—the best remedy for that *unhappy* disease is active employment, at least I find it so—avoid *books* and *reflection* as neither prove efficacious—you see I am an *able Physician* therefore beware of slighting my *advice*.[20]

Mary Telfair was charmed during the winter of 1837–1838 by the company of Robert and Anne Bolton. Anne was the daughter of the Reverend William Jay of Bath and the sister of the architect for the Telfair mansion. The Boltons had returned to Savannah from England only a few years earlier. While living abroad, Robert Bolton had served for twelve years as pastor of the Independent Chapel at Henley-upon-Thames following a period spent trying to revive his family's failing mercantile business in Liverpool. Mary thought the Boltons to be excellent people and commended them to Mary Few:

> I would rather encounter interesting people in Savannah than elsewhere because we can lay hold of them here without getting up *an entertainment*—the very name teems with heartlessness. Such people as the Boltons coming among us, so pious, so intellectual, so fresh & natural in their feelings (to those who appreciate character above all things)—resembles the feelings of the weary traveler who encounters an oasis in the *desert—They are just the people for you.* I wish such could oftener cross my dreary path of life. Every year, I may say every day, I feel less disposed to listen to *chatterers.* Mr. Bolton I hear recovered only 5,000 dollars from the wreck of his patrimony—but he is richer than those who count many thousands.[21]

Mary Few became acquainted with the Boltons when they moved to New York. Mr. Bolton received holy orders from the Episcopal bishop of the diocese and became the minister at St. Paul's Episcopal Church in East-Chester, New York. After disposing of his property in Savannah, he purchased an estate in New Rochelle, where in 1838 he constructed a stone house in the old English style following plans suggested by his friend Washington Irving. This fine residence came to be known as Pelham Priory. There he established a parish school, which became a highly regarded educational institution. Bolton caused to be built nearby a stone church, which was consecrated in 1843 as Christ Church. There he served a devoted congregation. Mr. and Mrs. Bolton returned to England in 1850, determined to be near the Reverend Jay in his declining years. Bolton became chaplain to the Earl of Ducie, a post that he held until failing health forced him to resign. He died in November 1857 at the age of sixty-nine. Anne Bolton died two years later at the age of sixty-five.[22]

With the passage of years, Anne Clay had grown in Mary Telfair's estimation. She wrote thus of her friend in the spring of 1838:

> Anne Clay passed several days in Town last week—She paid me two delightful *tête a tête* visits. The freshness and originality of her mind is delightful—her conversation equal to an instruc-

tive and entertaining book not *"French mémoires"* but a fine moral essay—She realizes my beau ideal of a *public* unmarried woman —The world has set her upon a high eminence & she has strength of character & mind enough to sustain her upon the elevated height without danger of becoming dizzy and tumbling head-long from it. I love a *matronly* single woman.[23]

When transatlantic steamships began to provide transportation to Europe on a regular basis, the Telfair sisters were eager to make the trip abroad. Some worried about hijackings, as Mary Telfair reported from Philadelphia in 1837: "A panic has been struck here by the report of a Pirate having boarded a ship for Liverpool. Several of the most respectable families here went in her—their relatives of course are in a state of suspense & misery." Mary and her sisters were invited in 1838 to join a group of their friends on a voyage to Europe, but at the time Sarah's health was too delicate for them to accept the invitation. "I suppose there is nothing talked of in New York but the great British Steamers," Mary wrote. "What an eventful age we live in!"[24]

Travel by steamship was not without its dangers. The *Pulaski*, named for the Polish count who died in the Siege of Savannah, was put on the route between Savannah and Baltimore. Justice and Mrs. Wayne and Harriett Campbell were on her maiden voyage, and Mary Telfair and her party had planned to take passage from Norfolk to Savannah in the fall of 1837, but wound up instead on the *South Carolina*. The following year, the *Pulaski* left Savannah on the afternoon of June 13, touching at Charleston before sundown to take on the rest of the passengers booked for the trip to Baltimore. At eleven o'clock on the warm, starlit night of June 14, while under steam off the coast of North Carolina, her starboard boiler exploded, killing many passengers outright while they slept in their berths and throwing others into the sea where they drowned. The vessel split in two, with the surviving passengers waiting in each half to be rescued and taken ashore to Wilmington, North Carolina. There was much anxiety as to the identity of the survivors when news of the tragedy reached Savannah several days later.[25]

Mary and Margaret Telfair had come close to being on this ship, and so might well have lost their lives in the accident at sea. In a reminiscence Charles Seton Henry Hardee gave one version of the ladies' close call:

I have heard it said that the two Misses Telfair, very wealthy young ladies belonging to one of the most prominent families of the city, had taken passage on the *Pulaski*, but finding that a gentleman and his wife, belonging also to another very prominent family of the City, with whom they were not on friendly terms, had also taken passage for the same trip, the Telfair young ladies canceled their engagement, and thereby perhaps saved their lives, while the lady and gentleman spoken of lost theirs.[26]

Letters to Mary Few confirm that Mary Telfair and her sisters did intend to be on the *Pulaski's* fateful voyage and that they had canceled their reservations and rebooked on the same ship for the sailing that was scheduled to depart from Savannah on June 27, 1838. There is no evidence, however, to support the rumor that their failure to leave as scheduled was motivated by the presence of the couple referred to by Mr. Hardee. Telfair's version of the event is set forth in a letter written shortly after the tragedy occurred:

I wrote to you my dear Mary that we expected to sail in the *Pulaski* for Baltimore on the 13th. We had even registered our names on the list of Passengers and were making every preparation to go when an unaccountable feeling came over me to wait for the 27th—the principal inducement for delaying was that Mrs. Jas. Hunter suddenly made up her mind to go on that day —And now that I look back upon the train of circumstances that operated to induce us to withdraw I can only say it was merciful Providence that arranged it all. I always feel a degree of sadness in leaving home & returning to it which I cannot express, but on this occasion it was overwhelming. I told my Sisters that I felt as if a calamity was impending over us, and that I felt that I could not leave home. How strange! how mysterious are our impressions at times. Is it not a convincing proof that there is a communion between the visible and invisible worlds.[27]

The daughter of Justice James Moore Wayne came close to making the voyage. According to Mary Telfair, "Nothing but Mary Wayne's irresolution kept her from going on the 13th. Her Parents urged it & she could not towards the last make up her mind to separate from them." The Clay sisters and their brother might have been on the *Pulaski* as well if they had chosen to wait a few weeks to take this modern steamboat to New York rather than sailing on the brig *Savannah* on May 28. Dr. John Cumming and his wife, who in years past had been the Telfairs' frequent traveling companions, were not so fortunate. They were among the passengers who did not survive the disaster. Mr. Hardee's reference to the prominent couple whose presence had led the Telfairs to cancel their trip probably was to Dr. and Mrs. Cumming. They had once been great friends of the Telfairs, but apparently there had been a falling out. Whatever ill will existed, it is highly unlikely that it caused the ladies to revise their travel plans. Mary Telfair appears to have been consistently honest with Mary Few, and it is doubtful that she would have told her friend of her foreboding if it had not been a true story. Mary had this to say concerning the death of Dr. and Mrs. Cumming: "I cannot tell you how their loss affects me. I have never harboured any feelings towards them of enmity, and truly can I say that sorrow not anger at the past was all I felt & my prayer was that they might be shielded from trials such as we have bitterly experienced."[28]

The people of Savannah were devastated over the loss of so many relatives and friends when the *Pulaski* went down. The Independent Presbyterian Church was clothed in black. Mary Telfair described her feelings and those of her fellow citizens:

> Our community is plunged into woe. Every countenance is sad—every heart is filled with grief. We can think and talk of nothing but the loss that we have sustained—so many precious souls in the twinkling of an eye ushered into the presence of their Creator. We look to second causes when we ought to look to the great first cause and say "*Thy will be done.*" It seems as if Death had entered every dwelling here so profound is the sympathy for those who perished as well as those who survive. The news papers will give you all the information. The most affecting circumstance of a private nature related here was the death of Mr. Woart the Episcopal Minister & his wife. They were five days on a fragment of the wreck and died of exhaustion he to the last moment exhorting & comforting them. His wife followed him in a few moments. They were lovely in their lives and in Death were not divided.[29]

The Telfair ladies finally did get to northern climes that year. They traveled in the Northeast and paid a visit to Niagara Falls. The return trip from New York to Savannah in the fall was made by the overland route. It was fatiguing, as usual, but as she described it to Mary Few, Mary Telfair endured it with good cheer:

We had a most fatiguing journey home due to mud & mire. The roads were in a wretched condition but we were enabled to catch three hours sleep every night which was most refreshing to wearied nature. When we got to Washington City we found some difficulties in the way of getting an extra & our party took the mail stage which was a fortunate circumstance for nothing but frequent changes of Horses could have enabled us to proceed. We bore the fatigue astonishingly well indeed are improved by it. We were detained a week in Augusta owing to the river being too low for steam boats to pass down from the City. So we plucked up courage to again take the stage. You will say could that be Mary Telfair riding all night. I have indeed changed my nature in some degree. Necessity is a Stern Master. I have found him so in many instances. I have often told you how much mental agony it has cost me to think and act for myself and for others. Sarah & Margaret always in cases of difficulty accord me the *right of primogeniture*. To return to our expedition we converted the *mail* stage into a female one and Mrs. Hunter & ourselves with Sarah Campbell, Mrs. Lloyd & Elizabeth Gardner with one young Lad who we never saw before filled it. When we got to the Spring Hill the way worn cavalry refused to pull the stage and three times they halted before they got to our gate. It poured down rain. Our servants espied our difficulty & came with umbrellas. What with extra clothing & close packing we had to be lifted out.[30]

As if Savannah had not seen enough of death in 1838, Dr. George Jones died in November shortly after Mary Telfair and her sisters had completed their exhausting journey home. Mary made no effort to conceal her grief in relating the sad news of her uncle's passing:

The sad feelings which we always experience at this season of the year in returning to a Home once so happy & so cheerful has been deepened by the death of our old & valued friend Dr. Jones—he expired two days after he landed; his disease became fixed upon his lungs—he was surrounded by all his family—

what a comfort to them to know that he died in his home and was received into the sepulcher of his Fathers. He was a good Man and died full of years; latterly he lived very much above the world and I believe was fully prepared for eternity. He had been a kind friend to us when we most needed sympathy & kindness and he seemed to be the only link to the past. He could talk to us of those we had never seen & those we remembered well. His children [Letitia, age fifteen, and George Frederick Tilghman, age eleven] were much afflicted at his loss and they are the finest pair I have ever seen. They watch over their Mother with unremitting care & devotion.[31]

Savannah was more quiet than usual following the *Pulaski* disaster. "I fancy there will be no gaiety here this winter," Mary wrote. "The loss of the *Pulaski* has thrown a gloom over this place that will not soon be dissipated and ought not—alas!" The magnitude of the loss was vividly brought home by the sight of the vacant seats in church. Mary spent much of the week before Christmas of 1838 engrossed in the writings of William Wilberforce, the British statesman and author. "What a man and what a Christian!" she thought. "I am perfectly in love with the character of Wilberforce," she had written earlier. "I feel as if I knew him intimately—his friendship with Miss Hannah More seemed so pure it seems to me his friendship must have been more valuable to her than all the fame gathered from her works." Books of a serious nature continued to be more appealing to Mary than novels. Charles Dickens' *Oliver Twist* had come out in serial form in 1837, but Mary had decided not to read it. She explained her reasons to Mary Few: "I know myself well enough to *avoid Oliver Twist*. My life is too secluded a one, and my temperament too excitable to allow myself to read works of absorbing interest—You may *venture* but I dare not, for my mind is still too undisciplined to permit me to wander into the fairy fields of Imagination—not even to peep into them." Later, when Sarah was reading *Nicholas Nickleby* and found it delightful, Mary reaffirmed her lack of interest in the works of Dickens: "I do not feel any more disposed for a humorous work than for a *Tea party*. I never was in my gay days fond of humorous reading. I loved it passionately in Conversation but it has lost its charm completely even as a spice on that ingredient." While Sarah laughed and wept over the adventures of Dickens' characters,

Mary immersed herself in a biography of Martin Luther, which she thought "a very sweet production." "I continually associate Luther with Dr. Franklin," she commented.[32]

Christmas of 1838 was celebrated at the mansion on St. James Square. On Christmas Eve, Mary wrote to Mary Few:

> This is Christmas Eve dear Mary when all the world here are preparing for their family feasts. We three are seated in our quiet parlour drawn close around a large wood fire for the weather is intensely cold and no sound invades my ear but the report of pop guns. Our Plants are all covered with moss which gives them a hoary look. They are my pets and I hope will reward me with their sweets when Spring unfolds her charms.

Catharine Bulloch's Christmas offering that year was a "pathetic little tale by Charles Lamb—she says to make me weep."[33]

Mary Telfair and her sisters had a Christmas tradition that they observed each year. It took precedence over all else:

> Catharine Bulloch invited me to dine with her & Mrs. Wimberly Hunter the gentlemen of the family having spent the day out of town but I declined. We also declined Mrs. Telfair. It is a custom with us to cook a large dinner for our Servants; each has the privilege of inviting their friends. So they keep the festival and are made happy by it.[34]

Visitors came to call during the holiday season. There was a delightful visit from Anne Clay. "She was in her happiest mood and she made me for several hours *forget myself,*" Mary wrote. Mary learned from Anne that Tom Clay's newborn son had been named Joseph Clay. "With what joy he must have been hailed," thought Mary, "reviving a name so venerated and loved by them all." Mary's conversation with Anne Clay was interrupted by the arrival of Justice James Moore Wayne, who was passing time in Savannah during the Supreme Court's Christmas recess. "Anne became *Stately* and he *Judicial,*" Mary wrote. Mary did not think that the Justice would ever call Anne "my child" as he did her. "She certainly inspires profound respect in the Lords of Creation," Telfair marveled.[35]

The years 1837–1838 had been eventful for Mary Telfair. There had been the financial turmoil that gripped the country, the *Pulaski* tragedy, and the death of Dr. Jones. But Mary had managed to maintain

1. Sarah Martin (Mrs. William) Gibbons, Mary Telfair's grandmother. Courtesy of the Telfair Museum of Art, Savannah.

2. Sarah Gibbons (Mrs. Edward) Telfair, Mary Telfair's mother. Courtesy of the Telfair Museum of Art, Savannah.

3. William Few, friend of Edward Telfair. Courtesy of V. & J. Duncan Antique Maps & Prints, Savannah.

4. Thomas Gibbons, cousin of Mary Telfair. Courtesy of V. & J. Duncan Antique Maps & Prints, Savannah.

5. Dr. George Jones, Mary Telfair's uncle. Portrait by Rembrandt Peale, c. 1838. Courtesy of the Telfair Museum of Art, Savannah.

6. Alexander Telfair, Mary Telfair's brother. Courtesy of
the Telfair Museum of Art, Savannah.

7. One-room Litchfield Law School in Litchfield, Connecticut, attended by Josiah and Thomas Telfair, and Tapping Reeve's house (1773), where classes were first held. Photograph by Charles J. Johnson, Jr.

8. Mantel in drawing room of Telfair mansion. Courtesy of the Telfair Museum of Art, Savannah.

9. Sarah Telfair (Mrs. George) Haig, Mary Telfair's sister. Courtesy of the Telfair Museum of Art, Savannah.

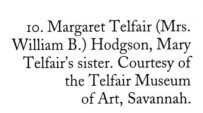

10. Margaret Telfair (Mrs. William B.) Hodgson, Mary Telfair's sister. Courtesy of the Telfair Museum of Art, Savannah.

11. Margaret Long (Mrs. Thomas) Telfair, wife of Mary Telfair's brother. Courtesy of the Telfair Museum of Art, Savannah.

12. Mrs. William Few, friend of Mary Telfair. Courtesy of the Telfair Museum of Art, Savannah.

13. John Macpherson
Berrien, United States
attorney general and friend
of the Telfair family.
Courtesy of V. & J. Duncan
Antique Maps & Prints,
Savannah.

14. SS *Savannah*, first steam-driven ship to cross the Atlantic. Courtesy of
V. & J. Duncan Antique Maps & Prints, Savannah.

15. William B. Hodgson, husband of Mary Telfair's sister. Courtesy of the Telfair Museum of Art, Savannah.

16. Medallion of Mary Telfair by Henry Dmochowski. Courtesy of the Telfair Museum of Art, Savannah.

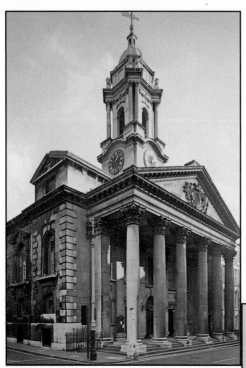

17. St. George's Parish Church, Hanover Square, London, where Margaret Telfair and William B. Hodgson were married on July 11, 1842.

18. Independent Presbyterian Church, Savannah. Courtesy of V. & J. Duncan Antique Maps & Prints, Savannah.

19. United States Supreme Court Justice James Moore Wayne.
Courtesy of V. & J. Duncan Antique Maps & Prints, Savannah.

20. Mary Telfair in advanced age. Courtesy of the Telfair Museum of Art, Savannah.

21. Hodgson Hall, Georgia Historical Society, Savannah.
Courtesy of V. & J. Duncan Antique Maps & Prints, Savannah.

22. General Alexander B. Lawton, lawyer who wrote Mary Telfair's will.
Courtesy of V. & J. Duncan Antique Maps & Prints, Savannah.

23. General Henry Rootes Jackson, law partner of Alexander R. Lawton. Portrait by Carl Ludwig Brandt. Courtesy of the Telfair Museum of Art, Savannah.

24. Chatham County, Georgia, Court House.
Courtesy of V. & J. Duncan Antique Maps & Prints, Savannah.

25. Carl Ludwig Brandt, artist and first director of the Telfair Museum of Arts and Sciences. Courtesy of the Telfair Museum of Art, Savannah.

26. Telfair and Hodgson memorials at Bonaventure Cemetery, Savannah. Photograph by Charles J. Johnson, Jr.

her routine of summers in the North and quiet winters in Savannah. Despite periods of depression, she had enjoyed her books and the company of old friends and had continued to find satisfaction in living a life that was wonderfully ordinary.

13

Ordinary Pleasures

The sober comfort, all the peace which springs
From the large aggregate of little things.
Hannah More, *Sensibility*

Mary Telfair once wrote, "Trifles make the sum of human life," and it was in trifles that she often found the most pleasure. She had the capacity to recognize beauty in those small, everyday events that might pass unnoticed by those consumed with ambition and material pursuits. For example, there was a charming little incident during the winter of 1838:

> This morning while arranging my new family [some new plants] upon the steps of the Portico, to catch the morning sun, a beautiful fugitive in the form of a canary bird lighted near me. I called Man Friday to my assistance and we got an empty cage and put sponge cake into it and the sweet warbler was enticed in it so my prize was secure. The rightful owner will no doubt soon apply for it.[1]

Mary marveled at the clear blue sky under which she drove one fine day in January 1838 on an excursion to the Isle of Hope:

> C. Bulloch took us to the Isle of Hope 9 miles from town to rusticate a day at a little cottage belonging to Mr. Bulloch. We formed a female group—The day was clear & very cold—a sky whose cloudless blue might *shame* even that of far famed Italy's. The ride was sweet & the number of druidical oaks with the

moss drooping mournfully from their branches made me wish for you [Mary Few] knowing that a dash of melancholy mingles with your admiration for Nature in all her forms.[2]

Apart from a fugitive canary or a crisp winter day, some pleasures that for Mary Telfair were ordinary were beyond the reach of most of her contemporaries in the South. The urban elite traveling in the Northeast each summer could enjoy pleasures unknown to planters and their wives who ventured no farther than the nearest market town. An ordinary pleasure for Mary Telfair, such as a visit to Niagara Falls, might be an impossible dream for a woman tied to the soil. When Mary visited the falls in August 1838, she was so moved by their beauty and power that she copied this poem into a commonplace book that she was keeping at the time:

> Niagara Hail! before thy watry shrine
> The high, the low, in humble rev'rence bow
> And all acknowledge that a hand divine
> Alone could form thee as we see thee now.
>
> Thy pearly crest and robe of silvery dew
> No art can equal, and no skill surpass
> While emerald green of hourly changing hue
> Spreads itself o'er thy ever moving mass.
>
> Thy rushing torrents never ending roar
> Shakes the huge rocks and makes the mountains quake
> But heedless of the whole thy waters pour
> From the bright bosom of the placid lake.
>
> But while upon thy verdant banks we stand
> And gaze enraptur'd on thy mighty fall
> We see in thee the great Creator's hand
> And pay him homage as the God of all.[3]

In planning their 1839 visit to the North, the Telfair ladies decided to take their niece Margaret with them once again. Margaret had been enduring "a most tedious illness" and looked "wretchedly." The plans were to sail on the *Trenton*, to pass a few days in New York, where they would visit the Fews and buy some summer clothes, and then proceed to Newport, where Margaret would have the benefits of a bracing climate. All went according to plan. Telfair and her party visited New York and then made the voyage through Long Island Sound to Newport:

> We had a very smooth and pleasant night on Monday my dear Mary, so very tranquil were the waves and so gentle the breeze that we passed Point Judith without the consciousness of turning that prominent point. At eleven o'clock the moon poured her calm light upon us and we landed at Newport at 7 o'clock and are now at Mrs. Rathbones where the Minises lodged in Thames Street—a horrid situation and noisy, but the house is clean and our Landlady very kind and obliging so much so that we dislike the idea of leaving her, particularly as she is a woman of limited means and has known better days.[4]

At that time, Newport was a favorite resort of Southerners. Indeed, it had long been a virtual Southern colony. It was just beginning to be discovered by New England intellectuals and the business leaders of New York. "We have received calls from all the Bostonians here who seem to be clever people some of the elite of Boston among them," Mary reported. "They are the only people that I feel *safe* in renewing old acquaintanceship with. The New Yorkers with the exception of *l'ancien régime* I steer clear of, they are so heartless and flippant."[5]

Newport was a town of unpretentious rooming houses and quiet cottages, a place to savor ordinary pleasures. There was not yet any of the ostentation that first came to Newport during the gilded age of the 1880's, when August Belmont and other captains of industry built their massive "cottages" along the cliffs on Bellevue Avenue. Newport was a place to enjoy sea breezes, the sound of the crashing surf, and expansive views from the cliffs. "The Margarets go into the surf and enjoy it," Mary wrote. "I have not ventured in yet, but have engaged an *old* man to duck me." Mary must have been speaking of Bailey's Beach, where mixed bathing was permitted. At First Beach, bathing was restricted to women in the morning and men in the afternoon. Newport was a place for picnics and leisurely carriage rides. The climate was ideal. "Newport is cool when every other place is warm," Mary wrote. "We wear our cashmere shawls, and find them very comfortable." Sarah Haig, however, sometimes found the Newport air too keen and occasionally would complain of rheumatism.[6]

It was during the summer of 1839 that George Noble Jones was making plans to build his Newport cottage. He struck a great bargain in the purchase of the lots on which he would build his summer house, no doubt aided by the continuing depressed state of the economy. The property was on a high ridge isolated from the center of town. Jones chose the property in part for its openness on all sides to the Atlantic breezes. Only farms and marshes surrounded the land, and no stands of trees interfered with the views west to the harbor and east to the sea. Jones chose as his architect Richard Upjohn, a founder of the American Institute of Architects and one of the country's leading exponents of the Gothic Revival style. It was Upjohn who designed the mansion that the Gardiners built in Maine to replace the one destroyed by fire in 1834. Jones specified a cottage containing eight chambers, besides two or three sleeping apartments for servants. He added the request that "the water closets be inside—also a bath." An interesting feature of the house was the aviary, a bow-windowed room over the front door that Jones would fill with parrots, macaws, and other colorful birds. The house was completed in 1841 and in years to come would be the scene of the relaxed, informal social life that Jones and his family so much enjoyed.[7]

Margaret Telfair and Sarah Haig decided that they should build a cottage as well. Instead of passing the time in Newport in a rooming house with a group of strangers, they could enjoy their stay in the comfort of their own home. Mary wanted no part of the scheme. She lacked the enterprise for such an endeavor: "The fact is I have lost all my enthusiasm and do not feel as if I could be *wound* up to any thing. I am like a watch that has lost its main spring—So the cottage will end in talk if it rests upon my decision—Milton said one *tongue* was enough for a woman & I think one *Home* enough for a woman— every *addition* where the affections are not enlisted gives trouble." Yet Mary could appreciate her sisters' point of view: "I am very sensible that a boarding house life however private 'chills the genial current of the soul' and domestic feelings can only flourish under the shelter of one's own roof." Perhaps if they did have a place of their own she could concentrate better on her reading: "Volumes are devoured in my own quiet room in Savannah where pages are read elsewhere. Does not that speak in favor of a cottage somewhere if not at this second Isle of Wight."[8]

According to Mary Telfair, there was an overabundance of women at Newport:

This is a *feminine* place fifty women to four men at Miss
Mumfords 9 women to *no man* in this house. This you will say
does not suit my *Capuchin* taste. What a gossiping must be kept
up. Mrs. Stout & Mrs. Gracie rumor allows (and you know she
has a forked tongue) are said to keep up a *brisk volley* at Mumfords—I heard a piece of wit of a Georgia Lady which I will give
for your edification—She said she disliked Newport because all
the Houses were *Hen* Houses—for my part unless *Roosters* have
ideas I would rather dispense with the flapping of their wings
and idle crowing.[9]

Mary Telfair must always have remembered Newport as it was in
the summer of 1839 when George Noble Jones paid tribute to Savannah and its ladies in a toast composed in a well-structured rhythm:

> Fill high the sparkling bowl,
> A rich repast is here,
> And music for the soul,
> With songs to mem'ry dear.
>
> Sweet friends we soon must part,
> The moments glide away;
> Yet whisperings of my heart,
> Bid you still longer stay.
>
> Wanderers from our home,
> In distant climes we are;
> But wheresoe'er we roam
> We'll think of Sav'na dear.
>
> Yes, Sav'na is my toast,
> And whether far or near,
> It still shall be our boast
> To drink to Sav'na dear.
>
> Another toast I'll give
> Before I take my chair,
> Long may ye happily live,
> Savannah's daughters fair.[10]

One can imagine the chuckles of the men and the blushes on the
cheeks of the Telfair ladies as they acknowledged this tribute from
their gallant cousin.

As planned, Mary Telfair and her party returned to New York after their stay in Newport. The heat of the summer had passed, and they wished to visit friends in the city. They went on to Philadelphia, where they spent the autumn waiting to receive a favorable account of health conditions in Savannah before returning home. As it was, the news brought reports of several cases of yellow fever and continued warm weather, which Mary knew would aggravate the disease. They passed the time serenely seeing only their cousins, who visited twice a day, and the widow of Noble Wimberly Jones II. While Mary, her sisters, and their niece Margaret were in Philadelphia, they received word that the other daughter of Thomas Telfair, Mary Cobb, had died on October 7, 1839. She was only twenty-six at the time of her death. The previous spring, as she was taking leave of her elder niece in Savannah, Mary Telfair had a presentiment that she and the young woman would never again meet on this earth. So it was. Mary Cobb's mother and her daughter Alberta had been seriously ill as well, but they were fortunate enough to recover. Mary Telfair regretted that she had not been there to afford Mrs. Telfair assistance and sympathy. Her niece Margaret grieved deeply over the loss of her sister and reproached herself for not having been at home when the end came. Telfair believed it fortunate that Margaret had not been in Georgia, however, for she probably would have fallen ill as well, and Dr. Joseph Clay Habersham had warned that she could not survive another attack of fever such as she had the previous spring. With her mother dead, little Alberta, a child of five, was left to the care of her grandmother.[11]

The trip from Philadelphia to Savannah was made in three and one-half days. "It seemed like the flight of a bird so rapidly were we whirled along by cars and steamers," Mary Telfair wrote of the journey. Always one to make fun of her own embarrassment, she related an incident that occurred along the way:

> Never commend me for tact again. I have forfeited all claims to it which the following *narrative* will fully testify. Curwan (good soul) or rather good *body* thinking one man to seven women was literally a fulfilment of prophecy brought a friend of his into the cars to introduce to us as a *Help* on the journey having the evening previous given me a biographical sketch of his friend in *the Briggs* style—"Clever man—lost his wife in the *Pulaski.*"

Without looking at him I bowed with my veil down. After we landed a man not exactly *comme il faut* in appearance approached me with an air of brusquerie and said do you keep on the boat? I replied yes—are you the agent? No I am the person Mr. Curwan introduced to you in the car. I lost my *balance* and began to *talk at random.* He gave me his arm and we trudged off together, I shocked yet internally convulsed with the ludicrous position I occupied. He shewed himself a man of sense not to keep aloof after my unfortunate blunder and was really useful in helping us up & down the steps of the car and carving for us at table.

Mary admired the courage of the Clay ladies in traveling home that fall without being accompanied by a man or a man servant. "How desirable it is to be able to act independently of the Lords of Creation," she thought. She admitted that the height of her courage was to ride alone in an omnibus.[12]

During her annual journeys up and down the East Coast, Mary Telfair frequently came upon interesting fellow travelers. With her Southern openness, she had no trouble striking up conversations with other passengers who appeared to be respectable. Mrs. and Miss Rutledge, of the Charleston Rutledges, had joined her party on the trip south in 1839. Mary informed Mary Few that she found Miss Rutledge quite delightful:

> I was charmed with her mind, character, and manners—none of that ridiculous pride which characterizes the *Aristocracy* of Carolina. Religion has given the finishing touch to a character naturally lovely. I should like you to know her; she is a woman after your own heart. There is an atmosphere about some people that reflects excellence. We feel our moral natures as much vivified after being with them as our physical after we leave the cold side of Broadway for the sunshine on the other or the cold north winds for the balmy South which now breathes a second spring.

A gentleman encountered on the same trip was not quite as charming:

> We met Mr. Legare in the steam boat and enjoyed his *"colloquy divine"* for several hours. He is very brilliant in conversation but a complete man of the world. It is impossible for a public character and a Belle to possess a heart. Where you will say is

Mary Telfair's *Mantle of Charity*? One of "the woes that wait on age" is to be able to read too clearly the volume of human nature.[13]

That winter, after their return to Savannah, the Telfair sisters often sat of an evening in the candlelight of the oak room and reminisced about their summer and fall in Newport, New York, and Philadelphia. There was something about the "incognito life" that Mary led in Newport that was very agreeable to her. She felt comfortable in New York as well. "A large City has many advantages over a small one," she thought. "The freedom from restraint, the consciousness of our actions not being commented upon, and our remarks repeated, gives a sort of independence to our movements." Mary Telfair would look back on the frequent trips by horse-drawn omnibus that she made that autumn from her New York lodgings to the Few residence, which since September 1833 had been at 239 Ninth Street. There she and Mary Few had many of the long "confabs" that they enjoyed so much.[14]

During her quiet periods that winter, Mary reflected upon her life and the sorrows that she had endured. Thus she wrote on a fine day in January 1840 when the pure white japonicas were in bloom:

> My enjoyments are now *few* and *simple*—It is very true that after we have known sorrow in its most blighting form, that circumstances the most agreeable have a depressing effect by recalling past happiness. "Trifles light as air" strike upon the chords of memory like the breeze upon the Aeolian Harp—So much is life made up of associations & recollections and happy they who are too much engrossed with active duties to dwell too intensely upon the past.[15]

At this stage of their life, Mary and her sisters were leading a quiet existence. "What shall I say to you to amuse or interest you," Mary wrote to Mary Few, "for we are so *detached* from the multitude that we are like people on an Island—an old friend steps in occasionally of an evening which interrupts our reading, and that is the extent of our *dissipation*." A rainy day in April could be spent pleasantly and usefully in the oak room. On one such day, Mary Telfair could be found musing over the character of Madame de Staël, whose intellect and talent for conversation she so admired:

A rainy day my dear Mary is favorable to darning stockings, gossip, and writing letters. I have just put a bobbinette dress upon Milton to protect him from the rude touch of *unpoetical* fingers and am tired of the society of Lord Brougham's great Men. Apropos what a sweet Portraiture he has drawn of Caroll of Carollton and he has given a more favorable sketch of Madame de Staël than any other of her Biographers—he has thrown the mantle of charity over her weaknesses and made her very interesting. There is something in deep attachments that always touch my heart, and hers for her Father seemed to be interwoven with her nature. You would not suppose that so worldly a woman and one so dazzled with her own brilliant reputation could have felt for any one so pure and strong an attachment not even for a Father, as holy as the tie is—Well I suppose every one has a redeeming trait in character if we can only discover the hidden treasure under the rubbish.[16]

Some days were "all business" consisting of "buying, shipping, cutting out work, etc." Of course there were visits to church:

I went in the morning and again at night to hear Mr. Fuller a Baptist clergyman once a Lawyer and highly esteemed at the Bar for his talent—He belongs to the *aristocracy* of Carolina and I recollect him fourteen years ago an Elegant fashionable young man just from College—about 6 years ago he became seriously impressed and has ever since devoted himself to the cause of Religion. He is a very solemn Preacher and appeals very strongly to the feelings—he relates anecdotes in the Methodist style and his zeal and animation exceeds any one's that I have ever heard.[17]

Mary Telfair's devotion to the Presbyterian Church did not keep her from helping out a friend in raising money at the Episcopal Fair. "I have been *coining* money," she wrote, "not nefariously with my hands, but *with my brain*—this enigma requires solution":

Louisa Bulloch applied to me to assist in writing letters for the Episcopal Fair. A Post office was established at one Table and she was *Post Mistress*. I took *the dignitaries* of the land to write to, and under the feigned name of Agnes was traced and had a beautiful note sent to me with a ten dollar bill. Another replied to another of my letters with a five dollar gold piece.[18]

Nor did her Presbyterian faith prevent Mary from attending the consecration of the new Episcopal church on Johnson Square. The magnificent Greek revival structure with its six Ionic columns had been two years in the building under the direction of the rector, the Reverend Edward Neufville, and a building committee of distinguished parishioners. The day of consecration was the third Sunday in Lent, March 22, 1840, and the inclement weather did not prevent the church from being filled to capacity with members of the Christ Church congregation and representatives of the other churches in town. Bishop Ives of North Carolina and old Bishop Chase of Illinois led the celebration along with other members of the clergy. Bishop Chase had called on the Telfairs while in town. "Bishop seems to be very evangelical and perfectly devoted to his calling," Mary wrote, "but he is *tinctured* with the bigotry of his sect." The discourse that Bishop Ives delivered on the occasion was eloquent and appropriate according to Telfair. She took umbrage, however, at his assertion "that the Episcopal was the true Church handed down from the Apostles." She went on to write with tongue in cheek, "I think if we go to the *root* of things that the Baptist is the true Church for our Lord himself was baptized & his Herald was a Baptist." She probably was expressing her true feelings when she concluded that "form is nothing—it is the spirit alone that can purify the heart."[19]

Mary continued to laugh at her own foibles. This always had been one of her most attractive traits. She enjoyed telling this little tale:

> I attended a meeting for forming a society to get a domestic Missionary for the neighboring counties where I met an *old acquaintance* who had changed her name twenty years ago. I proposed her name as a member of the board and addressed her by her first husband's name—Catharine Bulloch shook her head. I thinking that she objected to the woman insisted upon Mrs. King being put down. The woman looked aghast first, then angry. Still I persisted until Catharine pinched me & whispered her name is Lewis—A *reaction* took place, and I burst into a fit of laughter and set off several others to the amazement of the *Changeable* Lady—who must have thought me in a state of Rip Van Winkle who had been asleep twenty years.[20]

Ann Wallace arrived in town during the spring of 1840. Mary's enthusiasm at seeing her old friend was evident from her description of their meeting and the pleasure that they shared during Ann's stay in Savannah:

> You may imagine our surprise at seeing Ann Wallace a few mornings since in the Market Square walking up with Ben Stiles—We hailed her and tried to lure her home with us but as she had decided upon going out to the Clays the following morning she consented to take a drive with us to Bonaventure and returned & passed the evening with us—She enjoyed the sight of our shrubbery (the roses being in full bloom) and seemed to have enjoyed her visit to the Cummings at Augusta.

While Ann Wallace was in town, she went with the Telfair sisters, Catharine Bulloch, and Mary Gray on an expedition to the Isle of Hope. This excursion led Mary to joke with Mary Few, "You will say I thought that Mary had done with *hope & anticipation* and so I have for believe me that I live upon *realities* and the only *romance* that is left in me is my love for my friends."[21]

The Telfair ladies returned to the newly consecrated Christ Church in May to attend the marriage of George Noble Jones to Mary Wallace Savage Nuttall, a Savannah heiress who was the daughter of Thomas Savage and the widow of William B. Nuttall. Mary Telfair called her the "Empress of Florida" and joked that her "roll of Lovers [was] even *longer* than her *rent roll*." Jones's first wife, Delia Gardiner, had been dead for several years. Mrs. Nuttall's little girl was at the wedding, and Mary Telfair thought it was the dearest thing ever when young Mary Nuttall said that she wanted to be called Mary Jones so that she would continue to have the same name as her mother. Mary Telfair described the wedding in some detail:

> On Monday at 8 o'clock in the morning before our breakfast we were at the Episcopal Church. *Toujours pret* being my motto we went at ½ past 7—the ceremony commenced at 8—There were 70 persons present below, and the Gallery pretty well filled with family servants—two of ours took advantage of kinsfolke & went. We were all seated in the pews near the altar in silent expectation when the chancel door was thrown open & the bridal pair locked arm in arm entered followed by the near relatives of each. Four generations stood before the Altar. I am losing my *nerves* for I was *unmoved* until a *thrill* came over me

when I saw the child looking like an Angel—its face bathed in tears and as white as the cambric frock it wore. Its Mother thought I will have other objects to share her love—it is better for you and yet its feeling was too touching. When Mr. Neufville pronounced George & Mary man & wife the dear little creature burst into tears & said afterwards that she had no mother unless people would call her Mary Jones—it was not right for her Mother to have a *name* different from hers.

The bride and groom went off to Charleston in the steamer an hour after the ceremony. The Telfair ladies, their great-niece Alberta, their maid Judy, and the bride's mother and daughter planned to follow and join them in Charleston the following Monday.[22]

The Telfairs made their 1840 journey to the "North Countrie" in early June. Sarah's doctor would have preferred for them to have waited a week or so for she had been quite ill with a fearful cough that she attributed to taking off the flannel handkerchief that she had worn all winter. "I am anxious about her," Mary wrote. "She is the thinnest person I have ever seen and so depressed yet she goes on fulfilling her domestic duties. She says that she must be occupied." Their great-niece Alberta accompanied them on the journey. She had been ill as well, suffering from a bilious fever, and Mary hoped that the trip would be good for her health. She was eager to get the little girl into the surf at Newport. A portion of the journey was made by rail. Mary found it tedious and lacking in privacy:

> Car traveling is very stupid no conversation nothing to beguile the time. Mrs. Walburgh said she turned to look at me in the night and there was my head and Bishop Donne's together —he was my neighbor and unconsciously *sharing* my pillow— it happened to be a *clean* head—but there were some I should not like to come in contact with. A rail road car is a perfect democracy.[23]

The Telfair sisters and their great-niece visited friends in Baltimore and then passed a week in Philadelphia in order to spend time with their cousins, who were leading a "monastic life" in rooms looking out upon a stable. Mary had developed a dislike for Philadelphia: "The very atmosphere (don't think me uncharitable) breathes formality, stiffness, & coldness, an atmosphere ungenial to my nature for every day I value freedom from the trammels of conventional form more & more." As much as she loved her cousins, Mary was glad when the week was over and she and her party could head for the tranquil climes of Newport, where young Alberta would spend part of each day in a small school run by a most respectable lady.[24]

Alberta was proving to be a handful for the Telfair sisters that summer, but Mary felt that the girl had real potential. Her grandmother had been far too indulgent with her. Mary, in the role of the wise maiden aunt, felt that she was in a position to exert a strong positive influence on her great-niece:

> She has been so accustomed to have her own way that we find it very difficult to manage her. Sarah throws it on me and I am pretty firm. I reason with her but can neither bribe or coax her but she requires nothing but firmness for she is a very good child and wonderfully obedient to us considering that she has been so indulged. Her precocity of mind amazes me. The little creature seemed so delighted on the journey. The ocean seemed to fill her with wonder. She asked me if I did not think it a monstrous world to be made in six days. She is very fond of reading and in good hands would make a solid character.

The ideal place for Alberta, Mary thought, would be the Boltons' school in New Rochelle. "How I wish the Boltons could have her for 10 years," she wrote, "but her Grand Mother will never part with her & the climate would be too severe for her."[25]

During the autumn of 1840, Mary had the opportunity to spend some time with Mary Few at her home on Ninth Street in New York. The hours spent with her oldest and dearest friend were precious, ranking among the best of life's small pleasures. "I left New York and Ninth Street this autumn with more than usual regret," Mary later wrote to Mary Few. "Every year binds me closer to the friends I love—My spirit is with you every evening as you surround the tea table where we were wont to enjoy ourselves so much." The return trip to Savannah was made through Philadelphia and then to Baltimore, where the ladies passed a few days receiving visits from old acquaintances. There Mary ran into a gentleman on whom she had once had a crush, "the beau ideal of [her] youthful imagination Commodore Warrington." She was shocked by the way he had changed over the years: "Time is a sad innovator and changes the human Form as much as it ravages the human heart. The hero of other days looks like a round tower—as broad as he is long."[26]

The overland passage to catch the boat at Wilmington, North Carolina, had its usual discomforts:

> We left Baltimore on Tuesday and traveled rapidly under a serene sky by day and a refulgent moon by night—"Sleep that knits the revelled sleeve of care" chained me so completely that I lay upon the floor of the car with a carpet bag for my pillow and slept profoundly to the amazement of our little party which occupied a small car with seats so narrow that we could scarcely preserve our equilibrium. My *Natural Tournure* was in my way for the first time in my life.[27]

Mary's description of the remainder of the journey and her arrival in Savannah reflects the joyless feelings that so often gripped her upon returning to an empty house after a long absence:

> We found the Wilmington Boat full to overflowing and were glad to rest our wearied limbs upon the Cabin floor—This going to & fro prevents fixed habits if no other good results from it—We tarried one night in Charleston and reached our home on Friday night between 8 and nine o'clock—No one to welcome us but servants—Silent, dreary, and desolate it always is for weeks—We three took our tea around the hearth—You might have heard a pin drop—About 8 o'clock Catharine Bulloch & her husband came in—Hall & Mrs. McAllister. We tried to rally our spirits but could not—Every change is saddening—What in youth gives buoyancy in after life depresses.[28]

Mary's spirits continued to be low the following winter. Mary Few had come up with the idea of printing a weekly newspaper to which her friends could contribute. She called it "The Whisperer." She asked Mary Telfair to submit something original. Telfair did send her friend a poem by Joseph John Gurney called "The Evening Star," but her mood was such that she did not feel up to composing a piece of her own:

> I need not tell you my dear Mary that the first page [the Gurney poem] is intended for your weekly paper. If you would send me a number I might contribute, but I do not know exactly

whether grave or gay, moral or severe suits best the character of the Whisperer—My imagination is so limited in its range now, that I find it difficult to unlock the portal of my brain so much are its hinges *rusted* by sadness—If you could peep at our trio *planted* down in one spot, with no cheerful associations you would wonder how I could even *squeeze* any thing so *huge* as an *Omnibus* out of my contracted brain—I believe that I have not laughed but once this winter, and that was elicited by some droll remarks by Catharine Bulloch.[29]

Mary did come up with a poem for her friend's paper, and it was a poem about an omnibus. Indeed, it was a much-improved version of a poem that she had written years earlier and had preserved in her commonplace book. This time she worked into the verse the theme of the omnibus as a leveler, an instrument bringing together all members of society:

The Omnibus

The praises of the omnibus I sing
Tis such a glorious independent thing—
It lessens distance by its wondrous speed
And to the weary proves a friend indeed
There old acquaintances we often greet
And much loved friends with great delight we meet
Tis true the Canaille gentle folks annoy
But where is comfort found without alloy?
Not on this wide Earth fair, and ample bound,
Can pleasure free from sorrow long be found
A picture it presents of human life
Its *ups and downs*—its toil and strife
All classes seek this wonder of the age
The high, the low, the silly, and the sage—
Fit emblem for our Democratic Nation
Where no regard is paid to rank or station—
The Laundress there her basket holds with care
Next to the States Man proud with lofty air
The hapless Emigrant from Erin's shore
In filthy garb and miserably poor
Sits next a belle in pride of youthful bloom

Deck'd in a velvet hat and waving plume
Ye patrons then continue to be kind
And always bear the Omnibus in mind.[30]

Mary had matured and mellowed in her assessment of people, for in this version of *The Omnibus* the "hapless Emigrant" sitting next to the young belle is a symbol of democracy rather than the object of scorn that he was in the poem that Mary had written as a young woman.

Happily, Mary Telfair had not mellowed so much as to have lost any of her acerbic wit. She kept her tongue in her cheek as she reported to Mary Few on a visit from a mutual acquaintance:

We had a *reminiscence* of Sing Sing this morning in a call from Genl. Ward the *cidevant* Colonel. Father Time has added flesh or more *genteelly* speaking corpulence to his figure but not impaired his good looks. Entre nous in *mannerism* he is almost equal to Judge C but no *soft, low tones*, he is no *Whisperer* though he might furnish some sketches for the *Whisperer*. I was afraid to ask after Mrs. Ward as "*men get into the habit of losing wives*" and he did not advert to her.

Telfair merrily continued her discourse on General Ward:

The General intends calling to see you and politely offered to be a bearer of my letter. I have too much of *Scotch* sincerity to send this by him—you remember the old Highlander's remark, "I canna break bread in a Mon's house & laugh at him afterwards." So after my *free* account of the *Soldier & Statesman* I would not dare to make a *Mail* of him.[31]

On Sunday morning, February 28, 1841, at the new Christ Church, Mary attended the consecration of the Reverend Stephen Elliott as the first Episcopal bishop of Georgia. Anne Clay was a friend of the new bishop, and she had come to Savannah from her family's plantation in Bryan County to attend the ceremony. Bishop Meade gave the sermon, and it had a powerful impact on the congregation:

Bishop Meade's sermon was *perfect*. He is a plain Evangelical Preacher and thrills the heart while he awakens the conscience —not one metaphor and scarcely any gesture. Yet the attention is riveted by the solemn truths that he declares. I have never heard a Presbyterian or Methodist Preacher denounce the pomps

and vanities of the world more than he does all public amusements and private revelings and banquetings as he styles evening
parties and quite justly. He denounces fine furniture and orna-
ments in dress as unbecoming the professor of religion. I told
Margaret I felt as if I could have *gouged* the solitary diamond out
of my brooch. Anne Clay from her account was undergoing the
same process at the same time. She said shall I take the flowers
out of my bonnet but on reflection she thought that she would
continue to wear them.[32]

Later that winter, Mary had the pleasure of having Bishop Elliott
as her dinner partner. She described the evening to Mary Few:

> We emerged from our winter's seclusion last week and took
> a family dinner at Mr. Robt. Habershams. . . . It was my good
> fortune to have Bishop Elliott next to me (he is a nephew of
> Mr. Rich. Habersham) and the very best specimen of a Southern
> Gentleman that I have seen for years. He talked delightfully on
> a variety of topics, religion blending with them all. It seems
> uppermost in his thoughts—As a Preacher I think him superior
> to Mr. Kirke, Dr. Hawkes or Mr. Bethune—Simplicity & sin-
> cerity mark him for their own—He is just the sort of Man that
> you would approve of for in him is taste, genius and sensibility
> —all consecrated to religion—His Wife is congenial in every
> thing *but looks*—she is very plain & he very handsome—but I
> have lived long enough in the world to estimate the treasures of
> a pure heart and a fine intellect beyond all personal ambitions.[33]

On March 4, 1841, William Henry Harrison was inaugurated President of the United States. The hero of Tippecanoe, with his running mate on the Whig ticket, John Tyler, had ousted the incumbent
Democrat, Martin Van Buren, with a successful campaign that built
up the old general as a man of the people who lived in a log cabin
and drank hard cider. Inauguration Day was the coldest in history,
and Harrison refused to wear a hat or overcoat as he addressed the
crowd for an hour and forty minutes. The cold that he caught at his
inauguration turned to pneumonia, and exactly a month later old
Tippecanoe was dead and John Tyler was President. Mary Telfair
thought the public mourning for the late President to be overdone:

Yesterday the obsequies of President Harrison were *performed* —for it seemed a *performance*. A little child observed that it was the first *false* funeral that she ever attended. I have an instinctive aversion to parade and always feel sad at the season of public celebrations. I understand that Judge Berrien delivered an eloquent eulogy at our church and that Braham sang a requiem. If departed spirits are permitted to witness the scenes of earth how insignificant must the homage of mortals to a mortal appear, particularly if he whom they eulogize is enjoying the glories and honors of the eternal world.[34]

The following summer, Mary Telfair and her two sisters had the honor of being presented to President Tyler, a pleasure beyond the ordinary even for women of the Telfairs' elite standing. This event took place through the good offices of the President's daughter-in-law, to whom the Telfair ladies had formed an attachment when she visited Savannah some years before.[35] It must have been a cherished moment. The new President was a Southern aristocrat, a champion of states' rights who held that the Constitution did not empower the federal government to interfere with the institution of slavery. He was a man with whom the ladies could identify.

The time spent in Washington in the summer of 1841 before moving on to New York was interesting in other respects. Hours were spent in the Senate chamber by Mary, Margaret, and their friend Catharine Bulloch, who with her husband had accompanied the Telfair ladies to the capital. At this time the Senate was sitting in the old chamber that it would use until 1859, when the new Senate wing that was added to the Capitol was ready for occupancy. The Senate was still a small body. With only twenty-six states in the Union, it had fifty-two members. Sarah had no interest in spending her time in this fashion. She could not understand how her sisters could sit for five hours listening to men wrangle. As prominent Georgians and daughters of a late governor and member of the Continental Congress, the Telfair ladies were not ignored by the political leaders of their state:

> The Georgia delegation have been very attentive in calling & offering to conduct us to see the Lions. I have been satisfied in hearing them *roar* in the Senate. The Bank question is now discussing with great warmth. We have heard Mr. Clay—Benton,

Rives, Buchanan, and several others of inferior note. Mr. Clay I prefer to any—he is clear & concise & perfectly natural—I now wish to hear Mr. Calhoun & then I shall be satisfied with *Senatorial* eloquence.[36]

Mary was saddened by her brief visit to the House of Representatives:

> We went for 10 minutes to the House of Representatives and there witnessed a *melancholy* sight—John Quincy Adams seated among boys—he seems determined to swallow the *dregs* of public life. How much more dignified to act *the Patriarch* and "*sit under his own vine & fig tree.*" Retirement is good for the young, but to the aged its blessings seem indispensable.[37]

Mary had no confidence in politicians. "*Cunning & intrigue* are their *watch words,*" she wrote. What she called the "empty honors" of public life did not move her:

> Were I a Man I would rather be Washington Irving beautifying my grounds and *raising chickens* than Mr. Clay receiving the plaudits of admiring crowds—There is an excitement in political life that seems to swallow up the finer feelings—I doubt if Politicians love their wives and children as much as other men.[38]

Washington was a small town in 1841. There was a sense of intimacy between the leaders and the public that would be all but impossible today. The great Senator Rives was staying at the same rooming house as the Telfairs. Mary reported that he "sits next to me at dinner and gives me his *cheek music* freely." She liked him. "He is very agreeable and *free from flourish,*" she wrote. Mary established a nodding acquaintance with the First Lady:

> I received a bow of recognition from Mrs. Tyler in the lobby of the Senate chamber yesterday. She looked sad. I heard a friend of hers say that she had no enjoyment in the grandeur that surrounds her & that she behaves sweetly in her new situation, very modest & retiring—I do love people who can bear prosperity meekly.[39]

The intellectual stimulation of her visit to Washington seemed to have snapped Mary Telfair out of her blue funk. The adventure that she was about to undertake, moreover, would be the most stimulating experience of her life to date. It would leave her with little time to be gripped by ennui. There was a major surprise in store for her as well.

14

Travel and Romance

Travel, in the younger sort, is a part of education; in the elder, a part of experience.

Francis Bacon, "Of Travel," in *Essays* (1625)

On September 30, 1841, a passport was issued by the State Department to "Miss Mary Telfair and two sisters—attended by a servant."[1] The ladies were off for Europe on a trip that Mary had dreamed of for years. Before leaving on the journey, she arranged for three servants at the Savannah residence—Judy, the cook; Coomba, Judy's chambermaid-daughter; and Coomba's husband, George—to temporarily enter the service of William Neyle Habersham and his bride of just over a year. They could be a big help at the Habershams' new home at the corner of Harris and Barnard streets. A mild illness that Mary incurred in New York prevented her from sailing on the *George Washington* on October 7 as planned. Albert and Frances Chrystie and their two children, Mary and William, with whom the Telfair sisters were to travel, would not hear of leaving without them. Instead, the entire party sailed for Portsmouth on the *Quebec* a few weeks later.[2]

The trip abroad had not been long in the planning. Young Mary Chrystie, a student at the Boltons' academy in New Rochelle, had been in dreadful health. She had been forced to leave school because of her illness. Her parents had planned to take her to Savannah for the winter, but Mr. Chrystie changed his mind and decided that a longer sea voyage would be more beneficial to his daughter's health. The family would go to Europe instead. The Telfairs, with whom the Chrysties were to have stayed in Savannah, decided to go with them rather than break up the party. Frances Chrystie's great desire was to spend the winter at Montauban in the south of France. This had been a bastion of French Protestantism, a Huguenot stronghold where three congresses of the reformed churches of France had been held in the sixteenth century and where in 1621 the people of the town withstood a siege by Catholic troops under the command of Louis XIII. There was a religious society there to which Frances hoped to obtain an introduction. Her alternative plan, should the weather not be propitious in Montauban, was to spend the winter in Nice, then a city within the Kingdom of Sardinia.[3]

The November crossing of the North Atlantic was marked by squalls and calms and storms, but the ship was strong and the captain skillful. Frances Chrystie felt no fear until she and her companions entered the small boat that transported them from ship to shore in Portsmouth. The approach to the port was made through the Needles and the Solent, the narrow passage between the English mainland and the Isle of Wight. The passengers could see ivy-covered Norris Castle in the distance to starboard. They knew that Victoria had resided there before ascending the throne. The Telfair sisters and the Chrysties stayed in the best inn in Portsmouth and then took a post coach to Southampton. Along the way, they passed Salisbury plain, which Mary Telfair thought a "dreary moor." Frances Chrystie thought that there could be nothing more picturesque than the "thatched cottages with the green moss growing on the thatch & the ivy running on the walls." Mary Telfair found "a poetical beauty thrown around every object, from the simple vine-covered lodge up to the lordly Castle." The travelers made an excursion from Southampton to the ruin of Nettley Abbey, which Mary Telfair thought "a noble specimen of Gothic architecture." Frances picked a few leaves of ivy, two daisies, and a buttercup and pressed them in her Bible as a memento of the place.[4]

The weather in England was cold and overcast, and Frances knew that she could not expect her daughter's health to improve in such a climate. Although young Mary's cough persisted, she was eating and sleeping well and enjoying herself exceedingly. After four days of sightseeing in England, the travelers crossed the English Channel to France on the night steamer. The cabins were small and close and the bunks lacked sheets. They all were glad to put their feet on the quay at Le Havre. They continued on to Rouen, where Joan of Arc had been burned at the stake, and arrived in Paris on November 21. There they took up residence at the Hotel Wayram at 28 Rue de Rivoli.[5]

Little did Margaret Telfair dream when she arrived in Paris that it was there that she would meet her future husband, the scholar-diplomat William Brown Hodgson. Hodgson was in Paris at the time on his way to his new post as consul general in Tunis, the capital of one of the Barbary States. According to Hodgson, the meeting was accidental. The two were immediately attracted to one another, and soon, as Hodgson quaintly put it in Victorian fashion, the lady "accepted the offer of my affections." She imposed one condition, however. She would not marry him unless he resigned his post in Tunis. Margaret Telfair was not about to take up residence on the Barbary Coast.[6]

Hodgson was a remarkable person, and it is easy to understand why Margaret found him to be fascinating company. Born in 1801 in Virginia, he was left fatherless as a young boy. He never attended college. His formal education was limited to studies in Georgetown, principally under the Reverend James Carnaham, a future president of the college at Princeton. While there, young Hodgson lived in the household of Georgetown lawyer Francis Scott Key. Books were his teachers and, at the age of thirteen, he completed reading Lucian's *Dialogues in Greek and Latin*.[7] He had an unusual facility for foreign tongues and ultimately would master thirteen languages. Although he never studied at Princeton, in 1824 the College of New Jersey granted him an honorary A.M. degree. Undoubtedly his former teacher had something to do with the award, for the Reverend Carnaham had become the president of the college in May 1823.

As a young man, Hodgson attracted the attention of Henry Clay, then a member of Congress, who secured for him a position in the State Department. There he pursued his studies of Hebrew and Sanscrit as the basis of the Oriental languages. When Clay became secretary of state under President John Quincy Adams, he assigned Hodgson to the Barbary States to assist William Shaler, the consul general at Algiers, and to receive linguistic training. It was Clay's firm belief that it was essential to have language experts in the State Department. Algiers was a walled city, a veritable fortress with guns mounted on the walls and on the citadel that towered above it. It was a maze of narrow streets. Small houses with whitewashed walls and interior courtyards sheltered a population of 50,000. Hodgson arrived in Algiers in 1826. There the young diplomat began his lifelong fascination with the Berbers and their ancient language.

Shaler resigned as consul general in 1828 because of ill health, and for the next year Hodgson was acting consul in Algiers. He returned to Washington in 1830 after Major Henry Lee, son of Light-Horse Harry Lee, was nominated for the post of consul general, a position he would never actually fill. In the spring of 1831 Hodgson was sent to Constantinople with instructions to return with a ratified treaty with the Turks. He was successful in his mission and while in Constantinople attracted the attention of the American chargé d'affaires, Commodore David Porter, a hero of the War of 1812. Porter requested that Hodgson be assigned to his legation as dragoman or interpreter. Hodgson returned to Constantinople in the summer of 1832, having survived along the way a treacherous hail storm on the Bosporus. Porter proved a difficult man to work with. When he sought to have his nephew replace Hodgson as dragoman, Hodgson bitterly complained to the State Department that the young man was unqualified. When Porter cut off his salary, Hodgson countered by selling in the bazaar a horse that the Pasha of the Dardanelles had asked him to deliver to Porter as a gift.

In 1834 Hodgson was relieved of his post in Constantinople and sent on a secret mission to Egypt. Porter was happy to see him go. He wrote to his wife, "my mind is more at ease, I have not that puppy Hodgson to vex me." Hodgson was assigned the task of ascertaining how far it might be desirable and practicable to form commercial relations with Egypt. His mission resulted in a comprehensive report on the Egyptian economy and the relationship of Pasha Mehemet Ali to the Sultan of the Ottoman Empire. Hodgson sailed for Morocco in 1835 bearing gifts to mark the renewal of a treaty between that country and the United States. In 1836 he was serving in London, and the following year he was back at a desk in Washington. In October 1837 he was dispatched on a mission to Lima carrying with him in an hermetically sealed tin box a treaty of peace, friendship, and commerce with the new Peru-Bolivian Confederation. After another stint in Washington, Secretary of State Daniel Webster appointed Hodgson to his first consular post. He was to go to Tunis as consul general.[8]

After receiving Margaret Telfair's promise of marriage, Hodgson went to Tunis to temporarily take up his post. Mary Telfair and her sisters then traveled to Switzerland. "I should like to pass a whole summer in & near Geneva," Mary wrote to Mary Few. "Lausanne is the sweetest spot I ever beheld," she continued. "The hotel that we stayed at was built upon Gibbon's domain, and we saw the tree under which he studied." The sisters toured northern Italy, including the Lake District, and by March 1842 had made their way as far south as Naples. "The state of Religion in Italy is an objection to that country," Mary wrote, revealing once again her Protestant bias. Yet nothing interested her more than the ancient cathedrals that she and her sisters visited during their journey.[9]

In the meantime the Chrysties had taken up residence in Nice. Mary Chrystie died there during the winter. She was only eighteen. As her Aunt Matilda related it to her friend Mary Garrettson, the girl's death was "triumphant." "I never heard of a more peaceful close," Matilda wrote, "her last words were Jesus is with me." Matilda went on to describe her niece's final days: "She spoke of Heaven as her home. My little body she said will rest in that grave yard, but it is no matter—the resurrection day will unite soul & body. Peace she said comes whenever I pray."[10]

Mr. Hodgson joined the Telfair sisters in Rome, head over heels in love with his bride to be. They went together to the Vatican to see the art treasures, but Hodgson only had eyes for Margaret. He later would write in his notebook, "How many of the chef d'œuvres of the Vatican did I fail to see, whilst they were before my eyes. I was in the gallery of the Vatican with Margaret, but I did not see the Belvedere Apollo nor that powerful pomp of statuary the Laocoön. Such is the blindness of Lovers."[11] These were not the words of a lovesick twenty-year-old. Hodgson was over forty at the time, and, though he may not have known it, his future wife was several years his senior.

Two months later Hodgson returned to Italy once again. Traveling from Tunis by way of Malta, he landed in Naples in May 1842 and immediately contacted his friend Mr. Boulware, the American consul general. Boulware had a letter for him from Margaret, written from Florence. "What conflicting emotions did it excite!" Hodgson wrote in his pocket notebook. "After a long and anxious absence of two months, I again have intelligence of the Gentle Being, who is the sole object of my thoughts as she is of my affections." The morning after Hodgson's arrival, Boulware presented him to the king of Naples at a levee held in honor of his majesty's birthday. They arrived at the palace in company with the Chevalier Barbozo, the minister from Brazil who had just negotiated a treaty of marriage between his emperor and the sister of the king. One can picture Hodgson and his friend in court dress, complete with gold lace, knee breeches, and silver-buckled shoes, their swords at their sides. The gentlemen took their places among the members of the diplomatic corps, which was headed by the Papal Nuncio. The dowager queen entered the chamber and was followed by the king and his queen. Shortly thereafter, the count of Syracuse, brother of the king, joined the assembly in the company of his countess and his sisters. At this point, Hodgson and Boulware had exactly the same reaction:

> Mr. Boulware and myself immediately exclaimed what an exact resemblance does the Countess of Syracuse bear to Miss Margaret Telfair! It would scarcely be possible for two persons to be more alike. The same *stature, person, complexion* and *expression.* I confess that I felt proud of *my Margaret—my Countess of Syracuse.* With what intense interest did I gaze upon this noble lady and dwell upon her features, which kindled in my bosom feelings of tender recollection of her the idol of my heart, whom I love so exclusively, so ardently. Ah me! What an age has passed in the two months of my absence! When shall I again see & embrace *my* Countess of Syracuse.[12]

The couple was reunited in Florence, where Hodgson feared he would have little interest in the paintings at the Pitti Palace so enchanted was he with his Margaret. They went with the others to Geneva, where they planned to marry, arriving in mid-June. They discovered, however, that the civil code required a residence of six months for a marriage license to issue, so they all headed for London, where residence in a parish for fifteen days (the time necessary to publish the bans of marriage on three successive Sundays) was the only requirement for a marriage to be solemnized by a dignitary of the established church. From London, Hodgson tendered his resignation in a dispatch to Secretary of State Daniel Webster. He did advise the secretary of state that he would be willing to serve as secretary of legation at the Court of St. James or a continental court. The marriage ceremony took place on July 11, 1842, at St. George's Parish Church on London's Hanover Square and was presided over by the Very Reverend Robert Hodgson, the long-time rector of the parish and the nonresident dean of Carlisle Cathedral. Margaret's sisters and the Chrysties attended the wedding as did Edward Everett and his daughter Anne. The noted orator and statesman was then serving as minister plenipotentiary to the Court of St. James.[13]

Margaret's engagement and marriage were difficult for Mary Telfair to accept. The two sisters had been inseparable for ages, and now a man had entered the picture to alter the balance of Mary's life. How would her relationship with her sister be changed? During the preparations for the wedding, Mary received another blow. News arrived in Europe of the death of her niece, the young woman who also bore the name Margaret Telfair. Young Margaret died at the age of twenty-five, almost the same age that her sister had been at the time of her death. As she did so often when she needed a release for her emotions, Mary Telfair wrote to Mary Few. Mary's letter to her friend told of "the overwhelming shock of our bereavement." The news of the young woman's death was a complete surprise and had come at a time when Mary Telfair had begun to think that her niece might turn out quite well after all:

> It was difficult to believe that one who in the course of nature we thought would survive us should so suddenly so unexpectedly have been torn from us & life so full of hopes and promises to her, who had not experienced the bitter sorrows and disappointments that have clustered around my path. She was the last and only Representative of a beloved Brother—the link that bound me to the world—Her character had sobered down and improved during the last two years, and I hoped to see her a useful and happy Woman contributing too to the happiness of another who fully merited her love & respect—It was a mysterious Providence that snatched her away at this interesting period and laid low the hopes of many—and made desolate her Mother.[14]

The shock of young Margaret's death and the dislocation occasioned by sister Margaret's impending marriage were almost too much for Mary Telfair to bear. "I feel as if I had lived twenty years in the last nine months," she wrote to Mary Few. "Such changes! Two such unexpected events succeeding each other." She had hopes for the success of the marriage, however:

> Frances has written to you respecting Margaret's engagement & marriage and all the circumstances attending it—therefore I

will not enter into particulars—suffice it to say that *I am satis-fied*—She appears to be very much attached to Mr. Hodgson and he has been devoted in his attentions to her—I trust that it will be productive of happiness and if she survives Sarah & myself she will not stand alone in the world. I try to take the most favorable view of it though I find it difficult to look to the bright side of things in this world of care, anxiety, and sorrow— Fears with me preponderate over hopes—Mr. H. is a well edu-cated man and a gentleman in his habits, feelings & manners— His domestic character is yet to be proved—I have promised to let Frances know how that develops.[15]

Immediately following the wedding ceremony, Albert and Frances Chrystie and their son William went their own way. They took the train to Liverpool and from there embarked for New York on July 15. Hodgson and the ladies went directly to Oxford. Mary had been tempted to return to America with the Chrysties:

> I do not allow myself to think of a separation from Frances— it is very trying, and I feel ready to go with her, but taking all things into view I do think it best to remain a year longer—I view Europe as only a School of improvement to the mind, and for that reason I force myself to see sights.[16]

When news of Margaret's marriage reached America, there were smiles and a few raised eyebrows. There also were flutterings of renewed hope in the breasts of some of the spinsters. Upon learning of the match, George Noble Jones wrote from Newport to George Kollock in Savannah, "What is thought of Miss Margaret Telfair's marriage? I presume it must have caused much surprise. The ladies of a certain age are carrying everything before them and are certainly the greatest belles." Mary Few did not know what to make of the marriage and expressed her doubts to Mary Garrettson:

> You have no doubt heard that Margaret is married. She is now Mrs. Hodgson. Mr. H. was Am. Consul at Tunis. She met him immediately after her arrival in Paris & he has been de-voted to her ever since. He is said to be amiable & intelligent. To me it appears a hazardous experiment but perhaps it is only the views of an "Invariable." We must hope that he will add to

the happiness of our dear friends. "A three-fold cord is not easily broken." One of four fold may be still more durable.[17]

For the next several months, Hodgson, his new wife, and his sisters-in-law toured England, Ireland, and Scotland. Before the wedding, they had taken day-trips out of London to Windsor Castle and Hampton Court. On the way to Hampton Court they visited Richmond, which Mary thought the "most beautiful and picturesque spot in England." Mary was charmed by the view of Oxford from a distance. In touring the Oxford colleges, Mary was particularly struck by the beauty of Christ Chapel. She strolled beneath the elm trees lining Addison's Walk and thought it "a fit retreat for the elegant and refined mind of Addison to meditate in." Before leaving Oxford, the travelers visited Blenheim Palace, the seat of the Duke of Marlborough. Blenheim was far too grand for Mary's taste:

> All these things I view with a *Republican* eye and feel disposed to exclaim with Cowper, "Riches have wings and grandeur is a dream." I would rather be Mary Few or Mary Telfair than the Duchess of Marlborough—there is something in the trammels of state most obnoxious to my *free* born spirit, and after all what are the enjoyments of this world at best. I have lived to find it an empty shew.[18]

Time spent in England gave Mary a greater appreciation of the religious freedom in her native land:

> I am more and more struck with the formality of the Church of England and shall return a better Presbyterian and a better Republican than I left it. The liveried footmen bearing the prayer books is too ridiculous, and yet I have heard several most spiritual Preachers in the Episcopal Church—they are like Angels visits few & far between. Mr. Birch [a dissenting preacher] thinks that there is no field for him here [Paris] and returns to England in November. I wish that we could get him to our free land. He mentioned that a Congregation in England threatened to displace a Clergyman for preaching against public amusements. He thinks that the dissenters are persecuted for their zeal. I am rejoiced that we have no established church and that all are permitted to worship God in their own form.[19]

Mary and her party visited the city of Bath and its environs. The Reverend William Jay, at the age of seventy-three, was still drawing large crowds at the Argyle Independent Chapel, where he had been pastor since the year of Mary Telfair's birth. Mary had the privilege of meeting the famous preacher. She described the visit to Mary Few:

> We arrived in Bath this morning and this afternoon I went to see Mr. Jay with my letter of introduction. The servant at the door of the sweet little manse with its flower garden in front took it up & returned to say he was at home and would be glad to see us. We sat an hour with him and I was charmed with his conversation, his countenance, & his manner. He talks in a most unstudied style and you never forget for a moment his sacred calling—for he looks & talks like a minister of the Gospel. I wish that I could remember his beautiful compliment to the Wesleyans—it was to this purpose that at a time when there was great deadness among the Episcopalians and the Dissenters the Wesleyans flew about like angels disseminating the truth.[20]

Hodgson and the ladies went on to Bristol and then to Leamington, where they saw the ruins of Kenilworth Castle. Mary thought Cheltenham the most beautiful town in England, presumably surpassing Richmond. As was always the case when she traveled, Mary could carry herself back into the past. She felt this sense of history quite keenly when she visited "the mouldering abbeys and antiquated mansions of England":

> We identify ourselves with the Poets, Statesmen, and Heroes of the past by visiting their birthplaces. We trace their footsteps in their favorite walks, and enjoy the shade of the same trees under which they wrote and meditated. What a privilege to be able to revive those emotions created by early reading from pilgrimages to the haunts of departed genius![21]

Hodgson and the ladies were back in London before the end of September having first revisited Paris. They shipped some of their belongings to Savannah, care of Robert Habersham. As her tour drew to an end, Mary Telfair reflected on her feelings about Europe and her native land: "I feel towards it [Europe] as I do to a new and delightful acquaintance who refreshes my intellect with *outpourings* of new and brilliant ideas—but to America I have the feeling of an old & cherished friend—I love it with all its faults."[22]

Mary had met a number of interesting people during her year abroad. Mary Few asked her what acquaintances she had made, and Mary attempted to answer her "in as graphic a manner as possible":

Mr. Jay in Bath an hour with him delightfully spent—Dr. Chalmers in Belfast—a green spot in memory's waste—Dr. Wild in Dublin, an author of some repute and an eminent surgeon—Col. Wilson in Paris, British Minister to Lima—a frank social Englishman—he quite won my heart by bringing into our room under his arm a flat band box to shew us an elegant gift he had just purchased for his wife—Most men of his rank would have had a *liveried footman* at his heels, to carry the burden—My measure of greatness is an exemption from *littlenesses*. The trammels of state are to me what a harness is to a wild horse. We were one day in Havre made the acquaintance of a most agreeable Irish Baronet who called early the next morning to see us being on the wing for Paris. Saw Mr. Beasly and liked him very much—he bears the impress of two valuable *commodities* Truth & Honesty. He paid us a very long visit, talked much of Mr. Gallatin and of Washington Irving who he seems much attached to—He called him *Wash*—how unpoetical![23]

Mary Telfair and her new brother-in-law had become better acquainted during their travels and had come to accept one another on their own terms: "Mr. Hodgson is very English in his tastes and habits. He thinks me I believe a perfect *outlaw* from the Court of Fashion—a *very plebeian* in my notions." "There is much in him to like," Mary wrote of Hodgson, "and I hope that he will give up diplomacy and become a useful private character." The two were different from one another in many ways, but they were becoming friends.[24]

Hodgson and the ladies sailed for New York in October 1842, and after spending several days in the city in the company of friends, began to wend their way in the direction of Savannah. They went first to Philadelphia, where Hodgson was introduced to Cousin Eliza and Cousin Margaret. They were very much pleased with him. While Mary was with her cousins, Mr. Bethune paid a call, and Sarah entertained him. Hodgson took Margaret to meet his mother in Virginia, and Mary and Sarah made a pleasant journey to Baltimore in the company of Percival Drayton, the brother of William Drayton. Mary found him a "delightful specimen of a Natural Gentleman." "If I had met with his facsimile at eighteen my heart would have been in imminent danger," she wrote. Mary and Sarah took rooms at a hotel in Richmond, Virginia, where they later were joined by the newlyweds. "Margaret was very much pleased with Mr. Hodgson's Mother and family," Mary later wrote. "She says that they are guileless, unpretending people and very pious, refined in their sentiments and feelings, and very fond of each other." A day and a night were spent in Charleston before making the last leg of the journey to Savannah.[25]

The ladies and Hodgson finally arrived at the mansion on St. James Square, where they were greeted by the servants. Mary found her people to be quite overcome by the sight of her and her sisters after such a long absence. "They said it seemed to them as if we had all passed away," she reported. "I never knew before how much they valued us." The servants were curious to get a look at the new member of the family. "They greeted Mr. Hodgson with great cordiality," Mary wrote, "and were glad to see him look *so old*, for Gossip had spread its wings very wide in this direction, and some pronounced him to be 22 while others stopped at 35."[26]

Hodgson and his bride settled into the residence. The upstairs southeast corner room at the front of the house had always been Mary Telfair's chamber. The room adjoining it was the spare bedroom. Mr. and Mrs. Hodgson moved into the bedroom across the way at the rear of the house, and Hodgson moved his books into the northeast corner room, which became his study. It was a most comfortable arrangement. Mary, however, quickly fell into that period of sadness that she always experienced upon returning to her home after being absent for an extended period of time. She likened it to the "desolate feeling which pervades the heart of a Bankrupt when he is driven from his long cherished home."[27]

The first person that Mary got in touch with upon her return to Savannah was her sister-in-law, Mrs. Thomas Telfair. Mary found her in deep mourning over the death of her daughter Margaret:

> Poor Mrs. Telfair arrived a few days since. She looks very miserably—it seemed a comfort to her to unburden her sorrows, and they have been heavy indeed—Her House is desolate—

and she is bowed down with grief and ill health. She says her heart must have been very hard to have required such chastisement.[28]

Mary Telfair was required to come to terms with another death when word reached Savannah that fall that her dear friend Anne Clay had passed away at her sister's home in Boston. The end came for Anne on October 28 while Mary, Sarah, and the Hodgsons were en route to Savannah. Anne Clay was only forty-six years of age at the time of her death. She had for several years suffered from an enlargement of the heart and in the months preceding her death had developed dropsy, an accumulation of serous fluid in the chest. The Reverend Charles C. Jones, who had supported Anne in her efforts to instruct the slaves on her family's plantation, delivered a heartfelt tribute to his friend at a memorial service held at the Presbyterian Church in Bryan County the following January. The Reverend Mr. Jones praised the majesty and elegance of Miss Clay's person and the dignity in her manners. He dwelled at length upon many of the same qualities that Mary Telfair had so admired in Anne Clay: her strong and vigorous intellect, her powers of conversation, her ready and searching wit, and her Calvinistic piety that led her to work tirelessly for the moral and spiritual improvement of her family's slaves. Mary Telfair had once compared Anne Clay to Queen Elizabeth, and the Reverend Mr. Jones echoed this comparison when he referred to her "queenly person." Mary Telfair may have been one of those that he had in mind when he proclaimed that the circle of Miss Clay's intimate friends and acquaintances "embraced many of the most talented as well as pious individuals of our country." Mary Telfair was loaned by a friend a copy of the Reverend Mr. Jones's tribute to Anne Clay, and she found it "a beautiful and faithful sketch of her character." Telfair was particularly struck with the sentiment: "He who shapes my fortunes gives me the impress of time; he who shapes my character gives me the impress of eternity." She wished that the family would have a limited number of copies published for the benefit of the friends of Anne Clay.[29]

Mary Telfair decided to personally take over the education of her great-niece Alberta. The girl was nine, and Mary feared for her welfare if no one but her bereaved grandmother looked out for her interests. Initially all went well:

Berta is installed as my pupil for the winter—She took her first lessons yesterday and seemed interested in them. She is to come to me every morning from 9 to 1 o'clock. I wish to interest her early in History, sacred and profane, so as to lead her mind from fiction entirely. After her lesson in Geography I shewed her Engravings of the places she read of and traced on the map. She listened with a great deal of pleasure to my description of Rome and I would not desire better materials to work upon. Her affections want cultivation as well as her intellect but nature has done a good deal for her. I have enlisted Mr. Hodgson's aid to teach her French, but I am afraid his patience will fail for he has never taught the young idea how to shoot—I think that the Bible ought to be the basis of Education and it may be made interesting to a child.[30]

Mary later sought to become Alberta's guardian, but Mrs. Telfair did not take kindly to the idea. Also, Mary ultimately did not succeed as the girl's tutor:

Mrs. Telfair has not given her to me except in the event of my surviving her—she came during the winter to say her lessons and read to me but I found it impossible with her positive dislike to learning to do her justice in any way—so entirely undisciplined too that I found it necessary to recommend her being sent to school where she would stand in fear of her Teacher and have her mind drawn out by the spirit of emulation—poor child just as she was getting into proper training she was taken ill. She is ten years of age and perfectly ignorant. She can never enjoy health so entirely is her physical education neglected. She sits all day in a close room by her Grand Mother's side working on canvas or reading fairy tales—no exercise in the fresh air— no intercourse with children. Left entirely to her own guidance, she must become thoroughly selfish—her habits and opinions are as confirmed now as that of a woman of forty. Her precocity in some respects is wonderful such caution and distrust I have never known in childhood before. Her mind is excellent but I can compare it to a garden choked with weeds.[31]

Apparently Mrs. Telfair agreed at one point that her sister-in-law should become Alberta's legal guardian, for in the September 1843 term of the Chatham County Court of Ordinary, letters of guardianship were issued, without opposition, naming Mary Telfair guardian to the person of Alberta Cobb, a minor. It appears, however, that Mary was unable to control the girl and the arrangement later was terminated.[32]

After Mary Telfair failed in her attempts to tutor Alberta, the girl was enrolled in a religious school, the Montpellier Female Institute founded by Bishop Elliott and located in the vicinity of Macon, Georgia. There the teachers were well-educated religious women from England, all selected by one of the bishop's friends in London. Shortly after her return from Europe, Mary spent a week at Montpellier and attended the girls' examinations morning, noon, and night for three days. On the whole, Mary approved of the institute and found Alberta much improved. The teachers said that the girl had a great deal of talent, and the superintendent of the boys' institute said that he had never seen such phrenological development in a female head. "I was astonished to find her *chanting* at morning and evening service," Mary wrote, "for she could not raise a note before she went there."[33]

During the year following their return from Europe, the Chrysties struggled to come to terms with the death of their daughter. Frances shared her grief with Mary Garrettson: "I miss my beloved child every day & every hour. I feel sick to see her, to talk to her, to sleep with her. There is a dreadful void in my heart which only God can fill." The only means of coping was to go on leading a normal and active life. Frances wrote to Mary Telfair in December 1843 with news from New York. Perhaps inspired by Mr. Hodgson, Mr. Chrystie was attending a series of lectures on Egypt and had become absorbed in hieroglyphics. His wife marveled at the tales of this ancient civilization that he would relate to her each evening when he returned home. "They seem to have had all the arts & contrivances which we considered modern & some ended which we do not know, even rail roads were used by them," she wrote to her friend. Frances herself was spending her evenings with her mother in the back parlor "reading & talking & trying to find out all that we can of our future inheritance." Frances' son William was having serious problems with his throat and was obliged to leave Columbia College on account of it. The doctors had been unsuccessful in curing him, and his mother had decided on a new course of treatment. "I will let you know how homeopathy succeeds," she promised Mary Telfair. "I have much faith in it. Mrs. Clinton, who is a regular attendant at our prayer meeting, would give me no rest 'till I tried it & Will did not object." [34]

Memories of her travels enriched Mary Telfair's life after her return to Savannah and stimulated her intense intellectual curiosity:

> My visit to Scotland has inspired me with a wish to become better acquainted with John Knox whose life lately published by McRie I have just commenced, and I find that he is disposed to be more indulgent to the stern Reformer than other of his Biographers. How completely we identify characters with places! Calvin with Switzerland, Luther with Germany, and Knox with "Caledonia stern and wild." Songs bring certain people before us —and flowers too—I shall never look at a beautiful sunset in a pleasant land of hill and dale without thinking of the last rays of a glorious sun resting upon the ruins of "Alloway's auld haunted Kirk" and the Brigg of bonnie Doon—the most romantic of all classic streams. I am ashamed to say that my mind often reverts to those scenes when the *local talk* is going on and when I ought to be listening to "He said so, and she said, and they said."[35]

Hodgson adapted well to his new way of life. He was making friends in Savannah. But, as his sister-in-law described it, the adjustment was not entirely easy:

> Mr. Hodgson finds our quiet & retired life here a great contrast to New York with which he was delighted as well as with our friends and acquaintances. He accommodates himself wonderfully though at first seeing us so depressed he seemed to feel lost. But he has been kindly received and I think that he is very grateful for attention. When he goes out he says that he is very glad to get home to us—I am sure that I hope the feeling will continue.[36]

Hodgson could not help but become restless, however. In the year following his move to Savannah, he gave some serious thought to reentering the diplomatic service. He was feeling bored and was itching for adventure. There was a post open in Constantinople that he coveted, but his wife would have no part of it, no more so than she would think of living in Tunis. Mary understood the feelings of both her sister and her brother-in-law:

> Constantinople so long the *gilded* dream of Mr. Hodgson's imagination is relinquished. Margaret put her veto upon it and

he would not apply for it. He viewed it as the *promised* land and associates it with all that is attractive to an Oriental Scholar— while his fellow traveler in life views it as the land of Plague and Mohammadanism. I am glad to find that she takes a decided stand in some things. He has accommodated himself to our retired way of living better than I expected and seems quite happy —but ambition will peep out sometimes and the *Linguist* and *Diplomatist* stand out in *bold* relief—as I am a *tongueless* woman and I may, *if I knew myself,* add a perfectly unambitious one there is no sympathy on that subject. I can enjoy with him the beauties of nature, books & paintings but not society. I have lost all relish for that beyond an interesting tête a tête companion.[37]

Hodgson took over the supervision of the Telfair plantations and in time became caught up in the intellectual life of Savannah. Having left the consular service, he had time to concentrate on the scholarly work that had first captured his interest as a young man. When only twenty-eight years of age, he had contributed to the American Philosophical Society a study of the language and ethnology of the Berbers. He concluded that the language of these North African tribesmen was in most respects the same as that of the natives living in the region of Carthage during its days of glory. In 1833 he had supervised the translation of twelve chapters of St. Luke's Gospel into Berber, a work that was published by the British and Foreign Bible Society. He relished the opportunity to return to stimulating projects of this kind.[38]

Hodgson joined the Georgia Historical Society shortly after his arrival in Savannah. The committee appointed to arrange the Society's 1843–1844 winter lecture series invited him to deliver one of the talks on a subject of his choosing taken from the whole range of American history and biography. He was elected to the Board of Curators of the Historical Society in 1845 and served on that body for twenty-five years. Hodgson's scholarly work in Georgia included studies in the physical sciences. In 1843 he was delegated by the Historical Society to attend a meeting of the National Institute at Washington to present a paper on the organic remains and geology of the Georgia coast. He subsequently presented another paper to this organization entitled "The Foulahs of Central Africa and the American Slave Trade," and in 1844 Wiley and Putnam published his "Notes on Northern Africa, the Sahara and Soudan." This study included a number of Berber proverbs that Hodgson found to be "almost identical with those in use among the most polished nations": "When the cat is out, the rats will play." "You are like one that strikes cold iron." "Profit comes not from sleep." In succeeding years other works followed on equally exotic subjects: 1844, "Remarks on the Past History and Present Condition of Morocco, Algiers and the Barbary Regencies"; 1846, "Memoir on the Megatherium and Other Extinct Gigantic Quadrupeds of the Coast of Georgia"; 1857, "The Gospels Written in the Negro Patois of English, with Arabic Characters, by a Mandingo Slave in Georgia"; 1858, "Remarks on the Recent Travels of Dr. Barth in Central Africa or Soudan"; 1868, "The Science of Language," a paper read before the Georgia Historical Society that compared the ancient written languages of Sanskrit and Hebrew.[39]

Hodgson based much of his ethnological and linguistic scholarship on his contacts with the slaves on the Telfair plantations. He found a great deal of ethnic diversity among these Africans, a diversity which he declared to be common on all plantations along the coast of Georgia and the Carolinas. He could distinguish between Mandingoes, Eboes, Goulahs, people from Guinea, and Foulahs, the latter being people of a "powerful warlike nation." Hodgson numbered a Foulah among his own slaves. Through his knowledge of African languages, he was able to converse with the slaves in their native tongues. Hodgson wrote of some interesting individuals whom he met in the course of his studies. Among them was a Mandingo belonging to the Maxwell family of Savannah who made a curious translation of Genesis. He also wrote of Bilali, a slave who belonged to the Spaldings of Sapelo Island, who died unconverted to Christianity clasping to his breast passages from the Koran. William Harden, for many years the librarian of the Georgia Historical Society, recalled the story of a slave owned by his grandfather who, though thought to be illiterate, filled a notebook with strange characters. When the writing was shown to Mr. Hodgson, he saw that it was Arabic. The man could indeed read and write, but only in his own language.[40]

Hodgson's studies brought him into contact with a number of Sea Island planters in addition to the Spaldings. He was a friend of Pierce Butler of Philadelphia and St. Simons and Butler islands, whose wife, the English actress Fanny Kemble, wrote of the evils of slavery in her *Journal of a Residence on a Georgia Plantation in 1838–1839*. Among Hodgson's papers can be found a letter from Butler thanking him for a gift of Madeira, "which I shall taste with due deliberation." Hodgson also counted among his friends Thomas Butler King, who had moved to Savannah from Pennsylvania in 1822 and later married Anna Matilda Page, the only daughter of Major William Page, the owner of the Retreat Plantation on St. Simons Island. After King embarked on a career in government, he kept Hodgson apprized of national affairs.[41]

Another well-known planter of the Altamaha River estuary, James Hamilton Couper, carried on a lively correspondence with Hodgson on ethnological subjects and the fossil remains on the Georgia coast. They shared a deep interest in all things scientific. Couper passed on to Hodgson information received from Bilali on the Spalding estate. Hodgson sent Couper his pamphlet on the Felatah of the Sudan, and Couper promised to give Hodgson a copy of a paper that he was preparing for the Academy of Natural Sciences of Philadelphia on the fossils that he had discovered during the excavation of the Brunswick-Altamaha Canal. The two men shared an interest in the fossils found by Dr. Joseph Clay Habersham on Skidaway Island. When Sir Charles Lyell, the eminent British geologist, visited Savannah in December 1845, Hodgson accompanied him on an excursion to Skidaway, an event that Lyell described in *A Second Visit to the United States of North America:*

> While in Savannah I made a delightful excursion, in company with Dr. Le Conte, Captain Alexander, and Mr. Hodgson, to Skiddaway, one of the sea islands, which may be said to form part of a great delta on the coast of Georgia, between the mouths of the Savannah and Ogeechee rivers. The alluvial region consists of a wide extent of low land elevated a few feet above high water, and intersected by numerous creeks and swamps. I gave some account in my former tour of my visit to Heyner's Bridge, where the bones of the extinct mastodon and mylodon were found. Skiddaway is five or six miles farther from Savannah in the same south-east direction, and is classical ground for geologists, for, on its north-west end, where there is a low cliff from two to six feet in height, no less than three skeletons of the huge *Megatherium* have been dug up, besides the remains of the *Mylodon, Elephas primigenius, Mastodon giganteus,* and a species of the ox tribe.[42]

James Hamilton Couper spoke the same language as Mr. Hodgson and Sir Charles: "The claws which were, at first, supposed to belong to the Megalenyx, I am *nearly* convinced are of the Megatherium; but I require a more minute examination of the large one of Maj. Williams' collection to satisfy me." And again: "Mr. Lyell writes me that having submitted the supposed tooth of the *hippopotamus,* and the jaw bone described by Harlan as the *Sus Americana,* to Mr. Owen, he pronounces the first to be a lower tooth of the mastodon giganteus." It was a language spoken by few others. An 1814 graduate of Yale College, Couper was not only a scholar but a highly successful planter and businessman. He developed his family's estate, Hopeton, into one of the finest and most productive rice plantations in the South. He was one of the principals in the company that cut the canal in which he found his fossils. He also was a skilled architect. Indeed, he was the architect for Christ Episcopal Church in Savannah. Couper was a survivor of the *Pulaski* disaster and behaved with great courage and resourcefulness in saving not only himself but also his sister Ann Fraser and her five-year-old son and a woman from Cumberland Island and her infant.[43]

After Hodgson joined the family, he and the ladies spent a good deal of time in the North, for his studies required his presence there. Hodgson was constantly on the go. In September 1843 Mary Telfair was in New Haven with Hodgson and her sisters. She was introduced to Benjamin Silliman, professor of chemistry and natural history at Yale College, and found him to be a "pure and lofty spirit, one of Nature's Noblemen." "He is very playful in conversation and his manners are perfectly charming," she wrote of the great scientist. Hodgson was opening new doors for the ladies in the academic community. "I have never a summer before made so many interesting acquaintances," Mary wrote that September. Mary's guide in New Haven was Miss Hillhouse, one of a distinguished Connecticut family. Mary found infectious her enthusiasm for her native city. "She loves the very soil of New Haven, and she ought to do so for independent of the advantages of literature and Religion, it affords much to gratify her—and she is so revered among all classes. She is a *genuine Republican.*" Mary was told by Miss Hillhouse that there were no extremes of wealth and poverty in New Haven. "Education is bestowed upon the poor as well as the rich—One Hundred and 38 thousand dollars annually expended upon free schools—Miss Hillhouse is to take me to one of them. She says there are not 5 children of 10 years of age in the State who cannot read." "This seems to me a most desirable spot to live in," Mary continued. "If I had children to educate I would prefer this place to any in America—In Europe Geneva would be my choice."[44]

During the winter of 1843, Hodgson and the ladies had discussions on the desirability of having a place of their own in New York. According to Mary Telfair's report to Mary Few, they were unable to reach an agreement:

> We have given up all idea of purchasing or renting a house in New York—Mr. Hodgson's ideas are too *grand* for me. He likes *double* houses while my standard is such a one as yours—a *single* three story house—I look upon a fine spacious establishment as a Task for Care, and of all cares, housekeeping cares are the most uninteresting—What we shall eat and what we shall drink seem uppermost to the mind—If persons could command the same aid from well trained Servants as in England and had the same revenues then they might inhabit fine Mansions without having their minds enslaved—I am every day more and more convinced that simplicity carried throughout in living, in character, habits & manners is conducive to virtue.[45]

William Hodgson received many honors during his lifetime. He was a member of the American Philosophical Society and the American Oriental Society. He belonged to the Royal Asiatic Society and the Asiatic Society of Paris. He was elected to membership in the ethnological societies of New York, London, and Paris and the geographical societies of London and Paris. Princeton awarded him an honorary LL.D. in 1856. He was one of the first Americans to receive the French Legion of Honor.[46]

Hodgson's entry into the family had enlivened and enriched the entire household. Although the Hodgsons' marriage had been a true love match, the differences in their ages and personal wealth led some outsiders to guess otherwise. A young socialite who shared the Hodgsons' table at a dinner party in Philadelphia recorded this cynical observation in his diary:

> Have been to three parties, at Mr. Binney's last Tuesday & at Mrs. Edwd. Biddle's on Thursday. The first given to Mrs.

Swann, the last to Mrs. Rush. Enjoyed them all very well. There was also a dinner at Mr. Atherton's on Thursday given to Mr. and Mrs. Hodgson and Miss Telfair from Savannah, whom the Athertons met last summer in Saratoga. Hodgson is a well educated man, who spent nearly all his life in the East, where he was a dragoman. He married Miss Telfair two or three years ago, she an old maid very plain, he, comparatively a young man & well looking, she very rich, he very poor, the old story.[47]

The young observer was quite mistaken in his assessment. The Hodgsons' love was strong and enduring and would last a lifetime. Mary Telfair would always be close at hand to share their sorrows and joys. The Hodgsons and Mary and Sarah were the "four-fold cord" of which Mary Few had written. Mary's fears that her sister's marriage would change their relationship proved in the long run to be unfounded.

15

Middle Age at Mid-Century

That time of year thou mayst in me behold
When yellow leaves, or none, or few, do hang
Upon those boughs that shake against the cold,
Bare ruined choirs where late the sweet birds sang.
William Shakespeare, Sonnet 73

As Mary Telfair entered middle age, she continued to deal with life's inevitable crises. There was the financial disgrace of the husband of one of her closest friends, the disgraceful behavior of her great-niece Alberta, and the deaths of her sister Sarah and her beloved cousins in Philadelphia. Pleasure and mental stimulation would come with a second trip to Europe, where Mary and the Hodgsons would spend a year savoring a rich cultural feast. The years flanking the mid-century mark were to Mary Telfair the worst of times and the best of times.

Although by the early 1840's economic conditions in Savannah had improved greatly over the years of depression that followed the panic of 1837, many of the banks were in dire financial straits as a result of imprudent lending practices. The Telfairs were stockholders in a number of these financial institutions. Mary complained in the winter of 1843, "In consequence of the misconduct of Bank officers and the immense draughts made by certain individuals upon our banks, they give no Dividends." The problem, she believed, was that people were living beyond their means. She deplored the situation:

The love of shew and the spirit of vying is the ruin of character as much as of fortunes in this Country. To *appear* rich is the acme of ambition with the majority of persons in America. The national character has been deeply injured by it. In this place the most luxurious livers are those who live by their *wits*. The facility with which money could be borrowed from Banks and can still by individuals possessing scarcely the means of procuring a daily support has had a most corrupting influence. Endorsers have been ruined and we *harmless* stockholders made to pay for it.[1]

Mary likened the state of affairs to an epidemic:

There are times for moral epidemics as well as physical. The Cholera seems to have been the forerunner of the Stealing *Mania* so diffused throughout our land. William Drayton was talking to me a few evenings since on that subject. He says the same immorality prevailed in Great Britain during the reign of George the first. I suppose that human nature is depraved every where but our laws for the punishment of crimes are not enforced. I believe that the fear of punishment *in this world* prevents many, who have no fear of God, from committing crimes.[2]

Financial distress came close to home when Jones Bulloch, the husband of Mary's friend Catharine Bulloch, suffered financial ruin. Mary Telfair had not approved of the marriage in the first place. As a result of his financial difficulties, Bulloch decided to leave his wife and seek employment in the West. He got as far as Philadelphia on his way to Michigan, but was discouraged from proceeding further. Apparently there was some chicanery involved in his dealings, for Mary felt strongly that Catharine's husband should be far removed from Savannah:

Here he ought not to remain. If I were in her situation, I would rather be where I was unknown and pursue the humblest occupation than live here with suspicion resting upon him. One false step in life brings such a train of evils upon those who depart from the path of integrity. How true is the hackneyed proverb that "Honesty is the best policy."[3]

Catharine missed her husband and gave some thought to going to Philadelphia with her sister-in-law to open a boarding house. They were most anxious to leave Georgia. Mary Telfair thought it a bad idea. Philadelphia was filled with boarding houses. Mary thought that her two friends were competent to run such an establishment and that they might succeed in St. Augustine. "It is a place of great resort in winter," she wrote, "and families who would go there are prevented from the want of a comfortable boarding house." Also, they could take their own servants there as well as their furniture. They would find it a cheap residence. "The Climate though warm is said to be quite pleasant," Mary observed, "for they are fanned in Summer by the Lea breezes." St. Augustine would be just the place the more that Mary thought of it. "They will have no Savannahians there *to gossip about them,* and poor Catharine may look up a little there—Here she never can, and much as I shall miss her, I feel anxious for her to go."[4]

"I have never been able to converse with C B relative to the subject of her Husband's disgrace," Mary Telfair confessed to Mary Few. "Whenever she alludes to it I am dumb." "Do you not sometimes feel a degree of shame for people who do wrong as if you yourself had committed the act?" she inquired. "I am unfortunate in this respect and wish that I could overcome it and learn more to blush for myself and not to be thinking so much of the feelings of others." Mary kept in close touch with Catharine Bulloch after her husband left Savannah in disgrace. She was, after all, one of her closest friends. Mary said of her to Mary Few, "I feel that she is as much my strong hold in Savannah as you are in New York." Although Catharine Bulloch's life appeared serene, Mary could recognize that her husband's embarrassment continued to cause great pain:

> I spent yesterday with Catharine Bulloch. She seems *contented* and sometimes cheerful. Her children are a source of perpetual interest to her. Johnny her Nephew caught the fish & crabs for dinner. Lydia raised the chickens. Martha keeps a regular school for the two younger girls and makes herself very useful. The garden looked sweetly, and the old moss covered trees may vie with some of those that grace the ancestral domains of England.

Deep down, however, Catharine was not at peace. Mary could see this quite clearly: "The scene is often peaceful without but within corroding cares and sorrows prey. This world can never be to her what it has been. There is a blight on every thing around her and I do pity her." The old gaiety that had existed between Mary and Catharine was gone. "Where we had fifty jokes we meet & part now without one," Mary wrote.[5]

Cousin Eliza Telfair died in Philadelphia in the spring of 1844. She had been indisposed as a result of the epidemic ravaging that city, but had been well enough to go out for walks. She was not confined to her bed until the day of the night that she died. Her niece, Mary Ewing Ritchie, was with her when her time came. Mary Telfair recorded the circumstances of her cousin's death, as related to her by Mrs. George Noble Jones, who was staying at the time with her family in Philadelphia:

> Mary Ritchie heard her knock and went into her room found her suffering from oppression at her chest, and seated her in a chair and while Mary was supporting her, she embraced her very tightly (as if to bid her farewell) which induced Mary to look into her face. She saw that she was dying. Cousin Margaret who was ill in bed hearing a noise went into the room, and on seeing her Sister fainted away and was taken up and carried to her bed—they never met again. *What a separation!* Margaret is now the last of her name on that side of the family. I trust that Mary Ritchie will be a comfort to her as long as the feeble pulse of life remains in her.

Mary was saddened by the death of her cousin. She had been a tie to the past:

> As far back as my memory can go, I remember Cousin Eliza. Every member of our family loved her, but there were two that she seemed most particularly to distinguish and I was one of them. My Father I have always heard loved her as if she had been his own child. I always associated her with past happenings, and I still unite her with "the loved and the lost." The other night I dreamed of seeing her among them cheerful and happy.[6]

Eliza had been a woman of sterling character and deep religious convictions. Mary had held her in high esteem:

> I feel that a strong tie has been severed and when I look back upon the period of childhood when I first learned to love her, it seems that my attachment "grew with my growth." I have

corresponded with her ever since I was fourteen years of age. My esteem for her Character was very great. She had striking virtues—a strict regard to truth the most prominent. I never knew her guilty of a subterfuge, and even when the world had many attractions for her she seemed to rise above the petty feelings that govern so many of its votaries. Mary Ritchie told me last autumn that my Cousin's mind, she thought, was much exercised on religious subjects, that she read her Bible a great deal.[7]

Cousin Margaret Telfair came close to death herself the evening that her sister died. She was attended by a physician who predicted that she would not last the night. But the painkillers that she was given induced sleep, and she managed to pull through. Several days later, young George Jones (the son of George Noble Jones) wrote to Mary Telfair to inform her that Cousin Margaret was better but he thought her composure forced. Mary was quite taken by the young man:

Little George Jones bids fair to be a most useful and estimable character if his life is spared. He is only 16 and performs already duties with a fidelity and ability that few men of riper years could do. His religious and moral education has been most strictly attended to. He has been every thing to my Cousins, and his sympathies seem to have been deeply enlisted in their sufferings. They wrote to me in the winter that his tender care and watchfulness over his Mother was beautiful. He never left her but from necessity. Good Children are the staff of age.[8]

The loss of her sister was a burden almost too great for Cousin Margaret to bear. "They were so united in life," Mary Telfair wrote of her cousins, "so dependent upon each other for support and happiness, that in this case 'the Survivor dies.'" Cousin Margaret did die later in 1844. She breathed her last in Philadelphia on November 23. Mary Ewing Ritchie received half of her estate. Mary Telfair had always approved of Mary Ritchie, and she was a welcome guest at the residence on St. James Square: "Mary Ritchie is on a visit to us—she is a rational companion—she both reads and reflects and is perfectly independent of society—she sets a high value upon the intellectual and took at an early age a decided stand not to mingle in the amusements of fashionable life."[9]

Mary Ritchie later married Ambrose Thompson of Litchfield, Connecticut, a widower with five children. The marriage did not last. According to Mary Telfair, the husband "treated her so inhumanly that she was compelled to leave her home." "Her Husband was never unkind," Mary explained, "but he would not acknowledge that his children were wrong. She is broken hearted and rendered very unhappy by being separated from the two youngest who loved her as much as she loved them." In Mary Telfair's later years, Mary E. Thompson (née Ritchie) became her close companion. Mrs. Thompson legally adopted the daughter of one of her brothers, Margaret Ewing Ritchie, called "Maggie." According to Maggie's stepson, William K. Wallbridge, her father had turned out to be a "very bad egg," and Mary Telfair had rescued her from that situation and had her brought up by Mrs. Thompson. Mary E. Thompson and her niece and adopted daughter resided for long periods of time at the Telfair mansion and were living there at the time of Mary's death.[10]

Mary Telfair, as a middle-aged woman of fifty-three, had lost none of her fascination with politics. "I agree with you in thinking that Mr. Frelinghuysen's election to the Vice Presidency will be a good thing for our Country," she wrote to Mary Few of Henry Clay's running mate on the Whig ticket in the campaign of 1844. "A Christian Ruler is always desirable," Mary wrote of the gentleman from New Jersey. "We want such men in power to redeem a nation from those calamities produced by party spirit and intrigue." Clay's and Frelinghuysen's opponents were the Democratic candidates, James K. Polk and George M. Dallas, who ultimately won the election.[11]

Why was a Telfair supporting a candidate running in opposition to the Democrats, the descendants of the party of Jefferson? The answer is that party alignments had altered radically since Mary's father and brothers were part of the political scene. The men supporting Andrew Jackson for the presidency some twenty years earlier nominally were still Democratic-Republicans, as were those supporting John Quincy Adams. At the time of Jefferson, the party that the Telfairs supported had definite principles, but in time it became a hodgepodge and split into two factions, those who adhered to Jacksonian Democracy and those who opposed Old Hickory. Those who supported Adams and Clay called themselves National Republicans. Adherents to this party came to be called Whigs. Mary Telfair noted this political transformation in a letter to Mary Few:

Times are changed since you & I used to mount the fence at Greenwich and call out to passers by—Federalist or Republican—Now it is Whig or Democrat. Do you remember one Man replied to our question Tory—that ought to have silenced us but we kept up the nightly cry for some time until I suppose our *political ardour* was quenched.[12]

Mary Few had become fascinated with mesmerism, a form of hypnosis developed by the German-Swiss physician, Friedrich Anton Mesmer. In February 1845 she wrote to Mary Telfair describing a demonstration put on by one of their circle, Professor Bush, a scene "worthy of the pencil of Hogarth." Agreeing to demonstrate his mesmeric powers, Professor Bush brought a young woman with him to the house, "performed the usual manipulations and soon pronounced her in a profound slumber." Mary Few continued with her description of the scene and the reactions of those witnessing it, including herself:

Her eyes were bandaged, and cotton stuffed beneath them so as to exclude any ray of light—& certainly there were some very remarkable exhibitions of her sympathy with him. She, however, was a stranger to us—yet I cannot help thinking that there was something more than accident in some of the coincidences—be that as it may—if I had given you the gift of clairvoyance you would have enjoyed the groups of spectators to this scene. We were about twenty. Some were inclined to believe with Dr. B himself that the "science of mesmerism" was about to open a communication with the heavenly world. Others were firmly persuaded that it was connected with magic & sorcery & were regarding the exhibition with horror. Others again believing that an artful girl was imposing upon a credulous enthusiast were overcome with laughter—while the intense curiosity painted in many countenances (quite unconscious of being the objects themselves of observation) completed the grouping. What was the result? you will ask. I can only answer—It is so contrary to all my preconceived ideas that one human being should possess such a power over another that I do not want to believe it—but as Christians we must not fear the truth & I am anxious to have my doubts satisfied either for or against. Who knows but it may bring us into contact with the world of the spirits?

Professor Bush, according to Mary Few, was writing a book on the Resurrection "in which he maintains that we carry about us now as the germ of our resurrection body some special fluid connected with the nervous system, which develops the moment the spirit leaves its clay tenement—& just as the butterfly expands its wings and leaves its shell behind, so shall we bid an eternal farewell to our shell and soar upwards in our spiritual body." "He is a firm believer in the scripture," Few wrote, "but I believe much learning has made him mad."[13]

Mary Telfair became concerned over the propriety of dancing and sought out the opinion of Mary Few. Apparently Alberta had resolved against dancing, and her grandmother, a great belle in her day, had tried to convince her otherwise. "I hardly know how to answer your question about dancing my dear Mary," Few responded. "In itself I consider it an innocent and healthful recreation—but it is connected with so much that is evil, and is so much condemned by the best people, that I feel as if I could wish to have nothing to do with it." As for Alberta's resolve, as far as Mary Few was concerned, it seemed "almost a providence."[14]

Sarah Haig died on April 3, 1845, at the age of fifty-two.[15] She had become very feeble in the years before her death. Indeed, in May 1843 her sister Mary reported that she had been "so feeble as scarcely to leave a hope that she could live to see the spring." The following year Mary reported that Sarah had regained some strength and was able to attend church and walk and go out for rides in the carriage. Then she became unwell again in consequence of going twice to church on Sunday and walking home in the heat. Sarah was ill during the following winter as well, but in February Mary Few had been able to write to Mary Telfair that she was glad to hear of Sarah's improvement. "She has shown great strength of constitution and may yet survive us all." This was not to be. Sarah had her ups and downs during the spring, but at last she expired. Madame Utilite no longer would be around to think up new ways to be useful.[16]

Mary Telfair had long enjoyed a warm friendship with Eliza Rhodes Terrell of Sparta, Georgia. It was she who Mary had attempted to comfort at the time of her elder daughter's death in 1840. Mrs. Terrell was the wife of Dr. William Terrell. A graduate of the Medical College of the University of Pennsylvania, where he studied under the eminent Dr. Benjamin Rush, Dr. Terrell practiced medicine for many years in Sparta. He was a statesman as well as a physician.

He served in the state legislature (1810–1813) and was a member of Congress (1817–1821). He declined renomination in 1821, having tired of politics, and took up the planting of cotton. He remained a planter for the rest of his life and developed an interest in scientific farming. He devoted much time to the promotion of agricultural science and, through a grant of $20,000, endowed a professorship in agriculture at the University of Georgia. Dr. Terrell suffered from a lesion on his face that did not heal and caused him much discomfort. He traveled extensively in Europe seeking a cure for his affliction.[17]

Eliza Terrell also was a friend of Thomas Telfair's widow, and she and her husband shared Mary Telfair's concern over Alberta's behavior. Alberta's conduct in the winter of 1848 and in the ensuing years became so unacceptable to her great-aunts that it would end in a permanent rift in their relationship. That winter Alberta announced that she intended to marry Charles S. Arnold, a clerk and later a partner at the firm of Padelford & Fay, and a respectable young man in the eyes of his friends. Alberta was not quite fourteen at the time, much too young to marry as far as Mary Telfair and the Hodgsons were concerned. Besides, Arnold was considered by the family to be far beneath a girl with Telfair blood.[18]

Dr. Terrell advised Mr. Hodgson that he was quite sure that no amount of persuasion would deter Alberta from going forward with her marriage. "You cannot persuade her that the man she professes to love will ruin her," he wrote. "She knows better than you do, for during her short life she has never been persuaded to do any thing she did not like—and why should she now?" As far as Dr. Terrell was concerned, there was only one way to save Berta and that was to "remove her from the object that threatens her destruction, either carry her away or secure her so that she cannot escape or have intercourse with the man implicated." Dr. Terrell admitted to Hodgson that "the latter is considered cruel and is difficult to execute," but he thought it entirely justifiable, "as justifiable as confinement for lunacy." Indeed, he considered Alberta to be suffering from a mental aberration worse than some who are treated by solitary confinement for a few weeks or months. Terrell was particularly outraged when he learned that Alberta had said that she did not love the man but was doing this to "humble a certain family pride." "A pretty thing indeed at fourteen to be a judge of what ought to be rationally considered love," he fumed to Hodgson, "and quite wonderful to talk of humbling family pride especially by degrading her own." In Terrell's opinion, this was a case "which justifies a resort to the most coercive means."[19]

On February 1, while Mary Telfair was visiting her sister-in-law, the family's worst fears came to pass. There was anguish in every word as Mary wrote to Eliza Terrell of Alberta's elopement:

> The deed is over, and Berta's fate is sealed, and a miserable one it will be if I have any *prescience*. Her conduct ever since you left has been most cruel to her Grand Mother. This morning she told Philis and Ephraim [slaves] that her Grand Mother had given her permission to walk out. She dressed herself and while I was seated in your cousin's room walked off, and at 8 o'clock this evening with her cloak & bonnet on went into her Grand Mother's room—told her that she had been married in the morning by Justice Bruen, and that Arnold was at the door in a Carriage to take her to the Charleston boat—hoped her Grand Mother would forgive her, and tripped off. She left a note for me which I have preserved for your *edification*. I feel as if she were dead to every feeling of humanity as well as decency, but what else could be expected from such a training—the pupil of Sarah and companion of Negroes—no moral principles inculcated—permitted to run wild like an animal. Indeed I have often said to my Sister—it is the education of an animal allowed to eat, drink, sleep, and frolic. She has neither sensibility or refinement consequently will be insensible to neglect, but when she is restricted in her purse and thwarted in her will—she will *feel*.[20]

Mary Telfair had always disapproved of Alberta's behavior and could have predicted the outcome. Some years before, she had written, "Alberta, Mary's child sits up until ten every night, and already talks of her beau—I tell them that she will be an old woman at fifteen." Mary had made every effort to improve the child. But nothing would change Alberta. Mary concluded that Alberta's nature had been "bad, self willed, and artful from the cradle."[21]

Telfair was not alone in her general disapproval of the girl. Dr. Terrell was completely in accord, as indicated by the thoughts that he shared with Mr. Hodgson:

> Berta has always appeared to me a little different from most girls of her age at all times when I have seen her. A remarkable

confidence in her own opinions and an impatience of restraint added to a wilfulness of temper have produced in her a disregard of the convenience if not the happiness of others old or young, and having been indulged in all her whims and follies and perhaps the childish vices of her age she has become entirely selfish and being courted and flattered supposes herself the object of universal admiration by everybody, but her real friends, who of course are wrong and whom she ought to disregard and disobey.[22]

Even so, Terrell was shocked when he learned of the elopement. He wrote Hodgson that he could not "imagine anything more cruel than the deliberation with which she bid defiance to age, infirmity and filial affection." Nothing in his experience equaled such behavior:

I have had a good many romances in times gone by and from my present recollection of the dramatis personae I have no recollection of any such character considering her birth and breeding. The scene when she left her grandmother for the Charleston boat I must consider as one of the most remarkable which has ever been enacted considering all the circumstances, and the wonder is that one so young, so tenderly treated, so caressed, so doted on, could have carried it through. Psychologically considered she appears to me to be one of the rarest specimens of humanity I have ever been acquainted with and if I should live I shall be exceedingly curious to know her future history.[23]

However inconsiderate of her family that she may have been, the overriding fact was that Alberta liked men—and men liked Alberta. She enjoyed a good time and was as uninhibited as Mary Telfair and her friends were reserved. Her unconventionality reminds one of Henry James's Daisy Miller. Alberta was not exactly pretty, but everyone thought her face remarkable. No less a judge than Bishop Elliott commented that Berta's eyes were like none that he had ever seen and reminded him of those of "the Enchantresses of Eastern tales."[24] Quite simply, the girl had sex appeal. Men were attracted to her, and she was not one to reject their attentions.

Mary felt sorry for her sister-in-law, but thought that it was her own fault. Thomas' widow had always been too lenient with Alberta:

Her poor Grand Mother feels it deeply, but I think will probably live through it. I think *(between us)* that she wavered much about giving her consent to the marriage. It was better for the poor wretched child that she did not yield to her wishes—As for the property not being secured (which seemed to trouble her greatly) I consider as *dust in the balance* with the reputation of both Grand Mother & Child. The former would justly have been condemned for permitting a child of fourteen to marry and the reputation of the child would have been sacrificed to a marriage settlement. It is better as it is. If she had been my charge I would have had her taken away by force to save her from an union with a villain, but Mrs. Telfair's want of decision & firmness has been the bane of her existence.

Mary believed that Alberta's power over her grandmother was "super human." "She could make her hate or love whom she chose but I hope that she will never make her love the Wretch who has torn her child from her & blighted all her earthly hopes."[25]

On the surface Mary Telfair dealt with her great-niece and her despised husband in the only way she found possible. She ignored them. Alberta, who in happier days had had the run of the Telfair mansion, no longer was welcome there. Mary did not speak of Alberta except to her sister and Eliza Terrell, and her friends knew enough to avoid the subject of the girl's elopement. "This is a subject I never talk on," she told Eliza Terrell, "and banish as much as possible from my mind." "When an evil can not be remedied it ought to be forgotten. Why should I have my happiness embittered by one who never loved me nor would admit of any influence?" On the inside, it was a different matter. Two months after Alberta's marriage, Mary was still stewing and fretting over the affair and decrying her great-niece's ingratitude. She shared her resentment with Mrs. Terrell, her chief confidant on the subject of Alberta:

> The scenes through which we passed in January appear to me now like a frightful storm, and I do regret that I took any part in trying to prevent an elopement which to every person of common sense & delicacy must have appeared a moral obliquity. As such I shall ever view it. I regret too ever taking Berta to the North with me—the gentle restraint I imposed upon her was viewed as tyranny & I have almost certain proofs that she

misrepresented me to her Grand Mother over whom she ever
has & ever will exercise a *super human* power. Sally Rembert's
letter *(I speak confidentially to you)* which we received three weeks
ago unfolds a great deal, which combined with subsequent
circumstances, convinces me that my *last service* in striving to
snatch her from a marriage at fourteen would indeed be my last
effort to promote her good. I cannot for one moment imagine
that our countenance & society could be any loss to Berta, when
it was freely offered to her and every mark of kindness shewn—
we were repulsed. Then my influence might have been beneficial and had I been permitted to have taken her to the North
& superintended her education until seventeen, she might have
been a respectable & a useful & a happy woman. You know
what has been the fatal result of growing up like a weed & I
very much fear from all that I hear a baleful influence will be
spread wherever she goes.[26]

Mr. Hodgson and Dr. Terrell shared many interests besides the
affairs of young Alberta. Anyone who had an interest in science, as
Dr. Terrell did, was welcomed as a companion by Hodgson. The two
men kept up a lively correspondence in which they exchanged views
on the issues of the day. Terrell had a wry sense of humor, and
Hodgson, no doubt, had many a chuckle over the words that flowed
from his friend's pen without pause for a period. Terrell's account of
a delay in a journey which was caused by flooding and was spent at
an inn operated by a Mr. Wilder is typical of his wit:

I had a remarkably bad time of it at Raytown though Wilder
did his best and so did his wife, but things went badly from the
beginning so I found an old Bible and read from Job which
surely might have reconciled me to my lot for there was an
infinite disparity in our condition, but Job was a Philosopher
and I am not, and it sometimes happens strangely enough how
unreasonable we are in refusing to be comforted, for the only
other book that I found Wilder owned was the adventures of
Archibald Robbins who was wrecked on the coast of Africa &
fell into the hands of the Arabs of the desert and a horrible account he gives of his suffering and captivity, but it still rained &
the river continued to rise and the wind blew and the children

cried and the dogs & cats wanted to warm themselves & I could not drive them out in the cold rain and so we passed the best or worst of three days.[27]

In February 1848 there were barricades in the streets of Paris, and France's reform party was able to force the abdication of Louis Philippe. "The present is not the time to visit Europe," Mary wrote. "A year hence I suppose tranquility will reign." That winter she satisfied her craving for the sights of Europe by attending a series of lectures on European history delivered by a Dr. Bayard. She also was studying French. She had begun her studies in 1845 under the tutelage of one Madame Lanney and continued to work with this teacher until 1850. Mary had studied the language as a young girl and quite probably had continued her French lessons through her teenage years. It is unlikely that she would have copied an excerpt from Balzac in her commonplace book in 1822 had she not been able to comprehend its meaning. Telfair kept French notebooks in which she would write short sketches in English and then translate them into French. She loved to sprinkle French words throughout her letters and other writings. A woman that she met during her trip abroad had with her a *"petit chien,"* and, based upon the frequency with which she used it, her favorite French word was *"recherché."*[28]

Georgia's economy required improved transportation if it was to flourish, and by mid-century it was obvious that the future lay with the railroads. As early as 1833 a rail line had been constructed from the seaport of Charleston 136 miles to the town of Hamburg across the Savannah River from Augusta. At the time it was the longest railroad in the world, and it threatened to divert commerce from Savannah. The Central of Georgia Railroad was organized to run a line from Savannah to Macon, deep in the heart of the central cotton belt. It was begun in 1836 and, despite the depression, was completed in 1843. William Hodgson took a burning interest in the development of Georgia's railroad system. He was particularly interested in a connection between Augusta and Savannah, and in 1848 he corresponded with the editor of the Augusta newspaper on the best means of accomplishing this. In 1849 he and Dr. Terrell were debating the best routes for Georgia's rail system and the means of financing their construction, and the following year Alexander R. Lawton, then president of the Savannah and Augusta Railroad, was writing to Hodgson on the progress of the spur from the central line to Waynesboro.[29]

In 1849 Mary Telfair and the Hodgsons bought a house in New York. It was located at 19 Brevoort Place in the neighborhood of their friends and the church that they attended when they were in the city. Mary reported to Eliza Terrell that it was "a delightful house just large enough for our family." She advised her friend that they had "furnished it for comfort." "Nothing for show," she insisted. Hodgson resigned from the board of the Georgia Historical Society in April 1849 because of his intention to spend most of the year in New York. During the remainder of 1849 and throughout the year 1850, his friends addressed mail to him at the Brevoort Place address. Presumably the ladies were there as well throughout this period.[30]

Dr. and Mrs. Terrell had a daughter named Lucy, and Mary Telfair took a keen interest in her welfare. Telfair felt strongly that the young lady should be sent to school in New York. Her experience with Alberta, no doubt, had confirmed her views that an education in the North was best for a young girl from Georgia. Lucy had studied French and music in New York during the summer of 1846, but this was but an interlude in her education. Assuming the role of the wise aunt, Mary Telfair visited New York's Spinger Institute on the Terrells' behalf and interviewed its principal, Mr. Gorham Abbot. The school had a good reputation, and Mary found the arrangement of the house excellent: "There is a Hall in the Attic for Calisthenics taught by a Lady, and a Chapel where lectures are delivered." She believed, however, that Mrs. Terrell should travel to New York and judge for herself whether the school was the right one for Lucy. Nonetheless, Mary was certain that Lucy should not stay in the South for her schooling:

> I wish that Savannah could be emptied of its Girls. The precious period from 7 to 13 years is passed there in frivolous amusements, flirting, & total idleness. Next to sacrificing a child on the car of Juggernaut or throwing it into the Ganges is to bring it up without moral responsibilities, or intellectual advantages. When we consider that Women form the character of Men too much cannot be done to strengthen & discipline their minds for such a task. Many generations suffer from the errors of one Woman. A weak minded mother particularly if she is opinionated and indolent is like a moral upas [a tree with

a poisonous sap]—she destroys the germ of what is naturally good & nourishes the evil propensities of a fallen nature. I do not wonder at your anxiety respecting your daughter. I should esteem you less if you did not feel it & I perfectly agree with you that at her age a Mother's care is more necessary even than in infancy. You are right to come on with your child. You have the means, and you cannot employ them better than in promoting her future happiness & respectability by enabling her to reap the advantages which New York affords.[31]

It was Mary Telfair who first introduced young Ward McAllister to New York society. This was the same Ward McAllister who became the renowned social arbiter and who in 1892 made up the list of "the 400," those members of society who could fit into Mrs. Astor's ballroom and feel at ease there.[32] Born in Savannah in 1827, McAllister always believed in the natural superiority of Southerners. His grandmother was Hannah Gibbons, sister of Thomas Gibbons and a first cousin of Mary Telfair's mother. At the age of fifteen, Ward opposed his younger brother Hall at a meeting of the Springfield, Georgia, debating society on the question, "Which is the stronger passion, Love or Ambition?" Hall advocated ambition, Ward love. So it would be. Hall intended to become a great lawyer. After passing the Georgia bar, he set off on a trip around the world. Upon reaching San Francisco, he heard of the discovery of gold and settled there to practice his profession. Ward, in pursuit of Venus, went to New York.[33] He described his arrival in the city in his 1890 book *Society As I Have Found It:*

> I myself soon left Savannah for New York after Hall's departure, residing there in Tenth Street with an old maiden lady, my relative and godmother, whom I always felt would endow me with all her worldly goods, but who, I regret to say, preferred the Presbyterian church and the Georgia Historical Society to myself, for between them she divided a million. At that time Tenth Street was a fashionable street; our house was a comfortable, ordinary one, but my ancient relative considered it a palace, so that all her visitors were taken from garret to cellar to view it. Occupying the front room in the third story, as I would hear these visitors making for my room, I often had to scramble into the bath-room or under the bed, to hide myself. Having a large

fortune, my relative, whom I called Aunt (but who was really only my father's cousin), was saving to meanness; her plantations in the South furnished our table; turkeys came on in barrels. "It was turkey hot and turkey cold, turkey tender, and turkey tough, until at grace one would exclaim, 'I thank ye, Lord, we've had enough.'" As the supposed heir of my saving godmother, the portals of New York society were easily opened to me, and I well remember my first fancy ball, given by Mrs. John C. Stevens in her residence in College Place. A company of soldiers were called in to drill on the waxed floors to perfect them for dancing. A legacy of a thousand dollars paid me by the New York Life Insurance and Trust Company I expended in a fancy dress, which I flattered myself was the handsomest and richest at the ball. I danced the cotillion with a nun, a strange costume for her to appear in, as "I won't be a nun" was engraved on every expression of her face. She was at that day one of the brightest and most charming young women in this city, and had a power of fascination rarely equaled.[34]

Although not mentioned by name, the "old maiden lady" is certainly Mary Telfair. Presumably the house referred to is the Brevoort Place residence, which was in the neighborhood of Tenth Street.

Ward pursued Venus just as he said he would. He would find her, and a fortune as well, when he proposed marriage to his cousin Sarah Gibbons. Sarah was the daughter of William Gibbons, the son of Thomas Gibbons. When Thomas Gibbons died in 1826, he was said to be the richest man in the South. He disinherited his son-in-law John M. Trumbull (and Trumbull's offspring) in the most violent of terms as a punishment for the gentleman's failure to testify on Gibbons' behalf in one of his several lawsuits, and Sarah's father inherited the bulk of Thomas Gibbons' estate.[35] It was Sarah's father who in 1836 built in what is now Madison, New Jersey, a mansion designed to resemble the White House. This structure later became Drew University's Mead Hall. Sarah Gibbons and Ward McAllister were married in 1853. His wife financed his brilliant social career for the rest of his life, although she herself had no interest in society.

McAllister found Newport charming in the years before the war. He remembered his uncle and his father "building bonfires on Paradise

Rocks on the Fourth of July and flying kites from Purgatory." He described the island resort as it was before the arrival of the *nouveaux riches*:

> Newport was now at its best. The most charming people of the country had formed a select little community there; the society was small, and all were included in the gaieties and festivities. Those were the days that made Newport what it was then and is now, the most enjoyable and luxurious little island in America. The farmers of the island even seemed to catch the infection, and they were as much interested in the success of our picnics and country dinners, as we were ourselves. They threw open their houses to us, and never heeded the invasion, on a bright sunny day, of a party of fifty people, who took possession of their dining-room, in fact of their whole house, and frolicked in it to their heart's content. To be sure, I had often to pacify a farmer when a liveried groom robbed his hen house, but as he knew this fashionable horde paid their way, he was easily soothed.[36]

McAllister liked the simplicity of Newport:

> The charm of the place then was the simple way of entertaining; there were no large balls; all the dancing and dining was done by daylight, and in the country. I did not hesitate to ask the very crème de la crème of New York society to lunch and dine at my farm, or to a fishing party on the rocks. My little farm dinners gained such a reputation that my friends would say to me: "Now, remember, leave me out of your ceremonious dinners as you choose, but always include me in those given at your farm, or I'll never forgive you."[37]

McAllister made his mark in Savannah as well as in New York and Newport. He developed a love of French cuisine, and his dinner parties became the talk of the town. When the son of the duke of Devonshire and the son of the earl of Shaftesbury visited Savannah, McAllister managed to have them accept his invitation to dinner. The menu for the evening included *filet de boeuf aux truffles et champignons*. The dinner was a great success:

> My *filets de boeuf*, and the scions of noble English houses placed me in the front social rank of that little, aristocratic town,

and brought forth from one of its oldest inhabitants the exclamation, "My dear boy, your aunts, the Telfairs, could give breakfasts, but you, you can give dinners."[38]

The entertainment that Ward McAllister provided his English guests the following day was of a sort that would have been familiar to the gentlemen in the society of which the Telfairs were a part. After a good breakfast, they all went to the river where they boarded the *Rice Bird*, a ten-oared boat owned by Ward's brother-in-law. Ward took the tiller, and the oarsmen, decked out in their yachting rig, pulled for dear life singing all the while their plantation songs. McAllister described the rest of the day as follows:

> Reaching the plantations, of which there were three, Fairlawn, Argyle, and Shaftsbury, well equipped with admirable dogs (for my brother-in-law was a great sportsman), we would shoot snipe over the rice lands until 2 P.M., then lunch elaborately in his plantation house, and row back in the cool of the afternoon, dining at 8 o'clock, and having as my guests every pretty girl within a hundred miles or more of the city. The flowers, particularly the rose called the Cloth of Gold, and the black rose, I was most prodigal with. I had given a fee to the clerk of the market to scour the country for game and delicacies, so our dinners were excellent, and the old Southern habit of sitting over Madeira until the small hours was adopted, and was, with the bright minds I had brought together, most enjoyable.[39]

Another entertainment that McAllister provided his guests would have been familiar to the Telfair ladies:

> I was then able to show my guests a Savannah picnic, which is an institution peculiar to the place. Leaving the city in a river steamer our party consisting of one hundred people, after a little over an hour's sail we reached an island in the Atlantic Ocean, known as Dawfuskie, a beautiful spot on which stood a charming residence, with five acres of roses surrounding the house. The heads of families carried, each of them, huge baskets containing their dinner, and a full table service, wine, etc., for say, ten or a dozen people. On our arrival, all formed into groups under the trees, a cloth was laid out on the ground, dishes, plates and glasses arranged on it, and the champagne at once

frapped in small hand pails. There was then a dance in the open air, on a small platform, and in the afternoon, with cushions as seats for the ladies, these improvised dinner-tables were filled. Each had its separate hostess; all was harmony and pleasure. As night approached, the people re-embarked on the steamer and returned home by moonlight.[40]

Changes were taking place in Savannah at mid-century. In 1848 a telegraph line was run between Augusta and Savannah. In 1850 the Savannah Gas Works was established, and the street lamps, formerly fueled by whale oil, were converted to gas. The lamp lighter still had to make his nightly rounds, only now he would be lighting a gas jet. That year, legislation was enacted authorizing the appropriation of funds for the construction of the Savannah Public Waterworks, which would be completed in 1854 and would render obsolete the pumps and cisterns that stood in each of the city's squares. The water tower built on Franklin Square as part of the new system would remain a Savannah landmark until the turn of the century, when a change in the water system rendered it useless. In 1850 the Andrew Low mansion was completed on Lafayette Square and the new Custom House on Bay Street, at the intersection of Bull, was placed in operation. It was in the 1850's that the stone retaining walls were built along the riverfront and the sloping ramps of ballast stone were constructed to provide access to River Street. The cotton boom of the 1850's brought prosperity to Savannah, and Georgia was becoming increasingly industrialized. It was a period of growth for Savannah. The free population of the city, which stood at 9,081 in 1850, grew to 14,540 in 1860.[41]

Mary Telfair and the Hodgsons had something to do with the changing face of Savannah. They constructed a building on the southwest corner of Bull and Broughton Streets that was known as the Hodgson Building. It replaced the old Lyceum Hall that had stood on the site for decades. It was this building that years later Mary Telfair would devise to the Independent Presbyterian Church. But much of Savannah had not changed by 1850. The two-story clapboard inn where Washington had stayed on his trip to Georgia in 1791 still stood across the square from the Telfair mansion and would remain there throughout Mary Telfair's lifetime. The streets remained sandy and unpaved, making walking unpleasant particularly during periods of drought. It could be even worse during periods of heavy rain when the streets turned to mud. It was William B. Hodgson who came up with the idea that the pine woods to the south of Gaston Street should be made into a public park. He erected at his own expense a rude wooden fence around the twenty-six-acre tract for the purpose of keeping trespassers from cutting the trees. Originally known as Hodgson Park, it was an immediate success. Alexander R. Lawton mentioned the park favorably in a letter addressed to Hodgson in New York City: "The ladies make great use of 'Hodgson Park' & the 'German Band' plays there twice a week. They say it will need a more substantial railing to secure it against depredations." The area was renamed Forsyth Place in 1851 to honor John Forsyth, the well-known statesman who was governor of Georgia in the late 1820's and under whom Hodgson served after Forsyth was appointed secretary of state by President Jackson in 1834. At the time the park was renamed, a cast-iron railing was built around the site. Later, in 1858, the lovely white cast-iron fountain was installed, and the surrounding area became a favorite gathering spot for the people of Savannah. Hodgson loved to walk in the park in pleasant solitude thinking his scholarly thoughts.[42]

On May 30, 1851, Mary, Margaret, Mr. Hodgson, and their servant George left on a tour of the Continent that would keep them away from home for over a year.[43] They sailed from the port of New York on the steamship *Franklin*, and after a voyage of twelve days, during which they spotted icebergs, arrived in Le Havre on June 12. They were greeted at the quay by a crowd of thousands out to see the great ship from America, the men in their peasant blouses and the women in their high Normandy caps. They visited Rouen and then were off to Paris for shopping and sightseeing. They toured the Low Countries, a place that Margaret was glad to leave for she found the people of Holland to be uncouth.

The travelers headed south through Germany, traveling part of the way on a Rhine steamer. Near Bonn, Mary Telfair was enchanted to view the ruin of the castle of Roland, the illustrious nephew of Charlemagne who wooed and won the hand of the beautiful Hildegarde. Before they could wed, he was called to war by his uncle. After performing prodigious feats of valor, he was wounded at the hand of a Saracen infidel and was taken for dead. A spark of life appeared, however, and he was taken to the cottage of a shepherd, where in time he recovered. When news of his supposed death reached his beloved, she entered the Ursuline Convent on Nuns Island, never to emerge again. Roland returned and learned that his betrothed had taken the veil. He built a castle on the mountain overlooking the convent so that he could be close to his only love. When she died and was taken to her final resting place, Roland sat for hours with his eyes fixed upon the cemetery and then expired. Mary loved tales such as these. She may have remembered that it was the songs of this same Roland that the minstrel Taillifer had sung as he entered the fray against the English at the Battle of Hastings.

Although Mary liked the beauty and romance of Germany, there was much that she disapproved of in the conduct of the people of that country. She believed that a woman, married or single, should be able to stand on her own two feet and come and go as she pleased. This was not true of the women in Germany: "In Germany a married woman can only walk with her Husband. What a commentary upon the state of Society! The English and Americans do not adopt their customs—they walk and talk with whom they please, which is their 'Declaration of Independence.'"

Soon the travelers found themselves in Switzerland. They were detained in Lausanne for twelve days while their servant George recovered from an illness. Perhaps he suffered from exhaustion as a result of the pace set by his masters. He was strong and young (in his early thirties at the time), but after all, he was only human. When George was well enough, the travelers set off for Vienna. They stayed for several weeks at the famous Windsor Hotel, where Eliza Terrell also was staying.[44] The two woman enjoyed their time together in a city that Mary thought magnificent. Trieste was the next stop and then Venice. Mary was much taken with Venice. She wrote upon first viewing the city: "Rising with her tiara of proud towers—it seemed like the embodiment of a dream, for everything is *dreamy* in it. A universal stillness reigns, its *Streets* are canals—its *Coaches* Gondolas." She loved the architecture of Venice, which she noted had been compared to "Poetry in Stone." She thought that the architecture of the Piazza San Marco fully illustrated Madame De Staël's notion of architecture as "Frozen Music," for "its unbroken line of arcades in their marble beauty are as harmonious as the dulcet tones of Jenny Lind." She also was happy to visit the piazza with an acquaintance to eat ice cream and listen to the band that played in the evening.

The family was in Florence in November and found the weather

extremely cold. They endured a severe snow storm on the last day of
the month. In Florence, in addition to viewing the masterpieces in
the Uffizi, Mary purchased an oil painting of Mary Magdalen by an
unknown artist. Senor Petrini, the dealer from whom she purchased
the painting, assured her that it was at least a hundred years old. With
its ornate gold frame, it would be one of the paintings bequeathed by
Mary Telfair to the Georgia Historical Society for the Telfair Academy of Arts and Sciences.

In mid-December the family set out for Rome, then part of the
Papal States. In a letter to the Habershams from Florence, Hodgson
expressed the hope that they would find warm accommodations
there and that they would have a safe journey:

> If we are fortunate enough to escape banditti and accidents in
> the Mediterranean, we shall have cause of congratulation. Several
> families, traveling, have recently been robbed in the Papal States,
> and one adventure of this kind took place four days before we
> set out from Boulogne to Florence. But the rule is that greater
> security exists immediately after an accident. Two steamers ran
> into each other some short time ago, and one went down carry-
> ing with her entire families.[45]

Hodgson also had some gossip to pass on to the Habershams:

> Henry Wyckoff, well known at home for his connection with
> Fanny Elssler, is in prison at Genoa for having attempted forcibly
> to compel an heiress to marry him. The lady is Miss Gamble,
> niece of the Florida Gambles. She was traveling alone with a
> maid & courier. This last was a bribed accomplice. The whole
> story would make a romance. It is said that he will be sent to the
> galleys. It is difficult in such cases to arrive at truth.[46]

The Christmas holidays were spent in Rome, and it was there that
Margaret sat for the marble bas-relief profile by the sculptor Shakespeare Wood that is now at the Telfair Academy. Hodgson was impressed by the pageantry in Rome:

> During these Christmas holidays, we have witnessed many
> imposing spectacles in the great Catholic churches here. At St.
> Peter's the wonder of the world, the Pope, Pius IX, was carried

through the long aisle in a chair under a canopy on the shoulders of twelve of his people. On either side of him were borne two huge ostrich fans. There were two rows of soldiers through which he passed the whole length of the Church. I suppose there were 500 soldiers under arms. At High Mass, on the elevation of the Host, there was a grand flourish of trumpets. The whole scene was vastly grand and imposing; but I could not perceive its connection with religious devotion.[47]

Hodgson reported to the Habershams on an audience with the Pope and on Protestant worship in the Papal States:

Mr. Cass our chargé d'affaires has presented us to his Holiness. He appears to be a very mild, amiable man. You are aware that since his return from Naples he granted to Americans the liberty of having a place of worship within the walls of the City. Lately that privilege has been annulled because all other Protestant nations demanded the same right, and we now have to worship in a room of Mr. Cass' private residence. The English have a Church just outside of the walls.[48]

The family left Genoa for Marseilles in mid-April and then made its way through the south of France and on by steamer to Bordeaux. Four miles from the city, near the village of Blanquefort, Mary and her companions visited the ruins of the palace of the Black Prince, the same knight who years later would be depicted by the artist, Julian Story, standing over the body of blind King John of Bohemia after the Battle of Crécy in a painting that now hangs in the Telfair Academy.

After passing through the Loire Valley, the travelers crossed the channel to England and visited the site of the Battle of Hastings, where the minstrel Taillifer had lost his life in 1066. They went on to London, in Mary's opinion "the most gloomy & uninteresting place in the old world." Mary hated injustice, and the $1.50 per day "service charge" imposed by the Ellis Hotel in London infuriated her because not one cent of it was given to the servants. Mary had no patience with the pretensions of the English nobility with their coaches driven by wigged coachmen and with liveried footmen hanging on behind. Upon meeting a charming acquaintance and later learning that she was the Dowager Viscountess of Ashbrook, Mary sniffed, "It made no difference in my opinion of her having had the Organ of *Reverence for Rank* left out of my head." On another occasion she minced no words in stating, "The servile devotion to rank in the English Character is disgusting." After seeing Queen Victoria pass by in London, Mary wrote with disapproval, "She is a coarse looking woman with rather a cold countenance, but she *wears a crown,* and that wins the homage of her subjects."

A trip to the Isle of Wight followed the stay in London. Then the family returned for another visit to Paris, where Napoleon's tomb was being constructed at the Invalides. Mary disapproved of smoking, and the sight of a *"defense de fumer"* sign during this stay in Paris inspired her to sound off on the deplorable smoking habits of the Germans and the Dutch. On August 22, 1852, Mary and her companions sailed from Liverpool to New York on the steamship *Arctic,* tired but fulfilled by the wonders of their tour. One can only marvel at the amount of energy expended over the preceding year by the sixty-one-year-old Mary Telfair. There was plenty of good entertainment during the crossing, as well as food for the soul:

> Madame Sontag, the charming vocalist, gave a concert in the upper Saloon for the benefit of the Fire Men. She delighted the audience by her soul-thrilling melodious voice which some connoisseurs say is superior to Jenny Lind's. Miss Keen, a young actress, recited the Maniac and the evening's entertainment closed with a Mesmeric Exhibition. Sunday, the last day aboard the *Arctic,* the Revd. Dr. Johns of Baltimore preached a beautiful and affecting sermon from the text "and Jesus wept"—he described in a most touching manner the deep sympathy manifested by our Lord towards the sorrowing Sisters of Bethany, and introduced several examples in Holy Writ of the efficacy of grief upon the human heart.

It had been a grand trip, and Mary Telfair had much to report to her friends upon her return to America. Surely she would tell them of seeing Louis Napoleon reviewing twenty thousand troops on the Champs de Mars in Paris, the great man distinguishable from his officers by the white plume in his hat. Her friends would be amused by the story of the trip by rail to Versailles and how Mr. Hodgson had left the train at one of the stations along the way and was stranded as it unexpectedly pulled away. Unfortunately he had with him the passport that the ladies would have to show to the concierge upon entering the palace. The good news was that Mary was sufficiently fluent in French to explain their plight to a respectable-looking couple who insisted that she and Margaret enter the palace under their wing. There would be smiles in the drawing room when Mary described how Hodgson finally turned up breathless and flustered halfway through the tour.

There was much more to report: the "world of fashion" that one saw along the Champs Élysées; the thrill at spotting the "fine head" of de Tocqueville in the French Chamber of Deputies; how lovely it was to drive through the Bois de Boulogne; the beauty of the botanic gardens in Brussels; the grandeur of the castle at Heidelberg; the sight of the great seaport of Rotterdam. Mary's friends would be interested to hear of "the miserable house from which the great banker Rothschild issued" and of how Mary had seen the house in Frankfurt in which Martin Luther had lived. Surely they would have understood the emotion that Mary felt at the time when they learned that she and her sister actually had set foot in the room overlooking Lake Geneva, where Lord Byron had written "The Prisoner of Chillon."

Mary Telfair loved to travel in Europe and had no use for anyone who did not. Of an acquaintance who disliked Europe, her only comment was that this was "proof that she is neither a woman of taste or high education."[49] Mary found inspiration in visiting the sites where the great events in history had taken place. Upon seeing the old palace in Innsbruck, she could conjure up in her mind the "tempestuous night" in 1552 when Charles the Fifth escaped from that place in a litter with his prisoner, the Elector of Saxony. After writing in her journal of the rocky mountain in the Tyrol where the Emperor Maximilian had fallen and was saved by a hunter from a horrible death, Mary reflected eloquently on her love for the romantic past: "It is these reminiscences of bygone ages which invest European travel with such a charm. History and Poetry give their colouring to all that we see, and the imagination is hourly gratified by the beautiful and grand in Nature being rendered more interesting by the legends of those powerful auxiliaries."

Nowhere did Mary Telfair feel as deep a communion with the past than at Westminster Abbey, "that glorious pile, where the dead of feudal ages sleep." Of this sacred place she wrote in her journal:

There are enshrined the marble Forms of those who taught us in childhood and early youth to love the historic page—The statesman too, whose eloquence, "listening senates could command." I thought that I could trace the genius of Gray in his elegant face, worthy of the author of his Elegy. Henry the Seventh's Chapel is a gem indeed, set in a gothic frame. I thought of Mr. Webster's comparison of it to Nature's Cathedral at Bonaventure. The tomb of Mary Queen of Scots with her beautiful form stretched upon it—the pale hue of death resting upon her finely chiseled features occupies the centre of that Royal Mausoleum.

Mary enjoyed meeting people during her travels. She was far from shy. She would strike up a conversation with anyone who appeared to be a refined person of her own class. She liked to make use of her knowledge of French and on occasion would converse in their own language with French-speaking people with whom she became acquainted. In Tours she chatted with her neighbor at the table d'hôte who turned out to be a most interesting gentleman. He had traveled all over the world after fighting with Wellington at the Battle of Waterloo. In Baden-Baden she met the sister of Lord Metcalf, the governor-general of Canada. On another occasion she met a lady whose brother was the physician who accompanied Florence Nightingale to the Crimea. These encounters were all faithfully recorded in her travel journal.

Mary Telfair, for her entire life, found pleasure in the visual arts and the beauties of nature. "Taste," she wrote, "may be defined the power of receiving pleasure from the beauties of nature and of art." During her European travels, she had seen some of the world's greatest paintings. In Venice she marveled at the works of Titian, Tintoretto, Bellini, and Paolo Veronese. While there, she gazed in awe at Tintoretto's immense painting of Paradise in the Doge's Palace. She especially admired an Adoration of the Magi that she saw in Freyburg, Germany. In Nuremberg she saw several paintings by Albrecht Dürer. She visited the picture gallery in Antwerp dedicated to the Dutch Masters and found remarkable *The Young Bull* by the seventeenth-century Dutch painter Paul Potter. In Antwerp's old cathedral, she found inspiration in Rubens' *Descent from the Cross*. She had seen paintings by Rembrandt, Raphael, and Holbein. She had seen the

great marbles of antiquity and particularly admired the Dying Glad-
iator in Rome's Capitoline Museum for, she wrote, "so true to nature
is the expression of suffering in his manly face." At times, when she
came upon a scene in nature that stirred her, she could become poetical: "It is harvest season and to see the reapers in the field (men and
women) forms a sweet picture of rural life such as the English Poets
have described, and such as the lovers of Nature love to gaze upon."

Leaving Louvie Juzon, in the south of France in the shadow of the
Pyrenees, Telfair wrote of "blooming valleys, smiling in their dewy
freshness, and the near mountains with their Shepherds and Dogs
following their flocks." She marveled at "the lofty chain of the Pyrenees covered with snow." "How elevating are such scenes to the mind!"
she wrote, "How cheering to the spirits!" Often the beauty of nature
would inspire Mary Telfair to thoughts of God. To her the French
Alps seemed to say, "the hand that made me is divine." After gazing
upon them, she returned to her hotel to write in her journal: "Who
can look upon those snowy Alps and their glaciers descending like
frozen waterfalls, and looking like monumental pillars in a graveyard,
without elevating their thoughts above this Earth—for they seem a
feeble emblem of Eternity for they can never disappear until Time
shall be no more."

When traveling abroad, Mary Telfair always managed to find a
Protestant church to attend on Sunday, whether it was the Huguenot
church in Rouen, where the minister gave the sermon in French, or
the Wesleyan Chapel in Paris, a "humble little sanctuary in the heart
of a gay metropolis." The Huguenot church in Rouen had once been
Catholic, and Mary did not appreciate the remnants of popery that
were still part of the ornamentation. She particularly admired a church
that she visited in Switzerland because, "It looks Protestant." In re-
marking on a woman with a sweet smile she did not merely compare
her to an abbess or a nun, but to a "Directress of a Protestant Society
of Sisters of Charity." Gazing upon the ruin of Tintern Abbey, Telfair mused over the destruction of ecclesiastical buildings during the
Reformation and found it an acceptable necessity: "We should call it
cruel in the Reformers to have destroyed such exquisite specimens of
human skill, if we were not satisfied that it was essential to the establishment of a purer religion to efface those splendid shrines of an
idolatrous worship."

Mary Telfair had passed through some of the worst and some of the best times of her life. She had emerged with her soul cleansed by a year immersed in the history and beauty of Europe. She would return home to a country that was becoming ever more deeply divided over the issue of slavery and that in another decade would find itself involved in a tragic sectional conflict.

16

Advancing Years and the Approach of War

When musing on companions gone
We doubly feel ourselves alone.

Sir Walter Scott, *Marmion* (1808)

After returning from Europe, the family spent the fall of 1852 at the house on Brevoort Place in New York. In November, Mary Telfair wrote to Eliza Terrell in Vienna sending her news from America. She reported on the marriage of George Frederick Tilghman Jones (who at the time was calling himself George Wymberley-Jones) to Mary Nuttall: "Wimberly Jones was united to Mary Nuttall a fortnight since and they sailed yesterday on the *Baltic* for Liverpool and anticipate passing the winter in Italy." "We were not invited to the Jones Wedding for more reasons I suppose than *one*," Mary added with a suggestion of disappointment. It is difficult to fathom why invitations were not issued to Mary and her sister for they were cousins of the groom and appeared to be on good terms with him and his bride. Mary also reported on Mary Jones's happiness since her marriage to the Reverend William Harison, a man eight years her junior. She thought the disparity "a vast difference on the woman's side for Father Time usually claims her for his own sooner than the Man, unless he says with the Poet 'Thou never canst decay in Soul, Thou always wilt be fair.'" Men with "evergreen affections," she added, are "like angels visits few and far between."[1]

Telfair knew that Eliza Terrell would be interested in hearing news

309

of Alberta. The girl's marriage to Charles Arnold had not worked out, as Mary Telfair could have predicted. Two years after her elopement, she was living in the upcountry and her husband was living in Savannah. The two were still married, but as Telfair reported, "Arnold holds out in not returning," and Alberta was complaining that she could not get any money out of her husband. Telfair became rather worked up in informing Mrs. Terrell of another instance of Alberta's infamy:

> Berta told Mrs. McAllister that you invited her to go with you to Europe but that she could not leave her Grand Mother. I *denied the fact* knowing you too well to believe it and I may add knowing her equally well. Unfortunate Being thus to persevere in untruth. That propensity has been her ruin joined with her ungovernable passions.[2]

During Alberta's estrangement from Arnold, she engaged in some type of scandalous behavior so dark that Mary Telfair could not bring herself to describe it in writing, even to Eliza Terrell:

> I paid Mrs. Telfair a visit this morning. "Her Chaplain" (as Mr. Preston calls *the old Mariner*) was by her side, and Mrs. Lincoln near her bed. Her brother had just left her, and she seemed though glad to see us, very dull. There is a report in town that her illness was occasioned by Berta's imprudence. Whether it is so I know not, for I know less of the proceedings in that house than any one in Savannah for I never ask a question. Mrs. Jackson (*entre nous*) made some disclosures to me that corresponded with the *feats* performed at Athens summer before the last. If I was not afraid to trust what she told me to pen, ink, and paper, I would write it to you. All Savannah is talking of it, but I prefer your hearing of it from another source. I would not believe it when Mrs. J told it to me but set it down to Savannah gossip but it was afterwards communicated to me by a person of high Character and whose truth I have entire confidence in. She knew *all the circumstances*, which look pretty dark. *Sappho* will yet be her ruin, if I am any Prophetess. The next imitation of Mrs. W. B. will be *a Divorce*. I look upon the first, *Charioteering*, as innocent but the *Jehu boldness* which is displayed invites coarse remarks, and there are Men always ready to say vulgar things of Women who dare to

depart from the path of Delicacy. I have a vague notion that Mrs. Harden told you of it, for she I am sure has heard it. I trust that Mrs. Telfair's life will be prolonged for Berta's sake. When she pays her debt of Nature there will be no restraint. There is no act that she may perform that will astonish me, and I sometimes think she must be deranged. She attended the Theatre every night when Persons were sitting up with her Grand Mother unattended by *Spouse* or *Ciresbeo*—though the world gives her three. I thought that there was something very mysterious in the insinuations of the two *old crones* Mom Sally & Mom Clarissa, when they talked of the wanderings of their Mistress's mind—the latter pointed to her heart saying, "*trouble lies there*."[3]

Alberta and Charles Arnold finally were divorced in early 1856. Mary Telfair learned from the newspaper that he had obtained leave of the legislature to marry again. He had been engaged for some time to a young widow from Boston who had spent the previous three or four years in Savannah for the benefit of the health of her eight-year-old son. She was a woman of independent means and well educated. Mary was incredulous. "Can we wonder at the sneering manner in which some Men talk of Women for so many lower themselves by marrying in every way beneath them," she wrote. The widow's devotion to Alberta's husband was "an Enigma." Mary wondered how this woman could marry a man so "dissolute and uneducated." She thought the man a disgrace. "Certainly," she wrote, "his first step in life, eloping with a Child for the sake of her money was very disgraceful, and the evils which have resulted to both incalculable."[4]

Alberta celebrated her divorce by immediately going off with no protection but that of her maid to the Charleston races, behavior nothing short of scandalous. Now that she was no longer Mrs. Arnold, Alberta decided to take the name Telfair rather than revert to her maiden name, Cobb. Mary Telfair was vehement in her disapproval when she heard this shocking news:

> I was perfectly amazed several days since to hear a gentleman say Mrs. Telfair was going that night in the Boat to Charleston. I said impossible—He replied Mrs. *Addison* Telfair. Who is she I replied for I never heard of such a person. Mrs. Arnold that was. I said has she taken the name of Telfair. Why did she not resume as is always done her own name. He made no response

to my question. I am sure that Cobb is a more popular name in the State than Telfair and suits her better since it was her Father's name. I feel provoked at her taking a name she is no way entitled to but I hope that she will change it soon.

Mary was inclined to think that Alberta's grandmother had encouraged her to take the name Telfair. "If she thinks that is any recommendation to me she is mistaken," Mary assured Eliza Terrell. "I am truly glad that she is not a Telfair. I never could discover one quality in her that resembled her Grandfather." As far as the grandmother was concerned, "Some people are no more calculated to train children than they are to head Armies."[5]

Lucy Terrell enrolled in school in New York as Mary Telfair had insisted she must. She was accompanied there by her mother. "What I shall do with myself while they are resident in New York I know not," her father wrote to William Hodgson. As far as Mary Telfair was concerned, Lucy was everything that Alberta was not, and she and the Hodgsons welcomed the young woman into their home. The warm regard that Mary and her family felt for Lucy was reciprocated in full and was appreciated by her parents. Dr. Terrell wrote approvingly of this relationship in a November 1853 letter to Mr. Hodgson:

> I received your very kind letter by Lucy and also the one previous referring to the young lady's health. For your kind and considerate attentions to her we are under the greatest obligations, you and the ladies of your family have so won her affections that she refers to you rather as relatives than as friends and in the little narratives of circumstances about New Port and New York she speaks of our house or our parlor quite as readily as if you had adopted her. I am now glad that she spent so much time with you which I did not quite like at first supposing that she would be troublesome, desirous as most young people are of strolling about in search of trifling amusements, if in this particular she had any penchant I have the confident belief that the ladies put her to rights and indeed it was this belief that reconciled me to her long absence.[6]

A letter to Lucy Terrell written in April 1854 reveals that as Mary Telfair grew older she had lost none of her delight in expressing her opinions on affairs of the heart:

> Prepare yourself for a *shock*. You have a *Deserter* from your corps of Admirers. Barnwell has sought and won the heart of Miss Clarkson of New York best known as grand daughter to Edwd. P. Livingstone. She is très jeune, très belle, et très riche. What more could an *amateur* of worldly advantages desire. I presume that by & by he will erect une très belle maison in Fifth Avenue that will rival *"Uncle Tom's Cabin."* If I had an only daughter (which Miss C. is) I should be very unwilling to give her to such a mere man of Society. The *fag* end (as a Lady once said of a beau) of an old family. Miss Clarkson has only a brother, so I suppose Barnwell will join the domestic group.

Margaret interrupted as Mary wrote and charged her to tell Lucy that Barnwell had at last found "the Crock of Gold."[7]

Mary's friendship with Lucy Terrell was one of the bright spots in her life at this time. The pleasure that she received from her relationship with the daughter of her friend stands in sharp contrast to the anguish that she felt as a result of Alberta's scandalous behavior. One receives the impression that knowing Lucy made her feel young again. Her letters to the young woman were always bright and cheerful and devoid of any of the neurotic ramblings that frequently crept into her correspondence with others during her blue periods. The chatter in her letters to Lucy is almost girlish, as in the case of her description of a bonnet that she had picked out for the girl in Savannah:

> As soon as I had received your letter, and order, I went to *the Toombs* not as a *Culprit* but as a Purchaser and made choice of a neat traveling Bonnet. I told her not to let it rest upon the neck, but to make it to shelter the face from the too ardent rays of Sol. I hope like the Milk Maid in the Fable that you have a *passion for green* as the only ribbon which we considered comme il faut in her shop was of that hue. I hope that you will like it. The price was 5 dollars, and 50 cts. for the box. I ordered it sent last evening to Mr. Duncan to direct & send it. I sent him a note by making assurance doubly sure, as I was ignorant whether to address it to Terrell or Sparta. The bill as you directed was put in the box.

Mary couldn't wait to hear whether her young friend approved of her choice:

Let me hear about all your projected movements and how you like your Bonnet and *green* ribbon. Laura, the pride of woman-kind, was dressed in green when Petrarch, the matchless Petrarch, first beheld her as he leant against that noble column in the old Cathedral and saw her rise like Thetis from her devotions. You must be wearied ma chère petit with this illegible scrawl.

Mary requested Lucy to direct her next letter to her care of J. R. Habersham at 13 Broadway in New York for she was about to head for the North and expected to spend five days in "that Bedlam or Babel whichever you esteem most poetical." She expected to be in some new and quiet place in July and August and to spend September in Newport after the "Matrimonial Speculators" leave.[8]

Mary took a great interest in Lucy Terrell's romantic life and, even as a woman in her sixties, liked to exchange views with the young woman on men and love, as she had with Mary Few in earlier years:

I can understand that a young Lady may like the society of a Gentleman without being *in love*. I have been delighted with the conversation of Men that I never could in mes beaux jours have *loved* so I comprehend fully your feelings toward the *Cavaliero*—L'Âme de Paris et *le compagnon de voyage* to the Mammoth Cave—what *Romances* people invent.[9]

Telfair also liked to share with Lucy news of the rumored attachments of their mutual friends, however unreliable they might be:

A few evenings since Cooper, your Mother's favorite Savannah beau, came to see us. He is very natural & intelligent—Mr. Coleman comes frequently to see us. Report has appropriated him to Miss Berrien and Miss Ellen Habersham—a good [match] for either, but perhaps it has not yet entered his head for the origin of reports are very mysterious. We have no old Dowagers here who make matches on commission as in Paris but we have a set of Gossips "in the land of the *free*" who, as like the Fates, amuse themselves with *weaving* destinies. No one is exempt from their *toils*.[10]

The new year brought gifts from Lucy Terrell. Mary was quick to extend her thanks:

Yesterday, my dear Lucy, your beautiful New Years offerings were received, and we regard them with pious care, as Pilgrims do their holy relics—Thank you for those valued specimens of your taste and industry. The Mat shall grace the new Library table which is [to be in] the large Drawing room after it is painted, and when you come to visit us you will see it in *bold relief.* The Slippers will be sported next summer, where I know not, for we have learned to form no distant plans. "He builds too low who builds beneath the skies."[11]

In 1854 Mary Telfair suffered the loss of one of her dearest friends, Mrs. Catherine Few, the mother of the Few ladies and a second mother to Mary. Mary and her sisters visited her at her home at 10 Park Place and later on Ninth Street whenever they were in New York. It was Mrs. Few who in 1818 made the very first entry in young Mary Telfair's commonplace book, a somewhat rambling expression of affection full of Christian piety. Mrs. Few also had been a dear friend of Mary Telfair's mother, and the two ladies corresponded on a regular basis while Mrs. Telfair was alive. Mrs. Few died on August 7, her ninetieth birthday, in Hastings-on-Hudson at the home of her son-in-law Albert Chrystie. She had been born Catherine Nicholson in New York City in 1764. As a young woman, she joined the Dutch Reformed Church and gave herself to God. Each day she read her Bible, and when her eyes finally gave out, the Scriptures were read to her by others. The hours at dusk were spent in prayer. Mrs. Few loved her daughters' close friends as if they were her own children. Of Mary Telfair and Margaret Hodgson, she said to her daughter Frances Chrystie shortly before her death, "I have always loved them; tell them I send my love to them. I think often of them; I pray for them; they have a heavy responsibility; I trust they will be shown the best way." After Mrs. Few died, Frances composed a memoir of her mother with particular emphasis on her last days. Mary Telfair copied it into a notebook and kept it among her treasures.[12]

Young William Chrystie was married in January 1855 to Emily Thomas of Augusta. The son of Albert and Frances Chrystie, the boy who had traveled through Europe with his parents and the Telfair ladies in 1841 and 1842 had grown to be a man. Mary wanted to be at the wedding, but an indisposition kept her at home:

Our young friend Wm. Chrystie spent three days with us on his way to Augusta to claim his betrothed and on the Evening of the 11th "He called her his, before the holy man" and the bridal party leave for Cuba on Tuesday next. We were all packed for the wedding intending to take Jefferson Plantation on the way back, but I was seized with a sick head ache, and Mr. Hodgson went without us.[13]

Mary Telfair managed to get out a bit that winter. One evening she dined en famille with her friend Miss Campbell, and on the same day she had tea with Mrs. James Hunter. She was at Christ Church to witness the marriage of Frederick Habersham and Miss Elliott. She dined with George Wymberley Jones (then called) at Wormsloe (the new style spelling). The sight of the old oaks there, wreathed with moss, made her heart expand towards "Nature, a mother kind alike to all." Her visit led her to muse, "What would become of us in the Sunny South if we had not the communion of woods and wild flowers, with a Carriage & horses to drive about and breathe the balmy air." Savannah society frequently was enlivened by the arrival of an interesting visitor. "We are to have the honorable Miss Murray with us this spring," Mary wrote to Lucy Terrell. "She is maid of honor to Victoria and said to be a Geologist, Botanist, Musician and Linguist—Where will she find her equal in the New World." Other visitors were not so welcome: "We have had the Northern *hordes* pouring down upon us all winter. Letters of introduction compel people to be civil to the *Barbarians* against their will. Some of them no doubt will pass us in Broad Way with a *well bred stare*."[14]

Mary Telfair was in Savannah during the spring of 1855 enjoying her simple pleasures in reasonably good spirits. She cherished the company of Sarah Cecil, as she had for so many years: "Miss Cecil and myself like Darby & Joan took seats vis à vis at the 'hearth stone' and no visitor interrupted our tête a têtes. We enjoyed our seclusion and talked over past and present." One evening that spring, a sacred concert was performed at the Methodist Church next door to the mansion on St. James Square, and Mary and her sister were able to hear the melody distinctly in their parlor as the organist's pipes "were tuned to concert pitch." Mary was reading *The Preacher and the King*. "It is full of talent," she wrote, "and my favorite Fénelon appears to great advantage among the Saints and sages of the age of Louis

Quatorze which was certainly the Augustan Age of France." The rain that descended in torrents that spring did not seem to bother Mary, for she passed it off as a "blessing to the Husband Man."[15]

There would be another trip to Europe in 1855.[16] On June 27 the Hodgsons and Mary Telfair sailed from New York to Liverpool aboard the steamer *Atlantic*. They saw no sun for eleven days. From Liverpool they went by steamer to Chester. They headed south and in Gloucester visited the cathedral and saw the monument to Dr. Edward Jenner, the discoverer of the smallpox vaccine. They saw the seaside towns of Torquay and Dartmouth in Devon and then traveled to Bath and London. Having been to London on two previous trips abroad, Mary and her sister were content to spend their time driving in Hyde Park each day and revisiting Westminster Abbey.

The steamer from Dover took them to Calais. Traveling in Germany, they visited Bonn, Frankfurt, Worms, Munich, and the Tyrol, a region that Mary loved. They visited Zurich and spent some time in Basel. They went on to Paris, where they enjoyed drives in the Bois de Bologne. There Mary saw the Empress Eugénie driving in her open barouche. She spotted her again in the Palais de l'Industrie. Margaret Hodgson wrote of the Empress, "She is not beautiful but exceedingly refined in appearance and looks so sensitive as if a *rude blast* would destroy her delicate frame." Mary found Paris "marvelously improved" under Louis Napoleon. Margaret noted that "his great aim at present next to the distinction of the great alliance with England is to embellish Paris." She found the Louvre "marvelously extended" since her last visit. She described the most beautiful boulevard in Paris: "The Champs Élysées is embellished with parterres of flowers refreshed by fountains which sparkle like precious gems when the bright beams of the sun reflect upon them." Sister Mary thought the Bois de Bologne the rival of Hyde Park and found the Rue de Rivoli "splendidly built up." Nonetheless, she preferred old Paris to the new.[17]

The Paris Exposition of 1855 was in progress at the time of Mary Telfair's visit to that city, and William Hodgson attended as commissioner from the State of Georgia. In this capacity he was presented with a certificate and a handsome silver medallion bearing a likeness of Napoleon III in profile. Hodgson delivered a speech in French in the Congress, which was highly commended. He was not a little pleased to find that an English lord who preceded him at the podium required some occasional prompting. On October 21, 1855, Hodgson and the ladies left the City of Lights for Dover and the trip home. The passage by sea to New York was uneventful.[18]

By this time, rail transportation had been established along the Eastern seaboard, but Mary Telfair and her sister preferred to make the journey from New York to Savannah by steamship. Travel by steamship had become increasingly comfortable. "The Steamers now are like floating Hotels," Mary wrote, "so comfortable and so much cleaner than the Collins Line." Besides, Mary had a fear of trains. "We heard of so many awful railroad accidents that we decided to embark upon the sea," she explained. "After all we are as safe there as upon land if we realize the protecting care of a Providence that never sleeps." Mr. Hodgson had left for Savannah immediately after docking in New York, but Mary and Margaret tarried there for a few days to rest. It was cold in the city, and snow fell on the day before the ladies departed for Savannah. The sea passage was half rough and half smooth as Mary poetically described it: "We left New York in a storm and it blew a gale until we turned Cape Hatteras, then a change came over the sea and sky. The azure of the latter recalled that of Italy and the moon reigned in full majesty—not a cloud darkened the refulgent lamp of night."[19]

Shortly after their return to Savannah, Mary and Margaret made plans to travel to Sparta to visit Eliza Terrell and her daughter. Hodgson was to go off on his own to check on the properties in Burke County. Dr. Terrell had died on the preceding Fourth of July. Mary had valued and respected his character and intellect and was pleased to learn that before his passing he had made his peace with God. The sorrow over her father's loss had affected Lucy's health. Mary, in preparation for the trip, wrote to Eliza Terrell that "though our meeting will be sad remembering the past linked by so many associations it will I am sure do us all good." "It is better to go to the House of Mourning than to the House of feasting," she assured her friend, "and I am more at Home with the afflicted than with the gay." "On an average I have not slept more than five hours each night since I left England," she told Mrs. Terrell, "and you must expect to see me looking haggard & thin." The program called for the Telfair ladies to pass two nights at the Retreat Plantation in Jefferson County, forty miles from Sparta, on the way to the Terrell residence. From there, they were to proceed to the Terrell plantation on the Ogeechee River, and Mrs. Terrell was to send a carriage there to pick them up.[20]

Mary Telfair's well-laid plans went awry, for she suffered one of her bouts of illness and was unable to make the trip. Her explanation and expressions of regret to Eliza Terrell give a picture of the health problems that Mary was undergoing at this stage of her life:

> It is impossible for me to express my regret at the very great disappointment I experienced in not being able to leave this morning. Our Trunk was strapped and every arrangement made for our departure but I have had a recurrence of that affection of my head, which an Eminent Physician I consulted in Paris told me proceeded from the heart. It always depresses me, and I cannot keep it off by medicine. The two sea voyages occurring so near each other and the furnace heat of the Cabin of the *Augusta* no doubt produced it. I am suffering from an entire derangement of the digestive organs. It was imprudent of me not to have rested longer, but I felt anxious to see you and thought if we deferred it later in the Season the road might be bad and you know I am very timid in a Carriage, more so I think than in a Ship. It is "Hope deferred" and it has made "the heart sick" but I was afraid of being detained by illness at the Retreat where there is no good Physician and I knew that Margaret would be miserable if she were placed in such a situation. We are the only two left of a once large and united family and as is natural bound up in each other, but you who have such strong affection, can comprehend all without my expressing it. How I regret next to not seeing you and dear Lucy that your Carriage should have been sent such a great distance for nothing. Mr. Hodgson says that he will try when we can go, to get us nearer Sparta with *our Donkeys*.

By the time she reached the end of her long letter, Mary's indisposition had progressed, for just before signing off she wrote, "It is most fortunate that I did not go this morning as my attack seems to have fallen on my bowels."[21]

Upon returning to Savannah from Europe, Mary received an earful concerning the disgraceful behavior of her great-niece Alberta. She wondered whether Mrs. Terrell had heard the same:

Did you hear of the *war whoop* given at the Fancy Ball? I hear that the *distinguished* character who *gave her away* says that she is deranged poor Child! She might by proper training have made a respectable woman. Habits are too confirmed now for any improvement unless the grace of God effects it. How entirely she governs her Grand Mother who seems to doat upon her more than she did upon her own children.[22]

Judge John M. Berrien died on New Year's Day, 1856, at the age of seventy-four. The old man, a former United States attorney general and senator, had suffered from a painful illness for two weeks before his death. He was attended by his children, except for his two youngest daughters who were at school in Philadelphia. His wife had died four years earlier. "Now our prominent men are all passing away," Mary lamented, "Soon a new race will act their part upon the Theatre of life." The experience of the Berrien girls in attempting to get to their father's funeral confirmed Mary's distrust of travel by rail. She related the near disaster to Eliza Terrell:

We hear of nothing but Railway collisions. The little Berriens, Sarah & Kate, had a narrow escape of their lives. Coming from Philadelphia by land a collision took place & one of them was dashed from her seat & thrown down. They arrived two days after their Father's funeral, and are now with Mrs. Hunter waiting for the Philadelphia steamer to get out of the blockade of ice in the Delaware.

"I have become an advocate for the sea," Mary concluded. "Fewer accidents happen in good steamers with good Commanders than on Rail Roads left to the mercy of drunken Engineers."[23]

That winter, Mary was paying particular attention to her health. "Thanks to Nux Vomica I am rid of my giddiness and for the last three days feel perfectly well," she reported to Lucy Terrell in mid-December. "I obey the injunction of my *Medicin* and walk every morning. I take no interest in it, but persevere in following good advice. I will *live* in the open air until the weather becomes too warm to permit it." Mary had experienced some problems with her eyes and was taking care not to overtax them. Fortunately she had a friend who was happy to come by and read to her:

Martha Hunter comes once a week to read Sidney Smith to me. We take our *"elemental Tea"* first, and after our reading, wind up with de la crème de glace not equal to Tortoni's Boulevards des Italiennes, but superior to *Sue Jackson's*. Sidney Smith realizes my beau ideal of a wit and a domestic character—a kind Husband and loving Father, but I cannot fancy him a Clergyman.[24]

It was cold and rainy in Savannah that winter, but according to Telfair, the weather was mild compared to that in New York: "My friends in New York write as if they were in Siberia. Mrs. Bulloch goes dressed in wrappers and a Basque to bed, and no fire can warm them. All intercourse with friends arrested by the depth of the snow and the slippery pavements." Mary E. Thompson, now separated from her husband, was expected to arrive in Savannah to spend the winter at the Telfair mansion. She was blocked by the snow on her way to New York and was forced to return to Buffalo where she was residing at the time. The arriving steamers were checked every day, and whether Mary Thompson ever made it to Savannah is not a matter of record. An item of interest in Savannah that winter was the organization by William Neyle Habersham of a society of amateur musicians. Habersham was president of the group and played the flute. The other musicians were ladies, Miss Sorrel, Miss Stoddard, Miss Parkman, and Mrs. School. "Twice a month they give musical soirees," Mary Telfair noted. "I hear they are very pleasant and they must be very improving."[25]

A chatty letter to young Lucy Terrell reveals Mary Telfair's cheerful mood and the goings-on in Savannah during the winter of 1856:

Ma Chère Lucie,

How have you been able to resist the cold in Sparta? I hope not by the warmth of a wood fire, but by riding on horse back and long walks. The American Women destroy themselves from want of exercise in the open air and irregular hours. We receive terrific accounts of the weather in New York. Snows of Alpine depth wall up the Houses and Rail roads in the interior of the state [are] impassable. I am too happy not to be there. Savannah is now very gay. Mrs. Gordon has had a brilliant party. Mrs. Stoddard followed her example. Miss Johnson's was on Tuesday night. Mrs. Green and Mrs. Lovell are each to give one before

Lent. As we never go to such places, it does not add to our gaiety. An Hungarian Count brought a letter from Mrs. A. Barclay to Mr. Hodgson and Mrs. Wallburgh to me. We have had him twice to tea. He is very animated, well bred and agreeable— Appears to be about 35. I think he resembles Charles Stuart in face. I asked him if he did not esteem Mrs. Wimberly Jones a handsome woman—He remarked, "She *has been* beautiful, but she is passé." I said how old do you think she is. He replied thirty. He was amazed when I informed him that she was not quite twenty-one. There is to be a Bachelors Ball on Tuesday. The Band from Charleston is to play for the disciples of Terpsichore to dance. Those things seem "flat, stale and unprofitable" to me but how many depend upon them for enjoyment.

Several Demoiselles have made their entrée into Society this winter. Miss Mollyneaux educated in Paris—Miss Gordon a pupil of Madame Candor's—Miss Waring—Miss Jane and Miss Augusta Kollock both educated at Montpellier. I have heard of no new beaux. One of the old ones (as I am in America, I am privileged to use the word *old* on all occasions) Miller paid us a visit a few evenings since. He inquired most *affectionately* after Miss Terrell. . . . Thackeray is expected here next week to give four lectures on the Georges. The Historical Society has invited him.[26]

Thus life went on in Savannah in those halcyon days before the South was ravaged by war. There were sad events as well to disturb the flow of life. Albert Chrystie, Frances' husband, died in New York on April 23, 1856, shortly after returning from a visit to Savannah made to benefit his declining health.[27]

Mary had sent to Lucy Terrell a piece of wedding cake that had been given to her and accompanied it with the comment, "The idea of chaining two Doves on the Icing is a pretty symbol, and you must take it as a model when you commission me to get your bridal Cake." No matter that there was a slight delay in the delivery of the cake to Lucy, for as Mary assured her, "Wedding Cake you know never becomes stale, and the *Doves* will never cease *cooing*." It would not be long before Lucy would need a wedding cake of her own, for during the year 1856 she married Edgar Gilmer Dawson and moved to Columbus, Georgia, where her husband was engaged in the practice of law. Shortly thereafter, Dawson gave up his practice and concentrated his efforts on his large plantations in southwest Georgia. Mary knew that Mrs. Terrell would miss her daughter and tried to console her: "How you must feel her absence, but we all learn to live out of ourselves in others. 'Perfect love' to God 'casteth out fear' and perfect love to the creature casteth out selfishness. Let those we love make their own happiness even if it is independent of us." In time, the Dawsons had a little boy. They named him Terrell. Later Lucy gave birth to a little girl.[28]

Mary tried her best on numerous occasions to persuade Eliza Terrell to accompany her on her excursions to the North, but her friend had no taste for the watering spots that the Southerners frequented during the summer months. She tried once again in January 1857 to interest Mrs. Terrell in joining her:

> Are you *rooted & grounded* in your dislike for Northern Travel? I confess that the crowds that we meet there, and the *uproar* of knives & forks with the Black March attendant upon a Table d'hôte, is *killing* to those who love quiet and conversation. Still we shall continue to go to the Fountain of Saratoga in June. The comfort of Union Hall does not atone for the water we had to drink there, its propinquity to *you know what* is repugnant to two important senses, *Taste & Smell.*[29]

Mary's great-niece Alberta was remarried on April 21, 1857, this time in the German Lutheran Church. The ceremony was performed by the Reverend William Epping. The man that Alberta married was Augustus Peter Wetter, a handsome German from Mainz in the duchy of Hesse, a leader in Savannah's German community, and an engineer by profession. Mary Telfair, as could be expected, disapproved of the match. "I have never trusted much to ink & paper," she wrote to Eliza Terrell, "but if we were tête a tête I might tell you much that public rumor asserts respecting the Dutchman as his neighbor calls him." Mary could only shake her head over her great-niece's situation:

> The History of poor unfortunate Berta always reminds me of the fable of the frogs who cried to Jupiter for another king, not satisfied with a log—and he sent them a serpent. Arnold was

too good natured to govern her, and what was the result—you
know as well as I do. She must needs take a foreigner and a
stranger to her—pursuing the same clandestine course, marrying him without the knowledge of her Grand Mother who ought
never to have delegated power to him.

Whatever Mary Telfair might say of her sister-in-law's knowledge of
the marriage, this was not a "runaway match" (to use the vernacular
of the time and place). Wetter was twenty-seven, and Alberta was
twenty-three. They knew what they were doing and were married in
a religious ceremony, unlike the Arnold marriage which was performed by a justice of the peace.[30]

Referring to Alberta's grandmother in her letter to Mrs. Terrell,
Mary wrote:

I believe that you & myself are her best & most disinterested
friends. No one can aid her, but I believe for the first time in her
life she has been controlled by *a double chord*. I hear from public
report that W has broken B's marriage settlement and is "Mon-
arch of all he surveys." What a misfortune wealth is to a woman,
even the reputation of it brings often calamity & misery.[31]

According to Augustus Wetter, he and Alberta wrote to Miss
Telfair and Mrs. Hodgson following their marriage but received no
reply. The sisters refused to be introduced to Wetter and would not
speak to him or to Alberta. If he and Alberta were at the home of
Alberta's grandmother when Mary Telfair and Margaret Hodgson
came to call, the sisters would pass them by as though they did not
exist. Mary Telfair's friends, however, paid calls on the newlyweds.
Sarah Cecil, in particular, called on them frequently. Later, when the
couple had children, Mary Telfair took no notice of them either. Even
though Wetter and his family occupied a pew near to that of Mary
Telfair and the Hodgsons at the Independent Presbyterian Church,
their presence at church was totally ignored. Alberta's estrangement
from her aunts was complete, and according to her husband, it upset
her greatly for "she loved both of her aunties."[32]

Thomas Telfair's widow apparently suffered a stroke in 1857. "Mrs.
Telfair has been very ill of paralysis," Mary reported to Eliza Terrell.
"One morning that I sat by her bed I thought that at any moment

her spirit might pass from her frail body. Her mind does not appear to be more weakened than it was but her articulation is much affected." She lived for another several years in a state of ill health. Another of Mary's friends was having medical difficulties at the same time. Mary Few had her eyes operated on for cataracts, and the report that reached Savannah was that the procedure had not been successful. "It makes me very sad when I think of the possibility of her being deprived of that most precious gift—sight," Telfair wrote to Mrs. Terrell, "but her mind is in such a heavenly frame that she will bear it better than those who look only to this world as their portion."[33]

Margaret and William Hodgson never had a child of their own. Margaret's age at the time of their marriage, forty-five, probably was the deciding factor. Hodgson, however, kept up a warm relationship with the sons of his brother Joseph. Joseph Hodgson had a farm in Columbia, Virginia, a small town on the James River between the cities of Richmond and Charlottesville. His elder son, Joseph, Jr., was graduated from the College of New Jersey in June 1856 and delivered the class poem at commencement. He studied law at the University of Virginia. His uncle proudly kept among his possessions a copy of young Joseph's address to the Jefferson Society delivered in Charlottesville in April 1857. He was admitted to the bar in Virginia, but decided to settle in Kansas City, Missouri, where he became active in politics and business.[34]

Telfair Hodgson, the younger son, also attended the College of New Jersey. He was a member of the class of 1859. There his junior oration was on the Puritan and the Cavalier. He went on to take theological studies at the General Theological Seminary in New York. From there he would proudly write to his uncle of his rapid progress in the study of Hebrew. He would go on to be ordained in the Episcopal Church. In 1878 he became dean of the theology department at the University of the South, Sewanee, Tennessee, and a year later was appointed vice-chancellor of the university. He served as managing editor of *The Sewanee Review*, which he had helped to found. William B. Hodgson delighted in walking with his nephews along the wharves of New York during his summer visits to that city. He would point out to them the people arriving from other nations and would describe their customs and manners. He would surprise the foreign visitors by striking up a conversation with them in their native tongue, whether it be Chinese, Arabic, Parsee, or Russian. Telfair Hodgson wrote of a visit to New York to see the Hodgsons and Mary Telfair in the diary that he kept during his sophomore year at the College of New Jersey:

SEPT. 27 [1856]. New York, the city of cities, "the town" of the United States and worthy of its fame. On the fourth story of my hotel about four o'clock I was awakened by the usual noisy crowd of people and things rushing through Cortlandt Street but after a time I got used to the noise and went to sleep again. I woke about eight, dressed and went down to breakfast. I went up Broadway and visited the Anatomical Museum. Returned to my hotel and after packing my "impedimenta" left. Went to the barbers. Was shaved and had my hair cut. Then I went out to Broadway and got into an omnibus and went up to the Clarendon Hotel. Sent my card up to Aunt's room but she was out. Uncle in the reading room where he saluted me with sundry questions concerning the length of my shoes and if I wore suspenders or if I kept a toothbrush, etc. Together we went down Broadway and he purchased a vest and dresscoat for me and then sent me down to Mr. Habersham's office to get his letters at 8th Street. Went to the Clarendon where I saw Aunt and Miss Telfair and at five we dined. We remained about an hour and a half at dinner. We then went to our several rooms and prepared to make a fashionable call. So when dressed we took a Bowery car and went down to Bond Street and called on Mrs. and Miss Barclay, the wife and daughter of the British Consul. We returned about ten. Took supper by myself for the ladies had retired and then retired myself to dream over the sayings and actions of fashionable people and to awaken with the satisfaction that the day before I had enjoyed myself and to spend another day at the Clarendon.[35]

When the year 1858 began, Mary Telfair decided to keep a daily journal.[36] She stuck with it for little more than a month, but from it one can obtain an idea of her daily routine while in Savannah. It also suggests that, as she approached her sixty-seventh birthday, she had lost much of the zest for life that had been rekindled by her trips abroad. Or perhaps she just was having one of the "somber fits" that frequently came upon her during the holiday season when she wrote the entry for the first day of January:

"Happy New Year" is a sound like music to the ear of Child-hood and of youth; but after Sorrow has cast its blight upon the heart, and the ungentle tide of Time has swept with restless force our budding joys, and full blown blossoms of Hope away, we regard the wish as belonging to the Past, and yet we thank the Giver of all good for preserving us "through hidden dangers, toils and deaths" to the present period of our lives.

The evening of New Year's Day had been spent at prayer meeting at the sabbath school room of her church. A few days later Mary enjoyed "a sweet drive" in her pony chaise out the Thunderbolt Road, but deplored the number of live oaks that had been cut down. "The primeval forests are fast disappearing, and soon very soon no traces of the Monarchs of the forest will remain." On a dark and gloomy day when "deprived of walking and driving as in weeks past" she turned to "our Mute associates books, to relieve us from ennui." According to her journal, her reading included Mr. Winthrop's speech on the occasion of the dedication of the Boston Public Library and Dr. James Alexander's letters from Baden-Baden in the *New York Observer*. There were friends to entertain. "We had a small dinner party consisting of five guests—more than the Graces and less than the Muses. Conversation was general and occasionally playful."

When the weather cleared, Mary and her sister took a long and pleasant drive on the White Bluff Road. It was out on the White Bluff that William Neyle and Josephine Habersham had their home on the Vernon River. They called it "Avon" after the river associated with Josephine's favorite poet. On the drive, Mary plucked several branches of the yellow jasmine that was in full bloom. She noted that it rarely bloomed before February, but that the mild weather that year had brought it to full perfection.

On Sunday night, January 17, 1858, Mary went to hear Bishop Elliott preach at Christ Church. His sermon was based on the text, "How long shall thy vain thoughts lodge within thee?" There was nothing that Mary appreciated more than a good sermon. A few days later she drove out to Wormsloe, the estate facing on the Skidaway Narrows founded by Noble Jones. There she visited for two hours, probably with Mary Nuttall De Renne, then mistress of the estate.[37] "The air was delicious, and the sky without a cloud," she wrote. "It reminded me of a winter's day in Nice." The return trip was made on the White

Bluff Road. Mr. and Mrs. Hallowell Gardiner were in town escaping from the snows of Maine, and they dined at the mansion on St. James Square. A few days later Mary drove out the Louisville Road to Sabine Fields, the family plantation nearest to Savannah on the site of the present Amtrak railroad station. On some days there was shopping to be done and calls to be made in town. One morning she planted roses in the back garden. She noted her birthday on January 28, and called it a milestone that marked her "journey through the Pilgrims road to a final home." On the following day she mentioned receiving a letter from Matilda Tillotson. Then the journal ended, and the spaces for February are taken up with musings on such subjects as prayer, conversation, war ("the greatest scourge that can be inflicted upon poor human nature"), peace (which "can only be appreciated by those who have experienced the horrors of war"), and faith. These are followed by short pieces on flowers, shells ("the flowers of the ocean"), and trees. Hope, memory, happiness, fear, and imagination are the subjects of the final entries in this strange little book.

William B. Harden, librarian of the Georgia Historical Society, recalled years later that Mary and Margaret were inseparable companions and frequently took carriage rides together. Their servant George was their chauffeur as well as the butler at the residence. According to Harden, when the Telfair sisters were out in their carriage they wore an air as if inviting people to behold them as the most important people in town. People would point them out as "characters," he said. He remembered that they bore themselves with "an air of superiority and aloofness," but that they always dressed plainly. It was generally said that the Telfair ladies considered themselves socially superior to everyone else in Savannah, that they were much taken with their own self-importance, and that they associated only with a small, select group of the socially elite. After Mary's death, the *Savannah Morning News* would comment that she and Margaret were "noted for their peculiar exclusiveness." Mr. Harden was of the view that the Telfairs' notion of their family's superiority was based on their father's position as governor of Georgia, on the fact that the family's roots went back to colonial times, and also on their Gibbons blood. He would remember them in their later years as unattractive "dried up old women."[38]

Mrs. Thomas Telfair died at Madison Springs, Georgia, on September 10, 1859. She left her entire estate to Augustus P. Wetter, as trustee, and named him executor of her will. As much as Mary Telfair disapproved of Wetter, he was perfectly acceptable to Alberta's grandmother. In fact, Wetter was a thoroughly respectable citizen of his adopted city. An architect by training, he had found a good job in Savannah as a civil engineer. For a time he worked as the manager of a cotton press. He joined the Chatham Artillery, and when the war came, he served the Confederate cause as captain of the DeKalb Infantry. Besides, while Mrs. Telfair was still living, he fathered two sons, a boy called Telfair, born June 22, 1858, and another called Conrad, born April 22, 1859, and thus the old lady had two great-grandsons to love during the last year of her life. Wetter made Alberta happy, so why should her grandmother not approve of him?[39]

In the spring of 1860 Mary Telfair and her sister had the remains of Sarah Haig removed from the family vault at the Sharon Plantation and interred in an underground vault at Bonaventure Cemetery. They did not attempt to remove the remains of their father or others. The new family burial plot, which Mary had purchased on January 10, 1857, was surrounded by an iron enclosure, and the sisters erected within its confines a monument in the shape of a sarcophagus. On one side they caused to be inscribed the words, "In Memory of Edward Telfair of Georgia / Died Sept. 17, 1807, Aged 64 / and of His Sons / Edward Telfair Josiah G. Telfair / Thomas Telfair Alexander Telfair." The ladies caused to be inscribed on the opposite side the name of their mother, who had been buried in Philadelphia, and "Sarah G. Haig Widow of Capt. George Haig U.S.A." At one end of the monument can be found the notation, "Erected by His Surviving Daughters / 1860." After their deaths, the names of Margaret Telfair Hodgson and Mary Telfair would be added to the female side of the monument. The notation on the monument that Edward Telfair died at the age of sixty-four is inaccurate. He actually died at the age of seventy-one or seventy-two. Mary and her sister never were very accurate when it came to ages. Indeed, the 1860 census lists William B. Hodgson as fifty (he was fifty-nine), Margaret as fifty (she was sixty-five), and Mary as forty-eight (she was sixty-nine).[40]

Mary Telfair and the Hodgsons continued to spend their summers in the North even as war approached. In August 1859 they were staying at the Ocean House in Newport, that monument to Victorian splendor that stood on Bellevue Avenue just across from George Noble Jones's cottage. They were in Saratoga during the summer of 1860, but in

August 1861, after the firing upon Fort Sumter, they were escaping the heat in Flat Rock, North Carolina. In the years leading up to the war, life in the North was not as pleasant for Southerners as it had once been. The hotels at Madison Springs, Georgia, advertised that ladies and gentlemen from the South could take the waters there without being subject to abuse by rude Yankees.[41]

Mary had read enough history to appreciate the horrors of war. As for the preservation of the Union, she remained sanguine as late as February 1860. "Are you apprehensive of disunion?" she asked Eliza Terrell. "I am not," she allowed. "The North cannot do without us."[42] Her views on slavery were the same as those of her sister and brother-in-law and her friends in the South. Slavery was part of the natural order of things, as far as these Southerners were concerned. Had not Bishop Elliott said that slavery had been ordained by God as a means of bringing a benighted people to the throne of Grace? The Telfairs had owned slaves since they first established their plantations. After all, field hands were required for the cultivation and harvesting of crops. The census figures for both 1850 and 1860 show William B. Hodgson as the largest slaveholder in Burke County. In 1850 he is shown as owning 135 slaves, and in 1860 he is listed as the owner of 240 slaves. All families of refinement and means had servants to attend upon them, whether they lived in the North or the South. Indeed, in the agitation of the 1850's to reopen the slave trade, which had been abolished by the federal government in 1808, the argument actually had been made that it was unfair for the North to benefit from the free immigration of cheap labor from Europe while the South was forbidden to import labor from Africa.

Mary believed that servants should be treated kindly and with the utmost consideration for their well being. But slavery was a fact of life that she did not choose to question. Indeed, Negro slaves made up almost half of Georgia's antebellum population. Nowhere in her letters does Mary indicate that she found the South's peculiar institution morally repugnant. Mary believed that the people who served her family liked and appreciated her. The slaves on her family's plantations must have shared the resentment of slaves on other plantations in the South, but Mary never perceived it or at least refused to admit it:

> We had a satisfactory visit to our Plantation. The people looked well & happy and seem disposed to *worship* me. One said,

"Do get up and let me see if you have *grown.*" I said yes grown old. Another said, "You look mighty *steady*" meaning *grave*, for I felt too sad in revisiting a spot where I had passed so many happy days & months, with those who were the lights of other years, and gave a charm to Earth & Earthly things that can never, never be renewed.[43]

Mary's world was in a state of flux, and she was finding it difficult to deal with the many changes that were taking place: "Savannah is improving in size but alas! not in society. I walk and rarely meet a familiar face. In a few years it will be a Yankee town and the Georgia character be like a tale that is told." She mourned the passing of some of the leading figures of the day, men who had enriched her intellectual life:

How many great and good men have lately exchanged Time for Eternity. Macaulay and Irving's magic pens will write no more. Yesterday's paper announced the death of Dr. Joseph Alexander, a professor in the Theological Seminary of Princeton. He was a learned Divine, an eloquent Preacher and the greatest linguist in this Country. He soon followed his brother who died only four months ago universally lamented, for he was as unrivaled as a minister of the gospel and a scholar as he was lovely in his domestic circle.

Mary also noted the death of a lesser figure, Jones Bulloch, who years before had gone to the West in financial disgrace. "He died in St. Louis of softening of the brain," she reported. "I dare say that his mental anguish for past deeds weighed heavily on his conscience. He died with his bible near to him and her [his wife Catharine's] Daguerreotype on his breast." Mary hoped that he would be forgiven: "The Physician of Souls could alone give peace in death, and as the dying thief on the cross was pardoned so may he have been."[44]

Affairs of state came to a head in the presidential election of 1860. Abraham Lincoln received the nomination of the young Republican party on the third ballot. Senator Hannibal Hamlin of Maine, once a Jacksonian Democrat, was picked as the vice-presidential candidate. The Democrats convened in Charleston in April, but were unable to agree on a candidate. Stephen A. Douglas adhered to the party's 1856 doctrine of popular sovereignty, the right of the people in the territories to decide on the issue of slavery. After the convention refused to adopt an extreme proslavery platform, including a plank proposed by Jefferson Davis requiring Congress to protect slavery in the territories, the delegates of eight Southern states withdrew along with a few Buchanan Northerners. The convention moved to Baltimore and there the diminutive Douglas received the nomination. Herschel V. Johnson, a moderate from Georgia, ran on the ticket with Douglas. The convention held by the seceding delegates nominated John C. Breckinridge of Kentucky, who was then serving as United States vice-president, and named Senator Joseph Lane as his running mate. The plan conceived by Jefferson Davis was to throw the election into Congress for want of a majority in the electoral college.

In an attempt to steer a middle-of-the-road course and avoid the conflict that could lead to the dissolution of the Union, conservatives from the North and South formed the National Constitutional Union, the only party, it was said, that a gentleman could belong to. The names placed in nomination by this party of conciliation were John Bell and Edward Everett, the same gentleman who had attended the Telfair-Hodgson wedding in London. Bell was a senator from Tennessee, and Everett had been president of Harvard and a four-time governor of Massachusetts. He was considered the country's greatest orator. It was Everett who, several years later, would speak for two hours at the dedication of the cemetery at Gettysburg immediately before President Lincoln rose to make a few remarks. Writing to his uncle from Kansas City under date of September 4, 1860, Joseph Hodgson, Jr., made clear his support of the new Constitutional Union party:

> I left the Democracy because I foresaw its dissolution & the rise of a great third party which must rest upon the adjustment of 1850 and settle the "Slavery Question" in a spirit of conciliation. Else the dissolution of the Union is merely a matter of time. I recognize in the nominees of the Union party gentlemen of ability & conservatism; and can accept Mr. Bell upon his States-Rights record. Whether Bell & Everett will be elected I cannot predict. The movement was made in their favor not so much with a present hope of success as of an ultimate establishment of a peace party.
>
> I am sick of the Slavery agitation. We in West Missouri have

an interest in the discussion so far as it affects our own interests. But at the same time we will not acknowledge the right of Congress over the matter in the Territories nor will we that Mr. Douglas presents a true issue in his squatter sovereignty-dogma, nor will we yet acknowledge that Mr. Breckenridge can establish his "protection" system. With the National Democratic party as it was in 1856 we might have stood, but now as you say very properly, parties are in a state of transition & we feel at liberty to mark out a new road. If it leads to nowhere we have lost nothing. The other roads would most certainly have led to dissolution an the one hand or centralization on the other.

Young Hodgson ended by saying that if Bell or Everett were elected, he would request, as a reward for services, an appointment as consul or secretary of legation abroad. He stated that Missouri had a claim upon such an appointment and that he had as many influential friends in the state to back him as any other young man.[45]

Hodgson replied to his nephew's letter in a positive vein, and under date of September 24, 1860, the young man again wrote to his uncle, this time from St. Louis, where he had business to transact and where he was attending the State Fair for pleasure. With respect to the political situation, he wrote:

I am happy to know that your own convictions politically & those of my father accord with my own. I shall fight for Bell & Everett until the elections, and then I shall advocate the cementing of a party whose cardinal doctrines shall be those of Mr. Clay, as they related to the questions of internal policy, & whose settlement of the slavery agitation shall be the adjustment of 1850. I see no other solution of our difficulties but a dissolution. The evils of that I fully appreciate from a perusal of the letters of the Federalist. Mr. Breckinridge's policy will never be conceded by the anti-slavery sentiment of the North. Mr. Lincoln's policy is obnoxious to the dignity of Southern states. Mr. Douglas' policy is based upon socialistic ideas which threaten the integrity of government, especially Republican government. I can endorse none of them, & hence I will vote for Mr. Bell whom D.I.W. Alexander called "a last branch of the old trunk" and Mr. Everett whom I know as a patriot & can reverence as a man of letters. Our country has had enough of rail-splitters like Lincoln, itinerant demagogues like Douglas, & callow stump-speakers like Breckinridge. I beg their pardon for such disrespectful language, but I believe them all to be second-rate men.[46]

Mary Telfair, the Hodgsons, and other Southerners of their class represented the establishment, an established order that wanted nothing more than to maintain the status quo. The elite of Savannah had strong ties to the North. To these people, it was not a case of them against us. They had little more patience with the hot-heads agitating for secession than with those who advocated the abolition of slavery. More than anything else, they yearned for peace. These sentiments were shared generally by their friends in the North. Letters arriving from New York expressed deep concern over the threatened conflict. Mary Telfair's friend Matilda Tillotson wrote of her own deep feelings:

> We are all anxious to know how this terrible excitement in our Country will end. Mr. T is still sanguine & thinks the South slow in coming to a decided stand & all here pray to the Almighty to avert this threatened evil. Frances hates Lincoln as the *cause* of trouble, though his character and talents are undisputed. These infamous penny papers the *Herald* and the *Post* are in receipt of high pay to foment the troubles, and these find their way over the world.[47]

It would not be long before the entire troubled country, both the North and the South, would know how the "terrible excitement" would end.

In 1860 Mary Telfair began a little notebook in which she recorded ideas that were meaningful to her as she became older. By now she was almost seventy. The talk of secession that was gripping Savannah was disturbing to her household. Meetings urging dissolution of the Union were held throughout the city, and many evenings there were torchlight parades. A secession flag bearing the representation of a large rattlesnake and the inscription *"Noli Me Tangere"* was unfurled at the Greene monument on Johnson Square. Men wore palmetto rosettes on their hats in support of secession. It must have been a distressing time for an older woman such as Mary Telfair who so loved quiet and calm and the beautiful things that until then had filled her life. In this time of trouble, even her humor took on a political edge: "Why should Abraham Lincoln find it difficult to have his life insured? Because no one can make out his policy."[48]

The rail-splitter that young Hodgson deplored and Mary Telfair could not fathom won the election, but only with thirty-nine percent of the popular vote. Mr. Bell came in last. As soon as Lincoln's election was certain, South Carolina voted to secede from the Union. Jefferson Davis wished to give the Lincoln administration a fair trial, but there was too much pressure from the small planters, lawyer-politicians, and journalists who took up the cause of secession. Alabama, Florida, and Mississippi followed South Carolina's lead and left the Union as well. As talk of secession turned into action, Mary Telfair was finding the situation more and more difficult to accept. On New Year's Day, 1861, she wrote to Mary Few:

> We were delighted with O'Connor's speech [Charles O'Conor]. I express my admiration of it in a letter to Matilda. He exhibited a noble mind, clear and strong, and a true Union spirit. Himself and Stephens are the great men of these times. I am glad to hear that you enjoyed Christmas day and the sports of the Children. We are so isolated, and so sad, when festal days come round that we shut ourselves up and pass them like Sunday.

Mary had spent the last days of the year reading *The Vale of Baca*, a book that "seems to have been written for me so much do I sympathize with every line in it." Illness in the family did not help her mood: "Margaret is suffering from Influenza and Mr. Hodgson has been confined to his room with a cough for some days. His health is very delicate."[49]

Georgia seceded from the Union on January 19, 1861, and then Louisiana and Texas, the latter despite old Sam Houston's pleas for delay. On February 8 representatives of the states that had left the Union met in Montgomery, Alabama, and organized the Confederate States of America with Jefferson Davis as President. The die was cast. There was no turning back. With the Southern states out of the Union, war was inevitable. The sons of Mary Telfair's friends soon would take up arms, many to die or to have their lives changed forever. The two sons of Neyle and Josephine Habersham signed up in the Confederate cause. So did Mr. Hodgson's nephews. Telfair Hodgson left the General Theological Seminary to join the 44th Virginia Infantry (the Richmond Zouaves) as a private. He later transferred to the 1st Alabama, where he served under his brother, Colonel Joseph Hodgson. He ultimately would be promoted to the rank of major and serve on the staff of General Joseph Wheeler.

As soon as Georgia seceded from the Union, young Thomas Carolin Clay, the son of the late Thomas Savage Clay, Anne Clay's brother, left Yale to join the Confederate Army. Years later Tom Clay's Yale classmate, Dr. Thomas E. Satterthwaite of New York, would relate the circumstances of his leaving to Clay's son, who in turn lovingly recorded the tale for posterity:

> Dr. Satterthwaite asked me, "Did your father ever tell you of the time he left Yale?" I replied, "No. My father rarely spoke of himself." "Well," said he, "I want to tell you about it."

And tell the story he did:

> Your father was the most popular boy I ever knew. I am not afraid to say that he was probably the most popular boy who ever attended Yale. He was loved by everybody, teachers and boys alike. He was a boy of such fine qualities and lovable character.
>
> You know he had decided to study for the ministry. This was in a very trying period. Heated arguments, political and religious, were being heard on every side. It was evident that a climax must soon be reached.
>
> We had learned that your father had been informed that his state of Georgia had seceded and he felt that he should return to his Georgia home at once. Our class was thrown into despondency. We could not see Tom Clay leave us. We visited him as a class and argued with him, hoping to dissuade his mind and have him remain with us, but he said it was not what he wanted to do, but what he should do.
>
> We talked with him about his desire to prepare for the ministry; told him it was not to reduce the force forming against the North, for in his case, it would be but one man and no one would know the difference. We argued that if God saw fit to remove him from the scene of action and start him in a college course for the ministry, was it not his duty to stay and continue his preparation. Was it not probable that the struggle would be a very bitter one and ultimately result in the loss of much prop-

erty, especially in the South, and looking to this point, the class of '64 pledged itself in such an event to stand by and furnish him all needed funds to see him through college and seminary and landed in a pastorate able to carry on for life.

Clay's son continued the story:

This was indeed a noble evidence of affection and worthy tribute to the character of my father, but duty seemed clear to him and he told them he was sorry but that he must return in the hour of trial of his native state. Accordingly a few days later he appeared at the station to catch his train for New York and thence by boat to Savannah. Says Dr. Satterthwaite, "Every boy in his class was at that train to see him off and among all of those boys there was not a dry eye, and I am not ashamed even today to admit that I cried too, for we loved him."[50]

Stories such as this were legion. It was a time for patriotism and idealism. For the young men of the South, a way of life was being threatened. From their standpoint, the Yankees were the aggressors, and they were about to teach them a lesson that they would never forget.

Lincoln was inaugurated on March 4, 1861, and declared, "I hold that, in contemplation of the universal law and of the Constitution, the Union of these States is perpetual." By the time of Lincoln's inaugural address, the Confederates had seized all forts and naval installations in the seceded states, except Fort Pickens in Pensacola and Fort Sumter in Charleston harbor. On April 12 the Confederate forces fired upon Fort Sumter. The Civil War had begun.

Mary Telfair's reaction to the outbreak of hostilities was as could be expected. It was all the fault of the Yankees:

We are jogging on in our quiet way as usual, absorbed in the events of the times, sad enough and we may expect worse for the Republicans of the North seem to be as black in *heart* as in *name*, and their cry is war & subjugation. You are fortunate in being removed from the sea board. We may expect a blockade and then the defenders of Fort Pulaski will pour their fire upon them. While we are shewing courtesy & kindness to Northerners they are shooting, imprisoning & threatening to hang our Citizens. Greiner who was a volunteer at Fort Pulaski and *caught* in Kentucky will be hung for treason. Mr. Gus Lamar has been compelled to resign his presidency of a bank in New York, and ordered home. I am not sorry for those who clung to the North after the Bombardment of Fort Sumter. They displayed not only a want of patriotism but a mean servile spirit.[51]

Mary was disgusted when her once close friend, Justice James Moore Wayne, chose to retain his seat on the United States Supreme Court rather than return to the South to embrace the cause of the Confederacy. She could attribute such behavior to nothing but base motives. "What think you of Judge Wayne's *apostasy?*" she inquired of Eliza Terrell. "Like Genl. Scott he loved the almighty dollar better than his Country."[52]

Mary had nothing but praise for Jefferson Davis and nothing but scorn for Abraham Lincoln:

> What a noble Message is *our* President's—so clear, so patriotic, so dignified, so full of every thing that is great & good. The North must contrast it with old Abe's "Nothing hurt." *Aunt Abe* will not *secede* from the White House, like "Uncle Abe" she loves distinction. When Lord Lyons was introduced to Lincoln he gave him an *embrace* and *whispered in his ear.* Lord L's English blood must have curdled in his veins and no doubt he *mentally* if not *bodily* recoiled from such familiarity.[53]

Mary Telfair's beloved Savannah soon would be in turmoil. The city's established militia units took up arms. The Chatham Artillery, the Jasper Greens, the Republican Blues, the Oglethorpe Light Infantry, and the Pulaski Guards paraded through Savannah led by Alexander R. Lawton, then a colonel, the same gentleman who would write Mary Telfair's will years later. The men of Savannah marched off to fight in Virginia, and before long some two hundred of them would die in the first battle of Manassas. It was the beginning of a tragic struggle that would last for four long years.

17

Clouds Over Georgia

And I looked and, behold; a pale horse; and his name that sat on him was Death.

Revelation: 6:8

By December 1861 the port of Savannah was completely bottled up by the blockade imposed by the Union fleet under the command of Admiral Samuel Francis DuPont. Commerce stagnated, and many businesses closed their doors. Food and other necessities were in short supply. Prices soared. Mary Telfair thought that these economic woes were nothing compared to the grief brought on by the ravages of war and disease:

> The stores here are *naked* and every thing enormous both *eatables & wearables*. Mr. H. says that if the Banks fail to give dividends we shall have to live upon air. Rents have fallen to nothing and cotton cannot and *ought not* to sell. Poverty is the least to be dreaded in these times. The wail of sorrow is over our land like a requiem. Miss Rodgers who married Mr. Wade last July is now a widow. He died of typhoid fever & his remains were brought out today. She reached him just as his spirit was departing. He did not recognize her. Hamilton Couper too died of typhoid fever after escaping death in the battle of Manassas.[1]

William B. Hodgson worried over the legality of the blockade, as if the legal niceties really mattered. His mental gymnastics served as a distraction from the realities of war. In June 1861 he wrote to his friend, William Henry Trescot of Charleston, formerly of the State Department, seeking his expert opinion on the status of the Union navy's actions under international law. Trescot assured Hodgson that an incident that Hodgson had cited involving the seizure of two United States vessels while loading guano at facilities in Caleta Pabellón de Pica and Punta Lobos during a civil disturbance in Peru did not raise the question of blockade. It really was not a precedent. At Hodgson's request, Trescot also passed on to him his best recollection of the details of an event that had occurred while he was acting secretary of state involving the capture at sea by a Neopolitan man of war of an American vessel cleared out of Genoa on the ground that she was supplying troops to Sicilian rebels.[2]

In a subsequent letter, referring to the previous one, Trescot wrote to Hodgson:

> I am glad to learn from your letter that the information sent you was what you desired. That the Government of the U.S. is acting in direct contradiction to that interpretation of international law which it has always maintained and the maintenance of which has always been considered the chief merit of its diplomacy is undeniable. It can be very easily demonstrated, but what then? It is only using the privilege of every strong handed belligerent and the only reply worth making must be at the mouth of the cannon rather than from the mouth of the publicist.[3]

Thus did Mr. Hodgson occupy himself as news of war fatalities arrived in Savannah daily, and the ladies of the city put on their mourning black.

With the war now begun, notes of deep pessimism began to appear in Mary Telfair's notebook: "The characters that can stand the test of daily intimacy are about as numerous as four-leaved clovers in a meadow; in general, those who do not annoy you with positive faults love you with their insipidity." The young Mary Telfair, who so reveled in the joys of friendship, would never have written those words. Nor would she have written, "How small a thing is a human heart! You might grasp it in your little hand; and yet its strifes and agonies are enough to distend a skin that should cover the whole world." And only the bitter taste that came with war could have moved Telfair to write, "Life has three elements to most of us, Joy, Sorrow & Work."[4]

The women of the South rolled up their sleeves and gave their all for the war effort. There was little that Mary Telfair could do, however. She was seventy when the Confederates fired on Fort Sumter, and her energy level was not what it once was. She was too old for nursing, and besides she had no practical training. There is no evidence that she did any coarse sewing, stitching uniforms and tents, as did thousands of women in the South. She may well have done so, however. Nor is there any evidence that she engaged in fund-raising efforts for the Confederate cause, although she and her sister contributed many thousands of dollars to the Georgia Relief Association ($50,000 by Mary and $25,000 by Margaret) and also contributed to the Soldiers' Relief Fund. The most that she had to offer was her prayers.[5]

In mid-July 1861 Mary and her family left for the mountains of Western North Carolina. A trip to the old watering spots of the North was, of course, out of the question. They passed a day and two nights in Augusta and the same length of time in Columbia County. They arrived at Flat Rock, North Carolina, on July 26. It was a lovely spot far from the turmoil of war: "The scenery is beautiful, the lights and shades upon the mountains charming, and the crystal streams remind me of 'God's Masterpiece' as Mr. Tappan styled Switzerland." The accommodations, however, left much to be desired. "The Hotel like all Southern Hotels is *vile*," Mary wrote. "The beds like rocks— the food heavy as lead." At least there was a church nearby for the family to attend, an Episcopal one. It was presided over by a very good preacher whom Mary said the Presbyterians would style "low Church" but whom the Episcopalians called "evangelical." Mary found Flat Rock to be quite a fashionable place: "The *aristocracy* of Charleston have country seats around Flat Rock. They number 25. Some are cultivated with great taste and command extensive views of mountains. The *elite* of Carolina are at the Hotel." The horrors of war, however, were not far from the minds of those staying at this idyllic spot. Mary related their activities and thoughts to Eliza Terrell:

> The Ladies are all engaged in knitting stockings for our poor Soldiers. Some of them are so beautifully done that Beauregard might wear them. We cannot imagine their sufferings camping out without blankets to cover them. I wonder that more of them have not died from exposure as well as sickness. Both of Mr. Hodgson's nephews, whom you saw at Saratoga, are in the army and both have been ill.[6]

Mary's letter to Mrs. Terrell from Flat Rock reveals that, at this early stage of the conflict, she remained optimistic that the South would prevail. Why shouldn't the Confederate forces be victorious? That July, they had routed the Union Army in the Battle of Manassas (called by the Yankees the Battle of Bull Run after the small stream that flowed nearby). The letter also underscores Mary's abiding dislike of Lincoln:

> You perhaps have heard the joyous intelligence of the arrival of the new Steamer belonging to the Charleston Line laden with Blankets, cannon powder, and Enfield rifles. It was thought most prudent not to publish it for two more are on the way and the Blockading Steamers might capture them. I rather think that we shall soon be recognised by England & France, as a Minister has been appointed for each capital, Slidell for France & Mason for England. I hope that the same President and Vice President will be elected for 7 years. Jefferson Davis as far as my feeble political knowledge allows me to judge has acted his part nobly.
>
> Did you read his obituary notice in a Philadelphia paper? I have no doubt that the *Lincolnites* are anxious to *kill* him and all of our Confederate Men who possess wisdom & valor—they have so little of it on their side. The winter campaign will no doubt be a severe one. I have been reading Motley's Dutch Republics and fear that if our war continues that we shall have as sanguinary one as those of the Netherlands. They fought against a *Royal* Despot. We are fighting against an *upstart vulgar Despot* whose reign will last only 4 years. The Northern Men in their love of lucre have lost all sense of manliness and independance to submit to such tyranny as is exercised by the *Autocrat* and his prime Minister Seward.[7]

The dispatch of Senators John Slidell and James M. Mason to their European posts, to which Telfair referred, gave rise to the famous Trent Affair, which strained, almost to the breaking point, the relationship between Great Britian and the Union. The two diplomats were proceeding on a British mail steamer, the *Trent*, on their way to Southampton when, on November 8, 1861, Captain Charles Wilkes, in command of USS *San Jacinto*, ordered the vessel boarded, arrested the envoys and their secretaries, and had them placed in confinement. This was viewed as an insult to the British flag, and cries of outrage poured out of London. A breakdown in the transatlantic cable prevented an immediate exchange of insults. When President Lincoln, at the urging of Senator Charles Sumner, ordered the prisoners released, the honor of the British was satisfied.

One of the consequences of the war was that the people of the South were unable to communicate with their friends in the North. Mary felt particularly sorry for those who had lost contact with close relatives: "How completely has the Despot cut us off from our friends in the North. Years may pass before we hear from them. I feel very much for Mrs. Bulloch & the Hunters. The former can now hold no Epistolary Communication with her brother. What a situation to be placed in!"[8]

While in North Carolina, Mary and her sister continued to enjoy their drives in the open air. Instead of driving in a coach and four, they had the servants hitch up a pair of mules, for they were swift-footed and better suited than horses to ascend and descend the high mountains. As the water courses were high and some bridges had been swept away, the ladies were prevented from visiting nearby Asheville as they would have liked. At the end of September, they left the mountains, passed a few days in Greenville and Augusta, paid a visit to Eliza Terrell, and then returned to Savannah.[9]

The family would not be long at their home before they were again disrupted. Early in November, Union forces captured Port Royal on Hilton Head Island. The mosquito fleet and the few river boats under the command of Commodore Josiah Tattnall were no match for a superior naval force, and Fort Pulaski and Savannah itself were threatened. The family took a house on Broad Street in Augusta. "We shall go up as soon as we are ready," Mary informed Eliza Terrell under date of November 23:

> You can imagine the trial it is for us to leave our comfortable home and embark in housekeeping. If Savannah is attacked women ought to be away from it in order for the men to do their duty in defending the city. Miss Campbell goes to the Harisons. Several families have gone to Augusta, some to Macon. The panic was terrible but it has subsided a little. The enemy have triumphed and New York has been illuminated in consequence of the capture of Port Royal.[10]

The cautious optimism that had flowed from Mary's pen two months earlier had vanished. The fortunes of the Confederacy had taken a turn for the worse, and she was less than sanguine as to the outlook for a Confederate victory:

O this dreadful war it overwhelms me with sorrow when I think of the result of it. Memphis it is thought will be taken. The blood thirsty wretches are for booty. I think that the Carolina Planters ought to have applied a torch to their Cotton to keep it from the ruthless invaders. The silly Editors of Newspapers have been indeed our ruin. Our ambassadors [Slidell and Mason] would have reached England if there had been secrecy observed, but *blabbing & boasting* is the order of the day.[11]

"We have not laughed or smiled since we left your hospitable Mansion," Mary wrote to Eliza Terrell before leaving Savannah for Augusta. "The gloom of this place is overpowering. No one visits, and yet there was a marriage a few days hence, Capt. Morris of the Navy to Miss Clem McAllister. He was in the battle of Port Royal." Mary allowed herself to think the unthinkable. "If we are conquered can you live under the old government?" she asked her friend. "I feel as if I could never unite with the North again." For Mary, thoughts of war were all consuming. "My mind dwells too much upon war. I can neither read, work, or think of any other subject."[12]

Lucy Terrell's husband, Edgar Gilmer Dawson, was serving as an officer with the Confederate forces. At the outbreak of the war, he organized and equipped a battery of artillery that he named the Terrell Light Artillery in honor of his late father-in-law. In November 1861 Lucy went to visit her husband in camp. She and her two children had been staying with her mother while Dawson was away. Her young son, Terrell, talked of nothing but becoming a soldier and fighting the Yankees. "Tell Terrell not to forget his friends and to take good care of his little Sister," Mary Telfair wrote to his grandmother.[13]

On April 11, 1862, Colonel Charles Olmstead surrendered Fort Pulaski after enduring thirty hours of bombardment by rifled cannon fired by Union artillery forces based on Tybee Island over 1,700 yards away. Robert E. Lee had worked as an engineer on the construction of Fort Pulaski as his first assignment after graduating from West Point. The fort had been taken over by Confederate forces from

Savannah in the early stages of the conflict, and it had been declared impregnable from such a distance by none other than Lee himself. But Union General Quincy A. Gilmore's revolutionary new rifled cannon was up to the job, and the Stars and Stripes was raised over Fort Pulaski.

The war continued in the North. In September 1862 Confederate General "Stonewall" Jackson captured Harpers Ferry. Two days later, Lee's forces were driven back into Virginia in the Battle of Antietam in Maryland. On the first day of 1863, President Lincoln issued the Emancipation Proclamation. Union forces were defeated by the Confederates at Chancellorsville in the first days of May, but in July the Union victory at Gettysburg set the pattern for the rest of the war. Meanwhile, Savannah served as a garrison for Confederate troops and suffered under soaring inflation. Mary Telfair's heart must have gone out to William Neyle and Josephine Habersham that day in July 1864 when she learned to her horror that the Habershams' sons, Joe Clay and Willy, has been killed within an hour of each other fighting off Union forces in the Battle of Atlanta. Joe Clay's last words were, "Tell my mother I die happy. I died at my post fighting for my country." Both young men were buried at Laurel Grove Cemetery under a single marker bearing the words, "In Their Death They Were Not Divided."[14]

As 1864 drew to a close, Union forces under the command of General William T. Sherman were advancing from Atlanta toward Savannah, leaving in their wake a swath of destruction. Soon they would occupy the city. William B. Hodgson kept a handwritten journal during the period November 22, 1864, to January 29, 1865, providing a first-hand account of the impact of the occupation on his family.[15] On the evening of November 22, the overseer at the Retreat plantation in Jefferson County sent a message to Hodgson stating that the approach of General Sherman's army compelled him to leave the plantation immediately and join up with the Confederate forces. On the morning of November 24, Hodgson and George Noble Jones set out for Jefferson County to visit their plantations. At the town of Millen, Hodgson found that he had been cut off by enemy forces from proceeding on the road leading to the Retreat. He returned to Savannah, but Jones was able to take a different route and reach Olivinia, his plantation near Louisville. Judson Kilpatrick's cavalry forces had reached the place and had burned the house and its contents. Sherman's infantry passed through the Retreat on the way to Louisville burning and laying waste to everything on the plantation. Hodgson had given orders for the horses and mules, along with wagons loaded with household effects, to be moved to the River Plantation in Burke County upon the approach of the Union Army. There is no evidence that this order was carried out.

Sherman stayed at Louisville until December 5, at which time his forces advanced toward Savannah. The army required supplies, and to obtain them Sherman needed to link up with his navy. The guns of Fort McAllister guarding the Ogeechee River barred the way. The earthwork compound was manned by some 150 Confederate soldiers under the command of George W. Anderson. After a valiant defense, the fort was overrun by superior Union forces. The capture of Savannah was by then a foregone conclusion.

Sherman's troops appeared before Savannah on December 8. Hodgson's friend, Anthony Barclay, the former British consul general in New York, moved with his family to the residence on St. James Square on the 10th of December. Enemy fire had made it too dangerous for them to remain at their place outside the city. At the same time, Hodgson began to remove to the city everything that he could from the Sabine Fields Plantation, furniture from the cottage there as well as corn, rice, and vegetables. On December 15 Hodgson noted in his journal that it had been nineteen days since Sherman's army had marched through the Retreat and that while the road to Augusta was open, he had heard not a word from the plantation. He went on to write, "It is believed that our plantation on the Savannah River has not been visited by the enemy—By and by, we shall know."

General William J. Hardee commanded the 9,000 men based in Savannah. Morale was low. The heat had been oppressive, the sand flies were a nuisance, measles and yellow fever were epidemic, and the people of the town were unfriendly. With the end in sight, Hardee impressed over a thousand slaves to construct a pontoon bridge across the Savannah River to Hutchinson Island and beyond it to South Carolina and to build a road to the Back River. Dismounted men, some five hundred strong, of the Ferguson Brigade of General George Wheeler's cavalry, left their encampment in Hardeeville to man the trenches before Savannah.

On December 17 General Hardee received Sherman's written demand for the surrender of the city, with its threat of bombardment.

Three days later, the pontoon bridge having been completed, the evacuation of the Confederate troops began. That evening the Board of Aldermen met and invited Hodgson and several other prominent citizens to join with them to consider the state of affairs. Dr. Richard D. Arnold, the mayor, announced that the evacuation of troops would be completed during the night and that at daybreak he and two of the aldermen would proceed to the enemy lines and surrender the city.

There was looting by the retreating Confederates and by the lower orders in the city who took advantage of the chaos that prevailed on the day and night of the evacuation. During the day the Confederates seized all horses and mules by impressment and carried them off at nightfall. Hodgson noted in his journal the loss of one horse and three mules. Having been alerted to be on guard against Confederate soldiers who proposed to search the house for gold and silver, the family sat up all night with the lights burning. Mr. Barclay and the ladies took the first watch and Hodgson the second. The ladies, however, refused to go to bed. One can envision Hodgson, with his pistol in his lap, sitting with the ladies as the night wore on, fearful that at any moment the house would be entered. He was ready to resist should it be necessary. Margaret Hodgson later would describe that fearful night and how she had her gold and jewelry quilted into her clothing.[16] Fortunately no attempt at robbery was made.

In the morning the formal surrender was made to Sherman's representative, General John W. Geary. Union forces immediately began to enter the city. They continued to pour in throughout the day, by companies and regiments, until there were approximately six thousand men encamped in the squares. Mr. Barclay had his two carriage horses at a neighbor's stable, and they were taken by Union soldiers. On December 22 Sherman dispatched his famous telegram to President Lincoln presenting him with the City of Savannah as a Christmas gift.

Charles Green, a wealthy English merchant, offered his spacious home on Madison Square to Sherman as his headquarters. Barclay called upon General Sherman and General Geary and was assured of every protection. Sherman offered to place a picket at the residence, a courtesy that Barclay gladly accepted. He was promised that his horses would be returned. Some Union soldiers, seeking food, made an effort to enter the kitchen of the mansion, but Hodgson pointed to the British flag that had been flying in front of the house since the former British consul general had taken up residence and invoked the name of General Sherman. The soldiers were persuaded to leave. General Geary's men restored order and put an end to the looting. Although Hodgson observed that the soldiers encamped in St. James Square across from the house were killing all the chickens found at large, he wrote in his journal that "property is well protected, and the officers have given stringent orders to enforce that protection." "Citizens pass to and fro unmolested," he added.

Christmas came and went. Federal officers and soldiers thronged to the churches and filled the pews of individual Savannahians. Mr. Axton, the Presbyterian minister, prayed "for the restoration of peace to our distracted land." Hodgson wrote in his journal, "The usual festivities of the season were suspended." "But, in our own family," he continued, "we had plum pudding and egg nog." Two Union officers called on the family on Christmas night. They brought a band to serenade the ladies. Hodgson noted that he "declared this professed courtesy as liable to misconstruction in the present condition of things."

Hodgson wanted badly to visit the family plantations in Burke and Jefferson counties. He applied in person to General Sherman for a safe conduct under a parole of honor to enable him to do so, as well as to return to his family after completing his tour of inspection. General Sherman replied with much kindness that his military rule did not allow anyone to return to Savannah who had left the city. According to Hodgson, "He suggested, and I sincerely believe with kind motives, that I had better not leave the city just now."

With the arrival of the Union army, throngs of black men and women flocked to the city and congregated in the streets. Some came from neighboring plantations and others had followed the Union army on its march through Georgia. Hodgson found it a "painful spectacle." He despaired as to what would become of these people. "The future conditions of these poor creatures is a problem which no wisdom can solve," he wrote. "It is at least certain that unless they be placed on plantation & compelled to work, they must soon starve." Hodgson noted that the servants of many families had "deserted their kind owners." The servants of his own family, however, remained at the residence on St. James Square.

Hodgson predicted serfdom would replace slavery, a prediction that unfortunately came true in the years immediately after the Civil War:

After the War is over, this African race will still be here. If it lives it must work. A state of serfage, or ascription to the soil is a necessity from which there is no escape. Slavery as it has existed may be modified. But if the European race cannot contract the labor of the African under some forms, the African must die out or the white race be transported to another soil. Even then the African would not till his own soil. This would be a barren result of Northern interference.

In a conversation with General Hatch, second in command to General Foster and based at Hilton Head, Hodgson inquired of the conditions of labor by the former slaves. He was told that they worked five days a week for $10 a month, out of which they were required to feed and clothe themselves. Each had an allotment of land or garden for himself. "Are they compelled to work?" Hodgson asked. "The Provost Marshal has control of that," was the reply. This was the peonage of Mexico or the serfdom of the thirteenth century, as far as Hodgson was concerned.

Hodgson received word that an order had been issued to General Sherman allotting to former slaves all the Sea Islands and all the abandoned rice plantations on the rivers to a distance of thirty miles from the sea. Each black man was to have forty acres of land. No white person would be permitted to settle among them. In Hodgson's opinion, "The chances of Negroes settling such places makes the order a 'mauvaise plaisanterie.'" Sherman, he wrote, "can control but not create a social order. He has destroyed but cannot restore it or introduce a substitute."

The gravest fear of the white people of Savannah, according to Hodgson, was that black troops would be sent in to garrison the city. This, he believed, would excite feelings of undying hatred of the Northern states. "It would be evidence of a design to crush out the proud spirit of mankind, and check the tendency of Citizens to return to the Union—Savannah would be abandoned by our best people." In a meeting with General Sherman two days after Christmas, Hodgson advised him that the people of Savannah were "dreadfully frightened" by the rumor that the city would be garrisoned with black soldiers and that he personally shared that apprehension. "I have not a Negro soldier in my army," Sherman assured him. "That is true," Hodgson replied, "but General Foster, now at Beaufort, has many, and he is military commander of these two states." The rumor persisted. In a conversation with General Hatch, second in command to General Foster, Hodgson learned that Mrs. Foster and her family desired to live in Savannah. Hodgson inferred from this that General Foster would move here and garrison the city with black soldiers. "This would be painful and humiliating," Hodgson wrote.

William Hodgson had nothing but good things to say about Sherman and his treatment of the people of Savannah during the occupation. He found the general's mind to be "quickly perceptive." "I am impressed with what I really believe to be his individual character, that of innate benevolence," Hodgson wrote. According to Hodgson, Sherman was "social" and "genial" and liked to talk of families and people in the town. Hodgson noted that the general laughed heartily at certain remarks that he had made concerning an eccentric woman that the general had met. Sherman loved children and enjoyed playing with the young people of Savannah. The door of his headquarters was never closed to the little ones. He was an officer and a gentleman, and despite the destruction left behind on his march to the sea, the people of Savannah came to respect him as such.

Sherman issued general orders giving to the people of Savannah the option of remaining in the city or joining their friends in Augusta or Charleston, neither of which had as yet fallen into Union hands. Most citizens chose to stay. Those families that registered as wishing to be transported within the Confederate lines left on January 10 for Charleston by steamer under a flag of truce. On the third day of the occupation, Sherman established a new newspaper in the city, *The Savannah Daily Loyal Georgian*. Its motto was "Redeemed, Regenerated and Disenthralled—The Union it must and shall be preserved." In Sherman's opinion, it was a simple matter for the Union to be restored. All that was required was for the representatives from Georgia to appear in Congress and answer to their names when called. Georgia would then resume her equal and sovereign rights under the Constitution. Hodgson, on the other hand, believed that there should be a convention of the states as a means of settling differences. This "would save the dignity of all," he thought.

Secretary of War Stanton arrived at Sherman's headquarters on January 11 and insisted that General Sherman execute an order to expel from the city the family of every man who had anything to do with the war or the Confederate Army. Sherman replied, "Mr. Secretary, if you wish such an order carried out, you will have to do it yourself. You know that by your own order there is not a house standing within fifty miles of Savannah. Is not the weather cold? I shall not send women and children out to perish."[17] Hodgson saw Sherman's refusal to obey the order as evidence of his humanity and good feeling. As Hodgson stated, "It would have been more humane to shoot all such than to send them out at this season, homeless and destitute." It was cold enough at home as it was. "We have no wood & no teams to haul it if we had wood," Hodgson wrote in his journal. Later, after Sherman's departure, he wrote, "Order by Genl. Grover the new Post commandant that no one shall pass the picket line in the canal for any purpose even to cut wood. This will give us raw food & cold toes. Chill blains are common."

Mary Telfair's seventy-fourth birthday began quite unpleasantly. At one-thirty in the morning on January 28, the cry of fire was raised. A blaze of unknown origin spread to the Confederate arsenal on West Broad Street, to the rear of the mansion, where the retreating army had abandoned a thousand charged shells and a quantity of ammunition. An explosion of ammunition shook the house as if there had been an earthquake. The shells burst unceasingly until 4:00 A.M., and fragments were thrown all over the city. The family and guests anxiously watched the approach of the flames; and when it appeared that danger was imminent, Hodgson, Barclay, and the ladies packed several trunks of clothing and placed them near the front door, ready for removal. By 4:30 the following afternoon, the flames had sufficiently died down that it become evident that it would not be necessary to abandon the house. Hodgson wrote in his journal, "We should have left behind us all bedding and all furniture, and thus we should have been reduced to absolute want." The experience was traumatic. It had a profound effect on Hodgson, and the ladies must have been terrified. Hodgson put down in his journal the emotions that he felt: "Never while I live shall I cease to remember this night of horrors. It was the coldest night of the season, shells were every instant bursting in mid-air and no bombardment could have been more awful, save in the more destructive fall of bombs."

Many citizens who heard the explosions that night had believed that the Confederates had mounted an attack in an effort to recapture the city. Anthony Barclay, who knew that ammunition was stored in the arsenal, immediately surmised the source of the explosive outburst.

The fear was that something like this would happen again. The following night, two or three pounds of coarse cannon powder were laid at the front door of one of Hodgson's friends. A curfew was imposed, and anyone found on the street after 9:00 P.M. was arrested. "Our anxieties are painful," Hodgson wrote in his journal. "Certainly, it cannot enter into the designs of the most *infernal, hellish* heart than to destroy a town with all its women & children." There was nothing to do but hope that the military authorities would effectively guard the homes and lives of the people.

On February 1, 1865, Sherman's army marched out of Savannah to crush whatever resistance remained in the Carolinas. With Lee's surrender to Grant at Appomattox Court House on April 9, 1865, the war came to an end. The laying down of arms, however, did not bring an end to the South's misery. If the military men had had their way, matters might have been different. The utmost courtesy was shown to the defeated officers, and Confederate soldiers were provided with free rail and shipboard transportation to their homes. Matters might have been different too if the assassin John Wilkes Booth had failed in his foul deed at Ford's Theater and President Lincoln had been able to make good on the words of his second inaugural address:

> With malice toward none; with charity for all; with firmness in the right, as God gives us to see the right, let us strive on to finish the work we are in; to bind up the nation's wounds; to care for him who shall have borne the battle, and for his widow, and his orphan—to do all which may achieve and cherish a just and lasting peace among ourselves, and with all nations.

But this was not to be. Although President Andrew Johnson adopted Lincoln's policy of forgiveness, the smell of hate and revenge was in the air fostered by the gloomy and ill-mannered Secretary of War Edwin Stanton and the Republican "Radicals" led by Thaddeus Stevens. If Grant had not prevented it, Lee and the other Confederate generals would have been arrested and tried as conspirators against the Union. As it was, Jefferson Davis was imprisoned for two years, and Captain Henry Wirz, commandant of the Andersonville stockade, was tried and hanged.

The people of Savannah deplored the assassination of Lincoln. William Hodgson was one of the organizers of a meeting held on

Johnson Square to publicly denounce the deed. He was on the committee that drafted the resolutions decrying "with deepest pain and sorrow" Booth's dreadful crime as "a calamity to the whole country."[18]

Several years before the defeat of the Confederacy, Mary Telfair had decided that she would set her slaves free upon her death. Even after the institution of slavery had been put to a decisive end at the cost of the blood of thousands of young men, Mary still thought it necessary to take legal steps to make certain that this would be the case. She and others like her could not fully appreciate that the fate of their servants was no longer in their hands. In June 1865, two months after Lee had agreed to the terms of surrender laid down by General Grant, Mary had her lawyers draw up a will (apparently never signed) which included this rather curious clause:

> *Item* 10th. Whereas by a former Will made by me some few years since, I emancipated all my negro slaves, now it is my will and desire that, should the institution of slavery in any way be continued or restored in the State of Georgia, I hereby direct that all my slaves be and remain emancipated and forever set free, in any manner consistently with the laws of the State of Georgia, and which will not invalidate this my Will on account of this clause, it not being my intention to violate any law of the State; notwithstanding the new condition of the institution.[19]

Apparently the lawyer who acted as Telfair's scrivener was as divorced from reality on the issue of slavery as she was.

Although Savannah had not been sent up in flames by Sherman's troops, the spirit of the city had been crushed. A deep sadness took hold of its people. Hodgson observed "marked effects of moral depression." "The minds of men are stupefied," he wrote in his journal. "A state of some barbarism has succeeded to active intelligence." He found the effect of conquest to be "brutifying." He observed that, under these conditions, the minds of men turned inwardly upon themselves and their emotions, whether it be fear, hope, or mistrust, make them "distrait or absent." "You converse with a man pleasantly as you suppose," Hodgson wrote, "and imagine that you gained his attention. Not at all! He has not heard your remarks and asks a second & third time to have your remarks repeated." Hodgson would reply to such persons, "I have forgotten what I said," and the conversation would come to an end.

There were some in the South who left the country rather than endure the indignities imposed by the occupation. A Confederate colony was established in São Paulo, Brazil, and many Southerners with London bank accounts sailed for Europe. Mary Telfair advised her friend Mrs. Isabella C. Hamilton, living in France a year after the surrender of Savannah, that Commodore Josiah Tattnall intended to move with his family to Canada and that Alexander R. Lawton would be sending his family to live in France. As for Mary and the Hodgsons, they made plans to spend a year or two in Europe. While observing the same sadness that Hodgson noted, Mary Telfair sounded a note of hope in writing to Isabella Hamilton:

> We have all passed through a sad ordeal since subjugation took place. The South has been shorn of its beams. The climate is all that is left of its glory. The inhabitants look very sad. Some young men belonging to the old aristocracy of South Carolina are supporting themselves by fishing and cutting wood for the government. I admire them as heros. I admire them still more as *Woodcutters* and *Fishermen*. How nobly do they bear adversity! What an exhibition of real strength and character.[20]

The basis for the South's economy had been destroyed. Southerners for whom slavery had been a way of life did not see the change as the propitious end of a cruel and dehumanizing economic system. Hodgson, in his journal entry for January 24, 1865, lamented the passing of the old order:

> I observe that all values are destroyed which had been created by long years of peaceful industry. Values will never be restored but by the same princeps which created them. Perhaps the most ingenious and cruel device of the Federal is that of destroying our system of labor, on which all values depend. Land, houses, Bank & railroad stocks, Corporate & State Bonds, are annihilated by unsettling the bases on which they rest. Not only the interest which these last yielded is lost, but the accumulated capital, itself, derived from labor & economy.
>
> In this state of things, as a final analysis, the aged must lose the accumulated labor of their lives, and the young must begin their toils without any of the important assistance generally derived from it.

In other words, Leisure the result of accumulation will not be the inheritance of any: and without Leisure there can be no intellectual progress, no civilization.

Alberta Wetter, the great-niece whom Mary continued to regard with stern displeasure, died on July 21, 1866. She was thirty-two. In addition to her husband, she left four children, her boys Edward Telfair (called "Telfair") and Conrad, six-year-old Meta, and her baby Louisa Alberta Mina, who had been born during the occupation of Savannah in the year before her mother's death. In the years before Alberta's passing, the Wetters had established themselves as prominent and respected Savannahians. They lived in one of the most beautiful houses in the city. Their residence, which was located on the southeast corner of West Broad Street and Oglethorpe Avenue, had been built originally in 1840 by William Hodgson's friend, Anthony Barclay, on land that had been owned by Mrs. Thomas Telfair. Augustus Wetter completely remodeled the place just before the war. After the war, he adorned the balconies with ironwork featuring medallions depicting statesmen and poets in profile. The ironwork originally had been ordered for the State Capitol building in Milledgeville, but had never been installed there. After he returned from the war, Wetter was nominated for alderman on the Democratic ticket but declined to be a candidate. He was a leader of the city's German community and, in July 1865, made a trip to Germany for the purpose of making arrangements for immigration from that country to Georgia. At one time he was reputed to be one of the wealthiest citizens of Savannah and was noted for his princely hospitality. [21] Mary Telfair had no reason to be ashamed of Alberta's husband, but she persisted in her scorn for the man and never became reconciled with Alberta or her children.

Mary Telfair and the Hodgsons left for Le Havre on July 14, 1866, aboard the steamship *Napoleon III*.[22] They sailed just one week before Alberta Wetter's death. They were in Paris two weeks later. This was not as much a trip of discovery as a chance to escape from the consequences of war and to find peace and contentment once again amid the familiar sights of France. There would be no frenetic sightseeing in Paris, as in earlier years, but rather quiet drives and walks in the Bois de Bologne. Part of the summer was spent traveling in Normandy, where they viewed the Bayeux tapestry and visited the insane asylum where Beau Brummel had spent his last days. Mary found the newly fashionable watering place of Dieppe to be less than amusing. "A frequenter of Saratoga or Newport would find it a dull place," she wrote in her travel journal. She did enjoy the sea views and found the drives in the environs of Dieppe "very sweet." She also enjoyed seeing the ladies in the old costumes of Normandy who appeared from time to time on the grounds of the casino.[23] Margaret had not been "sorry to bid adieu to by-gone ages in Caen for a gay scene which Dieppe presented." She found the ruins of the old castle looking down upon the casino to be "truly picturesque."[24]

Mary and the Hodgsons returned to Paris in early September. The weather was wretched. Despite an agreeable summer in Normandy and comfortable quarters in a hotel on the Place Vendôme, Mary's spirits were low. Writing to Isabella Hamilton and expressing regret that her friend's young daughter had been indisposed, Mary suggested that a removal to Paris might benefit the girl both physically and intellectually. She revealed her mood in writing, "There is much in this magnificent City to enchant the eye of a young person to whom 'life is new,' but oh! to those who have experienced the sorrows and vicissitudes of life there is little to satisfy the heart."[25]

Margaret Hodgson remained bitter over the outcome of the recent war. In a letter penned in Paris that fall, she wrote of being in "La Belle France sojourning under the French flag which I *revere more highly* than I do the Stripes and Stars." She went on to reveal her feelings toward the Yankees:

> Paris is filled with Americans. We only associate with Confederates, with the exception of the Gallatins who return to New York next month. I was interrupted a few moments since by a visit from an old Boston acquaintance. She greeted us so affectionately I for a moment forgot she belonged to Yankee land.[26]

Plans were made to spend the winter in Pau in the shadow of the Pyrenees. The choice may have been inspired by cousin Ward McAllister, who loved Pau for "a climate where the wind never blows hard enough, even in winter, to stir a leaf on the trees, the best cooks in the world, and where people appeared to live but to eat well and sleep." Of their trip to Pau, Mary wrote to Mrs. Hamilton:

The climate of the south of France is more congenial with our constitutions and we hope to live much in the open air and enjoy the grand and beautiful in nature. The snow-capped Pyrenees will be always in sight and we can sit on the margin of the romantic Gave in the park where there are "many seats beneath the shade" and within sight of the venerable historic castle—the birthplace of the heroic Henri Quatre, whose memory is still revered by the interesting peasantry.[27]

From a letter to Isabella Hamilton written by candlelight in Biarritz, it is apparent that the winter in Pau was not a success: "We did not enjoy the climate of Pau—it was too cold & damp for our Southern Constitutions. I have been an invalid all winter owing to taking repeated colds. On an average it must have rained every third day for six month in Pau." In early April, Mary and the Hodgsons moved to a hotel in Biarritz on the Bay of Biscay, where they could "enjoy the sight of the boundless ocean and the dash of the waves over high picturesque rocks as well as the roar of its music." They made an excursion into Spain and were delighted with San Sebastian. On a trip to St. Jean de Luz, they visited the cathedral where the Infanta of Spain had been married to Louis the Fourteenth. They also visited Cambo, "a pretty rural place" twelve miles from Biarritz.[28]

The time came to return to Savannah and the "poor old Mansion, stripped of those beautiful specimens of art which adorned its walls." As she prepared to leave France for the last time, Telfair bemoaned the changes that had taken place in the country that she loved more than any other in Europe: "France is becoming Anglicized and *Americanized*. When I first visited it, I was enchanted with the romance of the Country. The servants were different, the Cuisines perfect. Posting was favorable to refinement. Alas! Alas! Change is the lot of humanity and 'there is nothing true but Heaven.'" Passage was booked on the *Europe*, a side-wheel steamer departing from Le Havre later in May. Mary preferred side-wheelers to screw-driven vessels because she believed them to be much more stable.[29]

In the congressional elections of 1866, Republican Radicals, bent on revenge against the South, and Copperhead Democrats (Northerners who had been sympathetic to the South during the war) were in many cases the only choices before the voters. The new Congress imposed military rule on the South. Five military districts were created, and the governors, Union Army generals, ruled with a firm, if not arbitrary, hand. An army of occupation made up of some 20,000 Federal troops enforced their edicts. The Radical leaders of the Republican party in Congress were intent upon putting President Andrew Johnson in his place. A Democrat elected with Lincoln on the National Union party ticket, Johnson was not the smoothest of politicians. Lacking in tact and popular appeal, he was fair game for the Radicals. The Tenure of Office Act, passed in March 1867 over the President's veto, required the advice and consent of the Senate for removals from office as well as appointments. Convinced that the act was unconstitutional, as it later was held to be by the Supreme Court, President Johnson ordered the resignation of Secretary Stanton, though nominally a Democrat, a supporter of the Radical cause. In retaliation, on February 24, 1868, the House of Representatives impeached the President before the Senate, and but for the courage of seven Republican senators who voted for acquittal, Johnson would have been out of office and succeeded by Ben Wade, president pro tem of the Senate and an ardent Radical. On May 20, 1868, four days after Johnson's acquittal, the Republican convention, meeting in Chicago, named General Ulysses S. Grant as the party's nominee for President.

In July 1868 Mary Telfair was enjoying the delightful climate of Newport and watching the early morning fogs that rolled in from the sea over the town, which, according to Mary, were "said to be as favorable to beauty of complexion as to the living green of its exquisite lawns." One evening she and her companions drove to the farm of Governor Arnold, several miles from town, and Mary found his unpretentious "cottage" refreshing when compared to the "Palatial Edifices on Bellevue Avenue." "I admired primitive old Newport much more than I do modern Newport," she wrote. "I believe that I have an *inborn* love of antiquity." Her impressions of Newport in the summer of 1868 paint an interesting picture of this old resort by the sea:

> Some of the society here is polished and agreeable, and morning visits are almost "as thick as leaves in Volambrosa." The Husbands always visit with the wives, and the young girls drive their pony chaises on the Margellina of New Port in English style—the coach man seated in the Rumble behind. If I had never driven on the Margellina of Naples and seen Vesuvius

and the lovely isles of that enchanting Bay, I might share the enthusiasm of the people here who *rave* about the new road along the margin of the Ocean.[30]

The Democratic presidential convention took place in New York in July 1868. The party's platform called for "the immediate restoration of all States to their rights in the Union under the Constitution." It also called for the reinstitution of civil government, amnesty for all past political offenses, and "the regulation of the elective franchise in the States by their citizens." In other words, the federal government would not interfere to afford voting rights to black people. Horatio Seymour, a New York politician sympathetic to the South who was then serving as governor of that state, was nominated on the twenty-second ballot. His protests that he would not accept the nomination earned him the nickname "The Great Decliner." His running mate was General F. P. Blair of Missouri. Mary Telfair was delighted at the choice: "I am very glad to hear that the Democratic convention has nominated a man of ability & principle for President. I passed an evening in company with Mrs. Seymour several years ago and thought her very Ladylike, so there is the prospect of the White House at last being occupied by a *Gentleman & Lady*." Mary "felt strongly disposed to espouse his cause, for he is said to be not only a man of high moral worth but also religious and conscientious." Not everyone in Newport shared her views. She was distressed to hear a "Black Republican" call Seymour an "Artful Dodger." "We hear much and say little," she wrote with resignation.[31]

It was frustrating to Telfair when others failed to appreciate the difficulties being faced in the South under a military government:

> I read with interest the speeches of Genl. Hampton and Judge Perry of South Carolina. The Northerners cannot or *will not* believe in the oppression of the South. I feel that if I had been a man and a member of the Convention I should have *thundered* against Radical rule, but it is difficult to preserve a medium course.[32]

As concerned as Mary Telfair might be with the state of the South under Reconstruction, public affairs would often take a back seat to personal concerns. This was the case in June 1869, when Mary Telfair, suffering from the heat and a wound to her leg that would not heal despite the daily ministrations of Dr. Lemuel Kollock, mourned the passing in April of Fenwick Jones Gardiner, wife of Hallowell Gardiner of Gardiner, Maine. Fenwick's health had been very delicate for the preceding two years, and Margaret Hodgson was convinced that the rigorous climate of Maine had accelerated her end. Margaret had considered Fenwick her favorite relation and was convinced that Hallowell had been a devoted husband. Mary Telfair commented that Fenwick was "an excellent wife" and "a blessing to the poor & afflicted in Gardiner." "She had a lovely disposition," Mary wrote, "and the life of profound retirement she led for years past developed the best feelings of her heart."[33]

Despite her advancing years, Mary Telfair continued to take an interest in the romantic involvements of her young friends. She shared a bit of harmless gossip with Mary De Renne:

> My *Intelligencer* informed me that Mr. Geo. Fenwick Jones was the escort of Miss Anna Habersham to the picnic given at the McAlpin Plantation by the gallants of the day. Wallace did not go to it. He seems to be less of a beau than his Brother, and more admired by the middle aged Mammas.[34]

Margaret, despite her happy marriage, could rival her sister Mary in making sarcastic remarks about the opposite sex:

> The Merchant Prince Green sent a letter of introduction to Mr. Hodgson by the Le Marquis de Bourbel. All Mr. H. could do was to give him a sight of Bonaventure & bring him to eat waffles which he highly extolled. He is genteel looking, has a most indistinct voice, quite intelligent, & so *over bred* as to annoy *me by it,* as I had to rise to see about the ice cream he rose, & whenever I did so he was on his feet. His Mother I rather think is English. His Father was a great Naturalist, and was lost on one of his scientific expeditions. His residence is 30–miles from London. He is a Captain in the Royal Engineers. His bow reminded me of Wymberley's when a child placing his hand on his chest with the due reverence. I wish he could give a few lessons on deference to the male kind in this place.[35]

William Hodgson continued to attend to his business affairs and maintained a strong interest in the operation and expansion of Georgia's rail system. In November 1869 he was complaining to the

Savannah, Skidaway & Seaboard R.R. Co. about the injury to his property on the north side of Bay Street occasioned by the running of the street cars there.[36] In July 1870 a friend proposed that he fill a vacancy on the board of directors of the Central Railroad & Banking Company, but he did not receive the appointment, ostensibly because of his customary absence from Savannah during the summer months. He was, however, elected to the board of directors of the Atlanta and Savannah Railroad in December 1870.[37]

Hodgson's intellectual interests never flagged. In the spring of 1870 he received from his old friend Anthony Barclay a book of plays by Plautus accompanied by a charming note demonstrating the refined taste of a gentleman who could appreciate puns in Latin:

> I send herewith a little volume for your acceptance. It contains three of Plautus' plays, more modest in thought and language than any of his others, full of wit, humor, puns, and moral maxims. His ancient Roman dialect, so different from the refined formation of later days, resembles the simple north Devonshire compared with the elegant English of the present age. I think that the perusal will afford you much pleasure. The fact that the taste and scholarship evinced in the editing of this book belong to an American student marks a new era in the literature of this country.[38]

William Brown Hodgson died on Monday, June 26, 1871, while in New York City. He was seventy. His remains, accompanied by his bereaved widow, were taken to Savannah on the steamship *Leo*. Despite a heavy downpour, a number of friends were at the wharf to extend their condolences to Margaret and to escort the body to the residence on St. James Square. Generals Alexander R. Lawton and Henry Rootes Jackson, who in later years would play a major role with respect to Mary Telfair's legacy, were among his pallbearers when he was laid to rest in the Telfair family crypt at Bonaventure Cemetery. There Margaret erected a splendid monument as a memorial to her husband. Words of praise issued in the press following Hodgson's death, not only with respect to his scholarship and learning, but also his human qualities. The anonymous author of Hodgson's obituary in the *New York Home Journal*, a "friend who, with trembling hand, records this tribute of his love," wrote, "His manners had that singular charm of aristocratic polish, of genial, comical responsiveness which result from the rare combination of high organization, ripe scholarship, and courtly cultivation, which, if history not be a fable, once existed at St. James and St. Cloud." In a most interesting observation, the author of the obituary refers to Hodgson marrying into the family of the Telfairs of Savannah "whose well-known consideration for their inherited Africans has associated their names with humanity."[39] The author, writing in a New York paper, perhaps was attempting to justify his late friend's association with a family of slave owners.

The following summer, while Mary Telfair and her sister were staying in Morristown, New Jersey, at the home of Catharine Bulloch, Margaret took a serious fall while coming down a flight of stairs. She broke no bones nor was there any dislocation, but the sprain that extended from her shoulder down her entire side caused her extreme pain that was mitigated only by a treatment involving the use of electricity. She was confined for three weeks to her "chambre à coucher," as her sister called it. All the strength of an Irish maid was required to turn her in bed and lift her out of it. Margaret was unable to use her right hand and called upon sister Mary to handle her correspondence, as she did in responding to a letter from Mary De Renne. The incident caused Mary much anguish. All in all, it was "a bad summer made up of memories and associations," and matters were not helped by the extreme heat in the Northeast that Mary found worse than any experienced in the South.[40]

The respect and affection in which Margaret held the man to whom she had been married for almost thirty years was evidenced by her decision after his death to have his portrait painted and to construct, in his memory, a new headquarters and library for the Georgia Historical Society in which the portrait would be hung in a place of honor. Hodgson had served for twenty-five years as a member of the Board of Curators of the Historical Society, and, as stated in the resolutions adopted by the society to mark his death, he had been "one of its most useful, active, and important members."

The artist chosen by Margaret to paint William Hodgson's portrait was Carl Ludwig Brandt, N.A., a German-born painter who in 1852 emigrated to America and settled in New York City. Brandt had spent some time in Savannah prior to the war and had become a friend of Mr. Hodgson. He was a well-known artist whose paintings had appeared in numerous exhibitions in New York and who had received high praise from critics in the United States and abroad.

Among his patrons were members of the Roosevelt family and Justice Samuel Nelson of the United States Supreme Court. Born in Holstein in 1831, Brandt began his study of drawing under his father at the age of six. From the age of eleven until he was fourteen, he studied under Professor Bauer of the Copenhagen Academy of Art. In later years he would say that it was there that he learned to work with patience and care following the motto, "If it is worth doing, do it well." Brandt then became a pupil of the president of the Guild of Master Painters at Hamburg. The normal term of apprenticeship at the guild was five years, but Brandt completed his studies in three, a feat that the members of the guild celebrated by drinking to his health from a jeweled goblet of Rhine wine.[41]

Although Margaret Hodgson's motivation in building Hodgson Hall was to create a memorial to her late husband and a shrine in which his portrait could be displayed, the Historical Society did need new quarters. The society had been founded in 1839 at the suggestion of Israel Keech Tefft, a Savannahian who had devoted many years of his life to the collection of autographs and other historical documents. The following year, the first volume of its collections was published. In 1842 the City Council of Savannah granted to it a lot on Liberty Street for the erection of a library building. Its location was considered unsuitable, and in 1847 efforts were made to purchase from the United States Government the lot on Bryan Street on which the Custom House formerly stood, that building having been destroyed in the great fire of 1820. The negotiations were successful, and to enable the society to pay for the property, the City Council conveyed to it the Liberty Street lot, with permission to sell it and devote the proceeds to the purchase of the lot on which the old Custom House stood. A building was completed, and the society took possession in 1849. By the summer of 1870, the number of volumes in the library had increased to such an extent that it was evident that more room was required. The following spring the Historical Society made arrangements with the Chatham Artillery by which the two upper floors of Armory Hall were leased, and the library was moved to that location. This, however, was no substitute for a building of its own. Land was acquired on the corner of Gaston and Whitaker streets on which to locate the building that would honor William Hodgson. It was altogether fitting that the site should overlook the park that Hodgson had established. The architect commissioned to design the structure was Detlef Lienau, one of the early fellows of the American Institute of Architects. In 1873 construction was commenced on the elegant structure that would be called Hodgson Hall.[42]

On March 2, 1874, Margaret Telfair Hodgson died. The heavy cold that had confined her to her chamber had turned into a fatal case of pneumonia. The funeral was held at the residence on St. James Square, and the gentlemen of the Georgia Historical Society attended as a body. With Margaret gone, it was lonely at the old mansion. Mary had lost her closest companion, a sister who had become her only tie to life. Never again would the sisters come together in the late afternoon before a fire in the oak room to engage in quiet conversation and enjoy the tea and cakes that their servant Friday brought to them on a silver tray. The deep sorrow that Mary experienced found expression in a letter to George Noble Jones written less than three months after Margaret's death. "My dear George," she wrote, "My health is improving slowly; but I can never recover my cheerfulness after my overwhelming affliction which leaves me the last of my family on Earth." She may have recalled the lines of verse that she had penned years earlier:

> What are the worst woes that wait on age?
> What stamps the wrinkle deeper on the brow?
> To view each lov'd one blotted from life's page,
> And feel alone on Earth as I do now.[43]

When Margaret died, work on Hodgson Hall was still in progress. She had made no provision for its completion. Mary Telfair, wishing to carry out her sister's intention to honor her late husband, ordered that work continue and, as residuary legatee under Margaret's will, conveyed in trust to her lawyer and confidant, General Alexander R. Lawton, for the use of the Historical Society, the building under construction, and the lot on which it was located. By the terms of the deed of trust, Telfair charged the entire residuum of her sister's estate in her hands, or in the hands of her executors after her death, "to such extent as will furnish the means and funds necessary to finish and complete such structure." She also contributed $10,000 of her own funds toward the furnishing of the building.[44]

Mary's thoughts often turned to her own death. A few months after Margaret's passing, she drew up a memorandum specifying how her silver plate was to be divided among her friends, including Mary Harison, Mary De Renne, Sarah H. Kollock, and Mary Elliott. Mary's lifelong friends Frances Chrystie and Matilda Tillotson were to receive a selection of flatware, but there was no mention of their sister Mary Few. She had died in 1873, ever the old maid as she had predicted. Nor was there any mention of Eliza Terreli for she had died in August 1866. The remaining silver plate was to go to Mary E. Thompson, who had become Mary's companion at the residence.[45]

In late April 1874 the three younger Wetter children returned to Savannah to live with their father after having spent five years in the North and in Germany. Wetter came down from his plantation to meet them at the boat. Their brother Telfair, who also had been living in Germany, arrived three weeks later. By that time, Alberta Mina, the youngest, was nine years old. While in Germany, the children had been cared for for six months by Mrs. Margaret F. Donker, Captain Wetter's housekeeper in Savannah, and later by a Mrs. Hutching of Stuttgart. After their return to Savannah, the Wetter children never were sent for by Mary Telfair nor did she ever come to see them. Indeed, the Wetter children had never once spoken to Mary Telfair nor were they ever inside of her home.[46]

Mary managed to make her customary trip to the North in the summer of 1874. She left Savannah in the middle of June, bringing along a book given to her by George Noble Jones which she intended to read when she got herself settled. In September she was in Hastings with Frances Chrystie. She spent some time there with Matilda Tillotson. She received at Hastings a letter from William Neyle Habersham describing with enthusiasm his salmon and speckled trout fishing. He told her of his plans to be in the White Mountains in October. She was pained to receive a letter from Isabella Hamilton advising that her mother was very ill. As September drew to a close, she made plans to move on to New York. George Noble Jones would come down from Troy and would escort her from Hastings to the city by train. She let him know quite clearly that she wished to take the train to the 30th Street station rather than 42d Street, the former being nearer to the hotel at which she would be staying. She seemed to have her life under control at this point and indeed was a bit bossy in writing to Jones, "You had better take the early train for Hastings as I shall be ready to leave as soon as I can get my Trunks and Bags taken down."[47]

During the spring of 1875, Mary was despondent. Nothing seemed to console her. In May she wrote to her friend Sophie Clinch, the second wife of General Duncan Lamont Clinch:

> I thank you for your kind affectionate letter which quite soothed my weary mind. I never leave my desolate home but to drive on the shell road and to attend Church once every Sabbath. We have had a beautiful spring, its leafy splendor unusually rich, and the roses have been magnificent, but I can take no interest in the objects that surround me and realize more fully every day that I am a lonely pilgrim in a vale of Tears.

It was not easy for Mary to get about. Two years earlier, she had written to Isabella Hamilton that the fine weather had improved her physical condition. "I hope to walk as far as Mrs. Kollocks today by way of prelude to a longer walk." It is unlikely that she was able to walk a greater distance as age crept up upon her.[48]

The changes taking place in postwar Savannah were unsettling to Mary Telfair, as she complained to Sophie Clinch: "Savannah is increasing in size and old buildings are giving their place to new ones, but I hear only of *new people* which I have no taste for." It was the continuation of a trend that she had deplored years before when she wrote in her 1858 journal, "The Americans with few exceptions have no love of antiquity—old houses are demolished with an unsparing hand. Old furniture destroyed or sent to auction." She complained that "Yankees and Highlanders" were moving to her city and that the land that "was formerly covered with noble forests" was now being converted into "Lilliputian Plantations." The lady who so loved the ruins of antiquity, the moonlight on the Coliseum, and the mystery of Tintern Abbey was finding it increasingly difficult to cope with the changes taking place at such a rapid pace: "The northern people are flying like migrant Doves from snow & ice to Orange Groves and it is predicted that Florida will be as celebrated a winter watering spot as Newport is a summer one."

Mary at least had her books to keep her company. Fortunately her eyesight was sufficiently unimpaired that she was able to read. She reported to Mrs. Clinch that she had been reading a charming book lent to her by Mary De Renne, *The Memoirs of Robert Chambers* written by his brother, whose autobiography was included in the same volume. "The rise and progress of those intellectual men," she wrote,

"proves how much can be acquired by patient industry & economy."
Books had always been a source of comfort to Mary Telfair. Some
years earlier she had noted that Leigh Hunt, the English poet and
friend of Lord Byron, had remarked in his autobiography that the
love of nature and of books are the best accomplishments for a
woman. Mary added, "They are certainly the most durable." Mary
went on to tell Mrs. Clinch that, if the heat were not so intense, she
would prefer to stay at home in Savannah that summer, "sad &
dreary as it is." She had made plans, however, to leave for the North
on or about the 12th of June.[49]

She would not make the trip. Indeed, she would never leave Savannah again.

18

The Telfair Will Contest

It is a laudable ambition to wish to transmit one's name to posterity by deeds of beneficence.
Justice Joseph P. Bradley, Jones v. Habersham (1879)

Mary Telfair died on June 2, 1875, the day after she signed her last will and testament. Her physician, Dr. James B. Read, had paid her a visit at 5:00 A.M. He paid a second visit later in the morning. When he called a third time, he found her dead. Years before, Mary Telfair had written, "Many an individual leaves this world after a long sojourn in it, a stranger in the most emphatic sense."[1] How many of those who had passed through her drawing room appreciated the depth of her intellect or sensed the poetry in her soul? How many people other than her sisters, perhaps, and her "Siamese twin," Mary Few, really had known and understood this complex women?

William Neyle Habersham, one of the executors named in Mary Telfair's will, took charge of her papers on the day that she died. The tin box that contained her valuable documents, two bags of papers, and three or four trunks were taken to his office and given a preliminary perusal in the presence of Margaret Ritchie, the niece and adopted daughter of Mary E. Thompson, and George Noble Jones, Telfair's cousin. They were turned over to William Marshall, Habersham's bookkeeper, who spent several weeks poring through them and discarding those papers that he thought worthless. In the process he unfortunately discarded many personal letters written to Mary Telfair.[2]

Little did Mary Telfair's lawyer, Alexander R. Lawton, and the executors know as they attended the funeral service at the residence on June 4 and the burial at Bonaventure Cemetery that they were about to become involved in a will contest that would consume much of their lives for the next eight years. Surely General Lawton never dreamed that he was about to become involved in a legal controversy that would take him all the way to the Supreme Court of the United States. If anyone was up to the task, however, it was Alexander R. Lawton. He was a formidable figure in the Savannah community and one of the leaders of the Georgia Bar. Lawton was graduated from the United States Military Academy at West Point in 1839 and was commissioned second lieutenant of the First Artillery. He resigned his commission in 1841 and commenced the study of law at Harvard. He established himself in Savannah and practiced his profession until 1849, when he became president of the Savannah and Augusta Railroad, a position that he held until 1854. He was elected to the Georgia General Assembly in 1855 and became one of the strongest members of the legislature. An advocate of secession, he offered his services to the Confederacy and was placed in charge of a brigade, the famous Lawton, or Georgia, Brigade. He was commissioned a brigadier general and placed in charge of defending the Georgia coast from Savannah to the Florida border. In 1862 he was ordered to Virginia and led his troops in the "seven days fight" around Richmond and in the Second Manassas Campaign. In 1863 Lawton was made quartermaster general of the Confederate Armies. After the war, he returned to his legal practice in Savannah and served in the Georgia legislature from 1870 until 1875. In years to come he would receive many honors. He was elected president of the American Bar Association in 1882, and in 1887 President Grover Cleveland named him United States minister to Austria. Now, however, it was his job to have the Telfair will admitted to probate.[3]

Shortly after Mary Telfair's death, General Lawton produced the will to George Noble Jones, as one of the heirs at law, and to William Neyle Habersham and William Hunter, the named executors, and read it aloud to them word for word.[4] When General Lawton completed reading the will, it was clear to George Noble Jones that he was to receive from his late cousin no more than a few parcels of Savannah real estate and that his sister, Mary Harison, was to receive but a token bequest from an estate that would be valued at more than $640,000. He noted that Telfair had followed his urging and, notwithstanding her aversion for her late great-niece Alberta, had established a trust for the education and support of her daughters. The income from $29,000 in United States bonds would be of substantial help to the girls, particularly in light of their father's financial reversals. There is nothing to indicate one way or another whether Jones raised any question at that time as to the validity of the will or whether he expressed surprise that the bulk of the estate would go to the Georgia Historical Society to establish an academy of arts and sciences at the mansion on St. James Square, to a trust to build a hospital for women, and to the Independent Presbyterian Church and other charities. One can be quite sure, however, that after learning of the contents of the will he wasted little time in having a chat with his family lawyer, Joachim R. Saussy.

As could be expected of any good lawyer, General Lawton went promptly to work to have the Telfair will admitted to probate. A few days after Mary's death, he caused the will, together with the memorandum listing her silver plate referred to in Article Sixteen thereof, to be filed with the Court of Ordinary of Chatham County (the equivalent of today's Probate Court). Affidavits were presented by the subscribing witnesses proving the will and the collateral memorandum, and on June 7, 1875, upon the application of Mr. Habersham and Mr. Hunter, as executors, the Chatham County Ordinary ordered that the will, including the memorandum, be admitted to probate in common (or preliminary) form and that letters testamentary be issued to Mr. Habersham and Mr. Hunter confirming them as executors.[5]

When it became known that the Telfair will had been placed on file and thus had become a public document, many curious persons visited the courthouse for the purpose of discovering what provisions the rich old lady had made for the disposition of her fortune. A reporter from the *Savannah Morning News* prepared a summary of the will that was published in the newspaper. There was much speculation at the time over the reaction of the heirs and whether there would be a challenge to the will.[6]

On June 17 General Lawton's law firm filed a petition with the Court of Ordinary on behalf of the executors requesting that the will that had been admitted to probate in common form be admitted to probate in solemn form and that due notice be given to the heirs at law in accordance with the relevant statute. The heirs named in the petition were George Noble Jones of Savannah, Mary G. Harison of

Newark, New Jersey (George's sister and the wife of the Reverend William Harison), Mary E. Thompson of Savannah and William A. Ritchie of Holly, Michigan (both grandchildren of William Telfair), and Alfred Cuthbert, Jr., of Newark, New Jersey, the son of the late Alfred and Sarah Jones Cuthbert. The notice ordered by the court and published cited the named heirs to appear in court on November 1, 1875, at 10:00 A.M., to attend the probate of the will in solemn form and to make any objections that they might have.[7]

J. R. Saussy advised George Noble Jones that he had reasonable grounds to challenge Mary Telfair's will. Jones was presented with a hard choice. Should he try to overthrow Mary Telfair's charitable bequests? He had always been close to his late cousin and had the highest respect for her. If she wished to leave the bulk of her fortune to charity, was it right for him to interfere? He had little to gain personally from a legal battle that would be anything but pleasant. He was sixty-four years of age and was wealthy in his own right. But did he not have an obligation to his sister Mary and cousin Alfred to say nothing of his own children? He weighed his options and authorized his lawyer to do what he could to invalidate the charitable bequests.

J. R. Saussy called in his fellow lawyer W. W. Montgomery to assist him on the matter. Mr. Montgomery, acting on behalf of George Noble Jones, Mary G. Harison, and Alfred Cuthbert, Jr., filed with the Ordinary a so-called "caveat," dated October 5, 1875, challenging the probate of the will "so far as the so-called charitable bequests therein contained are concerned." At this point the caveators did not contest the validity of the entire will. They did not claim that Mary Telfair had died intestate. The first basis for their challenge was that the charitable bequests were made in a will executed within ninety days of the date of death, an obvious reference to a Georgia statute invalidating a bequest so made by a person leaving a "wife or child, or descendants of a child." Certain of the charitable bequests were challenged as too indefinite or uncertain or because the charity did not have a legal existence or the power to receive the bequest. In the case of the Historical Society, the caveators claimed that it was "incapable, under its charter, of taking the bequest given and executing the trust provided for." The basis for this claim was a clause in the society's charter limiting the amount of income that it could receive annually. The income from the railroad stock bequeathed to it under the will, when added to its current income, would bring it over this limit.[8]

Mary E. Thompson and her brother William A. Ritchie did not join in the challenge to the will at this point. Ritchie was a party to the later equity proceeding in the federal court, but Mrs. Thompson never took part in the litigation, perhaps in deference to the testamentary wishes of the lady with whom she had lived for a number of years. Of course, if the charitable bequests had been set aside, Thompson would have benefitted with the others, for she and her brother were related to Mary Telfair in the same degree as George Noble Jones, Mary G. Harison, and Alfred Cuthbert, Jr., and his sister Mary.

At the time of Mary Telfair's death, there were three surviving children of the marriage of Augustus P. Wetter and Alberta Cobb: Edward Telfair Wetter, Mary Martha Wetter ("Meta"), and Louisa Alberta Mina. Their mother had died in July 1866. The children were not named as heirs at law in the petition seeking to have the Telfair will admitted to probate in solemn form. It is evident that counsel for the executors believed the Jones group, rather than the Wetter children, to be the heirs at law of Mary Telfair. Augustus Wetter, having learned of Mary Telfair's death and the probate proceedings, hired a team of lawyers—Rufus E. Lester, Thomas M. Norwood, and N. C. Collier—and petitioned the Court of Ordinary, alleging that his children, all minors, were the next of kin and praying that a guardian *ad litem* be appointed to protect their interests in the proceeding for probate. Wetter had no qualms about seeking to protect the interests of his children. Mary Telfair would not even speak to him when she was alive, so why should he concern himself with her testamentary intent? It was a matter of money pure and simple. On reading Wetter's petition in open court at the November 1, 1875, hearing, the Ordinary appointed Wetter guardian *ad litem* for his three children.[9]

Upon his appointment as guardian, Wetter, with the assistance of counsel, proceeded to file a caveat against the probate of the will claiming that, at the time she executed her will, Mary Telfair was not of sound and disposing mind and memory and that the charitable bequest in the residuary clause was void as too indefinite and uncertain. Here the will itself was called into question, for if Mary Telfair had not been competent to execute it, the heirs at law, whomever they might be, would be entitled to the entire estate. The propounders of the will moved to strike out all of the grounds of the Jones and Wetter caveats, save that questioning the competency of Mary Telfair, because the Court of Ordinary had no jurisdiction to entertain any question other than "the factum of the execution of the will, and its being the will of Miss Mary Telfair." The Ordinary agreed and granted the motion under date of November 27, 1875.[10]

Subsequently, on November 29, 1875, Wetter amended his caveat to add a further basis for invalidating the will—namely, that Mary Telfair was "unduly influenced by the will of her deceased sister Margaret T. Hodgson and by the divers other persons and so did not execute the same freely and of her own account nor with perfect liberty of action."[11] General Lawton, as counsel for the propounders of the will, must have scratched his head at a claim of undue influence based upon the wishes of a deceased sister.

After a hearing on November 29, 1875, in the Court of Ordinary, a judgment was entered overruling the caveats of George Noble Jones, *et al.*, and Augustus Wetter and admitting the Telfair will to probate in solemn form. The parties challenging the will entered an appeal, which meant that there would be a trial on the merits in the Superior Court of Chatham County sitting in the old Doric-columned courthouse on Wright Square. At the same time, Wetter amended his caveat once again to include certain technical objections similar to those in the Jones caveat. The documents on file with the Court of Ordinary were certified by the clerk and filed with the Superior Court under date of February 3, 1876.[12]

Hodgson Hall was dedicated on February 14, 1876, the thirty-seventh anniversary of the founding of the Georgia Historical Society. The proceedings began with the singing of "Mighty Jehovah" and a prayer by the Reverend Dr. Axton. This solemn introduction was followed by the singing of Verdi's "Spirit Immortal" by a chorus and a bass soloist. General Alexander R. Lawton then formally delivered possession of the handsome building to the Historical Society. The president of the Society, General Henry Rootes Jackson, made the formal acceptance. The portrait of William B. Hodgson by Carl Brandt was unveiled, and General Jackson delivered a stirring oration in praise of the ladies whose generosity had made Hodgson Hall possible and the gentleman in whose honor it had been constructed. This was followed by a piece by Mendelssohn, an address by Dr. Richard Arnold, the chorus from "Lucretia Borgia" by Donizetti, and the benediction.[13]

The case was not heard in the Superior Court until June 6, 1877.

Two years had elapsed since Mary Telfair's death. By this time, George Noble Jones had died. Upon his death in May 1876, his two sons, Wallace Savage Jones and Noble Wimberly Jones, who were their father's executors, took over the conduct of the litigation. Mary E. Thompson and her niece, Margaret Ewing Ritchie, were living under straightened circumstances at the time due to the failure of the Central Railroad to pay dividends and their being kept out of Mary Telfair's legacy due to the lawsuit. Mrs. Thompson wrote to a friend at the time that she and her niece were "living incognito" in their own cottage "seeing no one & doing their own work."[14]

Before the trial began, the Jones group amended its caveat to add a half-dozen additional clauses of a technical nature. Wetter also amended his children's caveat to make more specific the claim that Mary Telfair was not of sound and disposing mind at the time of the execution of her will. He alleged that Telfair was "laboring under a monomania" as to the children that caused her to be greatly prejudiced against them. The theory was that Telfair's disapproval of the behavior of her great-niece Alberta, which led to her estrangement from Alberta and her children, had been a fixation that rose to the level of insanity. It was this insane fixation or monomania, so the argument went, that led Mary Telfair to leave the bulk of her estate to charity rather than to the Wetter children.[15]

Judge Henry B. Tompkins presided over the trial in the Superior Court after overruling an objection to his doing so made by Wetter's lawyers. They had made the claim that he could not be impartial because of his membership in the Georgia Historical Society, an allegation not likely to win the judge's favor.[16] Judge Tompkins was a close friend of the Lawton family, frequently dining or taking tea at their home at 135 Perry Street, but no one in Savannah's close-knit legal fraternity would dare to question his impartiality on this basis.[17] Wetter's lawyers tried to postpone the trial until they could subpoena G. W. J. De Renne to appear as a witness on behalf of the Wetter children. De Renne was in the North, as was his custom at that time of the year, and a subpoena issued on May 31 had been returned without having been served. In a sworn statement in support of the motion for a postponement, Wetter set forth what he expected to prove by De Renne's testimony. It was an exposition of the theory that Mary Telfair was suffering from monomania or an insane delusion with respect to Alberta and her children:

That for a period of about thirty years said De Renne had been intimately conversant with the testamentary intentions of Mary Telfair, and during said period had counseled and advised with her as to the disposition of her property by will; that for a number of years immediately succeeding the marriage of Alberta Cobb, the mother of deponent's children, the testamentary intentions of said Mary Telfair were vague, wavering and uncertain, she being constant only in the determination to exclude said Alberta from all share in her bounty; that this said determination was the result of the hostility aroused by the marriage of said Alberta, first to Charles Arnold and afterwards to this deponent; that said hostility was so intense and unreasoning as to cause said Mary Telfair to refuse to recognize said Alberta as a member of the Telfair family as long as the marriage with said Charles Arnold continued, and was revived with the same or greater intensity upon the marriage of said Alberta to this deponent; that this hostility was visited upon the children of the said Alberta and this deponent, and carried the said Mary Telfair to such extremity that she, jointly with her sister Margaret Hodgson, caused the remains of their sister Sarah G. Haig to be removed from Sharon vault, the family burying place, in the year 1860, and intended to remove from said Sharon all the remains there buried, so as to prevent Alberta or all or any of the said children from being buried by the side of any member of the Telfair family; that said Mary Telfair was laboring under the insane delusion that the said marriages of said Alberta had dishonored and disgraced the Telfair family, and that the interment of the remains of said Alberta or any one or all of her children in the same vault or tomb with her the said Mary Telfair would be dishonoring to the said Mary Telfair; that disgrace and dishonor would attach to the Telfair name if the dwelling house or residence of her the said Mary Telfair should descend to or be occupied by the said Alberta or any of her said children; and further, deponent expects to prove by said De Renne that the marriages aforesaid so wounded the pride of the said Mary Telfair that the determination to exclude the said Alberta and some of her children from all share in her testamentary bounty amounted to a monomania, out of which it was impossible to reason her the said Mary Telfair, and that said monomania affected the last will of said Mary Telfair to the injury of these said children, the heirs at law.[18]

According to the sworn statement of the executors, De Renne had indeed testified before the Ordinary that he had used whatever influence he had with Mary Telfair to induce her to make a bequest to the Wetter children. He also had testified that the testatrix was of perfectly sound and disposing mind and memory at the time of the execution of her will. It appears to have been generally known that he had rendered advice to the lady concerning her charitable bequests, including the establishment of an academy of arts and sciences. He had been a confidant of the family, a close friend of William Hodgson, and had consulted with Margaret Hodgson concerning the construction of Hodgson Hall. The executors opposed any postponement of the trial, arguing that the condition of De Renne's health had been such for the past several months that his personal attendance in court could not have been secured and that his testimony should have been taken in writing, especially as his absence from the state was to extend beyond the present term of the court.[19] Judge Tompkins agreed, and the trial went forward as scheduled.

The case was to be heard before a jury, and General Lawton had brought in his partner General Henry Rootes Jackson to assist him. General Jackson's career had been equally as distinguished as that of General Lawton. His election to the presidency of the Georgia Historical Society spoke volumes as to the respect in which he was held in the Savannah community. In addition to being a fine lawyer, Jackson was a poet, an orator, and a diplomat. A member of the Yale class of 1839, and the Yale secret society Skull and Bones, he had read law in Savannah, was admitted to the bar at the age of twenty, and was appointed United States district attorney at the age of twenty-three. In 1846 and 1847 he served in the Mexican War as colonel of the First Georgia Regiment. In 1849 he was made a judge of the Superior Court and served as such until 1853 when, at the age of thirty-three, he was appointed United States minister to Austria, a post that he held until 1859. That year he served as one of the government lawyers who unsuccessfully prosecuted the captain and owners of the slaveship *Wanderer*, which had been seized during an attempt to bring African slaves into Savannah. Jackson's book of poetry, *Tallulah and Other Poems*, was published in 1851. He served as a brigadier general in the Confederate Army. He was captured in 1864 at the Battle of Nashville and remained a prisoner until the end of the war. Later, during the administration of President Grover Cleveland, he served as the United States minister to Mexico.[20]

The firm of Hartridge & Chisholm acted as cocounsel for the executors. William Grayson Mann represented the Independent Presbyterian Church on a *pro bono* basis. The presentation of testimony began on the morning of Wednesday, June 6, and continued through Friday afternoon, when further hearings were scheduled for Monday morning.[21] The principal evidence introduced by counsel for the Wetter children in an effort to demonstrate Mary Telfair's alleged monomania was the testimony of Augustus Wetter himself concerning the estrangement between his wife and her aunts and the removal of Sarah Haig's remains from the Sharon vault. Hardly did it demonstrate that Mary Telfair was irrational on the subject of Alberta and her children:

> *Question.* There has been something said about an estrangement between them; can you tell what caused it?
>
> *Answer.* I can only tell what my wife told me.
>
> *Question.* Was there no intercourse between your wife and the family?
>
> *Answer.* There was an estrangement as to Mr. Hodgson and his wife and Miss Telfair. They never spoke to me or my wife, but they refused to be introduced to me. I only knew from my wife what this estrangement was. This estrangement, I understand, took place before her marriage to [Charles] Arnold, as she informed them that she would marry him and they forbade it. My wife lived with her late grandmother. She worried herself to death about this feeling of Miss Telfair's, as she was her only relative; in fact she loved both of her aunties. My wife wrote several letters to her aunties, she only got one answer, that answer we have here, that is the only reply. It is not exactly a reply but it came in answer to an advertisement I put in the paper. "That if any one disturbed our family vault, I would take legal steps." That note did not come in reply to the letter, but in reply to the advertisement. Sharon vault was the burying place of the Telfairs and the Gibbons. It was established in 1754, if I am right from an old will. I noticed all were buried there except

one, that one was the wife of Gov. Telfair; she was I heard buried in the North. I had control of this vault in 1860. I was executor of Mrs. Margaret Telfair. She was my wife's grandmother. I got notice about 20th December, 1860, that the vault had been broken into. Mrs. Wetter got notice from a Mr. Hutchings that the vault had been broken open and that hogs could go into her family vault. She sent a servant to find out the truth. He reported that the last remains of Mrs. Haig, who died in 1845, that her remains or a portion of her remains had been taken out of the vault and a small part of the shroud had been left. Mrs. Wetter wrote a letter to her aunts stating that she would try to find out who had done this. I offered a thousand dollars to find out the person. I never supposed it was Miss Telfair herself. Then this note was received. Mrs. Wetter also wrote inquiring what they did with the remains, and received no reply.

At this juncture, the letter, which bore the date of December 30, 1860, was read aloud and was introduced into evidence. It was curt and to the point:

> Miss Telfair and Mrs. Hodgson have to say to Mrs. Wetter that, in the month of May last, acting under legal advice, they instructed a highly respectable white man to open the Gibbons and Telfair vault at Sharon and remove the remains of their sister, Mrs. Haig, from it. No other was touched. The vault was secured after the removal.

Wetter continued with his testimony. He disputed the contention that the vault had been secured: "The vault had not been closed up after they had taken those remains out. The vault was opened in May and left so until December." Wetter then testified with respect to a bill in equity seeking to have the Sharon vault closed for all time: "I received notice from Judge Harden. He was Miss Telfair's lawyer. He said it was a bill in equity. I acknowledged service as Executor of Mrs. Margaret Telfair and for my wife. The bill was for the purpose of forever closing up Sharon vault." At this point, counsel for the executors objected. No bill in equity fitting this description appeared upon the docket or record of the court where it was purported to have been filed; no foundation had been laid for the introduction of this secondary evidence; and besides the testimony was irrelevant. The objection was overruled, and Wetter continued with his tale:

This bill in equity was by Robert Habersham, as next friend for Miss Telfair, and for others. I acknowledged service on the bill, or brief, or bill, or whatever you may call it in law. I paid Jones and Ward one hundred dollars retaining fee to attend to that case. I also wrote to Mr. Cobb, my wife's relative, to come and defend it. I don't know if this bill was ever filed or not; we have tried to find it but could not. I got a copy of this bill, it was given to me by Mr. Harden, this I gave to Ward and Jones, they said their papers had been destroyed during the war, and scattered, and that this paper had been lost.

It was evident to all that most of Mary Telfair's charitable bequests were motivated, at least in part, by a desire to perpetuate and honor the Telfair name. The academy of arts and sciences was to have a marble slab high on its facade bearing the Telfair name. The hospital was to carry the Telfair name. There were gifts to churches in Telfairville and on Telfair Street in Augusta. In an effort to demonstrate that Mary Telfair's pride in her family was in some way unnatural, the caveators introduced into evidence an excerpt from an undated letter written by her years before to her brother Thomas:

It is a common practice with me to answer a letter immediately after receiving it, when the feelings are warm, for delay never fails to obliterate those impressions conceived on the perusal of an epistle from one we esteem and love. On this occasion I rise superior to the Telfair Coat of Arms, *Pride* and *Indolence*, and boast myself proudly pre-eminent in point of *Punctuality*. Inclination has frequently prompted me to write you a congratulatory letter; but Pride, *the ruling passion of my soul*, deterred me from again attempting to draw something from you, as my former endeavors had proved fruitless, and this morning I was extremely gratified by receiving a letter from you, although a laconic one. We were all rejoiced at hearing of the arrival of your son in the *world of woe*. I hope he will be a prodigy, *the Phoenix of the age*. You know my veneration for *Talents*, and the first wish (after naming him) was that he might be eminently endowed with wisdom. Beauty is not essential in a man, though in a child it is all that renders them interesting. I hope that you will not, by overindulgence, crush *young genius in the bud*, but permit it to bloom and *enlighten the land which gave him birth*; kiss the little fellow for me. I very often think and talk of him, but have not affianced him yet.

To anyone familiar with Telfair's bantering style and fondness for word-plays, this letter would prove nothing, but perhaps it had some effect on the jury.

The caveators also offered in evidence a copy, written on the back of another document, of a letter dated September 19, 1859, purported to have been sent by Alberta Wetter to her aunts upon the death of her grandmother. The propounders of the will objected to the introduction of this document on the ground that there was no evidence that such a letter had ever been sent. The judge overruled the objection and allowed it to be admitted solely for the purpose of aiding the jury in arriving at the state of feelings entertained by Alberta Wetter toward her great-aunt at the time that the letter was stated to have been written. The text of the document in dispute follows:

Oh, Aunts, I feel so wretched, so lonely and so miserable without her tender love and affectionate heart to lean on, that I know not what to do. Earth and life seems a blank. I have so few to love and cherish me that *one* from that number, and that one such as her, must ever leave an aching void and cheerless blank in heart and life, and when I think of how few relations I have whom I have known and loved thro' life, I would that I had power to draw them all around me and encircle my life with their love and kindness. Oh, my dear Aunts, may I not in this hour of affliction lean upon your love; may I not trust that all unkind feelings, all causes of alienation or faults you may deem I have committed, will be buried in the past, and from this time forth I may claim your love and regard as one of the few bright spots of existence. If you knew how much I feel this terrible trial and the terrible loneliness of heart *as well as* clinging of soul to those so dear to me from early childhood, as you are (for I view you as almost part and parcel with her being connected so closely by early ties and fond recollections), you would not, I am sure, refuse me your sympathy and love in such a trying hour as this.[22]

After all the evidence was in, counsel for the executors moved to dismiss the Wetter caveat on the ground that the Wetter children were not the next of kin, but that the heirs of George Noble Jones and those joining with them were. In considering the motion, Judge Tompkins looked to the section of the Georgia Code dealing with inheritance and degrees of kindred and found that both classes of caveators bore a relationship to the testatrix more remote than that covered by the specific terms of the statute. Accordingly, the question would be governed by the sweeping provisions of the final clause of the section, which provided: "The more remote degrees shall be determined by the rules of the canon law, as adopted and enforced in the English courts prior to the 4th day of July, A.D. 1776." The reference to canon law was puzzling. Despite arguments to the contrary in support of the motion to dismiss, Judge Tompkins could not believe that the Georgia legislature intended to apply in an instance such as this the canons of the Church of England relating to kinship or blood relationships that were designed primarily to prevent incestuous marriages and that never had been adopted and enforced by the courts of England as rules of inheritance. If these provisions of the ecclesiastical law, as set forth in Blackstone, were to be applied, the Wetters would be out of luck.

The judge believed that the true construction of the Georgia statute required the application in this case of the "canons of inheritance," as adopted and enforced in England and not the "canons of consanguinity" as administered in the ecclesiastical courts in dealing with marital relations. The judge's reasoning made a good deal of sense:

> Neither propinquity nor consanguinity govern absolutely in the decision of who is the heir; and the gist of the question is not one of blood, but of legal designation as to who is an heir. The framers of the Code, even if they did not inadvertently put "canon law" for "common law" or "canons of the law," could yet have meant nothing but to refer to English law "as adopted and enforced in the English courts," as a means of who inherited an estate, after the special rules laid down in the Code were exhausted.

This being the case, and applying the arcane doctrine of representation, the Wetter children moved up one degree in relationship "placing them on an equal footing, at least, with the second cousins of the testatrix." On this basis, the judge handed down his decision on

Tuesday, June 12, denying the motion to dismiss the Wetter caveat.[23]

With the evidence in and the motion to dismiss denied, counsel delivered their closing arguments to the jury. Each of the lawyers spoke at length. The presentations went on until Wednesday evening when the court took a recess until nine o'clock the following morning.[24] At that time Judge Tompkins delivered his charge to the jury. The reading of the charge took about an hour. The judge had no doubt as to the due execution of the will. The only issue was the competency of the testatrix. The judge put six questions to the jury:

First. At the time of the execution of the will in dispute, by Miss Mary Telfair, on 1st June, 1875, was she of sound and disposing mind and memory, and entirely free from any kind of insanity?

Second. At the time of the execution of the paper purporting to be the will of Mary Telfair, was she a monomaniac upon any subject, which in any degree affected the fairness and validity of said will?

Third. If Miss Mary Telfair, at the time of executing the will, was a monomaniac, was the will in any way a result of or connected with that monomania?

Fourth. Was the will of Mary Telfair procured or executed by reason of misrepresentations of any kind to the injury of the heirs at law?

Fifth. Do you find in favor of the propounders and executors of the will, or in favor of the caveators?

Sixth. If you find in favor of the caveators, do you find in favor of the caveat of A. P. Wetter, as guardian, etc., of his children; or in favor of the caveat of Jones and others—one or both.

The questions were placed before the gentlemen of the jury in writing, and they were asked to come up with the answers and put them down in the spaces left on the paper for that purpose.[25]

The jury retired at ten-thirty that morning and deliberated throughout the day and into the evening. As time wore on, the feeling of those present in the courtroom, including the representatives of the press, was that there would be a mistrial. At ten o'clock that night, the jurors reentered the courtroom. To the surprise of many, the foreman announced that the jury had agreed upon a verdict. Weary after long hours of deliberation, he read out the answers to the six questions propounded by Judge Tompkins:

To the first—She was not.

Alexander R. Lawton and his colleagues must have slumped in their chairs as they heard these ominous words. The jury had found that Mary Telfair was not of sound and disposing mind at the time that she executed her will. The will would not be admitted to probate in solemn form. The best that could be hoped for was that the judge would order a new trial. This was a major setback indeed.

Wetter and his counsel and Jones and his legal team listened intently as the foreman continued to read the jury's responses to the judge's remaining questions:

To the second—She was a monomaniac upon the subject of Alberta Wetter and her children.

To the third—It was.

To the fourth—It was not procured by misrepresentation.

To the fifth—In favor of the caveators.

With respect to the sixth question, whether it would be the Wetter children or the Jones group, or both, who would prevail, the judge had not given the jury any guidance in his charge. In denying the motion to dismiss the Wetter caveat, he had held that "the children of Wetter stand on an equal footing with the other caveators in this case." And yet, he had given the jury the option of choosing between the two. How would the jury decide? The answer was not long in coming:

To the sixth—In favor of the caveat of A. P. Wetter, guardian, etc., of his children.

The reading of the general verdict came as an anticlimax:

W e, the jury, find in favor of the caveat of A. P. Wetter, guardian, etc., and against the caveat of Jones and others and we further find that at the time of the execution of the will the testatrix, Mary Telfair, was a monomaniac upon the subject of Alberta Wetter and the children of Alberta Wetter, who were her great-grand nephews and nieces.[26]

This was not only a setback to the charities named as beneficiaries of the Telfair fortune but to the Jones group as well. If the jury verdict were to stand, it would be as if there had never been a will, and the Wetter children would inherit the entire Telfair fortune. The all-male jury had based its verdict on the most flimsy evidence supporting Mary Telfair's alleged lack of testamentary capacity. Perhaps they were influenced by the reputation for being somewhat eccentric that the Telfair sisters had acquired during their later years. One can be certain that many of their fellow members of the Historical Society collared General Jackson and General Lawton the following day to ask how this outrage could have occurred and to inquire as to their strategy in seeking a reversal of this distressing verdict.

The propounders of the will promptly moved for a new trial. The motion was argued on August 1, 1877. Although Judge Tompkins had charged the jury that it was incumbent upon the propounders to prove not only that the testatrix was of sound and disposing mind and memory at the time of the execution of her will, but also that she did not suffer from monomania, he granted the motion for a new trial on the substantive basis that, despite the findings of the jury, he could find nothing in the evidence that amounted to proof of monomania.[27] One can only wonder why he allowed the question to go to the jury in the first place.

The parties challenging the Telfair will took exception to Judge Tompkins' ruling and appealed to the Supreme Court of Georgia. The appeal was heard in the January Term, 1878, and the court affirmed the judgment below granting a new trial. On the issue of monomania, Judge Hillyer, writing for the court, stated:

> As the case is to be tried again, we do not indulge in any extended commentary on the evidence. We will only say that looking carefully through the evidence in the record, we all agree thoroughly with Judge Tompkins, that there is nothing in it which amounts to proof of monomania, and we have no hesitation in affirming the judgment granting the new trial on that ground.

More significantly, in this appeal the highest court in the State of Georgia was called upon to face up to the thorny issue of whether George Noble Jones (who was still alive at the time of Mary Telfair's death) and the others who claimed with him or the Wetter children were the legal heirs of Mary Telfair entitled to continue to challenge the validity of her will. The court was required to consider and decide who were the next of kin, the grandchildren of an aunt of the testatrix or the great-grandchildren of her brother. As noted by Judge Hillyer, this was "a question much mooted at the trial, and the subject of the most elaborate argument and research in this court." Judge Hillyer had no difficulty finding the applicable rule in the adjudicated cases. Simply count up from the decedent to the common ancestor and then count down the collateral line to the person claiming to be the heir at law, assigning one degree to each generation. The number of degrees in the longer of the two lines was the degree of kindred. It was all quite simple as far as Judge Hillyer was concerned. In the case of George Noble Jones, the common ancestor was Mary Telfair's grandfather, William Gibbons the elder, who stood two degrees above her. Counting down from there, Mary's aunt (George's grandmother), George's father, and then George himself, placed George and the others similarly situated in the third degree. In the case of the Wetter children, the common ancestor was Edward Telfair, Mary's father. Counting down the collateral line to brother Thomas, then to his daughter, next to his granddaughter, Alberta, and finally to Alberta's children, four generations were included and thus the Wetter children were related to Mary Telfair in the fourth degree. But the court also had to decide whether the doctrine of "representation" applied, whether the Wetter children would be deemed to stand in the shoes of their great-grandfather for the purpose of counting degrees of kindred. After considering at great length the proper application of this arcane doctrine, the court concluded that it did not apply in this case and that the members of the Jones group were the true heirs at law to the exclusion of the Wetters.[28] So Wetter was out of the fight with nothing to show for his efforts but his legal bills.

The second trial was held in Chatham Superior Court at May Term, 1878. Prior to trial, the Jones group amended its caveat by striking out all former grounds for objecting to the will and by substituting the following objections: First, that the will was not attested and subscribed by three competent witnesses. Second, that Mary Telfair "was under a mistake of fact as to the existence of her heirs at law." Third, that she was not of sound and disposing mind and memory. Finally, that at the time of her death she did not know that the caveators, George Noble Jones and others, and Mary E. Thompson, were her heirs at law. The challenge to the competency of General Lawton and Dr. Read as witnesses was based on the fact that both of these gentlemen were members of the Historical Society, and thus interested in the bequest to that institution, as well as taxpayers in Chatham County who would benefit from those of Telfair's gifts that would help the poor. An issue also was made over the fact that General Lawton was a pewholder in the Presbyterian Church. The court gave short shrift to these arguments and held that Lawton and Read were indeed competent witnesses to the execution of the will. The court refused to charge the jury in a manner favorable to the Jones group with respect to the three other legal points in the amended caveat. On June 26, 1878, the jury returned a verdict up-holding the validity of the will.

A motion was made for a new trial; and after briefs were filed and oral arguments presented, the motion was denied. There was an appeal once again to the Supreme Court of Georgia, and once again Judge Hillyer handed down an opinion favorable to the proponents of the will. He held that the witnesses were competent no matter what their interest. On the issue that Mary Telfair did not know who her heirs were, Judge Hillyer said that she well knew how all the parties were related to her and if she did not know that the Joneses were heirs in the third degree and the Wetters in the fourth, well so be it: "It would indeed be strange, if the testatrix had not had the same doubts by which lawyers and courts were so long troubled, and for her to have been able, by herself to solve this intricate and difficult problem, would have argued a degree of capacity and men-tal power far beyond that which the law requires as sufficient to make a will." The judge concluded his opinion with these eloquent words:

> The testamentary scheme contained in the will, displays, on the part of the testatrix, a broad philanthropy, great knowledge of the times and society in which she lived, deep foresight in choosing the objects of her bounty, and the measures for its faithful and enduring application, in fact, unmistakably the product of a well-ordered and strong mind. It would be hard to find a will in which so large an estate (over $600,000) is be-stowed to varied objects of culture, charity and religion, personal

regard and kinship, though remote and collateral, and in which will, and every clause of it, *judgment* is more apparent.[29]

This was not the end of the matter. The heirs at law, led by George Noble Jones's executors, his sons Wallace Savage Jones and Noble Wymberly Jones, were unwilling to concede defeat. Their lawyers, Messrs. Montgomery and Saussy, devised a strategy. There was some interesting language in the opinion handed down by Judge Hillyer in the previous decision of the Georgia Supreme Court that provided them with a good deal of comfort:

> When a will is propounded for probate . . . the object of the investigation is to determine the question of testacy or intestacy, and it can never be said that the litigation is ended, unless all persons have been heard or have had an opportunity to be heard, who either really have an interest or *bona fide* claim to have an interest.

The syllabus, which Judge Hillier incorporated into his opinion, contained even stronger language to the effect that if the fact of a will's execution and testamentary capacity be proven to the satisfaction of a jury, they should find for the will and the court should order it to record, "leaving all questions of construction and the fate of charitable or other particular bequests for action of the parties or future direction in the proper court, as the case may require." "Where the executors are propounding an alleged will for probate in solemn form," the syllabus continued, "the issue, and the only issue, is *devisavit vel non*," that is whether the document propounded is or is not the last will and testament of the decedent.[30] All that the courts of Georgia had decided was that the will should be admitted to probate in solemn form. Was it not open to further challenge?

The lawyers for the heirs realized that they would not get far in the Georgia state courts, so they turned their attention to the federal courts. The Judiciary Act, in accordance with Article III, Section 2 of the Constitution, provided that federal courts had jurisdiction, concurrent with the state courts, with respect to all suits of a civil nature, at common law or in equity, involving a specified sum or value, where the suit was between citizens of the state in which it was brought and citizens of other states. George Noble Jones's two sons were at the time citizens of Florida, and there were other heirs at law scattered throughout the country outside of Georgia. Federal jurisdiction could thus be based on diversity of citizenship. At that time a principle of federal jurisdiction was evolving to the effect that while federal courts do not have jurisdiction to probate a will or administer an estate, where jurisdiction can be based on diversity of citizenship, federal courts may entertain suits by heirs and other claimants against a decedent's estate to establish their claims, at least where such claims could be made in the state court.[31] Messrs. Montgomery and Saussy concluded that a suit in the federal court was worth a try. Accordingly, they filed a bill of complaint in equity with the United States Circuit Court for the Southern District of Georgia, the federal court of original jurisdiction, seeking to have the devises and bequests under the Telfair will adjudged inoperative and void and a resulting trust in all of her estate declared in favor of the heirs. In drafting their complaint, the lawyers were careful to set forth the citizenship and residence of each of the claimants and defendants in order to establish diversity of citizenship. They alleged that the will had been duly admitted to probate in the Court of Ordinary in Chatham County (this was not a probate matter) but that the will undertook to dispose of the property of the testatrix "in an illegal fashion." The executors demurred to the bill. The demurrer did not raise the issue of federal jurisdiction, and accordingly there was no argument on that question as there might well have been. Arguments on the merits were made before the great Justice Joseph P. Bradley of the United States Supreme Court, sitting as a circuit justice, and District Judge Erskine.[32]

Some of the issues raised in the bill in equity were new. Some were old chestnuts that had been argued before in the state courts, including the rule against perpetuities. Every law student learns the intricacies of the rule against perpetuities, but seldom does a lawyer in practice have the opportunity to use this rule to challenge the validity of the provisions of a will. The rule, which is intended to prevent trusts from continuing in perpetuity, provides in effect that a bequest or devise must vest within a period measured by lives in being plus twenty-one years. When Mary Telfair had General Lawton draw up her will, she wished to be very sure that Hodgson Hall would be completed. To this end, her will provided that "none of the legacies bequests and devises in this my will shall be executed or take effect" until Hodgson Hall was completed and entirely paid for out of her estate. Messrs. Montgomery and Saussy seized upon this provision in challenging the legality of the devises and bequests. At the time of Mary Telfair's death, Hodgson Hall was still under construction. In theory, at least, the building might never be completed, and so, the lawyers argued, the gifts might never vest. As they might never vest, they claimed, the gifts violated the rule against perpetuities.

General Lawton may have had a few moments of concern. On the surface, the argument had a certain ring of validity. If the court accepted this argument, Lawton would be remembered at the bar as the lawyer who drafted the Telfair will that violated the rule against perpetuities. He would be the laughing stock of Savannah. He need not have worried, however. Although he was required to split a few hairs in holding that the rule was not violated, Justice Bradley found a way to reach the proper result. He reasoned his way through the contending arguments and concluded, "It seems to us, therefore, that the gift itself is not suspended upon the completion of Hodgson Memorial Hall and the payment thereof, but only the execution and carrying into effect thereof." The distinction may have been difficult to grasp by any but the most subtle of minds, but the result was the one that General Lawton and the executors had hoped for.

The court also had to deal with the old arguments raised in the state courts that the charitable bequests were void for uncertainty and that certain of the charities lacked capacity to accept the gifts made to them. These arguments were dismissed in a manner favorable to General Lawton's clients. The objection raised in the original caveat that the Historical Society could not accept the bequest of railroad stock because it would provide it with more income than was permitted under its charter was raised again in the federal court. Never mind that the legislature had amended the Historical Society's charter in 1877 to eliminate this restriction. According to the parties challenging the will, under the Georgia Constitution, the legislature had no power to do so. And, in any event, they argued, the law at the time of the testatrix's death must govern. Justice Bradley had a ready answer. If the Historical Society was in violation of its charter, the legislature could revoke the charter or ignore the violation as it saw fit. In no event would it affect the validity of the gift.

Messrs. Montgomery and Saussy seemed to be grasping at straws when they argued that the devise to the Historical Society must fail because it was not in fact a charitable devise. "It is 'a monument to vanity' to donee's name," they argued. "It is no charity at all." Justice Bradley was eloquent in his finding that this claim was not tenable when he handed down the court's opinion in the April Term of 1879:

> It is a laudable ambition to wish to transmit one's name to posterity by deeds of beneficence. The millionaire who leaves the world without doing anything for the benefit of society, or for the advancement of science, morality or civilization, turns to dust, and is forgotten; but he who employs a princely fortune in founding institutions for the alleviation of suffering, or the elevation of his race, erects a monument more noble, and generally more effectual to preserve his name, than the pyramids. Thousands of the wealthy and the noble, in the early days of English civilization are deservedly forgotten; but the founders of colleges in Oxford or Cambridge will be borne on the grateful memories of Englishmen as long as their empire lasts. Harvard and Yale, in our own country, are pertinent examples of this truth.

Having dealt at length with all of the objections raised by counsel for the Jones group, the justice held that all of the gifts were valid and dismissed the bill in equity with costs.[33]

There was one more avenue open to those seeking to overturn Mary Telfair's charitable bequests: an appeal to the Supreme Court of the United States. Unlike today when the Circuit Courts of Appeal stand between the Federal District Courts and the Supreme Court, in 1879 the only appeal from a federal court of original jurisdiction was to the Supreme Court. Messrs. Montgomery and Saussy made the requisite application to Justice Bradley. The Justices of the Supreme Court, sitting in the old courtroom in the United States Capitol, ordered in open court on June 5, 1879, that the appeal be allowed. Then, as now, the wheels of justice turned slowly, and more than three and one-half years would elapse between the day that Justice Bradley handed down his opinion upholding the Telfair will and November 1882, when the lawyers for both the appellants and the appellees filed their briefs with the Supreme Court.

The gentlemen of the Georgia Historical Society had become hardened to delay. While the lawyers engaged in judicial combat, the Telfair mansion had remained empty, and any efforts to establish there an academy of arts and sciences were placed on hold. Mary Telfair's "faithful colored servant" George, who had been bequeathed $1,000 under the contested will and had taken on the surname Gibbons after emancipation, had stayed on in the servants' quarters after Mary Telfair's death. He had done his best to keep the house and its contents in decent condition. It was difficult, however, to maintain an empty house, unprotected against constant changes in temperature, a moist climate, and dusty air. But George Gibbons was intelligent and resourceful. While acting as custodian at the old mansion, he studied for the ministry and was named pastor of Bethlehem Baptist Church. He was a man of considerable learning. He had traveled throughout Europe with Mary Telfair and the Hodgsons and with them had absorbed the culture of the old world. In 1878 the Reverend George Gibbons became pastor of the First African Baptist Church, a venerable place of worship located a short distance from the Telfair mansion.[34]

In addition to the arguments in the primary brief for the appellees filed in November 1882, the Justices of the Supreme Court had the benefit of reading those arguments beautifully set forth in a separate brief prepared by counsel for the Presbyterian Church in Augusta, the eminent lawyer Charles C. Jones, Jr., whose father had years before presided at the memorial service for Mary Telfair's friend Anne Clay. Jones did his best to impress the Justices with the importance of the Telfair bequests to the people of Georgia:

> In the history of wills Georgia has never known charitable bequests of such magnitude and of such liberal scope. They stand apart, and whole communities yearn for the advent of the time when, this litigation ended, they may enjoy the benign and far-reaching benefits which will flow from their judicious and enduring administration. Art, science, religion, the orphan, the widow, the sick and indigent female, with united voice and confident entreaty pray your Honors by final decree to sustain the provisions of this most beneficent will.

Oral arguments were heard on November 13 and 14, 1882. On March 5, 1883, Mr. Justice Gray delivered the opinion of the court holding that all of the devises and bequests in Mary Telfair's will were valid as against the heirs at law.[35]

The struggle was over. The highest court of the land had spoken, and there could be no further appeal. Mary Telfair's wishes would be carried out. The gentlemen of the Georgia Historical Society would establish the Telfair Academy of Arts and Sciences. The Telfair Hospital for Females would be built to serve the women of Savannah. The other charitable bequests would be implemented as well. Years later, a writer for the *Savannah Morning News Magazine* would write of Mary Telfair, "No one since Oglethorpe has done as much for the people of Savannah as this one woman."[36]

Appendix A: Last Will and Testament of Mary Telfair

I Mary Telfair of the City of Savannah and State of Georgia being of sound and disposing mind and memory do hereby make publish and declare this my last will and testament hereby revoking and making null and void any and every will by me at any time heretofore made.

First I hereby give devise and bequeath to George Noble Jones, son of the late Noble Wymberly Jones, all that full lot of land in the City of Savannah on Bryan Street East of and near Drayton Street, with the buildings and improvements thereon commonly known as "Oglethorpe Hall," to him and his heirs forever. And I also give devise and bequeath to the said George Noble Jones, to him and his heirs forever, all those lots of land on Farm, Poplar, and Harrison Streets, in the City of Savannah, of which I am seized and possessed, or of which I am at present the *bona fide* owner.

Second I hereby give devise and bequeath to Mary Harison, wife of the Reverend William Harison, at present residing in Newark, New Jersey, for her sole and separate and only use, and subject to her exclusive control and disposition, one hundred shares of the capital stock of the South Western Rail Road of the State of Georgia.

Third I give devise and bequeath to Mary E. Thompson, a resident of Litchfield, Connecticut, one hundred shares of the capital stock of the Camden and Amboy Rail Road of New Jersey, each share of the par value of one hundred dollars, the dividends on said stock to be paid by my Executors regularly to the said Mary E. Thompson during her life and the shares to be subject to disposition at her death by the last will and testament of the said Mary E., or any instrument in the nature thereof to be executed by her.

Fourth I give devise and bequeath to Margaret Ewing Ritchie, niece of the said Mary E. Thompson, also one hundred shares of the capital stock of the Camden and Amboy Rail Road Company, the dividends arising from the same to be paid by my Executors regularly to the said Margaret Ewing Ritchie, for her sole and separate use, and the shares to be subject to disposition after her death by the last will and testament of the said Margaret Ewing Ritchie, or any instrument of writing for that (for that) purpose made and executed by the said Margaret.

Fifth I give devise and bequeath to Kentwyn De Renne, son of G. W. J. De Renne of Savannah, fifty shares of the capital stock of the South Western Rail Road of Georgia.

Sixth I give devise and bequeath to Catherine Jones Bulloch, now residing in Morristown, New Jersey, fifty shares of the capital stock of the South Western Rail Road Company of Georgia, to receive the dividends regularly from my Executors during her life, and from and after her death said shares to be held by my Executors and their successors in trust for the use and benefit of the three nieces of the said Catherine Jones Bulloch, to wit: Martha Hunter, Lydia Hunter, and the present wife of William T. Gould of Augusta, formerly named Hunter, and for the use and benefit of the survivor of them.

Seventh I give devise and bequeath to my friend Frances F. Chrystie, of Hastings on the Hudson River, one thousand dollars should she survive me and not otherwise.

Eighth I give devise and bequeath to my friend Matilda F. Tillotson, if she survives me and not otherwise, one thousand dollars.

Ninth I give devise and bequeath to my faithful colored servant George, now in my service, twenty-five shares of the capital stock of the South Western Rail Road of Georgia, provided said servant George be in life at the time of my death.

Tenth I hereby give devise and bequeath to the Trustees of the Independent Presbyterian Church of the City of Savannah all that full lot of land in the City of Savannah, on the southwest corner of Broughton and Bull Streets, with the buildings and improvements thereon, to have and to hold the same on the following terms and conditions and not otherwise, to wit: *First.* that the Trustees of the said Independent Church shall appropriate annually out of the rents and profits of said lot and improvements the sum of one thousand dollars to one or more Presbyterian or Congregational Churches in the State of Georgia, in such destitute and needy localities as the proper officers of said Independent Presbyterian Church may select, so as to promote the cause of Religion among the poor and feeble Churches of the State. *Second*. This gift and devise is made on the further condition that neither the Trustees nor any other officers of said Independent Presbyterian Church will have or authorize any material alteration or change made in the pulpit or galleries of the present Church Edifice on the corner of Bull and South Broad Streets, but will permit the same to remain substantially as they are, subject only to proper repairs and improvements, nor shall they sell or alien[ate] the lot on which the Sabbath School Room of said Church now stands but shall hold the same to be improved in such manner as the Trustees or pewholders may direct. *Third*. Upon the further condition, that the Trustees of said Independent Presbyterian Church will keep in good order and have thoroughly cleaned up every spring and autumn, my lot in the Cemetery of Bonaventure, and that no interment or burial of any person shall ever take place either in the vault or within the enclosure of said lot, and for the purpose of having the same protected and cared for, I hereby give devise and bequeath my said lot in the Bonaventure Cemetery to the Trustees of the Independent Presbyterian Church and their successors.

Eleventh I give and devise to the Union Society of Savannah all that lot or parcel of land in the City of Savannah on the north side of Bay street and at or near its intersection with Jefferson Street extended or prolonged, known in the plan of said City as lot "Letter B," with the buildings and improvements thereon; but on the express condition that said Society shall not sell or alienate said lot, but shall use and appropriate the rents and profits of the same for the support of the school and charities of said Institution, without said lot being at any time liable for the debts or contracts of said Society.

Twelfth I give devise and bequeath to the Widows Society of Savannah all that lot or parcel of land in Savannah on the corner of President and West Broad Streets on which the improvements now consist of four brick tenement buildings, the rents and profits of the same to be appropriated to the benevolent purposes of said Society, but this devise is made on condition the said Savannah Widows Society shall not sell or alienate said lot or improvements, nor hold the same subject to the debts contracts or liabilities of said Society.

Thirteenth Should either one or more of the corporate bodies or Institutions named in the preceding items of my will attempt to sell alienate or otherwise dispose of the property and Estate therein devised contrary to the terms and conditions therein set forth, or should there be any levy on the same to satisfy the debts of said corporations then I hereby direct my Executors or legal representatives to repossess and enter upon said property or Estate as to which the conditions may be so broken or violated, and in that event I do hereby give and devise the said property so entered upon and repossessed unto the Savannah Female Orphan Asylum.

Fourteenth I hereby give devise and bequeath to the Georgia Historical Society and its successors all that lot or parcel of land, with the buildings and improvements thereon, fronting on Saint James' Square in the City of Savannah and running back to Jefferson Street, known in the plan of said City as Lot Letter N Heathcote Ward, the same having been for many years past the residence of my family, together with all my books, papers, documents, pictures, statuary, and works of Art or having relation to Art or Science, and all the furniture of every description in the dwelling house and on the premises (except bedding, and table service such as china, crockery, glass, cutlery, silver, plate, and linen) and all fixtures and attachments to the same, to have and to hold the said lot and improvements, books, pictures, statuary, furniture and fixtures, to the said Georgia Historical Society and its successors, in special trust to keep and preserve the same as a Public Edifice for a Library and Academy of Arts and Sciences, in which the books, pictures and works of Art herein bequeathed and such others as may be purchased out of the income rents and profits of the bequest hereinafter made for that purpose, shall be permanently kept and cared for, to be open for the use of the public on such terms and under such reasonable Regulations as the said Georgia Historical Society may, from time to time prescribe; but this devise and bequest is made upon condition that the Georgia Historical Society shall cause to be placed and kept over and against the front porch or entrance of the main building on said lot a marble slab or tablet, on which shall be cut or engraved the following words, to-wit:————

Telfair
Academy of Arts and Sciences,

the word "Telfair" being in larger letters and occupying a separate line above the other words, and on the further condition that no part of the buildings shall ever be occupied as a private residence or rented out for money, and none but a Janitor and such other persons as may be employed to manage and take care of the premises shall occupy or reside in or upon the same, and that no part of the same shall be used for public meetings or exhibitions, or for eating, drinking, or smoking, and that no part of the lot or improvements shall ever be sold alienated or encumbered, but the same shall be preserved for the purposes herein set forth. And it is my wish that whenever the walls of the building shall require renovating by paint or otherwise the present colors and designs shall be adhered to as far as practicable.

For the purpose of providing more effectively for the accomplishment of the objects contemplated in this item or clause of my will, I hereby give devise and bequeath to the Georgia Historical Society and its successors one thousand shares of the capital stock of the Augusta and Savannah Rail Road, of the State of Georgia, in special trust to apply the dividends income rents and profits arising from the same, to the repairs and maintenance of said buildings and premises, and the payment of all expenses attendant upon the management and care of the Institution herein provided for, and then to apply the remaining income rents and profits in adding to the Library and such works of Art and Science as the proper officers of the Georgia Historical Society may select, and in the preservation and proper use of the same, so as to carry into effect in good faith the objects of this devise and bequest.

Fifteenth Such of my household furniture as is not included in the above bequest to the Georgia Historical Society (except silver and silver plate, which is hereinafter provided for) and all kitchen furniture proper, and wearing apparel, I hereby give and bequeath to Mary E. Thompson hereinbefore named, to be disposed of as she may think most proper.

Sixteenth I hereby give and bequeath to such persons as I may name and indicate on a list to be signed by me and folded up with this my will, and in the proportions and of the classes therein set forth, all my silver-ware and plate of every description, said list to be taken as part of this my last will and testament, and said persons therein named to be legatees under this clause or item of my will.

Seventeenth I hereby give devise and bequeath to the Presbyterian Church of the City of Augusta which has its Church Edifice on Telfair Street in that City, or to the Trustees thereof, and its or their successors, the sum of thirty thousand dollars in United States currency, to be appropriated to and expended in the building and erection of a suitable and commodious Sunday School House and Library on a portion of said lot fronting on Telfair Street. And I hereby request and direct my Executors to pay over said sum of thirty thousand dollars from the funds in the hands of Baring Brothers and Company of London, which funds are to be by them withdrawn after my death.

Eighteenth In addition to the gifts and bequests to Mary E. Thompson and to her niece and adopted daughter Margaret Ewing Ritchie contained in the third and fourth items or clauses of this my will, I do hereby further give and bequeath to each of them one hundred and twenty-five shares of the capital stock of the South Western Rail Road Company of Georgia, to be held upon the same trusts uses and conditions as are set forth in said third and fourth clauses respectively.

Nineteenth I hereby give devise and bequeath to my Executors hereinafter named, and to the survivor of them, twenty-nine thousand dollars in the Registered Bonds of the United States at their par value, In Trust to hold the same for the only use and benefit of Mary Martha Wetter and Louisa Alberta Wetter children of the late Alberta Wetter formerly Alberta Cobb, to pay the income rents and profits arising from the same directly for the support and education of the said Mary Martha Wetter and Louisa Alberta Wetter and the survivor of them, not into or through the hands of their father or any other person for them, until both of them, or the survivor of them, shall arrive at twenty-one years of age. And after they or the survivor of them shall have arrived at the age of twenty-one years, to pay the income arising from this bequest to the said Mary Martha Wetter and Louisa Alberta Wetter or the survivor of them, directly and not into or through the hands of any other person, during the natural lives of them or the survivor of them, and from and after the death of the survivor to divide the same, with any accumulations of income or interest that may have been invested, equally among the children of the said Mary Martha Wetter and Louisa Alberta Wetter who may be then living, and in default of any such children then living, to return the corpus of this bequest with any accumulations thereon to the body of my Estate, to be disposed of as directed and provided for in the residuary clause of this my will.

Twentieth It is my wish and desire, and I do hereby so request, that my friend Mary E. Thompson hereinbefore named shall remain in my dwelling house a sufficient time after my death to assort and arrange the furniture, wearing apparel and other articles of value, and to take away such as are not included in the devise and bequest to the Georgia Historical Society, and I desire that no formal Inventory be taken or made of said furniture, apparel and other articles in any dwelling house to be returned to the Court of Ordinary, and that no auction or sale of any kind shall take place in the house or on the premises.

Twenty-first All the rest and residue of my Estate of whatever the same may consist, real, personal, and mixed, and wherever situated, I hereby give devise and bequeath to my Executors hereinafter named and to the survivor of them, and to the successors in this Trust of said survivor, In Trust to use and appropriate the proceeds arising from the same to the building and erection and endowment of a Hospital for females within the City of Savannah, on a permanent basis, into which sick and indigent females are to be admitted and cared for in such manner and on such terms as may be defined and prescribed by the Trustees or Directresses provided for in this item or clause in my will, the income rents and profits of such portion of the residuum of my Estate as may not be expended in the building, erection and furnishing said Hospital shall be annually appropriated to the support and maintenance of the same. My desire and request is that a thoroughly convenient Hospital of moderate dimensions suited to the wants of the City of Savannah, and capable of enlargement if necessity should require, may be built and erected, with no unnecessary display connected with it. And I do hereby nominate as the first Trustees, managers, or Directresses, of said Hospital Mrs. Louisa F. Gilmer, Sarah Owens, Mary Elliot formerly Habersham, Susan Mann, Florence Bourquin, Eva West & Eliza Chisholm, all of Savannah, Georgia, and do request and instruct my Executors to advise and consult with the ladies named as to the construction, arrangement, and furnishing of said Hospital. It is further my wish and desire, and I do hereby request, that a suitable and proper Act of Incorporation for said Hospital shall be obtained from such Tribunal in the State of Georgia as may have jurisdiction in the premises, to be called and known as the *"Telfair Hospital for Females,"* with the ladies above named, or such of them as may consent to serve, and such others as they may apply for to be associated with them, as the first trustees, managers, or directresses, under said Act of Incorporation, with power to fill any vacancies that occur in their number. And for the purpose of accomplishing the objects contemplated in this item or clause of my will I do hereby authorize and empower my Executors or the survivor of them to sell and convey all or any portion of the real Estate, or any interest in the same, which I may have or be entitled to, and not given or devised in any of the previous items or clauses of this my will, using their discretion as to private or public sales, and as to whether and at what time such sales shall be made.

Twenty-second It is my wish and I hereby so direct that none of the legacies bequests and devises in any of the clauses of this my will shall be executed or take effect until the building and other improvements on the lot on the corner of Gaston and Whitaker Streets, and known as the "Hodgson Memorial Hall," which I have conveyed in trust to the Georgia Historical Society, shall be completed and entirely paid for out of my Estate.

Twenty-third I hereby give and bequeath to the First Christian Church erected or to be erected in the Village of Telfairville in Burke County or to such persons who may become the trustees of the same the sum of one thousand dollars, and a like sum of one thousand dollars to the Hodgson Institute in the same village.

Lastly I hereby nominate William Neyle Habersham and William Hunter, both of the City of Savannah, as the Executors of this my last will and testament and trustees under the provisions of the same.

In Witness Whereof I do hereby and hereto set my hand and seal this first day of June in the year Eighteen Hundred and Seventy-five.

/s/ Mary Telfair [LS]

Signed Sealed declared and published by Mary Telfair the testatrix as and for her last will and testament in our presence, who in her presence and at her request and in the presence of each other have subscribed the same as attesting witnesses—(the word "not" being erased and written again in nineteenth clause) fifteen pages of writing, the seventh page being blank.

/s/ A. R. Lawton

/s/ Jas. B. Read

/s/ William J. Marshall

Memorandum of Silver Plate
Incorporated by Reference into Will

Savannah May 29th, 1874

Memorandum of Silver Plate &c to be divided as herein set forth among my Friends named and to be taken as part of my Last Will and Testament.

I give to Mrs. Mary Harison, Wife of the Revd. W. H. Harison of Newark, New Jersey, a plain silver Tea Set consisting of a Tea Pot, Milk Pot, Sugar Dish, and Bowl marked W.G. also a pair of small wrought silver waiters without any Initials upon them.

I give to Mrs. Mary De Renne, Wife of G. W. J. De Renne of Savannah, an ancient carved Coffee Pot of Silver, also a Silver Tureen and a pair of carved Oyster Dishes with covers to them, also a small carved Cake Basket.

I give to Mrs. Frances Chrystie of Hastings on the Hudson, State of New York, a large silver Cake Basket with a handle across the top marked Telfair, also two plain silver Dishes for vegetables with covers to them without a mark.

I give to Mrs. Matilda Tillotson of New York a dozen desert silver knives and forks and one dozen silver table spoons marked MT also a silver saucepan with a cover to it.

I give to Mrs. Sarah H. Kollock a silver Chocolate Pitcher, with a top to it.

I give to Mrs. Mary Elliott of Savannah, Orleans Square, one large Silver Cake Knife.

I give to the Revd. Telfair Hodgson one dozen Tea Spoons marked with the Hodgson Crest, a Bird on the handle of each Spoon. I also give to him a gold Watch worn by his Uncle William B. Hodgson.

The remainder of my silver plate not herein before named I give to Mary E. Thompson for and during her natural life, and after her death to her Niece Margaret Ewing Ritchie.

In presence of   In duplicate

/s/ A. R. Lawton

/s/ William J. Marshall   /s/ Mary Telfair

/s/ John S. Coburn

Appendix B: Rules and Directions for the Operation of Thorn Island Plantation

1. The allowance for every grown Negro, however old and good for nothing, and every young one that works in the field, is a peck of Corn each week, and a pint of Salt, and a piece of meat, not exceeding fourteen pounds, per month.

2. No Negro to have more than Fifty lashes inflicted for any offense, no matter how great the crime.

3. The sucking children, and all other small ones who do not work in the field, draw a half allowance of Corn and Salt.

4. You will give tickets to any of the Negroes who apply for them, to go anywhere about the neighborhood, but do not allow them to go off it without, or suffer any strange Negroes to come on it—without a pass.

5. The Negroes to be tasked when the work allows it. I require a reasonable day's work, well done—the task to be regulated by the state of the ground and the strength of the Negro.

6. The Cotton to be weighed every night and the weights set down in the Cotton Book. The product of each field to be set down separately—as also the produce of the different Corn fields.

7. You will keep a regular journal of the business of the plantation; setting down the names of the sick; the beginning, progress, and finishing of work; the state of the weather; Births, Deaths, and everything of importance that takes place on the Plantation.

8. You are responsible for the conduct of all persons who visit you. All others found on the premises who have no business, you will take means to run off.

9. Feed everything plentifully, but waste nothing.

10. The Shade Trees in the present clearings are not to be touched; and in taking in new ground, leave a thriving young Oak or Hickory Tree to every Five Acres.

11. When picking out cotton, do not allow the hands to pull the Boles off the Stalk.

12. All visiting between this place and the one in Georgia is forbidden, except with Tickets from the respective overseers, and that but very seldom. There are none who have husbands or wives over there, and no connections of the kind are to be proposed.

13. No night-meeting and preaching to be allowed on the place, except on Saturday night & Sunday noon.

14. Elsey is allowed to act as midwife, to black & white in the neighborhood, who send for her. One of her daughters to stay with the children and take charge of her business until she returns. She draws a peck of corn a week to feed my poultry with.

15. All the land which is not planted, you will break up in the month of September. Plough it deep so as to turn in all the grass and weeds which it may be covered with.

16. If there is any fighting on the Plantation, whip all engaged in it—for no matter what the cause may have been, all are in the wrong.

17. Elsey is the Doctress of the Plantation. In case of extraordinary illness, when she thinks she can do no more for the sick, you will employ a Physician.

18. My cotton is packed in Four & a half yard Bags, weighing each 300 pounds, and the rise of it.

19. Neither the Cotton nor Corn stalks to be burnt, but threshed and chopped down in every field on the plantation and suffered to lie until ploughed in the course of working the Land.

20. Billy to do the Blacksmith work.

20. [numbered as in document] The trash and stuff about the settlement to be gathered in heaps, in broken, wet days to rot: in a word make manure of everything you can.

21. A Turnip Patch to be planted each year for the use of the Plantation.

22. The Negroes measured for shoes to be sent down with the name written on each, by my Raft hands, or any other certain conveyance, to me, early in October. All draw shoes, except the children, and those that nurse them.

23. Write me the last day of every month to Savannah, unless otherwise directed. When writing have the Journal before you, and set down in the Letter everything that has been done, or occurred on the Plantation during the month.

24. Pease to be planted in all the Corn, and plenty saved for seed.

25. When Picking Cotton in the Hammock and Hickory Ridge, weigh the Tasks in the field, and haul the Cotton home in the Wagon.

26. The first picking of Cotton to be depended on for seed. Seed sufficient to plant two Crops to be saved, and what is left, not to be thrown out of the Gin House until you clean it out before beginning to pick out the new Crop.

27. A beef to be killed for the Negroes in July, August and September. The hides to be tanned at home if you understand it, or put out to be tanned on shares.

28. A Lot to be planted in Rye in September, and seed saved every year. The Cowpens to be moved every month to tread the ground for this purpose.

29. When a Beef is killed the Fifth quarter, except the hide, to be given to Elsey for the children.

30. Give the Negroes nails when building or repairing their houses when you think they need them.

31. My Negroes are not allowed to plant Cotton for themselves. Everything else they may plant, and you will give them tickets to sell what they make.

32. I have no Driver. You are to task the Negroes yourself, and each Negro is responsible to you for his own work, and nobodys [sic] else.

33. The Cotton Bags are to be marked A. T. and numbered.

34. I leave my Plantation Shot Gun with you.

35. The Corn & Cotton stalks to be cut, and threshed down on the land which lies out to rest, the same as if it was to be planted.

Appendix C: Excerpt From Decision as to Heirs of Mary Telfair

The Jones group, who were grandchildren of an aunt of Mary Telfair, and the Wetter children, who were great-grandchildren of her brother, Thomas, did not come within the first eight clauses of Section 2484 of the Georgia Code, and thus the issue of who were Mary Telfair's lawful heirs was determined by the sweeping provisions of the ninth clause which provided "that the more remote degrees of kindred shall be determined by the rules of the canon law, as adopted and enforced in the English courts prior to the 4th day of July, 1776." The following excerpt from Wetter v. Habersham, 60 Ga. 193 (1878), gives the court's reasoning on the question of who are the heirs of Mary Telfair:

To ascertain the rules of the canon law we have but to refer to the adjudicated cases and authorities in England coming down to us from beyond the date in question, and from these it is impossible to err in the proposition that to ascertain the degree of kindred we must count from the intestate up to the common ancestor one degree for each generation, thence down the collateral line to the contestant: the number of degrees in the longer of these two lines is the degree of kindred between the intestate and the contestant. And by this rule the grandchildren of an aunt are in the third degree, and are heirs at law in preference to the great-grandchildren of a brother, who are in the fourth degree. This construction involves the proposition, that if Alberta Wetter, the grandchild of Thos. Telfair, the brother, had been in life at the time her grand-aunt Mary Telfair died, she would have inherited the whole estate to the exclusion of the Joneses.

Because by representation she would have been moved up to the position of her grandfather, Thos. Telfair, and then standing in the shoes of a brother she would of course have inherited to the exclusion of the descendants of an aunt (the Joneses); but that Mrs. Wetter having died before Mary Telfair, her line is cut off altogether; and though she left children they are postponed to the same grandchildren of an aunt, whom their mother would have completely outranked. For myself if not controlled by authority and precedent, I should have some hesitancy in so ruling. The doubt is as to whether the language, "There shall be no representation beyond the children and grandchildren of brothers and sisters," means that none but living persons shall be counted under, or take rank by, representation, or whether representation ought not to be admitted as far as Alberta Wetter (a brother's grandchild) although she be dead, but not "beyond" her, and thus in counting the degrees to move her up to the place of her grandfather, Thomas Telfair, and to count her and her mother and her grandfather, by "representation," as all one degree. If Alberta Wetter had been in life, the fact that her mother and grandfather were dead, would not prevent the degree of kindred from counting in her favor or prevent her from being moved up to and standing in the shoes of her dead grandfather; and why should her death prevent her children from standing in her shoes? Quite an ingenious argument might be made in favor of that view, and the subject made to furnish another of the curious and difficult problems incident to the whole doctrine of kinship and inheritance, than which perhaps no one branch of the law has been more fruitful of controversy, or had expended upon it more learning and research. But the safe course is to resort to authority, follow the beaten path of precedent. The doctrine of representation is not now in the laws of England.

From quite an ancient date representation was admitted in England as far as the children of brothers and sisters. And such was the law of Georgia down to the act of 1859. By that act representation was extended to grandchildren of brothers and sisters. But the ancient inhibition which came across the waters with our forefathers was retained, namely, "that further than this there should be no representation among collaterals." Now take the law as it stood in England prior to our adopting statute, where the rules of the canon law were of force, and in human experience such a contest as the present one would be apt to arise with some frequency, and accordingly we find quite a number of cases in which this and the like question did arise, and were decided in the English courts, and it was very early held, and the doctrine firmly established, that the language of the act: "There shall be no representatives admitted after brothers' and sisters' children," operated to cut off all who were in any more remote degree altogether from any benefit of the doctrine of representation; that is, that if the person entitled to representation within the words of the act, be dead, that all representation is at an end, and one who stands in the shoes of such a deceased person can thereby take no benefit of representation. We quote from the case of Pett *vs.* Pett, 1 Comyn's Reports, 87: "A libel was exhibited against the administrator, setting forth that the intestate had two brothers who had issue and died. The issue of one of the brothers had issue, a son and a daughter, and then the intestate dies; and his grand-nephew and grand-niece, the son and daughter of the issue of one of the brothers, wanted to have distribution with his niece, the issue of the other brother; but the spiritual court had denied it, for there is a proviso in the act of parliament that there shall be no representatives admitted after brothers' and sisters' children, which occasioned the motion for a *mandamus,* but it was denied." Can anything be plainer? This was decided in the twelfth year of William III, and in support of the doctrine there laid down may be cited [citations].

Concluding, then, as we do, that the doctrine of representation is not applicable to the case, and that by the rules of the canon law, the Joneses are in the third degree and the Wetters in the fourth, we hold that the former are heirs at law to the exclusion of the latter.

Family Trees

GENEALOGICAL CHARTS

Charts

1. The Gibbons Family
2. Edward Telfair and his Descendants
3. William Telfair (brother of Edward Telfair) and his Descendants
4. The Jones Family
5. The Few Family
6. Anne Clay and her Family

Definitions:

= or m. – Married
unm. – Died unmarried
n.c. – Did not have any children
+ – Had progeny not covered by chart
b. – Born
d. – Died

CHART I
The Gibbons Family

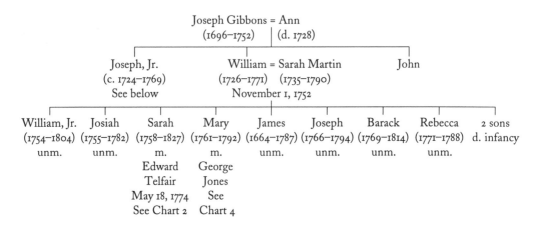

Joseph Gibbons = Ann
(1696–1752) | (d. 1728)

Joseph, Jr.	William = Sarah Martin	John
(c. 1724–1769)	(1726–1771) (1735–1790)	
See below	November 1, 1752	

William, Jr.	Josiah	Sarah	Mary	James	Joseph	Barack	Rebecca	2 sons
(1754–1804)	(1755–1782)	(1758–1827)	(1761–1792)	(1664–1787)	(1766–1794)	(1769–1814)	(1771–1788)	d. infancy
unm.	unm.	m.	m.	unm.	unm.	unm.	unm.	
		Edward	George					
		Telfair	Jones					
		May 18, 1774	See					
		See Chart 2	Chart 4					

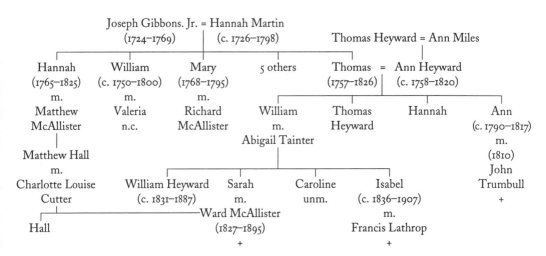

Joseph Gibbons. Jr. = Hannah Martin
(1724–1769) | (c. 1726–1798)   Thomas Heyward = Ann Miles

Hannah	William	Mary	5 others	Thomas =	Ann Heyward
(1765–1825)	(c. 1750–1800)	(1768–1795)		(1757–1826)	(c. 1758–1820)
m.	m.	m.			
Matthew	Valeria	Richard	William	Thomas	Hannah	Ann
McAllister	n.c.	McAllister	m.	Heyward		(c. 1790–1817)
			Abigail Tainter			m.
Matthew Hall						(1810)
m.						John
Charlotte Louise	William Heyward	Sarah	Caroline	Isabel		Trumbull
Cutter	(c. 1831–1887)	m.	unm.	(c. 1836–1907)		+
		Ward McAllister		m.		
Hall		(1827–1895)		Francis Lathrop		
		+		+		

CHART 2
Edward Telfair and his Descendants

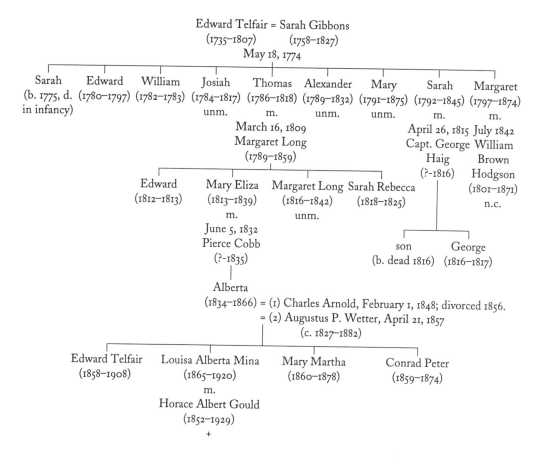

CHART 3
William Telfair (brother of Edward Telfair) and his Descendants

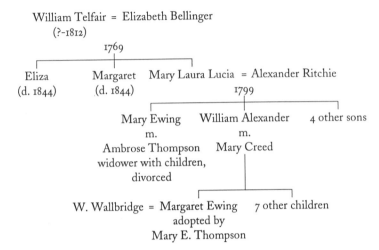

CHART 4
The Jones Family

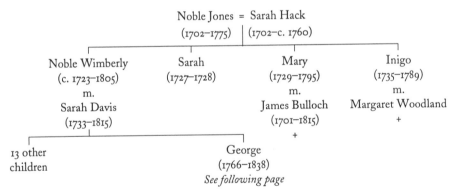

CHART 4 *(Continued)*
The Jones Family

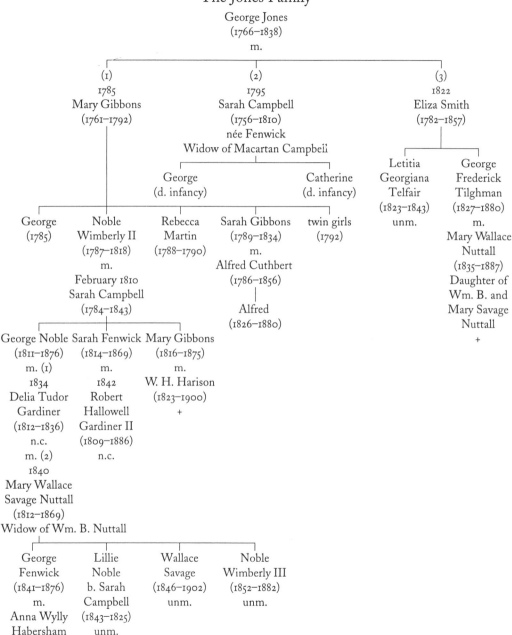

George Jones
(1766–1838)
m.

(1)
1785
Mary Gibbons
(1761–1792)

(2)
1795
Sarah Campbell
(1756–1810)
née Fenwick
Widow of Macartan Campbell

(3)
1822
Eliza Smith
(1782–1857)

George
(d. infancy)

Catherine
(d. infancy)

Letitia
Georgiana
Telfair
(1823–1843)
unm.

George
Frederick
Tilghman
(1827–1880)
m.
Mary Wallace
Nuttall
(1835–1887)
Daughter of
Wm. B. and
Mary Savage
Nuttall
+

George
(1785)

Noble
Wimberly II
(1787–1818)
m.
February 1810
Sarah Campbell
(1784–1843)

Rebecca
Martin
(1788–1790)

Sarah Gibbons
(1789–1834)
m.
Alfred Cuthbert
(1786–1856)
|
Alfred
(1826–1880)

twin girls
(1792)

George Noble
(1811–1876)
m. (1)
1834
Delia Tudor
Gardiner
(1812–1836)
n.c.
m. (2)
1840
Mary Wallace
Savage Nuttall
(1812–1869)
Widow of Wm. B. Nuttall

Sarah Fenwick
(1814–1869)
m.
1842
Robert
Hallowell
Gardiner II
(1809–1886)
n.c.

Mary Gibbons
(1816–1875)
m.
W. H. Harison
(1823–1900)
+

George
Fenwick
(1841–1876)
m.
Anna Wylly
Habersham
(1849–1888)
+

Lillie
Noble
b. Sarah
Campbell
(1843–1825)
unm.

Wallace
Savage
(1846–1902)
unm.

Noble
Wimberly III
(1852–1882)
unm.

FAMILY TREES

CHART 5
The Few Family

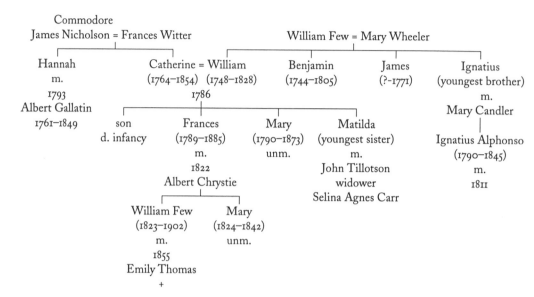

Commodore
James Nicholson = Frances Witter   William Few = Mary Wheeler

Hannah
m.
1793
Albert Gallatin
1761–1849

Catherine = William   Benjamin   James   Ignatius
(1764–1854) (1748–1828)   (1744–1805)   (?–1771)   (youngest brother)
1786   m.
                                                             Mary Candler

son   Frances   Mary   Matilda   Ignatius Alphonso
d. infancy   (1789–1885)   (1790–1873)   (youngest sister) (1790–1845)
             m.   unm.   m.   m.
             1822   John Tillotson   1811
             Albert Chrystie   widower
                                            Selina Agnes Carr

William Few   Mary
(1823–1902)   (1824–1842)
m.   unm.
1855
Emily Thomas
+

CHART 6
Anne Clay and her Family

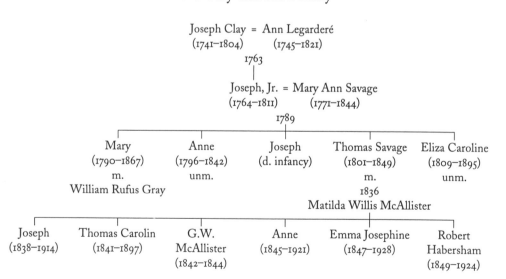

Joseph Clay = Ann Legarderé
(1741–1804)   (1745–1821)
1763

Joseph, Jr. = Mary Ann Savage
(1764–1811)   (1771–1844)
1789

Mary   Anne   Joseph   Thomas Savage   Eliza Caroline
(1790–1867)   (1796–1842)   (d. infancy)   (1801–1849)   (1809–1895)
m.   unm.   m.   unm.
William Rufus Gray   1836
                                            Matilda Willis McAllister

Joseph   Thomas Carolin   G.W.   Anne   Emma Josephine   Robert
(1838–1914)   (1841–1897)   McAllister   (1845–1921)   (1847–1928)   Habersham
                                 (1842–1844)   (1849–1924)

Principal Characters

The following thumbnail sketches relate to the principal family members, friends, and acquaintances who affected or passed through the life of Mary Telfair ("MT"). Authors and literary characters mentioned by MT are not included; nor are nationally known military or political figures not directly connected to the Telfairs. The intricate family relationships that pervaded MT's social sphere can best be untangled by reference to the accompanying genealogical charts.

Arnold, Charles: Clerk and later partner in Savannah mercantile firm; eloped in 1848 with Alberta Cobb (granddaughter of Thomas Telfair); divorced in 1856.

Arnold, Dr. Richard D. (1808–1876): Physician; mayor of Savannah; surrendered city to General Sherman.

Barclay, Anthony: Served as British consul general in New York; friend of William Brown Hodgson; stayed at Telfair mansion during occupation of Savannah by Sherman's forces.

Berrien, Eliza Ancieux (d. 1828): First wife of John Macpherson Berrien.

Berrien, Eliza Cecil (d. 1852) (née Hunter): Second wife of John Macpherson Berrien; niece of Sarah Cecil.

Berrien, John Macpherson (1781–1856): Distinguished Savannah lawyer; the "American Cicero;" United States senator; attorney general in cabinet of Andrew Jackson; resigned over Margaret Eaton affair; friend of the Telfairs.

Biddle, Nicholas (1786–1844): Wealthy financier from Philadelphia; president of the Bank of the United States; friend of MT with whom she exchanged poetry.

Bolton, Robert (1788–1857): Savannah native; married Anne Jay (1793–1859), daughter of Rev. William Jay of Bath; held pastorate in

Henley-upon-Thames; received holy orders in Episcopal Church in New York; built Pelham Priory; established highly regarded parish school there; friend of MT.

Bradley, Justice Joseph P. (1813–1892): United States Supreme Court justice; presided over equity proceeding challenging MT's charitable bequests in United States Circuit Court for the Southern District of Georgia.

Brandt, Carl Ludwig (1831–1905): Artist of German nationality; born in Holstein; painted portrait of William Brown Hodgson in Hodgson Hall, headquarters and library of Georgia Historical Society built by Margaret Telfair Hodgson as a memorial to her husband; first director of Telfair Academy of Arts and Sciences; painted posthumous portrait of MT.

Bulloch, Catharine (née Hunter): Satirical and amusing friend of MT in Savannah; married Jones Bulloch, who suffered financial reversal; spent later years in Morristown, New Jersey.

Bulloch, Jones (d. 1860): Grandson of patriot Archibald Bulloch; cousin and husband of Catharine Hunter Bulloch; forced by financial scandal to leave Savannah.

Butler, Pierce (1810–1867): Wealthy Philadelphian and Sea Island planter; grandson of Major Pierce Butler; married Fanny Kemble in 1834; friend of William Brown Hodgson.

Campbell, Harriett: Daughter of Macartan and Sarah Fenwick Campbell; half sister and close companion of MT's cousin Sarah Jones.

Campbell, Sarah ("Lillie"): See Jones, Sarah.

Campbell, Sarah (née Hull): Wife of Edward F. Campbell (1786–1861) (brother of Lillie and Maria); much admired friend of MT; taught slave children on plantation near Augusta.

Cecil, Sarah (1791–1878): Direct descendant of William Cecil, secretary of state and lord treasurer to Elizabeth I and his younger son Robert Cecil, Earl of Salisbury; close friend of MT in Savannah.

Chrystie, Albert (d. 1856): Prosperous New York merchant and farmer; married Frances Few in 1822; built mansion in Fishkill, New York; with wife Frances and two children traveled in Europe with Telfair sisters.

Chrystie, Frances (1789–1885) (née Few): Elder sister of Mary Few; friend with whom MT loved to exchange jokes; wife of Albert Chrystie.

Chrystie, Mary (1824–1842): Daughter of Albert and Frances Few Chrystie; died in Nice during European trip.

Chrystie, William Few (1823–1902): Son of Albert and Frances Few Chrystie; traveled with parents and Telfair sisters in Europe; married Emily Thomas of Augusta, Georgia, in 1855.

Clay, Anne (1796–1842): MT's intellectual friend; queenly in stature and bearing; strong Christian; taught slave children on family plantation; daughter of Joseph Clay, Jr.; never married.

Clay, Eliza Caroline (1809–1895): Sister of Anne Clay; never married and ran Bryan County, Georgia, plantations with brother Thomas Savage Clay.

Clay, Joseph (1741–1804): Patriarch of Clay family in Georgia; business partner of Edward Telfair; married Ann Legarderé in 1763; grandfather of Anne Clay.

Clay, Joseph, Jr. (1764–1811): Lawyer, judge, planter, ordained Baptist minister; married Mary Ann Savage in 1789; father of Anne Clay.

Clay, Mary: See Gray, Mary.

Clay, Mary Ann (1771–1844) (née Savage): Mother of Anne Clay.

Clay, Thomas Carolin (1841–1897): Son of Thomas Savage and Matilda Clay; left Yale to join Confederate forces out of a sense of duty.

Clay, Thomas Savage (1801–1849): Brother of Anne Clay; Harvard graduate; operated family plantation in Bryan County, Georgia; wrote *Detail of a Plan for the Moral Improvement of Negroes on Plantations.*

Cobb, Alberta: See Wetter, Alberta.

Cobb, Mary Eliza (1813–1839) (née Telfair): Daughter of Thomas and Margaret Telfair; tutored by MT and MT's sister Margaret; studied in New York; married Pierce Cobb in 1832; mother of Alberta.

Cobb, Pierce (d. 1835): Husband of Mary Eliza Telfair Cobb; father of Alberta.

Couper, James Hamilton (1794–1866): Leading planter on the Altamaha River estuary; shared with William Brown Hodgson interest in ethnological subjects and fossil remains; architect for Christ Church in Savannah; survivor of *Pulaski* disaster.

Cumming, Dr. John (d. 1838): Friend of Alexander Telfair; traveling companion of Alexander and his sisters; with Telfairs in Winchester, Virginia, during Alexander's last illness; went down with the *Pulaski.*

Cuthbert, Alfred (1786–1856): Eccentric classmate of Josiah Telfair at

College of New Jersey (Princeton); married in 1823 Sarah Jones; member of United States Congress; United States senator (1835–1843).

Cuthbert, Sarah (1789–1834) (née Jones): Sister of Noble Wimberly Jones II; cousin and lifelong friend of MT; wife of Alfred Cuthbert; died in childbirth leaving son Alfred, Jr.

De Renne, George Wymberley Jones (1827–1880): Born George Frederick Tilghman Jones; son of Dr. George Jones and Eliza Smith Jones; from 1847 to 1866 called himself George Wymberley Jones; inherited Wormsloe; married Mary Wallace Nuttall in 1852; changed name to De Renne in 1866.

De Renne, Mary Wallace (1835–1887) (née Nuttall): Daughter of William B. and Mary Wallace Savage Nuttall (Mrs. Nuttall was second wife of George Noble Jones); mistress of Wormsloe; friend of MT.

Elliott, Right Reverend Stephen (1806–1866): First Episcopal bishop of Georgia.

Few, Benjamin (1744–1805): Brother of Colonel William Few; fought with brother in Revolutionary War as an officer in the Richmond County, Georgia, militia.

Few, Catharine ("Kitty") (1764–1854) (née Nicholson): Mother of Mary Few and sisters; second mother to MT.

Few, Frances: See Chrystie, Frances.

Few, Ignatius Alphonso (1790–1845): Cousin of Mary Few; Methodist minister; a founder of Emory University.

Few, Mary (1790–1873): Daughter of Colonel William Few and Catherine Nicholson Few; MT's friend from school days in New York; lifelong soul mate of MF, her "Siamese Twin" with whom she carried on an extensive correspondence; lived in New York; never married.

Few, Matilda: See Tillotson, Matilda.

Few, Colonel William (1748–1828): Revolutionary War officer; delegate from Georgia to Constitutional Convention and signer of Constitution; one of first two United States senators from Georgia; close friend of Edward Telfair; banker, lawyer, and political figure in New York; father of Frances, Mary, and Matilda.

Gallatin, Albert (1761–1849): Married in 1793 Hannah Nicholson, Mary Few's maternal aunt; secretary of the treasury under Presidents Jefferson and Madison; United States minister to France.

Gardiner, Delia Tudor: See Jones, Delia Tudor.

Gardiner, Emma Jane (1785–1865) (née Tudor): Wife of Robert Hallowell Gardiner; entertained MT and her party in Gardiner, Maine.

Gardiner, Robert Hallowell (1782–1864): Founder and developer of Gardiner, Maine; father of Delia, first wife of George Noble Jones.

Gardiner, Robert Hallowell II (called "Hallowell") (1809–1886): Brother of Delia; married Mary Fenwick Jones.

Garrettson, Mary: Friend of Few sisters; lived in Rhinebeck, New York; daughter of Rev. Freeborn Garrettson, an important force in spreading the Methodist faith in America.

Gibbons, Barack (1769–1814): MT's maternal uncle; never married.

Gibbons, George (1819–1884): Slave in Telfair household; butler and chauffeur; traveled abroad with MT and Hodgsons; took last name Gibbons after emancipation; stayed on at Telfair mansion after MT's death; became pastor of First African Baptist Church.

Gibbons, Hannah (c. 1726–1798) (née Martin): Wife of Joseph Gibbons, Jr.

Gibbons, Joseph (1696–1752): Patriarch of Gibbons family in America; MT's great-grandfather.

Gibbons, Joseph, Jr. (c. 1724–1769): MT's great-uncle; married Hannah Martin; father of William and Thomas Gibbons.

Gibbons, Joseph (1766–1794): MT's maternal uncle; lawyer in Liberty County.

Gibbons, Sarah Martin (1735–1790): Grandmother of MT; wife of William Gibbons.

Gibbons, Thomas (1757–1826): Owner of Whitehall Plantation on Savannah River; mayor of Savannah; operated ferry from Elizabethtown, New Jersey, to New York; plaintiff in the case of Gibbons v. Ogden, a landmark in constitutional law decided by Supreme Court; MT's cousin.

Gibbons, William (1726–1771): Grandfather of MT; married Sarah Martin in 1752.

Gibbons, William, Jr. (1754–1804): Son of William and Sarah Martin Gibbons; uncle of MT; planter; never married but fathered three children of Sally, a mulatto woman whom he freed in 1796.

Gibbons, William (1750–1800): Son of Joseph Gibbons, Jr., and Hannah Martin Gibbons; member of the Sons of Liberty with Edward Telfair; a leading lawyer in Georgia; associate justice of Chatham County; speaker of the Georgia House of Representatives.

Gibbons, William (d. 1852): Son of Thomas Gibbons and Ann Heyward Gibbons; built mansion in New Jersey that is now on campus of Drew University; daughter Sarah married Ward McAllister.

Gray, Mary (1790–1867) (née Clay): Elder sister of Anne Clay; married to William Rufus Gray of Boston.

Greene, Caty (1753–1814): Wife of General Nathanael Greene; Eli Whitney invented cotton gin at Mulberry Grove, her plantation on the Savannah River.

Greene, General Nathanael (1742–1786): Commander of Continental armies in the South.

Habersham, James (1715–1775): Came to Savannah with the Reverend George Whitefield to establish Bethesda school and orphanage; established mercantile firm of Harris and Habersham; remained loyal to Crown; served as governor of Georgia colony while Royal Governor James Wright was in England.

Habersham, James, Jr. (1746–1799): Son of James Habersham; prominent Savannah merchant and political leader; helped finance revolutionary struggle against Great Britain; grandfather of Richard West Habersham.

Habersham, John (1754–1799): Son of James Habersham; major in Continental Army.

Habersham, Joseph (1751–1815): Patriot and member of Sons of Liberty; with Edward Telfair confiscated 600 pounds of powder from British arsenal; led band of revolutionaries that arrested Royal Governor James Wright.

Habersham, Dr. Joseph Clay (1788–1855): Son of Major John Habersham; Savannah physician; discovered fossil remains of mastodon.

Habersham, Richard West (1811–1878): Grandson of James Habersham, Jr.; artist; studied in Paris; friend of Samuel F. B. Morse; painted portraits of MT and sister Margaret.

Habersham, Robert (1783–1870): Son of Joseph Habersham; senior partner in firm that acted as Telfair family's factors and financial advisors.

Habersham, William Neyle (1815–1899): Son of Robert Habersham; graduate of Harvard; partner with father in firm of factors; married Josephine Clay Habersham; two sons killed in the Battle of Atlanta; noted for proficiency as fisherman, knowledge of fine wines, and skill on the flute; executor of MT's will.

Haig, Captain George (d. 1816): Married Sarah Telfair in 1815; soldier and planter; served in War of 1812.

Haig, Sarah (1792–1845) (née Telfair): Sister of MT; wife of George Haig; noted for her domesticity.

Harison, Mary Gibbons (1816–1875) (née Jones): Sister of George Noble Jones; married Rev. William Harison.

Harison, Reverend William (1823–1900): Married Mary Gibbons Jones.

Hodgson, Joseph: Brother of William Brown Hodgson; lived on farm in Columbia, Virginia.

Hodgson, Joseph, Jr.: Nephew of William Brown Hodgson; 1856 graduate of the College of New Jersey (Princeton); studied law at the University of Virginia; settled in Kansas City, Missouri.

Hodgson, Margaret (1797–1874) (née Telfair): Youngest sister of MT and her closest companion; married William Brown Hodgson in London in 1842.

Hodgson, Telfair (1840–1893): Nephew of William Brown Hodgson; 1859 graduate of the College of New Jersey (Princeton); studied at General Theological Seminary in New York; ordained in the Episcopal Church; dean of theology department and vice-chancellor, University of the South; managing editor of *The Sewanee Review*.

Hodgson, William Brown (1801–1871): Scholar-diplomat; master of thirteen languages; appointed consul general at Tunis; husband of Margaret Telfair Hodgson; member, Board of Curators of Georgia Historical Society.

Hunter, Catharine: See Bulloch, Catharine.

Hunter, Eliza Cecil: See Berrien, Eliza Cecil.

Hunter, William (d. 1892): Savannah businessman; executor of MT's will.

Jackson, Henry Rootes (1820–1898): Savannah lawyer; law partner of Alexander R. Lawton; minister to Austria; Confederate brigadier general; poet; president of Georgia Historical Society at time of MT's death.

Jay, William (1792–1838): Son of Rev. William Jay of Bath; architect; designed Telfair mansion on St. James Square and other Savannah buildings.

Johnson, William (1771–1834): Supreme Court justice from South Carolina appointed by President Jefferson; friend of MT; played Captain John Smith to MT's Pocahontas at masquerade.

Jones, Reverend Charles Colcock (1804–1863): Presbyterian minister; participated with Anne Clay in educating slaves; delivered tribute to Anne Clay at her memorial service.

Jones, Charles Colcock, Jr. (1831–1893): Noted lawyer; filed brief with United States Supreme Court in Telfair will case; son of Rev. Charles Colcock Jones.

Jones, Delia Tudor (1812–1836) (née Gardiner): Daughter of Robert Hallowell and Eliza Gardiner of Gardiner, Maine; first wife of George Noble Jones.

Jones, Eliza (1782–1857) (née Smith): Third wife of Dr. George Jones; daughter of Thomas and Letitia Van Deren Smith of Philadelphia; mother of Letitia and George Frederick Tilghman Jones.

Jones, Dr. George (1766–1838): Uncle of MT; married MT's aunt Mary ("Polly") Gibbons (1785), Sarah Fenwick Campbell (1795), Eliza Smith (1822); father of Noble Wimberly Jones II and grandfather of George Noble Jones.

Jones, George Noble (1811–1876): Grandson of Dr. George Jones and Mary Gibbons Jones and son of Noble Wimberly Jones II and Sarah Campbell ("Lillie") Jones; planter; married Delia Tudor Gardiner (1834), Mary Savage Nuttall (1840); cousin and friend of MT; challenged validity of charitable bequests in MT's will.

Jones, George Wymberley: See De Renne, George Wymberley Jones.

Jones, Mary ("Polly") (1761–1792) (née Gibbons): First wife of Dr. George Jones; MT's maternal aunt.

Jones, Mary Gibbons: See Harison, Mary Gibbons.

Jones, Mary Wallace Savage Nuttall (1812–1869): Second wife of George Noble Jones; widow of William B. Nuttall.

Jones, Noble (1702–1775): Came to Georgia colony with Oglethorpe in 1733; built tabby fortified house called Wormslow (original spelling); fought in Battle of Bloody Marsh; patriarch of Jones family in Georgia.

Jones, Noble Wimberly (c. 1723–1805): Son of Noble Jones; physician; member Sons of Liberty with Edward Telfair; father of Dr. George Jones and thirteen other children.

Jones, Noble Wimberly II (1787–1818): Son of Dr. George Jones and Mary Gibbons Jones; at Princeton with Telfair boys, his cousins; closest friend of Alexander Telfair; married Sarah Campbell in 1810.

Jones, Sarah: See Cuthbert, Sarah.

Jones, Sarah ("Lillie") (1784–1843) (née Campbell): Daughter of second wife of Dr. George Jones by her first husband Macartan Campbell; married in 1810 to Dr. George Jones's son Noble Wimberly Jones II; lived as a widow in Philadelphia.

Jones, Sarah Fenwick (called "Fenwick") (1814–1869): Sister of George Noble Jones; married in 1842 to Robert Hallowell Gardiner, brother of Delia Tudor Gardiner Jones.

Jones, Sarah Fenwick Campbell (1756–1810): Second wife of Dr. George Jones; first husband Macartan Campbell by whom she had Sarah ("Lillie") and Maria.

Kollock, George Jones (1810–1894): Cousin and friend of George Noble Jones; lawyer and planter; son of Dr. Lemuel and Maria Campbell Kollock.

Kollock, Rev. Henry (1778–1819): Pastor of Independent Presbyterian Church in Savannah; sermons much admired by MT; cousin of Dr. Lemuel Kollock.

Kollock, Dr. Lemuel (1776–1823): Savannah physician; married in 1802 Maria Campbell, daughter of Macartan and Sarah Fenwick Campbell.

Kollock, Mary Fenwick: See Neufville, Mary Fenwick.

Lawton, Alexander R. (1818–1896): West Point and Harvard Law School graduate; lawyer and railroad executive; Confederate brigadier general; quartermaster general of Confederate army; drafted MT's will; principal lawyer for her estate; appointed minister to Austria in 1887; president American Bar Association.

Long, Colonel Nicholas (d. 1819): Father of Margaret Long Telfair, wife of Thomas Telfair; served as dragoon officer in Revolutionary War and as Colonel in War of 1812.

McAllister, Ward (1827–1895): Cousin of MT; son of Matthew Hall McAllister; introduced to New York society by MT; supported by his wife, Sarah Gibbons McAllister, granddaughter of Thomas Gibbons; wrote *Society As I Have Found It;* established "the 400."

Milledge, John (1757–1818): Liberty Boy with Edward Telfair; officer in Revolutionary War; United States congressman; governor of Georgia; United States senator.

Montgomery, W. W.: Cocounsel with J. R. Saussy on behalf of George Noble Jones and other caveators in Telfair will contest.

Neufville, Reverend Edward (1802–1851): Beloved rector of Christ

Church, Savannah; married Mary Fenwick Kollock, daughter of Dr. Lemuel and Maria Campbell Kollock.

Neufville, Mary Fenwick (1806–1885) (née Kollock): Wife of Rev. Edward Neufville.

Nicholson, Commodore James (c. 1736–1804): Commander in United States Navy; leader of Republican Party in New York; grandfather of Mary Few.

Read, Dr. James B. (1827–1908): Physician who attended MT during her last illness.

Ritchie, Margaret Ewing: Great-granddaughter of Edward Telfair's brother William; adopted by Mary Ewing Ritchie Thompson, her aunt; living at Telfair mansion at time of MT's death.

Ritchie, Mary Ewing: See Thompson, Mary Ewing.

Saussy, Joachim R.: Principal lawyer for George Noble Jones and other caveators in Telfair will contest.

Savage, Mary Ann: See Clay, Mary Ann.

Scarbrough, William (1776–1838): Savannah merchant; built mansion designed by William Jay; sponsored SS *Savannah,* first oceangoing steamship to cross Atlantic; wife Julia noted for elaborate parties she called "blowouts."

Smith, Eliza: See Jones, Eliza.

Telfair, Alexander (1789–1832): Youngest brother of MT; graduate of College of New Jersey (Princeton); planter, business leader, and man of culture; built mansion on St. James Square; never married.

Telfair, Edward (1735–1807): Father of MT; came to America from Scotland in his early twenties; settled in Savannah in 1866; partner in mercantile business with brother William; planter with extensive land holdings; patriot in struggle against King George III; member Sons of Liberty; member Continental Congress; three-term governor of Georgia; married Sarah Gibbons in 1774.

Telfair, Edward, Jr. (1780–1797): Eldest son of Governor Edward and Sarah Telfair; died at age sixteen.

Telfair, Eliza (d. 1844): MT's cousin; lived with sister Margaret in South Carolina and then Philadelphia; daughter of William and Elizabeth Bellinger Telfair; never married.

Telfair, Josiah (1784–1817): Brother of MT; received B.A and M.A. from College of New Jersey (Princeton); studied at Litchfield Law School; spent all of his time on his plantation; never married.

Telfair, Margaret (1789–1859) (née Long): Famous belle from Washington, Georgia; married Thomas Telfair in 1809; mother of Mary and Margaret; grandmother of Alberta.

Telfair, Margaret (1797–1874). See Hodgson, Margaret.

Telfair, Margaret Long (1816–1842): Daughter of Thomas and Margaret Telfair; tutored by MT; studied in New York; never married.

Telfair, Margaret (d. 1844): MT's cousin; lived with sister Eliza in South Carolina and then Philadelphia; daughter of William and Elizabeth Bellinger Telfair; never married.

Telfair, Mary Eliza: See Cobb, Mary Eliza.

Telfair, Sarah ("Sally") (1758–1827) (née Gibbons): Mother of MT; married Edward Telfair in 1774 at age sixteen; died and buried in Philadelphia.

Telfair, Sarah: See Haig, Sarah.

Telfair, Thomas (1786–1818): Brother of MT; graduate of College of New Jersey (Princeton) and Litchfield Law School; member of United States Congress (1813–1817); husband of Margaret Long Telfair; father of Mary and Margaret and grandfather of Alberta.

Terrell, Eliza Rhodes (d. 1866): Friend and correspondent in later life of MT; shared MT's concern over MT's great-niece Alberta; resident of Sparta, Georgia; wife of Dr. William Terrell.

Terrell, Louisa (c. 1825–1840): Daughter of William and Eliza Terrell; attended at her deathbed by MT.

Terrell, Lucy: Daughter of William and Eliza Terrell; admired fondly by MT; married Edgar Gilmer Dawson of Columbus, Georgia.

Terrell, Dr. William (1778–1855): Graduate of the Medical College of the University of Pennsylvania; practiced medicine in Sparta, Georgia; United States congressman; agronomist; endowed chair at University of Georgia.

Thompson, Mary Ewing (née Ritchie): Granddaughter of Edward Telfair's brother William; married and later divorced Ambrose Thompson of Litchfield, Connecticut, a widower with children; adopted niece Margaret Ewing Ritchie; companion of MT at Telfair mansion during MT's last years.

Tillotson, Matilda (née Few): Youngest sister of Mary Few; married John Tillotson, a widower with children.

Tompkins, Judge Henry B.: Trial judge in Georgia Superior Court in Telfair will contest.

Tondee, Peter (1723–1775): Operated tavern in Savannah with his wife

Lucy Mouse in which meetings of patriots were held prior to Revolutionary War.

Wallace, Ann: Friend of MT from childhood days; had home in Montgomery, community on Vernon River south of Savannah; moved to New York.

Wayne, James Moore (1790–1867): Mayor of Savannah; appointed to United States Supreme Court in 1834 by President Jackson; friend of the Telfairs; remained on Supreme Court throughout Civil War.

Wetter, Alberta (1834–1866) (née Cobb): Granddaughter of Thomas Telfair; caused MT great pain by eloping at the age of thirteen with Charles Arnold, divorcing him eight years later, and marrying in 1857 Augustus P. Wetter, a German immigrant; her children, through their father as guardian *ad litem*, challenged the validity of MT's will.

Wetter, Augustus P. (c. 1829–1882): Second husband of Alberta Long Wetter; born in Mainz in the duchy of Hesse; leader of the German community in Savannah; engineer by profession.

Wetter, Conrad Peter (1859–1874): Second son of Alberta and Augustus P. Wetter; died of drinking contaminated well water prior to Telfair will contest.

Wetter, Edward Telfair (1858–1908): Elder son of Alberta and Augustus P. Wetter.

Wetter, Louisa Alberta Mina (1865–1920): Second daughter of Alberta and Augustus P. Wetter.

Wetter, Mary Martha (1860–1878): Elder daughter of Alberta and Augustus P. Wetter.

Wright, Sir James (1716–1785): Royal governor of Georgia.

Telfair Chronology

1726 Birth of William Gibbons, Sr., Mary Telfair's maternal grandfather, in Bear Bluff, South Carolina (April 5).

1730 King George II signs charter for Georgia (April 21).

1733 James Oglethorpe sails up the Savannah River (February 12); Noble Jones a passenger.

1734 Salzburgers arrive in Savannah (March 12).

1735 Edward Telfair, Mary Telfair's father, born in Scotland; birth of Sarah Martin, Mary Telfair's maternal grandmother (October 14).

1739-48 War of Jenkins' Ear.

1740 Bethesda Orphanage founded by Rev. James Whitefield and James Habersham.

1742 Battle of Bloody Marsh (July 7).

1744 Founding of firm of Harris and Habersham.

1748 Birth of William Few.

1750 St. Andrew's Society founded in Savannah.

1751 Savannah becomes a Royal Crown City.

1752 William Gibbons, Sr., marries Sarah Martin (November 1).

1754 Birth of William Gibbons, Jr., Mary Telfair's maternal uncle (February 1).

1756-63 French and Indian War.

1758 Edward Telfair sails for English colonies with brother William; birth of Sarah Gibbons, Mary Telfair's mother (August 26).

1760 George III takes English throne; James Wright becomes royal governor of Georgia colony; birth of Mary Gibbons, Mary Telfair's aunt who marries Dr. George Jones (November 14).

1765 First Stamp Act (March 22).

1766 Edward Telfair settles in Savannah; birth of Joseph Gibbons, Mary Telfair's uncle (April 18); birth of Dr. George Jones, son of Noble Wimberly Jones and grandson of Noble Jones (February 23).

1767 Townshend Acts (June 29).

1768 Edward Telfair elected to Georgia Commons House of Assembly.

1769 Birth of Barack Gibbons, Mary Telfair's uncle (February 9); William Telfair, brother of Edward, marries Elizabeth Bellinger of South Carolina.

1770 Boston Massacre (March 5).

1771 Death of William Gibbons, Sr. (February 10).

1773 Boston Tea Party (December 16).

1774 Edward Telfair marries Sarah Gibbons at Sharon Plantation, west of Savannah (May 18); Continental Congress in Philadelphia (September 5 to October 26) attended by representatives of all colonies except Georgia.

1775 Battles of Lexington and Concord (April 19); Sons of Liberty, including Edward Telfair, seize British powder in Savannah (May 10); Second Continental Congress opens in Philadelphia (May 10); Edward Telfair named to Council of Safety (June 22); George Washington appointed commander-in-chief of Continental Army (June 15); Battle of Bunker Hill (June 17).

1776 Royal Governor James Wright placed under house arrest at Government House in Savannah (January 18) and later flees to England; Declaration of Independence (July 4); Americans defeated in Battle of Long Island (August 27); Battle of White Plains (October 28); Washington crosses Delaware and defeats Hessians (December 26).

1777 Battle of Princeton (January 3); Battle of Saratoga (October 7–17); Congress adopts Articles of Confederation (November 15).

1778–82 Edward Telfair in Continental Congress.

1778 British occupy Savannah (December 29).

1779 William and Benjamin Few fight British in Georgia upcountry in skirmish at Burke County jail; Battle of Kettle Creek, Georgia (February 14); Governor Wright returns to Savannah (July); Siege of Savannah (September-October); Count Casimir Pulaski and Sergeant Jasper killed in action (October 9).

1780 Birth of Edward Telfair, Jr., Mary Telfair's brother (March 13).

1781 Surrender of Cornwallis at Yorktown (October 19).

1784 Birth of Josiah Telfair, Mary Telfair's brother (June 24).

1785 Dr. George Jones marries Mary Gibbons, sister of Sarah Gibbons Telfair, thus joining Telfair and Jones families.

1786 William Few marries Catherine ("Kitty") Nicholson of New York; birth of Thomas Telfair, Mary Telfair's brother (March 2); Edward Telfair elected governor of Georgia for one term; Georgia state capital moved to Augusta; death of General Nathanael Greene from sunstroke suffered at William Gibbons' plantation (June 12).

1787 Birth of Noble Wimberly Jones II, son of Dr. George Jones and Mary Gibbons Jones (January 2); first meeting in Philadelphia of Constitutional Convention with William Few in attendance (May); delegates, including William Few, sign Constitution (September 17).

1788 Constitution becomes operative upon ratification by New Hampshire (June).

1789 Birth of Alexander Telfair, Mary Telfair's brother (January 25); birth of Margaret Long, who marries Thomas Telfair (January 31); birth of Frances Few; George Washington takes office as President (April 30); Bastille stormed by Paris mob (July 14); birth of Sarah Gibbons Jones, daughter of Dr. George Jones and Mary Gibbons Jones (August 15).

1790 Birth of Mary Few.

1790–93 Edward Telfair's second and third terms as governor of Georgia.

1791 Mary Telfair born in Augusta in seventeenth year of parents' marriage (January 28); Governor and Mrs. Telfair entertain George Washington in Augusta (May); September massacres in Paris.

1792 Eli Whitney arrives at Mulberry Grove Plantation, home of Caty Greene; birth of Sarah Telfair, Mary Telfair's sister (September 28); death of Mary Gibbons Jones, wife of Dr. George Jones.

1793 Louis XVI loses head on guillotine; cotton gin invented at Mulberry Grove Plantation by Eli Whitney.

1794 Robespierre executed ending Reign of Terror (July 27); Dr. George Jones marries Sarah Fenwick Campbell, widow of Macartan Campbell.

1796 Great fire in Savannah; birth of Anne Clay.

1797 Death of Edward Telfair, Jr., age 16 (January 18); John Adams inaugurated as President (March 4); birth of Margaret Telfair, sister of Mary Telfair (March 28).

1799 Few family moves to New York; Mary Laura Lucia Telfair, daughter of William Telfair, marries Alexander Ritchie in Bahamas (December).

1801 Thomas Jefferson inaugurated as third President (March 5); Mary Telfair arrives in New York to attend school and live with Few family (July); Mary enters Miss Dow's classes in fall with Few girls, Mary and Frances; birth of William Brown Hodgson, future husband of Margaret Telfair.

1802 Mary Telfair enters Newark Academy; Alexander Telfair enters Bergen Academy.

1803 Marbury v. Madison; Louisiana Purchase; Josiah Telfair graduates College of New Jersey (Princeton).

1804 Death of William Gibbons, Jr. (April 15); Josiah Telfair a student at Tapping Reeve's law school in Litchfield, Connecticut; Napoleon proclaimed emperor and places crown on own head (May 18); Alexander Hamilton slain in duel with Aaron Burr (July 11).

1805 Thomas Telfair graduates College of New Jersey; Battle of Trafalgar and death of Lord Nelson (October 21).

1806 The Reverend Henry Kollock resigns from the faculty of the College of New Jersey and accepts call to Independent Presbyterian Church, Savannah.

1807 Thomas Telfair a student at Tapping Reeve's law school; rebellion by students at Princeton (spring); American warship *Chesapeake* boarded by British sailors from HMS *Leopard* (June 22); Alexander Telfair graduates College of New Jersey; Governor Edward Telfair dies (September 17).

1808 Thomas Telfair helps organize Georgia Foresters (April) and delivers Fourth of July oration in Savannah.

1809 James Madison inaugurated President (March 4); Thomas Telfair marries Margaret Long of Washington, Georgia (March 16); Alexander Telfair delivers Fourth of July oration in Savannah.

1810 George Wimberly Jones II marries Sarah Campbell (February).

1811 Birth of George Noble Jones (May 25).

1812 Congress declares war against Great Britain (June 18); William Telfair, Edward's brother, dies in Surinam; Napoleon begins retreat from Russia (September 19).

1813 Chatham Academy opens in Savannah; British attack on Hampton, Virginia (spring); birth of Mary, daughter of Thomas and Margaret Telfair (August 9); Admiral Perry defeats British in Battle of Lake Erie (September 10).

1813–17 Thomas Telfair in United States Congress.

1814 Napoleon abdicates and is exiled to Isle of Elba (April 11); Lord

Byron writes *The Corsair*; death of Barack Gibbons (August 14); British burn Washington (August 24); Treaty of Ghent ends War of 1812 (December 24).

1815 General Andrew Jackson defeats British in Battle of New Orleans before receiving word of treaty (January 8); Sarah Telfair marries Captain George Haig (April 25); Napoleon defeated at Battle of Waterloo (June 18).

1815–24 Reign of Louis XVIII of France.

1816 Steamboat service inaugurated on Savannah River; birth of Margaret, second daughter of Thomas and Margaret Telfair (June 24); death of George Haig (December 4).

1817 Josiah Telfair dies, age 32 (March 13); James Monroe inaugurated President; architect William Jay arrives in Savannah (December 29).

1817–18 Seminole War; cession of Florida to United States by Spain.

1818 Thomas Telfair dies, age 31 (February 18); Noble Wimberly Jones II dies (December); Mary Telfair's cousin Thomas Gibbons establishes ferry service between New York City and Elizabethtown, New Jersey; Alexander Telfair retains architect William Jay to design mansion; Jay-designed Savannah Theater opens (December 4).

1819 President Monroe attends reception at Jay-designed home of William and Julia Scarbrough (May 18); new Independent Presbyterian Church consecrated; SS *Savannah* sails for England; Telfair mansion completed.

1820 Fire wipes out two-thirds of homes in Savannah (January); George III dies (January 20) and is succeeded by his son, George IV; Missouri Compromise (March 3); Frances Few visits Telfairs in Savannah; Sir Walter Scott writes *Ivanhoe*.

1821 Architect William Jay leaves Savannah.

1822 Frances Few marries Albert Chrystie; Dr. George Jones marries third wife, Eliza Smith (October).

1823 Birth of William Few Chrystie ("Willie"); Monroe Doctrine (December 2).

1824 Gibbons v. Ogden decided by United States Supreme Court; birth of Mary Chrystie.

1825 John Quincy Adams inaugurated sixth President (March 4); Lafayette visits Savannah (March 19).

1826 William Brown Hodgson posted to Algiers.

1827 Birth of Ward McAllister, Mary Telfair's cousin; Sarah Gibbons

Telfair, mother of Mary Telfair, dies at age 69 in Philadelphia (October 13).

1828 Tariff Act—"tariff of abominations."

1829 Andrew Jackson inaugurated President (March 4); John Macpherson Berrien of Savannah named attorney general.

1830–48 Reign of Louis Philippe as king of France.

1831 Matilda Few visits Telfairs in Savannah; John James Audubon in Savannah; construction of Fort Pulaski begun.

1832 Alexander Telfair delivers oration for centennial of George Washington's birth (February 22); William Brown Hodgson assigned to Constantinople as dragoman; Alexander Telfair dies in Winchester, Virginia, at age 43 (October 9); South Carolina Ordinance of Nullification.

1833 Birth of Alberta Cobb, daughter of Pierce Cobb and Mary Telfair Cobb and granddaughter of Thomas and Margaret Telfair.

1834 Death in childbirth of Sarah Jones Cuthbert (August); George Noble Jones, son of Noble Wimberly Jones II, marries Delia Gardiner of Maine (September 2); Catharine Hunter, close friend of Mary Telfair, marries Jones Bulloch (October 29); Telfair sisters have portraits painted by Richard West Habersham (December).

1835 Phrenology the fad in Savannah; death of Pierce Cobb (February); James Moore Wayne of Savannah sworn in as associate justice of United States Supreme Court by Chief Justice John Marshall.

1836 Death of Delia Gardiner Jones (January 8); Battle of the Alamo (March 6); Sam Houston defeats Mexicans in Battle of San Jacinto (April 21).

1837 Martin Van Buren becomes eighth President of United States; financial panic; Queen Victoria takes the throne of England at age eighteen (June).

1838 Sinking of SS *Pulaski* off coast of Wilmington, North Carolina (June 14); death of Dr. George Jones (November); *Oliver Twist* published.

1839 Georgia Historical Society founded; death of Mary Telfair Cobb, daughter of Thomas and Margaret Telfair and mother of Alberta (October 7).

1840 Consecration of new Christ Church in Savannah (March 22); George Noble Jones, then a widower, marries Mary Wallace Savage Nuttall (May 18).

1841 Reverend Stephen Elliott consecrated first Episcopal bishop of

Georgia (February 28); Vice-President John Tyler becomes President upon death of President William Henry Harrison (April 14); Telfair sisters presented to President John Tyler; George Noble Jones's Newport cottage completed (summer); Telfair sisters, with Albert and Frances Chrystie and their children, William and Mary, sail on their first trip to Europe (October 24); Margaret Telfair and William Brown Hodgson meet in Paris (November).

1842 Death of Mary Chrystie in Nice (winter); death of Margaret Telfair, daughter of Thomas and Margaret Telfair (February 5); William Brown Hodgson marries Margaret Telfair in London (July); Telfairs and Hodgsons return to America after completing tour (October); death of Anne Clay.

1843 Rail line from Macon to Savannah completed by Central of Georgia Railroad.

1844 Death of cousin, Eliza Telfair, daughter of William Telfair (April 4), and her sister Margaret Telfair (November 23).

1845 Sarah Haig dies (April 3); James K. Polk inaugurated President.

1846 Beginning of Mexican War.

1847 Mormons, led by Brigham Young, settle in Utah.

1848 Victory over Mexico; Treaty of Guadalupe Hidalgo (February 2); gold discovered in California; telegraph line run between Augusta and Savannah; revolutions in Europe; Louis Napoleon Bonaparte becomes President of French Republic; Alberta Cobb elopes with Charles Arnold at age thirteen (February 1).

1849 Mary Telfair and Hodgsons buy house in New York; Zachary Taylor inaugurated President.

1850 Compromise of 1850; Custom House completed in Savannah; Savannah Gas Light Company organized; Millard Fillmore becomes President upon death of Zachary Taylor (July 10).

1851 Mary Telfair and Hodgsons leave on trip to Europe (May 30); spend Christmas in Rome; Margaret Hodgson poses for bas-relief by Shakespeare Wood now at Telfair Academy; audience with Pope Pius IX.

1852 Napoleon III Emperor of France; Mary Telfair and Hodgsons return to America from Europe (August 22).

1853 Thackeray lectures in Savannah; Franklin Pierce becomes President; Worlds Fair at Crystal Palace in New York.

1854–56 Crimean War.

1854 Death of Mrs. Catherine ("Kitty") Few (August 7).

1855 William Chrystie, son of Albert and Frances Chrystie, married in Augusta to Emily Thomas (January); Mary Telfair leaves on third trip to Europe, traveling with the Hodgsons (June 27); William Brown Hodgson commissioner from the State of Georgia to Paris Exposition; death of Dr. William Terrell, a close friend of Mary Telfair and Hodgsons and husband of Eliza Terrell (July 4).

1856 Death of John Macpherson Berrien (January 1); death of Albert Chrystie, husband of Frances (April 23); William Brown Hodgson awarded honorary LL.D. by Princeton; Alberta and Charles Arnold divorced; Lucy Terrell, daughter of William and Eliza Terrell, marries Edgar Gilmer Dawson.

1857 James Buchanan becomes President (March 4); Dred Scott decision (May 7); Alberta remarried to Augustus P. Wetter (April 21).

1858 Cast-iron fountain erected in Savannah's Forsyth Park.

1859 Death of Thomas Telfair's widow (September 10); John Brown leads raid on Harper's Ferry (October 19).

1860 Mary Telfair and Margaret Hodgson erect monument on family plot at Bonaventure Cemetery and remove remains of Sarah Haig from Sharon Plantation for burial there; Abraham Lincoln elected President; South Carolina secedes from Union (December 20).

1861 Georgia secedes from Union (January 19); Jefferson Davis inaugurated President of Confederate States (February 22); Confederate forces fire upon Fort Sumter (April 12); First Battle of Manassas (Bull Run) (July 21).

1862 Union ironclad *Monitor* defeats Confederate ironclad *Merrimac* (March 9); surrender of Fort Pulaski (April 11).

1863 Emancipation Proclamation (January 1); Battle of Gettysburg (July 1–3); Gettysburg Address (November 19).

1864 Sherman takes Atlanta (September 2); surrender of Savannah to Sherman's forces (December 21).

1865 Sherman's army leaves Savannah to crush resistance in Carolinas (February 1); Lee surrenders to Grant at Appomattox Court House (April 9); Lincoln assassinated (April 14) and Andrew Johnson succeeds to Presidency.

1866 Mary Telfair and Hodgsons leave for Europe (July 14); Alberta Wetter dies (July 21).

1867 United States acquires Alaska from Russia (March 30).

1868 President Andrew Johnson impeached, tried by Senate, and acquitted (February 24–May 26); Fourteenth Amendment to Constitution ratified (July 28).

1869 Ulysses S. Grant inaugurated President.

1870 Third Republic established in France upon defeat of Napoleon III (September 4).

1870–71 Franco-Prussian War.

1871 Unification of Germany (January 18); William Brown Hodgson dies at age seventy (June 26).

1873 Construction of Hodgson Hall begins.

1874 Margaret Hodgson dies (March 1); Henry Rootes Jackson elected President of Georgia Historical Society.

1875 Death of Mary Telfair at age eighty-four (June 2); will establishes Telfair Academy of Arts and Sciences with Georgia Historical Society as trustee; will challenged by children of Augustus P. Wetter and group led by George Noble Jones.

1876 Hodgson Hall dedicated (February 14); death of George Noble Jones (May 9).

1877 Rutherford B. Hayes inaugurated President; Telfair will found invalid by Superior Court jury on ground that Mary Telfair a monomaniac on the subject of Alberta Wetter and her children (June 15).

1878 Supreme Court of Georgia affirms grant of new trial and finds Jones group, and not Wetter children, to be the heirs at law of Mary Telfair (January); jury in second trial upholds Telfair will (June 26); Supreme Court of Georgia affirms.

1879 Federal Circuit Court rejects challenges to will.

1881 President James A. Garfield shot (July 2) and is succeeded by Chester A. Arthur.

1882 Oral arguments heard before United States Supreme Court in Telfair will case (November 13–14).

1883 United States Supreme Court upholds Telfair will.

$\mathcal{N}otes$

Preface   *pages xi–xix*

1. "Women worthies" neglected by history: Gerda Lerner, "Placing Women in History: Definitions and Challenges," *Feminist Studies* 3, nos. 1–2 (Fall 1975): 5–14.

2. Catherine Clinton, *The Plantation Mistress: Woman's World in the Old South* (New York: Pantheon Books, 1982); "wonderfully ordinary": Christine Jacobson Carter, ed., *The Diary of Dolly Lunt Burge, 1848–1879* (Athens: University of Georgia Press, 1997), xi; trifles: Mary Telfair ("MT") to Mary Few ("MF"), April 29 [1833], William Few Collection ("WFC"), Georgia Department of History and Archives, Atlanta, Accession No. 55–101, Item 37. Dates that appear in brackets are missing from the text of a letter, but can be determined with reasonable certainty from internal evidence. Photocopies of most of Mary Telfair's letters to Mary and Frances Few in the William Few Collection are among the Mary and Frances Few Papers, Georgia Historical Society Manuscript Collection No. 1,201. Hannah More wrote in her poem "Sensibility": "Since trifles make the sum of human things, / And half our misery from our foibles springs."

3. Barbara Welter, "The Cult of True Womanhood, 1820–1860," *The American Quarterly* 18 (1966): 151–74.

4. Susan Conrad, *Perish the Thought: Intellectual Women in Romantic America, 1830–1860* (Secaucus, N.J.: Citadel Press, 1978); Drew Gilpin Faust, *A Sacred Circle: The Dilemma of the Intellectual in the Old South, 1840–1860* (Baltimore: Johns Hopkins University Press, 1977); Bertram Wyatt-Brown, *Southern Honor: Ethics & Behavior in the Old South* (New York: Oxford University Press, 1982), 201; Clinton, *The Plantation Mistress*, 181; MT to MF, postmark December 22 [1835], WFC, Item 166.

5. Glenda Riley, *Inventing the American Woman: A Perspective on Women's History* (Arlington Heights, Ill.: Harlan Davidson, Inc., 1986), 7; Gerda Lerner, *The Grimké Sisters from South Carolina: Pioneers for Women's Rights and Abolition* (New York: Shockton Books, 1971). Sarah Grimké's lifespan (1792–1873) closely approximated that of Mary Telfair (1791–1875). Angelina Grimké was younger; she was born in 1805 and died in 1879.

6. Joan E. Cashin, ed., *Our Common Affairs: Texts from Women in the Old South* (Baltimore: Johns Hopkins University Press, 1996), Introduction: "Culture of Resignation." Another scholar has questioned whether the diary entries and letters selected by Ms. Cashin support her thesis. Frederick A. Bode, Review of *Our Common Affairs, Georgia Historical Quarterly* 81, no. 3 (Fall 1997): 776–78. Lerner, "Placing Women in History," 6.

7. C. Van Woodward, ed., *Mary Chesnut's Civil War* (New Haven: Yale University Press, 1981); Elizabeth Muhlenfeld, *Mary Boykin Chesnut: A Biography* (Baton Rouge: Louisiana State University Press, 1981); Wylma Wates, "Precursor to the Victorian Age: The Concept of Marriage and Family as Revealed in the Correspondence of the Izard Family of South Carolina," in Carol Bleser, ed., *In Joy and in Sorrow: Women, Family and Marriage in the Victorian South, 1830–1900* (New York: Oxford University Press, 1991); Carol Bleser, ed., *Tokens of Affection: The Letters of a Planter's Daughter in the Old South* (Athens: University of Georgia Press, 1996); Daniel P. Kilbride, "Philadelphia and the Southern Elite: Class, Kinship, and Culture in Antebellum America" (Ph.D. diss., University of Florida, 1997). I am grateful to both Christine Jacobson Carter and Professor Bertram Wyatt-Brown for calling my attention to this dissertation. It was written under Professor Wyatt-Brown's direction.

8. Lee Virginia Chambers-Schiller, *Liberty, A Better Husband, Single Women in America: The Generations of 1780–1840* (New Haven: Yale University Press, 1984), 2, 10; Riley, *Inventing the American Woman, 44; Mary Ryan, Womanhood in America* (New York: New Viewpoints Press, 1980), chap. 3; Nancy F. Cott, *The Roots of Bitterness: Documents of the Social History of American Women* (New York: E. P. Dutton, 1972), 11–14; Welter, "The Cult of True Womanhood," 151.

9. Joan E. Cashin, " 'Decidedly Opposed to the Union': Women's Culture, Marriage, and Politics in Antebellum South Carolina," *Georgia Historical Quarterly* 78, no. 4 (Winter 1994): 735.

10. E.g., Christie Anne Farnham, *The Education of the Southern Belle: Higher Education and Student Socialization in the Antebellum South* (New York: New York University Press, 1994), chap. 7, "Lovers: Romantic Friendships"; Carol Lasser, "'Let Us Be Sisters Forever': The Sororal Model of Nineteenth-Century Female Friendship," *Signs: Journal of Women in Culture and Society* 14, no. 1 (1988): 158–81; Blanche Wiesen Cook, "'Women Alone Stir My Imagination': Lesbianism and the Cultural Tradition," *Signs: Journal of Women in Culture and Society* 4, no. 4 (1979): 718–39; Carroll Smith-Rosenberg, "The Female World of Love and Ritual: Relations between Women in Nineteenth-Century America," *Signs: Journal of Women in Culture and Society* 1, no. 1 (1975): 1–29; Lilian Faderman, *Surpassing the Love of Men: Romantic Friendship and Love between Women from the Renaissance to the Present* (New York: William Morrow & Co., 1981), 15–16; Drew Gilpin Faust, *Mothers of Invention: Women in the Slaveholding South in the American Civil War* (Chapel Hill: The University of North Carolina Press, 1996), 142–45.

1. The Legacy   *pages 1–15*

1. Biographical information on Alexander R. Lawton: George T. Ness, Jr., "Georgia's Confederate Dead," *Georgia Historical Quarterly* 25, no. 4 (December 1941): 367; William B. Hesseltine and Larry Gara, "Georgia's Confederate Leaders After Appomattox," *Georgia Historical Quarterly* 35, no. 1 (March 1951): 13; William J. Northern, ed., *Men of Mark in Georgia*, 7 vols. (Atlanta: A. B. Caldwell, 1907–12), 3:185; William Harden, *A History of Savannah and South Georgia* (Atlanta: Cherokee Publishing Company, 1969, reprint of 1913 edition), 570–74.

2. The account of Mary Telfair's illness and the circumstances surrounding the preparation and execution of her will, including direct quotations, is taken from the

testimony of Dr. James B. Read, William J. Marshall, and Alexander R. Lawton, as subscribing witnesses to the will, as set forth in the Brief of Testimony (hereinafter "Brief of Testimony") filed June 23, 1877, in the office of the Clerk of the Superior Court, Chatham County, Georgia, 1–16, which constitutes a part of the Record on Appeal (hereinafter "Record") in the matter of Augustus P. Wetter, guardian *ad litem*, and George Noble Jones, *et al.* v. William Hunter and William Neyle Habersham, Executors of the will of Mary Telfair, which document is in the files of the Georgia Department of History and Archives in Atlanta (Accession No. 9621, Box 122, Loc. 110–04). The original of Mary Telfair's will, protected by a plastic coating, including a memorandum concerning the disposition of her silver plate, and the papers relating to its probate are in the files of the Chatham County Probate Court, Savannah. A copy of the will is set forth as Appendix A. The diagnosis of pneumonia by Dr. Read is noted in the records of the Chatham County Department of Health. Mary Telfair's attendance at church on the Sunday before the execution of her will: Testimony of Mrs. C. H. Cumming, Brief of Testimony, 69. Wetter's financial reversal: *Savannah Morning News*, April 6, May 4, and May 18, 1875, reporting on sheriff's sales. Codicil dated June 13, 1866: Telfair Family Papers, Georgia Historical Society Manuscript Collection No. 793 ("TFP"), Box 9, Folder 76, Item 305. Recollection of Margaret E. Harden: Brief of Testimony, 69–70. William Hunter obituary: *Savannah Morning News*, January 13, 1892.

3. W. J. Cash, *The Mind of the South* (New York: Alfred A. Knopf, 1941; reprint, New York: Random House, Vintage Books, 1991), 4–5.

4. Elizabeth Fox-Genovese, "Family and Female Identity in the Antebellum South: Sarah Gayle and Her Family" in Bleser, ed., *In Joy and In Sorrow*, 19. Genealogical information on the Cecils: J. M. Berrien Papers, Georgia Historical Society Manuscript Collection No. 67, Folder 3, Item 650.

5. Biographical information on Governor Edward Telfair: E. Merton Coulter, "Edward Telfair," *Georgia Historical Quarterly* 20, no. 2 (June 1936): 99–124; James F. Cook, *The Governors of Georgia* (Huntsville, Ala., Strode Publishers, 1979), 68; Charles C. Jones, Jr., *Biographical Sketches of the Delegates to the Continental Congress* (Boston and New York: Houghton Mifflin & Company, 1891), 161–67; *The National Cyclopaedia of American Biography*, 14 vols. (New York: James T. White & Company, 1892), 1:219; *Men of Mark in Georgia*, 1:310; Kenneth Coleman & Charles Stephen Gurr, eds., *Dictionary of Georgia Biography*, 2 vols. (Athens: University of Georgia Press, 1983), 2:965; genealogical and biographical records of the Telfair family in the vertical files of the Georgia Historical Society. For a detailed account of Edward Telfair's political and business career, see Sharon Wells Kemper, "Edward Telfair and Early Nationalism in Georgia" (M.A. thesis, Armstrong State College, 1987) [copy in library of Armstrong Atlantic State University]. Information on Edward Telfair's participation in the revolutionary struggle and his public service: William B. Stevens, *A History of Georgia*, 2 vols. (Savannah: Beehive Press, 1972, reprint of 1847 [vol. 1] and 1859 [vol. 2] editions), 80, 100–05, 335, 340–41, 367–98. William Harden, "Basil Cowper's Remarkable Career in Georgia," *Georgia Historical Quarterly* 1, no. 1 (March 1917): 24–35, provides information on Edward Telfair's business partner. Kenneth Coleman, *Colonial Georgia: A History* (New York: Charles Scribner's Sons, 1976), furnishes a picture of economic and social conditions in the colony as well as information on the Revolutionary War. Important sources of information on the events leading up to the Revolution and the conduct of the war

in Georgia: Carl Solana Weeks, *Savannah in the Time of Peter Tondee* (Colombia, S.C.: Summerhouse Press, 1997); Ronald G. Killion and Charles T. Waller, *Georgia and the Revolution* (Atlanta: Cherokee Publishing Company, 1975). The latter book is especially valuable for the documents therein set forth in full, including the Disqualifying Act of 1780 (with a list of names and positions, including Edward Telfair). For a chronological account of the Revolutionary War in the Georgia upcountry, see Edward J. Cashin, Jr., and Heard Robertson, *Augusta and the American Revolution: Events in the Georgia Back Country, 1773–1783* (Darien, Ga.: Ashantilly Press, 1975). Telfair's ouster of the Reverend Haddon Smith: Roger K. Warlick, *As Grain Once Scattered: The History of Christ Church, Savannah, Georgia (1733–1983)* (Savannah: State Printing, 1987), 43.

6. *Georgia Gazette,* May 25, 1774.

7. Among the Telfair Family Papers is a "Family Record" listing the governor's children (and spouses where relevant) and grandchildren with dates of birth, marriage, and death. TFP, Item 660, removed from Box 19, Folder 174, and microfilmed. Substantial independent evidence supports its accuracy. See also Telfair genealogical chart and paper "The Telfair Family of Georgia," Walter Charlton Hartridge Collection, Georgia Historical Society Manuscript Collection No. 349 (hereinafter "Hartridge Collection"), Box 145, Folder 2,624.

8. The genealogical studies in the Hartridge Collection were relied upon for data on the Gibbons family. See the charts in Box 103, Folder 1,925, and the biographical information on various members of the Gibbons family in Folders 1,925 and 1,926. William Gibbons, the son of Joseph Gibbons, is described in *Men of Mark in Georgia,* 1:102, and *Dictionary of Georgia Biography,* 1:345. Death of General Nathanael Greene: Mary Granger, ed., *Savannah River Plantations* (Savannah Writers' Project, Georgia Historical Society, 1947; reprint, Savannah: The Oglethorpe Press, Inc., 1997), 74. Whitehall Plantation is the subject of a three-part article in the *Georgia Historical Quarterly* 25, no. 4 (December 1941): 340; 26, no. 1 (March 1942): 40; 26, no. 2 (June 1942): 129.

9. Gibbons v. Ogden, 9 Wheat. 1, 6 L.Ed. 23 (1824). Thomas H. Gignilliat presented a paper on Thomas Gibbons at the October 29, 1955, meeting of the Madeira Society, a copy of which is in the Hartridge Collection, Box 103, Folder 1,925. See also Lee Griffen, "Savannah's Meanest Man," *Savannah Morning News Magazine,* April 9, 1961; *Dictionary of Georgia Biography,* 1:343.

10. Hartridge Collection, Box 103, Folder 1,925.

11. Biographical information on Dr. George Jones and the Jones family: E. Merton Coulter, *Wormsloe: Two Centuries of a Georgia Family* (Athens: University of Georgia Press, 1955); William Harris Bragg, *De Renne: Three Generations of a Georgia Family* (Athens: University of Georgia Press, 1999); *Dictionary of Georgia Biography,* 1:547; *Men of Mark in Georgia,* 2:342.

12. President Washington's visit to Augusta: Edward J. Cashin, Jr., *The Story of Augusta* (Augusta: Richmond County Board of Education, 1980), 48–50; Archibald Henderson, *Washington's Southern Tour, 1791* (New York: Houghton Mifflin & Company, 1923), 231–51.

13. MT to MF, June 1 [1834], WFC, Item 200.

14. *Ibid.*

15. MT to MF: July 28, 1833, WFC, Item 58; March 18, 1834, WFC, Item 59.

16. The tale of the minstrel Taillifer appears in the Telfair family genealogical

records at the Georgia Historical Society. The story also is related in Keith Feiling, *History of England* (New York: McGraw-Hill, 1948), 93. Mary Telfair knew the legend of Taillifer, for pinned to the inside front cover of her 1816–20 commonplace book (TFP, Box 6, Folder 57, Item 255) is the following handwritten quotation from Volume I, Chapter V, of Keightly's *History of England*:

> At the battle of Hastings, Oct. 15th 1066, a Norman Knight, named Taillifer, preceded the army, mounted on a stately horse, tossing his sword up in the air with one hand and catching it with the other, and singing aloud the deeds of the hero Roland. He slew two English warriors, but fell by the hand of a third.

17. Commonplace book, 1816–20, TFP, Box 6, Folder 57, Item 255.

2. Building Minds for the Republic   *pages 16–36*

1. MT to MF: February 17 [1828], WFC, Item 207; July 9, 1833, WFC, Item 57; June 19, 1839, WFC, Item 83.

2. William Few: Allen Johnson, ed., *Dictionary of American Biography,* 11 vols. (New York: Charles Scribner's Sons, 1964) 3:352; *Men of Mark in Georgia,* 1:81; *Dictionary of Georgia Biography,* 1:307; Florence Fleming Corley, "William Few, Jr.: Georgia's Silent Signer of the U.S. Constitution," *Georgia Journal of Southern Legal History* 1, no. 1 (Spring/Summer 1991): 223–28; *William Few Autobiography,* WFC, Item 994. Participation of William and Benjamin Few in Revolution: Otis Ashmore and Charles H. Olmstead, "The Battles of Kettle Creek and Brier Creek," *Georgia Historical Quarterly* 10, no. 2 (June 1926): 85–125. Benjamin Few: *Men of Mark in Georgia,* 1:75; *Dictionary of Georgia Biography,* 1:304. Mrs. Few's obituary: TFP, Box 5, Folder 52, Item 213.

3. *Columbian Museum & Savannah Advertiser,* January 24, 1797.

4. Mary Beth Norton, *Liberty's Daughters: The Revolutionary Experience of American Women, 1750–1800* (Boston: Little, Brown and Company, 1980), chap. 9, "Vindicating the Equality of Female Intellect." See also Clinton, *The Plantation Mistress,* 123–26.

5. William Few to Edward Telfair, July 12, 1801, Edward Telfair Papers, Special Collections Library, Duke University (hereinafter "ETP Duke").

6. Thomas Telfair to Alexander Telfair, March 12, 1807, ETP Duke.

7. William Few to Edward Telfair: July 12, 1801, July 30, 1801, ETP Duke.

8. Eric Homburger, *The Historical Atlas of New York City* (New York: Henry Holt and Company, 1994). Helen M. Morgan, ed., *A Season in New York (1801): Letters of Harriet and Maria Trumbull* (Pittsburgh: University of Pittsburgh Press, 1969), captures the essence of New York at the time that Alexander and Mary Telfair arrived there.

9. William Few to Edward Telfair, July 30, 1801, ETP Duke.

10. *Ibid.*

11. *Ibid.*

12. Catherine Few to "My dear sister" [Hannah Nicholson Gallatin]: no date [May 1795], October 1, 1793, Gallatin Collection 1802, Item 167, New-York Historical Society; William Few to Edward Telfair, July 30, 1801, ETP Duke.

13. Mary Telfair's 1855 Travel Journal (two volumes, unpaginated), TFP, Box 7,

Folder 65, Item 265 (volume one); MT to MF: postmark February 17 [1828], WFC, Item 207; November 10, 1822, WFC, Item 21; January 17 [1814], WFC, Item 124; postmark July 1 [1814], WFC, Item 14; October 28 [1814], WFC, Item 5.

14. MT to MF, September 18, [1819], WFC, Item 12.

15. MT to MF: August 20, 1811, WFC, Item 3; August 14, 1836, WFC, Item 71; November 10, 1822, WFC, Item 21. Richmond Hill's origins go back to 1767, when Major Abraham Mortier, paymaster-general of the British Army, acquired from Trinity Church a ninety-nine-year lease on a tract of land along the Hudson River just south of what is now the Greenwich Village section of New York. Here Mortier erected a large wooden dwelling, a mansion with a lofty portico supported by Ionic columns. The land, which no longer adjoins the river, is roughly outlined by Clinton Place and Varick and Charlton streets. During the brief period that New York was the seat of the federal government, it was the home of Vice-President John Adams. In May 1797 Trinity Church leased the estate to Aaron Burr for sixty-nine years. In 1803 Burr sold the Richmond Hill lease, save the mansion itself and a few surrounding acres, to John Jacob Astor, who filled in swamps, leveled hills, and created over 450 building lots. When Burr's daughter Theodosia was married in February 1801, she spent her honeymoon at Richmond Hill, and she and her infant son spent August to November 1802 there. Milton Lomask, *Aaron Burr, The Years from Princeton to Vice President, 1756–1805* (New York: Farrar, Straus & Giroux, 1979), 108–9, 117, 286, 329. Mary Telfair mentions Mary Few becoming "an inhabitant" of Richmond Hill in 1815 (MT to MF, June 9 [1815], WFC, Item 138) and of visiting the Fews "at Richmond Hill" (e.g., MT to MF, postmark December 8, no year, WFC, Item 139). Presumably the Fews lived in a house on land developed by Astor.

16. MT to MF: no date [spring 1815], WFC, Item 128; postmark February 10, no year, WFC, Item 171; postmark March 22 [1823], WFC, Item 219; postmark July 1 [1814], WFC, Item 14; June 12 [1813], WFC, Item 272.

17. MT to MF: February 6 [1831], WFC, Item 180; August 20, 1811, WFC, Item 3; June 9 [1815], WFC, Item 138. Ignatius Few: *Men of Mark in Georgia*, 2:362; *Dictionary of Georgia Biography*, 1:305.

18. Edward Telfair to Alexander Telfair: September 26, 1801, January 30, 1802, ETP Duke.

19. William Few to Edward Telfair, April [1802], Edward Telfair Papers, Georgia Historical Society Manuscript Collection No. 791, Folder 3, Item 23–A; Edward Telfair to Alexander Telfair, April 26, 1803, ETP Duke.

20. Edward Telfair to Alexander Telfair, May 8, 1802, ETP Duke.

21. Invoice for French lessons: TFP, Box 19, Folder 174, Item 662; exercise book: TFP, Box 19, Folder 174, Item 663; Edward Telfair to Alexander Telfair: May 8, 1802, January 30, 1802, ETP Duke.

22. Edward Telfair to Alexander Telfair, January 30, 1802, ETP Duke; Alexander Telfair to Edward Telfair [typed copy], TFP, Box 19, Folder 174, Item 664.

23. MT to MF, postmark December 13 [1836], WFC, Item 116.

24. Edward Telfair to Alexander Telfair: September 26, 1801, January 30, 1802, April 5, 1805, ETP Duke.

25. Edward Telfair to Alexander Telfair: January 28, 1804, July 1802, September 26, 1801, ETP Duke.

26. Thomas Telfair to Alexander Telfair, January 10, 1806, ETP Duke; Records of Litchfield Law School, Litchfield Historical Museum. Samuel H. Fisher,

The Litchfield Law School, 1775–1833 (New Haven: Tercentenary Commission of the State of Connecticut, Yale University Press, 1933). Tapping Reeve: *National Cyclopaedia of American Biography*, 6:175; *Dictionary of American Biography*, 8:468–70. *Princeton University General Catalogue, 1746–1906*, 114.

27. Historical information and a picture of life at Princeton at the time that the Telfair boys attended the college can be found in Thomas Jefferson Wertenbaker, *Princeton: 1746–1896* (Princeton: Princeton University Press, 1946). Academic records from this period are not available.

28. *Princeton University General Catalogue, 1746–1906* lists all classmates of the Telfair boys and members of other classes graduating in the early 1800's. *Men of Mark in Georgia* contains biographies of certain of the Telfairs' contemporaries at Princeton, including Alfred Cuthbert (2:235), John A. Cuthbert (2:343), Richard Wylly Habersham (2:106), and James Moore Wayne (2:426). See also Alexander A. Lawrence, *James Moore Wayne, Southern Unionist* (Chapel Hill: University of North Carolina Press, 1943).

29. Edward Telfair to Alexander Telfair, September 20, 1905, ETP Duke.

30. Thomas Telfair to Alexander Telfair, January 10, 1806, ETP Duke.

31. *Ibid.*

32. Records of Litchfield Law School, Litchfield Historical Museum.

33. Edward Telfair to Alexander Telfair, June 18, 1806, ETP Duke.

34. *Ibid.*

35. Edward Telfair to Alexander Telfair, July 19, 1806, ETP Duke.

36. Edward Telfair to Alexander Telfair, September 6, 1806, ETP Duke.

37. *Ibid.*

38. *Ibid.* Americans in the Republican Era were unwilling to recognize England's unwritten constitution as a real constitution. The theory that the English had no constitution was expounded by Thomas Paine in *Common Sense* (1776) and later in *The Rights of Man* (1791).

39. Edward Telfair to Alexander Telfair: February 12, 1807, ETP Duke; March 16, 1807, Alexander Telfair Papers, Georgia Historical Society Manuscript Collection No. 790, Folder 1, Item 1.

40. Thomas Telfair to Alexander Telfair, December 2, 1806, ETP Duke.

41. Thomas Telfair to Alexander Telfair, April 2 [1807], ETP Duke.

42. Thomas Telfair to Edward Telfair, July 18, 1807, TFP, Box 19, Folder 174, Item 665.

43. Edward Telfair to Alexander Telfair, August 6, 1807, ETP Duke.

44. Thomas Telfair to Alexander Telfair, June 26, 1807, ETP Duke; Edward Telfair to Alexander Telfair, June 4, 1807, ETP Duke.

45. Thomas Telfair to Alexander Telfair, May 2, 1807, ETP Duke. Details of the Princeton rebellion of 1807 are recounted in Wertenbaker, *Princeton: 1746–1896*, 138–44, and in excerpts from faculty minutes furnished to the author by the staff of the Princeton University Archives.

46. Edward Telfair to Alexander Telfair, June 4, 1807, ETP Duke. Among the Telfair papers at the Georgia Historical Society is Alexander's diploma issued upon his graduation from the College of New Jersey, the ribbon and seal all but disintegrated, and a certificate evidencing his membership in "Societas Cliosophica." TFP, Box 9, Folder 79, Items 312 and 313. Clio and Whig were the college's two debating societies. All three of the Telfair boys were members of Clio, as were their uncles,

Barack and Joseph Gibbons, both of whom were members of the class of 1790. Barack's society name was Aristides and Joseph's was Shandy, for the hero of Laurence Sterne's novel *Tristam Shandy*. There are brief biographical notes on Barack and Joseph Gibbons in Ruth L. Woodward and Wesley Frank Craven, *Princetonians, 1784–1790, A Biographical Dictionary* (Princeton: Princeton University Press, 1991), 477–79.

47. MT to MF, October 28 [1814], WFC, Item 5.

48. TFP, Box 16, Folder 76, Item 305.

49. October 1, 1808, entry, Frances Few Diary, 1808–1809, WFC, Items 940 and 941, reprinted with introduction and editorial notes by Noble E. Cunningham, Jr., in *Journal of Southern History* 29, no. 3 (August 1963): 345–61 (hereinafter "Frances Few Diary").

3. The Torch Is Passed   *pages 37–55*

1. Edward Telfair to Alexander Telfair, February 12, 1807, ETP Duke; Thomas Telfair to Alexander Telfair, September 17, 1807, ETP Duke. When Thomas wrote this letter, he had not yet learned of his father's death.

2. Register of Deaths, Savannah, Georgia, 1807–1811, Chatham County Department of Health; codicil dated July 19, 1802, to will of Edward Telfair: Edward Telfair probate file, Chatham County Probate Court; *The Counties of the State of Georgia* (Savannah: Georgia Historical Society, 1988); removal to Bonaventure Cemetery: *Savannah Morning News*, April 1, 1976.

3. Last will and testament of Edward Telfair dated November 6, 1799 and codicil dated July 19, 1802: Edward Telfair probate file, Chatham County Probate Court.

4. Entry on Thomas Telfair in GBS Notebook [file of military records], Georgia Historical Society.

5. Edward Telfair to Alexander Telfair, August 28, 1807, ETP Duke.

6. William Few recognized Edward Telfair's strong Republican sentiments in a letter reporting on the reaction in New York to Alexander Hamilton's death at the hand of Aaron Burr in their duel in July 1804 under the New Jersey Palisades and also on the general state of the Republican Party in the Northeast. William Few to Edward Telfair, December 17, 1804, ETP Duke. William Few's father-in-law was the head of the Republican Party in New York. Mary's politics: MT to MF, November 26 [1814], WFC, Item 7; Thomas' election: *Columbian Museum & Savannah Advertiser*, October 5, 1809. Biographical data on Thomas Telfair: *Men of Mark in Georgia*, 2:446.

7. Notebook: TFP, Box 9, Folder 81, Item 311; MT to MF, March 25, no year, WFC, Item 113.

8. Eliza A. Bowen, *The Story of Wilkes County* (Marietta, Ga.: Continental Book Company, 1950), 106–7; document containing data on Thomas Telfair's marriage and children: TFP, Box 9, Folder 81, Item 317A; MT to MF, December 3 [1813], WFC, Item 134.

9. MT to MF, postmark February 21 [1810], WFC, Item 155.

10. *Ibid.*

11. MT to MF, August 4 [1813], WFC, Item 142; entry on Alexander Telfair in GBS Notebook, Georgia Historical Society.

12. MT to MF, June 12 [1813], WFC, Item 272.

13. MT to MF, January 17 [1814], WFC, Item 124.

14. MT to MF, July 1 [1814], WFC, Item 14.

15. *Ibid.*

16. MT to MF, November 26 [1814], WFC, Item 7; no date [spring 1815], WFC, Item 128; MF to Mary Garrettson, February 1815 [postmark February 22], WFC, Item 391. Mary Garrettson was the daughter of the Reverend Freeborn Garrettson. Rev. Garrettson was a native of Maryland. After being ordained a Methodist minister in 1784 and having freed his slaves, he traveled through New England and parts of Canada establishing new churches before settling in Rhinebeck on the Hudson River. He was considered an important force in spreading the Methodist faith in America. In 1791 he wrote *The Experience and Travels of Mr. Freeborn Garrettson.* His wife was greatly admired for her piety by both the Fews and the Telfairs.

17. Joan E. Cashin, "The Structure of Antebellum Planter Families: 'The Ties that Bound Us Was Strong,'" *Journal of Southern History* 56, no. 1 (February 1990): 55–70.

18. MT to MF, March 30, no year, WFC, Item 17; Joseph Gaston Baillie Bulloch, *A History and Genealogy of the Families of Bellinger, De Veaux and Other Families* (Savannah: The Morning News Print, 1895), 6–13. Data on William Telfair's progeny is taken from genealogical studies in the Hartridge Collection. See charts in Box 145, Folder 2,624.

19. Bulloch, *History and Genealogy of the Families of Bellinger, etc.,* 13.

20. MT to MF, February 17, 1816, WFC, Item 9

21. MT to MF: October 28 [1816], WFC, Item 10; June 19 [1817], WFC, Item 8; biographical data on Colonel Long: *Men of Mark in Georgia,* 2:246.

22. Last will and testament of William Gibbons dated September 21, 1803: Brief of Testimony, 54.

23. Register of Deaths, Savannah, Georgia; last will and testament of Barack Gibbons dated July 28, 1814: Brief of Testimony, 60.

24. MT to MF: August 4 [1813], WFC, Item 142; dated "29th," no month or year, WFC, Item 123; January 31, no year, WFC, Item 191.

25. MT to MF: August 4 [1813], WFC, Item 142; June 6 [possibly 1813], WFC, Item 135.

26. Genealogical Committee of the Georgia Historical Society, *Marriages of Chatham County, Volume 1, 1748–1852,* 139; MT to MF: October 28 [1814], WFC, Item 5; no date [spring 1815], WFC, Item 128; June 9 [1815], WFC, Item 138.

27. MT to MF, June 1 [1816], WFC, Item 11. Captain Haig's desire for a child is evident from the language of his will dated December 3, 1816, on file at the Chatham County Probate Court. George Haig obituary: *Savannah Republican,* December 12, 1816. The author of the obituary wrote of Haig, "By his death his family are deprived of a valued friend; society of a virtuous citizen; the republic of a gallant soldier." Frances Few to Mary Garrettson, postmark January 24 [1817], WFC, Item 638; MT to MF, January 6 [1817], WFC, Item 13.

28. MT to MF, January 6 [1817], WFC, Item 13.

29. MT to MF: June 19 [1817], WFC, Item 8; December 6 [1817], WFC, Item 130.

30. MT to MF: May 1 [1817], WFC, Item 282; June 19 [1817], WFC, Item 8.

31. MT to MF: December 6 [1817], WFC, Item 130; November 2, no year, WFC, Item 186.

32. Affidavit of Noble W. Jones dated March 2 1818; last will and testament of Thomas Telfair (unsigned and undated): Thomas Telfair probate file, Chatham County Probate Court.

33. MT to MF, March 28 [1818], WFC, Item 131.

34. MT to MF, May 24 [1818], WFC, Item 129; document containing data on Thomas Telfair's marriage and children: TFP, Box 9, Folder 81, Item 317A.

35. MT to MF, December 23 [1818], WFC, Item 127.

36. 4 Johns. Ch. 150 (1819).

37. 9 Wheat. 1, 6 L.Ed. 23 (1824).

38. Information on William Cliffton and his house: *Colonial Records of Georgia*, 7: 108, 175. In 1786, the Georgia Assembly directed that a new town, to be called Louisville, be established as Georgia's capital. The capital was to be moved from Savannah to Augusta until Louisville was ready for occupancy, which was not until 1795. In this connection, Nathan Brownson, William Few, and Hugh Lawson were appointed Commissioners for the Town of Louisville to effect the change in the seat of government and were authorized to sell Government House and the lot on which it was situated. The property was purchased from the Commissioners by William Gibbons, Jr., and Major John Habersham, as joint owners. When Gibbons died in 1804, his moiety or undivided one-half interest in the house and lot passed under his will to his sister, Sarah Telfair, for her use during her natural life with the remainder to vest in his nieces and nephews living at the time of her death, share and share alike. Will set forth in Brief of Testimony, 54. After the death of John Habersham, his half interest in the property was auctioned by the marshal to satisfy a judgment against his estate, and Alexander Telfair was the high bidder, taking title under date of November 1, 1810. Chatham County Land Records: Deed Book 2C, 710. By instrument of conveyance dated June 3, 1818, Alexander acquired for $5,000 his mother's life estate and the remainder interests of his sisters and his cousins, Noble Wimberly Jones II and Sarah Jones, in the other undivided one-half interest in Trust Lot Letter N and the improvements thereon, thereby becoming the owner of the entire fee simple interest. Chatham County Land Records: Deed Book 2H, 480; Alexander Telfair's ledger indicating payments for lot, TFP, Box 4, Folder 34, Item 89.

39. Information on William Jay: Hannah H. Lerski, *William Jay, Itinerant English Architect, 1792–1837* (Lanham, Md.: University Press of America, 1983); James Vernon McDonough, "William Jay—Regency Architect in Georgia and South Carolina" (Ph.D. diss., Princeton University, 1950); Thomas Gamble, "Romance of Wm. Jay, Savannah Architect," *Savannah Morning News*, May 8, 1932. Biographical data on William Scarbrough: *Dictionary of American Biography*, 2:237. President Monroe's visit to Savannah: E. Merton Coulter, "Presidential Visits to Georgia During Ante-Bellum Times," *Georgia Historical Quarterly* 55, no. 3 (fall 1971): 339–42.

40. John Frazee was born in New Jersey and as a young man was apprenticed to a bricklayer. He took up stonecutting and, with his brother William, bought a marble shop in New York City in 1818. He specialized in mantels, tombstones, and lettering. Later he carved statues and busts of such famous persons as John Marshall and Daniel Webster. He was a founding member of the National Academy of Design.

41. Lerski, *William Jay, Itinerant English Architect,1792–1837*, Appendix D. A plan

of the mansion drawn by architect Detlef Lienau prior to its conversion to a museum is in the possession of the Telfair Academy.

42. MT to MF, no date [spring 1844], WFC, Item 109.

43. Harden, *History of Savannah and South Georgia*, 386; MT to MF, postmark June 6 [1840], WFC, Item 241; deed from Trustees of Independent Presbyterian Church to Alexander Telfair, May 15, 1818, Mary Telfair Papers, Georgia Historical Society Manuscript Collection No. 792 (hereinafter "Mary Telfair Papers"), Folder 1, Item 3.

44. Harden, *History of Savannah and South Georgia*, 288.

4. A Coastal Aristocracy *pages 56–72*

1. MT to MF, October 28 [1816], WFC, Item 10.

2. MT to MF, May 5, 1829, WFC, Item 34.

3. Richard H. Haunton, "Savannah in the 1850's" (Ph.D. diss., Emory University, 1968), 326.

4. MT to MF, April 25, 1837, WFC, Item 75. Another example was the visit of a Miss Verplanck to Charleston and Savannah. MT to MF, March 14 [1825], WFC, Item 24.

5. Commonplace book, 1816–20, TFP, Box 6, Folder 57, Item 255.

6. Kilbride, *Philadelphia and the Southern Elite*, 1, 5, 78.

7. Richard H. Shryock, ed., *Letters of Richard D. Arnold, M.D., 1808–1876* (Durham, N.C.: Seeman Press, 1929), 9.

8. Lollie Belle Wylie, ed., *Memoirs of Judge Richard H. Clark* (Atlanta: Franklin Printing and Publishing Company, 1898), 94.

9. MT to MF, postmark November 9, no year, WFC, Item 141.

10. MT to MF, February 6, no year, WFC, Item 125.

11. MT to MF: postmark December 8, no year, WFC, Item 139; February 5, no year, WFC, Item 183.

12. MT to MF, February 25, no year, WFC, Item 178.

13. March 8, 1809, entry, Frances Few Diary.

14. October 1, 1808, entry, Frances Few Diary.

15. MT to MF: October 28 [1816], WFC, Item 10; dated "29th," no month or year, WFC, Item 123; MF to Mary Garrettson [?], October 9 and 16, 1812, WFC, Item 4; MT to MF, October 14, 1827, WFC, Item 30.

16. Alexander Telfair to Robert Habersham, July 10, 1823, R. & J. Habersham Papers, Georgia Historical Society Manuscript Collection No. 342 (hereinafter "Habersham Papers"), Item 10.

17. MT to MF: October 28 [1814], WFC, Item 5; November 10, 1822, WFC, Item 21; August 20, 1811, WFC, Item 3; no date [spring 1815], WFC, Item 128.

18. MT to MF, August 22, no year, WFC, Item 250.

19. MT to MF: August 22, no year, WFC, Item 260; postmark September 6, no year, WFC, Item 220.

20. MT to MF, June 1 [1816], WFC, Item 11.

21. MT to MF, no date [spring 1815], WFC, Item 128.

22. MT to MF, October 11 [1818], WFC, Item 258.

23. MT to MF, March 28 [1818], WFC, Item 131.

24. MT to MF, December 3, 1823, WFC, Item 22.

25. MT to MF, August 3, no year, WFC, Item 221.

26. MT to MF: postmark July 14, no year, WFC, Item 223; July 4, no year, WFC, Item 222.

27. MT to MF: May 12 [1834], WFC, Item 206; September 28, no year, WFC, Item 246.

28. Jack Fruchtman, Jr., writing of Kitty Nicholson Few in his biography, *Thomas Paine, Apostle of Freedom* (New York: Four Walls Eight Windows, 1994), 37, speculates that Paine "might well have been in platonic love with this beautiful young woman."

29. Anne Hollingsworth Wharton, *Salons Colonial and Republican* (New York: J. B. Lippincott Company, 1900), 348–49.

30. TFP, Box 5, Folder 53, Item 229.

31. MT to MF, October 19 [1812], WFC, Item 6.

32. MT to MF, no date [spring 1815], WFC, Item 128.

33. Nancy Goyne Evans, "The Sans Souci: A Fashionable Resort Hotel in Ballston Spa," *Winterthur Portfolio* 6 (Charlottesville: University Press of Virginia, 1970), 114. Life at Ballston Spa was not unlike that at the Virginia Springs as described in Charlene Marie Lewis, "Ladies and Gentlemen on Display: Planter Society at the Virginia Springs, 1790–1860" (Ph.D. diss., University of Virginia, 1997).

34. MT to MF: August 6, no year, WFC, Item 147; postmark August 13, no year, WFC, Item 144; July 20 and 24, no year, WFC, Item 143; no date [1815 or 1816], WFC, Item 146.

35. MT to MF: no date [1815 or 1816], WFC, Item 146; August 6, no year, WFC, Item 147; postmark November 9, no year, WFC, Item 141.

36. Commonplace book, 1822–29, TFP, Box 6, Folder 58, Item 256.

37. TFP, Box 5, Folder 53, Item 245. Meta was Margaret Telfair's nickname.

38. Robert Mackay to Eliza Anne Mackay: July 20, 1816, July 22, 1816, July 23, 1816, Walter C. Hartridge, ed., *The Letters of Robert Mackay* (Athens: University of Georgia Press, 1949), 239, 241, 242.

39. MT to MF: February 5, no year, WFC, Item 183; June 19, no year, WFC, Item 279.

40. MT to MF, November 12, no year, WFC, Item 208.

5. Single Blessedness   *pages 73–96*

1. MT to MF, October 11 [1818], WFC, Item 258. The phrase "single blessedness," so popular in the early nineteenth century, has its origin in Act I, Scene 1, of *A Midsummer Night's Dream.* As used by Shakespeare, it bears no connotation of bliss. Hermia, in love with Lysander, refuses to marry Demetrius, her father's choice for her husband. She asks Theseus, duke of Athens, to tell her the worst that may befall her if she persists in her refusal. Death or a nunnery is his reply. He entreats her to consider whether she could endure the "livery of a nun" and "live a barren sister" all her life "chanting faint hymns to the cold and fruitless moon." Those who can "undergo such maiden pilgrimage" are "thrice blessed," but the duke would not recommend such a life to Hermia: "But earthlier happy is the rose distill'd, / Than that which withering on the virgin thorn / Grows, lives, and dies in single blessedness."

2. Wyatt-Brown, *Southern Honor*, 201–4; MT to MF: May 5, 1829, WFC, Item 34; Saturday 30th, 1837 [postmark September 30], WFC, Item 78; October 20, [1833], WFC, Item 54; October 3 [1823], WFC, Item 291; postmark October 3 [1823], WFC, Item 216; Eliza Bowne, *A Girl's Life Eighty Years Ago, Selections from the Letters of Eliza Southgate Bowne* (New York: Charles Scribner's Sons, 1887), 38, quoted in Chambers-Schiller, *Liberty: A Better Husband*, 36. For information on courtship practices generally, see Helen K. Rothman, *Hearts and Hands: A History of Courtship in America* (New York: Basic Books, 1984).

3. MT to MF, March 5, 1835, WFC, Item 67; "Wedlock, wedlock": Carrie A. Roland to Emily Howlands, August 7, 1842, Cornell University, quoted in Chambers-Schiller, *Liberty: A Better Husband*, 52.

4. MT to MF: June 19, 1839, WFC, Item 83; August 11, no year, WFC, Item 153; postmark November 11 [1840], WFC, Item 89; postmark May 14 [1841], WFC, Item 213; December 3 [1813], WFC, Item 134; postmark July 1 [1814], WFC, Item 14. According to a traditional story, as Sir Philip Sidney lay dying on the field of battle, he refused a cup of water and passed it to another wounded man whose need, he said, was greater than his own. Mary Telfair copied Sidney's dying words into her commonplace book. Commonplace book, 1816–20.

5. MT to MF, November 26 [1814], WFC, Item 7.

6. MT to MF: September 18 [1819], WFC, Item 12; postmark December 24, no year, WFC, Item 190; April 5, 1840, WFC, Item 88.

7. John Wallace to "My Dear Mag," September 1, 1814, Mary Savage Anderson, ed., "The Wallace Letters," *Georgia Historical Quarterly* 18, no. 2 (June 1934): 189; MT to MF, November 12, no year, WFC, Item 137.

8. MT to MF: postmark April 16 [1816 or earlier], WFC, Item 133; November 25 and December 10, no year, WFC, Item 136; June 9 [1815], WFC, Item 138; January 14 [1814], WFC, Item 1. "But let concealment . . ." is from *Twelfth Night*, Act II, Scene iv.

9. MT to MF, February 17, 1816, WFC, Item 9.

10. MT to MF, postmark March 22 [1823], WFC, Item 219.

11. MT to MF, January 17 [1814], WFC, Item 124.

12. MT to MF: February 17, 1816, WFC, Item 9; postmark April 16 [1816 or earlier], WFC, Item 133; November 22, 1826, WFC, Item 27; October 1, no year, WFC, Item 244; March 30, 1839, WFC, Item 82; June 9 [1815], WFC, Item 138; postmark March 21, no year, WFC, Item 199; January 14 [1814], WFC, Item 1.

13. Biographical data on Jabez Jackson: *Men of Mark in Georgia*, 2:446; MT to MF: September 19 [1818], WFC, Item 238; December 23 [1818], WFC, Item 127.

14. MT to MF, September 19 [1818], WFC, Item 238.

15. MT to MF, December 23 [1818], WFC, Item 127.

16. MT to MF, dated "22d" [fall 1818], WFC, Item 126.

17. MT to MF: April 14, no year, WFC, Item 132; dated "22d" [fall 1818], WFC, Item 126.

18. MT to MF: September 19 [1818], WFC, Item 238; no date [1815 or 1816], WFC, Item 148.

19. MT to MF, September 18, 1819, WFC, Item 12.

20. MT to MF: November 25 and December 10, no year, WFC, Item 136; June 1 [1816], WFC, Item 11; September 18 [1819], WFC, Item 12; November 26 [1814], WFC, Item 7; February 5 [1828], WFC, Item 32.

21. MT to MF: January 6 [1830], WFC, Item 204; postmark April 29 [1823], WFC, Item 18.

22. MT to MF: May 5, 1829, WFC, Item 34; March 30, 1839, WFC, Item 82; postmark October 19, no year, WFC, Item 120; no date [1815 or 1816], WFC, Item 148; April 13, 1840, WFC, Item 92.

23. MT to MF: August 6, no year, WFC, Item 147; July 20 and 24, no year, WFC, Item 143.

24. MT to MF: September 18 [1819], WFC, Item 12; January 14 [1814], WFC, Item 1.

25. MT to MF: August 6, no year, WFC, Item 147; July 23, no year, WFC, Item 225.

26. MT to MF, no date [1815 or 1816], WFC, Item 148.

27. MT to MF, January 14 [1814], WFC, Item 1.

28. MT to MF, November 26 [1814], WFC, Item 7.

29. MT to MF: October 3, no year, WFC, Item 288; November 25 and December 10, no year, WFC, Item 136; October 28 [1814], WFC, Item 5; October 19 [1812], WFC, Item 6.

30. MT to MF, postmark February 21 [1810], WFC, Item 155.

31. MT to MF: January 14 [1814], WFC, Item 1; postmark December 8, no year, WFC, Item 139; November 12, no year, WFC, Item 137; June 6 [possibly 1813], WFC, Item 135.

32. MT to MF, October 13, no year, WFC, Item 295.

33. MF to Mary Garrettson, postmark June 29, 1814, WFC, Item 382.

34. MT to MF: October 28 [1814], WFC, Item 5; January 17 [1814], WFC, Item 124; October 13, no year, WFC, Item 295; small book: TFP, Box 8, Folder 70, Item 283; MT to MF, April 6 [1825], WFC, Item 25.

35. MT to MF: January 26, 1840, WFC, Item 86; November 22, 1826, WFC, Item 27; postmark February 17, no year, WFC, Item 114; October 19 [1812], WFC, Item 6; postmark April 24, no year, WFC, Item 182; postmark December 15 [1839], WFC, Item 161; postmark April 24, no year, WFC, Item 196; October 13, no year, WFC, Item 295.

36. MT to MF: January 17 [1814], WFC, Item 124; December 2, 1829, WFC, Item 38; postmark June 6 [1838], WFC, Item 164.

37. Commonplace book, 1822–29, TFP, Box 6, Folder 58, Item 256.

38. MT to MF, January 17 [1814], WFC, Item 124; Commonplace book, 1816–20; MT to MF, June 9 [1815], WFC, Item 138.

39. MT to MF, November 26 [1814], WFC, Item 7.

40. *Men of Mark in Georgia*, 2:362; *Dictionary of Georgia Biography*, 1:305; MT to MF: April 3, 1831, WFC, Item 44; February 6 [1831], WFC, Item 180.

41. MT to MF: March 17, 1829, WFC, Item 36; May 5, 1829, WFC, Item 34.

42. MT to MF, January 26, 1840, WFC, Item 86.

43. MT to MF, June 19, 1839, WFC, Item 83.

44. MT to MF, postmark December 24, no year, WFC, Item 190.

45. MT to MF, January 29, no year [pre-1832]. Letter in files of Telfair Museum of Art, gift of Mrs. Rita Trotz of Savannah.

46. MT to MF, July 24, no year, WFC, Item 292.

47. MT to MF: January 25, 1828, WFC, Item 31; March 27 [1828], WFC, Item 281.

48. MT to MF, January 7, 1827, WFC, Item 28.

49. MT to MF, April 6, 1832, WFC, Item 45.
50. MT to MF: October 1, no year, WFC, Item 244; January 7, 1827, WFC, Item 28.
51. MT to MF, September 11, 1836, WFC, Item 72.
52. MT to MF, April 6 [1825], WFC, Item 25.
53. MT to MF, March 22, 1833, WFC, Item 50.
54. MT to MF, January 31, no year, WFC, Item 191.
55. Cashin, "'Decidedly Opposed to the Union'", 746, 750–51, 753, 757.
56. *Ibid.*, 746.

6. The Sisterhood *pages 97–115*

1. Smith-Rosenberg, "Female Role of Love and Ritual," 9; Suzanne Lebsock, *Free Women of Petersburg: Status and Culture in a Southern Town, 1784–1860* (New York: W. W. Norton and Co., 1983).
2. Cashin, "'Decidedly Opposed to the Union,'" 737, 745–46.
3. MT to MF: January 29 [1830], WFC, Item 201; January 6 [1830], WFC, Item 204; Matilda Few to Mary Garrettson, September 7, 1809, WFC, Item 313.
4. MT to MF, September 18, no year, WFC, Item 105 (The punning reference to a "point" probably was to a tagged ribbon or cord, once used in dress, as for tying or fastening parts.); MT to MF, August 5, no year, WFC, Item 226.
5. MT to MF, January 29 [1830], WFC, Item 201.
6. MT to MF: July 24, no year, WFC, Item 292; August 20, 1811, WFC, Item 3; October 28 [1814], WFC, Item 5; June 9 [1815], WFC, Item 138.
7. MT to MF, May 26 [1823], WFC, Item 15.
8. MT to MF: February 28, 1826, WFC, Item 26; January 3, no year, WFC, Item 189; postmark December 8, no year, WFC, Item 139; March 27 [1828], WFC, Item 281; April 3, 1831, WFC, Item 44; October 20 [1833], WFC, Item 54; August 1 [1834], WFC, Item 63; September 11, 1836, WFC, Item 72.
9. Information on Anne Clay, her family, and the family plantation: Carolyn Clay Swiggart, *Shades of Gray: The Clay & McAllister Families of Bryan County, Georgia* (Darien, Conn.: Two Bytes Publishing, Ltd., 1999); anonymous 1848 genealogical memorandum, 1880 article on Thomas S. Clay by Rev. John Winn, and 1937 sketch of life of Thomas Carolin Clay by his son Thomas Savage Clay, each in Clay Family Papers, Georgia Historical Society Manuscript Collection No. 125 (hereinafter "Clay Papers"); genealogical information on Clay family in Joseph Gaston Baillie Bulloch, *A History and Genealogy of the Habersham Family* (Columbia, S.C.: R.L. Bryan Company, 1901), 37–41; biographical information on Joseph Clay: *Men of Mark in Georgia* 1:48; *Dictionary of Georgia Biography* 1:195. The Richmond plantation passed from the Clay family in 1919 and was eventually acquired by Henry Ford. Ford built there a mansion of Savannah grey brick taken from the Hermitage plantation on the Savannah River. The property is now being developed as an upscale golf community called "The Ford Plantation." See also Buddy Sullivan, *From Beautiful Zion to Red Bird Creek: A History of Bryan County, Georgia* (Bryan County Board of Commissioners, 2000), 65–76 (Clay family), 297–330 (Henry Ford era).
10. Matilda Few to Mary Garrettson, December 8, 1812, WFC, Item 355; MT to MF, June 29 [1828], WFC, Item 104.

11. MT to MF: January 7, 1827, WFC, Item 28; postmark December 10, no year, WFC, Item 243; March 27, no year, WFC, Item 205; December 23 [1818], WFC, Item 127.

12. MT to MF, July 24, no year, WFC, Item 292; Edith Duncan Johnston, ed., "The Kollock Letters, 1799–1850," *Georgia Historical Quarterly* 30, no. 3 (September 1946): 221; MT to MF: March 30, 1839, WFC, Item 82; postmark September 11 [1833], WFC, Item 55.

13. MT to MF: postmark September 11 [1833], WFC, Item 55; July 9, 1833, WFC, Item 57; March 25, no year, WFC, Item 113; April 29 [1833], WFC, Item 37.

14. MT to MF: June 6 [1813], WFC, Item 135; November 25 and December 10 [1818 or earlier], WFC, Item 136; June 9 [1815], WFC, Item 138; postmark April 16 [1816 or earlier], WFC, Item 133.

15. Biographical data on Dr. Terrell: *Men of Mark in Georgia*, 2:377; *Dictionary of Georgia Biography*, 2:967; MT to MF, March 1 [1840], WFC, Item 106.

16. MT to MF, April 13, 1840, WFC, Item 92.

17. MT to MF: October 28 [1814], WFC, Item 5; March 27, no year, WFC, Item 205; April 25, 1837, WFC, Item 75.

18. MT to MF: March 30, 1839, WFC, Item 82; postmark April 23, no year, WFC, Item 162; no date, WFC, Item 280; no date and a week later, December 8 [1819], WFC, Item 289; September 16 [1824], WFC, Item 23; no date [summer 1826], WFC, Item 265.

19. MT to MF, postmark March 22 [1823], WFC, Item 219.

20. MT to MF, postmark August 28, no year, WFC, Item 234.

21. MT to MF: June 19 [1817], WFC, Item 8; May 15, no year, WFC, Item 194; January 26, 1840, WFC, Item 86; April 5, 1840, WFC, Item 88; postmark December 13 [1836], WFC, Item 116; postmark February 17 [1828], WFC, Item 207; January 26, 1840, WFC, Item 86; April 13, 1840, WFC, Item 92.

22. MT to MF, postmark April 16 [1816 or earlier], WFC, Item 133; Commonplace book, 1816–20; MT to MF, February 17, 1816, WFC, Item 9.

23. MT to MF: December 3 [1813], WFC, Item 134; September 18 [1819], WFC, Item 12; November 10, 1822, WFC, Item 21; MF to Mary Garrettson: July 1816, WFC, Item 401; October 1816, WFC, Item 403.

24. MT to MF: postmark July 1 [1814], WFC, Item 14; April 5, 1840, WFC, Item 88; September 16 [1824], WFC, Item 23; postmark December 24, no year, WFC, Item 190.

25. MT to MF: September 18 [1819], WFC, Item 12; postmark July 14, no year, WFC, Item 223; September 18, no year, WFC, Item 105; postmark July 1 [1814], WFC, Item 14; postmark April 29 [1816 or earlier], WFC, Item 133; November 26 [1814], WFC, Item 7; October 28 [1814], WFC, Item 5.

26. MT to MF: postmark December 8, no year, WFC, Item 139; postmark November 9, no year, WFC, Item 141; June 1 [1816], WFC, Item 11.

27. MT to MF, September 18 [1819], WFC, Item 12.

28. Nancy F. Cott, "Passionless: An Interpretation of Victorian Sexual Ideology, 1790–1850," *Signs: Journal of Women in Culture and Society* 4, no. 2 (1978): 233; Farnham, *Education of the Southern Belle*, 155; MT to MF: postmark December 24, no year, WFC, Item 190; March 18, 1838, WFC, Item 49; Faderman, *Surpassing the Love of Men*, ch. 2, "The 'Fashion' of Romantic Friendship in the Eighteenth Century"; MT to MF, December 13 [1843], WFC, Item 108.

29. Smith-Rosenberg, "Female World of Love and Ritual," 4–8.

30. Farnham, *Education of the Southern Belle*, 162–63; Smith-Rosenberg, "Female World of Love and Ritual," 27–28.

31. Farnham, *Education of the Southern Belle*, 165–66; Wyatt-Brown, *Southern Honor*, 251.

32. MT to MF: May 15 [1823], WFC, Item 217; postmark August 9 [1815 or 1816], WFC, Item 146; February 6, no year, WFC, Item 125.

33. MT to MF: postmark February 17 [1828], WFC, Item 207; postmark December 13 [1836], WFC, Item 116; April 5, 1840, WFC, Item 88; May 23, 1834, WFC, Item 61.

34. MT to MF: postmark December 8, no year, WFC, Item 139; April 14 [possibly 1818], WFC, Item 132.

35. MT to MF, January 3, no year, WFC, Item 189.

36. MT to MF: November 22, 1826, WFC, Item 27; December 16, 1828, WFC, Item 33; June 19 [1817], WFC, Item 8; no date and a week later, December 8 [1819], WFC, Item 289; December 6 [1817], WFC, Item 130; May 5, 1829, WFC, Item 34; December 12, 1837, WFC, Item 80; January 3, no year, WFC, Item 189.

37. MT to MF: May 5, 1829, WFC, Item 34; March 30, 1839, WFC, Item 82; January 7, 1827, WFC, Item 28; March 22, 1833, WFC, Item 50; January 9, 1844, WFC, Item 101.

38. Commonplace book, 1822–29.

7. Matters of the Mind   *pages 116–137*

1. MT to MF: October 14, 1827, WFC, Item 30; postmark October 19, no year, WFC, Item 120.

2. MT to MF, May 24 [1831], WFC, Item 174. The term "blue stocking" had its origin in the mid-eighteenth-century literary gatherings held in London at the home of Mrs. Elizabeth Montagu. Many of the participants eschewed full dress, including a Mr. Benjamin Stillingfleet, who habitually wore blue worsted stockings instead of the formal black silk. This coterie of intellectuals came to be known as the "Blue Stocking Society." Hannah More wrote a poem "Bas Bleu, or Conversation" on the subject.

3. Conrad, *Perish the Thought*, 5; Wyatt-Brown, *Southern Honor*, 173; MT to MF: postmark April 24, no year, WFC, Item 182; January 7, 1827, WFC, Item 28; January 17 [1814], WFC, Item 124.

4. Chambers-Schiller, *Liberty: A Better Husband*, 206; Conrad, *Perish the Thought*, 19, 54–55.

5. Chambers-Schiller, *Liberty: A Better Husband*, 176; MT to MF, December 1, no year, WFC, Item 187.

6. MT to MF: April 14 [possibly 1818], WFC, Item 132; postmark April 24, no year, WFC, Item 182; postmark March 22 [1823], WFC, Item 219; April 6, 1837, WFC, Item 74.

7. Wyatt-Brown, *Southern Honor*, 54; MT to MF, postmark April 24, no year, WFC, Item 182.

8. Alexis de Tocqueville, *Democracy in America*, abridgment of translation by Henry Reeve published in two volumes in 1835 and 1840 (London: Oxford Univer-

sity Press, 1952), 475, 476; MT to MF: postmark October 19, no year, WFC, Item 120; Saturday 30th [postmark September 30], 1837, WFC, Item 78.

9. MT to MF: April 29 [1835], WFC, Item 197; postmark March 6 [1832], WFC, Item 202.

10. Commonplace book, 1816–20.

11. MT to MF, January 3, no year, WFC, Item 189.

12. MT to MF: May 5, 1829, WFC, Item 34; postmark February 17, no year, WFC, Item 114; October 19 [1812], WFC, Item 6; January 26, 1840, WFC, Item 86.

13. MT to MF, March 17, 1829, WFC, Item 36.

14. MT to MF: March 27, no year, WFC, Item 205; June 1 [1834], WFC, Item 200; postmark March 21, no year, WFC, Item 199.

15. MT to MF: February 28, no year, WFC, Item 181; March 14 [1825], WFC, Item 24; postmark March 22 [1823], WFC, Item 219.

16. MT to MF: January 17 [1814], WFC, Item 124; postmark July 14, no year, WFC, Item 223; postmark March 22 [1823], WFC, Item 219.

17. MT to MF: postmark December 13 [1836], WFC, Item 116; March 15, 1820, WFC, Item 19; June 9 [1815], WFC, Item 138; April 14 [possibly 1818], WFC, Item 132; November 12, no year, WFC, Item 137.

18. MT to MF: October 28 [1816], WFC, Item 10; October 11 [1818], WFC, Item 258.

19. MT to MF, February 28, 1826, WFC, Item 26.

20. MT to MF, March 27, no year, WFC, Item 205.

21. MT to MF, April 6, 1832, WFC, Item 45.

22. MT to MF, April 29 [1833], WFC, Item 37.

23. MT to MF: November 28, 1837, WFC, Item 79; May 5, 1829, WFC, Item 34; March 18, 1838, WFC, Item 49; March 27 [1828], WFC, Item 281; July 23, no year, WFC, Item 225.

24. MT to MF, March 17, 1829, WFC, Item 36.

25. MT to MF: February 17, 1816, WFC, Item 9; February 6, no year, WFC, Item 125.

26. MT to MF: January 14 [1814], WFC, Item 1; postmark July 1 [1814], WFC, Item 14.

27. MT to MF: postmark April 16, no year, WFC, Item 133; October 28 [1814], WFC, Item 5; March 27, no year, WFC, Item 205; postmark December 13 [1836], WFC, Item 116; April 25, 1837, WFC, Item 75; April 5, 1840, WFC, Item 88; Commonplace book, 1816–20.

28. MT to MF, October 19 [1812], WFC, Item 6; October 28 [1814], WFC, Item 5.

29. Commonplace book, 1816–20.

30. MT to MF: postmark April 24, no year, WFC, Item 182; April 6, 1832, WFC, Item 45; August 4 [1823], WFC, Item 142; postmark December 22 [1835], WFC, Item 166.

31. MT to MF: November 28, 1837, WFC, Item 79; November 14, 1836, WFC, Item 73; January 31, no year, WFC, Item 191; October 11 [1818], WFC, Item 258; no date [winter 1828], WFC, Item 56 (Anacreon [ca. 570–ca. 480 B.C.] was a Greek writer of love songs and drinking songs.); November 12, no year, WFC, Item 137; June 19, 1839, WFC, Item 83; March 15, 1820, WFC, Item 19; July 1 [1820], WFC, Item 239; postmark March 22 [1823], WFC, Item 219; May 23, 1838, WFC, Item 81.

32. MT to MF, postmark November 25 [1837], WFC, Item 165. Greenough (1805–1852) designed the Bunker Hill monument while a student at Harvard and later executed busts of such famous persons as Lafayette, Henry Clay, James Fenimore Cooper, and John Jacob Astor. In 1835 he was commissioned by the United States Congress to create a statue of George Washington, which was placed in front of the Capitol. Mr. Gilmor's collection is considered in detail in Lance L. Humphries, "Robert Gilmor, Jr. (1774–1848): Baltimore Collector and American Art Patron" (Ph.D. diss., University of Virginia, 1998). Greenough's Medora, just as lovely today as when Mary Telfair described the marble figure, can be seen at the Baltimore Museum of Art.

33. Commonplace books, 1816–20, 1822–29; drawings: TFP, Box 5, Folder 56, Item 249; MT to MF, November 2, no year, WFC, Item 186.

34. MT to MF: December 12, 1837, WFC, Item 80; March 18, 1838, WFC, Item 49; postmark August 30, no year, WFC, Item 254.

35. MT to MF: February 24, no year, WFC, Item 198; postmark November 8 [1839], WFC, Item 249.

36. MT to MF postmark: December 23 [1818], WFC, Item 127; March 27 [1828], WFC, Item 281; no date [winter 1828] WFC, Item 56; no date, WFC, Item 280; June 19, 1839, WFC, Item 83.

37. MT to MF: November 28, 1837, WFC, Item 79; December 2, 1829, WFC, Item 38; October 28 [1816], WFC, Item 10.

38. MT to MF: March 21, no year, WFC, Item 173; November 25 and December 10, no year, WFC, Item 136; postmark August 27, no year, WFC, Item 145; September 28, no year, WFC, Item 246; April 24, no year, WFC, Item 182.

39. TFP, Box 5, Folder 53, Item 231.

40. TFP, Box 5, Folder 55, Item 247B.

41. TFP, Box 5, Folder 53, Item 233.

42. Album containing enigmas and anagrams, TFP, Box 6, Folder 62, Item 260.

43. MT to MF: September 18 [1819], WFC, Item 12; June 19, 1839, WFC, Item 83; postmark March 22 [1823], WFC, Item 219; March 17, 1829, WFC, Item 36.

44. MT to MF, postmark October 19, no year, WFC, Item 120.

45. MT to MF, postmark March 22 [1823], WFC, Item 219. The Black Dwarf is the protagonist in Sir Walter Scott's novel of the same name. Called Elshander the Recluse or Cannie Elshie, the Wise Wight of Mucklestane Moor, the dwarf is in reality Sir Edward Mauley. Embittered by his deformity, he lives alone, but eventually wins many friends through his kindness to all who seek his help.

46. MT to MF: May 26 [1823], WFC, Item 15; postmark December 10, no year, WFC, Item 243.

47. MT to MF, postmark December 10, no year, WFC, Item 243.

48. MT to MF, April 14 [possibly 1818], WFC, Item 132.

49. MT to MF, March 21, no year, WFC, Item 173. The reference is to *Saint's Everlasting Rest* (1650) by the English divine Richard Baxter (1615–1691).

50. MT to MF: July 28, 1833, WFC, Item 58; August 22 [1833], WFC, Item 122; July 3, 1833, WFC, Item 53; July 28, 1833, WFC, Item 58. Reginald Heber (1783–1836) wrote, among other hymns, "From Greenland's Icy Mountains" and "Holy, Holy, Holy, Lord God Almighty."

51. Commonplace book, 1816–20; MT to MF, April 29 [1835], WFC, Item 197; Commonplace book, 1822–29.

52. MT to MF, January 25, 1828, WFC, Item 31.

53. MT to MF, April 6, 1832, WFC, Item 45.

54. MT to MF, April 17, no year, WFC, Item 185; album containing enigmas and anagrams.

55. MT to MF: postmark September 27, no year, WFC, Item 257; April 5, 1840, WFC, Item 88.

56. MT to MF, January 31, no year, WFC, Item 191.

57. MT to MF, November 12, no year, WFC, Item 137.

58. MT to MF, February 28, 1826, WFC, Item 26.

59. MT to MF, April 29 [1833], WFC, Item 37.

60. MT to MF, postmark February 17, no year, WFC, Item 114.

61. MT to MF, July 9, 1833, WFC, Item 57.

8. The Wise Aunt   *pages 138–152*

1. MT to MF: postmark April 29 [1823], WFC, Item 18; December 23 [1818], WFC, Item 127.

2. MT to MF, postmark March 22 [1823], WFC, Item 219.

3. MT to MF: October 13, no year, WFC, Item 295; "21st," no month or year, WFC, Item 225; May 31, 1830, WFC, Item 42.

4. MT to MF, May 24 [1818], WFC, Item 129.

5. Chambers-Schiller, *Liberty: A Better Husband*, 40; MT to MF, January 29 [1830], WFC, Item 201.

6. Chambers-Schiller, *Liberty: A Better Husband*, 25–26; MT to MF: October 13, no year, WFC, Item 295; May 24 [1818], WFC, Item 129.

7. MT to MF, no date [summer 1826], WFC, Item 265.

8. MT to MF, January 17 [1814], WFC, Item 124.

9. MT to MF, no date [summer 1826], WFC, Item 265.

10. MT to MF: postmark February 17 [1828], WFC, Item 207; January 7, 1827, WFC, Item 28.

11. MT to MF, January 7, 1827, WFC, Item 28.

12. MT to MF: postmark July 14, no year, WFC, Item 223; June 21, 1830, WFC, Item 43; no date [summer 1826], WFC, Item 265; postmark February 17 [1828], WFC, Item 207.

13. MT to MF, March 30, no year, WFC, Item 17.

14. MT to MF, May 15, 1837, WFC, Item 76.

15. MT to MF: February 28, 1826, WFC, Item 26; April 6, 1837, WFC, Item 74.

16. MT to MF, postmark July 14, no year, WFC, Item 223.

17. MT to MF, April 6, 1837, WFC, Item 74.

18. MT to MF, April 25, 1837, WFC, Item 75. For a time, the raising of silkworms was a fad among the children of Georgia.

19. MT to MF: postmark July 14, no year, WFC, Item 223; no date [summer 1827], WFC, Item 290.

20. MT to MF: October 13, no year, WFC, Item 295; July 4 [1827], WFC, Item 222; no date [summer 1827], WFC, Item 290; postmark February 17 [1828], WFC, Item 207.

21. MT to MF: January 25, 1828, WFC, Item 31; no date [summer 1827], WFC, Item 290.

22. MT to MF: February 5 [1828], WFC, Item 32; March 29, 1830, WFC, Item 40; March 27 [1828], WFC, Item 281.

23. MT to MF, December 16, 1828, WFC, Item 33.

24. MT to MF, postmark February 17 [1828], WFC, Item 207.

25. MT to MF, March 5, 1829, WFC, Item 35.

26. MT to MF, December 2, 1829, WFC, Item 38.

27. MT to MF, January 29 [1830], WFC, Item 201.

28. MT to MF, December 11, 1834, WFC, Item 65.

29. MT to MF, March 5, 1835, WFC, Item 67.

30. *Ibid.*

31. MT to MF: November 28, 1837, WFC, Item 79; December 12, 1837, WFC, Item 80.

32. MT to MF, April 13, 1840, WFC, Item 92.

33. MT to MF: March 27 [1828], WFC, Item 281; February 26 [1843], WFC, Item 112; Kenneth Coleman, ed., *A History of Georgia* (Athens: University of Georgia Press, 1991), 182; 1880 article on Thomas S. Clay by Rev. John Winn, Clay Papers; Robert Manson Myers, ed., *The Children of Pride: A True Story of Georgia and the Civil War* (New Haven: Yale University Press, 1972), 1567; Thomas S. Clay, "Detail of a Plan for the Moral Improvement of Negroes on Plantations" (1833). I am grateful to Dr. R. F. Saunders, Jr., for calling to my attention and sharing with me a copy of this pamphlet by Thomas S. Clay.

34. MT to MF, July 28, 1833, WFC, Item 58.

35. MT to MF, February 26 [1843], WFC, Item 112.

9. The 1820's *pages 153–178*

1. MT to MF: August 20, 1811, WFC, Item 3; March 28 [1818], WFC, Item 131; April 14, no year, WFC, Item 132; October 11 [1818], WFC, Item 258; March 15, 1820, WFC, Item 19; no date and a week later December 8 [1819], WFC, Item 289; Chambers-Schiller, *Liberty: A Better Husband*, 112; MT to MF, March 15, 1820, WFC, Item 19 (The reference undoubtedly was the old path at Wormsloe, which runs along the marsh, for the mile-long avenue of live oaks extending from the entrance archway was not planted until the 1890's.); Frances Few to Mary Garrettson, January 27 [1820], WFC, Item 150.

2. MT to MF, March 15, 1820, WFC, Item 19.

3. Mary Few Journal of European Tour, WFC, Items 373, 374, 375. William Few to His Excellency Albert Gallatin, October 12, 1821, Gallatin Collection 1821, Item 83, New-York Historical Society; MF to Albert Gallatin, Jr., October 14, 1822, Gallatin Collection, Box 77, Item 77, New-York Historical Society.

4. MT to MF, December 3 [1813], WFC, Item 134.

5. Family History, Chrystie Family Papers, New-York Historical Society; MT to MF: postmark April 29 [1823], WFC, Item 18; May 15 [1823], WFC, Item 217; postmark March 22 [1823], WFC, Item 219.

6. MT to MF, March 27, no year, WFC, Item 205.

7. MT to MF, November 10, 1822, WFC, Item 21.

8. Cuthbert: *Men of Mark in Georgia*, 2:235; Coulter, *Wormsloe*, 282, n. 51; MT to MF: postmark October 3 [1823], WFC, Item 216; October 3 [1823], WFC, Item 291; December 3, 1823, WFC, Item 22.

9. MT to MF, May 26 [1823], WFC, Item 15.

10. MT to MF, December 3, 1823, WFC, Item 22.

11. MT to MF, December 26 [1823], WFC, Item 16.

12. MT to MF: September 16 [1824], WFC, Item 23; May 26 [1823], WFC, Item 15.

13. Records bearing the names of the Telfair plantations are among the Telfair family papers at the Georgia Historical Society. TFP, Box 4, Folder 36, Items 91, 92, Folder 37, Items 93, 94; Box 5, Folders 38–51, Items 95–211. Albert M. Hillhouse, *A History of Burke County, Georgia, 1777–1950* (Swainsboro, Ga.: Magnolia Press; Spartanburg, S.C.: The Reprint Company, 1985), provided data on the place where the Telfairs had their most extensive land holdings as did Sherwin Cooper, "The Rural Settlement of the Savannah River Basin in Georgia" (Ph.D. diss., University of Michigan, 1959). The precise location of the Telfair plantations in Burke County was ascertained from a 1780 map that appears on the endsheets of Cashin and Robertson, *Augusta and the Revolution.* Independent evidence makes it clear that "Telfare's Plan" and "Telfare's Saw Mill," as written on this map, constituted spelling errors by the cartographer. A visit to the area revealed that once thriving plantations have been replaced by a second growth of trees, except on the site of a nuclear-powered electric generating facility on the Savannah River. An early nineteenth-century map of Chatham County at the Georgia Historical Society shows the precise locations of the Sharon and Sabine Fields plantations.

14. Eugene Genovese, "'Our Family, White and Black': Family and Household in the Southern Slaveholder's World View," in Bleser, ed., *In Joy and In Sorrow*, 69; 1880 article on Thomas S. Clay by Rev. John Winn, Clay Papers.

15. MT to MF, postmark January 15, no year, WFC, Item 169.

16. Elisha Cain to Alexander Telfair: February 7, 1830, TFP, Box 5, Folder 39, Item 113; August 3, 1830, TFP, Box 5, Folder 40, Item 117a; June 1, 1828, TFP, Box 5, Folder 38, Item 96; August 18, 1829, TFP, Box 5, Folder 39, Item 105; September 11, 1829, TFP, Box 5, Folder 39, Item 106; October 10, 1829, TFP, Box 5, Folder 39, Item 107; June 2, 1826, TFP, Box 5, Folder 38, Item 95; February 18, 1831, TFP, Box 5, Folder 40, Item 119; May 4, 1830, TFP, Box 5, Folder 40, Item 115; July 22, 1829, TFP, Box 5, Folder 38, Item 104; June 2, 1826, TFP, Box 5, Folder 38, Item 95; May 4, 1831, TFP, Box 5, Folder 40, Item 122; November 17, 1829, TFP, Box 5, Folder 39, Item 110, November 22, 1829, TFP, Box 5, Folder 39, Item 111; reward: *Georgian*, January 22, 1831.

17. MT to MF: December 3, 1823, WFC, Item 22; March 14 [1825], WFC, Item 24; April 6 [1825], WFC, Item 25.

18. MT to MF: February 28, 1826, WFC, Item 26; postmark July 1 [1814], WFC, Item 14; June 9 [1833], WFC, Item 52.

19. MT to MF: no date [winter 1828], WFC, Item 56; January 25, 1828, WFC, Item 31; February 5 [1828], WFC, Item 32.

20. MT to MF, January 25, 1828, WFC, Item 31. The gentleman referred to probably is Mr. David Urquhart, a wealthy planter who was born in Scotland in 1779. His wife was Catharine Brooks Garterey MacGhee of Prince Edward County, Virginia. One of their ten children, Dr. John A. Urquhart, became a prominent physician in Columbus, Georgia. Urquhart genealogical file, Hartridge Collection.

21. MT to MF, November 12, no year, WFC, Item 137.

22. MT to MF, February 5, no year, WFC, Item 183.

23. *Ibid.*

24. MT to MF: January 29 [1830], WFC, Item 201; January 6 [1830], WFC, Item 204.

25. MT to MF, June 11, 1832, WFC, Item 46.

26. MT to MF, July 24, no year, WFC, Item 292.

27. TFP, Box 5, Folder 58, Item 209. A copy of the Thorn Island rules is set forth in full as Appendix B.

28. Elisha Cain to MT, October 25, 1833, TFP, Box 5, Folder 40, Item 123; Cooper, "The Rural Settlement of the Savannah River Basin in Georgia," 86.

29. Joseph Gaston Baillie Bulloch, M.D., *A History and Genealogy of the Habersham Family* (Columbia, S.C.: R. L. Bryan Company, 1901).

30. Alexander Telfair to Robert Habersham, July 10, 1823, R. & J. Habersham Papers, Georgia Historical Society Manuscript Collection No. 243 (hereinafter "R. & J. Habersham Papers"), Item 10.

31. Alexander Telfair to Robert Habersham, August 25, 1823, R. & J. Habersham Papers, Item 18.

32. *Georgian*, March 30, 1831.

33. Telfair appointed Associate Justice: *Georgian*, May 6, 1828; member of Union Society: *Bethesda: A Historical Sketch* (Savannah: J. M. Cooper, 1860), 17 [pamphlet at Georgia Historical Society]; member of St. Andrew's Society: Thomas H. Gignilliat, John A. Varnedoe, and A. Leopold Alexander, *History of the St. Andrew's Society of Savannah, Georgia* (Savannah: Kennickell, 1950), 15; dueling: Thomas Gamble, Jr., *Savannah Duels and Duelists, 1733–1877* (Savannah: Review Publishing & Printing Co., 1923; reprint, Spartanburg, S.C.: The Reprint Company, 1974), 186.

34. MT to MF, September 16 [1824], WFC, Item 23.

35. MT to MF, March 14 [1825], WFC, Item 24.

36. Lafayette's visit: Harden, *History of Savannah and South Georgia*, 297–310.

37. *Men of Mark in Georgia,* 2:140; Alexander R. MacDonell, "John Macpherson Berrien," *Georgia Historical Quarterly* 17, no. 1 (March 1933): 1–12. One of Berrien's sons related a tale involving Justice James Moore Wayne and his father. As a boy, the younger Berrien suffered from a speech impediment. When Berrien mentioned his son's problem to Wayne, the Justice lifted the little fellow to his knee, saying: "Let the boy alone. He'll talk all right. His tongue will wag in the middle and honey will drip from his lips." For years, young Berrien awaited the literal fulfillment of the miracle of honey dripping from his mouth, not realizing until later that it was a sly dig at Chief Justice Marshall's comment on his father's eloquence.

38. *Georgian*, May 6, 1831

39. The Eaton affair: Samuel Eliot Morison, *The Oxford History of the American People* (New York: Oxford University Press, 1965), 427–29; John F. Marszalek, *The Petticoat Affair: Manners, Mutiny, and Sex in Andrew Jackson's White House* (New York: The Free Press, 1997).

40. MT to MF, July 7, 1834, WFC, Item 62; Kollock incident and Snodgrass: Lowrey Axley, *Holding Aloft the Torch: A History of the Independent Presbyterian Church of Savannah, Georgia* (Savannah: Pigeonhole Press, 1958), 33–35, 52; Alexander Telfair named chairman: *Georgian*, January 28, 1828, March 4, 1828.

41. MT to MF, December 3, 1823, WFC, Item 22; Axley, *Holding Aloft the Torch*, 52–57; MT to MF, March 27 [1828], WFC, Item 281.

42. Rev. Daniel Baker to James Handy, May 12, 1828, quoted in Axley, *Holding Aloft the Torch*, 58; MT to MF, March 27 [1828], WFC, Item 281.

43. MT to MF, January 29 [1830], WFC, Item 201.

44. MT to MF, February 5, no year, WFC, Item 183.

45. MT to MF, no date [summer 1827], WFC, Item 290; MT to "the firm of Few," no date, WFC, Item 293.

46. MT to MF, August 9, 1827, WFC, Item 29.

47. MT to MF, August 28, no year, WFC, Item 234.

48. MT to MF, October 14, 1827, WFC, Item 30.

49. Mrs. Telfair: Christ Church records; Colonel Few: *Augusta Chronicle and Georgia Advertiser*, August 2, 1828; MT to MF, June 19 [1817], WFC, Item 8.

50. MT to MF: March 5, 1829, WFC, Item 35; January 29, no year [pre-1832], files of Telfair Museum of Art.

51. MT to MF, June 29 [1828], WFC, Item 104.

52. *Ibid.*

53. MT to MF: April 3, 1831, WFC, Item 44; February 6 [1831], WFC, Item 180; March 15 [1831], WFC, Item 214.

54. MT to MF: March 15 [1831], WFC, Item 214; February 6 [1831], WFC, Item 180.

55. MT to MF: March 15 [1831], WFC, Item 214; April 3, 1831, WFC, Item 44; February 6 [1831], WFC, Item 180; March 15 [1831], WFC, Item 214; May 24 [1831], WFC, Item 174.

56. Obituary: *Georgian*, October 20, 1832.

57. Chatham Academy address: TFP, Box 9, Folder 78, Item 310F. The charter granted to Chatham Academy on December 8, 1791, was signed by William Gibbons as speaker of the house (son of Joseph Gibbons and brother of Thomas) and by Edward Telfair as governor.

58. Mary Savage Anderson et al., *Georgia: A Pageant of Years* (Richmond, Va.: Garrett & Massie, 1933; reprint, Spartanburg, S.C.: The Reprint Company, 1974), 100 (page citation is to the reprint edition).

59. George Washington centennial address: TFP, Box 9, Folder 78, Item 310; MT to MF, postmark March 6 [1832], WFC, Item 202; J. Marshall to Alexander Telfair, February 24, 1832, TFP, Box 9, Folder 78, Item 310B. Washington had actually been born on February 11, 1732, as reckoned by the old Julian calendar. When Pope Gregory XIII set the calendar straight in 1572 by bringing it into line with the solar year, he ordained that October 4 was to be followed by October 15. Because the reform came from Rome, Protestant England, and later the American colonies, refused to go along and adopt the Gregorian calendar. Not until 1752 were they persuaded to make the change. It was only then that George Washington began celebrating his birthday on February 22.

60. MT to MF: June 11, 1832, WFC, Item 46; July 7, 1832, WFC, Item 47; July 23 [1832], WFC, Item 225; August 5 [1832], WFC, Item 226; August 12 [1832], WFC, Item 227.

10. A Season of Sorrow, a Time to Heal
pages 179–195

1. MT to MF, [September] 25, 1832, WFC, Item 48; obituary: *The Georgian*, October 20, 1832.

2. TFP, Box 9, Folder 78, Item 308. Alexander's gravesite is Plot No. 198 in the old section of Mount Hebron Cemetery. There is a raised ledger monument over

the grave, a flat marble tablet on which the inscription has been largely worn away by the elements.

3. MT to MF, November 11 [1832], WFC, Item 283.

4. "Extract from Miss Eastburn's Journal sent to me in a season of sorrow by my friend Mary Few, 1832": TFP, Box 5, Folder 53, Item 227; MT to MF, January 4 [1833], WFC, Item 179; meditation: TFP, Box 5, Folder 53, Item 227.

5. MT to MF: March 22, 1833, WFC, Item 50; April 29 [1833], WFC, Item 37; July 9, 1833, WFC, Item 57.

6. MT to MF, July 9, 1833, WFC, Item 57.

7. MT to MF: June 9 [1833], WFC, Item 52; July 28, 1833, WFC, Item 58. Eliza Cecil Hunter was the daughter of James Hunter and Eliza Tuten Cecil Hunter.

8. MT to MF, July 3, 1833, WFC, Item 53.

9. *Ibid.*

10. MT to MF, July 9 1833, WFC, Item 57.

11. MT to MF, August 29 [1833], WFC, Item 152.

12. *Ibid.*

13. MT to MF, August 22 [1833], WFC, Item 122. John Milledge (1757–1818) served as governor of Georgia from 1802 to 1806. He had been an officer in the Revolutionary War and was attorney general of Georgia (1780) and a member of the United States House of Representatives (1795–99) before becoming governor. Later (1806–09) he represented Georgia in the United States Senate. *Men of Mark in Georgia*, 1:262; *Dictionary of Georgia Biography*, 2:714.

14. MT to MF, July 28, 1833, WFC, Item 58.

15. MT to MF: August 22 [1833], WFC, Item 122; October 20 [1833], WFC, Item 54.

16. Last will and testament dated June 26, 1828, of Alexander Telfair: Alexander Telfair probate file, Chatham County Probate Court; letters from overseer at the Retreat plantation (1833–40), TFP, Box 5, Folders 40, 41, Items 124–27; letters from overseers at the Mills plantation (1833–40), TFP, Box 5, Folders 45, 46, Items 157–72.

17. Elisha Cain to MT, December 14, 1840, TFP, Box 5, Folder 41, Item 127; MT to MF, March 29 [1835], WFC, Item 176; women and slaves: Clinton, *The Plantation Mistress*, 187; Elisha Cain to MT, December 14, 1840, TFP, Box 5, Folder 41, Item 127; MT to MF: postmark September 27, no year, WFC, Item 257; postmark January 15 [1838], WFC, Item 169; February 23, no year, WFC, Item 203.

18. George Jones to "My dear Cousin," TFP, Box 5, Folder 52, Item 216.

19. Habersham obituary: *Savannah Morning News*, September 21, 1899; Spencer Bidwell King, ed., *Ebb Tide: As Seen Through the Diary of Josephine Clay Habersham, 1863* (Athens: University of Georgia Press, 1958), introductory chapter entitled "Avon." On the sensitivity of Habersham's palate, see Malcolm Bell, Jr., "The Romantic Wines of Madeira," *Georgia Historical Quarterly* 38, no. 4 (December 1954): 335. None other than Henry Wadsworth Longfellow recognized Habersham's musical ability. They both occupied quarters at Mrs. Craigie's rooming house on Brattle Street in Cambridge. The poet, then a Harvard professor, had this to say of the young Harvard student: "Young Habersham, of Savannah, a friend of Mrs. Craigie, occupied the other front chamber. He was a skillful performer on the flute. Like piping birds, he took wing for the rice fields of the south when the cold weather came, and I remained alone with the widow in the castle." Samuel Longfellow, ed., *Life of Henry Wadsworth Longfellow With Extracts From His Journal*

and Correspondence (Boston, 1891), 1:264. See also William Harden, *Recollections of a Long and Satisfactory Life* (Savannah: Review Printing, 1934), 72.

20. MT to MF, January 3 [1834], WFC, Item 188. John Tillotson was first married in 1816. MF to Mary Garrettson, July 1816, WFC, Item 401.

21. MT to MF, April 29 [1833], WFC, Item 37: "Mary Telfair, now Mrs. Cobb, has a daughter."

22. MT to MF, April 6, 1832, WFC, Item 45. The reference is to John Gay (1685–1723), the English poet and playwright best known for *The Beggar's Opera*, a satire of Sir Robert Walpole and the court of George II.

23. MT to MF: August 22 [1833], WFC, Item 122; postmark September 11 [1833], WFC, Item 55.

24. MT to MF, May 12 [1834], WFC, Item 206.

25. MT to MF, May 23, 1834, WFC, Item 61.

26. MT to MF: March 18, 1834, WFC, Item 59; May 12 [1834], WFC, Item 206.

27. Her husband erected over her grave a white marble slab with the inscription, "Sacred to the memory of Sarah G. Cuthbert, Wife of Albert Cuthbert, who died 12th July 1834, at the age of 45 years." Edward F. Campbell to George J. Kollock, July 26, 1834, Kollock Letters, *Georgia Historical Quarterly* 31, no. 2 (June 1947): 155.

28. MT to MF, August 1 [1834], WFC, Item 63; Edward F. Campbell to George J. Kollock, July 26, 1834, Kollock Letters, *Georgia Historical Quarterly* 31, no. 2 (June 1947): 155.

29. MT to MF: August 20, 1834, WFC, Item 64; August 1 [1834], WFC, Item 63.

30. Mary Fenwick Kollock to George J. Kollock, August 2, 1834, Kollock Letters, *Georgia Historical Quarterly* 31, no. 3 (June 1747): 156. George Kollock was the younger son and Mary Kollock the daughter of Dr. Lemuel Kollock and Maria Campbell Kollock.

31. MT to MF, August 20, 1834, WFC, Item 64.

32. Biographical information on Justice Johnson: *Dictionary of American Biography,* 5:128–29; MT to MF, July 7, 1834, WFC, Item 62. It would not be until 1842 that Georgia's own Dr. Crawford Williamson Long would become the first surgeon to use ether as an anesthetic in a surgical procedure. He had observed the effects of the gas as a source of entertainment and decided to use it while removing a tumor from the neck of a patient. He succeeded in performing the surgery with little discomfort. He continued to use ether in surgical procedures and in 1849 published his findings in the *Southern Medical and Surgical Journal.* In recognition of his achievement, Dr. Long is one of two Georgians whose statues are on display in the United States Capitol.

33. MT to MF, August 1 [1834], WFC, Item 63.

34. MT to MF, July 7, 1834, WFC, Item 62.

35. MT to MF, August 1 [1834], WFC, Item 63.

36. *Ibid.*

37. MT to MF, May 23, 1834, WFC, Item 61; George Noble Jones to George J. Kollock, July 26, 1834, Kollock Letters, *Georgia Historical Quarterly* 31, no. 2 (June 1947): 156; Delia's health: Robert Hallowell Gardiner, *Early Recollections of Robert Hallowell Gardiner, 1782–1864* (Hallowell, Maine: White & Horne Company, 1936), 188–9; MT to MF: January 30, 1835, WFC, Item 66; May 18 [1835], WFC, Item 195.

38. MT to MF, May 18 [1835], WFC, Item 195.

39. MT to MF, August 20, 1834, WFC, Item 64.

11. So Many Changes   *pages 196–219*

1. MT to MF, November 3 [1834], WFC, Item 177; Bulloch biographical data: Joseph Gaston Baillie Bulloch, *A History and Genealogy of the Families of Bulloch and Stobo and Irvine of Cults* (Washington, D.C.: Byron S. Adams, 1911), 17–24; Joseph Gaston Baillie Bulloch, *A History and Genealogy of the Families of Bulloch, Stobo, Irvine, Douglass, Baillie, Lewis, Adams, Glen, Jones, Davis, Hunter, Etc.* (Savannah: Braid & Hutton, 1892), 11, 21, 111; Bulloch biographical file, Georgia Historical Society, including papers by Armstrong State College students Jan Flores and Angela M. Yglesias.

2. MT to MF: March 18, 1834, WFC, Item 59; November 3 [1834], WFC, Item 177.

3. MT to MF, December 11, 1834, WFC, Item 65.

4. MT to MF: January 30, 1835, WFC, Item 66; March 29 [1835], WFC, Item 176.

5. Biographical information on Richard West Habersham: Habersham biographical file, Georgia Historical Society; Hartridge Collection, Box 106, Folder 1,977. The person at the easel wearing a red hat in the foreground of Morse's painting is believed to be Richard West Habersham. David Tatham, "Samuel F. B. Morse's *Gallery of the Louvre*: The Figures in the Foreground," *The American Art Journal* 13, no. 4 (April 1981): 44.

6. MT to MF, December 11, 1834, WFC, Item 65.

7. MT to MF, January 30, 1835, WFC, Item 66.

8. Richard West Habersham, article on the Telfair Academy, *The Savannah Daily Times,* February 9, 1885.

9. Richard West Habersham, "The Telfairs Again," *Savannah Morning News,* October 26, 1884.

10. Richard West Habersham, "The Telfairs," *Savannah Morning News,* October 19, 1884.

11. MT to MF: postmark September 11 [1833], WFC, Item 55; January 31 [1834], WFC, Item 188.

12. Habersham, "The Telfairs."

13. Habersham, "The Telfairs Again."

14. MT to MF: postmark March 21 [1834], WFC, Item 199; June 1 [1834], WFC, Item 200.

15. MT to MF: February 23, no year, WFC, Item 203; postmark June 3, no year, WFC, Item 210.

16. MT to MF: January 30, 1835, WFC, Item 66; March 5, 1835, WFC, Item 67.

17. MT to MF, April 29 [1835], WFC, Item 197.

18. MT to MF, March 5, 1835, WFC, Item 67.

19. MT to MF, January 30 1835, WFC, Item 66.

20. MT to MF, March 5, 1835, WFC, Item 67.

21. MT to MF, March 30, 1839, WFC, Item 82.

22. MT to MF, April 29 [1835], WFC, Item 197.

23. Joseph Frederick Waring, *Cerveau's Savannah* (Savannah: Georgia Historical Society, 1973), 69; Mary Fenwick Kollock to George J. Kollock, Kollock Letters, *Georgia Historical Quarterly* 31, no. 2 (June 1947): 162; MT to MF, postmark September 28 [1835], WFC, Item 235.

24. Gardiner, *Early Recollections,* 189.

25. MT to MF, January 30, 1836, WFC, Item 68.

26. MT to MF: postmark September 28 [1835], WFC, Item 235; postmark December 22 [1835], WFC, Item 166. "Master Humphry's Clock" was a proposed series of tales by Charles Dickens, purporting to be told by Master Humphry, an old deformed clockmaker, who later appeared in *The Old Curiosity Shop*.

27. MT to MF: January 1836 [postmark January 16], WFC, Item 69; January 30, 1836, WFC, Item 68.

28. MT to MF, postmark December 22 [1835], WFC, Item 166. Martin Van Buren was Andrew Jackson's heir-apparent, and in the 1836 presidential campaign ran with Richard M. Johnson against Whig candidates William H. Harrison and Francis Granger. Mary Telfair's position favoring a National Bank may well have been influenced by her friendship with Nicholas Biddle, president of the Bank of the United States. The charter of that bank was scheduled to expire by its terms in 1836, and the issue was whether it would be renewed. Justice Moore's term briefly overlapped that of John Marshall, for 1835 was the last year that the great Chief Justice would sit on the Court.

29. MT to MF, November 12, no year, WFC, Item 137. Mrs. Wayne was the former Mary Johnson Campbell, daughter of Alexander Campbell of Richmond, Virginia, and stepdaughter of her mother's second husband, the Reverend Dr. Henry Kollock, the much beloved pastor of the Independent Presbyterian Church.

30. MT to MF: November 12, no year, WFC, Item 137; February 24 [1836], WFC, Item 198.

31. MT to MF, February 24 [1836], WFC, Item 198. The references are to William Ellery Channing, *Essays on Slavery* (Boston, 1835) or *Slavery* (Boston, 1836) and James T. Austin, *Remarks on Dr. Channing's Slavery* (Boston, 1835).

32. MT to MF, June [May] 18, 1836, WFC, Item 70.

33. *Ibid.*

34. George Noble Jones to George J. Kollock, May 31, 1836, Kollock Letters, *Georgia Historical Quarterly*, 31, no. 3 (September 1947): 195–96.

35. MT to MF, July 30 [1836], WFC, Item 264.

36. MT to MF, August 14, 1836, WFC, Item 71.

37. MT to MF, July 30 [1836], WFC, Item 264; Danny D. Smith and Earle G. Shettleworth, Jr., *Gardiner on the Kennebeck* (Dover, N.H.: Arcadia Publishing, Images of America Series, 1996), 7–10.

38. MT to MF, August 14, 1836, WFC, Item 71.

39. MT to MF: August 14, 1836, WFC, Item 71; September 11, 1836, WFC, Item 72; postmark August 22 [1836], WFC, Item 261; September 5 [1836], WFC, Item 262.

40. William Douglass Branch, *The Sentimental Years: 1836–1860* (New York: Appleton-Century, 1934), 73–83.

41. MT to MF, September 11, 1836, WFC, Item 72.

42. MT to MF: postmark April 25, no year, WFC, Item 196; June [May] 18, 1836, WFC, Item 70; November 14, 1836, WFC, Item 73; May 23 [1844], WFC, Item 110.

43. MT to MF: November 14, 1836, WFC, Item 73; postmark December 13 [1836], WFC, Item 116.

44. MT to MF: April 6, 1837, WFC, Item 74; June 1, 1837, WFC, Item 77.

45. MT to MF: April 25, 1837, WFC, Item 75; March 18, 1838, WFC, Item 49.

12. Financial Panic and Tragedy at Sea
pages 220–237

1. MT to MF: April 25, 1837, WFC, Item 75; December 13 [1843], WFC, Item 108; March 1, [1840], WFC, Item 106; June 1, 1837, WFC, Item 77.

2. MT to MF: June 1, 1837, WFC, Item 77; April 25, 1837, WFC, Item 75; November 28, 1837, WFC, Item 79.

3. MT to MF: May 15, no year, WFC, Item 194; postmark June 3, no year, WFC, Item 210; May 23, 1838, WFC, Item 81.

4. MT to MF, postmark December 15 [1839], WFC, Item 161.

5. MT to MF: June 1, 1837, WFC, Item 77; May 23, 1838, WFC, Item 81.

6. MT to MF, January 26, 1840, WFC, Item 86.

7. MT to MF, postmark December 13 [1836], WFC, Item 116.

8. MT to MF, April 13, 1840, WFC, Item 92. Coelebs is the hero of a novel by Hannah More entitled *Coelebs in Search of a Wife* (1809), and "Coelebs' Wife" was a term for a bachelor's ideal of a model wife.

9. Frances Few Chrystie to MT, postmark March 2, no year, TFP, Box 5, Folder 52, Item 221.

10. MT to MF, June 1, 1837, WFC, Item 77.

11. MT to MF: Saturday 30th [postmark September 30], 1837, WFC, Item 78; June 1, 1837, WFC, Item 77; Martha Gallaudet Waring, ed., "Charles Seton Hardee's Recollections of Old Savannah," Part 1, *Georgia Historical Quarterly* 12, no. 4 (December 1928): 376, 378–79.

12. MT to MF: May 12 [1834], WFC, Item 206; April 25, 1837, WFC, Item 75; November 16 [1839], WFC, Item 157; March 18, 1841, WFC, Item 96; Saturday 30th [postmark September 30], 1837, WFC, Item 78.

13. Biographical data on Bethune: *Dictionary of American Biography*, 1:229; MT to MF: January 3, no year, WFC, Item 189; Saturday 30th [postmark September 30], 1837, WFC, Item 78; postmark October 23, no year, WFC, Item 242; Wednesday 25th [postmark October 26] [1837], WFC, Item 247; October 27 [1842], WFC, Item 240.

14. MT to MF, postmark October 23, no year, WFC, Item 242. *Old Mortality* is a novel by Sir Walter Scott published in 1816.

15. MT to MF: Saturday 30th [postmark September 30], 1837, WFC, Item 78; August 2, 1839, WFC, Item 84.

16. MT to MF, October 29, no year, WFC, Item 118.

17. MT to MF: November 28, 1837, WFC, Item 79; December 12, 1837, WFC, Item 80.

18. MT to MF: April 6, 1837, WFC, Item 74; November 12, no year, WFC, Item 137; June 6 [possibly 1813], WFC, Item 135; November 26 [1814], WFC, Item 7; June 19 [1817], WFC, Item 8.

19. Carroll Smith-Rosenberg and Charles Rosenberg, "The Female Animal: Medical and Biological Views of Woman and Her Role in Nineteenth-Century America," *Journal of American History* 60 (1973): 332; MT to MF, October 14, 1827, WFC, Item 30.

20. MT to MF: postmark February 17, no year, WFC, Item 114; June 6 [possibly

1813], WFC, Item 135; November 12, no year, WFC, Item 137; December 26 [1823], WFC, Item 16; October 13, no year, WFC, Item 295.

21. MT to MF, February 7 [1838], WFC, Item 209.

22. MT to MF, March 30, 1839, WFC, Item 82. Bolton biographical data: Henry Carrington Bolton and Reginald Pelham Bolton, *The Family of Bolton in England and America, 1100–1894* (New York: privately printed, 1895), ch. 17.

23. MT to MF, March 18, 1838, WFC, Item 49.

24. MT to MF: Wednesday 25th [postmark October 26] [1837], WFC, Item 247; May 23, 1838, WFC, Item 81.

25. MT to MF: Wednesday 25th [postmark October 26] [1837], WFC, Item 247; postmark November 25 [1837], WFC, Item 165; Waring, ed., "Hardee's Recollections of Old Savannah," Part 1, 376–77; Harden, *History of Savannah and South Georgia,* 336. For an eyewitness account by a survivor, see Rebecca Lamar McLeod, "The Loss of the Steamer *Pulaski,*" *Georgia Historical Quarterly* 3, no. 1 (March 1919): 63–95.

26. Waring, ed., "Hardee's Recollections of Old Savannah," Part 1, 377–78.

27. MT to MF: June 20, 1838, WFC, Item 167; postmark June 6 [1838], WFC, Item 164; postmark June 27 [1838], WFC, Item 160.

28. MT to MF: postmark June 27 [1838], WFC, Item 160; June 20, 1838, WFC, Item 167.

29. MT to MF, postmark June 27 [1838], WFC, Item 160.

30. MT to MF, postmark November 21 [1838], WFC, Item 158.

31. *Ibid.*

32. MT to MF: [December 24, 1838], WFC, Item 163; February 7 [1838], WFC, Item 209; postmark December 15 [1839], WFC, Item 161.

33. MT to MF, [December 24, 1838], WFC, Item 163.

34. MT to MF, postmark January 15, no year, WFC, Item 169. Mrs. Hunter, the former Ann Bulloch, was the sister of Catharine Bulloch's husband. The gentlemen may have been enjoying the custom of hunting on Christmas Day.

35. MT to MF, [December 24, 1838], WFC, Item 163.

13. Ordinary Pleasures   *pages 238–257*

1. MT to MF: April 29 [1833], WFC, Item 37; postmark November 21 [1838], WFC, Item 158.

2. MT to MF, February 7 [1838], WFC, Item 209.

3. Commonplace book, 1833–40, TFP, Box 6, Folder 60, Item 258.

4. MT to MF, August 2, 1839, WFC, Item 84. The Minis family traced its origin in Georgia to July 11, 1733, when a ship filled with Jews financed by a London synagogue was allowed by Oglethorpe to anchor in Savannah harbor.

5. *Ibid.*

6. *Ibid.*

7. *Ibid.* George Noble Jones's Newport cottage is described in *A Guide to Newport Mansions* (The Preservation Society of Newport County, 1984). A visit to the house, now called Kingscote, provided few insights into Jones's lifestyle as the contents on display belonged to the King family, the subsequent owners of the house. Design of Gardiner mansion: Smith and Shettleworth, *Gardiner on the Kennebec,* 35.

8. MT to MF, August 2, 1839, WFC, Item 84. The town of Newport is the county seat of the Isle of Wight.

9. *Ibid.*

10. TFP, Box 5, Folder 55, Item 243.

11. MT to MF, postmark October 27 [1839], WFC, Item 236.

12. MT to MF: postmark November 17 [1839], WFC, Item 157; postmark December 15 [1839], WFC, Item 161.

13. MT to MF, postmark November 17 [1839], WFC, Item 157.

14. MT to MF, January 26, 1840, WFC, Item 86.

15. *Ibid.*

16. MT to MF: January 25, 1840, WFC, Item 85; April 13, 1840, WFC, Item 92. Henry Peter Brougham, Baron Brougham and Vaux (1778–1868), who served in Parliament and rose to be Lord Chancellor of England, wrote *Historical Sketches of Statesmen in the Time of George III*. He is best known as one of the founders of the *Edinburgh Review*. The brougham, a one-horse closed carriage, was named for him.

17. MT to MF, January 25, 1840, WFC, Item 85.

18. MT to MF, April 5, 1840, WFC, Item 88.

19. *Ibid.*

20. MT to MF, May 28, no year, WFC, Item 170.

21. MT to MF, April 5, 1840, WFC, Item 88.

22. MT to MF: postmark May 17 [1840], WFC, Item 94; May 27, 1840, WFC, Item 93. As indicated by Mary Telfair's description of the ceremony, it was not the custom at the time for a bride to be escorted down the aisle by her father to be joined by the groom at the altar. Two years later, George's sister Fenwick married Robert Hollowell Gardiner II, his first wife's brother. The wedding took place at Trinity Church in Newport on May 28, 1842.

23. MT to MF: May 27, 1840, WFC, Item 93; postmark June 6 [1840], WFC, Item 241.

24. MT to MF: May 27, 1840, WFC, Item 93; postmark June 6 [1840], WFC, Item 241.

25. MT to MF: postmark June 14 [1840], WFC, Item 237; May 27, 1840, WFC, Item 93.

26. MT to MF, postmark November 11 [1840], WFC, Item 89.

27. *Ibid.*

28. *Ibid.*

29. MT to MF, February 22, 1841, WFC, Item 95.

30. Accompanies MT to MF, postmark January 15, no year, WFC, Item 169.

31. MT to MF, March 18, 1841, WFC, Item 96.

32. MT to MF, postmark March 3 [1841], WFC, Item 211. The Reverend William Meade, third bishop of Virginia, had been a year behind Alexander Telfair at Princeton. When Bishop Meade died in March 1862, Bishop Elliott would become the senior active, and thus "presiding," bishop in the Protestant Episcopal Church in the Confederate States.

33. MT to MF, February 22, 1841, WFC, Item 95.

34. MT to MF, postmark May 14 [1841], WFC, Item 213.

35. William Hodgson to President John Tyler (edited preliminary draft), TFP, Box 17, Folder 144, Item 577.

36. MT to MF, postmark July 2 [1841], WFC, Item 121. The references are to

Senators Henry Clay of Kentucky, Thomas H. Benton of Missouri, William C. Rives of Virginia, and James Buchanan of Pennsylvania.

37. *Ibid.*

38. *Ibid.*

39. *Ibid.*

14. Travel and Romance   *pages 258–279*

1. TFP, Box 5, Folder 52, Item 212. Unlike the passports issued today, this document consisted of a large, single sheet that was folded several times and, in the words of the printed form, offered the protection of the various United States consulates. There being no passport photographs at the time, the document contained a form to fill out with a description of the person to whom it was issued. Thus is Mary Telfair described: "Age - 40; Stature - 5 Feet . . . Inches; Forehead - High; Eyes - Black; Nose - Roman; Mouth - Medium; Chin - Prominent; Hair - Black; Complexion - Dark; Face - Oval." Age 40? Mary Telfair was born in 1791. Even a Christian lady such as Telfair was not above fibbing about her age.

2. MT to Wm. Neyle Habersham, October 8, 1841, TFP, Box 19, Folder 174, Item 668. (Habersham was married to his cousin Josephine C. Habersham on June 23, 1840, at Christ Church by the Reverend Edward Neufville.); Frances Chrystie to Mary Garrettson, November 19, 1841, WFC, Item 517.

3. Albert Chrystie and Frances Chrystie to Mary Chrystie at school in New Rochelle: July 30, 1840, WFC, Item 501; September 5, 1840, WFC, Item 504; Albert Chrystie to Mary Chrystie, September 29, 1840, WFC, Item 508; MF to Mary Garrettson, September 28, 1841, WFC, Item 315.

4. Frances Chrystie to Mary Garrettson, November 19, 1841, WFC, Item 517; entry under picture of Nettley Abbey, Southampton, in Mary Telfair's 1841–42 Travel Journal (unpaginated), TFP, Box 7, Folder 63, Item 261.

5. Frances Chrystie to Mary Garrettson, November 19, 1841, WFC, Item 517; visa on Telfair passport.

6. William B. Hodgson to President John Tyler (edited preliminary draft), TFP, Box 17, Folder 144, Item 577.

7. Hodgson's personal copy of *Lucian's Dialogues*, with the inscription "Begun and finished Lucian's dialogues in three months, 1814," TFP, Box 17, Folder 140, Item 563.

8. Biographical information on William Brown Hodgson: Leonard L. Mackall, "William Brown Hodgson," *Georgia Historical Quarterly* 15, no. 4 (December 1931): 324–45; Thomas A. Brazen, *An American Consular Officer in the Middle East in the Jacksonian Era: A Biography of William Brown Hodgson, 1801–1871* (Atlanta: Resurgent Publications, 1979); David H. Finnie, *Pioneers East: The Early American Experience in the Middle East* (Cambridge, Harvard University Press, 1967); Thomas A. Brazen, "William Brown Hodgson's Mission to Egypt, 1834," *West Georgia College Studies in the Social Sciences* 11 (June 1972): 10–17; *Dictionary of Georgia Biography*, 1:464; Hodgson's 1835 Journal of trip to Morocco: TFP, Box 17, Folder 142, Item 567. The biographical file on Hodgson at the Georgia Historical Society contains two unpublished term papers on the man and his career by Charles J. Morley, then a history student at Armstrong State College: "William B. Hodgson, Too Much to Summarize" (1985) and "I However Shall Do My Duty: the Diplomatic Career of

William Brown Hodgson" (1986). Among the Floyd Papers at the Georgia Historical Society is a manuscript by Dolores Boisfeuillet Colquitt (Floyd) entitled "W. B. Hodgson had Claim to Other Distinctions than as Husband of Margaret Telfair" (hereinafter "Colquitt Manuscript"), Papers of Marmaduke Hamilton Floyd and Dolores Boisfeuillet Floyd, Georgia Historical Society Manuscript Collection No. 1,308 (hereinafter "Floyd Papers"), Folder 623.

9. MT to MF, July 2, 1842, WFC, Item 97. The itinerary of the Telfair sisters can be determined from dated visas on the Telfair passport.

10. Family History, Chrystie Family Papers, New-York Historical Society; Matilda Tillotson to Mary Garrettson, postmark May 9 [1842], WFC, Item 150A.

11. Hodgson's pocket notebook: TFP, Box 17, Folder 144, Item 576.

12. *Ibid.*

13. Pitti Palace: *Ibid.* Hodgson's itinerary from Malta to Geneva, where he arrived on June 16, 1842, can be traced by visas on his passport issued in Malta on May 24, 1842, TFP, Box 17, Folder 144, Item 574. The circumstances of Hodgson's meeting with Margaret Telfair and his marriage to her in London are set forth in edited drafts of his letters addressed to Secretary of State Daniel Webster, dated July 2, 1842, and to President John Tyler, dated July 3, 1842, in which Hodgson explains the reason for his resignation as counsel general in Tunis, TFP, Box 17, Folder 144, Items 575, 577. Marriage ceremony: Marriage records of St. George's Church on microfiche at City of Westminster Archives, London; MT to MF, July 13 [1842], WFC, Item 98; *Savannah Daily Georgian*, August 5, 1842; *Dictionary of Georgia Biography*, 1:464. It was the same St. George's on Hanover Square that Alfred P. Doolittle in *My Fair Lady* asked his friends to get him to on time. Act Two, Scene 3: "I say, you want to come and see me turned off this mornin'? St. George's, Hanover Square, ten o'clock." Other notables who were married at St. George's Church include Benjamin Disraeli and, for the second time, Theodore Roosevelt.

14. MT to MF, July 13 [1842], WFC, Item 98.

15. MT to MF, July 2, 1842, WFC, Item 97.

16. MT to MF, July 13 [1842], WFC, Item 98; Catherine Few to Mrs. Garrettson, August 6, 1841 [1842], WFC, Item 521; MT to MF, July 2, 1842, WFC, Item 97.

17. George Noble Jones to George J. Kollock, August 15, 1842, Kollock Letters, *Georgia Historical Quarterly* 31, no. 4 (December 1947): 311; MF to Mary Garrettson, August 6, 1842 [add-on to mother's letter to Mrs. Garrettson], WFC, Item 521.

18. Entries under pictures of Windsor Castle and Oxford in Mary Telfair's 1841–42 Travel Journal; MT to MF July 13 [1842], WFC, Item 98.

19. MT to MF, September 25 [1842], WFC, Item 259.

20. *Ibid.*

21. Entry under picture of ruins of Kenilworth Castle and entry under picture of Nettley Abbey, Southampton, both in Mary Telfair's 1841–42 Travel Journal.

22. MT to MF, September 25 [1842], WFC, Item 259; William B. Hodgson to Charles Durand of M. M. Goodhue & Co., New York, September 20, 1842, William B. Hodgson Papers, Georgia Historical Society Manuscript Collection No. 388 (hereinafter "Hodgson Papers, GHS"), Folder 1, Item 1; MT to MF, October 18 [1842], WFC, Item 90.

23. MT to MF, October 18 [1842], WFC, Item 90.

24. *Ibid.*; MT to MF, September 25 [1842], WFC, Item 259.

25. MT to MF: postmark October 27 [1842], WFC, Item 240; November 13

[1842], WFC, Item 168; postmark November 21 [1842], WFC, Item 245; December 12 [1842], WFC, Item 156.

26. MT to MF, December 12 [1842], WFC, Item 156. With respect to Mary Telfair's perception of the attitude of the house slaves to the family, without minimizing the indignity inherent in being placed in involuntary servitude, it should be noted that Mary Telfair did treat her servants kindly. Referring to an occasion when Judy, a household servant, accompanied the family to the North, she wrote: "She tells her comrades here that she was very much pleased with her northern summer—every body was kind to her—I hope that it will be an inducement to her to repeat it. We never compel any of them to do what will make them unhappy." MT to MF, postmark November 17 [1839], WFC, Item 157.

27. Notes taken by Mrs. Dolores Floyd in an interview with William Harden, February 20, 1934, in regard to his recollections of the Telfairs (hereinafter "Harden interview"), Floyd Papers, Folder 620; MT to MF, November 13 [1842], WFC, Item 168.

28. MT to MF: November 13 [1842], WFC, Item 168; postmark December 12 [1842], WFC, Item 156.

29. Charles C. Jones, "Life and Character of Miss Anne Clay" (Boston: Press of Crocker and Brewster, 1844), collection of Carolyn Clay Swiggart; MT to MF, February 26 [1843], WFC, Item 112. I thank Ms. Swiggart for sharing with me a transcript of the pamphlet in her collection containing the tribute to Anne Clay.

30. MT to MF, postmark December 12 [1842], WFC, Item 156.

31. MT to MF, May 23 [1843], WFC, Item 110.

32. Brief of Testimony, 62.

33. MT to MF: July 4 [1843], WFC, Item 111; December 13 [1843], WFC, Item 108.

34. Frances Chrystie to Mary Garrettson, March 3, 1843, WFC, Item 518; Frances Chrystie to MT, December 23, 1843, TFP, Box 5, Folder 52, Item 217.

35. MT to MF, February 10, 1843, WFC, Item 100.

36. MT to MF, postmark December 12 [1842], WFC, Item 156.

37. MT to MF, May 23 [1843], WFC, Item 110.

38. Mackall, "William Brown Hodgson," 326–27.

39. Hodgson's January 9, 1843, Certificate of Membership in Georgia Historical Society: TFP, Box 17, Folder 146, Item 579; invitation to lecture at Historical Society, September 15, 1843: William B. Hodgson Papers, Special Collections Library, Duke University (hereinafter "Hodgson Papers, Duke"); William Harden, "The Georgia Historical Society," *Georgia Historical Quarterly* 1, no. 1 (March 1917): 8; Mackall, "William Brown Hodgson," 327; Brazen, *An American Consular Officer in the Middle East in the Jacksonian Era*, 138–41.

40. Colquitt Manuscript; information on Bilali: William S. McFeeley, *Sapelo's People* (New York: W. W. Norton and Co., 1994); Harden, *Recollections of a Long and Satisfactory Life*, 83.

41. Pierce Butler to William B. Hodgson, July 13, 1861, Hodgson Papers, GHS, Folder 1, Item 3; biographical data on King: Stephen Berry, "More Alluring at a Distance: Absentee Patriarchy and the Thomas Butler King Family," *Georgia Historical Quarterly* 81, no. 4 (Winter 1997): 863–96; T. Butler King to William B. Hodgson, February 28, 1848, Hodgson Papers, Duke.

42. J. Hamilton Couper to William B. Hodgson, November 22, 1843, February

18, 1844, March 12, 1844, June 9, 1844, Hodgson Papers, Duke; Sir Charles Lyell, *A Second Visit to the United States of North America*, 2 vols. (New York: Harper & Brothers, 1868), 1:234.

43. J. Hamilton Couper to William B. Hodgson, February 18, 1844 and November 18, 1846, Hodgson Papers, Duke; biographical data on Couper: T. Reed Ferguson, *The John Couper Family at Cannon's Point* (Macon, Ga.: Mercer University Press, 1994); *Men of Mark in Georgia*, 2:215; *Dictionary of Georgia Biography*, 1:223.

44. MT to MF, September 2 [1843], WFC, Item 154. Rev. James Hillhouse came to America from County Londonderry, Ireland, about 1720. His son William married Sarah Griswold, the sister of Matthew Griswold, and she bore James Hillhouse (1754–1832), who served in the Second, Third, and Fourth Congresses and was a three-term United States senator from Connecticut. His son, James Abraham Hillhouse (1789–1841), was a well-known poet. The family had strong ties to Georgia, as well as Connecticut. In 1787 the senator's brother, David Hillhouse, and his wife, the former Sarah Porter, moved from New Haven to the town of Washington in Wilkes County and there established a newspaper, the *Monitor and Impartial Observer*. Upon her husband's death, Mrs. Sarah Hillhouse became Georgia's first woman newspaper publisher and editor. She also ran her late husband's printing business and for a time published the Journal of the House of Representatives of Georgia. David and Sarah Hillhouse had a daughter, also named Sarah. She and Felix Gilbert were wed after the young man journeyed to New Haven to ask her late father's brother for permission to marry his niece. The Gilberts also had a daughter. Her education was perfected in New Haven, where she spent time with her intellectual and highly cultivated cousins. There she met Adam Alexander, a young Georgian who was studying at Yale. The two, she fourteen and he seventeen, soon were engaged. Three years later, on April 28, 1823, they were married at the old Gilbert home in Washington. They had ten children, and the second, Sarah Gilbert Alexander, married Alexander R. Lawton, the gentleman who years later would write Mary Telfair's last will and testament. Marion Alexander Boggs, ed., *The Alexander Letters, 1787–1900* (Savannah: privately printed, 1910; reprint, Athens: Brown Thrasher Books, University of Georgia Press, 1980), Introduction.

45. MT to MF, February 10, 1843, WFC, Item 100.

46. Mackall, "William Brown Hodgson," 327–28.

47. Entry dated December 12, 1847, Nicholas B. Wainwright, ed., *A Philadelphia Perspective: The Diary of Sidney George Fisher Covering the Years 1834–1871* (Philadelphia: Historical Society of Pennsylvania, 1967), 203.

15. Middle Age at Mid-Century   *pages 280–308*

1. MT to MF: February 10, 1843, WFC, Item 100; January 26, 1843, WFC, Item 99.

2. January 26, 1843, WFC, Item 99.

3. *Ibid.*

4. MT to MF, February 26 [1843], WFC, Item 112.

5. MT to MF, April 14 [1844], WFC, Item 102.

6. MT to MF, April 28 [1844], WFC, Item 103. See also Mrs. Jones to MT, April 1844 [postmark April 10], TFP, Box 5, Folder 52, Item 218. The April 28 [1844]

letter is the last dated or datable letter from Mary Telfair to Mary Few in the William Few Collection. The correspondence of the two friends did not terminate at this point. It is likely that subsequent letters have been lost. There is correspondence in February 1845 as evidenced by two letters from Mary Few to Mary Telfair among the Telfair Family Papers (Folder 52, Items 219, 220). There is a letter from Margaret Hodgson to Mary Few dated October 1, 1855, in the Hartridge Collection (Box 145, Folder 2,624), one from Matilda Tillitson to Mary Telfair dated November 21 [1860] among the Telfair Family Papers (Box 5, Folder 53, Item 223), and one from Mary Telfair to Mary Few dated January 1, 1861, in the Hartridge Collection (Box 145, Folder 2,624). Telfair writes of Mary Few's mind being in a "heavenly frame" in a 1858 letter to Eliza Terrell (Terrell Papers, Duke). Mary Few died in 1873, and Telfair continued her friendship with Frances Chrystie and Matilda Tillotson. She stayed at the homes of Frances and Matilda during the summer of 1874 (see Chapter Sixteen) and remembered both sisters in her will.

7. MT to MF, April 14 [1844], WFC, Item 102.

8. *Ibid.*

9. *Ibid.*; MT to MF, March 21, no year, WFC, Item 173.

10. MT to Eliza Terrell, February 9, 1856, William and Eliza Rhodes Terrell Papers, Special Collections Library, Duke University (hereinafter "Terrell Papers, Duke"); William K. Waldbridge to Jane A. Wright, Owens-Thomas House, May 27, 1958, Files of Telfair Museum of Art.

11. MT to MF, [spring 1844], WFC, Item 109. Frelinghuysen was a distinguished lawyer, attorney-general of New Jersey (1817–29), United States senator (1829–35), mayor of Newark (1837–38), and later chancellor of the University of the City of New York (1839–50) and president of Rutgers College (1850–61). He was noted for his Christian piety. Although never ordained, he usually was portrayed in political cartoons dressed in clerical garb. He studied at Princeton with Josiah and Thomas Telfair and was graduated second in the class of 1804. Biographical data on Frelinghuysen: *National Cyclopaedia of American Biography*, 3:401.

12. MT to MF, [spring 1844], WFC, Item 109.

13. MF to MT, February 5, 1845, TFP, Box 5, Folder 52, Item 219.

14. MF to MT, February 1845, TFP, Box 5, Folder 52, Item 220.

15. Obituary: *Georgian*, April 7, 1845: "DIED, on the 3d inst., at her residence in this town, Mrs. SARAH G. HAIG, relict of Captain George Haig, and daughter of the late Edward Telfair, Esq. of this State.

"The memory of the deceased is embalmed in the affections of her bereaved and afflicted family, and she will live in the remembrance of her friends. Sorrow and suffering had shed their blight upon her early life. Her constitution, by nature delicate, was gradually impaired; but under long and protracted disease, she evinced an unrepining and submissive patience. She gently sunk to rest, full of faith and trust in her Creator and Redeemer."

16. MT to MF: May 23 [1843], WFC, Item 110; [spring 1844], WFC, Item 109; MF to MT, February 5, 1845, TFP, Box 5, Folder 52, Item 219.

17. Biographical sketches of Dr. William Terrell: *Men of Mark in Georgia*, 2:377; *Dictionary of Georgia Biography*, 2:967. Terrell's affliction: William Terrell to William B. Hodgson, February 1845, Hodgson Papers, Duke. The Terrell Chair, oldest at the University of Georgia, is still occupied. The university's Terrell Hall is named in honor of Dr. Terrell.

18. Testimony of E. A. Soullard, Brief of Testimony, 35; testimony of Margaret E. Harden, Brief of Testimony, 70.

19. William Terrell to William B. Hodgson, January 26, 1848, Hodgson Papers, Duke.

20. MT to Eliza Terrell, February 1, 1848, Terrell Papers, Duke.

21. MT to MF, postmark February 17, no year, WFC, Item 114; MT to Eliza Terrell, February 1, 1848, Terrell Papers, Duke.

22. William Terrell to William B. Hodgson, January 26, 1848, Hodgson Papers, Duke.

23. William Terrell to William B. Hodgson, February 8, 1848, Hodgson Papers, Duke.

24. MT to MF, January 26, 1843, WFC, Item 99.

25. MT to Eliza Terrell, February 1, 1848, Terrell Papers, Duke.

26. Testimony of Augustus P. Wetter, Brief of Testimony, 37–39; testimony of George Gibbons [Telfair servant], Brief of Testimony, 35; testimony of Mrs. C. H. Cumming, Brief of Testimony, 68–69; testimony of Margaret E. Harden, Brief of Testimony, 69–70; testimony of Mrs. L. E. Waldburg, Brief of Testimony, 70; MT to Eliza Terrell, November 29 [1849], March 27, 1848, Terrell Papers, Duke.

27. William Terrell to William B. Hodgson, February 28, 1848, Hodgson Papers, Duke.

28. MT to Eliza Terrell, March 27, 1848, Terrell Papers, Duke; Mary Telfair's French notebooks: TFP, Box 5, Folder 56, Items 250–53; Mary Telfair's 1855 Travel Journal (two volumes, unpaginated), TFP, Box 7, Folder 65, Item 265 (volume one).

29. James Gardner, Jr., to William B. Hodgson, February 17, 1848; William Terrell to William B. Hodgson, August 19, 1849; Alexander R. Lawton to William B. Hodgson, June 20, 1850, Hodgson Papers, Duke.

30. MT to Eliza Terrell, November 29 [1849], Terrell Papers, Duke; concerning resignation: I. K. Tefft to William B. Hodgson, April 25, 1849, Hodgson Papers, Duke; mail to Brevoort Place: e.g., W. B. Daniell to William B. Hodgson, July 16, 1849; John R. Bartlett to William B. Hodgson, October 1849, March 21, 1850, Hodgson Papers, Duke.

31. William Terrell to William B. Hodgson, August 25, 1846, Hodgson Papers, Duke; MT to Eliza Terrell, November 29 [1849], Terrell Papers, Duke.

32. Cleveland Amory, *Who Killed Society?* (New York: Harper & Brothers, 1960) 118–21. The list of "the 400" appears in the forepart of Amory's book.

33. Gibbons genealogy: Hartridge Collection, Box 103, Folder 1,925; Ward McAllister, *Society as I Have Found It* (New York: Cassell Publishing Company, 1890; reprint, New York: Arno Press, 1975), 3–9.

34. McAllister, *Society*, 13–15.

35. Thomas Gibbons' will is on file at the Chatham County Probate Court. As if he had not made it sufficiently clear in the dozen prior statements that John M. Trumbull and his descendants were to have no part of his estate, Gibbons added near the end of his will, "And I do pray to that God before whom I am shortly to appear that I have been enabled so to devise and bequeath my whole Estate real and personal that no events may or possibly can arise in all the changes of this changing world that will enable John M. Trumbull or any one of his children or any person descended from him to be benefitted one cent or the value thereof from my Estate meaning, resolving and intending that they shall be forever excluded to the end of

time in as conclusive a manner as if the said John M. Trumbull had never been married and as if all his children by Ann Gibbons were illegitimates." Such bitterness hardly befitted a man who began his will with the pious words, "Being now weak in body but of sound mind preparing to meet the King of Terrors when he shall assail me in the feeble moments of departing life in the last severe and trying period that labouring hour of nature I do make this my last Will and Testament. First I recommend my soul to the mercy of my God through the intercession of my blessed Redeemer. Second I submit my body to the grave to be sealed up in expectation of a happy resurrection."

36. McAllister, *Society*, 7.

37. *Ibid.*, III.

38. *Ibid.*, 81–83.

39. *Ibid.*, 81–83.

40. *Ibid.*, 102–3.

41. In general, Richard H. Haunton, "Savannah in the 1850's" (Ph.D. diss., Emory University, 1968); gas works and waterworks: Harden, *History of Savannah and South Georgia*, 392–95; Martha Gallaudet Waring, ed., "Charles Seton Henry Hardee's Recollections of Old Savannah," Part 2, *Georgia Historical Quarterly* 13, no. 1 (March 1929): 46–47; riverfront improvements: Waring, *Cerveau's Savannah*, 14

42. Harden, *Recollections of a Long and Satisfactory Life*, 67–68, 80; Haunton, "Savannah in the 1850's," 27; Harden, *History of Savannah and South Georgia*, 410; Alexander R. Lawton to William B. Hodgson, June 20, 1850, Hodgson Papers, Duke.

43. This trip to Europe is described in detail in Mary Telfair's 1851–52 Travel Journal (three volumes, unpaginated), TFP, Box 7, Folders 63 and 64, Items 262, 263, 264. Except as otherwise indicated, descriptions and quotations relating to this trip are from this source.

44. MT to Eliza Terrell, January 17, 1857, Terrell Papers, Duke.

45. William B. Hodgson to Messrs. R. Habersham & Son, December 1, 1851, Hodgson Papers, Duke.

46. *Ibid.* The reference is to Henry Wikoff, the ward of a wealthy Philadelphian who was expelled from Yale as a young man, moved to Europe in 1834, and became an intimate of Fanny Elssler, the famous dancer. Jane Gamble was in her early forties when Wikoff pursued her. Milton Rugoff, *America's Gilded Age: Intimate Portraits from an Era of Extravagance and Change, 1850–1890* (New York: Henry Holt and Company, 1989), 180–81.

47. William B. Hodgson to Messrs. R. Habersham & Son, January 1, 1852 [continuation of December 1, 1851, letter], Hodgson Papers, Duke.

48. *Ibid.*

49. MT to Eliza Terrell, no date [1855], Terrell Papers, Duke.

16. Advancing Years and the Approach of War
pages 309–338

1. MT to Eliza Terrell, November 1, 1852, Terrell Papers, Duke.

2. *Ibid.* On Alberta and Arnold, see also MT to Eliza Terrell [at Mrs. Van Allen's, Murray Street, New York], no date [1850, Alberta sixteen], Terrell Papers, Duke.

3. MT to Eliza Terrell, May 4, no year, Terrell Papers, Duke. The Women's

Studies Archivist at the Special Collections Library at Duke University has included this letter and others written by Mary Telfair to Eliza Terrell in a list of "possible primary sources for the history of sex, sexuality and the construction of gender." Undoubtedly because of the reference to Sappho, the ancient poetess from the Greek island of Lesbos, some of Telfair's letters are said by the archivist to "allude to the scandalous conduct and lesbian tendencies of a particular acquaintance." In view of her demonstrated interest in men, it seems highly unlikely that a lesbian attachment on Alberta's part was the scandal of which all Savannah was talking. Although many of Sappho's love poems are addressed to women, she actually married and had a daughter. It is far more likely that Alberta's indiscretion was of a heterosexual nature. The reference to Jehu is to a king of Israel known for his furious chariot attacks.

4. MT to Eliza Terrell, February 9, 1856, Terrell Papers, Duke. Georgia law at the time prohibited the guilty party to a divorce suit from remarrying, but the legislature by granting a "relief" could remove the disability. These were granted routinely, as in the case of Charles Arnold. See Eleanor M. Boatwright, "The Political and Civil Status of Women in Georgia, 1783–1860," *Georgia Historical Quarterly* 25, no. 4 (December 1941): 301–24.

5. MT to Eliza Terrell, February 9, 1856, Terrell Papers, Duke.

6. William Terrell to William B. Hodgson, November 2, 1853, Hodgson Papers, Duke.

7. MT to Lucy Terrell, April 20, 1854, Terrell Papers, Duke.

8. MT to Lucy Terrell, June 18, 1854, Terrell Papers, Duke. Laura was the inspiration for Petrarch's series of poems, *Canzoniere*, or *Rime in Vita e Morta di Madonna Laura (Verses on the life and Death of My Lady Laura)*. Thetis was the chief of the Nereids, the sea nymphs of Greek mythology.

9. MT to Lucy Terrell, June 18, 1854, Terrell Papers, Duke.

10. *Ibid.*

11. MT to Lucy Terrell, January 13, 1855, Terrell Papers, Duke.

12. Obituary of Catherine Few by the Reverend Dr. DeWitt and Memoir by Frances Chrystie: TFP, Box 5, Folder 52, Item 213.

13. MT to Lucy Terrell, January 13, 1855, Terrell Papers, Duke; Family History, Chrystie Family Papers, New-York Historical Society.

14. MT to Lucy Terrell, January 13, 1855, Terrell Papers, Duke; MT to Eliza Terrell, no date [1855], Terrell Papers, Duke.

15. MT to Lucy Terrell, April 6, 1855, Terrell Papers, Duke. François de Salignac de La Mothe Fénelon was a French churchman and author who was attached to the royal court as a tutor to the Dauphin until exiled for his unorthodox advocacy of the mystic doctrines of Quietism. He was the author of a short treatise on the education of women.

16. This trip to Europe is described in Mary Telfair's 1855 Travel Journal (two volumes, unpaginated), TFP, Box 7, Folder 65, Items 265, 266. Unless otherwise indicated, descriptions and quotations relating to this European trip are from this source.

17. MT to Lucy Terrell, December 13 [1855], January 2, 1856, Terrell Papers, Duke. Margaret Hodgson to MF, October 1, 1855, Hartridge Collection, Box 145, Folder 2,624.

18. Certificate and medallion: TFP, Box 17, Folder 147, Items 586, 587; MT to Lucy Terrell, December 13 [1855], Terrell Papers, Duke.

19. MT to Eliza Terrell, [November] 31 [1855], November 24 [1855], Terrell Papers, Duke.

20. MT to Eliza Terrell, November 24 [1855], [November] 29 [1855], Terrell Papers, Duke.

21. MT to Eliza Terrell, [November] 31 [1855], Terrell Papers, Duke.

22. *Ibid.*

23. MT to Eliza Terrell, January 2, 1856, February 9, 1856, Terrell Papers, Duke.

24. MT to Lucy Terrell, December 13 [1855], January 2, 1856, Terrell Papers, Duke.

25. MT to Lucy Terrell, February 9, 1856, January 2, 1856, Terrell Papers, Duke.

26. MT to Lucy Terrell, February 1, 1856, Terrell Papers, Duke.

27. Family History, Chrystie Family Papers, New-York Historical Society.

28. MT to Eliza Terrell, December 13 [1855], January 2, 1856, January 17, 1857, Terrell Papers, Duke. On February 16, 1856, by legislative act, Terrell County, Georgia, was created from Lee and Randolph counties. The new county was named in honor of Dr. William Terrell, and its county seat, Dawson, was named for William Crosby Dawson, Edgar Dawson's father. This gentleman was a resident of Greensboro, Georgia, a distinguished lawyer and judge, a member of Congress (1836–41), and a United States senator (1849–55). Thus, the Terrell and Dawson families were joined geographically as well as by marriage.

29. MT to Eliza Terrell, January 17, 1857, Terrell Papers, Duke.

30. Chatham County Marriage Records; biographical information on Augustus P. Wetter: Hartridge Collection, Box 72, Folder 1,372; Wetter obituary, *Savannah Morning News*, September 9, 1882; MT to Eliza Terrell, no date [1858], Terrell Papers, Duke; testimony of Augustus P. Wetter, Brief of Testimony, 39.

31. MT to Eliza Terrell, no date [1858], Terrell Papers, Duke.

32. Testimony of Augustus P. Wetter, Brief of Testimony, 37–39.

33. MT to Eliza Terrell, no date [1858], Terrell Papers, Duke.

34. Joseph Hodgson to "My Dear Brother," Columbia, August 14, 1860, Columbia, August 21, 1860, Richmond, September 6, 1860, TFP, Box 17, Folder 148, Items 594, 595, 596; Joseph Hodgson, Jr., Pamphlet "Delivered at the Commencement of the Class of 1856 of the College of New Jersey, June 25," TFP, Box 17, Folder 149, Item 602; address to Jefferson Society: TFP Box 17, Folder 129, Item 602.

35. The Puritan and the Cavalier: TFP, Box 18, Folder 150, Item 608; study of Hebrew: Telfair Hodgson to William B. Hodgson, September 5, 1860, November 18, 1860, TFP, Box 17, Folder 149, Items 606, 607; walks with nephews: Hodgson obituary, TFP, Box 19, Folder 171, Item 652–2; Telfair Hodgson, "A Notebook of Facts and Gems," Hodgson biographical file, Georgia Historical Society. An introduction to this diary provided biographical information on Telfair Hodgson. See also Moultrie Guerry, *Men Who Made Sewanee*, ch. 5, "Telfair Hodgson, Third Vice-Chancellor" (as republished by Arthur Ben Chitty and Elizabeth Chitty; Sewanee, Tenn.: The University Press of the University of the South, 1981).

36. Mary Telfair's 1858 Journal: TFP, Box 7, Folder 66, Item 267.

37. Mary Telfair's friend was the wife of George Frederick Tilghmam Jones, who in 1847 changed his name to George Wymberly-Jones. In 1866, by order of the Superior Court of Chatham County, he added De Renne to his name. The new surname was a variant on the name of his maternal grandmother, Letitia Van Deren. It was in the 1850's that Jones changed the spelling of the name of the estate from "Wormslow" to "Wormsloe." Mary Telfair always used the old form.

38. Harden interview; "The Great Will Case," *Savannah Morning News*, January 15, 1877.

39. Biographical information on Augustus P. Wetter: Hartridge Collection, Box 72, Folder 1,372; Wetter obituary: *Savannah Morning News*, September 9, 1882.

40. Removal of Sarah's remains: Testimony of Augustus P. Wetter, Brief of Testimony, 37–39; MT and Margaret Hodgson to Alberta Wetter, December 30, 1860, Brief of Testimony, 92. Purchase of plot: Bonaventure Cemetery Records.

41. E. Merton Coulter, "Madison Springs, Georgia Watering Place," *Georgia Historical Quarterly* 47, no. 3 (December 1963): 391.

42. MT to Eliza Terrell, February 5, 1860, Terrell Papers, Duke.

43. MT to Eliza Terrell, no date [1853], Terrell Papers, Duke.

44. MT to Eliza Terrell, February 5, 1860, Terrell Papers, Duke.

45. Joseph Hodgson, Jr., to William B. Hodgson, September 4, 1860, TFP, Box 17, Folder 149, Item 600.

46. Joseph Hodgson, Jr., to William B. Hodgson, September 24, 1860, TFP, Box 17, Folder 149, Item 601.

47. Matilda Tillotson to MT, November 21 [1860], TFP, Box 5, Folder 53, Item 223.

48. Mary Telfair's 1860 Notebook: TFP, Box 7, Folder 66, Item 268; Harden, *Recollections of a Long and Satisfactory Life*, 86–87.

49. MT to MF, January 1, 1861, Hartridge Collection, Box 145, Folder 2,624. Charles O'Conor, a New York–born Roman Catholic lawyer, was popular with Southern Democrats because of his belief that slavery was a "just, benign and beneficent" institution and his firm conviction, often expressed, that there was no constitutional warrant for coercing seceding states. After the Civil War, he served as senior counsel for Jefferson Davis when the former president of the Confederate States was under indictment for treason. The title of the book that Mary Telfair was reading comes from the Book of Psalms and means the valley of tears.

50. Thomas Savage Clay, "Sketch of Life of Thomas Carolin Clay" [his father], Clay Papers, Folder 2, Item 15.

51. MT to Eliza Terrell, May 6 [1861], Terrell Papers, Duke.

52. MT to Eliza Terrell, September 29, 1861, Terrell Papers, Duke. General Winfield Scott ("Old Fuss and Feathers") was a native Virginian who remained loyal to the Union and, as general-in-chief of the United States Army, planned the defenses of the capital city of Washington upon the outbreak of hostilities. Although Justice Wayne remained on the Supreme Court during the war, there was another Southerner who did not. Justice John Archibald Campbell was born in Washington, Georgia, and was graduated from Franklin College (the University of Georgia) with first honor at the age of fourteen. He practiced law in Alabama, and was appointed to the Supreme Court by President Pierce in 1853. He openly and persistently opposed secession and acted as an intermediary between Secretary of State Seward and the Confederate commissioners in an effort to avoid war. He was misled by Seward's promises that Fort Sumter would be evacuated, while in fact its supplies were being replenished. Having failed in his attempts to save the people of the South from catastrophe, he resigned his judicial post and joined forces with them, eventually serving as assistant secretary of war for the Confederate States.

53. MT to Eliza Terrell, May 6 [1861], Terrell Papers, Duke.

17. Clouds Over Georgia   *pages 339–367*

1. Undated fragment of letter signed MT, presumably to Eliza Terrell, Terrell Papers, Duke. Hamilton Couper was the son of William B. Hodgson's friend James Hamilton Couper.

2. William Henry Trescot to William B. Hodgson, June 16, 1861, TFP, Box 19, Folder 173, Item 658.

3. William Henry Trescot to William B. Hodgson, June 23, 1861, TFP, Box 18, Folder 150, Item 617.

4. Mary Telfair's 1860 Notebook: TFP, Box 7, Folder 66, Item 268.

5. Women's war efforts: Faust, *Mothers of Invention*, 23–29, 92–113; Telfair financial contributions: *Savannah Morning News*, January 1, 1862, October 23, 1862.

6. MT to Eliza Terrell, September 29, 1861, Terrell Papers, Duke.

7. *Ibid.*

8. *Ibid.*

9. *Ibid.*

10. MT to Eliza Terrell, November 23 [1861], Terrell Papers, Duke.

11. *Ibid.*

12. *Ibid.*

13. MT to Eliza Terrell, September 29 [1861], Terrell Papers, Duke.

14. King, ed., *Ebb Tide*, 111–16.

15. A typewritten transcript of Hodgson's faded handwritten journal, prepared by the Georgia Historical Society in 1985, is in the Charles Colcock Jones Collection, Hargrett Library, University of Georgia Libraries, Athens, Georgia, Manuscript Collection No. 215, Folder 93. Unless otherwise noted, descriptions during this period are from the Hodgson journal. See also Alexander A. Lawrence, *A Present for Mr. Lincoln: The Story of Savannah from Secession to Sherman* (Macon, Ga.: Ardivan Press, 1961).

16. Excerpt from Benjamin Taloe's *Anecdotes and Reminiscences,* as copied by William Hartridge. Hartridge Collection, Box 145, Folder 2,624.

17. *Ibid.*

18. *Savannah Daily Republican*, April 21, 1865.

19. Unsigned 1865 will: Brief of Testimony, 95–98.

20. MT to Isabella Caroline Hamilton (née Delarocheaulion), no date [1865], I. C. Hamilton Papers, Georgia Historical Society Manuscript Collection No. 359 (hereinafter "I. C. Hamilton Papers"), Folder 2, Item 30 .

21. Funeral notice: *Savannah Daily Herald,* July 28, 1866; biographical information on Augustus P. Wetter and his children and information concerning his house: Hartridge Collection, Box 72, Folder 1,372; Wetter's obituary, *Savannah Morning News,* September 9, 1882; testimony of Augustus P. Wetter, Brief of Testimony, 36; *Savannah Daily Herald,* July 31, 1865, August 21, 1865, November 7, 1865, November 24, 1865. The Wetter mansion became the Savannah Female Orphanage in the early twentieth century and was demolished in 1949. A fragment of the ironwork can be seen in front of the building at 17 West McDonough Street (Chippewa Square) occupied by the law firm of Inglesby, Falligant, Horne, Courington & Nash, P.C. (formerly the Atlantic Mutual Fire Insurance Building).

22. This trip abroad is described in Mary Telfair's 1866 Travel Journal (three

volumes, unpaginated), TFP, Box 7, Folder 67, Items 269, 270, 271. Except as otherwise indicated, descriptions and quotations relating to this trip are from this source.

23. MT to Isabella Caroline Hamilton, October 6, 1866, I. C. Hamilton Papers, Folder 2, Item 37.

24. Margaret Hodgson to Isabella Caroline Hamilton, no date [1866], I. C. Hamilton Papers, Folder 3, Item 45.

25. MT to Isabella Caroline Hamilton, October 6, 1866, I. C. Hamilton Papers, Folder 2, Item 37.

26. Margaret Hodgson to Isabella Caroline Hamilton, no date [1866], I. C. Hamilton Papers, Folder 3, Item 45. The Gallatin reference is to a son of the late secretary of the Treasury and his wife.

27. McAllister, *Society*, 66; MT to Isabella Caroline Hamilton, October 6, 1866, I. C. Hamilton Papers, Folder 2, Item 37.

28. MT to Isabella Caroline Hamilton, May 4 [1867], I. C. Hamilton Papers, Folder 3, Item 46.

29. *Ibid.* Mary Telfair gives no indication of the fate of the art that adorned the walls of the mansion. Among the Telfair Family Papers is a paper, written in a scrawl that possibly is Hodgson's handwriting, that makes reference to a fire set by a Yankee and contains a list of books, possibly those burned. It also contains the statement, "All the boxes were opened Yankees may have taken the Paintings said I had no business to have my things away from Savh." TFP, Box 16, Folder 136, Item 551.

30. MT to Isabella Caroline Hamilton, July 11 [1868], I. C. Hamilton Papers, Folder 4, Item 63.

31. *Ibid.*

32. *Ibid.*

33. MT to Mary De Renne, "28ᵗʰ" [June 28, 1869], Margaret Telfair Hodgson to Mary De Renne, April 15, 1869, De Renne Family Papers, Hargrett Library, University of Georgia Libraries, Manuscript Collection No. 1064, Box 20, Box 1. I am grateful to Professor William Harris Bragg for informing me of the existence of these letters and providing me with copies.

34. MT to Mary De Renne, "28ᵗʰ" [June 28, 1869]. The McAlpin plantation was the Hermitage, a major tract on the Savannah River three miles to the west of Savannah. See Granger, ed., *Savannah River Plantations*, 419–50.

35. Margaret Telfair Hodgson to Mary De Renne, April 15, 1869, The "Merchant Prince" referred to was Charles Green.

36. J. P. S. Claghorn, President, to William B. Hodgson, November 30, 1869, January 5, 1870, Hodgson Papers, Duke.

37. Wm. M. Wadly to William B. Hodgson, July 10, 1870, Hodgson Papers, Duke; H. D. Capen, Secretary, to William B. Hodgson, December 29, 1870, Hodgson Papers, Duke.

38. Anthony Barclay to William B. Hodgson, April 28, 1870, Hodgson Papers, Duke.

39. Hodgson's obituaries: TFP, Box 19, Folder 171, Items 652–1 and 652–2.

40. MT to Isabella Caroline Hamilton, September 6, 1872. I. C. Hamilton Papers, Folder 4, Item 74; MT to Mary De Renne, September 4, 1872, De Renne Family Papers, Hargrett Library, University of Georgia Libraries, Manuscript Collection No. 1064, Box 23. I am again grateful to Professor William Harris Bragg for providing me with a copy of this letter to Mrs. De Renne.

41. *National Cyclopaedia of American Biography*, 3:432; see also David Willis McCullough, "Carl Brandt: Hasting's Other 19th-Century Painter," *Hastings Historian* (Summer 2000). Carl Brandt would go on to become, in 1883, the first director of the Telfair Academy of Arts and Sciences.

42. Historical information on the Georgia Historical Society: Harden, "The Georgia Historical Society," 3–13; biographical information on Lienau: Hartridge Collection, Box 71, Folder 1,322.

43. Register of Deaths, Chatham County Department of Health; *Savannah Morning News,* March 3, 1874; tea in the oak room: Louisa McAllister to Margaret Telfair, December 5, no year, TFP, Box 5, Folder 53, Item 226; MT to George Noble Jones, May 23, 1874, Jones Family Papers, Georgia Historical Society Manuscript Collection No. 440 (hereinafter "Jones Family Papers"), Box 1, Folder 17; verse: MT to MF, March 30, 1839, WFC, Item 82.

44. Harden, "The Georgia Historical Society," 11; *Savannah Morning News*, February 10, 1875.

45. Memorandum concerning disposition of silver plate: files of Chatham County Probate Court, Savannah. See Appendix A.

46. Testimony of Augustus P. Wetter, Brief of Testimony, 38–39; testimony of Alberta Mina Wetter, Margaret F. Donker [Wetter housekeeper], and Meta Wetter, Brief of Testimony, 71–72.

47. MT to George Noble Jones, May 23, 1874, September 21, 1874, September 17, 1874, Jones Family Papers, Box 1, Folder 17.

48. MT to Sophie Clinch, May 16, 1875, Mary Telfair Papers, GHS, Folder 2, Item 6. Duncan Lamont Clinch had been the Whig candidate for governor of Georgia in 1847. He lost the election to the colorful Democrat George Washington Bonaparte Towns. *Men of Mark in Georgia*, 2:312. MT to Isabella Caroline Hamilton, January 9, 1873, I. C. Hamilton Papers, Folder 4, Item 75.

49. MT to Sophie Clinch, May 16, 1875, supra; Mary Telfair's 1858 Journal, TFP, Box 7, Folder 66, Item 267.

18. The Telfair Will Contest   *pages 368–392*

1. Testimony of Dr. James B. Read, Brief of Testimony, 4; MT to MF, January 26, 1840, WFC, Item 86.

2. Testimony of William Marshall: Brief of Testimony, 4–8; Testimony of William Neyle Habersham: Brief of Testimony, 16–18.

3. Ness, "Georgia's Confederate Dead," 367; Hesseltine and Gara, "Georgia's Confederate Leaders After Appomattox," 13; *Men of Mark in Georgia*, 3:185; Harden, *A History of Savannah and South Georgia*, 570–74.

4. Jones v. Habersham, 63 Ga. 146, 150 (1879).

5. Order of Ordinary dated June 7, 1875, on file at Chatham County Probate Court.

6. *Savannah Morning News*, June 7, 1875, October 6, 1875.

7. Petition filed June 17, 1875: Record, 11; Orders dated June 18, 1875, of Ordinary: Record, 12–13; Certifications of publication by representatives of *New York Herald*, *Savannah Morning News*, and *Savannah Advertiser*, each dated November 1, 1875: Record, 16. Sarah Jones Cuthbert was the daughter of Dr. George Jones and Mary Gibbons. Alfred Cuthbert, Jr., bore the same degree of kinship to Mary Telfair as

George Noble Jones. His sister, Mary C. Cuthbert, should have been given notice as well. She later would appear as a party to the litigation.

8. Caveat dated October 5, 1875: Record, 13–14.

9. Petition of Augustus P. Wetter and Order of Ordinary dated November 1, 1875: Record, 14–15.

10. Caveat of Augustus P. Wetter filed November 1, 1875: Record, 15; Motion of propounders and Order of Ordinary dated November 27, 1875: Record, 20.

11. Amendment to Caveat filed November 29, 1875: Record, 20.

12. Order of Ordinary dated November 29, 1875: Record, 21; Order of Ordinary entering appeal: Record, 24; Amended Caveat filed November 30, 1875: Record, 21–22; Certification: Record, 25.

13. *Savannah Morning News*, February 13, 1876, February 18, 1876.

14. Kollock Letters, *Georgia Historical Quarterly* 34, no. 4 (December 1950): 327.

15. Amendment to Caveat of George Noble Jones, *et al.*: Record, 26–27; Amendment to Caveat of Augustus P. Wetter: Record, 27–28.

16. Record, 29–30.

17. Diary of Sarah Lawton, 1876–1884, Sarah Alexander Cunningham Collection, Georgia Historical Society Manuscript Collection No. 194, Box 2, Item 208.

18. Affidavit of continuance of Augustus P. Wetter dated June 6, 1877: Record, 30.

19. Affidavit of William Neyle Habersham and William Hunter in resistance of motion for continuance dated June 6, 1877: Record, 32; Remarks of Charles C. Jones, Jr., concerning Mr. De Renne, Georgia Historical Society Anniversary Address delivered in Hodgson Hall, Savannah, Georgia, February 14, 1881; G. W. J. De Renne to General Henry R. Jackson, De Renne Family Papers, Hargrett Library, University of Georgia Libraries, Manuscript Collection No. 1064, Box 13. I thank Professor William Harris Bragg for providing me with copies of Mr. Jones's remarks and Mr. De Renne's letter.

20. Jackson biographical data: *Men of Mark in Georgia*, 3:421–24; *Dictionary of American Biography*, 5: 543; poetry: *Savannah Morning News*, July 31, 1876; obituaries: *Savannah Morning News*, May 24, 1898, *Macon Telegraph*, May 24, 1898.

21. *Savannah Morning News*, June 15, 1877.

22. Testimony of Augustus P. Wetter: Brief of Testimony, 36–39; note from Mary Telfair and Margaret Hodgson to Alberta Wetter dated December 30, 1860: Brief of Testimony, 92; extract from undated letter from Mary Telfair to Thomas Telfair: Brief of Testimony, 91; extract from letter from Alberta Wetter to Mary Telfair endorsed on back of letter from Alberta Wetter to her husband dated September 19, 1859: Brief of Testimony, 91–92.

23. Decision of Judge Tompkins dated June 12, 1877: Record, 33–37.

24. *Savannah Morning News*, June 15, 1877.

25. Charge of Judge Tompkins to jury: Record, 42–44.

26. *Savannah Morning News*, June 15, 1877; Finding by jury dated June 14, 1877: Record, 50–51; General verdict: Record, 25.

27. Motion for new trial dated June 23, 1877: Record, 56–59; judgment on motion for new trial dated July 2, 1877: Record, 63–64.

28. Wetter v. Habersham, 60 Ga. 193 (1878). For the benefit of the few who may be interested, the court's reasoning on this issue is set forth in Appendix C.

29. Jones v. Habersham, 63 Ga. 146 (1879).

30. 60 Ga. at 202, syllabus at 194.

31. Case of Broderick's Will, 21 Wall 503 (U.S. 1874); Gaines v. Fuentes, 92 U.S. 10 (1875). See Note, "Federal Jurisdiction in Matters Relating to Probate and Administration," 43 Harv. L. Rev. 462 (1930).

32. Bill of complaint; demurrer of William Neyle Habersham and William Hunter, executors; order setting down demurrer for argument: Record on Appeal, United States Supreme Court.

33. Jones v. Habersham, 13 F. Cas. 957 (C.C.S.D.Ga. 1879) (No. 7,464); quoted portion at 969–70. Appointed to the Supreme Court by President Grant in 1870, Mr. Justice Bradley was a man of high intelligence and a lawyer of extensive learning. See Fairman, "What Makes a Great Justice? Mr. Justice Bradley and the Supreme Court, 1870–1892," 30 *B.U.L. Rev.* 49 (1950).

34. Obituary of Rev. George Gibbons: *Savannah Morning News*, November 24, 1884. The esteem in which Rev. Gibbons was held by his congregation is evidenced by the fact that when his remains lay in state before the pulpit of the First African Baptist Church the congregation kept vigil there throughout the night.

35. Briefs and Record on Appeal, United States Supreme Court; Jones v. Habersham, 107 U.S. 401 (1883).

36. Margaret Godley, "The Three Faces of Mary Telfair," *Savannah Morning News Magazine*, March 8, 1959.

Selected Bibliography

Manuscript Sources

Chatham County, Georgia, Department of Health Records.
Duke University, Special Collections Library (Durham, N.C.).
   William B. Hodgson Papers.
   Edward Telfair Papers.
   William and Eliza Rhodes Terrell Papers.
Georgia Department of History and Archives (Atlanta).
   William Few Collection. Accession No. 55–101.
   Record on Appeal in the matter of Augustus P. Wetter, guardian
      ad litem and George Noble Jones, *et al.* v. William Hunter and
      William Neyle Habersham, Executors of the will of Mary Tel-
      fair, including Brief of Testimony filed June 23, 1877, in the
      office of the Clerk of the Superior Court, Chatham County,
      Georgia. Accession No. 9621, Box 122, Loc. 110–04.
Georgia Historical Society (Savannah).
   J. M. Berrien Papers. Manuscript Collection No. 67.
   Clay Family Papers. Manuscript Collection No. 125.
   Sarah Alexander Cunningham Collection. Manuscript Collection
      No. 194.
   Mary and Frances Few Papers. Manuscript Collection No. 1,201.
   Papers of Marmaduke Hamilton Floyd and Dolores Boisfeuillet
      Floyd. Manuscript Collection No. 1,308.
   R. & J. Habersham Papers. Manuscript Collection No. 342.
   I. C. Hamilton Papers. Manuscript Collection No. 359.
   Walter Charlton Hartridge Collection. Manuscript Collection
      No. 1,349.
   William B. Hodgson Papers. Manuscript Collection No. 388.
   Jones Family Papers. Manuscript Collection No. 440.
   Telfair Family Papers. Manuscript Collection No. 793.

Alexander Telfair Papers. Manuscript Collection No. 790.

Edward Telfair Papers. Manuscript Collection No. 791.

Mary Telfair Papers. Manuscript Collection No. 792.

New-York Historical Society (New York City).

Chrystie Family Papers.

Gallatin Collection.

University of Georgia, Hargrett Library, University of Georgia Libraries (Athens).

De Renne Family Papers. Manuscript Collection No. 1864.

William B. Hodgson Journal kept during the period of Sherman's occupation of Savannah, November 22, 1864, to January 29, 1865. Charles Colcock Jones Collection. Manuscript Collection No. 215, Folder 93.

Books and Articles

Amory, Cleveland. *Who Killed Society?* New York: Harper & Brothers, 1960.

Anderson, Mary Savage, *et al. Georgia: A Pageant of Years.* Richmond, Va.: Garrett & Massie, 1933. Reprint, Spartanburg, S. C.: The Reprint Company, 1974.

Anderson, Mary Savage, ed. "The Wallace Letters." *Georgia Historical Quarterly* 18, no. 2 (June 1934): 176–97.

Ashmore, Otis, and Charles H. Olmstead. "The Battles of Kettle Creek and Brier Creek." *Georgia Historical Quarterly* 10, no.2 (June 1926): 85–125.

Axley, Lowrey. *Holding Aloft the Torch: A History of the Independent Presbyterian Church of Savannah, Georgia.* Savannah: Pigeonhole Press, 1958.

Bell, Malcolm, Jr. "The Romantic Wines of Madeira." *Georgia Historical Quarterly* 38, no. 4 (December 1954): 322–36.

Berry, Stephen. "More Alluring at a Distance: Absentee Patriarchy and the Thomas Butler King Family." *Georgia Historical Quarterly* 81, no. 4 (winter 1997): 863–96.

Bleser, Carol, ed. *In Joy and In Sorrow: Women, Family and Marriage in the Victorian South, 1830–1900.* New York: Oxford University Press, 1991.

———. *Tokens of Affection: The Letters of a Planter's Daughter in the Old South.* Athens: University of Georgia Press, 1996.

Boatwright, Eleanor M. "The Political and Civil Status of Women in Georgia, 1783–1860." *Georgia Historical Quarterly* 25, no. 4 (December 1941): 301–24.

Boggs, Marion Alexander, ed. *The Alexander Letters, 1787–1900.* Savannah: privately printed, 1910. Reprint, Brown Thrasher Books, University of Georgia Press, 1980.

Bolton, Henry Carrington, and Reginald Pelham Bolton. *The Family of Bolton in England and America, 1100–1894.* New York, privately printed, 1895.

Bowen, Eliza A. *The Story of Wilkes County.* Marietta, Ga.: Continental Book Company, 1950.

Bragg, William Harris. *De Renne: Three Generations of a Georgia Family.* Athens: University of Georgia Press, 1999.

Branch, Edward Douglas. *The Sentimental Years: 1836–1860.* New York: Appleton-Century, 1934.

Bryson, Thomas A. *An American Consular Officer in the Middle East in the Jacksonian Era: A Biography of William Brown Hodgson, 1801–1871.* Atlanta: Resurgens Publications, 1979.

———. "William Brown Hodgson's Mission to Egypt, 1834." *West Georgia College Studies in the Social Sciences* 11 (June 1972): 10–17.

Bulloch, Joseph Gaston Baillie. *A History and Genealogy of the Families of Bellinger, De Veaux and Other Families.* Savannah: The Morning News Press, 1895.

———. *A History and Genealogy of the Families of Bulloch and Stobo and Irvine of Cults.* Washington, D.C., Byron S. Adams, 1911.

———. *A History and Genealogy of the Families of Bulloch, Stobo, Irvine, Douglass, Baillie, Lewis, Adams, Glen, Jones, Davis, Hunter, Etc.* Savannah: Braid & Hutton, 1892.

———. *A History and Genealogy of the Habersham Family.* Columbia, S.C.: R. L. Bryan Company, 1901.

Burke, Emily P. *Reminiscences of Georgia.* Oberlin, Ohio: James M. Finch, 1850. Reprint, under title *Pleasure and Pain, Reminiscences of Georgia in the 1840's.* Savannah: The Beehive Press, 1978.

Carter, Christine Jacobson, ed. *The Diary of Dolly Lunt Burge, 1848–1879.* Athens: University of Georgia Press, 1997.

Cash, W. J. *The Mind of the South.* New York: Alfred A. Knopf, 1941. Reprint, New York: Random House, Vintage Books, 1991.

Cashin, Edward J., Jr. *The Story of Augusta.* Augusta: Richmond County Board of Education, 1980.

Cashin, Edward J., Jr., and Heard Robertson. *Augusta and the*

American Revolution: Events in the Georgia Backcountry, 1773–1783. Darien, Ga.: Ashantilly Press, 1975.

Cashin, Joan E. "'Decidedly Opposed to the Union': Women's Culture, Marriage, and Politics in Antebellum South Carolina." *Georgia Historical Quarterly* 78, no. 4 (winter 1994): 735–59.

————. "The Structure of Antebellum Planter Families: 'The Ties That Bound Us Was Strong.'" *Journal of Southern History* 56, no. 1 (February 1990): 55–70.

————, ed. *Our Common Affairs: Texts from Women in the Old South.* Baltimore: Johns Hopkins University Press, 1996.

Chambers-Schiller, Lee Virginia. *Liberty: A Better Husband, Single Women in America: The Generations of 1780–1840.* New Haven: Yale University Press, 1984.

Clinton, Catherine. *The Plantation Mistress: Woman's World in the Old South.* New York: Pantheon Books, 1982.

Coleman, Kenneth. *Colonial Georgia: A History.* New York: Charles Scribner's Sons, 1976.

————, ed. *A History of Georgia.* Athens: University of Georgia Press, 1991.

Coleman, Kenneth, and Charles Stephen Gurr, eds. *Dictionary of Georgia Biography*, 2 vols. Athens: University of Georgia Press, 1983.

Conrad, Susan. *Perish the Thought: Intellectual Women in Romantic America, 1830–1860.* Secaucus, N.J.: Citadel Press, 1978.

Cook, Blanche Wiesen. "'Women Alone Stir My Imagination': Lesbianism and the Cultural Tradition." *Signs: Journal of Women in Culture and Society* 4, no. 4 (1979): 718–39.

Cook, James F. *The Governors of Georgia.* Huntsville, Ala.: Strode Publishers, 1979.

Cooper, Sherwin. "The Rural Settlement of the Savannah River Basin in Georgia." Ph.D. diss., University of Michigan, 1959.

Corley, Florence Fleming. "William Few, Jr.: Georgia's Silent Signer of the U.S. Constitution." *Georgia Journal of Southern Legal History* 1, no. 1 (spring/summer 1991): 223–28.

Cott, Nancy F. "Passionless: An Interpretation of Victorian Sexual Ideology, 1790–1850." *Signs: Journal of Women in Culture and Society* 4, no. 2 (1978): 219–36.

————. *The Roots of Bitterness: Documents of the Social History of American Women.* New York: E. P. Dutton, 1972.

Coulter, E. Merton. "Edward Telfair." *Georgia Historical Quarterly* 20, no. 2 (June 1936): 99–124.

———. "Madison Springs, Georgia Watering Place." *Georgia Historical Quarterly* 47, no. 3 (December 1963): 375–407.

———. "Presidential Visits to Georgia During Ante-Bellum Times." *Georgia Historical Quarterly* 55, no. 3 (fall 1971): 329–64.

———. *Wormsloe: Two Centuries of a Georgia Family.* Athens: University of Georgia Press, 1955.

Evans, Nancy Goyne. "The Sans Souci: A Fashionable Resort Hotel in Ballston Spa." *Winterthur Portfolio* 6. Charlottesville: University Press of Virginia, 1970.

Faderman, Lilian. *Surpassing the Love of Men: Romantic Friendship and Love between Women from the Renaissance to the Present.* New York: William Morrow & Co., 1981.

Farnham, Christie Anne. *The Education of the Southern Belle: Higher Education and Student Socialization in the Antebellum South.* New York: New York University Press, 1994.

Faust, Drew Gilpin. *Mothers of Invention: Women of the Slaveholding South in the American Civil War.* Chapel Hill: University of North Carolina Press, 1996.

———. *A Sacred Circle: The Dilemma of the Intellectual in the Old South, 1840–1860.* Baltimore: Johns Hopkins University Press, 1977.

Feiling, Keith. *History of England.* New York: McGraw-Hill, 1948.

Ferguson, T. Reed. *The John Couper Family at Cannon's Point.* Macon, Ga.: Mercer University Press, 1994.

Finnie, David H. *Pioneers East: The Early American Experience in the Middle East.* Cambridge, Mass.: Harvard University Press, 1967.

Fisher, Samuel H. *The Litchfield Law School, 1775–1833.* New Haven: Tercentenary Commission of the State of Connecticut, Yale University Press, 1933.

Fox-Genovese, Elizabeth. "Family and Female Identity in the Antebellum South: Sarah Gayle and Her Family." In *In Joy and In Sorrow: Women, Family and Marriage in the Victorian South, 1830–1900,* edited by Carol Bleser. New York: Oxford University Press, 1991.

Gamble, Thomas. "Romance of Wm. Jay, Savannah Architect." *Savannah Morning News,* May 8, 1932.

———. *Savannah Duels and Duelists, 1733–1877.* Savannah: Review Publishing & Printing Co., 1923. Reprint, Spartanburg, S.C.: The Reprint Company, 1974.

Gardiner, Robert Hallowell. *Early Recollections of Robert Hallowell Gardiner, 1782–1864.* Hallowell, Maine: White & Horne Company, 1936.

Genovese, Eugene. "'Our Family, White and Black': Family and Household in the Southern Slaveholder's World View." In *In Joy and In Sorrow: Women, Family and Marriage in the Victorian South, 1830–1900,* edited by Carol Bleser. New York: Oxford University Press, 1991.

———. *Roll Jordan Roll: The World the Slaves Made.* New York: Pantheon Books, 1974.

Georgia Historical Society. *The Counties of the State of Georgia.*

———. *Letters of Joseph Clay, Merchant of Savannah, 1776–1793.* Savannah: Collections of the Georgia Historical Society, vol. 8, 1913.

———. *Marriages of Chatham County,* 2 vols.

———. *Registers of Deaths in Savannah, Georgia.*

Gignilliat, Thomas H., John A. Varnedoe, and A. Leopold Alexander. *History of the St. Andrew's Society of the City of Savannah.* Savannah: Kennickell, 1950.

Godley, Margaret. "The Three Faces of Mary Telfair." *Savannah Morning News Magazine,* March 8, 1959.

Godley, Margaret, and Lilian C. Bragg. *Stories of Old Savannah.* Savannah: privately printed, 1949.

Granger, Mary, ed. *Savannah River Plantations.* Savannah: Savannah Writers' Project, Georgia Historical Society, 1947. Reprint, Savannah: The Oglethorpe Press, Inc., 1997.

Griffen, Lee. "Savannah's Meanest Man" [Thomas Gibbons]. *Savannah Morning News Magazine,* April 9, 1961.

Habersham, Richard West. "The Telfairs." *Savannah Morning News,* October 19, 1884.

———. "The Telfairs Again." *Savannah Morning News,* October 26, 1884.

Harden, William. "Basil Cowper's Remarkable Career in Georgia." *Georgia Historical Quarterly* 1, no. 1 (March 1917): 24–35.

———. "The Georgia Historical Society." *Georgia Historical Quarterly* 1, no. 1 (March 1917): 3–13.

———. *A History of Savannah and South Georgia.* Atlanta: Cherokee Publishing Company, 1969. Reprint of 1913 edition.

———. *Recollections of a Long and Satisfactory Life.* Savannah: Review Printing, 1934.

Hartridge, Walter C., ed. *The Letters of Robert Mackay.* Athens: University of Georgia Press, 1949.

Haunton, Richard H. "Savannah in the 1850's." Ph.D. diss., Emory University, 1968.

Henderson, Archibald. *Washington's Southern Tour, 1791.* New York: Houghton Mifflin & Company, 1923.

Hesseltine, William B., and Larry Gara. "Georgia's Confederate Leaders After Appomattox." *Georgia Historical Quarterly* 35, no. 1 (March 1951): 1–15.

Hillhouse, Albert M. *A History of Burke County, Georgia, 1777–1950.* Swainsboro, Ga.: Magnolia Press; Spartanburg, S.C.: The Reprint Company, 1985.

Hodgson, Telfair. "A Notebook of Facts and Gems, 1856." *The Princeton University Library Chronicle*, 8, no. 2 (February 1947): 67–87.

Holmes, James. *Dr. Bullie's Notes: Reminiscences of Early Georgia and of Philadelphia and New Haven in the 1800s.* Atlanta: Cherokee Publishing Company, 1976.

Homberger, Eric. *The Historical Atlas of New York City.* New York: Henry Holt and Company, 1994.

Humphries, Lance L. "Robert Gilmor, Jr. (1774–1848): Baltimore Collector and American Art Patron." Ph.D. diss., University of Virginia, 1998.

Johnson, Allen, ed. *The Dictionary of America Biography*, 11 vols. New York: Charles Scribner's Sons, 1964.

Johnston, Edith Duncan, ed. "The Kollock Letters, 1799–1850." *Georgia Historical Quarterly* 30, no. 3 (September 1946): 218–58; 30, no. 4 (December 1946): 312–56; 31, no. 1 (March 1947): 34–80; 31, no. 2 (June 1947): 121–63; 31, no. 3 (September 1947): 195–233; 31, no. 4 (December 1947): 289–322; 32, no. 1 (March 1948): 32–67; 32, no. 2 (June 1948): 119–43.

Jones, Charles C., Jr. *Biographical Sketches of the Delegates to the Continental Congress.* Boston and New York: Houghton Mifflin & Company, 1891.

Jones, Charles C., Jr., and Salem Dutcher. *Memorial History of Augusta, Georgia.* Syracuse, N.Y.: D. Mason. Reprint: Spartanburg, S.C., The Reprint Company, 1980.

Kemble, Frances Anne. *Journal of a Residence on a Georgia Plantation in 1835–1839.* Athens: Brown Thrasher Books, University of Georgia Press, 1984.

Kemper, Sharon Wells. "Edward Telfair and Early Nationalism in Georgia." M.A. thesis, Armstrong State College, 1987 [copy in library of Armstrong Atlantic State University].

Kerber, Linda. *Toward an Intellectual History of Women*. Chapel Hill: University of North Carolina Press, 1997.

Kilbride, Daniel P. "Philadelphia and the Southern Elite: Class, Kinship, and Culture in Antebellum America." Ph.D. diss., University of Florida, 1997.

Killion, Ronald G., and Charles T. Waller. *Georgia and the Revolution*. Atlanta: Cherokee Publishing Company, 1975.

King, Spencer Bidwell, ed. *Ebb Tide: As Seen Through the Diary of Josephine Clay Habersham, 1863*. Athens: University of Georgia Press, 1958.

Kollock, Susan M. "Letters of the Kollock and Allied Families, 1826–1884." *Georgia Historical Quarterly* 33, no. 4 (December 1949): 331–54; 34, no. 1 (March 1950): 36–63; 34, no. 2 (June 1950): 126–56; 34, no. 3 (September 1950): 227–57; 34, no. 4 (December 1950): 313–27; 35, no. 1 (March 1951): 60–75.

Lasser, Carol. "'Let Us Be Sisters Forever': The Sororal Model of Nineteenth-Century Female Friendship." *Signs: Journal of Women in Culture and Society* 14, no. 1 (1988): 158–81.

Lawrence, Alexander A. *A Present for Mr. Lincoln: The Story of Savannah from Secession to Sherman*. Macon, Ga.: Ardivan Press, 1961.

———. *James Moore Wayne, Southern Unionist*. Chapel Hill: University of North Carolina Press, 1943.

Lebsock, Suzanne. *Free Women of Petersburg: Status and Culture in a Southern Town, 1784–1860*. New York: W. W. Norton and Co., 1983.

Lerner, Gerda, ed. *The Female Experience: An American Documentary*. Indianapolis, Ind.: Bobbs-Merrill, 1977. Reprint, New York: Oxford University Press, 1992.

———. *The Grimké Sisters from South Carolina: Pioneers for Women's Rights and Abolition*. New York: Shockton Books, 1971.

———. "Placing Women in History: Definitions and Challenges." *Feminist Studies* 3, nos. 1–2 (fall 1975): 5–14.

Lerski, Hannah H. *William Jay, Itinerant English Architect, 1792–1837*. Lanham, Md.: University Press of America, 1983.

Lewis, Charlene Marie. "Ladies and Gentlemen on Display: Planter Society at the Virginia Springs, 1790–1860." Ph.D. diss., University of Virginia, 1997.

Lorant, Stefan. *The Glorious Burden: The American Presidency*. New York: Harper & Row, 1968.

McAllister, Ward. *Society As I Have Found It*. New York: Cassell Publishing Company, 1890. Reprint, New York: Arno Press, 1975.

MacDonell, Alexander R. "John Macpherson Berrien." *Georgia Historical Quarterly* 17, no. 1 (March 1933): 1–12.

McDonough, James Vernon. "William Jay—Regency Architect in Georgia and South Carolina." Ph.D. diss., Princeton University, 1950.

McFeeley, William S. *Sapelo's People*. New York: W. W. Norton and Co., 1994.

Mackall, Leonard L. "William Brown Hodgson." *Georgia Historical Quarterly* 15, no. 4 (December 1931): 324–45.

McLeod, Rebecca Lamar. "The Loss of the Steamer *Pulaski*." *Georgia Historical Quarterly* 3, no. 1 (March 1919): 63–95.

Marszalek, John F. *The Petticoat Affair: Manners, Mutiny, and Sex in Andrew Jackson's White House*. New York: The Free Press, 1997.

Minnigerode, Meade. *The Fabulous Forties*. New York: G. P. Putnam's Sons, 1924.

Morgan, Helen M., ed. *A Season in New York (1801): Letters of Harriet and Maria Trumbull*. Pittsburgh: University of Pittsburgh Press, 1969.

Morison, Samuel Eliot. *The Oxford History of the American People*. New York: Oxford University Press, 1965.

Muhlenfeld, Elizabeth. *Mary Boykin Chesnut: A Biography* . Baton Rouge: Louisiana State University Press, 1981.

Myers, Robert Manson, ed. *The Children of Pride: A True Story of Georgia and the Civil War*. New Haven: Yale University Press,1972.

The National Cyclopaedia of American Biography, 14 vols. New York: James T. White & Company, 1892.

Ness, George T., Jr. "Georgia's Confederate Dead." *Georgia Historical Quarterly* 25, no. 4 (December 1941): 364–70.

Northern, William J., ed. *Men of Mark in Georgia*, 7 vols. Atlanta: A. B. Caldwell (1907–12).

Norton, Mary Beth. *Liberty's Daughters: The Revolutionary Experience of American Women, 1750–1800*. Boston: Little, Brown and Company, 1980.

Princeton University General Catalogue, 1746–1906.

Riley, Glenda. *Inventing the American Woman: A Perspective on Wo-*

men's History. Arlington Heights, Ill.: Harlan Davidson, Inc., 1986.

Rothman, Helen K. *Hands and Hearts: A History of Courtship in America*. New York: Basic Books, 1984.

Rugoff, Milton. *America's Gilded Age: Intimate Portraits from an Era of Extravagance and Change, 1850–1890*. New York: Henry Holt and Company, 1989.

Russell, Preston, and Barbara Hines. *Savannah: A History of Her People Since 1733*. Savannah: Frederic C. Beil, 1992.

Ryan, Mary. *Womanhood in America*. New York: New Viewpoints Press, 1980.

Scott, Anne Firor. *The Southern Lady: From Pedestal to Politics*. Chicago: University of Chicago Press, 1970.

———. "Women's Perspective on the Patriarchy." *Journal of American History* 61 (June 1974): 52–64.

Shryock, Richard H., ed. *Letters of Richard D. Arnold, M.D., 1808–1876*. Durham, N.C.: Seeman Press, 1929.

Smith, Danny D., and Earle G. Shettleworth, Jr. *Gardiner on the Kennebec*. Dover, N.H.: Arcadia Publishing, Images of America Series, 1996.

Smith, Julia Floyd. *Slavery and Rice Culture in Low Country Georgia, 1750–1860*. Knoxville, Tenn.: University of Tennessee Press, 1985.

Smith-Rosenberg, Carroll. "The Female World of Love and Ritual: Relations between Women in Nineteenth-Century America." *Signs: Journal of Women in Culture and Society* 1, no. 1 (1975): 1–29.

Smith-Rosenberg, Carroll, and Charles Rosenberg. "The Female Animal: Medical and Biological Views of Woman and Her Role in Nineteenth-Century America." *Journal of American History* 60 (1973): 332–56.

Stegeman, John F., and Janet A. Stegeman. *Caty: A Biography of Catherine Littlefield Greene*. Athens: University of Georgia Press, 1985.

Stevens, William B. *A History of Georgia*, 2 vols. Savannah: Beehive Press, 1972. Reprint of 1847 (vol. 1) and 1859 (vol. 2) editions.

Sullivan, Buddy. *From Beautiful Zion to Red Bird Creek: A History of Bryan County, Georgia*. Bryan County Board of Commissioners, 2000.

Swiggart, Carolyn Clay. *Shades of Gray: The Clay & McAllister Families of Bryan County, Georgia, during the Plantation Years (ca. 1760–1888)*. Darien, Conn.: Two Bytes Publishing, Ltd., 1999.

Talbott, Page, ed. *Classical Savannah: Fine and Decorative Arts, 1800–*

1840. Savannah: Telfair Museum of Art, 1995 [exhibition catalog].

Tocqueville, Alexis de. *Democracy in America*. Abridgment of translation by Henry Reeve published in two volumes in 1835 and 1840. London: Oxford University Press, 1952.

Trollope, Frances Milton. *Domestic Manners of the Americans*, edited by Robert Smalley. New York: Random House, Vintage Books, 1949.

Union Society. *Bethesda: A Historical Sketch*. Savannah: J. M. Cooper, 1860 [pamphlet at Georgia Historical Society].

Wainwright, Nicholas B., ed. *A Philadelphia Perspective: The Diary of Sidney George Fisher Covering the Years 1834–1871*. Philadelphia: Historical Society of Pennsylvania, 1967.

Waring, Joseph F. *Cerveau's Savannah*. Savannah: Georgia Historical Society, 1973.

Waring, Martha Gallaudet, ed. "Charles Seton Hardee's Recollections of Old Savannah." *Georgia Historical Quarterly* (Part 1) 12, no. 4 (December 1928): 353–89; (Part 2) 13, no. 1 (March 1929): 13–49.

Warlick, Roger K. *As Grain Once Scattered: The History of Christ Church, Savannah, Georgia (1733–1983)*. Savannah: State Printing, 1987.

Wates, Wylma. "Precursor to the Victorian Age: The Concept of Marriage and Family as Revealed in the Correspondence of the Izard Family of South Carolina." In *In Joy and In Sorrow: Women, Family and Marriage in the Victorian South, 1830–1900*, edited by Carol Bleser. New York: Oxford University Press, 1991.

Weeks, Carl Solana. *Savannah in the Time of Peter Tondee: The Road to Revolution in Colonial Georgia*. Columbia, S.C.: Summerhouse Press, 1997.

Welter, Barbara. "The Cult of True Womanhood, 1820–1860." *The American Quarterly* 18 (1966): 151–74.

Wertenbaker, Thomas Jefferson. *Princeton: 1746–1896*. Princeton: Princeton University Press, 1946.

Wharton, Anne Hollingsworth. *Salons Colonial and Republican*. New York: J. B. Lippincott Company, 1900.

Woodward, C. Van, ed. *Mary Chesnut's Civil War*. New Haven: Yale University Press, 1981.

Wyatt-Brown, Bertram. *Southern Honor: Ethics & Behavior in the Old South*. New York: Oxford University Press, 1982.

Wylie, Lollie Belle, ed. *Memoirs of Judge Richard H. Clark*. Atlanta: Franklin Printing and Publishing Company, 1898.

Index

Abbot, Gorham (principal of Springer Institute), 294

Abolition and abolitionists, 212, 213

Academy of Natural Sciences of Philadelphia, and James Hamilton Couper, 276

Adams, John Quincy, 256, 260, 285

Alabama, secedes from Union, 335

Albany, N.Y., as stop on route to Ballston Spa, 69

Alden, Rev. Timothy, 36

Alexander, D. I. W., on presidential candidate John Bell, 333

Alexander, Dr. James, and letters from Baden-Baden read by MT, 327

Alexander, Dr. Joseph (preacher and linguist), 331

Algiers, and W. B. Hodgson, 260–61

Altamaha River estuary, Ga., and James Hamilton Couper, 276

American Anti-Slavery Society, 212

American Bar Association, and presidency of A. R. Lawton, 369

American Institute of Architects, and Richard Upjohn, 241; and Detlef Lienau, 364

American Oriental Society, and W. B. Hodgson, 278

American Philosophical Society, and W. B. Hodgson, 274, 278

Anderson, George W., and Fort McAllister, 364

Andersonville stockade, 352

Anne (Oglethorpe's ship), 13

Anti-Dueling Association, Savannah, 166

Antietam, Battle of, 1, 345

Antwerp, Belgium, MT visits picture gallery in, 306

Apollo Belvedere (statue in Vatican), 262

Appalachian Mountains, as boundary for East Coast aristocracy, 58

Appomattox Court House, and Lee's surrender, 352

Arabic language, and W. B. Hodgson, 275, 326

Arctic (steamship), 304

Argyle Independent Chapel, Bath, England, and Rev. William Jay, 267

Argyle Plantation (on Savannah River), and Ward McAllister, 298

Armory Hall, Savannah, and Georgia Historical Society, 363

Arnold, Charles S. (first husband of great-niece Alberta Cobb), 288, 289, 310, 311, 324, 375, 377

Arnold, Governor (of Rhode Island), Newport, R.I., farm of visited by MT, 358

Arnold, Dr. Richard D., letters of, 58–59; and surrender of Savannah to General Sherman, 347; and dedication of Hodgson Hall, 373

Arnold, R. J. (Bryan County planter), 193, 217

Articles of Confederation, signed by Edward Telfair, 11

Ashbrook, Dowager Viscountess of, MT on rank of, 303

Asheville, N.C., MT wishes to visit, 343

Asiatic Society of Paris, and W. B. Hodgson, 278